Family Violence

an international and interdisciplinary study

John M. Eekelaar
Sanford N. Katz

With an Introduction by Anthony Storr

BUTTERWORTHS

Family Violence

an international and interdisciplinary study

With an Introduction by
ANTHONY STORR

·3476 Int.

edited by

JOHN M. EEKELAAR
LL.B., B.C.L., M.A., Fellow of Pembroke College, Oxford, England

SANFORD N. KATZ
PROFESSOR of LAW, Boston College Law School,
United States of America

BUTTERWORTHS

TORONTO

CANADA: BUTTERWORTH & CO. (CANADA) LTD.
                    TORONTO: 2265 Midland Avenue, Scarborough, M1P 4S1

UNITED KINGDOM: BUTTERWORTH & CO. (Publishers) LTD.
                    LONDON: 88 KINGSWAY, WC2B 6AB

AUSTRALIA: BUTTERWORTH PTY. LTD.
                    SYDNEY: 586 Pacific Highway, Chatswood, NSW 2067
                    MELBOURNE: 343 Little Collins Street, 3000
                    BRISBANE: 240 Queen Street, 4000

NEW ZEALAND   BUTTERWORTHS OF NEW ZEALAND LTD.
                    WELLINGTON: 77-85 Custom House Quay, 1

SOUTH AFRICA: BUTTERWORTH & CO. (SOUTH AFRICA) (PTY.) LTD.
                    DURBAN: 152/154 Gale Street

Canadian Cataloguing in Publication Data

International Conference on Family Law, 2d, Montreal, Que., 1977.
   Family violence

Proceedings of the second International Conference on Family Law held
in Montreal in June 1977.

Includes index.
ISBN 0-409-87460-4 pa.

1. Conjugal violence — Congresses. 2. Child abuse — Congresses. I.
Eekelaar, John. II. Katz, Sanford N. III. Title.

HQ518.I58 1977   301.42'7   C78-001379-4

PREFACE

It can come as a shock to discover how the most sensitive minds in past ages could accept racial oppression and conflict with equanimity, even approval. It has taken the horror of the Nazi holocaust to raise public consciousness of the evils and dangers of racial conflict to a significant level and has led to programs on both national and international levels to combat its threat. But family violence and oppression have been with the human race equally as long as racial violence. Yet its existence has been buried in the subconscious, glimpsed only in nursery stories, literature and black humor.

Family violence usually takes place in secret. It does not have the public face which racial conflict wears. The sufferings of its victims take place in silence. They are not recorded on the pages of our history books. Indeed, the society around them hardly considers their injuries and the deprivations inflicted on them as acts of violence at all. Rather, they are often considered right and legitimate. Worse still, the victims themselves often accept them to be so.

It has only been in very recent years that public realization that violence and oppression within our families exists at all and that it is an evil has become significant; and the degree of this realization still varies sharply from country to country. The work of Dr. Henry Kempe and his medical colleagues in Denver revealed to an incredulous world, that parents can and do inflict violent and fatal injuries on their young children. The significance of the truth, known but hardly appreciated, that children are far more likely to be injured by their parents and immediate family than by anyone else, is still in the process of being absorbed. Dr Kempe's work has dealt mostly with very young children. Yet we are becoming aware that the network of family conflict extends much wider than this. It includes generational conflicts between parents and their older children, conflicts between children themselves, violence and ill-treatment between spouses, sexual oppression and self-inflicted injury. The full implications of the Freudian revelation of the significance of family relationships and experiences on the later life of individuals are slowly being assimilated. We are asking how far individuals can become locked into a pattern of destructive behavior by reason of their family experiences. We are searching for new ways of understanding these processes and responding to them. New and challenging problems in medicine, psychology, social work and law have emerged and our societies are only feeling their way to their solution.

In June 1977 a conference was arranged by the International Society on Family Law at McGill University in Montreal. Convened by Professors H.R. Hahlo and Alastair Bissett-Johnson, the conference brought together experts in various fields from many different countries who were concerned with these issues. The Canadian Government, the Government of Quebec, the Canada Council and McGill University gave generous support to the meeting. There was a strong feeling among the participants that much still needed to be done to stimulate public and, particularly, official awareness of the fate of family members who suffer violence and oppression. This volume represents one attempt to do that. It endeavors to present evidence of family violence in its many different forms from widely different parts of the world. It tries to demonstrate how the social and legal systems of various countries have reacted to it. We hope that countries will be able to learn from the successes and failures of others. We do not believe that family violence is unique to any particular social system, although we recognize the contribution which societal organization can make to various of its manifestations. Societies which profess to take to heart the happiness and well-being of their individual citizens must be receptive to investigation of the quality of their citizens' lives in the family surroundings which dominate them. They must give full consideration to all the evidence which is available and must be prepared to devote resources to improving conditions of family life. Society expects much from families. It must give them something in return.

JOHN M. EEKELAAR,
Pembroke College, Oxford, England.

SANFORD N. KATZ,
Boston College Law School, Newton Centre, Massachussetts.

July, 1978

TABLE OF CONTENTS

Introduction

*Anthony Storr**

Although most people would probably agree in supposing that the family is the best milieu in which to rear children, it must nevertheless be recognized that home is a dangerous place. For it is within the family that the majority of homicides occur. On both sides of the Atlantic, "murder is overwhelmingly a domestic crime, in which men kill their wives, mistresses and children, and women kill their children."[1] As Norval Morris has put it: "You are safer on the streets than at home; safer with a stranger than with a friend or relative."[2]

We like to think of the family as the abode of love; of home as a safe retreat where any member of the family is sure of support and protection; of grandparents, parents, aunts, uncles and children as a closely-linked network of individuals who will stand united in the face of threat. The reality is rather different. Whenever human beings are held together by ties of love, whether that love is primarily erotic or supportive, aggressive tensions are also inescapable. It is our nearest and dearest who are most notably capable of provoking our intensest rage; and many of us find ourselves more easily capable of sympathetically identifying ourselves with murderers than with any other type of criminal.

Of course, it can be argued that serious violence within the family is abnormal; and I am not suggesting that homicide can be looked upon as an habitual ingredient of domestic life. But I do maintain that violence within the family is not in a category apart: that it is an exaggeration of aggressive tensions of a normal kind which are to be found in every home; and that we shall only understand violence if we also understand something about the ordinary aggressive impulses which operate within us all.

Human childhood, compared with that of other animals, is enormously prolonged relative to the total life-span of the human being. We take an unconscionable time to become grown-up. Moreover, human infants are born into the world in a peculiarly helpless state. The biological reason for this is, of course, the fact that human adaptation to the world is largely through learning, rather than by means of instinct. Human young need to be, for a very long time, both dependent and malleable, if they are to have the maximum opportunity of learning from those who are more experienced. But this helplessness and prolongation of dependency carries with it disadvantages as well as advantages. For helplessness can easily be made humiliating, and dependency necessarily involves restriction. Humiliation and restriction are potent instigators of violence in adults; but we can see their precursors in normal human infants.

---

* University of Oxford, England.

1

As psychoanalysts see it, the baby begins life as part of the mother and only gradually comes to realize his separate identity. As he gradually becomes aware of his own body boundaries, that is, the distinction between self and not-self, he also becomes aware that there is something or someone 'out there' who is essential to the fulfilment of his needs. Because of the way in which we in the West rear our infants, we are generally more aware of the baby's demands for closeness than of his demands for separateness. Babies who spend much of their time in a perambulator at the end of the garden would, if they could speak, be more likely to complain that they were not getting enough contact with their mothers than that they were getting too much. But the stage is soon reached when the baby becomes independently mobile, and at that point he begins to show resentment if his movements are interfered with. Although he needs to return to the mother to find support and warm contact, he also needs to differentiate himself from her and to define himself as a separate entity. For this purpose a certain amount of aggression is essential; and if even a very small child never showed any aggression toward those who protect, and therefore restrict it, we should rightly suppose that there was something essential missing from its make-up. The degree of restriction we impose upon very small children is intensified by the conditions of urban life, where many dangers, like automobiles, which are absent in primitive societies, threaten those who are not yet equipped to look after themselves.

What we might call 'normal' aggression shows itself even more obviously at around the age of three or four. Here, not only restriction, but feelings of humiliation, play their part. The small child who is just learning to do things for itself will normally resent adult interference, often stamping with rage when a well-meaning adult offers to do up a button or feed it unnecessarily. One of the most frequent complaints which adult patients in psychotherapy have against their mothers is that the latter were too much in a hurry, taking out of their hands tasks which, given time, they would perfectly well have been able to complete unaided, and from which they would have got a sense of achievement. Never to be allowed to do things for oneself is both restrictive and humiliating.

This kind of aggressive self-assertion which, if not handled wisely, may give rise to violence, continues throughout childhood to reach a peak in adolescence, when further separation from the parents is necessary if the child is to break free of the restrictions of home and make new relationships in order, eventually, to create his own new and separate family. A certain amount of aggressiveness necessarily underpins the sense of identity. For how can one affirm identity without asserting difference? Adolescents, who are notoriously insecure, tend to cause unnecessary strife within the family by asserting differences from parents with too strident a voice; but, however much we may resent our 'teen-age young', we ought to be even more worried if they show no aggression towards us at all. Adults who, in their anxiety to please and their fear of any disagreement, have repressed most of their aggression, become nonentities. Psychologically, they have no separate identities, simply echoing the opinions of whoever they happen to be with. Authoritarian parents used to be blamed by their adolescent children for being dogmatic and disciplinarian. Today, many adolescents blame their parents for being too understanding and compliant. For how can one differentiate oneself from a parent who never disagrees nor asserts his own opinions? Parents who are too understanding, and who identify too closely with their children's problems, create difficulties for them in that they make the process of rebellion and differentiation something which is hedged around with guilt.

Normal aggressiveness within the family is, of course, not simply a matter of tensions between parents and children. Children are notoriously quarrelsome between themselves. They compete with each other for the parents' affection, vie with one another physically, and play games in which the archetypal theme is one of conquest. The Victorians, who in their false idealization of childhood, supposed that children were as innocent of aggression as they were of sex, treated quarrels as sin. In that children's classic *The Fairchild Family,* when Mr. Fairchild found two of his children quarrelling, his first response was to whip them, and his second to take them to view the corpse of a criminal who had murdered his brother, suspended in chains from a gibbet. This was to serve as a warning; a demonstration of what happened to children who did not love their siblings.

Today we regard quarrelling as an inescapable and necessary part of growing up. Children who have no siblings to quarrel with are at a disadvantage when they reach the larger world of school because they have not learned the give-and-take of aggressive exchanges, and do not know how to stand up for themselves. Research with subhuman primates has demonstrated that rough-and-tumble play and other forms of aggressive interaction with peers are essential if the young primate is to learn how to interact socially; that is, when to stand up and fight and when to give in. Dominance-submission interactions are part of primate social life, including our own; but the individual's place in the pecking order has to be learned gradually, through repeated encounters. Neurotic human beings very often show inappropriate aggressive responses because they have not mixed with others at the appropriate stage in childhood. Such people tend habitually to be submissive, but, if they do finally become aggressive, grossly overdo it. A great deal of human violence seems to be the worm turning; the person who has felt comparatively weak and helpless suddenly reversing this role.

In a recently published book, *The Deadly Innocents,*[3] the psychoanalyst, Muriel Gardiner, tells the story of Tom. Tom was a rejected child whose mother banned him from mixing with the rest of the family. He was kept in a shed at the end of the garden, and whipped if he made any attempt to get in touch with his ten siblings. Eventually he became delinquent. When the facts of his family life came before the juvenile court, he was taken away from home and put in the care of an uncle and aunt. Unfortunately, the uncle turned out to be a violent alcoholic who resented Tom, and who treated him almost as cruelly as had his mother. Tom managed to find a stray kitten with a broken leg which he tended with great care and gentleness. The kitten was the first creature with whom he developed ties of affection. One afternoon his uncle came home early from work, and in a fit of rage, strangled the kitten in front of Tom. When Tom attempted to bury it, the uncle trod the little cross he had made into the ground, destroying the grave. At this point Tom seized one of his uncle's guns and shot his uncle, his aunt and another woman who was living in the house.

In this case, as in many others, the ultimate act of violence occurs against a background of repeated humiliation and cruelty. The trigger may or may not be something quite trivial.

The story of Tom illustrates several points which I want to emphasize. First, many violent acts are committed by persons who have been made to feel humiliated, ineffective, and of no account. Secondly, the resentment which finally issues in violence often goes back a long way, so that the person who is attacked represents not only himself, but a whole series of other persons who have caused humiliation. Thirdly, isolation in early childhood, whether it is physical, as in Tom's case, or emotional, as in the case of children who fail to make affective ties with their peers, makes it more likely that an aggressive response will be inappropriately violent.

Tom's case is not so exceptional as we would like to think. Throughout most of the history of Western civilization, children have been abominably treated. A recent book by ten American historians entitled *The History of Childhood* begins: "The history of childhood is a nightmare from which we have only recently begun to awaken. The further back in history one goes, the lower the level of child care, and the more likely children are to be killed, abandoned, beaten, terrorized, and sexually abused."[4] Some children who have been treated cruelly grow up into adults who are themselves habitually inconsiderate and cruel, and who adopt the defence of pretending that human relationships mean nothing to them. Others remain cowed and submissive. On analysis, both kinds of person are found to have a deep sense of inadequacy.

I think we must assume that human children have a built-in expectation of affection and personal regard. Even if children are not treated with actual cruelty, but merely somewhat impersonally, as happens in many institutions, they develop a tendency toward resentment of other human beings which is very hard to erase. The long period of helplessness which we all experience as infants demands a great deal of special attention, reassurance, and loving care to make us feel that we are worth anything at all. Looked at from the point of view of a detached observer, the praise which the average, loving mother lavishes upon the trivial achievements of her infant — his first steps, or his first words, for instance — is glutinously sentimental; but those who have never experienced the irrational delights of feeling themselves, however briefly, to be the most important person in the world, tend to spend the rest of their lives looking for precisely that experience. I remember one maternally deprived woman, for example, whose emotional life consisted in forming passionate attachments to one older woman after another, in the vain hope of finding the ideal mother whom she had never had. So intense was her desire to be 'special', the adored baby, the most important person, that she passionately resented any attention which her mother surrogate might pay to anyone else. In addition, she needed to know, every minute of the day, where her adored maternal substitute might be. Co-existent with this intense emotional dependence was an equally intense rage, which manifested itself in jealousy. She came to the attention of psychiatrists only because she received a prison sentence for making a murderous attack upon the woman to whom she was at that time attached, supposing that the woman was taking an interest in someone else.

The study of parents who batter their children bears out what I have said about the relation of violence with feelings of helplessness. For such parents seem to have been made to feel, in the words of Steele and Pollock, that all they did was "erroneous, inadequate and ineffectual."[5] Even more or less normal parents know what it is to be reduced to impotence by a child who will not stop crying; and I find it easy to understand that parents who themselves have been disregarded and humiliated very easily feel threatened even by a baby. Helplessness, in animals as well as humans, generally evokes protective and cherishing responses, and is inhibitory of aggression. But these basic biological behavior patterns are easily overridden in humans; and one of the most distasteful aspects of human psychology is the fact that, once violence has begun to be used against the helpless, helplessness not only loses its capacity to inhibit, but may actually increase the use of violence. When animals of the same species engage in contests, the loser is generally allowed to go free; but men seldom let their defeated enemies escape, and often treat their helpless victims with the utmost cruelty, as if they were still a threat.

There seems little doubt that those who have themselves been neglected or ill-treated as children are more prone to treat others likewise. This argues that much human cruelty is really revenge. Revenge requires a long memory, and it may be argued that those who have been neglected or ill-treated in infancy are incapable of revenge, since they cannot recall events which took place so early in life. I am not a Kleinian, and I have never convinced myself that patients can accurately remember the emotions which they experienced during the first few months of life. But this does not mean that neglect and ill-treatment leave no traces, and every analyst must have seen a number of tragically disturbed patients who, although they cannot recall their very early childhood, give evidence of having suffered considerable trauma in that they are unable to regard the analyst, or indeed any other human being, as anything other than a malignant persecutor. The surgeon, George Crile, in his book, *A Naturalistic View of Man,* suggests an explanation of how infantile trauma can continue to operate, although it cannot be consciously remembered.

The experiences of early childhood are firmly recorded in the lower centres of the old brain and exert a profound effect on subsequent behavior. However, they are isolated and inviolable. There is no way for them to become connected with the interpretive (temporal) cortex which has not yet developed, and hence they can never be either retrieved as memories or altered by comparison with subsequent experiences. They are like the patterns of behavior that are inherited as instincts, or are acquired as a result of imprintation.[6]

I find this explanation illuminating, although it sheds a depressing light upon some of our patients in that it implies that some basically pathological behavior patterns are incapable of modification by any means at our disposal.

However, although I believe that those who have been ill-treated are more prone to violence, I also think that a violent potential exists in every one of us. For each of us knows what it is to be entirely in the power of others; to be so helpless that our simplest physical needs have to be attended to by others; to be picked up, put down, moved around or left to cry entirely at the whim of others. However benign his parents, the small child cannot be unaware of his own helplessness, nor fail to resent the fact that he is entirely at the mercy of creatures much larger and more powerful than himself. No wonder Thomas Szasz begins his book of aphorisms, *The Second Sin,* by affirming that "childhood is a prison sentence of twenty-one years."[7]

Traces of our infantile experience persist in every one of us, and show themselves particularly in phantasies and other imaginative products. It is interesting that the horrific aspects of being in the power of others predominate, even when we might have supposed that a particular infant's experience was mostly benign. Swift, admittedly, was plagued by his obsessional temperament, and cannot be regarded as psychiatrically normal, but he is surely depicting a universal infantile experience when he writes of Gulliver visiting Brobdingnag, the land of giants. "That which gave me most Uneasiness among those Maids of Honour, when my Nurse carried me to visit them, was to see them use me without any Manner or Ceremony like a Creature who had no Sort of Consequence."[8] Kafka, in his terrifying novels, depicts a world in which authority is both inaccessible and capricious; in which decisions are taken with no reference to those whose lives are affected by them. In one passage in *The Trial* Kafka describes how a manufacturer and a bank official confer together about a scheme which the main protagonist of the novel, K., has put forward. "Then as the two of them leaned against his desk, and the manufacturer set himself to win the newcomer's approval for his scheme, it seemed to K. as though two giants of enormous size were bargaining above his head for himself."[9]

The fear of being at the mercy of malignant persecutors has become a reality in totalitarian states, where dissenters are treated in ways which one's worst phantasies have hardly encompassed; but, even when such a threat is neither real nor immediate, it is not difficult to persuade ordinary people that they are in danger from persons possessing evil powers. An infantile world, peopled not only by giants, but by demons and witches, exists below the surface in us all and can be brought to the surface when we are threatened by personal or collective disaster.

The history of anti-Semitism amply demonstrates that normal people can easily be persuaded, for example, that there is an international conspiracy of Jews dedicated to world domination. In the past, Jews have been viewed not only as potential dominators, but as poisoners, torturers, castrators, and ritual murderers, a collective embodiment of evil. At least some of the Nazi leaders had a megalomaniac sense of mission in which they were playing the noble role of exterminating evil.

It is easy enough to see the sinister role which paranoid projection plays in the case of people who are actually or potentially powerful. What is more difficult to understand is how the same mechanism operates in cases where the person conceived as evil is obviously weak, as in the case of a child, or a member of an outcaste group. However, there is no doubt that, in instances in which conventional power is lacking, the person designated as evil is often imagined to possess magical powers for harm. During the great European persecutions of the 15th, 16th and 17th centuries, countless old women were burned as witches whose actual potential for 'maleficium' — that is, for harm to others — was minimal. In Japan, the outcaste group called the Burakumin are at a considerable disadvantage economically and educationally compared with the ordinary Japanese. Yet these people are regarded as polluting, that is, as magically poisonous; and 'poisonous' is of course an adjective which any of us may apply to someone we particularly dislike, as if they have some kind of contaminating effect upon those with whom they associate.

Pariah castes act as scapegoats for the tensions within a society. They not only provide an outgroup to which even the lowliest legitimate members of the society can feel superior, but also can be blamed for everything evil within the society.

Exactly the same phenomenon occurs within families. Tom, the boy who killed his uncle and aunt, was not allowed to come into contact with his brothers and sisters, as if he was in some way contaminating. R.D. Laing and his collaborators have often drawn attention to the way in which psychotic symptoms are manifested by members of families who have been forced into the role of scapegoat. It has often been assumed that children are essentially evil, the embodiments of original sin. In order to subdue the devil within, severe restraint and savage punishment has been thought justifiable, almost from the moment of birth. In *The History of Childhood* one mother wrote of her son: "I whipped him till he was actually black and blue, and until I could not whip him any more, and he never gave up a single inch."[10] The boy was four months old.

The lower a person's sense of self-esteem, the more does he have recourse to paranoid mechanisms to sustain what little feeling of worth he possesses, and the more vulnerable he is to having that little undermined. It is the insecure and inadequate who most easily feel threatened, and who resort to violence as a primitive way of restoring dominance.

One way of making the inadequate feel even more so is to be critical or contemptuous of his sexual attractiveness or performance. For most human beings, self-esteem is inextricably linked with sexuality rather than with anything more rational, like intellectual achievement or goodness. Men, particularly, for obvious anatomical and physiological reasons, are vulnerable to disparagement. I do not know how many murders of women by men are the consequence of the victim taunting the murderer with his sexual inadequacy, but the number cannot be small.

The relation between sexuality and violence is one which I believe to be often misunderstood. Although violence may be the consequence of sexual frustration, violence itself seldom brings sexual fulfilment in a direct sense. There are, of course exceptions; Gilles de Rais, the mediaeval child-murderer, and Ian Brady and Myra Hindley, perpetrators of the 'Moors Murders' in Britain in the 1960's, are examples of persons in whom sexual satisfaction and murder appear to go hand in hand. But very few murders are 'lust murders'. The Kinsey team, in their book on *Sex Offenders,* write: "Child murders in connection with sexual activity receive great publicity which gives the impression that they are not infrequent; actually they are extremely rare. . . . The murder of a child as an integral part of sexual gratification is a one-in-a-million phenomenon. We discovered no such murders, but a few of the aggressors vs. children whom we interviewed had inflicted injuries that might easily have led to death."[11] And Mohr, Turner and Jerry, in their study of *Pedophilia and Exhibitionism,* write: "Although homicide of children resulting from pedophilic offences does occur, it is so rare that pedophilic offenders cannot be considered more homicidal than any other population group."[12]

In my view, human cruelty is not primarily a sexual phenomenon. The riot police wielding their clubs may become exhilarated by this manifestation of their power, but I do not believe they have erections whilst engaged in this activity. Torturers may certainly gain gratification from the torments they inflict upon their helpless victims, but this gratification is surely one of revenge; exhilaration at having a previously feared enemy at their mercy, and pleasure in retaliation for real or imagined injuries. I am not disputing the fact that men who are conscious of exercising power, even at the despicable level of inflicting pain upon others, may then become more confident in their potency in other situations, including the sexual. A certain amount of confidence is essential, especially for males, before sexual intercourse can be engaged in satisfactorily.

Persons who require the assistance of sado-masochistic phantasies, or who actually have to engage in sadistic activities before they can perform the sexual act, are persons who have no such confidence. Essentially, they believe themselves to be weak and helpless children, and other people to be grown-up and much more powerful; a belief which persists emotionally in spite of actual evidence to the contrary. Their sado-masochistic preoccupations reflect a failure to achieve an established place in a real and actual hierarchical structure with other human beings; a step which appears to be an essential prerequisite to becoming capable of a true love involvement. Although there are a few psychopathic people who act out their sadistic phantasies, by far the majority of patients who consult a psychiatrist on account of such phantasies are, in real life, passive, ingratiating, and fearful of women. Their phantasy life, split off from reality, contains in exaggerated and distorted form the active and dominant aspects of their masculinity which have been repressed and dissociated.[13]

The fact that about 80 percent of pornographic literature is sado-masochistic and that very large numbers of human beings show some interest in such writings, attests how widespread are feelings of male inadequacy. Indeed, such feelings can, without too much difficulty, be disinterred from the inner recesses of the minds of most of us. Violence, in many instances, seems to be a response to the activation of feelings of inadequacy and helplessness; and such feelings are an inevitable part of infancy and childhood, which none entirely escape. We are status-seeking creatures whose belief in our own status is easily overthrown and demands constant reinforcement. Most of us gain that reinforcement from the love and esteem of our fellows. But those who have never felt themselves to have had such love and esteem, or who cannot believe in its reality when proffered, easily resort to violence; and it is not surprising that the place where such violence most often makes itself manifest is within the family.

NOTES

1. Morris, T., and Blom-Cooper, L., *A Calendar of Murder*. London, Eng.: 1964.
2. Morris, Norval, and Hawkins, Gordon, *The Honest Politician's Guide to Crime Control*. Chicago: University of Chicago Press, 1970.
3. Gardiner, Muriel, *The Deadly Innocents*. London, Eng.: Hogarth Press, 1977.
4. De Mause, Lloyd, *The History of Childhood*. London, Eng.: Souvenir Press, 1976.
5. Quoted in: Renvoize, Jean, *Children in Danger*. London, Eng.: Routledge, 1973, p. 43.
6. Crile, George, *A Naturalistic View of Man*. Cleveland, Ohio: World Publishing Co., 1969.
7. Szasz, Thomas, *The Second Sin*. London, Eng.: Routledge, 1974.
8. Swift, Jonathan, "A Voyage to Brobdingnag" in *Gulliver's Travels and Selected Writings in Prose and Verse*. Hayward John (ed.), London, Eng.: Nonesuch Press, 1963.
9. Kafka, Franz, *The Trial*. (Trans. Willa and Edwin Muir) London, Eng.: Secker and Warburg, 1956, p. 136.
10. De Mause, Lloyd, *op. cit.*

11. Gebhard, Paul H.; Gagnon, John H.; Pomeroy, Wardell B.; and Christenson, Cornelia V., *Sex Offenders*. London, Eng.: Heinemann, 1965, p. 134.
12. Mohr, J.W.; Turner, R.E.; and Jerry, M.B., *Pedophilia and Exhibitionism*. Toronto, Canada: University of Toronto Press, 1964, p. 76.
13. Storr, Anthony, *Human Destructiveness*. New York, New York: Basic Books, 1972, p. 73.

PART ONE

FAMILY VIOLENCE -
PSYCHOLOGICAL AND
SOCIAL PERSPECTIVES

In his introduction to this volume, Dr. Anthony Storr draws attention to the normality of aggression. "If even a small child", he writes, "never showed any aggression toward those who protect, and therefore restrict it, we should rightly suppose that there was something essential missing from its make-up". Yet there comes a stage when natural aggressive instincts become pathological, when rough and tumble becomes sadistic, when self-assertion turns into violence. The borderline between acceptable, even desirable aggressive manifestations and those we stigmatize as 'violent' is not one which can be objectively established. The social acceptability of violence varies between cultures, within cultures and across time. The researcher into family violence is therefore forced to establish his own working criteria for identification of violence. In a paper published in 1975[1] Dr. Richard Gelles showed how important it was, in the area of child abuse, to examine "who does the public labelling of abuse, what definitions or standards are employed, under what conditions are labels successfully applied, and what are the consequences of the labelling process." The significance for social policy of the professional images of child abuse is further explored by Drs. Eli Newberger and Richard Bourne in Chapter 10 of this volume.

Differing perceptions as to what types of conduct constitute 'violence' (including family violence) is significant in theoretical discussion and partly accounts for the widely varying types of explanation given for it. Many of these theories are explored by Mr. Michael Freeman in the first part of Chapter 5. The major theories may be broken down, as Dr. Mary Lystad[2] does, into three groups. There are those which explain unacceptable violence in terms of psychological variables operating diversely on individuals. Dr. Storr's references in the Introduction to individual experiences of helplessness and humiliation and Dr. Richard Makman's account, in Chapter 3, of the prevalence of the related experiences of rejection and loss by persons known to have performed acts of abnormal violence provide further insight into the psychological aetiology of violence. Other explanations have looked to social variables, whether of cultural (class) or economic origin and have often seen the seeds of violence in the functioning of family life in the modern world. Many of these factors are considered by Professor Murray A. Straus in Chapter 2. It is also possible to look more widely across modern society and seek the causes of family violence in its fundamental cultural assumptions and values. In Chapter 1, Professor David G. Gil provides an analysis and critique of societal relations and argues that the institutional patterns and dynamics of western (especially American) society 'violate' essential processes of human development and that this "structural violence . . . tends to breed reactive or counter-violence on the personal level, leading to chain reactions with successive victims becoming agents of violence." The broad view taken by Professor Gil of the pervasiveness of violence reflects an equally broad perception of violence in terms of "acts and conditions which obstruct the spontaneous unfolding of innate human potential, the inherent human drive toward development and self-actualization."[3]

It is proper that the description and evaluation of legal and social techniques which have been developed to deal with family violence set out in subsequent pages of this volume should be read against this backdrop of theoretical diversity. Individual judgments on practical policies may reflect idiosyncratic assessments about the definition of the 'problem' (what counts as violence) and the corresponding conclusions as to the nature of its causes. While the chapters in this part of the volume are representative of some of the major developments in current thinking on this subject, it has not been possible to present the full range of contemporary theories in their richness and depth. Some writers have sought to show that our cultural patterns of violence tend to perpetuate the domination of men over women.[4] Others, such as Dr. James W. Prescott[5] and Ms. Mary van Stolk[6] have explained the phenomenon of violent behavior in humans as being a result of deprivation of sensory contacts either during infancy or adulthood. Repression of sexual desire, especially in children, is therefore seen as a major source of the violence which is integrated into modern cultural patterns. Of course, such explanations are not necessarily inconsistent with each other. They may simply represent alternative explanations of a complex phenomenon seen from the standpoint of different branches of science.

One specific feature of modern societies is given special attention in Chapter 4. There Judge Lucien Beaulieu, who was a member of the Canadian Royal Commission on Violence in the Communications Industry, examines the role of the media, especially television, in promoting the ethos of violence into family life. After his chapter was written a significant paper was delivered by Dr. William Belson to the British Association for the Advancement of Science.[7] This was a study of a representative sample of 1,565 London boys in the age range 13 - 16 years. The results provided strong evidence in support of the hypotheses that 'serious' violent *behavior* is increased by long term exposure to:

plays or films in which close personal relationships are a major theme and which feature verbal or physical violence;
programmes in which the violence seems just thrown in for its own sake or is not necessary to the plot;
programmes featuring fictional violence of a realistic kind;
programmes in which the violence is presented as being in a good cause;
Westerns of the violent kind.

However, the evidence did not support the hypothesis that television violence affected the boys' *attitudes* to violence by, for example, increasing callousness or leading them to accept violence as a way to solve problems or leading them to feel that violence was inevitable. Dr. Belson suggests that these apparently contrasting findings might be explained by the presence of an unconscious process caused by television violence whereby the boys' behavior patterns change without them being aware of it or feeling any different about violence. The evidence summarized by Judge Beaulieu and the findings presented by Dr. Belson's study seem sufficient to discharge any burden of proof that may lie on those who see the broadcasting media as major purveyors of a culture of violence and to cast the stigma of responsibility for the continuation of this culture on those who obstruct the administrative and legal measures necessary to bring broadcasters under control.

NOTES

1. Gelles, Richard J., "The Social Construction of Child Abuse" (1975), 45 *Amer. J. Orthopsychiat.* 363.
2. Lystad, Mary Hanemann, "Violence at Home: A Review of the Literature" (1975), 45 *Amer. J. Orthopsychiat.* 328.
3. See chapter 1.
4. See the discussion by Mr. Michael Freeman, chapter 5.
5. "A Culture of Violence: Philosophical, Religious and Psychosocial Foundations", paper presented to the Second World Conference of the International Society on Family Law, McGill University, Montreal, June 1977; see also Prescott, James W., "Body Pleasure and the Origins of Violence" (April 1975) *The Futurist* 70.
6. President of the Tree Foundation of Canada: see "The Sexually Abused Child", paper presented to the Second World Conference of the International Society on Family Law, McGill University, Montreal, June 1977.
7. "Television Violence and the Adolescent Boy", paper presented to the British Association for the Advancement of Science, Aston University, Birmingham, September 1977.

Chapter 1

Societal Violence and Violence in Families

*David G. Gil**

This chapter explores violence in society and in families from a holistic perspective, and suggests approaches to overcome such violence. My central thesis is that violence in families is rooted in societal violence, and therefore can be neither understood nor overcome apart from it. To study and treat violence in families as a discrete phenomenon with supposedly discrete dynamics and solutions, as is often done, rather than as a multi-dimensional phenomenon reflecting specific social contexts with which families interact, seems to me futile.

I will approach this exploration by clarifying first the concept 'violence', whose meaning varies in scholarly discourse. Since definitions of concepts are, however, not value-neutral, nor independent of assumptions, I note that I approach this exploration from an egalitarian, libertarian, humanistic and democratic value perspective, and that I accept the following assumptions concerning human nature.

Human life is a process of spontaneous unfolding of potential inherent in genetic material. This process appears to be self-motivated, tends toward expression and actualization, and does not seem to require incentives from outside forces. Yet the human life process is neither self-contained nor self-sufficient: it unfolds only through exchanges in interactions among individuals, and between them and their environments — a natural habitat and a human-created, culturally transmitted, social and psychological context. Exchanges among humans and their environments are oriented primarily toward satisfaction of biological, social, and psychological needs — a *sine qua non* of survival, health, and development. Humans seem, by nature, neither good nor evil. Their consciousness, attitudes, behavior, and relations evolve as they grow up in interaction with particular natural and social environments — historical products of the interplay among intrinsic human needs, perceived interests, emerging values, and policy choices.[1]

1. Violence

In accordance with these values and assumptions I view violence as acts and conditions which obstruct the spontaneous unfolding of innate human potential, the inherent human drive toward development and self-actualization. Such acts and conditions which 'violate' the process of human development may occur at

* Professor of Social Policy, Brandeis University, U.S.A.

inter-personal, institutional, and societal levels, and may differ in scope, intensity, and consequences. On the inter-personal level, individuals may act violently toward one another using physical and psychological means. They may also establish and enforce conditions which deprive, exploit, and oppress others, and which consequently obstruct their development. On the institutional level, organizations such as schools, hospitals, welfare agencies, and business enterprises, may through their policies and practices disregard developmental requirements of people and subject them consequently to conditions which inhibit the unfolding of their potential. Such policies and practices may be intentional or by default. Finally, on the societal level, institutional patterns and dynamics may be established and legitimated resulting in phenomena such as poverty, discrimination, unemployment, illness, *etc.*, which inevitably inhibit the development of some individuals and groups.

To distinguish collective forms of violence from personal violence, I will refer to conditions and acts obstructing development which originate on institutional and societal levels as 'structural violence'. Structural violence is usually a 'normal', ongoing condition reflected in socially sanctioned practices, whereas personal violence usually involves acts which transcend formal, social sanctions. Personal and structural violence should not be viewed as discrete phenomena, however. Rather, they should be understood as symptoms of the same social context, *i.e.*, the same values, institutions, consciousness, and dynamics. Personal and structural violence always interact with and reinforce one another. Personal violence is usually 'reactive violence' rooted in structural violence, rather than initiating violence, since experiences which inhibit a person's development will often result in stress and frustration, and in an urge to retaliate by inflicting violence on others. Structural violence thus tends to breed reactive or counter-violence on the personal level, leading to chain reactions with successive victims becoming agents of violence. Chains of violent behavior and attitudes on the personal level will, in turn, feed back into collective attitudes which reinforce structural violence.

2. Families as Agents and Arenas of Violence

Families are basic living units of societies whose functions include biological and social reproduction. In modern societies, families tend to undertake also another important task, namely, to restore the emotional stability of individuals who experience psychological strains in formal settings of everyday life. Social reproduction and restoration of emotional stability are relevant to an exploration of violence within families.

Social reproduction refers to processes through which children are prepared for adulthood. Whenever personal violence and submission to structural violence are normal aspects of adult life, families along with other agents of socialization, such as schools, reading materials, TV, and radio, will teach these tendencies and capacities to children through 'normal' child rearing and socialization practices, which include games, sports, cognitive learning, emotional milieu and relations, rewards, punishments, *etc.*

Restoration of emotional stability emerged as a significant role of families when people encountered emotionally unsettling experiences outside their homes, at places of work and in other formal settings of mass-societies, where humans are usually treated in an impersonal, dehumanizing, alienating manner. Families are now expected to compensate their members for these emotionally taxing experiences. They have become balance wheels or lightning rods for the stresses and strains of everday life, normative settings for uninhibited discharge of feelings of hurt, insult, frustration, anger and reactive violence, feelings which originate mostly outside the family, but can usually not be discharged at their places of origin. People tend to express and act out these feelings at home, rather than at their places of work or in other formal settings for several reasons. First, families are traditionally informal settings suited to emotional exchanges among members. Next, society in general, and law enforcement authorities in particular, tend to refrain from involvement in family tensions and conflicts, and risks of punitive sanctions are, therefore, limited. Finally, people tend to spend more time with their families than in formal settings, and time spent with the family tends to be less structured.

3. Propositions Linking Violence and Families

The discussion, so far, may be reduced to the following propositions:

(1) Violence comprises conditions and actions originated by humans, which obstruct the unfolding of human development throughout the life cycle.

(2) Violence, as defined here, may be a result of societal dynamics — 'structural violence', of acts of individuals — 'personal violence', and of interactions between societal and individual dynamics.

(3) Unfolding of human development tends to be obstructed when inherent biological, psychological, and social needs are frustrated or oversatiated beyond a variable level of tolerance.

(4) Whether, and to what extent, human needs are met in a particular society depends on its policies concerning resources, work, production, and rights, and on the values and consciousness, which shape and are recreated by these policies. These policies and values determine the quality of life and of human relations in societies, and, hence, the scope and limits of human development and self-actualization.

(5) When a society's normal institutional processes consistently frustrate human needs and, consequently, obstruct human development, energy thus blocked by structural violence will often erupt as reactive, personal violence by individuals and groups.

(6) Individuals will frequently discharge violent feelings and impulses in the informal setting of their families, rather than in more formal societal settings where these feelings often originate.

(7) Families will often endure discharges of displaced, personal violence from their members, as they are now the setting for restoring the emotional balance of

individuals who encounter unsettling experiences away from home, in the normal course of every-day life.

(8) Personal violence discharged within families will often set in motion chain reactions of violence within and beyond families.

(9) Families serve as unwitting agents of structural violence when rearing children in societies in which personal violence and submission to structural violence are normal aspects of life. In such societies, families tend to stress hierarchical patterns, irrational, arbitrary authority, discipline, and punishment including corporal punishment, patterns and practices which transmit to children attitudes and capacities they will require as adults in societies permeated with structural violence.

4. Structural Violence

It follows from these propositions, that if violence is to be overcome in a society and its families, obstructions to the unfolding of human potential need to be eliminated, and the institutional order needs to be transformed into a non-violent one conducive to human self-actualization in which all people can freely meet their intrinsic biological, social, and psychological needs. The written record of history does not mention many societies which succeeded in creating for themselves genuinely non-violent systems. This of course does not mean that such social systems did not exist, nor does it mean that such social systems cannot be conceived, designed and evolved now or in the future, using reason, philosophical insights and modern scientific knowledge. I have discussed elsewhere, and will summarize later in this chapter, some concrete requirements for the emergence of such societies.[2]

Many contemporary societies are, regrettably, permeated with structural violence, and so is the existing international order. Since my experiences and studies of these issues are limited largely to the United States, I will examine in the following discussion structural obstructions to human development in that country. To prevent misunderstanding, however, I hasten to note that structural and personal violence are and have been prevalent in many societies whose institutional orders are either similar to, or different from, that of the United States, including non-capitalistic and pre-capitalistic societies.

To understand the scope for human development, and the dynamics of structural violence obstructing that scope in particular societies, one must systematically examine policies regulating the key-processes of human existence: management of resources, organization of work and production, and distribution of rights in all existential spheres; and one must inquire into the nature of dominant societal values. In the United States, the dynamics of resource management, work, production, and rights distribution are rooted in the evolution and philosophy of capitalism, which emerged as a liberation movement from European feudalism and mercantilism and which gradually developed into a worldwide, social, psychological, economic, political, and ideological system. The United States became a leading force of this world system during the 19th and 20th centuries.

Because of the global structures and dynamics of capitalism, its central features and tendencies discussed below with reference to the United States, now permeate many societies linked into the capitalistic economy.[3]

Development and Control of Resources

A central feature of resource management in the United States is private ownership and control, by individuals and corporations, of most life-sustaining and life-enhancing, productive resources, including land, other natural resources, energy, human-created means of production, and human-generated knowledge, technology, and skills. Owners are relatively free from societal controls in the use of their resources. That use is directed, primarily, toward generating profits by producing goods and services for sale in markets, and investing parts of the profits in order to expand their share in the ownership and control of society's productive resources. Thus a major objective of ownership is to use what one owns and controls in a continuous process of further accumulation and concentration of property. Meeting the needs of people is not a direct objective of ownership and production but only an indirect consequence. Early theorists of capitalism assumed that in 'free markets', open competition among many self-interested, owner-producers would, in spite, or rather because, of the profit motive, result in improvements of products and productivity, decline of prices and of the rate of profit, satisfaction of people's needs rather than merely of 'effective demand', and stability and equilibrium of markets.

Actual developments in the United States did not, however, follow the theories of 'classical' economists, nor the more refined theories of 'neo-classical' economists. The powerful dynamics of profit, acquisitiveness, accumulation, and concentration resulted in gradual elimination from markets of many small owner-producers who failed in competition and whose property was absorbed by the winners. Moreover, large segments of the population, including freed slaves, never owned sufficient amounts of productive resources to participate on fair terms in market competition. At present a significant majority of the population in the United States is propertyless as far as control over productive resources is concerned, while a minority of less than twenty percent owns and controls almost all the productive resources. The majority depends consequently on the minority for access to, and use of, productive resources necessary for their survival. Oligopolies have, by now, effectively replaced whatever 'free enterprise' existed in the past in all important industries, and the economy is dominated by giant national and multi-national corporations, the results of mergers and conglomerations, whose economic resources and corresponding political influence enable them to control markets, horizontally and vertically.

Products of modern corporations are continuously being modified marginally, yet their quality is not being significantly improved. Wasteful obsolescence is built into them, forcing repairs and replacements and assuring continuous profits. Prices and profits tend to increase, and to achieve pseudo-gains in productivity. Workers are replaced by machines when such replacement is profitable. Basic needs for goods and services of large segments of the population remain unmet, while many workers are unemployed and productive capacity remains under-utilized. These latter phenomena are usually compensated partly by massive, wasteful production for present and future hot and cold wars, which are being fought to create and defend markets for economic expansion, and to assure steady sources for relatively cheap raw materials and labor. Yet in spite of compensatory tactics, the economy moves from crisis to crisis, rather than towards stability and equilibrium. To deal with recurrent crises, the government engages in 'fine tuning of the economy' and occasionally in more energetic measures such as wage and price controls, but not control over resources and profits.

A further intrinsic aspect of the economic system of the United States which results from the primacy of the profit motive is an all-pervasive, exploitative attitude, reflected in widespread waste of human potential, materials, and energy, and in frequently irreversible damage to the biosphere. Decisions by individuals and corporations concerning resource development, and types, quantities, and quality of products, are also shaped largely by profit criteria. This means that needs will not be met, when meeting them is not profitable, *e.g.,* urban mass transportation, and, on the other hand, that new, non-intrinsic needs, will be stimulated by manipulative advertising, when doing so is profitable. It also means that 'effective demand' by wealthy population segments for luxury goods and services will be satisfied through the market, while genuine needs of the poor population for essential goods and services will remain unmet.

Organization of Work and Production[4]

To understand the destructive consequences of the prevailing organization of work and production in the United States on human development, creativity and self-actualization, one needs to relate the current context to the original functions and meanings of work. Work evolved as a rational response to human needs, motivated by an innate drive to satisfy these needs. It became a *sine qua non* of human survival, self-reliance, independence, and freedom. Work used to mean all mental and physical activities through which humans produce life-sustaining and enhancing goods and services from their environments, and it involved, therefore, the integrated use of intellectual and physical capacities to conceive and design solutions to existential problems, and to try out, implement, and evaluate these solutions in the material world. It also involved the study and use by workers themselves of accumulated, transferable human experience, knowledge, and skills relevant to their respective crafts.

Being rooted in intrinsic human needs and drives, and being a central aspect of human existence, work is affected by, and affects, human emotions. Work has therefore, a significant psychological component and has evolved into a major constituent of human consciousness. Hence, it has implications for self-discovery, self-definition, self-expression, and self-actualization of humans, and for their relationships with one another.

In a dynamic sense, work and production mean the combination of past and present human capacities with natural resources in order to transform these resources into products needed by humans. Workers therefore require free access to, and use of, natural and human-created, concrete and abstract resources, including past discoveries, inventions, science, technology, tools, and other material products. To think of work apart from this fundamental requirement of using resources results inevitably in conceptual confusion. At this point, analysis of work in the United States intersects with the preceding analysis of resource control. That analysis revealed that the majority of the population is prevented from engaging in self-directed work to pursue their survival and development as they do not have the right of access to, and use of, necessary productive resources, most of which are owned and controlled by a small minority. The propertyless majority is thus dependent on securing employment from the minority, the owners of most productive resources, and on 'selling' to the owners their physical and mental capacities. In exchange for selling their productive capacities, their only marketable goods, workers receive wages, equivalent in value to a mere fraction of the goods and services they produce, while the surplus value generated by their work is appropriated by the owners of the productive resources as legitimate profits.

Yet, the propertyless majority is not merely prevented from working independently. They also do not have an effective right to employment. The scope of available employment, as all other decisions concerning the uses of productive resources, depends, primarily, on criteria of profitability, which is usually enhanced when a reserve pool of unemployed workers compete for scarce jobs, and when those ready to sell their labor for lower wages are hired. A surplus of workers in the market makes it also easier for owners and managers to control employees, and to assure discipline, submissiveness, and conformity in workplaces, in spite of the dehumanizing and alienating quality of most jobs.

The professional jargon of economists in the United States refers to workers as 'factors of production employed by capital'. There is no more revealing language to describe the antagonistic, exploitative, and alienating nature of the relationship between property owners and propertyless employees. The latter are considered and treated as means to the ends of the former, not as dignified subjects in their own rights, as self-reliant masters of their destiny and proud masters of production. Work is now designed and subdivided into minute, repetitive operations in a manner that denies workers democratic self-direction and the integrated use of their intellectual, emotional, and physical capacities, and transforms them from craftsmen into servants and attachments of machines. Whether they work with their hands or their heads, workers must always carry out someone else's instructions, since responsibilities for designing and monitoring products and work processes have been separated from persons doing the actual work. Hence, on the job, workers are not whole, fully developed and developing human beings. Only part of them, a specific function is bought and used. Employees are thus not only exploited in an economic sense by being deprived of a major share of their products; they are also oppressed psychologically, because of the dehumanizing dynamics of the prevailing organization of production which obstructs, *i.e.,* violates, the unfolding of their capacities in the work context.

A further essential feature of the division of labor and organization of production in the United States is found in the finely graded hierarchical structures which foster competition for advancement among members and segments of the work-force, inhibit solidarity among workers, and consequently protect the established order and its property and power relations. Consciousness shaped within these competitive, hierarchical contexts causes people to strive, selfishly, for upward mobility, and blinds them to the futility of these strivings in the aggregate. Human relations and experiences in competitive, hierarchical settings are deeply frustrating, since everyone is perceived as everyone else's potential adversary and ends up lonely and isolated. Selfish competition for entering the work-force in order to survive, and for advancing within it in order to improve one's lot, has become also a major source of prejudice and discrimination on the basis of sex, age, race, ethnicity, religion, *etc.*

It is important to realize that the exploitative and alienating dynamics of work in the United States affect and trap nearly everyone in and outside the work-force, and not only the economically deprived segments of the population. Unemployed and marginally employed workers, and workers who lack significant skills suffer objective economic hardships and social and psychological alienation, while steadily employed workers, be they technicians, professionals, academics, or administrators, may be less affected by objective, material deprivation, yet their social and psychological alienation is as real, if not more so, than that of the former group.

In summary, this discussion of the organization of work and production in the United States reveals that when workers are prevented from using productive resources freely, on their own responsibility, and under their own direction, and when labor is sub-divided into hierarchies of largely meaningless 'jobs', work loses its original, rational, potentially enriching and self-actualizing quality, and is transformed into forced and dehumanizing labor which obstructs human development. It is no longer aimed directly at the satisfaction of biological, psychological, and social needs of workers, but at securing wages, *i.e.,* purchasing power in markets whose goods and services are produced and sold to generate profits, rather than to satisfy intrinsic human needs. Rational, productive behavior, rooted in a logic of human survival, development, and enhancement of the quality of life for all, has been replaced by essentially irrational, pseudo-productive activities, rooted in the internal logic of capitalistic dynamics, according to which the perceived interests and profits of a minority are more important than the satisfaction of human needs and the unfolding of the inherent human potential of the entire population.

Socialization

Analysis of work and production needs to shed light also on the processes through which children are prepared for roles as citizens, wage-laborers, and surplus people. Settings for these processes are schools and, in a more subtle way, families. Schools, from nursery through graduate and professional, are formal mechanisms and families are informal training grounds, for the reproduction of a work force and an unemployed labor reserve.

Schools carry out their function mainly by shaping the consciousness and mind-sets of students within authoritarian, hierarchical structures which resemble, in many ways, the structures and dynamics of workplaces. Schools foster competitive dynamics and inculcate values, beliefs, and behavioral tendencies appropriate for adjustment to the prevailing reality of workplaces. Development of intellect, critical thought, talents, imagination, creativity, and individuality are usually minor objectives of schooling, since only small segments of the work-force are expected to use intellect and talents at work, and to be self-directing, imaginative and creative. Most workers are expected to be conforming organization-people, rather than independent, fully developed individuals.

Schools put emphasis on identifying the select few whom they channel into superior educational settings, *e.g.* elite colleges and universities. For the multitude of students, however, who are steered into average and below average educational tracks, schools serve essentially as holding patterns (reducing the count of official unemployment), until as 'graduates' or 'drop-outs' they are ready to enter the various layers of mindless jobs of the existing work structure, the armed forces, or the pacified cadres of the unemployed. What schools do for these young people does not fit the euphemism 'education'. It is more appropriately described as massive waste and destruction of human potential, or, in the terms used here, disguised violence. This is certainly not the conscious intent of teachers and others laboring hard in schools; but it is, nevertheless, the inevitable, aggregate outcome of schooling in the United States, as long as the established division of labor and the design of work do not require fully developed human beings.

It is often assumed, erroneously, that the selection process in schools is determined by objective, scientific measurements of human capacities, and that most students are guided into adult roles fitting their inherent potential. Yet, in spite of supposedly fair tests and guidance, the aggregate results of the student selection process seem biased in favor of students from a socially and economically privileged strata. These aggregate results of the educational and occupational selection process seem to be mediated in the United States through experiences in families and schools in socially occupationally homogeneous neighborhoods. Schools in different neighborhoods vary in style, expectations, and aspirations, and although they may have similar formal curricula, their subtle messages and their milieu will nevertheless vary significantly, and will reflect the dominant social reality of people living in their respective neighborhoods and communities. This aspect of homelife and schooling assures that the work-force is reproduced not only in its entirety, but that every layer is reproduced largely on its own social turf.

Families and schools interact and mutually reinforce their respective contributions to the process of social reproduction based on inter-generational continuity. As a result, children will end up within social, economic, and occupational ranges similar to those of their parents, although some individuals will transcend this general pattern and will thus reinforce the myths and illusions of democratic meritocracy, equal opportunity, and free mobility. The general pattern however has little to do with the actual distribution of innate capacities among children, nor does it reflect preferences of poor families and occupationally marginal workers and their children. Rather this pattern reflects powerful and durable dynamics which permeate societies stratified by wealth, occupation, and social prestige, dynamics which subtly force families and schools to play unwitting roles in reproducing a hierarchically structured work-force out of correspondingly structured social strata.[5]

Rights are social constructs, rather than 'natural' phenomena, as is sometimes erroneously and wishfully claimed. Legitimate rights of individuals and groups in a society are products of societal processes involving conflicts, choices, and decisions, before they become formalized in social policies.[6] The roots of rights are human needs, the more intense of which, such as needs for food and human relations, are natural in origin. However, which and whose needs will be satisfied out of a society's natural resources and human-created wealth, on what terms, when, and to what extent, depends always on societal choices. In short, rights are explicit or implicit societal sanctions, for satisfaction of specific human needs of certain individuals and groups, out of society's concrete and symbolic resources.

In the United States, rights tend to be linked to the prevailing distribution of control over productive resources, and the organization of work and production. The overall result of the links among resources, work, and rights is that the majority of the population who do not own productive resources and who depend on employment provided by owners, tend to be relatively disadvantaged in the distribution of every kind of right.

Legitimate rights to material goods and services are distributed in the United States mainly through market mechanisms, which means that those who can afford the price have an effective right to purchase the goods and services they desire. Purchasing power, a function of wealth, earned and unearned income, and credit, is, therefore, a rough index of rights available to individuals and groups. This index is certainly valid for such items as food, housing, clothing, health care, transportation, education beyond publically provided schooling, recreation, *etc.*, all of which are usually available for purchase, rather than as entitlements provided as public services. Only the most deprived segments of the population whose purchasing power falls below a defined level, are entitled to receive limited, and often inferior shares of these items through transfers of purchasing power or in kind from public welfare agencies.

Wealth, a major source of purchasing power, and hence of rights, tends to be highly concentrated. To illustrate, in the United States, in 1972, one percent of the population owned 56.5 percent of all corporate stock, and six percent owned 72.2 percent.[7] For the majority of the population, those without significant shares of wealth, money-income is consequently the main, and frequently the only, source of purchasing power. Credit, another important factor of purchasing power, tends to be related to wealth and income, and need not be examined separately here.

Perhaps the most pervasive, taken for granted, yet least acknowledged aspect, of 'making a living' in the United States by generating income and accumulating wealth is the competitive and thoroughly dehumanizing quality of these activities. To be sure, there are codes of civility and fairness which supposedly govern these processes, codes which are meant to soften and counter-balance the underlying dynamics of a jungle mentality. Yet these codes tend to be enforced primarily toward less powerful players in the competitive game of 'making a living', while the more powerful actors possess, and use, the means (money and lawyers), to get around the codes. For what matters in the end is the 'bottomline', and arguments for decency, morality, and constraints tend to be considered utopian, old-fashioned, or unmanly.

For most people income means wages or salaries, specific rewards for holding specific jobs. Different jobs command different levels of rewards, differences which are often assumed to reflect different levels of specialization, preparation, risks, difficulties, *etc.,* but which upon analysis appear to be related largely to social power and the internal logic and dynamics of competition. Most people prefer better paying jobs and the wider scope of effective rights attached to such jobs. People will, therefore, compete ruthlessly for scarce jobs, and for promotions to even scarcer, better paying jobs. As competition for jobs becomes a way of life, those involved in it come to relate to one another antagonistically, as objects to be used for selfish ends and overcome in competition. Such relations among people are the general model for success in the 'rational' drive for 'better' jobs, larger incomes, and a broader scope of effective rights but they are also the general model for all violence. One can thus not avoid two related conclusions, (1) that latent, and often not so latent, inter-personal violence is an essential, though not sufficient, requirement for success in the competition for incomes and rights, and (2) that legitimate rights in competitively organized societies tend to be rooted in latent or manifest violence.

The foregoing conclusions are reinforced when one recalls the history of wealth accumulation, the most potent source of rights. In the United States, the roots of this accumulation are complex processes of large-scale appropriations and expropriations of land and other resources. Without systematic, forceful expropriations which began in colonial times, a small minority could never have achieved the present levels of accumulation and concentration of wealth. This was not a voluntary process, as far as its victims are concerned, but was accompanied by overt and covert force and violence, until its results were rationalized, sanctified, and legitimated *ex post facto.* Once legitimated, accumulation through expropriation changed from a lawless, violent process into lawful, violent conditions or structures. To maintain the status quo, continue the process of accumulation and provide it with an appearance of legitimacy, two complementary processes were gradually perfected: a system of socialization-indoctrination, to shape people's consciousness and assure 'voluntary' adjustment to the structual violence of the established order, and a constant presence of latent, potential force and violence, often euphemistically referred to as a system of law-enforcement and criminal justice, to enforce compliance when socialization proves inadequate.

Violence was not only essential to initiate, defend, and maintain the process of accumulation of wealth. As indicated in the analysis of work and production, structural violence is also an essential aspect of preparing and controlling a work-force and a labor reserve pool which together assure the continuation of the accumulation process. Once more, it is inconceivable for humans to lend themselves voluntarily to the prevailing, dehumanizing and exploitative work processes, which are the norm in the United States. This paradox is explained by the fact that submission to the prevailing context of work is the lesser of two evils. The only available alternative for most people is unemployment and a severe reduction of the scope of rights. What is celebrated as 'free' labor is thus in reality a sophisticated variation of slavery, assured by the lack of viable alternatives. One is led to the same conclusion as before: the process of accumulating wealth through the 'voluntary' work of forced labor depends on the presence of structural violence and potentially overt violence; were this violence removed, people would not voluntarily participate in the process of wealth accumulation for a minority, but would take control of their own lives and of society's resources, and would redesign production in accordance with their real human needs.

Having concluded that in the United States the drive for effective rights through income from jobs and through accumulation of wealth involves a dehumanizing mentality and overt and covert violence, it is now necessary to note some results of this drive. The lop-sidedness of wealth distribution requires no further discussion, but some comments concerning the distribution of income are indicated.

Whatever yardsticks one chooses to describe the distribution of income, several facts stand out clearly. Incomes of large segments of the population fall below government defined levels of poverty and adequacy, which means levels precluding the purchase of adequate food, housing and clothing, health care and education, transportation and recreation, *etc.* In 1975, 26 million people, about one in eight persons or over 12 percent of the United States population, were classified by the government as 'poor'. Their incomes were about one-third of the Low Budget defined by the U.S. Bureau of Labor Statistics. During the same year, about 30 percent of the population lived in households with incomes below the Low Urban Family Budget of $9,588. In many of these families, one or more persons were employed full time, yet in spite of this, incomes did not exceed poverty or marginal levels. President Roosevelt noted in 1932 that "one-third of the nation were ill-fed, ill-clad, and ill-housed", which, in view of the foregoing sketch seems to be a continuing condition in the United States.

Income levels, purchasing power, and scope of rights were probably worst for the unemployed and their families, about eight million or 7.5 percent of the work-force throughout 1976 and 1977 by official count, and for the additional millions who are no longer counted in the work-force who must exist on meager support from government welfare agencies. To round out this sketch of income insufficiency as a measure of rights deprivation, one needs to note that the figures quoted here refer to the total U.S. population. When one examines the situation of minority groups, the incidence of income insufficiency and of deprivation of rights is significantly higher.

It seems hardly necessary to note that individuals of all ages whose rights to material necessities are as limited as reflected in this sketch, are likely to experience obstructions of varying intensity to the free unfolding of their innate human potential: they are constantly confronting structural violence which undermines their bodies and souls.

Economic and biological rights, *i.e.,* rights to material goods and services are fundamental in terms of human survival and development. Yet social, psychological, civil and political rights are not less important. These rights, though less concrete and more symbolic, are nevertheless as real as economic rights, and being deprived of them is likely to have equally destructive consequences for the unfolding of human potential.

Social recognition, human dignity, and social prestige tend to accrue in the United States to individuals and groups who possess material wealth, and to those who receive relatively large incomes related to knowledge and skills, such as professionals, academicians, administrators, some skilled crafts people, political leaders, athletes, artists, *etc.* The multitude of propertyless, low-skilled and unskilled, workers and unemployed on the other hand, receive relatively little or no recognition, dignity, prestige, and income. Social relations tend to be stratified by wealth and prestige. Those who are wealthy and prestigious associate with one another and avoid social intercourse with those who are materially and socially less advantaged or deprived. Less advantaged groups tend to follow the same patterns of social relations, participation, and segregation, stratum by stratum. These tendencies are reflected in residential patterns, social clubs, schools, and even religious congregations, all of which tend to be segregated by economic and social criteria. Racial segregation is merely one aspect of social and economic segregation, yet frequently the only form of segregation addressed by public policy. The result of these dynamics of social relations, participation, and segregation is a society deeply divided not just by skin-color, as noted by a Presidential Commission on Civil Disorders in 1967, but along multiple social and economic lines.

The pursuit of individual self-expression and self-actualization is less tied to wealth and income than other social and psychological rights, although a minimum level of economic security seems essential before people develop a sense of individuality and self-worth and are motivated to search for self-expression and self-actualization. Yet this issue defies simple, material solutions. In the United States, it seems that wealthy and privileged individuals do not attain satisfaction of these innate human needs to a significantly larger extent than poor persons and persons with adequate incomes. One is therefore, forced to conclude that the right to become an individual in the fullest sense, to explore, unfold, and express one's innate potential, has been sacrificed to materialistic ends, and is now effectively lost for nearly everyone. The inherently violent dynamics of competition, acquisition, domination, exploitation, and dehumanization seem to preclude this right for everyone trapped in these dynamics, be they agents or victims of violence.

Civil rights, individual liberties, and due process are in theory distributed equally in the United States, yet in reality it is more difficult for economically and socially disadvantaged individuals and groups to know, claim, and exercise these rights than it is for more privileged ones. Moreover, prevailing competitive dynamics among multiply divided, antagonistic groups tend to result in biased attitudes and discriminatory practices which interfere with the exercise of civil rights of economically and socially deprived and discriminated against groups. Actual practices concerning civil rights in the United States reveal that these rights are not separable from the economic and social context as is often erroneously assumed, and that equality of liberty depends on equality of economic, social and political rights. As for political rights, such as access to information, participation in decisions affecting one's life, and sharing responsibilities for public affairs, these too tend to be distributed in the United States in association with economic power and social rights. Similarly to civil rights, political rights are in theory distributed equally in a formal democracy, yet the same forces and processes which interfere with the exercise of equal civil rights result also in a skewed distribution of political rights and power.

Values

Values are culturally transmitted guides for human behavior and relations whose sources and rationale are usually widely repressed. These sources can always be traced however, to human needs and to efforts by groups of humans to meet these needs by trial and error and by conscious choices concerning universal existential processes. Values were evolved to encourage and enforce particular solutions and practices considered appropriate in terms of perceived interests of entire societies or sub-groups within societies.

The dominant values in the United States, which shape and are reinforced by policies and practices concerning resources, work, production, and rights, seem rooted in an early, unsophisticated view of human existence, according to which individuals ought to take care of their own needs and the needs of their kind. This, not unreasonable, concept of social reality led logically to practices and values of self-centeredness and acquisitiveness which seemed conducive to meeting the needs and ends of the self in sparsely populated environments. It also led to an attitude of suspicion toward others, especially strangers, who came to be regarded as potential threats to security and as adversaries against whom one had to compete in the constant drive for life-sustaining and life-enhancing resources and against whom one had to defend one's acquisitions and possessions. Implicit in these emerging attitudes and practices was a perception of the lives of others as less important or of lesser worth than one's own life and the lives of one's kin. This perception became the source of socially structured inequalities among people, and of the notion that others could and should be used as means for the ends of the self, rather than treated as equals, and that they can and ought to be dominated to assure their availability to serve the ends of the self.

These simple, internally logical notions, and practices and experiences derived from them, as well as reinforcing them, have resulted in the currently dominant values of selfishness, inequality, domination, competition, and acquisitiveness. No doubt, one can discern in the United States also alternative values, namely, equality, liberty, regard for the needs of others, cooperation, and sharing. However, this alternative paradigm, which derives from more sophisticated existential assumptions, plays, for the time being, only a minor role in shaping policies, institutions, attitudes, behaviors, and human relations. Given the dominance of the former values people tend to be concerned primarily with their own needs and development. The inevitable, paradoxical result is a progressive deterioration of everyone's scope for needs-satisfaction and self-actualization, an unintended consequence of competitive struggles for survival and success of all against all, and of uncritical conformity to the internal logic of the dominant values. Thus in a tragic twist of fate, the individualistic pursuit of well-being seems to have turned into a certain course toward collective insanity and suicide.

5. A Paradigmatic Revolution Toward Non-Violent Societies[8]

The foregoing examination of institutional patterns and values in the United States reveals that structural violence and its multi-faceted consequences are now inevitable, normal byproducts of the established way of life. Earlier, I noted specific, compelling links between structural violence and violence in families, and I argued that the latter cannot be eliminated unless the former is overcome. This hypothesis leads to the crucial question whether, and how, structural violence can be overcome — the issue of 'primary prevention', which must now be confronted.

Before examining this issue, however, it is important to note that much can, and should, be done short of primary prevention, to ameliorate the destructive consequences of structural violence and of violence in families. In my view, there is no insurmountable contradiction between primary prevention and amelioration, as long as one does not mistake the latter for the former. Moreover, as I have argued elsewhere, amelioration can actually be practiced in accordance with a radical, preventive perspective and could become an integral aspect of a comprehensive political strategy for fundamental transformations toward a non-violent societal existence.[9] Unfortunately, ameliorative work in the United States conforms to a conventional, supposedly politically neutral, model of professional practice, which, by implication, accepts the structurally violent status quo as a constant, and promotes adjustment to its patterns and dynamics, rather than conscious struggle for its transformation.

Turning to the issue of primary prevention of violence on all levels, reason seems to suggest, and a critical study of history reveals, that human existence can be, and has often been, organized in a manner conducive to the unfolding of everyone's innate potential, which means free from structural violence. Non-violent, cooperative and egalitarian societies of varying sizes have existed throughout humankind's history as constant counterpoints to the major themes of force, violence, domination, and exploitation, and have demonstrated their feasibility and viability in various parts of the globe, among diverse peoples, and at different stages of cultural, scientific, and technological development.[10]

Humans in such societies think of themselves as integral to nature, rather than apart from it and masters over it. They have an abiding respect for life, including human life, and they hold waste and destruction of life and of natural resources to a minimum. They consider one another of equal intrinsic worth in spite of individual differences. Hence they regard everyone's biological, social, and psychological needs of equal importance, and they treat everyone as entitled to equal rights and liberties in every sphere of life, and also subject to equal responsibilities and constraints, the latter necessitated by scarcities of resources and by equal entitlements for all. They value individuality (not the same as individualism), self-reliance and self-direction, as well as cooperation and mutual aid in collective pursuits of survival and improvements in the quality of life. They perceive no inevitable conflicts of genuine, human interest among individuals, and between individuals and collectivities, as their is not a zero-sum mentality of scarcity, but a plus-sum mentality of sufficiency created by cooperation and sharing. They reject selfishness, competition, domination, and exploitation in mutual relations. Their humanistic, egalitarian, democratic philosophy of life and society seems rooted in an idea of Protagoras, an early Greek philosopher, (480-410 B.C.): "Humans are the measure of all things".

To overcome structural violence in the United States and in similarly organized societies, prevailing policies concerning resources, work, production, and rights, need to be adjusted to the foregoing values. For these values, but not their opposites, seem to be compatible with the unfolding of everyone's inherent potential, and institutions shaped by these values are, therefore, likely to be conducive to free and full individual development. I am sketching below some concrete implications which follow from this proposition to indicate the direction in which societies need to move should they choose to overcome structural violence, rather than force people to adjust to it.

(1) Productive resources, be they concrete such as land, raw-materials, energy, and tools, or non-concrete such as knowledge and skills, should be liberated from prevailing, private controls and made accessible for use by all people. That use should be geared, rationally, toward meeting the needs of all humans, everywhere, those living now, and those yet to be born, with everyone's lifelong needs constituting a flexibly equal claim against the aggregate of resources. Criteria will have to be developed for priorities related to needs of different urgency, and for balancing current and future needs against requirements of conservation. Obviously also, waste, destruction and irrational uses of resources will have to be eliminated. Allocation decisions are difficult in any social context, but in a humanistic-egalitarian society these decisions can be made within a rational frame of reference, undistorted by narrow, selfish interests of powerful minority groups.

It is important to stress that, contrary to widespread assumptions, control over resources and their allocation must not be centralized and bureaucratized, to assure equal access and equal rights to needs-satisfaction. On the contrary, centralization and bureaucratization may themselves be serious obstacles to equal access and to equal rights to needs-satisfaction, since they involve hierarchically organized structures which tend to obstruct free and full development of individuals. The principle of free access to, and egalitarian use of, resources should therefore be implemented in a decentralized manner, involving democratic coordination and cooperation among self-directing, equally entitled, relatively small communities of producers and consumers. This means that each community should cooperatively use and control local resources, and should exchange its surplus with neighboring and distant communities on egalitarian, non-exploitative terms, so that the needs of people living in differently endowed localities can be met.

(2) Work and production will have to be redesigned thoroughly to overcome the dehumanizing quality and consequences of the prevailing modes of production and subdivisions of labor which are shaped primarily by profit considerations rather than by humanistic and egalitarian objectives. This means that work and production should once more become rational undertakings geared toward everyone's needs-satisfaction through the processes and products of work. Workers themselves should design, direct, and execute their work and should be thoroughly knowledgeable concerning all aspects of their work, so that they can become proud masters of their crafts, rather than merely 'factors of production'. Their work should not be a means toward the ends of others, but a means to

sustain their own existence and enhance the quality of their lives. Given such a redesigned context of production, workers will spontaneously develop a genuine work-ethic and work motivation, in place of the prevailing forced work-ethic which is motivated largely by fears of unemployment and starvation.

Unnecessary, unproductive, and wasteful work such as advertising, banking, insurance, real estate deals, military enterprises, *etc.,* should be eliminated, so that only work necessary for human well-being and enjoyment of life will be carried out, and individuals engaging in such necessary, productive work, will be regarded with respect for their contributions to the common good. People should be able to freely choose the kind of work they want to engage in. This would require that essential work not chosen voluntarily by enough people because of undesirable qualities should be carried out by everyone on a rotating basis. Similarly, work preferred by too many people should also be shared by rotation among all individuals selecting it. Life-long learning will be required and enjoyed by all to keep up with developments in one's work, and attain satisfactory mastery.

People will tend to cooperate at work when they are no longer forced to compete for jobs and promotions, and when everyone will have effective rights and responsibilities to participate in production as designer, decision maker, and executor. Coordination among workers and work groups should be achieved horizontally and cooperatively, rather than through vertical direction and supervision. Talents and competence of individuals should be acknowledged, and guidance from competent individuals should be sought and accepted. However, talents and competence should not become a basis for privilege, nor should knowledge and skills be monopolized. Rather, they should circulate freely, so that everyone could acquire them. Science and technology should be pursued vigorously, and disseminated widely among the population, so that workers should be able to apply scientific insights towards improvements of products and production processes.

Education and preparation for adulthood and work, in schools and at home, will be geared to everyone's full development, when a transformed mode of production will require and make use of the integrated intellectual, physical, and emotional capacities of every individual. Also, socialization at home and in the schools will no longer need to be authoritarian, competitive and punitive, when the context of work will be democratic, cooperative, and rewarding. Finally, schools will no longer be used as holding patterns for young people: they will not be needed to disguise the real scope of unemployment.

(3) Economic, social, psychological, civil, and political rights should be distributed equally as human entitlements, rather than through markets, where larger incomes, wealth, and economic power command larger shares of all kinds of rights. The distribution of rights should thus be separated from the specific roles of people in the social division of labor, and should be based instead on people's individual needs.

It should be noted though, that, contrary to widespread misconceptions, equality of rights does not mean mathematical equality, sameness, conformity, and uniformity. Rather, it means an equal right to develop and actualize oneself, and hence, to be unique and different. An egalitarian distribution of goods and services and other rights should, therefore, involve flexibility in order to allow for differences of innate and emerging needs among individuals.[11]

Equality of political rights should be implemented through open access to all relevant information, which requires, by implication, elimination of all secrecy concerning public affairs, and through participation in all decisions affecting one's life by direct participation in open meetings of one's community and indirect participation on trans-local levels through a network of assemblies representing genuinely democratic communities, rather than anonymous individuals. Service on representative and administrative bodies should be rotated and should not entitle those engaged in it to privileged circumstances of living. They should act as servants of their communities, executors of democratically evolved decisions, and not masters over people. It may be assumed that, given access to all relevant information and effective rights to participate in economic and political life, most people will develop capacities and skills to represent their communities in trans-local political assemblies, and to bring to the work on coordinating levels a perspective that integrates local and trans-local interests.

6. Epilogue

These comments on alternative values and policies concerning resources, work, production, and rights were not meant as a detailed blueprint for humanistic, egalitarian, libertarian, democratic, non-violent societies, but merely as a demonstration that such societies are not beyond the realm of reason and human potential, and that they are not 'unrealistic' and 'utopian' as is often claimed. It should also be stressed that there is no single correct model for such societies, and that different human groups would have to develop their own models, fitting their individuality by working together guided by the paradigm of alternative values. No one can claim with certainty that paradigmatic shifts in values and institutions are not possible, since human nature and natural conditions of human habitats do not preclude such paradigmatic shifts. There is also nothing inherently inevitable about presently dominant values and institutions, nor is there anything unnatural about the radical alternatives sketched here. One is therefore led to suspect that claims concerning the impossibility of paradigmatic shifts toward humanistic, egalitarian, libertarian, democratic and non-violent societies, reflect either ignorance or vested interests in the maintenance of the prevailing paradigm. Labelling alternative paradigms 'unrealistic' and 'utopian' seems to be a defensive maneuvre on behalf of the dominant paradigm, as it tends to discourage people from exploring alternatives systematically before forming an opinion about their feasibility and viability. After all, who would want to waste scarce time on unrealistic and utopian projects?

If indeed such societies are not beyond the range of human capability, as I have argued here, then people who value the free unfolding of human potential, and who want to eliminate violence from our lives, ought to participate actively in political movements which struggle for the emergence of such societies, in order to overcome structural violence at its roots, and to eliminate its 'normal' consequences and symptoms, including the destructive phenomenon of violence in families. In short, primary prevention of violence requires a political process, rather than merely professional, technical and administrative measures.

The main thesis of this chapter will remain problematic and its validity will be known only when presently dominant societal orders are transformed in accordance with the alternative paradigm sketched here. Based on experiences with collective life, on studies of anthropology and history, and on theoretical explorations, one can expect egalitarian, libertarian, democratic and non-violent societies to be conducive to satisfactions of intrinsic human needs, and hence to free development and self-actualization of their members. There is much evidence throughout history that humans can relate caringly and lovingly toward one another and that they can cooperate rather than compete, dominate and exploit as they tend to do under prevailing conditions. There are thus no genetic obstacles to caring and cooperative behaviors. Whatever obstacles interfere with such behaviors are results of social processes and social choices. Accordingly, social orders will have to be transformed if these possibilites are to become realities.

Human behavior will always be affected by socialization whatever the nature of a society will be. But processes of socialization will be liberating and enriching, rather than violent and oppressive when a society respects all individuals, considers and treats them equally entitled, and is committed to everyone's full development and participation.

Living in society will always involve limits on absolute individual freedom. Such limits are expected to reach an irreducible minimum for all individuals in genuinely egalitarian, libertarian, democratic and non-violent societies.

NOTES

1. These assumptions concerning human nature and development and the unfolding of human potential or self-actualization are based on studies and writings of humanist social and behavioral scientists, *e.g.,* Maslow, Abraham H., *Motivation and Personality.* New York, New York: Harper & Row, 1970; Fromm, Erich *The Sane Society.* Greenwich, Conn.: Fawcett, 1955; Fromm, Erich, *To Have Or To Be.* New York, New York: Harper & Row, 1976; Freire, Paulo, *Pedagogy of the Oppressed.* New York, New York: Herder & Herder, 1970; Kropotkin, Petr, *Mutual Aid.* Boston, Mass.: Porter Sargent, 1956 (originally published in 1902); Tawney, R.H., *Equality.* London, Eng.: Allen & Unwin, 1964 (originally published in 1931).
2. Gil, David G., *The Challenge of Social Equality.* Cambridge, Mass.: Schenkman Publishing Co., 1976. See especially the essay "Resolving Issues of Social Provision".
3. Wallerstein, Immanuel, *The Modern World System.* New York, New York: Academic Press, 1974.
4. Braverman, Harry, *Labor and Monopoly Capital.* New York, New York: Monthly Review Press, 1974; Gil, David G., "Social Policy and the Right to Work" (Winter, 1977) *Social Thought* Vol. III: 1.
5. Bowles, Samuel, and Gintis, Herbert, *Schooling In Capitalist America.* New York, New York: Basic Books, 1976.
6. Gil, David G., *Unravelling Social Policy.* Cambridge, Mass.: Schenkman Publishing Co., 1973.

7. *The New York Times,* July 30, 1976.
8. Gil, David G., "Overcoming Cultural Impediments To Human Survival" (Summer, 1977) *Humanity and Society* Vol. 1: 1.
9. Gil, David G., "Clinical Practice and Politics of Human Liberation", *Journal of Clinical Child Psychology* (Winter, 1976) Vol. V: 3.
10. Benedict, Ruth, "Synergy: Patterns of the Good Culture" (June, 1970) *Psychology Today;* Buber, Martin, *Paths in Utopia.* Boston, Mass.: Beacon Press, 1958; Kropotkin, Petr, *Mutual Aid.* Boston, Mass.: Porter Sargent, 1956.
11. Tawney, R.H., *Equality.* London, Eng.: Allen and Unwin, 1931.

Chapter 2

Wife-Beating: How Common and Why*

Murray A. Straus†

As the title of this chapter indicates, it has two main objectives: The first is to present some of the findings on violence between spouses from a recently completed study of American couples. These findings are unique because they are the first such data on a nationally representative sample. Although the findings have limitations, they give at least an indication of the extent to which wife-beating is part of the way of life of American families. The second objective is to help explain the paradox of why it is that the group to which most people look for love and gentleness is also the most violent civilian group or institution in our society.

The first of these objectives poses tremendous technical problems. The second objective, in addition to the technical problems, poses theoretical problems which are fundamental to our understanding of human society. Therefore, what follows should be taken as highly tentative, exploratory answers to these questions.

To be more specific about some of the problems, data will be presented on a sample of over 2,000 couples. This sample was chosen in a way which makes it extremely likely that they are representative of all American couples. Moreover, such things as the age, race, and socio-economic status of the couples in the sample correspond quite closely with census data for the nation as a whole. So far so good. But what about the data on wife-beating?

1. What is Wife-Beating?

To do research on the incidence of wife-beating, one must be able to define it in a way which can be objectively measured. Here one soon realizes that wife-beating is a political rather than a scientific term. For some people, wife-beating refers

* The materials in this chapter are presented more fully in Straus, Gelles and Steinmetz, *Violence in the American Family* (1978). The research program on intrafamily violence is supported by grants from the National Institute of Mental Health (MH 27557 and MH 13050). A program bibliography and description of current projects is available on request.
† Department of Sociology and Anthropology, University of New Hampshire, U.S.A.

only to those instances in which severe damage is inflicted. Other violence is treated as normal or is laughed off. For example, a joke I remember hearing as a child, and which I heard again on my car radio while driving across northern England, goes like this in the BBC version: One woman asks another why she feels her husband doesn't love her anymore. The answer: "He hasn't bashed me in a fortnight." Or take the following:

Concord, N.H. (AP) The New Hampshire Commission on the Status of Women has rejected a plan to help battered wives, saying that wife-beating is caused by the rise of feminism. "Those women libbers irritate the hell out of their husbands," said Commissioner Gloria Belzil of Nashua. At a meeting Monday, commission members, appointed by Gov. Meldrim Thomson, said any program to help battered wives would be "an invasion of privacy". (*Portsmouth Herald,* Sept. 13, 1977.)

This statement suggests that a certain amount of violence in the family is 'normal violence' in the sense that it is deserved (for example by 'irritating the hell' out of one's spouse) and that unlike violence outside the family, the state should not interfere.

The same conclusion is suggested by a recent conversation with a student who had decided to do a term paper on violence in the family. She came to see me for help on how to narrow the topic to something manageable. I suggested that she could choose to concentrate on either husband-wife violence, parent-child violence, or violence between the children in a family. She was astounded at the latter possibility and said "Well I never thought of my brother hitting me as violence." So there seems to be an implicit, taken-for-granted cultural norm which makes it legitimate for family members to hit each other. In respect to husbands and wives, in effect, this means that the marriage licence is also a hitting licence.

But at what point does one exceed the bounds of 'normal' family violence? When does it become 'wife-beating'? The solution to this problem which Suzanne Steinmetz, Richard Gelles and I took for our research, is to gather data on a continuum of violent acts, ranging from a push, to using a knife or gun. This lets anyone draw the line at whatever place seems most appropriate for their purpose.

2. Measuring Wife-Beating

But this 'solution' can also be a means of avoiding the issue. So in addition to data on each violent act, we also combined the most severe of these into what can be called a 'severe violence index' or, for purposes of this paper, a 'wife-beating index'.

The conflict resolution techniques (CRT) scales were used to gather this data (Straus, 1976b). These scales provide data on how family members attempt to deal with conflicts between themselves. The physical violence index of the CRT contains the following eight items:

K. Throwing things at the spouse
L. Pushing, shoving or grabbing

M. Slapping
N. Kicking, biting, or hitting with the fist
O. Hit or tried to hit with something
P. Beat up
Q. Threatened with a knife or gun
R. Used a knife or gun

The overall violence index consists of the extent to which any of these acts were carried out during the previous twelve months. The wife-beating index consists of the extent to which acts N through R occurred.

The choice of acts N through R as the wife-beating index does not reflect our conception of what is permissible violence. I find none of these to be acceptable for relationships between any human beings, including parent and child, brother and sister, husband and wife, student and teacher, minister and parishioner, or colleagues in a department. In short, I follow the maxim coined by John Valusek: "People are not for hitting".

What then is the basis for selecting items N through R to make up the wife-beating index? It is simply the fact that these are all acts which carry with them a high risk of serious physical injury to the victim. With these considerations in mind, we can turn to the question of trying to estimate the extent of wife-beating in the United States.

3. The Extent of Wife-Beating

Yearly Incidence

The most direct, but in some ways also a misleading, statistic emerging from the data on the 2,143 couples in our sample is that, for the twelve month period preceding the interview, 3.8 percent of the respondents reported one or more physical attacks which fall under our operational definition of wife-beating. Applying this incidence rate to the approximately 47 million couples in the U.S.A. means that in any one year, approximately 1.8 million wives are beaten by their husbands. But the figure can be misleading, because there are two other things which must be considered: how often these beatings occur, and how they fit in with the overall pattern of violence in the family.

Yearly Frequency

Among those couples in which a beating occurred, it was typically not an isolated instance, as can be seen from the 'Frequency In 1975' columns of Table 1. However, the mean frequency of occurrence overstates the case because there are a few cases in which violence was almost a daily or weekly event. For this reason the median gives a more realistic picture of the typical frequency of violence in the violent families. This is 2.4, *i.e.,* the typical pattern is over two serious assaults per year. But of course there is great variation. For about a third of the couples who reported an act which falls in our wife-beating category, it occurred only once during the year. At the other extreme, there were cases in which this occurred once a week or more often. In between are about 19 percent who reported two beatings during the year, 16 percent who reported three or four beatings, and a third who reported five or more during the year.

Table 1. Comparison of Husband and Wife Violence Rates

| | Incidence Rate | | Frequency* | | | |
| | | | Mean | | Median | |
CRT Violence Item	H	W	H	W	H	W
Wife-Beating and Husband-Beating (N to R)	3.8	4.6	8.0	8.9	2.4	3.0
Overall Violence Index (K to R)	12.1	11.6	8.8	10.1	2.5	3.0
K. Threw something at spouse	2.8	5.2	5.5	4.5	2.2	2.0
L. Pushed, grabbed, shoved spouse	10.7	8.3	4.2	4.6	2.0	2.1
M. Slapped spouse	5.1	4.6	4.2	3.5	1.6	1.9
N. Kicked, bit, or hit with fist	2.4	3.1	4.8	4.6	1.9	2.3
O. Hit or tried to hit with something	2.2	3.0	4.5	7.4	2.0	3.8
P. Beat up spouse	1.1	0.6	5.5	3.9	1.7	1.4
Q. Threatened with a knife or gun	0.4	0.6	4.6	3.1	1.8	2.0
R. Used a knife or gun	0.3	0.2	5.3	1.8	1.5	1.5

* For those who engaged in each act, *i.e.,* omits those with scores of zero

A more literal interpretation of the data can be obtained from looking at the figures in Table 1 for each type of violent act. By a more 'literal interpretation' I mean restricting the category of 'wife-beating' only to those who used the term 'beat up' to describe what happened (item P). This gives a figure of 1.1 percent during the year, with a median of 1.7 beatings per year among the couples who reported a beating. While this is much lower than the 3.8 percent figure taking into account all the severe, violent acts, it still represents over half a million families.

Duration of Marriage Rates

Another aspect of wife-beating which must be considered is the proportion of families in which a beating *ever* occurred. Unfortunately, our data for events before the year of the survey do not distinguish between who was the assailant and who was the victim. So all that can be reported is that 28 percent of the couples in the study experienced at least one violent incident and 5.3 percent experienced violence which we consider a beating.

In some of these cases it was a single slap or a single beating. However, there are several reasons why even a single beating is important. First, in my values, even one such event is intrinsically a debasement of human life. Secondly, there is the physical danger involved. Thirdly, is the fact that many, if not most, such beatings are part of a family power struggle. It often takes only one or two slaps to fix the balance of power in a family for many years — or perhaps for a lifetime.

Physical force is the ultimate resource on which most of us learn as children to rely if all else fails and the issue is crucial. As a husband in one of the families interviewed by Larossa (1977) said when asked why he hit his wife during an argument:

. . . she more or less tried to run me and I said no, and she got hysterical and said, 'I could kill you!' And I got rather angry and slapped her in the face three or four times and I said, don't you ever say that to me again! And we haven't had any problem since.

Later in the interview, the husband evaluated his use of physical force as follows:

You don't use it until you are forced to it. At that point I felt I had to do something physical to stop the bad progression of events. I took my chances with that and it worked. In those circumstances my judgment was correct and it worked.

Since superior strength and size gives the advantage to men in such situations, the single beating may be an extremely important factor in maintaining male dominance in the family system.

Accuracy of Estimates

How much confidence can be placed in these figures? I am reasonably confident that the sample is representative of American couples generally. But that is only one aspect of the accuracy question. The other main aspect is whether our respondents 'told all'. Here I have doubts for the following reasons:

(1) Under-reporting of domestic violence is likely to occur among two groups of people, but for opposite reasons. On the one hand, there is a large group for whom violence is so much a normal part of the family system that a slap, push, or shove (and sometimes even more severe acts) is simply not a note-worthy or dramatic enough event to be remembered. Such omissions are especially likely when we asked about things which had ever happened during the entire length of the marriage.
(2) Somewhat paradoxically, there is also under-reporting at the other end of the violence continuum — those who experienced such severe, violent acts as being bitten, hit with objects, beaten up, or attacked with a knife or gun. These are things which go beyond the 'normal violence' of family life. There is reluctance to admit such acts because of the shame involved if one is the victim, or the guilt if one is the attacker.
(3) A final reason for regarding these figures as drastic underestimates lies in the nature of our sample. Since a major purpose of the study was to investigate the extent to which violence is related to other aspects of husband-wife

interaction, we sampled only couples living together. Divorced persons were asked only about the current marriage (because of interview time limits and recall accuracy problems). Since 'excessive' violence is a major cause of divorce, and since our sample is limited to couples living together, our data probably omits many of the high violence cases.

These considerations, plus the higher rates in our pilot studies and informal evidence (where some of the factors leading to under-reporting were less) suggest that *the true incidence rate is probably closer to 50 or 60 percent of all couples than it is to the 28 percent who were willing to describe violent acts in a mass interview survey.*

4. Husband Beating

Now I come to some findings which may be surprising to some readers. This is the fact that the national sample data confirms what all of our pilot studies have shown: (Gelles, 1974; Steinmetz, 1977; Straus, 1974) that violence between husband and wife is far from a one way street. The old cartoons of the wife chasing a husband with a rolling pin or throwing pots and pans are closer to reality than most of us (and especially those of us with feminist sympathies) realize. This can be seen from an inspection of the wife columns in Table 1.

Violence Rates

The overall figures in the second row of Table 1 show that, for all violent acts during the survey year, there is only a slightly higher incidence for husbands than for wives (12.1 percent versus 11.6 percent). In addition, the overall violence index (K to R) for those wives who were violent indicates that they tended to engage in such acts somewhat more frequently than did the husbands in this sample (median of 3.0 times in the year compared to 2.5 times for the husbands). Moreover, the first row of Table 1, which gives the data on severe violence suggests that the wives were more violent even in this traditional sense of the word violence.

Specific Violent Acts

If we look at the specific types of violent acts sampled by the CRT, there is evidence for the pot and pan throwing stereotype since the number of wives who threw things at their husband is almost twice as large as the number of husbands who threw things at their wife. For half of the violent acts, however, the rate is higher for the husband and the frequency is higher for the husbands than for the wives for all but two of the items. The biggest discrepancy in favor of wives occurs in the kicking and hitting with objects. Such acts are less dependent on superior physical strength to be effective. This seems to be consistent with the view that a main difference between male and female domestic violence stems from the smaller size, weight, and muscle development of most women, rather than from any greater rejection of physical force on moral or normative grounds.

Policy Implications

Although these findings show high rates of violence *by wives,* this should not divert attention from the need to give primary attention to wives *as victims* as the immediate focus of social policy. There are a number of reasons for this:

(1) A validity study carried out in preparation for this research (Bulcroft and Straus, 1975) shows that under-reporting of violence is greater for violence by husbands than it is for violence by wives. This is probably because the use of physical force is so much a part of the male way of life that it is typically not the dramatic and often traumatic event that the same act of violence is for a woman. To be violent is not unmasculine. But to be physically violent *is* unfeminine according to contemporary American standards. Consequently, if it were possible to allow for this difference in reporting rates, it is likely that, even in simple numerical terms, wife-beating would be the more severe problem.

(2) Even if one does not take into account this difference of under-reporting, the data in Table 1 show that husbands have higher rates in the most dangerous and injurious forms of violence (beating up and using a knife or gun).

(3) Table 1 also shows that when violent acts are committed by a husband, they are repeated more often than is the case for wives.

(4) These data do not tell us what proportion of the violent acts by wives were in response to blows initiated by husbands. Wolfgang's data on husband-wife homicides (1957) suggests that this is an important factor.

(5) The greater physical strength of men makes it more likely that a woman will be seriously injured when beaten up by her husband than the reverse.

(6) A disproportionately large number of attacks by husbands seem to occur when the wife is pregnant (Gelles, 1975) thus posing a danger to the as yet unborn child.

(7) Women are locked into marriage to a much greater extent than men. Because of a variety of economic and social constraints, they often have no alternative to putting up with beatings by their husband (Gelles, 1976; Martin, 1976; Straus, 1976a, 1977b).

In short, wives are victimized by violence in the family to a much greater extent than are husbands and should therefore be the focus of the most immediate remedial steps. However, this data also indicates that a fundamental solution to the problem of wife-beating cannot be restricted to the immediate problem of assaulting husbands. Rather, violence is embedded in the very structure of the society and the family system itself (Straus, 1976a). The particularly brutal form of violence known as wife-beating is only likely to end with a change in the cultural and social organizational factors underpinning parent-to-child, child-to-child, and wife-to-husband violence, as well as husband-to-wife violence. Some of the specific steps to accomplish this have been outlined in another paper. (Straus, 1977b).

5. The Causes of Wife-Beating

Now I turn to the proposition that the causes of wife-beating are to be found in the very structure of American society and its family system. Demonstrating this, even in principle, is a vast undertaking. All that can be done in this chapter is to identify seven of the main factors and to give the general flavor of the argument. An overview of these factors and some of their interrelationships is given in Figure 1. These are:

(1) The fact that the family is a type of social group characterized by a high level of conflict. (2) The fact that the U.S.A. is a nation which is fundamentally committed to the use of violence to maintain the status quo or to achieve desirable changes. (3) The fact that the child rearing patterns typically employed by American parents train children to be violent. This in turn: (4) legitimizes violence within the family and (5) builds violence into the most fundamental levels of personality and establishes the link between love and violence. (6) The male dominant nature of the family system, with a corresponding tendency to use physical force to maintain that dominance when it is threatened. (7) The fact that the sexual inequalities inherent in our family system, economic system, social services, and criminal justice system, effectively leaves many women locked into a brutal marriage. They literally have no means of redress, or even of leaving such a marriage.

It is the combination of these factors, as shown in Figure 1 (plus others not diagrammed for lack of space) which makes the family the most violent of all civilian institutions, and which accounts for that aspect of family violence which we call wife-beating. Let us look at the first three of these factors in a little more detail, starting with the question of what makes conflict so much a part of family life.

6. High Level of Family Conflict*

Time at Risk

The most elementary family characteristic accounting for the high incidence of conflict and violence in the family is the fact that so many hours of the day are spent interacting with other family members. Although this is an important factor, the ratio of intrafamily violence to violence experienced outside the family far exceeds the ratio of time spent in the family to time spent outside the family. A moment spent comparing the family with other groups in which large amounts of time are spent, such as work groups, provides a concrete way of grasping the fact that far more is involved that just 'time at risk'.

---

* This section is adapted from Gelles and Straus (1978), to which readers are referred for a more comprehensive analysis of theories of violence in the family.

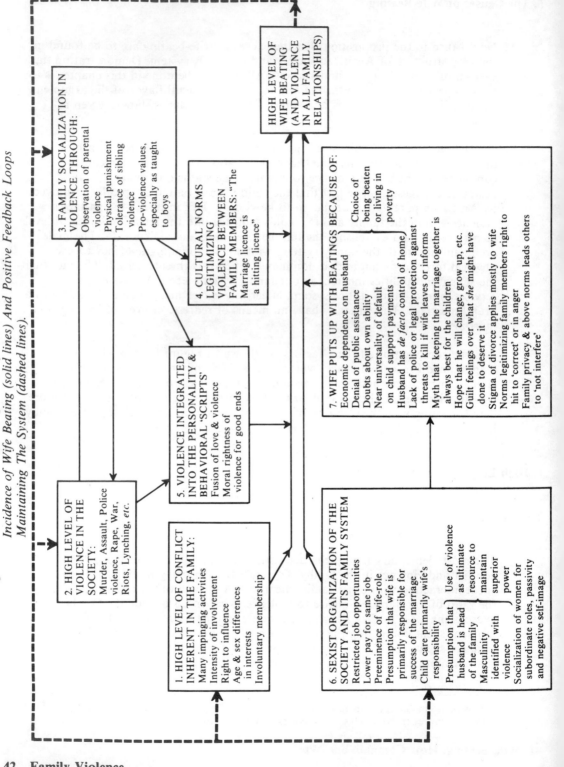

Figure 1. Flow Chart Illustrating Some Of The Factors Accounting For High Incidence of Wife Beating (solid lines) And Positive Feedback Loops Maintaining The System (dashed lines).

HIGH LEVEL OF WIFE BEATING (AND VIOLENCE IN ALL FAMILY RELATIONSHIPS)

3. FAMILY SOCIALIZATION IN VIOLENCE THROUGH:
Observation of parental violence
Physical punishment
Tolerance of sibling violence
Pro-violence values, especially as taught to boys

4. CULTURAL NORMS LEGITIMIZING VIOLENCE BETWEEN FAMILY MEMBERS: "The Marriage licence is a hitting licence"

7. WIFE PUTS UP WITH BEATINGS BECAUSE OF:
Economic dependence on husband
Denial of public assistance
Doubts about own ability
Near universality of default on child support payments
Husband has *de facto* control of home
Lack of police or legal protection against threats to kill if wife leaves or informs
Myth that keeping the marriage together is always best for the children
Hope that he will change, grow up, etc.
Guilt feelings over what *she* might have done to deserve it
Stigma of divorce applies mostly to wife
Norms legitimizing family members right to hit 'correct' or in anger
Family privacy & above norms leads others to 'not interfere'

Choice of being beaten or living in poverty

2. HIGH LEVEL OF VIOLENCE IN THE SOCIETY:
Murder, Assault, Police violence, Rape, War, Riots, Lynching, *etc.*

5. VIOLENCE INTEGRATED INTO THE PERSONALITY & BEHAVIORAL 'SCRIPTS'
Fusion of love & violence
Moral rightness of violence for good ends

1. HIGH LEVEL OF CONFLICT INHERENT IN THE FAMILY:
Many impinging activities
Intensity of involvement
Right to influence
Age & sex differences in interests
Involuntary membership

6. SEXIST ORGANIZATION OF THE SOCIETY AND ITS FAMILY SYSTEM
Restricted job opportunities
Lower pay for same job
Preeminence of wife-role
Presumption that wife is primarily responsible for success of the marriage
Child care primarily wife's responsibility
Presumption that husband is head of the family
Masculinity identified with violence
Use of violence as ultimate resource to maintain superior power
Socialization of women for subordinate roles, passivity and negative self-image

Broad Range of Activities and Interests

Most non-family social interactions are focused on a specific purpose. But the primary group nature of the family makes family interactions cover a vast range of activities. This means that there are more 'events' over which a dispute or a failure to meet expectations can occur.

Intensity of Involvement

Not only is there a wider range of events over which a dispute or dissatisfaction can occur, but in addition, the degree of injury felt in such instances is likely to be much greater than if the same issue were to arise in relation to someone outside the family. The failure of a work colleague to spell or to eat properly may be mildly annoying (or more likely just a subject for derision). But if the bad spelling or table manners are those of one's child or spouse, the pain experienced is often excruciating.

Impinging Activities

Many family activities have a 'zero sum' aspect. Conflict is structured into such things as whether Bach or rock will be played on the family stereo, whether to go to a movie or bowling, or a line up for use of the bathroom. Less obvious, but equally important is the impinging on one's personal space or self-image brought about by the life style and habits of others in the family, such as those who leave things around versus those who put everything away, or those who eat quickly and those who like leisurely meals.

Right to Influence

Membership in a family carries with it an implicit right to influence the behavior of others. Consequently, the dissatisfaction over undesirable or impinging activities of others is further exacerbated by attempts to change the behavior of the other.

Age and Sex Discrepancies

The fact that the family is composed of people of different sexes and age (especially during the child rearing years), coupled with the existence of generational and sexual differences in culture and outlook on life, makes the family an arena of culture conflict. This is epitomized in such phases as 'battle of the sexes' and 'generational conflict'.

43 Wife-Beating: How Common and Why

Ascribed Roles

Compounding the problem of age and sex differences is the fact that family statuses and roles are, to a very considerable extent, assigned on the basis of these biological characteristics rather than on the basis of interest and competence. An aspect of this which has traditionally been a focus of contention is socially structured sexual inequality, or, in contemporary language, the sexist organization of the family. A sexist structure has especially high conflict potential built in when such a structure exists in the context of a society with egalitarian ideology. But even without such an ideological inconsistency, the conflict potential is high because it is inevitable that not all husbands have the competence needed to fulfill the culturally prescribed leadership role (Kolb and Straus, 1974; Allen and Straus, 1975).

Family Privacy

In many societies the normative, kinship, and household structure insulates the family from both social controls and assistance in coping with intrafamily conflict. This characteristic is most typical of the conjugal family system of urban-industrial societies (Laslett, 1973).

Involuntary Membership

Birth relationships are obviously involuntary, and under-age children cannot terminate such relationships. In addition, Sprey (1969) shows that the conjugal relationship also has non-voluntary aspects. There is first the social expectation of marriage as a long-term commitment, as expressed in the phrase 'until death do us part'. In addition, there are emotional, material, and legal rewards and constraints which frequently make membership in the family group inescapable, socially, physically, or legally. So, when conflicts and dissatisfactions arise, the alternative of resolving them by leaving often does not, in practice, exist — at least in the perception of what is practical or possible.

High Level of Stress

Paradoxically, in the light of the previous paragraph, nuclear family relationships are unstable. This comes about because of a number of circumstances, starting with the general tendency for all dyadic relationships to be unstable (Simmel, 1955: 118-144). In addition, the nuclear family continuously undergoes major changes in structure as a result of processes inherent in the family life cycle: events such as the birth of children, maturation of children, aging, and retirement. The crisis-like nature of these changes has long been recognized (LeMasters, 1957).

7. High Level of Violence in the Society

These ten characteristics of the family, combined with the huge emotional investment which is typical of family relationships, means that the family is likely to be the locus of more, and more serious, conflicts than other groups. But conflict and violence are not the same. Violence is only one means of dealing with conflict. What accounts for the use of violence to deal with conflicts within the family? One fundamental starting place is the fact that we are talking about families which are part of a violent society. There is a carry over from one sphere of life to another, as I have tried to show in a paper comparing levels of family violence in different societies (Straus, 1977a). However, even granting the carry-over principle, this is by no means sufficient. Conflict is also high, for example, in academic departments. But there has never been an incident of physical violence in any of the six departments I have taught in during the past 25 years. In fact, I have only heard of one such incident occurring anywhere. Clearly, other factors must also be present.

8. Family Socialization in Violence

One of the most fundamental of these other factors is the fact that the family is the setting in which most people first experience physical violence, and also the setting which establishes the emotional context and meaning of violence.

Learning about violence starts with physical punishment, which is nearly universal (Steinmetz and Straus, 1974). When physical punishment is used, several things can be expected to occur. First, and most obviously, is learning to do or not do whatever the punishment is intended to teach. Less obvious, but equally or more important, are three other lessons which are so deeply learned that they become an integral part of one's personality and world view.

The first of these unintended consequences is the association of love with violence. Physical punishment typically begins in infancy with slaps to correct and teach. Mommy and daddy are the first and usually the only ones to hit an infant. And for most children this continues throughout childhood. The child therefore learns that those who love him or her the most, are also those who hit.

Second, since physical punishment is used to train the child or to teach about dangerous things to be avoided, it establishes the moral rightness of hitting other family members.

The third unintended consequence is the lesson that when something is really important, it justifies the use of physical force.

These indirect lessons are not confined to providing a model for later treatment of one's own children. Rather, they become such a fundamental part of the individual's personality and world view that they are generalized to other social relationships, and especially to the relationship which is closest to that of parent and child: that of husband and wife.

All of the above suggests that early experiences with physical punishment lay the groundwork for the normative legitimacy of all types of violence but especially intrafamily violence. It provides a role model, indeed a specific 'script' (Gagnon and Simon, 1973; Huggins and Straus, 1975), for such actions. In addition, for many children, there is not even the need to generalize this socially scripted pattern of behavior from the parent-child nexus in which it was learned, to other family relationships. This is because, if our estimates are correct, millions of children can directly observe and role model physical violence between husbands and wives (see also Owens and Straus, 1975).

9. Cultural Norms

The preceding discussion has focused on the way in which violence becomes built into the behavioral repertory of individual husbands and wives. Important as that is, it would not be sufficient to account for the high level of family violence if it were not also supported by cultural norms legitimizing such violent predispositions. Since most of us tend to think of norms which call for love and gentleness within the family, it is difficult to perceive that there are *also* both *de jure* and *de facto* cultural norms legitimizing the use of violence between family members. Once one is sensitized to the possibility that such rules exist, examples pop up all over. These rules are sometimes explicit or even mandatory — as in the case of the right and obligation of parents to use a 'necessary' and appropriate level of physical force to adequately protect, train, and control a child. In fact, parents are permitted or expect to use a level of physical force for these purposes that is denied even prison authorities in relation to training and controlling inmates.

In the case of husband-wife relations, similar norms are present and powerful, but they are largely implicit and taken-for-granted and therefore also largely unrecognized. But the fact is that, just as parenthood gives the right to hit, the marriage licence is also a hitting licence. The evidence can be found, for instance in everyday expressions and jokes, such as the ditty:

A woman, a horse, and a hickory tree
The more you beat'em the better they be

or the joke mentioned earlier in this chapter. Many of the men and women interviewed by Gelles (1974: 58) expressed similar attitudes, as represented by such phrases as 'I asked for it', or 'she needed to be brought to her senses'.

But the marriage licence as a 'hitting licence' is not just a matter of folk culture. More importantly, it also remains embedded in the legal system despite many legal reforms favoring women. In many jurisdictions, for example, a woman still cannot sue her husband for damages resulting from his assaults, because, in the words of a California Supreme Court judgment (*Self v. Self*, 1962) this "would destroy the peace and harmony of the home, and thus would be contrary to the policy of the law"!

Of course, criminal actions can be brought against an assaulting husband, but here too there is an almost equally effective bar inherent in the way the criminal justice system actually operates. Many policemen personally believe that husbands *do* have a legal right to hit their wives, provided it does not produce an injury requiring hospitalization — the so-called 'stitch rule' found in some cities. If a wife wants to press charges she is discouraged from every step in the judicial process, beginning with police officers (often the first on the scene) who will not make arrests, and going on to prosecuting attorneys who will not bring the case to court, and by judges who block convictions in the miniscule fraction of cases which do reach the court (Field and Field, 1973).

Finally, there is evidence from surveys and experiments also pointing to the implicit licence to hit conferred by marriage. Perhaps the most direct of this type of evidence is to be found in the survey conducted for the National Commission on the Causes and Prevention of Violence (Stark and McEvoy, 1970). This study found that about one out of four of those interviewed agreed with the proposition, that it is sometimes permissible for a husband to hit his wife. Equally cogent are the results of an unpublished experiment by Churchill and Straus. This showed that when presented with identical descriptions of an assault by a man on a woman, those who were told that the couple is married recommended much less severe punishment.

There is a great deal of other evidence supporting the existence of the 'marriage licence as a hitting licence' norm (Straus, 1976). What was just presented may at least make the case plausible and allow us to move on to a consideration of one other causal factor.

10. Sexual Inequality and the Violent Society

The last causal factor to be considered can be summarized in the proposition that the sexist organization of the society and its family system is one of the most fundamental factors accounting for the high level of wife-beating. Demonstrating this proposition is such a large undertaking that it would require an entire chapter in itself. Fortunately, much of the evidence has already been well documented (Dobash and Dobash, 1974; Martin, 1976; Straus, 1976a, 1977a, b). Some aspects have also been presented earlier in this paper. A summary of the main elements of sexism which lead to wife-beating is presented in boxes 6 and 7 of Figure 1.

Perhaps it is just as well that the combination of space limitations and the availability of previous work on sexism and wife-beating led to only summarizing the argument in Figure 1. Perhaps devoting an inappropriately small part of this chapter to one of the most important of the causal factors can serve to dramatize the fact that, important as is sexism in understanding wife-beating, it is only one part of a complex causal matrix. This can be seen from the fact that even though men are dominant, their dominance does not protect them from violence by other men.

If we imagine that true equality between the sexes were somehow to be achieved tomorrow, all forms of family violence (including wife-beating) would still continue to exist — perhaps at a somewhat lower incidence rate — unless steps are taken to also alter the factors identified in boxes 2, 3, 4, and 5 of Figure 1. This means steps to lower the level of *non*-family violence, and steps to end the training in violence that is part of growing up in a typical American family. Violence is truly built into the very fabric of American society, and into the personality, beliefs, values, and into behavioral scripts of most of our population. Elimination of wife-beating depends not only on eliminating sexual inequality, but also on altering the system of violence on which so much of American society depends.

REFERENCES

Allen, Craig M., and Straus, Murray A., "Resources, Power, and Husband-Wife Violence", paper presented at the National Council on Family Relations, 1975 Annual Meeting.

Bulcroft, Richard, and Straus, Murray A., "Validity of Husband, Wife and Child Reports of Intrafamily Violence and Power" (mimeographed).

Dobash, Russell, and Dobash, R. Emerson, "Violence Between Men and Women Within the Family Setting", paper presented at the VIII World Congress of Sociology, Toronto, Canada, August, 1974.

Field, Martha H., and Field, Henry F., "Marital Violence and the Criminal Process: Neither Justice nor Peace" (1973), 47 *Social Service Review* (2): 221-240.

Gagnon, John, and Simon, William, *Sexual Conduct: The Social Sources of Human Sexuality.* Chicago, Illinois: Aldine, 1973.

Gelles, Richard J., *The Violent Home: A Study of Physical Aggression Between Husbands and Wives.* Beverly Hills, California: Sage, 1974.

Gelles, Richard J., "Violence and Pregnancy: A Note on the Extent of the Problem and Needed Services" (Jan., 1975), 24 *The Family Co-ordinator* 81-86.

Gelles, Richard J., and Straus, Murray A., "Determinants of Violence in the Family: Towards a Theoretical Integration", in Burr, Wesley R.; Hill, Reuben; Nye, F. Ivan; and Reiss, Ira L. (eds.) *Contemporary Theories About the Family.* New York, New York: Free Press, 1978.

Gelles, Richard J., "Abused Wives: Why Do They Stay?" (Nov., 1976), 38 *Journal of Marriage and the Family* 659-668.

Huggins, Martha D., and Straus, Murray A., "Violence and the Social Structure as Reflected in Children's Books From 1850 to 1970", paper read at the 1975 Annual Meeting of the Eastern Sociological Society.

Kolb, Trudy M., and Straus, Murray A., "Marital Power and Marital Happiness in Relation to Problem Solving Ability" (Nov. 1974), 36 *Journal of Marriage and the Family* 756-766.

Larossa, Ralph E., *Conflict and Power in Marriage: Expecting the First Child.* Beverly Hills, California: Sage, 1977, chapter 4.

Laslett, Barbara, "The Family as a Public and Private Institution: a Historical Perspective" (Aug., 1973), 35 *Journal of Marriage and the Family* 480-492.

LeMasters, Ersel E., "Parenthood as Crisis" (Nov., 1957), 19 *Marriage and Family Living* 352-355.

Martin, Del, *Battered Wives.* San Francisco, California: Glide, 1976.

Owens, David, M., and Straus, Murray A., "The Social Structure of Violence in Childhood and Approval of Violence as an Adult" (1975), 1 *Aggressive Behavior* 193-211.

Simmel, Georg, *Conflict and the Web of Group Affiliations*. New York, New York: Free Press, 1955 (originally published 1908).

Sprey, Jetse, "The Family as a System in Conflict" (1969), 31 *Journal of Marriage and the Family* 699-706.

Stark, Rodney, and McEvoy III, James, "Middle Class Violence" (Nov., 1970), 4 *Psychology Today* 52-65.

Steinmetz, Suzanne K., *The Cycle of Violence: Assertive, Aggressive and Abusive Family Interaction*. New York, New York: Praeger, 1971.

Steinmetz, Suzanne K., and Straus, Murray A. (eds.), *Violence in the Family*. New York, New York: Dodd Mead, 1974.

Straus, Murray A., "Leveling, Civility, and Violence in the Family" (Feb., 1974), 36 *Journal of Marriage and the Family* 13-28.

Straus, Murray A., "Sexual Inequality, Cultural Norms, and Wife-Beating" (Spring, 1976a) *Victimology* 1: 54-76, also reprinted in Viano, Emilio C. (ed.), *Victims and Society*. Washington, D.C, Visage, 1976, and in Roberts-Chapman, Jane, and Gates, Margaret (eds.), *Women Into Wives: the Legal and Economic Impact of Marriage,* Sage Yearbooks in Women Policy Studies, Vol. 2. Beverly Hills, California: Sage, 1977.

Straus, Murray A., "The CRT Scales for Measuring Conflict in Families" (1976b), paper presented at the 1976 meeting of the National Council on Family Relations (mimeographed).

Straus, Murray A., "Societal Morphogenesis and Intrafamily Violence in Cross-Cultural Perspective", (1977a), 285 *Annals of the New York Academy of Sciences* 719-730.

Straus, Murray A., "A Sociological Perspective on the Prevention and Treatment of Wife-beating" (1977b), to appear in Roy, Maria (ed.), *Battered Women*. New York, New York: Van Nostrand-Reinhold.

Straus, Murray A.; Gelles, Richard J.; and Steinmetz, Suzanne K., *Violence in the American Family*. (1978) Book in preparation.

Wolfgang, Marvin E., "Victim-precipitated Criminal Homicide", (June, 1957) *Journal of Criminal Law, Criminology and Police Science* 1-11. Also reprinted in Wolfgang, Marvin E. (ed.), *Studies in Homicide*. New York, New York: Harper and Row, 1957, pp. 72-87.

Chapter 3

Some Clinical Aspects of Inter-Spousal Violence

Richard S. Makman*

1. Loss, Projection and Violence

Two concepts concerned with the normal growth and development of the
individual are particularly useful for an understanding of inter-spousal violence.
The first, that of attachment, has been elaborated most extensively by Bowlby in
his volumes on *Attachment*[1] and on *Separation*.[2] He considers attachment to be
an observable, biological process, innate to human and other animals and thus
independent of other developmental processes. Bowlby summarized attachment
theory as a "way of conceptualizing the propensity of human beings to make
strong affectional bonds to particular others . . .". "The key point of my thesis",
he states, "is that there is a strong causal relationship between an individual's
experience with his parents and his later capacity to make affectional bonds".[3]
Reviewing the evidence at the time, Scott[4] suggested "an almost absurdly simple
interpretation of the facts: that an individual at the proper period of life (six
weeks to six months) will become attached to anything in the surrounding
environment, both living and nonliving". All that is required is *prolonged contact.*
Not only is this "process of forming a social bond independent of the influences of
reward or punishment", but punishment produces anxious, clinging children 'over
dependent' and sensitive to absence of the attachment figure. The process of
attachment can readily be seen to underly the difficulty a woman has in leaving a
marriage, no matter how destructive. It also provides a way of understanding this
difficulty without misusing the concept of masochism, which has turned into a
useless, emotionally laden 'dirty' word. Thus the argument that a woman provokes
a beating, whatever its reality in a given situation, is not to the point. The issue
is the need for societal support in moving out of the relationship, including an
understanding of the necessity for overcoming an inbuilt biological system
operating in the direction of continued attachment. The question before courts
and legislatures is not how the relationship came to be, but how difficult it is to
leave it. Focus on attachment theory shifts us from an attitude of blame to one of
concern about the process of separation. Further, the time of separation itself is a
time of danger and of increased risk of violence and murder. Thus attachment

* Director, Quincy Court Clinic, Commonwealth of Mass., Department of Mental Health,
U.S.A.

theory offers a psychological rationale for the need for society to provide aid to a battered spouse during the process of separation.

The second important concept is that of projection, "the psychological process whereby a person (male or female) attributes to another (male or female) some features of his own self, especially some aspect of himself that he dislikes or is afraid of. This process must, almost inevitably, lead to false and unfavourable attributions being made about the other person and his motives . . . The most frequent usage of the term 'projection' is to denote our propensity to attribute our failings to others and to be blind to them in ourselves . . .".[5] Projection also underlies a paranoid style of thinking as well as the development of paranoid delusions. A relationship between projection, violence and paranoia is suggested. Mack et al,[6] analysing matricide, a rare crime, suggest that for the murderous act to occur a particular psychic mechanism is required. "If the son can devalue his mother sufficiently and find justification for the murder in convincing himself of the mother's perfidious nature, declaring to himself that she deserves to be killed, then the superego prohibitions and the ego controls may be overcome." Russell,[7] discussing the *Ingredients of Juvenile Murder,* further elaborates this mechanism, illustrating the development of a system of "self justification through paranoid construction" as an integral part of the trigger mechanism for the act of murder itself. In reviewing cases of assault evaluated in our court clinic I am struck by the regular appearance of this mechanism, so that I would propose that the commission of any violent act is preceded by a more or less well-formed belief in the badness of the other person. This paranoid-projective mechanism may be limited to the circumstances surrounding the act itself, the personality structure remaining intact, or part of a more global psychopathology, from paranoid personality to outright paranoid schizophrenia.

In persons who commit violent acts there is less uniformity of diagnosis than of background. The backgrounds are littered with rejection, loss, and family turmoil, providing a fertile ground for the experience of hate. Bowlby[8] drew attention to the frequency with which anger is aroused after a loss, not only in children but in adults. "In its functional form", he states, "anger is expressed as reproachful and punishing behavior" meant to "discourage further separation". In its dysfunctional form, anger is so intense and persistent that it weakens the bond and alienates the partner. "Whenever thoughts or acts cross the narrow boundary between being deterrent and revengeful, feeling ceases to be the hot displeasure of anger and becomes the malice of hatred." When sitting face to face with the intense rage that can issue forth, almost visibly, from a hateful person, one is struck by the power of this peculiarly human affect: a fifteen-year-old student, who ran from home, ground his teeth as he spoke of his father, "I want him dead. Either he dies or I leave home". His father, whom he described as 'more stubborn' than himself, would not allow him to leave home under any circumstances. An older brother had been shot at camp, probably a suicide. He stated further, "I have too much life instinct to kill myself, but I could kill someone else".

Any person may be viewed as the product of and a participant in several 'systems'. Not only is the individual personality such a system, but the marital dyad, the family, community, society, the culture — each has a structure and rules of its own, each its own influence on behavior and its own potential for pathology and, as luck would have it, for intervention. Inherent in the idea of a nuclear

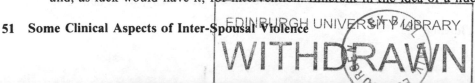

family is the assumption that the marital pair serves a central, vital function as the force relating these various systems, transmitting their particular influence on behavior through the interlocking life cycles of their parents and their children. Unconscious forces, reflecting childhood experiences, tend to perpetuate behaviors across generations; whereas conscious forces, reflecting adult capacity to will behavior, tend to modify such behaviors. To put it another way, to a greater or lesser extent, parents find themselves acting just like *their* parents despite their intention *never* to act that way *ever*. Considering this vital role of the marital couple, it is surprising to find that the special characteristics of the marital system have only recently been the subject of clinical investigation. Berman and Lief,[9] reviewing current concepts of marital therapy, outline a marital life cycle which parallels the tasks and stages of the individual adult life cycle. "It is crucial to recognize that critical stages in the marriage are intimately related to critical stages in the individual life cycle. Issues that appear to be either purely individual or purely dyadic are often actually the result of a complicated interaction between marital and individual crisis points." Pregnancy, for example, is identified as a critical point for both individual development and the marital dyad, straining the individual capacity for intimacy and caring while requiring a renewed commitment to the marriage. Using this framework, it is not surprising to see repeated reference to wife battering during pregnancy.

A middle aged, respected professional man, whose marriage is basically successful, became enraged at his wife by just thinking about her supposed deceit in becoming pregnant just as he finished his training. He did not beat her, but he 'treated her like dirt', acting nasty, going out with the boys and having a brief affair. On the individual level, he was the last and unwanted child of an older couple who basically ignored his needs and treated him as the bad child. He received a final punishment when his parents' will was read, for he received only a fifth as much of their estate as his siblings. On the marital level, his wife's pregnancy meant a withdrawal of support, for it meant depriving him of the chance to obtain those material things he had never been given and, more importantly, it meant his energy would be diverted from his own advancement, from the 'recognition' he needed to prove his own masculinity. He viewed the pregnancy as the result of her conservative Catholicism, which made her refuse to use contraceptives.

The psychological mechanism of projection has a special place in the development of a disturbed marriage. In the context of the marital relationship the process is modified to become the mechanism of projective identification. Basically, as described above, one or both partners has grown up with a residue of hateful or bad feelings that are not an acceptable part of his/her self image. As Zinner[10] puts it, "the projection of disavowed elements of the self onto the spouse has the effect of charging a marital relationship with conflict that has been transposed from an intrapsychic one to an interpersonal one. One woman whose cat and dog marriage was undergoing conjoint treatment states, 'I feel better when my husband hates me than when I hate myself.'" The characteristics of projective identification are summarized as follows: one partner perceives the other as possessing traits that are unacceptable in his/her own personality. Secondly, the partner works to evoke just those behaviors in the spouse, confirming suspicions; or has chosen a partner who in reality conforms to those expectations. Thirdly, this does not merely rid the person of these feelings; they are experienced vicariously, while denied as one's own, thus both lowering intrapsychic tension and intensifying the attachment to the partner. And finally, the marital partners are often in collusion with one another to sustain mutual projections.

2. Some Case Histories

The following case histories illustrate the central role of loss in precipitating violent behavior. 'A', a 24-year-old high school graduate, working irregularly as a landscaper, is before the court on charges of assault with a dangerous weapon, not against his wife. Mixed in with a lengthy record are two other assault charges. As an infant, a seizure left one arm and one leg crippled. He had compensated by adopting a pugnacious, rough and ready attitude, telling the world, "Don't assume there is anything I can't do". Family conflicts were prominent in his thoughts. His father, a military man, rejected him as a misfit; later bluntly saying, "Stay out of my life". 'A' recalled that at age eight, his father, drunk as usual, struck his mother, cutting her on the forehead. When he was ten years old, his mother came close to death from peritonitis complicating a hysterectomy. She died an alcoholic death one year ago. He held his father responsible for her death. Nevertheless, if his father would offer friendship, he would welcome it. Following his mother's death, he met his future wife, lived with her awhile and now has been married four months. He had several pet peeves, whose infraction would enrage him. Primary amongst these was the thought of a man hitting a woman.

The current incident had the following background. He had suffered two recent setbacks — an operation on his arm had failed to give him the hoped for increase in mobility; he was told at work he was not allowed to use a machine because of his physical handicap. He had had an argument with his wife that morning. He was on his way to pick her up at work. He knew she would be late. A car pulled sharply in front of him. He yelled; they swore at each other; they got out — the other guy was bigger, so 'A' grabbed a pipe from his car. 'A' wished he could treat other people like he did his wife: when he was angry with her, he 'bit his tongue'. It is of interest that 'A's' wife was close to a brother recently imprisoned for life on a charge of kidnapping and rape, for she had chosen a man who on principle would not be violent towards a woman, but who had difficulty not being violent.

'A' was a most cooperative subject. He was very like a wife-beater except that he decided not to hit a woman. Later he was back in court. He had changed his mind. He was charged with beating up his wife. His wife had left him. He was devastated. He did not know why she had left. He waits near her apartment. When she returns he abuses her and threatens her. The police say she has dropped charges twice before as she has this time.

Mr. and Mrs. 'B' were seen together. 'B' is 49, still smarting from embarassment at being brought to court, scowling at his wife and suspicious of my questioning. Although working steadily as a repairman for an electric company, he had a partial disability from shrapnel wounds, including a head injury, and a breakdown suffered during the Korean War. His wife, 35, appeared tearful, anxious and fearful. She was seven months pregnant. Married eight years, they have three children, ages eight, seven and eighteen months. This was the second time he had threatened to 'split her head open' and had hit her. The first time she was pregnant with their youngest child. She came to court not so much because she was hurt as because she had been holding the baby and both were struck. She believed the episode was caused by his taking a sleeping pill. He was a good husband and they loved one another.

Mr. 'B' was bitter: "Women are always right. They have it their way. They go out the door and kick the husband. If you don't like it, divorce me. I won't stop." He insisted that his wife did not look after the children adequately. His demands were obviously unreasonable. He complained he had to spend money on toys. He had just purchased his son a Big Wheels and his wife had allowed him to share it with other children. The tires were already worn out. He had watched for two hours and noted she had not prevented this. He was impervious to her argument — that the other children shared their bikes with his son, that she could not police his every move, not only because of her pregnancy but because she had been up all night with the baby, who had croup. As the interview went on his attitude changed markedly. He became calm and concerned about his behavior and expressed fondness for his wife. The focus changed as associations with loss came forth, suggesting a concern for his children's safety. An uncle had died 20 years ago, struck by a car and 'cut in two'. His father had died ten years ago after a year's struggle with cancer. 'B' had seen buddies blown to bits in the war; even now he was uncomfortable thinking about it. His work was dangerous — recently a fellow worker had touched a live wire and went up in flames. Although living in a well-to-do neighborhood, teenagers drove to and from the beach at the end of the street at 50 miles per hour.

Mrs. 'B' called after the interview was over to elaborate her husband's secretiveness: he had been married previously and had 'driven his wife insane'. He did not want more children, yet would not allow Mrs. 'B' a tubal ligation because it would 'give her cause to play around'. He had agreed to a vasectomy but his procrastination had resulted in the current pregnancy. Although his earnings were high, he spent money irrationally, especially for toys, and was in debt. Mrs. 'B' did not want a divorce: she dropped the charges. She did mention that there were severe problems in her growing up, but these were not elaborated. Her grandfather beat her mother, apparently with a sadistic flourish, tying her up. Her grandmother had 'driven her mother crazy'. These factors no doubt played into her choosing a disturbed husband and contributed to her tolerating a difficult marriage. However, it was clear that she did not need to provoke her husband to be the object of his suspicions, distortions and wrath.

The following case also illustrates the relationship between loss and violence, but focuses attention on the role played by the internal turmoil produced when unwanted feelings of weakness could no longer be denied through the belief that they were his partner's alone (projective identification). 'C' is a burly, affable 28-year-old mechanic, a former high school football star, who had come before the court after he had slapped his wife a second time. The first six years of marriage were satisfactory; 'we cooperated on everything'. 'C' had dropped out of high school to marry. His wife was pregnant but they had intended to marry soon. 'C's' mother called his wife a 'slut' accusing her of 'using her son to get out of her own family'. The pregnancy miscarried at three months. Three subsequent pregnancies miscarried; another infant died a few hours after birth. 'C's' wife wanted a funeral.

He refused, 'to spare her emotions'. The birth of their only child, five years ago, marked the decline of their relationship. The child was severely handicapped; the diagnosis of spastic quadraplegia was made after a year of medical indecision. 'C' quit his job, complaining of low pay for long hours; he was unable to find employment for a year. He looked after the child while his wife worked. Both began to abuse alcohol. At present 'C' is maintaining sobriety; he believes his wife's problem is more severe. Under its influence she has expressed resentments previously suppressed. The child's disability was particularly difficult for the wife, for she suffered herself from a congenital hip dysplasia which has required bilateral pinning. A brother suffered both from congenital hip dysplasia and congenital blindness. Although her disability is readily apparent she had not told her husband it was congenital for fear he would leave her.

More recently 'C's' mother-in-law developed rheumatoid arthritis. A severe gastrointestinal bleed precipitated by high doses of aspirin resulted in a heart attack. 'C' let his wife sleep off a drinking bout before telling her her mother was near death. She flew into a rage, 'screaming and scratching'. He slapped her. She took him to court. He moved back to his parents' home. She cut her wrists and begged him to come home. He returned. Another fight. The police were called. The cycle was repeated over and over, reaching a turning point only when he hit her a second time.

'C' painted a rosy picture of his home life, as he did of the first years of marriage. He was close to his parents. His parents never fought. In contrast, his wife's parents, both alcoholics, fought constantly. Her father 'put her mother in the hospital'. However, on further questioning the picture of 'C's' family unity becomes blurred: an older sister was divorced recently; her husband beat her. 'C' does not talk to a second sister. Their feud goes back to childhood. Their father had insisted that a man never hits a woman. The sister often attempted to get 'C' in trouble by claiming he had hit her. In the course of therapy, as 'C' learned not to respond to his wife's calls and as the separation became more complete, 'C' confided that he had been upset himself by his mother-in-law's illness, for he was 'closer to her than to his own mother'. He added, "I could be just like my wife, a whimpery child, unable to manage, if I allowed myself to feel things." In short, "I would lose my strength."

Finally, there is the case of 'D', 34, a black belt in karate, unemployed, charged with the murder of the 24-year-old girl he had been living with for five years. The relationship had been stormy, periods of calm alternating with separations, but it was the first and only relationship he had been able to maintain for any length of time and with any degree of trust. A month prior to the murder she had broken off the relationship. This time it felt final, for she was achieving some success as an entertainer and was burdened by his dependency. 'D's' background was grim. His earliest memory recalled his being tortured at age three by his father with a machine he had devized to shock the child. His mother, unable to care for him, left him in a boarding school at the age of eight, where he was beaten frequently. Once, because his hair was long, he was forced to dress as a girl and paraded in front of his classmates. He returned to his mother two years later; both his mother and her numerous boyfriends beat him. He dropped out of school in the fifth grade and managed as a loner. 'D' had an older brother, preferred by his mother, who died suddenly at age 23 from a cerebral hemorrhage. His mother 'never recovered from the shock' and died a year ago, her spirits broken. 'D's' girlfriend left him precipitously. Despairing, he made a suicide attempt by crashing his car. He still hoped for her return. Preoccupied with thoughts of her, he found where she was living, he called her repeatedly. She had bought a guard dog, so he took a pipe with him. Not finding her home, he sought her out and came upon her embracing a man in the park. His insistence that he was protecting her seemed delusional in its denial of reality. His thoughts were so far from killing her, that as he hit her he thought only of embracing her. He could not believe she was dead. Had he known, he would not have turned himself in, rather he would have forced a chase in the hope that the police would shoot him.

3. Conclusions

In summary, the psychological issue underlying the potential for violence is the dilemma of what to do with the need to maintain a positive attachment in the face of repeated experiences of rejection. A variety of characterological solutions to this dilemma exist: the position, 'I don't care about anybody' avoids the pain, but allows for actions without conscience; 'I hate them' maintains a precarious sense of self but without an ally moves easily to a paranoid, 'they are bad, look what they are doing to me' position, which can be overtly psychotic; another possibility is to take the blame, 'I'm awful', which exaggerates the anxiety of being left or alternatively focuses on control, 'I'll make them care', by suicidal threats or sadistic manipulation; again, the problem can be denied altogether, with the risk of a sudden expression of hatefulness under stress such as a real loss or under the influence of drugs or alcohol.

If one takes as a common denominator the experience of not being cared about, then it is apparent how depression and paranoia, jealousy and sadism, sociopathy and psychosis are interrelated: they all attempt to maintain an attachment against odds, to prevent a threatened loss. They all attempt to deal with the uniquely human response to hurt, the feeling of hate. The marital relationship is remarkable in its potential for either rejuvenation or destruction. In the fresh start that marriage offers, those past conflicts that lie dormant in the inner psychic depths, like personal Balrogs,[11] are incited to rise once more in the hope they can be put to rest once and for all. The destructive potential is there. These characterological resolutions leave the individual sensitive to renewed threats of loss as marriage fails to fulfill hopes. Anger soon becomes dysfunctional and a downward spiral results with increasing fears of loss and renewed attempts at control which finally includes violence.

In conclusion, I should comment on the issue of danger. When a marriage collapses, a man who is sensitive to loss and whose self esteem is dependent on control of a spouse, is likely to react to the actual loss of control by an increased effort to project blame or badness onto the spouse, thus becoming increasingly sadistic or paranoid. If his sense of adequacy is severely undermined, he may use this projection to justify violent behavior. This chapter has shown how separation is a stress that increases the risk of violence and of murder. This serves to emphasize the need for the courts to have adequate means to protect a woman throughout the process of separation and divorce.

NOTES

1. Bowlby, John, *Attachment and Loss,* Vol. 1, *Attachment.* New York, New York: Basic Books, Inc., 1969.
2. Bowlby, John, *Attachment and Loss,* Vol. 2, *Separation.* New York, New York: Basic Books, Inc., 1973.
3. Bowlby, John, "The Making and Breaking of Affectional Bonds" (1977), 130 *British Journal of Psychiatry* 201-210.
4. Scott, J.P., "The Process of Primary Socialization in Canine and Human Infants" (1963), 28 *Monographs of the Society for Research in Child Development* 1.
5. Bowlby, John, *op. cit.,* note 3, pp. 247-249.
6. Mack, John E.; Scherl, Donald J.; and Macht, Lee B., "Children Who Kill Their Mothers", in *The Child in His Family*, Anthony, E.J. (ed.), New York, New York: John Wiley and Sons, Inc., 1973, pp. 319-332.
7. Russell, Donald H., "Ingredients of Juvenile Murder", presented at the International Congress of Social Psychiatry, Athens, Greece, August, 1974.
8. Bowlby, J., *op. cit.,* note 3, p. 172.
9. Berman, Ellen M., and Lief, Harold I., "Marital Therapy from a Psychiatric Perspective: An Overview" (June 1975), 132 *The American Journal of Psychiatry* 583-592.
10. Zinner, John, "The Implications of Projective Identification for Marital Interaction", in *Contemporary Marriage: Structure, Dynamics, and Therapy.* Grunebaum, Henry, and Christ, Jacob (eds.), Boston, Mass.: Little Brown & Co., 1976, Chapter 12, pp. 293-308.
11. Tolkien, J.R.R., "The Bridge of Khazad - dum", in *The Fellowship of the Ring.* Boston, Mass.: Houghton, Mifflin Co., 1966, p. 342: "Something was coming up behind them, what it was could not be seen: it was like a great shadow, in the middle of which was a dark form, of man — shape maybe, yet greater; and a power and terror seemed to be in it and to go before it . . ."

Chapter 4

Media, Violence and the Family: a Canadian View

Lucien A. Beaulieu*

What is the impact of the mass media, especially television, in promoting, legitimizing and reinforcing violence in the home?

In approaching these important and complex questions, one confronts a curious paradox. On the one hand, there is overwhelming evidence of the complicity of the media in nourishing violence in society in a multitude of ways: role modelling, victimization, exaggerated fears, distorted perceptions of reality and desensitization, to name but a few.[1] On the other hand, the role of television has been almost wholly excluded from the mainstream study of violence in the family. A compounding paradox is that the literature of media violence rarely, if ever, deals directly with the question of television and family violence.

There are reasons why this is so, but there are more powerful reasons why it should not be so. Without doubt, there is insurmountable complexity in attempting to disentangle media effects from other variables influencing family violence. There are difficult problems in applying conventional methodologies to the study of family violence and the media. For example, it would hardly be ethical practice to attempt to elicit child abuse in a laboratory. Limitation of space precludes a full discussion of the recurring related debate about 'conclusive proof' and whether or not such onus should really be upon those who propound that there are no nefarious effects.

Less defensible, in my view, is the dismissal of the relevance of television by some commentators on purely theoretical grounds. They find it more appealing to concentrate on 'real' or 'hard' variables and dismiss television as ephemeral. They identify poverty, low prestige, the compulsive masculinity syndrome, the punitive personality, or violent life experiences as key governing factors.

It is in the impact of precisely these factors that television is most implicated.

---

* Senior Judge, Ontario Provincial Court (Family Division), Canada.

1. Television's Powerful Reach

Ninety-six percent of Canadian homes have television sets in use.[2] The average person watches television more than three hours per day: the average child watches more.[3] For a large and growing proportion of our population, only sleeping commands more of our time; but television is catching up quickly.

More than that, television is the principal source of information about the world beyond our direct, and therefore quite limited, experience.[4] Even where there are competing media such as newspapers and radio, television is the dominant source of information. Not only that, it increasingly pervades our basic social processes, from what we do together to what we talk about over coffee. It affects our basic socialization processes such as athletics, and it affects more and more of our education, both formal and informal.

Television reaches into virtually every home daily. And it reaches virtually every member of the family. If television can be therapeutic and pro-social, as the evidence overwhelmingly suggests it can,[5] television can reach into people's lives on a broader and more consistent basis than regiments from the helping professions. Conversely, if television and other media are a force for pernicious ill, we face a formidable and all-pervasive enemy.

2. The Roots of Family Violence[6] and the Role of Television

A preliminary Bill of Indictment on television and its role in family violence could be drawn up as follows. This is a list of charges, not necessarily a set of verdicts, though in some cases we are very close to that. There are, nonetheless, very serious grounds behind those charges. In many instances there is a substantial *prima facie* case. Part of that case but not all, is that much of the evidence is related to young persons. Be that as it may, young persons are the future adult spouses and parents.

The Frustration Syndrome

The link between frustration and aggression has been clearly established, and frustration has been identified as one of the roots of family violence. In many ways television is implicated as a causal factor in this syndrome. One dimension, the systematic under-representation and/or negative stereotyping of minorities[7] denies them the fundamental community statement of positive identity which television uniquely can confer. The crass commercial consumerism which is at the root of North American television is based on a concept of the individual as a market to be exploited.[8] The value of the individual, his personal worth and self-respect must take a second place.

Most important, television consistently portrays an attractive lifestyle which only part of the community can reasonably hope to obtain. Television thus makes an implicit statement about the cultural poverty of the low-income lifestyle, and the mean occupational status of the disadvantaged. Night after night, families and heads of households are told they don't measure up. Even where they do, by any reasonable standard, television may make people feel an even more glamorous lifestyle is imperative in terms of community status. The depicted culture is based on the belief that we are all in paradise and that self-gratification and self-admiration is our *raison d'être*.

Alienation

In many ways social alienation is closely related to frustration. Those who are deprived of a sense of participation and standing in the communities in which they live and work can become alienated. This breeds aggression against society, its institutions and symbols and sometimes against oneself. Here too the media can play a role. It is known, for example, that bad news reports stimulate negative and hostile feelings between groups and between individuals and their environment.[9] Realistic media fiction, much of it violence-based, can have similar results.

The Authoritarian Personality

The authoritarian personality has been identified as a recurrent perpetrator of family violence.[10] The authoritarian personality is persuaded to the extensive use of violence as a technique of social control, as a means of securing conformity to standards of behavior, even if those are set only by himself. Violence as a means to control and sanction others is richly nourished by the standard media diet.

The Compulsive Masculinity Syndrome and Male Aggression Stereotypes

The compulsive masculinity syndrome and male aggression stereotypes have been similarly identified as a recurrent variable in family violence.[11] They too are consistently nourished by television and by other media. Numerous content analyses and related studies have documented the prevalence on television of sex role stereotyping.[12] Both the consistent portrayal of aggression as a masculine value, as well as the contrasting and reinforcing portrayal of female stereotypes, aid and abet the compulsive masculinity syndrome. In turn, there are pressures to succeed in material, sexual, social and power terms. The media, especially television, are constantly feeding these destructive misconceptions.

Direct Stimulation of Aggression

Literally hundreds of laboratory and field studies, most involving children, but some involving adults, have shown that exposure to television and film violence consistently stimulates aggression — and not infrequently violence — in a significant minority of those exposed.[13] It is inconceivable that aggressive, and sometimes dangerous behavior is not elicited in the home by television violence. This has been corroborated by many parents. In many cases, it may be harmless. In extreme cases, it can lead to death.

Learning Criminal Technique

In addition to stimulating aggression, media violence can teach specific techniques of crime and violence. The Royal Commission on Violence in the Communications Industry has identified dozens of such alleged instances, and one of our research projects carefully examined, and confirmed, the validity of a number of them.[14] One example of family violence may suffice: in England it was recently reported that a young girl, imitating something she had seen in a popular television program, attempted to cut the brake lines in her parents' car to murder or injure them. Fortunately, she mistakenly cut only part of the brake cable. In many other instances, the potential victims of replications of media violence have not been so lucky.

Teaching Violence Norms

With specific reference to violence in the family, the most important, insidious and pervasive impact of television violence is undoubtedly its impact in fostering norms, values and attitudes which favor violence. I can identify seven main variations. In real life, they are frequently intermingled and mutually reinforcing.

One is the promotion of violent role models. Attractive and successful people are routinely shown using violence.

Secondly, violence is routinely portrayed as a standard method of conflict resolution. In a content analysis of a large sample of television programming conducted especially for the Royal Commission, non-violent means were rarely used to resolve conflict. Violence and attack were used overwhelmingly. Worse than that, more than 70 percent of the violence was gratuitous, or not necessary to the plot.[15]

Thirdly, television helps to legitimate the use of violence. It is widely known that television, including supposedly fictional television, is taken as a statement of 'reality'.[16] In connection with violence, it makes a powerful and repeated statement that violence is the way that problems are solved and objectives achieved. This serves to legitimate and reinforce an individual's inclination to commit violence, and to reinforce rather than counteract his or her violent life experiences.[17]

In a similar way, violence is favorably presented as an outlet for emotions such as frustration or vengeance. When these emotions, including vindictiveness and self-righteousness, are presented in dramatic form, violence is frequently used to give them satisfying expression.

61 Media, Violence and the Family: a Canadian View

Fifth, violence is routinely portrayed in the media as an appropriate and effective means to achieve desired ends. It is shown as a way to obtain material goods, such as through car theft or armed robbery, as a way to achieve success, to gain power over other people, or to obtain information or knowledge under compulsion.

Sixth, violence is portrayed as a standard technique of social control. One dimension of this was noted above in connection with the authoritarian personality. But in more general terms, both in what is portrayed as 'legal' and what is portrayed as 'illegal' ('honour among thieves') television entertainment promotes the idea that violence is an essential means to secure conformity to group, social or community norms. Furthermore, this is not necessarily done with much care for the validity of those norms.

Seventh, is the problem of athletics. This is an area of increasing concern, especially in Canada in connection with hockey. But it does not stop there. Professional sports violence has cropped up in supposedly non-violent sports like baseball and tennis.

Athletics is of particular concern because it has traditionally played an important role in the social and physical development of young people. If, instead of being taught the value of skill and teamwork, they are taught that violence is a way to succeed, we have a serious problem. Success may be defined narrowly in terms of making it to the major leagues. Those who succeed then become pernicious role models for a much larger audience. Alternatively, these values may spill over to other areas of personal interaction and social and community life.[18]

Intrafamily Abuse

In terms of social interaction, television may be seen to promote patterns of intra-family abuse. As the content analysis done for the Royal Commission documents, situation comedies are extensively based on sarcasm and verbal abuse. They teach us to abuse other members of our family, or our neighbours, and to think it's funny—and fun. The Fonz, the hero of 'Happy Days', is applauded for his smart-aleck interventions into other people's family affairs, usually at the considerable expense of the parents. Archie Bunker is a hero.

While it may be argued that such programs are opportunities to discuss topics which were hitherto taboo, there is an equal if not stronger case to be made for the possibility that their themes and messages are missed by the less sophisticated mass audiences and rather serve to reinforce existing biases, prejudices and negative views of traditional family life. The allegedly innocent afternoon 'soap dramas' and the recent phenomenon of 'punk rock' are an interesting commentary on the suggested means that individuals, particularly youth, can utilize to cope with adults, parents, and people in authority generally.

Victimization[19]

Television and other media teach people how to be victims. They teach patterns of provocation which are almost certain to lead to violence; they rarely teach techniques for diffusing explosive issues and interactions. They teach women and children patterns of submission. And they teach patterns of dramatic inevitability which can be re-enacted if the key properties of the real situation are right.

Expectations of Violence

The literature also shows that the use of physical punishment is frequently linked to parents' perceptions of the kind of world their children will live in as adults. Can one suppose that television is not the major source of information about what the world out there is like and is becoming? Is there any doubt that the television world is one which is overwhelmingly violent?[20]

The Role of Personality

The role of the authoritarian personality was noted earlier. More generally, the available research indicates, albeit without comprehensive specifics, that different people are affected in different ways. But almost everyone is affected. Two of the Royal Commission's research studies found,[21] among other things, that different personality types tend to perceive TV programs selectively in ways which reinforce their personality bias. Authoritarian personalities tend to see authoritarian messages in TV crime dramas. Alienated persons, watching the same shows, receive messages which reinforce their alienation. Other research done for the Commission suggests that TV-related personality and environmental patterns are established in childhood.

Catharsis

Finally, I conclude this outline with a reference to the question of catharsis, a pernicious myth which is only now being banished from empirical respectability, both in the study of family violence and in the study of media violence.[22] For reasons that have little to do with the facts, many people were ready to believe that family violence is cathartic (and therefore perhaps justifiable); and that media violence, operating vicariously rather than directly, was also cathartic. Part of the confusion has resulted from the 'blender-type' mixing of the classic Aristotelian concept of catharsis in tragedy with the Freudian concept of sublimation. However, as Geoffrey Wagner once said, "Intellectual balloonism funks that confrontation with reality demanded by intelligence". In any event these invented concepts have been shown in extensive empirical tests to be false.

3. The Pro-Social and Therapeutic Potential

Against this grim background of television and media complicity in helping to spread violence, there is a striking positive pro-social dimension which has been demonstrated.

A study conducted by the Royal Commission[23] outlined many ways in which non-didactic television has had positive effects. It can promote helping, sharing, learning useful information, overcoming unjustified fears, and learning not to cheat. In sum, the evidence suggests that entertainment television can have a very large positive effect.

This is reinforced by other studies. For example, a major study was conducted in California[24] with the cooperation of a local cable company to provide pro-social, anti-social and mixed programs to separate control groups. The most striking result was the significant improvement in pro-social behavior among those who had been exposed to the pro-social diet during the period of the study.

Another important study indicates that while bad news makes us bad, eliciting feelings of animosity and hostility, good news makes us good.[25] It is both economically and technically within our reach for people to be able to create their own home media environments, perhaps based on a videotape library. Future uses of television and related media provide new and constructive possibilities for positive social interaction.[26]

As noted at the outset, these elements have a specific relevance to family violence. Not only could the bad be eliminated or reduced but the good could be introduced. One of the studies for the Royal Commission indicated that journalists identified most with the helping professions such as teaching and social work.[27] That self-perception, if not practice, moves them close to the helping professions who earn their daily bread trying to cope with the problems of family violence. Television should be enlisted as part of our team, as an essential tool. In a treatment era where treating the family unit is increasingly emphasized — because the phenomenon of family violence grows out of the family system — there is no means to reach into homes as consistently or as extensively as with television.

Certainly, television cannot do it all. In particular it has the problem that it is only semi-interactive, and that it does not react to the audience's reactions. But it is an important supporting resource which we ignore at our peril. It has the potential to help, or to harm the social and mental health of both individuals and their families.

4. Changing the Media System

The media system, as it has evolved in North America, is elaborate, complex, cumbersome and overwhelmingly resistant to change. The kinds of changes which are needed will not come easily: it is easier to be diagnostic and prescriptive in the way I have outlined above, than to achieve the kind of change which is needed.

The Royal Commission has proposed a comprehensive program of recommendations to deal with all aspects of media violence. The main approaches were recommended in the hearings, the research and in foreign consultations.[28]

(1) Media accountability to the society it is serving and should be serving better.

(2) The restructuring of the television system.

(3) Ways of mobilizing available creative resources behind pro-social media objectives.

(1) One of the most frequently expressed concerns is for increased accountability of the media to society. The media however seem to feel that accountability is exclusively reserved to all *other* persons in society, regardless of status.

The dilemma is that there is extreme discomfort at the prospect of accountability mechanisms which either in form or substance signal government control. However, it is trite to say that this is not the only form of measuring and ensuring accountability. For this reason, it is not only important but essential that non-political community elements — especially those with a professional basis for concern — play a more aggressive role in calling the media to account and in seeking to participate in shaping it. The helping professions most concerned with key social problems are among those who should be most centrally involved, both by being more aggressive in forums which are now available to them, such as CRTC licence renewal hearings, and by participating in the debates on future directions for our media system. Hysterical denunciations and defensive cries of 'censorship' should be examined in the proper perspective of other professions and society in general.

(2) Part of that debate will be about ways to restructure mass media, especially television. Some of the possibilities merit our close personal and professional attention. For example, in a study conducted for the Royal Commission, it has been proposed that television be radically rearranged on a specialized channel basis.[29] This would involve eliminating the magazine-style television stations we now have, in favor of each channel being dedicated to a particular kind of program. For example, we might have one or more channels for light entertainment, another for serious entertainment, two or three for children at different ages, one for news and public affairs, and so on. Such a system could help Canada break the destructive commercial stranglehold of the American television system. It would provide a much richer and more convenient menu of programming for viewers of all kinds and present vastly improved opportunities for parents to use television more creatively and effectively in child development. Such things as video cassettes would also permit viewing important programs at any time and afford families the opportunity of planning the viewing diets more effectively.

(3) The larger problem is that the massive creative and financial resources of the television system are primarily geared to material which is at best harmless, but which is often harmful. The challenge to society is to find ways to mobilize those creative resources in ways which do substantially less harm and substantially more good at the same time. One of the reasons I make that point with conviction is that there is accumulating evidence that these goals do not need to be traded off against entertainment values. It is frequently alleged, of course, that such would be the case. We should not be readily fooled by simple rationalizations of the status quo. That everyone does it, hardly means it is right. That something happens does not mean it *should* happen.

What must change is the way society uses its mass media. At present the mass media primarily exists as servants of commerce. It is used to support business marketing, and the overall philosophy of entertainment programming, whether in fiction or in news, is geared to those ends. The medium is thus not only the 'message', the medium is also the 'MONEY'.

I do not question the need for the mass media to play an important informational role in our economy. But its position is far too exclusive. Individuals, professional groups and the larger community must work to find ways to harness the media for social ends as well. That we have barely begun to do. The helping professions, dealing with family violence and breakdown should be in the forefront of that social revolution.

NOTES

1. See Ontario, *The Royal Commission on Violence in the Communications Industry Report*, 7 vols. Toronto, Canada: Queen's Printer, 1977. See also Surgeon General's Scientific Advisory Committee on Television and Social Behavior, *Television and Social Behavior, Technical Reports to the Committee*, 5 vols. Washington, D.C.: U.S. Government Printing Office, 1972.
2. Statistics Canada, *Household Facilities Study, 1975.*
3. Various estimates are presented in the reports of the BBM Bureau of Measurement; by Statistics Canada; and by several studies done for the Royal Commission: Goranson, Richard, "Television Violence Effects: Issues and Evidence", in Ontario, *Royal Commission on Violence in the Communications Industry Report,* Vol. 5, *Learning from the Media.* Toronto, Canada: Queen's Printer, 1977. Fouts, Gregory, "Effects of Television on Children and Youth: A Developmental Approach", in Ontario, *Royal Commission on Violence in the Communications Industry Report,* Vol. 6, *Vulnerability to Media Effects.* Toronto, Canada: Queen's Printer, 1977. Tate, Eugene, "Viewer's Perceptions of Selected Television Programs", in Ontario, *Royal Commission on Violence in the Communications Industry Report*, Vol. 6, *Vulnerability to Media Effects.* Toronto, Canada: Queen's Printer, 1977.
4. See for example Bagdikian, Ben H., *The Information Machines.* New York, New York: Harper & Row, 1971.
5. For a contemporary review see: Rushton, J. Philippe, "Television and Pro-Social Behavior", in Ontario, *Royal Commission on Violence in the Communications Industry Report,* Vol. 5, *Learning from the Media.* Toronto, Canada: Queen's Printer, 1977.
6. Current reviews of theory and evidence on violence in the family can be found in: Arnold, A., *Violence and Your Child.* Chicago, Illinois: Henry Regnery Company, 1969. Brown, D.G., *Behavior Modification in Child, School, and Family Mental Health: An Annotated Bibliography.* Champaign, Illinois: Research Press Company, 1972. Gelles, R.J., *The Violent Home: A Study of Physical Aggression Between Husbands and Wives.* Beverly Hills, California: Sage Publications, 1974. Gil, D.G., *Violence Against Children.* Cambridge, Mass.: Harvard University Press, 1973. Helfer, R.E., and Kempe, C.H., *Child Abuse and Neglect: The Family and the Community.* Cambridge, Mass.: Ballinger Publishing Company, 1976. Madden, D.J., and Lion, J.R., *Rage, Hate, Assault and Other Forms of Violence.* New York, New York: Spectrum Publications, Inc., 1976. Mitchell, R., *Depression.* Harmondsworth, Middlesex: Penguin Books, 1975. National Institute of Mental Health, *Violence at Home.* Rockville, Maryland: U.S. Department of Health, Education and Welfare, 1974. Pasternak, S.A., *Violence and Victims.* New York, New York: Spectrum Publications,

Inc., 1975. Pizzey, E., *Scream Quietly or the Neighbours Will Hear.* Harmondsworth, Middlesex: Penguin Books, 1974. Steinmetz, Suzanne K., and Straus, Murray A. (eds.), *Violence in the Family.* New York, New York: Dodd Mead, 1974.

7. See in particular, Gerbner, George, and Gross, Larry, "Violence Profiles Numbers 1-7: Trends in Network Television Drama and Viewer Conceptions of Social Reality, 1967-1975", Phil., Penn.: University of Penn., Annenberg School of Communications, 1976.

8. A good discussion of the television business is to be found in Brown, Les, *Television: The Business Behind the Box.* New York, New York: Harcourt, Brace, Jovanovich, 1971.

9. See Holloway, S., and Hornstein, H.A., "How Good News Makes us Good" (1976) *Psychology Today* p. 76.

10. See Adorno, T.W.; Frenkel-Brunswik, Else; Levinson, Daniel J.; and Nevitt-Sandford, R., *The Authoritarian Personality,* New York, New York: Harper and Row, 1950. For interesting data on television and the authoritarian personality see Tate, Eugene, "Viewer's Perceptions of Selected Television Programs", in Ontario, *Royal Commission on Violence in the Communications Industry Report,* Vol. 6, *Vulnerability to Media Effects.* Toronto, Canada: Queen's Printer, 1977.

11. See for example, Jackson, Toby, "Violence and the Masculine Ideal" in Steinmetz, Suzanne K., and Straus, Murray A. (eds.), *Violence in the Family.* New York, New York: Dodd Mead, 1974.

12. See Gerbner and Gross, *op. cit.* and MacBeth-Williams, Tannis; Zabrack, Merle., and Joy, Lesley, "A Content Analysis of Entertainment Television Programming", in Ontario, *Royal Commission on Violence in the Communications Industry Report,* Vol. 3, *Violence in Television, Film and News.* Toronto, Canada: Queen's Printer, 1977.

13. For a contemporary survey, see Goranson, Richard, *op. cit.*

14. See Stanley, Paul, and Riera, Brian, "Replications of Media Violence", in Ontario, *Royal Commission on Violence in the Communications Industry Report,* Vol. 5, *Learning from the Media.* Toronto, Canada: Queen's Printer, 1977.

15. See Williams; Zabrack; and Joy, *op. cit.*

16. See Gerbner and Gross, *op. cit.*

17. See for example, Greenberg, B.S., and Dervin, B., *Use of the Mass Media by the Urban Poor.* New York, New York: Praeger, 1970.

18. See Ontario Ministry of Community and Social Services, *Investigation and Enquiry into Violence in Amateur Hockey* (McMurtry Report). Toronto, Canada, 1974 and a forthcoming report on hockey violence by Professor Gilles Néron of the Faculté de l'Education physique of the Université de Montréal.

19. See for example, Pasternak, Stefan (ed.), *Violence and Victims.* New York, New York: Spectrum Publications, 1975.

20. See Gerbner and Gross, *op. cit.* and Doob, Anthony, and Macdonald, Glenn, "The News Media and Perceptions of Violence", in Ontario, *Royal Commission on Violence in the Communications Industry Report,* Vol. 5, *Learning from the Media.* Toronto, Canada: Queen's Printer, 1977.

21. See Fouts, *op. cit.* and Tate, *op. cit.*

22. See Goranson, *op. cit.,* and Steinmetz, S.K., and Straus, M.A., "General Introduction, Social Myth and Social System in the Study of Intra-Family Violence", in Steinmetz and Straus, *op. cit.,* pp. 3-24.

23. See Rushton, *op. cit.*

24. Reported in private meetings by Dr. Robert Gorney of the University of California at Los Angeles.

25. Holloway and Hornstein, *op. cit.*

26. See Thompson, Gordon B., "Future Mass Media", in Ontario, *Royal Commission on Violence in the Communications Industry Report,* Vol. 7, *The Media Industries: From Here to Where?.* Toronto, Canada: Queen's Printer, 1977.

27. See Osler, Andrew M., "A Descriptive Study of Perceptions and Attitudes among Journalists in Ontario", in Ontario, *Royal Commission on Violence in the*

67 Media, Violence and the Family: a Canadian View

Communications Industry Report, Vol. 7, *The Media Industries: From Here to Where?.* Toronto, Canada: Queen's Printer, 1977.

28. Report of the *Royal Commission on Violence in the Communications Industry,* Publication Service, Ministry of Government Services, Queen's Park, Toronto or the Ontario Government Book Store, 880 Bay Street, Toronto.

29. See Griffiths, Stuart, "Alternatives for Canadian Television", in Ontario, *Royal Commission on Violence in the Communications Industry Report,* Vol. 7, *The Media Industries: From Here to Where?.* Toronto, Canada: Queen's Printer, 1977.

PART TWO

VIOLENCE BETWEEN ADULTS:
LEGAL AND SOCIAL RESPONSES

Mr. Michael Freeman closes Chapter 5 with the striking phrase: "At present, man's inhumanity to man is matched only by his inhumanity to wife." This part focuses primarily on relationships between men and women in marital and *quasi-marital* unions. The extent to which violence enters these relationships in modern United States society was shown by Professor Straus in the previous part. The subordination of a woman to her husband has a long history which is reflected in the social structures, judicial attitudes and legal frameworks of past times which survive to a greater or lesser extent in different countries today. Herein is to be found the juristic and social reinforcement which is common to both child abuse and inter-spousal violence. In later chapters it is made clear, in particular by Mr. M.C. Olmesdahl and Dr. Tahir Mahmood, how the power structure within the family, supported by legal norms, creates a framework which anaesthetizes society against perceiving violence against children as being anti-social behavior and promotes conditions in which it can flourish. So also in relations between husband and wife, Mr. Michael Freeman (in Chapter 5) Professor Marie-Thérèse Meulders (in Chapter 7) show how, in countries within both the common law and civil law traditions, legal doctrines underwrote the traditional dominance of the husband.

Of course, this dominance is not only a legal one. The dependent status of women was, and in many countries largely still is, a matter of general social organization. A redressing of the balance cannot be achieved simply by cosmetic changes to legal principle by such means as removing inequalities in the proclaimed rights and duties of husbands and wives. Insofar as the law is concerned, it is necessary to go further and to provide special mechanisms to protect women from the consequences of abuse by husbands of their role. Even this is of limited value. The chapters in this part will stress the importance of wider social measures, such as adequate housing policies and economic opportunities for women.

In this respect, the problems encountered by legal and social responses to violence between adults in the family are broadly similar to those which are relevant to violence to children. But Professor James B. Boskey (in Chapter 10) points to a potentially important distinction between them. In the case of children, he argues, the state's position as *parens patriae* has "long been seen as giving it the right to intervene in the manner in which a child was raised, at least in extreme circumstances." This is because a child cannot protect itself. But in the case of adults of full age and understanding, this model does not apply. It may be that the violence is to them "the appropriate way of dealing with the strains of daily living." The problem of what can be considered violent behavior was examined by Professor Murray A. Straus (Chapter 2) from the point of view of data collection of the incidence of wife-beating. With regard to the practical question about when society should intervene in cases of marital violence, it may be thought that the proposal made by Mrs. Susan Maidment (in Chapter 6) has much to commend it. She suggests that the degree of acceptability of the violence is to be set by the victim herself so that "a call for help by a wife to any outside body should be taken as (in itself) unassailable evidence that the violence suffered was unacceptable to that wife, and therefore to society at large". This criterion makes intervention in these cases in principle easier to defend than in some cases of child abuse where it is sometimes more difficult to resist the accusation that a particular section of society may be imposing alien values on another section (see in particular the remarks on this topic by Dr. Barbara Cohn Schlachet in Chapter 13).

Yet, in its practical application, the criterion suggested by Mrs. Maidment may not be easy. As Mr. Garry Bell says (in Chapter 11) "if I am not aware that I have a problem, do I have a problem?" The inhibitions felt by a wife against calling for help are very great and the reasons for them are well documented in this part. And to whom should the call be addressed? These questions raise the very important issue of identifying cases of spousal abuse and providing accessible agencies to which the relevant information will become available. In England it was not until Erin Pizzey opened Chiswick Women's Aid that the extent to which women needed protection became apparent. Mr. Bell specifies four criteria which must be met by any channel of communication for reception of information about spousal abuse (whether a 'crisis hot line, a rape center, a police department or a legal aid center'). They are credibility, visibility, accessibility and immediacy. In some countries it may be possible to adapt existing social welfare agencies to meet these requirements. Mr. Bell describes the Mobile Family Service Society in Regina, Saskatchewan, which has been largely successful in meeting them. Transition houses (refuges) may also be a necessary element in any network designed to meet those needs.

Having identified and confronted a case of spousal abuse, a myriad of other problems arise. At the most fundamental level, it must be decided whether a punitive or rehabilitative approach is to be taken, or perhaps some combination of the two. As a question of general principle, opinion is presently in some disarray as to the proper approach to take. In his earlier writings, which are referred to in detail by Mrs. Maidment (in Chapter 6), Professor Raymond Parnas advocated the 'treatment' model. However (in Chapter 8), Professor Parnas withdraws decisively from his earlier approach. There has been a failure to provide the services needed for the therapeutic process and a consequent demoralization of the police services. It is necessary, he argues, to make a break-through to people's consciousness that this behaviour is not to be tolerated and "only the coercive, authoritative harshness of the criminal process can do this". Mr. Freeman, too, is sceptical about a 'social welfare' orientation. "Too often in cases of domestic violence we are face to face with cases of brutal violence. Can mediation work in such a case?" Mrs. Maidment, on the other hand, while recognizing the need for the criminal process in the most serious cases, doubts whether that process "will achieve anything in terms of improving the marital relationship, the mutual respect which husband and wife should have for each other, or the husband's ability to understand and control his aggressions".

In this matter it is striking how attitudes diverge between what is considered the proper response to perpetrators of child abuse and strategies for dealing with those who inflict violence on their spouses. In the former case, the punitive model is widely thought to be inappropriate except in rare cases (see Part 4). Yet it is probable that the factors present in those cases which are usually thought to make the punitive response inappropriate are equally present in spousal abuse cases. It may also be remarked that in many countries there has been increasing recognition of the impossibility, in many cases, of making judicial assessments of the morality of inter-spousal behavior and this has been reflected in the growth of no-fault systems of divorce. The use of the criminal law in cases of inter-spousal violence (outside the most extreme cases) appears to run counter to this tendency. Perhaps the question whether the criminal law of rape should ordinarily be used where sexual violation within marital relations is alleged ought to be seen in this context. Undoubtedly the absolute immunity of a husband from prosecution for rape on his wife is symbolic of male domination, but, as Joanna McFadyen points out (in Chapter 9), the use of the criminal law, whether it be for rape or for some newly defined crime of sexual assault (which she proposes) is seldom an appropriate form of intervention in most families.

The option between punishment and mediation must also be made at a practical level. But who makes the decisions? The fact that most reports of domestic violence will usually be received in the first instance by the police (who are normally the only service open around the clock) might lead one to expect that the punitive model is the one usually applied. In fact, the result is usually a minimal response or none at all. In Brussels, Professor Meulders found that only seven of the (random) 155 inter-spousal violence cases on police records were prosecuted. The picture is little different in England, although Mr. Freeman gives the results of a particularly 'tough' prosecution policy adopted in Bedford, which resulted in 104 prosecutions from 288 cases. The reasons for the inadequacy of the police response appear in the following chapters. Even if there is a prosecution, the court might imprison (it did so in only three of the Bedford cases), fine, bind over, put the offender on probation and so on. But it is unlikely that the wife or family will benefit very much from this kind of intervention. It is for this reason that projects such as the Family Consultant Service, which assists the police force in London, Ontario (described by Peter Jaffe and Judy Thompson in Chapter 12) are of such interest. This service may be called upon by the police in the course of an investigation and is able to assist and advise on the further handling of the case. The Rapid Intervention Project of the New York Family Court (described by Dr. Cohn Schlachet in Chapter 13), also provided a specialized investigatory service into families beset by violence, but was called upon only when an individual came before a court.

Mrs. Maidment, drawing on some United States models, argues for the initial screening of such cases by an agency staffed by lawyers specialized in them. They would offer the victimized spouse advice as to the best way to proceed (whether by civil or criminal process, or merely by seeking help from other agencies), and they might perhaps even be given the power to act on her behalf in much the same way as agencies bring court proceedings on behalf of neglected or abused children. This approach goes far to integrate community responses to child abuse and to marital violence. It is surely right to see the problems as inter-related. In practice, they often co-exist, and a later chapter (Rob van Rees, Chapter 22) sees child abuse as simply a symptom of more general family problems. But this perception does not of itself provide the solutions for resolving those problems. Perhaps the first step of wisdom is the realization that many of them *cannot be solved.* If this is so, courts and other social agencies *can* play a practical role in helping the parties to make realistic arrangements for their (separate) futures. It is this dimension which the backward-looking punitive model misses or even obstructs. But forward planning does involve expenditure of time and resources. While the plans are being made, the victim (and children) will need accommodation and support; attention will need to be paid to the children's emotional attachments to both parents. It is again a question of how far society is ready to provide the resources for bridges to be built along which those family members unfortunate enough to be trapped in an intolerable cycle will be able to escape from it.

It will be evident that problems associated with family violence will be encountered across a wide range of professions. It is, therefore, fitting that this part should close with a chapter (14) in which Mr. Paul Havemann examines the attention which is paid to this topic in professional education and training in the United Kingdom and considers the difficulties involved in structuring courses to take it properly into account.

Chapter 5

The Phenomenon of Marital Violence and the Legal and Social Response in England*

Michael D. Freeman†

Madame Giroud, the French Minister for Women's Affairs, recently referred to wife-battering as an English malaise.[1] Like many politicians she must have been unaware as to what was going on about her, for some seven months later an article in *Le Monde*[2] indicated that women in Paris were organizing around the issue of wife-battering. The article informed us that that lady of many battles, Simone de Beauvoir, was president of the *Ligue du droit des femmes* which operates the *S.O.S. femmes - alternative* hotline finding battered women emergency housing. Nor was this the only group. The *Librairie des Femmes* maintained a phone service and moves were afoot to promote a refuge for battered women in Paris. Of course, the problem is not uniquely English, any more than it is a problem of the 1970s. It is a world-wide phenomenon and an age-old problem. It is true, though, that a re-awakening of concern for the plight of the battered woman appears to have hit the public conscience in England before it spread elsewhere. That it did is largely due to the crusading efforts of Erin Pizzey[3] in establishing the now world famous hostel at Chiswick in London.

This chapter is about legal and social responses to the problem. It concentrates very largely on the achievements and deficiencies of English law. But violence in the home cannot be eradicated by legislation. It is salutary to remember this for the 1970s is not the first occasion that the plight of battered women has surfaced to public attention. In an article in *The Sunday Times* of August 24, 1851 John Stuart Mill listed some of the cruelties inflicted by husbands and lovers: a bulldog set at the heels of a wife, attempted murder by hanging, stabbings, blows with a poker, murder in a fit of drunkenness. Dickens' novels *Bleak House* and *Oliver Twist* and the novels of Mrs. Gaskell[4] are replete with similar brutalities. The solution was thought to lie in the introduction of separation orders which could be obtained simply and speedily in magistrates' court. The case was put by Frances Power Cobbe in a pamphlet called *Wife Torture.*[5] She rejected the expedient of flogging the culprits, for "after they had undergone such chastisement . . . the ruffians would inevitably return more brutalized and infuriated than ever,

---

* The contents of this chapter appears in modified form as "Le Vice Anglais? — Wife-Battering in English and American Law", *Family Law Quarterly* (1977) 11: 199.
† Faculty of Laws, University College, London, England.

and again have their wives at their mercy."[6] It should be remembered that contemporaneously with the English reform the legislature of Maryland[7] passed legislation to whip wife-beaters and an attempt was made to copy this example in Pennsylvania.[8] The English reform may have helped some women. Certainly, the problem thereafter is no longer perceived as such,[9] though men clearly continued to batter their wives and mistresses. To-day's solutions must, therefore, be treated cautiously.

Solutions pre-suppose an understanding of the problem. Legal responses cannot operate *in vacuo*. Successful solvents require more than willingness to act. What is required is a thorough cognizance of the aetiology of wife-battering. Hasty measures passed in moral panics in reaction to the latest folk-devil,[10] whether that be football hooligans, squatters, brutal husbands or parents or whatever, are unlikely to grasp the problem by its roots. Of course, interim measures may be necessary. But one must then recognize them for what they are, and not expect them to emerge as panaceas.

1. Why Do Men Batter Their Wives?

The house of Commons Select Committee on Violence In Marriage which reported in 1975 recorded that "hardly any worthwhile research into either causes or remedies has been financed by the Government".[11] To put it more boldly there has been hardly any worthwhile research.[12] We do not know how much violence there is in marriage nor whether it is increasing. For even if we concentrate on indictable offences, official statistics only tell us about what the police and courts do,[13] not about the incidence of male violence to women and, outside of homicide, statistics are not available on the sex of the victim.[14] More interesting data was collected by the Dobashs in Scotland in 1974.[15] They examined the initial charge sheets for all offences in all precincts in Edinburgh and one in Glasgow. Violence and its threat accounted for only 11.1 percent of the offences reported to these police stations. More of this (6.31 percent) was non-family violence than violence within the family (4.79 percent). Within the family, wife assault accounted for 47.25 percent of the offences. Of non-family violence only 13 percent was directed by men against women, lending support to the view that to marry or cohabit is to increase the risk of physical attack. But the Dobashs' research cannot tell us how much violence is perpetrated on women in the home. So much depends upon the woman's reaction[16] and the response of the police to her cry for help. She can perceive the phenomenon of her husband's violence in a number of ways.[17] She can optimize and hope that his behaviour will improve.[18] She can accommodate to it in a way that obscures it.[19] She can normalize it and regard it as but a special case of normal behavior.[20] Only if she pessimises, accepts the worst and considers his deviance to be basically irreversible is she likely to alert control agencies. Her motivation to report is attenuated by her knowledge that the police traditionally do not interfere in domestic disturbances.[21] The police reluctance to arrest wife batterers is reflected in official statistics and research such as that conducted by the Dobashs: we cannot pretend that either gives us a true picture of the extent of the problem. In default we are forced to rely on speculation. Jack Ashley M.P., a champion of the cause of battered women, has suggested that between 20,000 and 50,000 women a year may be involved.[22] Marsden and Owens estimated the true incidence in Colchester (population 72,000) to be 1 in 200 wives/cohabitees or even 1 in 100.[23] Much depends on how we define battering.

But we do know that a woman is more likely to be killed by someone she knows than a total stranger.[24] This applies to rape[25] as well, and doubtless to other crimes of violence. We have some evidence that as the degree of violence decreases the percentage of strangers committing the offence goes up.[26] McClintock, in a study in London, accounted for 30 percent of homicides as domestic disputes.[27] Similar evidence is available from the United States,[28] Portugal,[29] Denmark[30] and Eire[31] and doubtless other countries as well. We know less about assault but there seems to be a basic similarity between patterns of assault and patterns of homicide. We also know that violence is often cited as a cause of marital unhappiness and divorce. Chester and Streather's[32] analysis of divorce petitions bears this out as does O'Brien's study.[33] He found spontaneous mention of overt violence in 25 of the 150 inverviews of 'divorce-prone families' he carried out. Eighty-four percent of the reports of violence emanated from women. Levinger[34] found that physical abuse was an important factor in one-fifth of middle-class divorces and twice as many involving working-class couples. There wives complained of physical abuse eleven times more frequently than did husbands.

There is thus more violence in marriage than many people suppose.[35] But, as Goode[36] has pointed out, all families are characterized by some degree of conflict. All conflictual situations do not, however, lead to violent behavior. The factors which lead to a conflictual family situation which ends in violence may not be radically different from those leading to other conflictual situations in the domestic setting. The concern is, therefore, with why some husbands respond violently to situations of conflict: indeed, why some, probably a minority, act violently when there appears to be no disagreement between themselves and their wives.

We do not know the answer. True, a number of myths has grown up as putative explanations of the phenomenon. These are a form of defence mechanism which have been constructed to protect the family as a social institution. They are well described by Steinmetz and Straus[37] in the introduction to their collection of essays, and will not be rehearsed here. As they say, each of the myths contains a scintilla of truth. None of them, however, adequately explains the phenomenon.

There are a number of theories as to why violence occurs in marriage. The dominant view emphasizes individual pathology: particular characteristics are isolated, they are found to exist in statistically significant numbers in husbands who have battered their wives and the battering is then attributed to possession of the particular pathological characteristic in question. This view individualizes the problem and locates its source in behavioral characteristics of 'official' deviants.[38] Thus, one commonly hears that battering husbands are alcoholics or have 'personality disorders' or that they are psychopaths. Violent behavior is said to be 'irrational' rather as other deviant behavior is labelled as 'mindless' or 'meaning-less' or 'stupid'.[39] Erin Pizzey subscribes to this view.[40] Thus, in a forthright article in *The Spectator* she wrote:[41] "no one likes the word 'psychopath', everyone is afraid of it, but that is exactly what he is — aggressive, dangerous, plausible and deeply immature".[42] Gayford's view is not far removed from this. When questioned by the Select Committee, he spoke of husbands' 'pathological jealousy' produced by alcohol which was not susceptible of being removed by 'logical reasoning'.[43] He has also emphasized pathological features of the women, notably that their disastrous marriages were often 'undertaken precipitately by a desire to leave home' resulting in short courtships and early and unplanned pregnancy.[44]

Such positivistic interpretations lead to suggestions of treatment-oriented solutions; more refuges, better medical provision, more social workers *etc.* The 'therapeutic state'[45] takes over and deviance is medicalized. Where this form of positivistic criminology differs from the usual is that it rarely examines the deviant.[46] Nearly all the research, and Gayford's is a good example, has concentrated on the wife-victims and has not examined the husband-batterers.[47] Conclusions about his pathology are often thus drawn from what his wife says about his personality and disposition.

A second view is to attribute violence to frustration, stress and blocked goals. Such a view is not novel and can be traced, in different contexts, to Durkheim[48] and Merton.[49] It stresses social structural factors. The British Association of Social Workers in a discussion document put it like this:

. . . economic conditions, low wages, bad housing, over-crowding and isolation; unfavorable and frustrating work conditions for the man; lack of job opportunities for adolescent/school leavers, and lack of facilities such as day care (*e.g.*, nurseries), adequate transport, pleasant evironment and play space and recreational facilities, for mother and children were considered to cause personal desperation that might precipitate violence in the home.[50]

To the Dobashs "numerous factors of a structural and interactional nature . . . might be considered as amplifying the potential for violence between spouses. Some of the structural elements which should be seen as important include socialization into a sub-culture of violence; limited access to and achievement of status within the larger social system; lack of effective sanctions on the part of the immediate social audiences and of relevant social agencies, and the general status of women."[51]

Gelles's researches led him to the conclusion that "violence is an adaptation or response to structural stress. Structural stress produces frustration, which is often followed by violence (expressive violence). Structural stress also produces role expectations (particularly for the husband) which, because of lack of resources, only can be carried out by means of violence (instrumental violence). The second major precondition . . . is socialization experience. . . . If an individual learns that violence is an appropriate behavior when one is frustrated or angry . . . then this will be the adaptation to stress employed".[52] In his study of 80 families, he found that violence was more likely to occur in the lower socio-economic groups. But this can partially be attributed to a sub-culture of violence. There is lack of privacy in lower-class families with the result that temporary escape from the other's clutches is more difficult and the violence more visible. It is also a fact that the poorer sections of the population tend to call in social control agencies like the police where the middle classes resort to social support institutions such as marriage guidance clinics and psychologists.[53] The effort this has on statistics and through this on theory cannot be underestimated.

More significantly it is the lower socio-economic classes who are most likely to suffer the anomie described by the Dobashs and Gelles. This is developed by Goode into a resources theory. He recognizes that "most people do not willingly choose overt force when they command other resources because the costs of using force are high".[54] He therefore hypothesizes that the greater the other resources an individual can command, the less he will use force in an 'overt manner'.

The husband in the middle or upper class family commands more force, in spite of his lesser willingness to use his own physical strength, because he possesses far more other social resources. His greater social prestige in the larger society and the family, his larger economic possessions, and his stronger emphasis on the human relations techniques of counter-deference, affection and communication give him greater influence generally, so that he does not have to call upon the force or its threat that he can in fact muster if he chooses . . .[55]

Some of Goode's ideas are developed in the research of O'Brien.[56] His assumption is that the family is a social system in which dominance patterns are based on social categories of age and sex. We find violence, he argues, where the male-adult-husband fails to possess superior skills, talents, resources on which his superior status is supposed to be legitimately based. So he expected violence to be prevalent in families in which the husband-father was deficient in relation to the wife-mother on achieved status characteristics. What he found, in a population in a mid-west standard metropolitan area largely devoid of the poor and blacks, was that husbands in his violent sub-group showed evidence of underachievement in work roles as well as being deficient in achievement potential: they were, for example, dissatisfied with their job or were education drop-outs. In 84 percent the husband's income was the source of serious and constant conflict. O'Brien's interpretation of his research is in terms of status inconsistency where superior ascribed status category fails to live up to achieved status characteristics. Violence, he suggests, results from a re-assertion of male dominance. O'Brien's research is open to a number of interpretations. Thus, as well as that suggested by O'Brien himself, his research may give support to those who see violence as a response to frustration, in this case of a low status job.

As the development of the Women's Movement has been a primary factor in sensitizing our consciences to the plight of the battered woman,[57] it is not surprising that theories as to the aetiology of male violence towards women should have developed within the ideology of their liberation politics. The Women's Movement sees battering as a function of woman's generally oppressed position. "The challenge of Women's Aid", states Weir, "is that it demands a fundamental change in the way in which women are defined".[58] No one has shown better than Kate Millett[59] how the patriarchal bias has operated in culture and is reflected in literature. The view is thus presented that the purpose of male violence is to control women. Nor is it a view unique to militant women. Whitehurst, whose own frame of reference is within social-structural theories of strain, admitted that a survey of his had shown that "threats of violence are frequent among husbands as a means of controlling wives".[60] He describes a case where a husband catching his wife *in flagrante delicto* "set upon the two of them in a jealous rage". Whitehurst interprets this in terms of "the husband's own need to control his wife and feel superior", and explains that this was "too much of an emotional burden for him to handle without recourse to violence."[61]

In Jalna Hanmer's recent piece,[62] this control thesis has evolved into a complete theory incorporating the whole state apparatus. In her view the state represents the interests of the dominant group who in this case are men. Thus, she says, "it is consistent that in domestic disputes the status of the victim determines the response of that section of the state given the task of controlling violence. That men unknown to the woman (the policemen) would back up the man known to her (the husband) in pursuit of their joint state-defined interest is to impartially enforce the law, for the state defines women as less equal."[63] Certainly the policies of the welfare state induce dependency. As Hanmer says: "law and law enforcement, housing policies, income maintenance, employment and earnings, interlock to trap the woman in dependence".[64] And it was the House of Commons Select Committee who asked the pertinent but rhetorical question in relation to a battering husband: "why should it be the wife and children who have to leave and not the husband? . . . Why should we not create hostels to receive the battering husband?"[65]

If male violence to women is to be seen in this way then there are no straightforward solutions, for what is being demanded is nothing less than a complete social revolution. This is recognized by Whitehurst and Hanmer. Whitehurst has put the case for 'alternative family structures',[66] families which contain more people than the traditional nuclear family, such as communes and group marriages. He rejects the hierarchical structure of the traditional family and looks to greater interpersonal openness. But, as Steinmetz and Straus recognize, there is no evidence that such families would be free of violence. There are anthropological findings that male violence to women antedates monogamy.[67] Hanmer recognizes that "male violence to women is not an unfortunate vagary of human nature called forth by class oppression".[68] Hanmer herself is less ambitious. She calls for women to challenge the use of force by males. She demands that "the problem of men" be "raised theoretically and with it the question of the extent to which men can be re-educated."[69]

Four explanations have thus been put forward to gain an understanding of the phenomenon of wife-battering. Most attention has been given to the pathological explanation and insofar as measures to reduce violence have been taken they have been directed towards the problem so conceived. This is hardly surprising. It is always easier to individualize a problem and to many it is preferable to psychologize it. It is comforting to think that violence in the family is abnormal. But so long as we think this way we are unlikely to solve the problem. On this pessimistic note I turn to consider how English law and English institutions have conceived the problem and what solutions have been offered.

2. Married Women In English Law

The Christian conception of man and wife as one flesh is the foundation of much of the common law on husband and wife.[70] And, as has been said, to the Pauline conclusion English law added the rider: "and I am he".[71] The very being of the married woman was suspended during coverture. Most of the disabilities have now been removed though significant vestiges remain: a married woman living with her husband, for example (indeed any woman living with any man) is not entitled to apply for supplementary benefits in her own right.[72] The strength of the

Volksgeist[73] in expressive relationships has often been commented upon:[74] law reform in family law does not guarantee a change in the mores.[75] This needs to be understood in this context.

Thus, for centuries husbands had the right to chastise their wives. Hawkins would allow a man to exercise 'moderate correction' upon his wife as he would 'correct his apprentices or children'.[76] In Bacon's Abridgment of 1736 a husband is said to have the right to 'beat' his wife.[77] Blackstone, in words reminiscent of contemporaries who believe wife-batterers to be confined to a working-class sub-culture, believed that the right was obsolete, having been doubted in the politer reign of Charles II, but that "the lower rank of people who were always fond of the old common law still claim and exert their ancient privilege and courts of law still permit a husband to restrain a wife of her liberty in case of any gross misbehavior".[78] In an aside he explained that this was for women's "protection and benefit . . . so great a favorite is the female sex of the laws of England." The right was "finally abolished"[79] in 1891 in *R. v. Jackson*: the Master of the Rolls doubted whether "it ever was the law"[80] and the Lord Chancellor referred to "quaint and absurd dicta".[81] There are, however, dicta as late as 1840 supporting a general right.[82]

More recently, judges have supported the right of a husband to correct his wife. In 1946 Henn Collins J. in *Meacher v. Meacher*[83] held a husband was within his rights in assaulting his wife because she refused to obey his orders not to visit her relations. The court of appeal reversed his decision. In 1959 a judge held that it was cruelty when a husband gave his adulterous wife the 'hardest smacked bottom she had ever had' but added that if he had punished her as one punishes a naughty child it would not have been cruel.[84] Only two years ago a sheriff in Scotland, on fining a husband for hitting his wife in the face, remarked: "it is a well known fact that you can strike your wife's bottom if you wish, but you must not strike her on the face".[85] He also expressed his support for the ancient principle that "reasonable chastisement should be the duty of every husband if his wife misbehaves." Do these judicial pronouncements, isolated as they are, reflect the common consciousness of a society ruled by the ethos of male domination? Do they go some way towards explaining the off-quoted rationalization of wife-battering that 'they deserve it'.[86] Gelles found women who subscribed to this view. One said: "he hit me once. It wasn't very long ago. The baby was about 2 months old . . . we were fighting about something. I have a habit of not keeping my mouth shut. I kept at him and at him. He finally turned round and belted me. It was my fault, I asked for it."[87] Parnas also observed occasions where wives believed that a husband should beat his wife 'every once in a while'.[88] The deviance has become normalized. Dunn J. though, got 'a wigging from wives' when he suggested that wives in the north of England didn't mind their husbands beating them but drew the line at adultery.[89] And Faulks J. confessed to having made 'an ass' of himself when he insinuated that the wives of Welsh miners accepted their husbands' right to spank them.[90]

3. The Problem of Rape

This ideology is reflected in the attitude of English law towards rape. By definition it cannot exist within marriage, though the behavior itself may be functionally equivalent to comparable behavior committed outside the bounds of marriage and given the official label of rape. A husband may, however, be convicted of raping his wife if magistrates have made a non-cohabitation order in favor of the wife,[91] if a decree *nisi* of divorce has been pronounced,[92] and possibly if they have agreed to separate, particularly if there is a separation agreement containing a non-molestation clause.[93]

In 1972 Cairns L.J. opined[94] that "the notion that a husband can, without incurring punishment, treat his wife . . . with any kind of hostile force is obsolete". He held that the crime of kidnapping could thus be committed by a husband against his wife. Kidnapping and rape are not *in pari materia,* but Cairns L.J.'s dictum is wide enough to cast doubt on the propriety of exempting husbands from prosecution for rapes upon their wives. Despite the existence of the immunity it is clear that a husband, though at liberty to have sexual intercourse with his wife, may not use force or violence to exercise that liberty. If he does he may be charged with assault or some other offence. The law rests on a fiction and is clearly inconsistent with civil law principles: a wife, for example, is not bound to submit to inordinate or unreasonable sexual demands by her husband,[95] and she may refuse sexual intercourse if he is suffering from a venereal disease.[96]

The privilege of a husband to rape his wife has been repudiated in the criminal codes of Sweden and Denmark and in the USSR and a number of other countries in the Communist bloc.[97] An attempt was made to abolish the exemption in England in 1976[98] but it ultimately failed. The logic of Soames in *The Forsyte Saga* is thus preserved: "women made a fuss about it in books, but in the cool judgment of right thinking men . . . he had but done his best to sustain the sanctity of marriage, to prevent her from abandoning her duty".[99] He had, of course, just raped Irene.

To many contemporary theorists the act of rape is a cameo of male-female relationships, forcible penetration being at one end of a spectrum of male sexual dominance.[100] Griffin refers to it as "a form of mass terrorism".[101] Davis believes that "a primary goal of the sexual aggressor . . . is the conquest and degradation of his victim"[102] and the Schwendingers see rape as "a power trip . . . an act of aggression and an act of contempt".[103] To these writers the motivation for rape is only secondarily sexual.[104]

4. The Protection of the Criminal Law

What protection is afforded the battered wife by the criminal law? With the exception of rape a husband can be prosecuted for all other offences against the person on his wife. It is unnecessary to list all these offences. Suffice it to say that any attack by a husband causing his wife any actual bodily harm constitutes a criminal offence.[105] To constitute 'actual bodily harm' the harm need not be really serious.[106] Lynskey J. said that "it includes any hurt or injury calculated to interfere with the health or comfort of the prosecutor."[107] This includes, so he held, a hysterical and nervous condition resulting from an assault. It seems to follow that many, if not most, acts of molestation[108] will come within the concept. A more serious offence is committed when 'really serious' bodily harm is caused.[109]

If criminal proceedings are brought, the wife is a competent and compellable witness against her own husband.[110] In fact, though, if she is an unwilling witness the police may well be hard put to prove the charge. Provocation is a defence only to a charge of murder (reducing it to manslaughter)[111] so a husband may not claim that he was driven to assault his wife. However, we know that juries do take account of such 'defences'[112] rather as they regard 'contributory negligence' as a defence to a charge of rape.[113] Furthermore, the injured wife's view of her own role in the event may enter into her decision not to mobilize the criminal justice system.[114]

There have been a couple of cases in England recently of wives who killed brutal husbands. To Mabel Bangert,[115] who killed her husband by stabbing him repeatedly in the back as he went to attack their crippled son, Milmo J. said: "you have lived your life with a tyrannical, violent and cruel husband. Your provocation was as severe as any I have come across". She was found guilty of manslaughter and received a suspended gaol sentence. In the popular press this decision was applauded and Mrs. Bangert became a folk hero — for a day or so. Valerie Pulling[116] shot her husband when she feared another beating from him. May J. told the jury it was important to assess the case without emotion but advised an acquittal if they felt it was not Mrs. Pulling's intention to kill or seriously harm her husband. The jury did not, it seems, put emotion aside and, in a perverse but arguably justifiable verdict, acquitted her. It is difficult to estimate how typical these cases are: my suspicion is that both judges and juries take a more lenient attitude to such cases than they would have done a decade ago.

In some legal systems, though not the English, wife-beating is a distinct nominate crime. Thus, in California a 1945 statute states: "any husband who wilfully inflicts upon his wife corporal injury resulting in a traumatic condition . . . is guilty of a felony"[117] punishable by a gaol sentence of between one year and ten. In *People v. Burns*[118] it was held that to satisfy this provision visible bruises and injuries had to be present. Apparently, "police and district attorneys are unwilling to charge an assailant [with wife-beating, which is a felony] because of the higher bail and longer jail sentence involved".[119] This statutory provision is currently under a cloud. It discriminates on the basis of sex and is therefore arguably unconstitutional. Indeed, in 1975 Judge Eugene Premo of the San Jose Superior Court dismissed a charge on this very basis: he said "a wife inflicting the same injury and trauma can be subjected to no more than misdemeanour prosecution under assault and battery sections".[120] In spite of Del Martin's forceful criticism that this decision "takes advantage of the existing male bias within the criminal justice system and denies the value of laws created to correct existing imbalances",[121] it is difficult to see what such laws achieve. If, as is generally accepted, the criminal law is a blunt instrument in the war against domestic violence, it is dubious if the creation of specific offences can improve the situation.

5. Compensation for Criminal Injury

In Great Britain since 1964 a scheme has existed whereby victims of criminal assaults can claim compensation from the state, through the Criminal Injuries Compensation Board (CICB). The idea originated in New Zealand and has since spread. California was the first state in the U.S.A. to introduce the concept. It has cost the British exchequer £30 million. Applications are going up all the time. In 1975-6 they were 17.3 percent up on the previous year.[122] Wives who suffer personal injury at their husband's hands are, however, excluded. Paragraph 7 of the scheme reads:

> Where the victim who suffered injuries and the offender who inflicted them were living together at the time as members of the same family no compensation will be payable. For the purpose of this paragraph where a man and a woman were living together as man and wife they will be treated as if they were married to one another.[123]

In the first twelve years of the operation of the scheme 335 applicants for compensation were ruled out of order on the basis of paragraph 7: that is, three percent of all applicants have failed because the injury was caused in a domestic setting. There were 76 cases in 1975-6 (four percent of the total number of applications). Many of these applications are made on behalf of children.[124]

The battered wife's plight was aggravated by a decision of the Divisional Court in 1972.[125] Lord Widgery held that the words "living together . . . as members of the same family" had their ordinary natural meaning and were not to be read in the light of general matrimonial law. He concluded that a couple were 'living together' although the wife, terrified for her own safety, slept in a bedroom with her two daughters leaving the husband to sleep on a sofa in the living room. There were no sexual relations. We do not know from the report whether meals were consumed together or whether she did his washing. But there is a good chance that he would be held to be in desertion and that they would be 'living apart' for the separation provisions of the divorce legislation.[126] In view of this the decision is to be deprecated. A wife who is separated from her husband is eligible for compensation as are divorced women. Thus, where a former husband slashed his former wife's hands lacerating tendons and ensuring that she was no longer able to work, the CICB paid her compensation (his behavior was also sufficiently 'obvious and gross' for it to be taken account of when the question of a transfer of property arose).[127] The British system is not alone in excluding victims of family violence. According to Shank, intrafamily crime or victim participation (a category also recognized for exclusion purposes in the British scheme) may disqualify one from compensation under the Californian scheme.[128]

How is one to explain the exclusion of victims of family violence from the scheme? Two popular explanations would cite the difficulties of proof in a family situation and the 'flood-gates' danger argument. Neither is a satisfactory explanation. In cases of impossibility of proof, otherwise eligible claims could be disallowed. The floodgates argument is also disingenuous as, with the number of violent crimes known to the police approaching 100,000 a year and nearly seven times more than the number of applicants for compensation, they are potentially open anyway, and it is only lack of knowledge and 'legal competence'[129] which cut access to the Board down. A better explanation is found (in another context) in Marx's recent study of violence in an Israeli township.[130] He argues that, in the case of inter-personal assaults in the privacy of the home, the "public interest is not at stake" with the result that "law organs tend to apply a more restricted definition of violence to them."[131] One could argue, as Hanmer does,[132] that male violence against women is in the public interest as presently defined in the sense that it is functional to preserving male dominance. If that is so, it is even more likely that the state would wish to exclude battered wives from the scope of the compensation scheme. So long as husbands can legally rape their wives and some judges are prepared to concede to them a liberty to spank them it is difficult to see how the state could compensate wives for injuries inflicted by their husbands.

6. The Non-Enforcement of the Criminal Law

In June 1973, in answer to a question tabled in the House of Commons by Jack Ashley M.P., a leading champion of battered women's rights, the Home Office said: "the law does not discriminate between assaults by a husband on his wife and other assaults. Any assault constitutes a criminal offence".[133] That is the theory but what happens in practice?

We know that wives are reluctant to report assaults by their husbands on themselves to the police. There are a number of reasons for this. They may expect to be degraded and humiliated. They may know (or half-know) about police attitudes towards domestic disturbances. If they are frequent victims they may tend to refrain from reporting because the burdens of such reporting and follow-up actions may be intolerably great. They may believe that, without a husband to support them, they will be worse off. They may sense that initiating police action is likely to cause them even greater distress: greater poverty or worse beatings.

But, given that they alert the police, what happens then? It is not generally realized that in cases of *common* assault (that is, where no bodily injury is incurred) the legal remedy is for the wife herself to initiate proceedings in the magistrates' court. A police officer is not entitled to act as informant on a charge of common assault[134] unless the person assaulted is so feeble, old and infirm as to be incapable of instituting proceedings because he is not a free agent but is under the control of the person committing the assault.[135] It is arguable that some battered women come into this category but the number is probably small. In cases of more serious assaults the police have the power of arrest as well as the duty to follow up and prosecute.[136]

The police attitude itself is fashioned by a number of factors. The Association of Chief Police Officers of England and Wales and Northern Ireland in its evidence to the House of Commons Select Committee cited as a consideration a factor that may well be at the root of the problem:

Whilst such problems take up considerable police time . . . in the majority of cases the role of the police is a negative one. We are, after all, dealing with persons 'bound in marriage', and it is important, for a host of reasons, to maintain the unity of the spouses. Precipitate

83 The Phenomenon of Marital Violence

action by the police could aggravate the position to such an extent as to create a worse situation than the one they were summoned to deal with.[137]

The association is favorable to the provision of refuges but it adds: "every effort *should be made to re-unite the family*[138] (its emphasis). In a similar way Parnas says of intrafamily violence that it is different from normal crime in that "preservation of family relationships may be deemed a very important social goal".[139] What is wanted is a restoration of the equilibrium with the minimum of change. It is taken as a 'given' that 're-uniting' the family, 'preserving' family relationships, is desirable.

The attitude of the police is formed also by their training and environment. In England the police recruit learns almost nothing about the dynamics of marital conflict during his sixteen-week crash induction. Courses tend to be legalistic and the social science content is sparse. In the United States, according to Parnas,[140] what police learn about most is the danger involved in intervening in marital conflict. Certainly, this is what remains in the policeman's memory. Since over 20 percent of police deaths in the U.S.A occur on domestic disturbance calls this is hardly surprising. Very few police are killed on duty in England, and to my knowledge no policeman has been killed when intervening in a domestic disturbance. But in England too a low profile policy is kept.

Parnas found that it is common for the wife to go to the aid of her husband so that "the danger quotient is high for both disputing parties".[141] Wives may attack the police: such a reaction being elicited by "emotional ties and habituated loyalty".[142] Furthermore, as the Metropolitan Police Memorandum to the House of Commons Select Committee points out: "the wife herself [in any subsequent prosecution] is an essential witness. Experience has shown that prosecutions have failed or could not be pursued because of a withdrawal by the wife of her complaint or because of her nervous reaction to the prospect of giving evidence against her husband. A woman no matter how cruelly treated is often reluctant to see her husband imprisoned or fined."[143] This can reach the point where the police can accept marital violence as violence between 'consenting adults' and hence a 'private affair'.[144] Even where the wife wants a prosecution to take place they may actively discourage her initiative.

Parnas has shown that in the U.S.A. the police in the marital violence situation act as support figures rather than instruments of control.[145] That they see their prime objective as adjustment rather than arrest. This is consistent both with general sociology of policing research[146] and with what has been found in England.[147] The public in England hold the police in high regard[148] and to many they are the first of the social services, acting as gatekeepers and filters to the other specialized services. No other agency is known to function for 24 hours a day. Arrests, however, do take place. What are the criteria for choosing between arrest and mediation or arrest and caution?

There will undoubtedly be local variations. These will largely reflect the differences in communities. A policeman cannot be an effective peace officer, he cannot act in a social support capacity, unless he understands, or better still participates in, the society he polices. Sub-cultural differences, also, affect patrol practices. Thus, Skolnick in his classic study of *Justice Without Trial* can write of the way the police interpret a stabbing in the white community as a 'potential homicide' which, in the black ghetto, is 'written off' as a 'North Westville battery'.[149]

The Association of Chief Police Officers of England, Wales and Northern Ireland in its Memorandum to the Select Committee lists a number of factors which militate for or against the decision to arrest and prosecute:

   (i) the seriousness of the assault;
  (ii) the availability of witnesses;
 (iii) the character of the alleged assailant;
 (iv) age, infirmity, *etc.,* of the complainant;
  (v) previous domestic history;
 (vi) the wishes of the complainant;
(vii) if prosecution ensued against the wishes of the complainant, would the domestic situation be adversely affected.[150]

Parnas[151] divides the decision-making into two levels in both of which discretion operates.

There is, he says, an initial screening undertaken by a dispatcher.[152] Many cases get no further. Cumming *et al.*[153] found that when a complainant reported a dispute she had only a one in two chance of getting more than advice. The interpretational latitude in a communications center is great. Surprisingly, it has not been commented upon at all in an English context, though it obviously exists.

Amongst the factors which Parnas[154] detects in decision-making in field operations are (a) the motivation for calling the police (does the victim want an arrest or does she rather wish to scare the offender, get him out of the house?); (b) the question whether the victim can afford to have the offender arrested (mainly the problem of support); (c) the sub-culture to which the disputants belong (is the conduct 'not seriously objectionable to the victim'?); (d) the danger that the offender may cause more serious harm upon his return; (e) the danger that it may cause temporary or permanent termination of family relationships or harm innocent family members; (f) the knowledge that the victim may change her mind; (g) reticence in the issuance of warrants and in prosecutions by prosecuting authorities; (h) the knowledge that the victim may choose not to prosecute; (i) the knowledge of the courts' leniency in sentencing; (j) the policeman himself having had similar experiences and his feeling that a 'man's home is his castle'.[155]

Suggestions as to the ways in which police performance can be improved usually take two forms. One view is that if the traditional role of the police in this area is adjustment and mediation, then one should increase the effectiveness of these techniques. The work of Bard[156] and the New York Family Crisis Intervention Unit[157] are the best known examples of this philosophy. An account of the New York scheme appears elsewhere in this volume (chapter 13). Chapter 12 describes similar experiments in London, Ontario.

A second view is to be found in the Report of the House of Commons Select Committee. They recommended that:

Chief Constables should review their policies about the police approach to domestic violence. Special instructions about this difficult and delicate subject should be given to all new recruits, and regular written guidance should be issued by the Chief Constable in the form of advisory leaflets.[158]

It is clear that what the committee wanted was a more vigorous prosecution policy. The Chief Constable of Bedfordshire, Mr. Anthony Armstrong, announced in February 1976 a tough new prosecution policy against husbands who battered their wives.[159] Under this policy, violent husbands were to be arrested, charged and taken to court whether or not their wives were prepared to give evidence against them. If the wife withdraws her complaint by the time the case gets to court, the police would invite the court to bind the husband over to keep the peace. If there were further incidents, the husband could be brought to court and dealt with for those as well as for breaking the order binding him over. At the same time Bedfordshire police force set up a special advisory service to help battered wives under which senior officers based at police stations in Dunstable, Luton and Bedford, the three main centres of population, are on a 24-hour call.

A report has been published on the results of the new prosecution policy during its first six months.[160] During the period, 288 acts of violence in the home came to the attention of the police. In 184 of the cases (63.9 percent), following the initial intervention of a police officer and a discussion with the parties to the assault, the complainants did not wish to pursue their complaints. No further action was taken as "any injuries visible did not justify police intervention". In 104 cases, complaints were substantiated, arrests were made and proceedings commenced. In 18 of those cases (17.3 percent), between the date the charge was preferred and the date set for the court hearing, the complainants withdrew their complaints and no further action was taken. Seventy-nine out of the remaining 86 cases had been disposed of by the time of the report. Only three men were given immediate custodial sentences. We are not told anything about the length of the sentences. Two hundred and eighty-five men (that is nearly 99 percent) responsible for acts of violence against their wives thus remained at liberty after the wives had apprised the police. Is it any wonder that battered wives are reluctant to invoke the criminal justice system against their husbands?

It may be useful to document the decisions taken in the remaining 76 cases. Two offenders were cautioned[161] by a senior police officer. In four cases no action was taken by the police. Five received suspended sentences and one a deferred sentence. Seventeen (that is 21.5 percent) were fined (this affects the wife and children as much as, if not more than, the husband). Another three were bound over as well as being fined. Five were put on probation. 15 were given conditional discharges and a further two absolute discharges. Eleven were bound over to keep the peace. A further three were bound over after the case had been dismissed and evidence heard and three more were bound over although the complaint was withdrawn. In one case a warrant was issued for arrest because the accused failed to appear. Four cases were dismissed and the men were not bound over. In total, 20 of the 79 cases resulted in men being bound over to keep the peace (that is, nearly 26 percent).

7. The Role of the Courts

Erin Pizzey has asserted that "the court is not the proper place to resolve problems of the battered wife".[162] She is critical of the willingness to grant bail and of the derisory sentences. She alleges that going to court is an ordeal, and that judges and officials are uncaring and unfeeling.[163] Field and Field have, however, pointed out that "the function of the criminal law is altered dramatically in the domestic-assault situation and the classical bases for the employment of the criminal process — deterrence, incapacitation, prevention, retribution or rehabilitation — do not apply in a substantial way to these cases."[164] In England this has barely been noted, and, although domestic violence has become an area for police experimentation, the traditional criminal process has remained intact. Unlike the U.S.A., where many attempts have been made to tailor the traditional process to take account of the special needs of spouses at war, in England the courts adjudicate upon domestic disputes and violence as upon other criminal behavior.

In the U.S.A. there have been a number of attempts to decriminalize domestic violence.[165] An account is to be found in chapter 6 of this volume. These experiments certainly appear bolder and more adventurous than anything being tried in England, and though they have the support of Susan Maidment (see chapter 6), I would enter a *caveat* against this counseling, social welfare orientation. We must ask ourselves with what we are dealing. Where we are confronted with petty violence, a couple who give as much as they take, with basically an ongoing relationship which needs sorting out, the family court approach may be desirable. Where parties are in a continuous state of social propinquity, resolution by adjudication is inconsistent with continuing viable social interaction.[166] Marital relations rest upon the social assumption that parties are ready and willing to accept and deal with each other: no amount of legal intervention can secure such a social basis.[167] But too often in cases of domestic violence we are face to face with cases of brutal violence. Can mediation[168] work in such a case?

The success of mediation depends on a number of variables, notably a common interest in having the conflict resolved to the satisfaction of each party. But what common interest do a brutal husband and a terrorized wife have in common? The standard answer is that they may have children and that it is important to stabilize the family. Mediation looks to the future whereas an adjudication measures the husband's behavior against criminal legislation.[169] Mediation looks towards a compromise solution: an adjudicator, employing traditional techniques, imposes what he regards as a just solution.[170] Once within the family court setting and a social welfare counselling orientation we may lose track of the fact that wife-beating may be a brutal criminal assault and not just the symptom of a troubled marriage.

The question that needs to be asked of those who see progress as lying with family courts and counselling services is what they conceive to be the causes of wife-beating. Their goal is clear: they want reconciliation and stability, they want the family to *function as it should*. They want to preserve the family. They rarely articulate a theory of family violence but implicit is one of two assumptions: (i) that the batterer has behaved 'irrationally' because he is disturbed in some way or (ii) he has problems resulting from inadequate resources. On either hypothesis the solution is seen in terms of the need for more social work intervention, courts developing welfare functions as well as better housing and improved employment prospects. But do these solutions speak to the right problem? Are they in the woman's interests? I doubt it. And even using the criterion of success employed by its proponents I would doubt whether the counselling orientation is successful.[171]

8. The Law of Tort

The act of battering constitutes the torts of assault and battery. In England until 1962 a spouse was not allowed to sue the other in tort.[172] Two reasons were given for this. First, the fiction that they were one flesh.[173] Secondly, that such litigation was "unseemly, distressing and embittering".[174] To quote Glanville Williams: "if a husband 'beats up' his wife, she cannot sue him, because to sue him would be unwifely".[175] Each of the parties to a marriage now has the same right of action in tort against the other as if they were not married. But, in order to prevent them from using the court as a forum for trivial domestic disputes, the proceedings may be stayed if it appears that 'no substantial benefit'[176] will accrue to either party from their continuation.

There are no statistics as to the number of spouses who sue each other in tort nor of the number of cases which are stayed. Nearly all cases will arise out of motor accidents and the spouse will only be a nominal defendant. "Nothing draws two people together like a mutual desire to get something out of one's insurance carrier."[177] Whilst the immunity was impossible to defend it would be folly to pretend that its removal has in any way helped the battered wife. But, though rarely if ever used for such purposes, it was potentially of use prior to the passing of the Domestic Violence and Matrimonial Proceedings Act 1976 as a way of obtaining an injunction against molestation or to exclude a brutal husband from the matrimonial home.[178]

The majority of American states have still to abrogate the doctrine of inter-spousal immunity.[179] California did so in the case of *Self v. Self*[180] in 1962: this case is instructive in that it arose out of an assault by a husband against his wife in the course of which her arm was broken. Again, there are no available statistics as to the use of a civil action for damages in any of the states which have abolished the immunity, but it is doubted that it is in common use anywhere.

9. Matrimonial Proceedings in Magistrates' Courts: the Non-Cohabitation Clause.

In England there are two types of matrimonial proceedings that can be brought. A spouse may seek the "summary, local and inexpensive relief"[181] offered by magistrates' courts. Provided an offence can be proved the court may make an order containing a non-cohabitation clause. This relieves the complainant of his or her obligation to cohabit with the defendant. It is, however, simply a declaration and is not enforceable. If granted it prevents the complainant relying on the defendant's desertion subsequent to the order, so that it may have positive disadvantages to the complainant.[182] On the other hand, forced sexual intercourse does amount to rape. Whether such a clause is inserted depends on the discretion of the court.[183]

Gibson found that many magistrates courts were overwilling to insert a non-cohabitation clause.[184] He noted that "in many instances the court in making a maintenance order inadvertently omits to strike out from the printed form, which is adaptable to different orders, the non-cohabitation clause".[185] He found in a survey of 1,200 orders in force in 1966 by 50 magistrates' courts that in 30 percent a non-cohabitation clause had been inserted. The proportion rose to 40 percent if orders made in 1964 and 1965 only were taken into account. Further, in only 62 percent of the cases where such a clause was found was persistent cruelty either the sole ground or one ground of two or more grounds for the wife's application. In 22 percent the ground was adultery, in 11 percent desertion and in five percent wilful neglect to maintain. Gibson also found a greater propensity to insert a non-cohabitation clause in courts in the north of England. Gibson blamed justices' clerks for the over-use of the non-cohabitation clause. It is possible also that they and the magistrates react to the policies of local authorities which show a greater willingness to transfer council tenancies where the wife has such an order.[186]

Many magistrates will not make a non-cohabitation order where a wife is still living with her husband. Others expect the impossible: that, although remaining in the matrimonial home, she lead a separate life from her husband. Magistrates have as yet no power to evict husbands, though the Law Commission has recommended[187] that such a power should be conferred on them where they are satisfied that the wife or a child of the family is in danger of being physically injured by the husband and that he has used violence against the wife or a child of the family, or he has threatened violence against the wife or a child of the family and also has used violence against some other person, or he has disobeyed a personal protection order. These recommendations are incorporated in the Domestic Proceedings and Magistrates' Courts Bill 1978.

Magistrates do not dissolve marriages. Only the superior courts, divorce county courts and the High Court, can grant a licence to remarry. So non-cohabitation orders do not affect status and the wife is left in a state of limbo. But something like 50 percent of the magistrates' court matrimonial orders remain the final orders for that marriage, leaving spouses neither properly married nor free to remarry.[188] Women in such cases invariably rely on state assistance and can form no regular sexual relationships unless the man concerned is ready and able to support them and their children, for the cohabitation rule (one of the best examples of the way in which the state controls women) prevents the payment of supplementary benefit where a woman lives with a man *as* his wife.[189]

The magistrates' courts "deal exclusively with what used to be called the lumpen proletariat . . . the poorest, the least literate, the worst informed section of the population".[190] Indeed, the domestic jurisdiction of the magistrates courts was designed for this very population. Magistrates' courts domestic juridiction is now under a cloud: attacked by McGregor *et al.* in *Separated Spouses,*[191] Marsden in

Mothers Alone[192] and most notably in the Finer Report.[193] There has been a considerable decline in recent years in the numbers of those using the courts for domestic proceedings. The Finer Report recommended family courts[194] but the British Government "see no prospect of accepting [this] recommendation".[195] The Law Commission's recent proposals for change take this into account and make suggestions for change in the substantive law within the existing structure of courts.[196]

The Law Commission proposes[197] that a magistrates' court should have power, if it is satisfied by evidence of violent behavior or threat of violent behavior on the part of the respondent against the complainant or a child of the family to make one or both of the following orders: (i) an order that the respondent shall not use or threaten violence against the complainant; (ii) an order that the respondent shall not use or threaten violence against a child of the family. It also recommends the power to make exclusion orders and emergency orders.

Although these proposals have been accepted in the Domestic Proceedings and Magistrates' Courts Bill 1978,[198] they are open to several criticisms. Protection is to be extended to husbands and wives but not to those who live together outside lawful wedlock. Since legislation has recently been passed enabling the county courts to do just this[199] it is difficult to defend their exclusion from magisterial domestic jurisdiction. Secondly, protection covers only 'children of the family'. This includes children 'treated' as such by a non-parent. But, whilst it may be reasonable to limit the provision of financial support to such children, it is difficult to see why a personal protection order should not extend to children who have not been 'treated' in this way. Thirdly, magistrates' courts will be able to act only when actual *violence* is used or threatened. Yet, as will be explained in section 10 of this chapter, recent legislation has allowed Superior Court judges to grant injunctions where husbands (or wives) merely pester, and can attach a power of arrest where psychological harm is perpetrated. The Law Commission defended its rejection of granting magistrates jurisdiction in this terrain by arguing that "adjudication on an allegation of psychological damage is a very difficult matter which may involve the assessment of evidence by psychiatrists. This is a highly skilled task which we do not think can appropriately be placed on magistrates".[200] It is difficult to accept this reasoning. Many magistrates will be better equipped to tackle psychiatric evidence than most judges. Fourthly, the Law Commission in my opinion, gave insufficient attention to the question of enforcement of the orders it proposes. It points out correctly the present deficiencies and then assumes that monetary sanctions and ultimately committal will ensure compliance with the new orders. Financial penalties, however, are unlikely to have an impact on the clientele of the domestic courts because quite simply the money is not there. Under the system proposed by the Law Commission the woman will have to go back to the court to ask it to enforce the order. It is not proposed to give magistrates the power to attach a power of arrest to the orders they make. Finally, it is suggested that the power to make emergency orders could be widened so that a single magistrate (or even a justices' clerk) might make a protection order out of court hours.[201]

The existing system is not satisfactory. The 1978 Bill, when enacted, will effect some improvement but is of limited value.

Another remedy open to a battered wife is to seek dissolution of her marriage. Not that she will necessarily live in peace if she accomplishes this. The Law Reports are replete with instances of post-dissolution batteries. Indeed, as will be shown in the next section, a divorced woman is at a disadvantage in seeking an injunction.

There is little doubt, however, that a woman battered by her husband can divorce him. Like many other systems, English law now bases divorce on the concept of irretrievable breakdown. Unlike some systems,[202] however, it does not leave the question at large but specifies facts,[203] proof of any of which raises a strong presumption that the marriage has broken down irreparably. One of these facts is "that the respondent has behaved in such a way that the petitioner cannot reasonably be expected to live with the respondent".[204] The courts consider not only the behavior of the respondent but "the character, personality, disposition and behavior of the petitioner".[205] The question asked is "can this petitioner, with his or her personality, with his or her faults and other attributes, good and bad, and having regard to his or her behavior during the marriage, reasonably be expected to live with this respondent?"[206] Bagnall J. gave as an example the following: "a violent petitioner can reasonably be expected to live with a violent respondent."[207] There are reported cases where wives have obtained decrees where husbands have treated them with violence.[208] In one case (*Bradley v. Bradley*)[209] the Court of Appeal accepted that a wife could not reasonably be expected to live with her husband "even though she [was] in the same house with him — and in fact living with him", as she had "no alternative open to her, nowhere else to go" It was "not reasonable to expect her to live there, but albeit unreasonable, she [had] no option but to be there".[210] Mrs. Bradley had seven children living with her and two non-cohabitation orders for persistent cruelty but the local public housing authority would not rehouse her until she secured a divorce against her husband. The case is thus particularly instructive.

It should be noted that in England one may only petition for divorce after three years of marriage.[211] A judge may, however, allow the presentation of a petition within this period if he considers the case one of exceptional hardship suffered by the petitioner or of exceptional depravity on the part of the respondent.[212] In determining the application the judge is to have regard to the interests of any child of the family and to whether there is a reasonable probability of reconciliation within the three years. This provision was first introduced 40 years ago and has been consistently defended by official committees[213] though it finds little support in academic literature.[214] It has never existed in Scotland or in most of the rest of the world. Its effect is to delay divorce, which in England reaches its peak after four years. As women who are going to be battered often find that this begins shortly after marriage, the bar to divorce is potentially a serious inconvenience. In the past the courts have construed serious cruelty coupled with physical injury as exceptional depravity.[215] In considering exceptional hardship, the courts have considered what effect the facts have had on the particular petitioner. So, if a nervous wife suffered a breakdown because of her husband's conduct, she might well get leave to petition within the three-year period.[216]

Because of such interpretations battered women should not suffer unduly from the bar. They did, however, suffer under the old law of injunctions when it was held that under a summons asking for leave to petition within three years the courts could not exclude the husband from the matrimonial home where this was in his name, although they could grant an injunction against molestation.[217] This is no longer the case since the passing of the Domestic Violence and Matrimonial Proceedings Act of 1976.

A further problem for the battered wife, and one which may have far-reaching implications, is the recent withdrawal of legal aid from undefended divorces.[218] She can still seek legal advice and assistance but she will have to negotiate the mechanics of the divorce herself.

Divorce is an obvious remedy and is usually efficacious. But it is final. Many women, distraught, bruised and battered, and doubtless endowed with beliefs about the necessity of trying to 'make a go of it', will lack the mental composure to consider the long-term decision of divorce. As Baroness Phillips said in the House of Lords in July 1976: "at the time of probably having been beaten, assaulted and thrown out of the house, bruised and frightened, the last thing a woman wants to do is start the complications of a divorce or separation proceedings."[219] Nor must one forget her 'romantic delusions',[220] the 'Beauty and the Beast syndrome';[221] she wishes to reform him and preserve the marriage for the sake of the family. Perhaps she also considers the alternatives; accommodation problems, living on state assistance, employment prospects, day-care facilities for children *etc.* These may be the real reasons why she stays and does not seek divorce: the romanticism may be merely rationalization. It may be predicted that divorce applications will increase as the alternatives to married life improve.

10. The Injunction Weapon

The injunction is the battered wife's best legal weapon. It is also the most popular legal remedy. In November 1975 there were 252 *ex parte* applications, three quarters of them in large cities.[222] According to the Lord Chancellor, speaking in the House of Lords in July 1976, "practically all of them involved physical violence to the person, and the very large majority related to couples who were still married".[223] This means that about 3,000 applications are made a year. When the President of the Family Division, Sir George Baker, gave evidence to the House of Commons Select Committee he noted that applications in the long vacation for injunctions had increased in London. In 1972 there had been 339 applications, in 1973, 468 and in 1974, 502. But outside London there was no evidence of any increase. With the introduction of the Domestic Violence and Matrimonial Proceedings Act 1976 the spiral may be expected to continue.

The High Court's power to grant injunctions is contained in the Supreme Court of Judicature (Consolidation) Act of 1925. Section 45 of this states that an injunction may be granted "in all cases in which it appears to the court to be just or convenient to do so". The jurisdiction of county courts is contained in section 74 of the County Courts Act of 1959 and is in every way as full as that of the High Court. The courts, however, cut down their jurisdiction. They decided that there had to be a sufficient nexus between the subject-matter of the main action and the relief sought by injunction.[224] It followed that an application for an injunction had to be ancillary to other proceedings. In theory these needed to be nothing more than an action for assault claiming £2 damages. In practice it tended to mean divorce proceedings. The courts also decided, though they hardly needed to, that an injunction could only be granted to support a legal right.[225] They then set about repairing some of the damage by holding that the wife's personal right to remain in the matrimonial home is such a right,[226] though this right ceased on termination of the marriage.[227] What jurisdiction they had they exercised most sparingly. The general attitude adopted until very recently was that to exclude a husband from the matrimonial home was a drastic step to be taken only in extreme circumstances. Thus, in *Hall v. Hall*,[228] the Court of Appeal said it would not order a husband out unless it was proved to be impossible for the spouses to live together. And in *Mamane v. Mamane*,[229] the Court of appeal said it would only make an order where it was "imperative and inescapable". An order was refused despite the fact that the husband was given to unbalanced emotional outbursts and acts of violence and there were two young children.[230] The question of jurisdiction has, however, been radically remoulded by the Domestic Violence and Matrimonial Proceedings Act of 1976. There is also evidence from the landmark decision of *Bassett v. Bassett*[231] that the way the court exercises its discretion has been liberalized.

The 1976 Act[232] provides that a county court shall have jurisdiction to grant injunctions against molestation and to exclude a spouse from the matrimonial home, whether or not any other relief is sought and irrespective of whether the man and woman involved are husband and wife or cohabitees. The jurisdiction of the High Court is not altered by the Act but this required only an amendment to Rules of Court and this has been made. The relevant section (s. 1) refers to applications "by a party to a marriage" and gives jurisdiction to grant an injunction against "the other party to the marriage". Husbands as well as wives can, therefore, apply for an injunction, so can cohabitees "living with each other in the same household as husband and wife" (s. 1(2)).[233] But former spouses cannot. This means that a county court which formerly had jurisdiction to issue injunctions restraining molestation of former spouses can no longer do so.[234] Further, county courts had been known to exclude former husbands from the former matrimonial home where they considered it necessary to protect children.[235] Such jurisdiction was dubious but there is no doubt it was exercised. They will no longer be able to do so. The High Court, in exercise of its inherent jurisdiction to protect children, will continue to be able to exclude husbands from their property where the marriage is already dissolved, where it is necessary to protect the welfare of children.[236]

Since injunctions may only be sought against "the other party to the marriage" (or cohabitation), a wife cannot exclude mistresses and husband's relatives from the matrimonial home, unless she has a proprietary interest in it, for otherwise a wife has no legal rights against such intruders.[237] An injunction not to molest is valueless if the offending party cannot be ejected. In the past courts have certainly ordered mistresses out of the matrimonial home.[238] On the plain language of the 1976 Act they will no longer be able to do so. This may not be of much practical significance since most mistresses will follow their lovers out of the matrimonial home, but problems could arise.

Another problem is that the Act is limited to, and does not define, the matrimonial home. English law is still founded upon separation of property.[239] A vindictive husband could thus on being excluded from the matrimonial home remove *his* furniture and leave the wife a miserable existence.[240] As the Act does not define 'matrimonial home' there must be considerable doubt as to whether a wife could exclude her husband from a home where she has never lived with him.[241] He may have sold the matrimonial home over her head and be threatening violence if she enters the house he has now bought. She could get an injunction against molestation but it is dubious if she could exclude him from the house. She certainly cannot do so under the Matrimonial Homes Act of 1967, even as amended by s. 3 of the 1976 Act.[242]

The Act is silent on the criteria for the exercise of jurisdiction. Its sponsor, Miss Jo. Richardson, thinks "the court will exercise its discretion along the lines of the policy it has already developed".[243] The courts were formerly most reluctant to order a man out. But in *Bassett v. Bassett*[244] the Court of Appeal took a more practical approach to the problem. Ormrod L.J. accepted that ordering a spouse to leave was a drastic order but he suggested that "to refuse to make such an order may have no less drastic results, if the consequences of refusing to make an order is to inflict severe hardship on the unsuccessful spouse".[245] He thought that, particularly in cases where the marriage has already broken down, the court "should think essentially in terms of homes, especially for the children, and then consider the balance of hardship"[246] likely to be caused by making the order against the hardship likely to be caused by refusing it. He believed that the husband would find it easier to secure accommodation for himself than the wife with a baby would. This is not necessarily so: local authorities are more willing to help mothers with young children than single men. Ormrod L.J.'s reasoning could, therefore, rebound.

Another decision which is particularly favorable to the wife is *Hunt v. Hunt*.[247] The wife made allegations of repeated violence on her by her husband. She left the home and wished to return. She sought an interlocutory order to exclude him on the ground that his violence made her fear for her safety and for that of the children who were also emotionally upset by the violence. The allegations were not substantiated. The Court of Appeal took the view that it didn't have to be satisfied that the wife's allegations were true, merely that they might be true. Their view was that the truth of the matter could be ventilated at the full hearing. But supposing the husband does not defend, for example, for reasons of cost?[248]

The courts are showing a much greater willingness to exclude a husband from the matrimonial home. The tendency is to think in terms of homes and personal rights rather than property rights.[249] The recent Court of Appeal cases of *Walker v. Walker*[250] and *Rennick v. Rennick*[251] also suggest that the *Bassett* approach is now prefered. But how easy is it to get an injunction and of what value is it once obtained?[252] First, the woman has to know how to set about getting it. She will almost certainly need a solicitor and legal aid. Finding a solicitor willing to act is not easy. If legal aid is required it will be needed urgently, so that emergency legal aid will have to be applied for. Many solicitors do not touch injunction cases and, if they do, will not get a legal aid certificate quickly enough. Pizzey reports that neighborhood law centers also usually exclude matrimonial matters, as these are allegedly served adequately by the private profession, though there is evidence of a greater willingness to help battered women secure injunctions than there was only a couple of years ago.[253] If these barriers can be overcome, matters can proceed very swiftly and an injunction can be obtained quickly. In the November 1975 survey, 88 percent of the orders were made within a day of the application and 58 percent within an hour. Eighty-four percent of the applicants obtained an interim injunction, although 20 cases were stood over to allow the respondent to attend.[254] Sir George Baker assured the House of Commons Select Committee that at 'the very worst' applications for injunctions were heard within 14 days.[255]

In the past, injunctions have not worked very well. Evidence such as that submitted to the Select Committee by the National Women's Aid Federation (NWAF) demonstrate this.[256] Things may now change as the Domestic Violence and Matrimonial Proceedings Act now gives a judge, for the first time, power to attach a power of arrest to an injunction.[257] Hitherto, many injunctions have not been worth the paper on which they were written. They are frequently broken and up till now this meant the woman returning to the court. The court could imprison or fine for breach of an injunction. It rarely did either. Pizzey tells us of 'Joan'[258] who took her husband before judges on eleven occasions before he was committed to prison. The police have looked to the civil authorities, bailiffs and tipstaffs, who work office hours and not weekends, to enforce an injunction after further proceedings to establish a breach.[259] Margaret Gregory tells us of "one case where the man contrived to avoid being served with the warrant for breach of injnction for six months, continuing all the time to commit further breaches".[260] Even when men are committed to prison for breach of an injunction their contempt can be purged relatively quickly, and the process starts all over again.

The reluctance of the police to get involved is as evident here as it is in the area of the criminal law. In answer to the sort of suggestions that led to section 2 of the 1976 Act, the Metropolitan Police in their evidence to the House of Commons Select Committee argued that: "the civil and the criminal law have always been separated for good reasons, and it would be wrong both constitutionally and practically to extend the criminal law to enable police to exercise powers to enforce orders made within the civil jurisdiction of the courts."[261] Section 2 has not extended the criminal law but it has brought the police into the enforcement of one aspect of the civil law. The Lord Chancellor could not "claim that this will make the job of a policeman easy, but it may well make it easier than it is now".[262] It is difficult to see the force of this argument: the policeman, contrary to what the Lord Chancellor thought, will have to exercise his own judgment. The statute says s. (2(3)): "a constable *may* arrest". How he will exercise his discretion remains to be seen.

Section 2 provides the police with powers of arrest for breach of injunctions in cases of domestic violence. It gives a judge power to attach a power of arrest to an injunction where (a) he grants an injunction containing a provision restraining the use of violence against the applicant or a child or makes an exclusion order *and* (b) he is satisfied that the addressee of the injunction has caused actual bodily harm to the applicant or the child *and* (c) he considers he is likely to do so again. The police are given the power of arrest without warrant where there is reasonable cause for suspecting breach of the injunction by reason of use of violence or entry into the excluded premises or area. Persons so arrested must be brought before a judge within 24 hours.[263] The police are not allowed to bail a person so arrested.[264]

This new provision may prove valuable. But one must not read too much into it. It does little, at least directly, to alter current police attitudes towards intervention in domestic violence. It only applies to the situation where there has been an injunction and it has been disobeyed. One must not lose perspective: most people, even violent husbands, obey the law.[265] Police operations at pre-injunction stage are not affected. There are also practical problems. How are the police to know about orders made in civil courts? There are 3,000 injunctions issued each year. It is impossible to tell us yet how many of them will have powers of arrest attached to them. Because of their policy of non-intervention they may not have been concerned hitherto in the spouses' domestic problems at all. Is there to be a register of matrimonial injunctions and are individual constables to be conversant with its details? The effective operation of this provision requires a centralized data bank. Is one to be set up? If not, how else are the police to know whether a particular alleged assailant is in breach of an injunction to which a power of arrest has been attached when the couple concerned come from a distant part of the country? She may have fled for refuge and he may have tracked her down but how are the police to know the details of the injunction?

Hitherto, injunctions have not been a particularly effective weapon. But with the passing of the Domestic Violence and Matrimonial Proceedings Act 1976 and the line of cases beginning with *Bassett v. Bassett* it may be that the injunction will prove useful protection for the battered wife. The Act could have been better drafted and some of its practical implications better thought through but it remains a distinct improvement on the previous situation.

11. The Problem of Accommodation

We have seen how English law in a rather hamfisted way sets about protecting the battered wife. The law sees protection as a primary need, for its ultimate goal is to keep her within the family and to rehabilitate it. The concern is less with rescue and refuge than with providing alternative accommodation, alternative life-styles. A good example of this ideology at work is the action taken in the mid-1960s over Part III accommodation.[266]

Until 1966 such accommodation, which is provided by local authorities for homeless families, was only open to wives and children. Husbands were not admitted. 'Battered women' did not 'exist' in 1965 but it was known that many of the women living in Part III accommodation were there because of their husbands' violence. But the campaign in 1965-6 to secure the entry of husbands into such accommodation was expressed in terms of the inhumanity of separating wives and husbands.[267] Of course, for many of these wives being separated from their husbands was not desirable. But for many it was a prime objective for coming to the accommodation. In the interests of the 'family' battered women were thus deprived of refuge. One wonders whether it is just coincidence that recognition of the problem of battered wives was to emerge in the four or five years following the opening of Part III accommodation to husbands.

A woman who leaves her husband is, it is frequently argued, not technically homeless. The law on homelessness hitherto provided that it was the duty of every local authority to provide residential accommodation for persons who by reason of age, infirmity or other circumstances were in need of care and attention which is not otherwise available to them, and to provide temporary accommodation for persons who were in urgent need of it, where the need had arisen in circumstances which could not reasonably have been foreseen.[268] A joint Department of the Environment/D.H.S.S. Circular in 1974 made the following recommendation:

Homelessness which results often very suddenly from the break up of family relationships can present particular difficulties for authorities in deciding what to do for the best. Accommodation for the mother and children may be required while the future of the relationship is in doubt, particularly when the future of the marriage itself has to be resolved.[269]

It was however not mandatory for local authorities to make provision for battered women. Evidence showed considerable variation in the way the provisions were made. Aylesbury claimed that battered women were voluntarily homeless: it refused to accept that she was homeless if her husband would have her back, regardless of her own choice and any danger she may have faced in returning.[270] Epping wanted evidence that she would not be accepted back before they would even consider accepting her on the housing list.[271] Indeed only 20 of 70 authorities, where the NWAF was a group, accepted battered women as homeless.[272] The Housing (Homeless Persons) Act 1977 could improve the status of battered women considerably. Although the Act does not single out battered women as a particular category with priority needs, it gives the Minister power to do so, and their case has been pressed in the Code of Guidance.[273] It remains to be seen what effect this has on housing authorities.

Local authorities adopt different attitudes towards the rehousing of battered women.[274] Some require that she has taken out legal proceedings against her husband. Some are satisfied that proceedings have been initiated, others insist that the divorce is completed. A number now do not require a battered wife to start proceedings before granting temporary accommodation. A common and reasonable requirement is that the children are in the woman's care. But this can lead to a 'Catch-22' situation when a woman is refused custody of her children because she is homeless and the local authority refuses to rehouse her as she does not have children in her care. Some impose residence qualifications. Some operate the 24-hour ruling under which the local authority ceases to have any responsibility towards rehousing when the person concerned has been out of the area for 24 hours. Both Cardiff and York apply this stringent rule.[275] In London an agreement operates between boroughs (the London Boroughs Association Agreement) under which it is recommended that "the authority in whose area the applicants were in residence the preceding night is the authority primarily responsible for the reception".[276] SHAC found that most Boroughs fulfilled at least some part of this agreement but some do not. In Redbridge, for example, the woman is referred to the "responsible borough".[277] Similar agreements operate outside London. NWAF found that 28 out of the 70 authorities under study operated this type of scheme.[278]

Many battered women will have been living in council (public housing authority) accommodation. There is an increasing tendency, at least in London, for this to be rented in joint names.[279] The majority of council tenancies are, however, still in the husband's name, and many local authorities do not grant joint tenancies at all. Bexley is one such example.[280] On a divorce the courts have a power to transfer council tenancies to the wife, though they are reluctant to exercise their powers unless the local authority is co-operative.[281] This is understandable. The attitude of most London Boroughs (and it is representative of the country as a whole) is to transfer tenancies to the wife's name where she has obtained custody of the children. As most of them require also that the wife has obtained a separation order or divorce before the tenancy transfer is effected, it implies that an interim custody order pending the divorce hearing will not of itself be sufficient. But final orders of custody can only be obtained at the stage of a decree *nisi* and then only in cases where the custody is not contested. Where it is, or where the divorce itself is contested, the entire case can take up to six months. Even an uncontested case may take three months.

Where is the battered woman to live during this period? Unless she has successfully excluded her husband from the matrimonial home by injunction, she will either have to live with him or with relatives or friends or in temporary accommodation or in a refuge. Another possibility is squatting but the courts have already held that 'necessity' is no defence,[282] and that reasonable force may be used to eject squatters.[283] The Criminal Law Act 1977, whilst not making squatting specifically illegal, has made it much easier for the police to effect instant evictions.[284] If she is on the streets with children and nowhere to go the children can be received into care (more children are in care because of parental homelessness than any other reason).[285] Local authorities' social services departments have a discretion to make payments to parents to diminish the need to receive their children into care.[286] Some local authorities make generous provision (ironically but not surprisingly those where the population as a whole is comparatively wealthy) and others hold the purse strings very tightly.[287] Some councils will pay to keep families or mothers and children in bed and breakfast accommodation. They are now cutting back on this, and the courts refuse to control the way they choose to make provision so long as it remains a lawful exercise of discretion. Thus Dorset County Council decline to accept or continue bed and breakfast commitments where there is only one child.[288] But, however generous authorities are, bed and breakfast accommodation in cheap hotels is no substitute for a home.

Many women thus fall back on the refuges such as that at Chiswick founded by Women's Aid or those established by the National Women's Aid Federation. There were hostels before Erin Pizzey established one in Chiswick. There was one in Pasadena, California in 1965: this was established by women from Al-Anon, a self-help group for families of alcoholics.[289] But the establishment of Chiswick Women's Aid in 1971 was the starting point for the current trend to create refuges specifically for battered women. To-day, there are more than 100 in Great Britain and shelters also exist in the U.S.A., Canada, the Netherlands (the one in Amsterdam is called 'Blijf van m'n Lijf' — stay away from my body), France, West Germany, Denmark, Australia and India, and doubtless in many other countries as well.[290]

The House of Commons Select Committee recommended that "the Department must ensure that refuges are provided by local authorities and/or voluntary organizations".[291] There should be "one family place per 10,000 of the population",[292] it recommended. The NWAF thinks that 15,500 family places or over 1,000 refuges will be needed to meet the Select Committee's "initial target". In its report *And Still You've Done Nothing,* published in 1976, it stated that there were only 504 family places in 73 refuges and that often the provision was inadequate.[293] By December 1976 the government was estimating that there were over 100.[294] But whichever figure is correct, by the Select Committee's standards Great Britain is at least 900 refuges short of the recommended 'initial' provision. The committee also recommended that local authorities make available to voluntary groups some of the larger houses they own or may acquire and stipulated that this should be regarded as a "priority category for local authority expenditure and acquisition and improvement".[295] Many local authorities have disregarded these recommendations and some, Hull, Leeds[296] and Great Yarmouth[297] being three notorious examples, have positively obstructed attempts to set up refuges. The government which has helped the spread of refuges by channelling in Urban Aid money has now announced that it cannot provide any more money for projects concerning battered wives. "Increased expenditure on services for the victims of violence in marriage can in practice only take place by a redeployment by the bodies concerned of resources already available to them".[298]

Perhaps the biggest blow and certainly the most insulting gesture came when the London Borough of Hounslow prosecuted Erin Pizzey for knowingly failing to comply with the requirements imposed on her by the 1961 Housing Act fixing 36 as the maximum number of individuals permitted to occupy the Chiswick refuge at any one time. At the date of the alleged offence the number of residents was 75 and it often exceeds 100. Pizzey's policy is never to turn away women who come for shelter. The House of Lords held,[299] with considerable regret, that, as the law now stood, the occupier of a house of refuge for battered mothers and their children was not a single household, so that when the residents at any time exceeded 36, the occupier of the house could be prosecuted. Lord Hailsham clearly indicated that the magistrates should exercise restraint and mercy in sentencing her and a conditional discharge was imposed. But the prosecution raises a number of important questions. Where were the other 40 persons to go on the night of January 14, 1976? Would the London Borough of Hounslow have provided alternative accommodation? What is a 'single household'? Certainly in 1961 Parliament did not have the problem of battered women in mind when it passed the statute. Is this perhaps an area where the decision to prosecute should be entrusted to another body? Perhaps it could be reserved to the Attorney-General.[300] As yet the effects of the decision cannot be ascertained but with money cut and limits enforced on numbers admitted the plight of the battered woman could, indeed, become grave. It is to be hoped that other local authorities will put their efforts into establishing hostels, not prosecuting energetic individuals who do so.

12. Advice

The complications in the law and the difficulties of securing accommodation point indubitably to one conclusion. To the battered woman it is "one vicious circle of a very large perimeter, with the woman in the middle and the husband and bureaucracy hitting out from all points."[301] What she needs above all else is advice to enable her to cope with her problems. This was recognized by the Select Committee of the House of Commons. It recommended the setting up of "well-publicized family crisis centers open continuously to which wives, husbands, and children can turn".[302] The centers would, it argued, have three primary roles:

Firstly, they should provide an emergency service, hence the 24-hour requirement. This means that they will need to develop very close liaison with the local medical, social, legal and police services. A very important link will be with the refuges . . . Secondly, they should be specially responsible for the co-ordination of the local arrangements already available to women and children in distress. We have been impressed by the fact that one of the prime problems for the family in stress is the need to consult with several different professionals, in different places, employed by different agencies, very often not relating together very effectively . . . The third and non-emergency role we see for the family crisis center is the development of specialist advisory services, education and publicity programes, group support and meetings for women with similar problems.[303]

There is currently a multiplicity of organizations which give advice and assistance to battered women. But one is struck, as the Select Committee was, by lack of co-ordination and by the fact that most advice is given when it is too late. For, just as many seek legal aid when, had they earlier sought legal advice, the need for aid would not have arisen, so too few battered women take advice as a preventitive measure. That they do not do so stems partly from their own lack of competence to do so but as such from the lack of provision of such advice. The Select Committee's proposal is, therefore, to be supported. But little has come of it. The Domestic Violence Matrimonial Proceedings Act has been passed, the Law Commission has reported that neither the Act nor the proposed measures can prevent much violence and neither does anything to provide alternatives to the woman in danger.

Of course, 24-hour crisis centers would cost a lot of money just as implementing the Finer Committee's recommendation of a guaranteed maintenance allowance would.[304] But then the Silver Jubilee has cost a lot too. It is a matter of getting priorities right.

A few 24-hour crisis centers have been set up, in Andover, Leicester, Ormskirk, and one is planned in Stoke. But we are not going to get 24-hour crisis centers on any nationwide basis. We should, therefore, consider whether improved advisory services could be worked into existing structures. To that end the proposal of SHAC deserves serious consideration. It recommends the establishment of a 'Primary Advisory Service' for battered wives.[305] Unlike crisis centers, the PAS would not necessarily require a fixed center but could be based in a particular local authority department, or in a Citizens' Advice Bureau or Housing Aid Center. This would cut down on the cost of establishing centers in separate premises. SHAC recognizes the need to publicize such a service widely. To be successful there would have to be duty officers on a round-the-clock basis similar to that which operates in social service departments.

Co-ordinated, expert and sympathetic advice is crucial if many of the women who suffer are to be relieved of their fears and feelings of impotence. At present in Great Britain it is its absence which should cause anxiety and disquiet.

13. Conclusion

There are no simple solutions. What is required is nothing less than a complete re-definition of the status of women in society. So long as women are perceived as inferior, so long also as preservation of existing family units is seen as the overriding consideration, force will be used to control women. So long as force and control are acceptable, violence will also occur. At root the problem, like so much else, is one of education and socialization.

In the meanwhile everything must be done to protect women from violence in the home. They must have ready access to sympathetic and integrated advice; there must be a proliferation of refuges; it must be made easier for wives to leave husbands. Current social policy is geared towards rehabilitation of the family. In many contexts that is right. But not here. Women stay, they do not report domestic violence because there are often no alternatives. We need improvements in child care facilities, better employment prospects for women with children, guaranteed income maintenance and alternative accommodation. Less women will then be battered.

At present, man's inhumanity to man is matched only by his inhumanity to wife.[306]

NOTES

1. Reported in *The Daily Express*, 21 April 1975.
2. Frappat, *Un Fleau Social: Les Femmes Battues*, 4 November 1975.
3. Pizzey, E., *Scream Quietly Or The Neighbours Will Hear*. Harmondsworth, Middlesex: Penguin, 1974.
4. Gaskell, E.C., *Mary Barton*. Harmondsworth, Middlesex: Penguin, 1970. Gaskell, E.C., *North and South*. Univ. of Oxford Press: Oxford: Eng., 1973.
5. See also Romeike, *The Wife-Beater's Manual* (1884) and Stead, *Maiden Tribute of Modern Babylon* (1882).
6. See her *Life* vol. 2, pp. 220-1, Bentley, 1894.
7. In 1883. It was abolished only in 1953. The English Judges at the time also favoured flogging.
8. See Steinmetz and Straus, *Violence In the Family*. New York, New York: Dodd, Mead, 1974, p. 45.
9. In the nineteenth century it was seen as a working-class problem: the solution was seen as two-fold (i) an improvement in working-class conditions so that the women could make 'homes' and their husbands respond by not beating them and (ii) a speedy, accessible remedy which resulted in the development of non-cohabitation orders. On (i) see Basch, Francoise, *Relative Creatures*. New York, New York: Allen Lane, 1974: on (ii) see Finer Report on One-Parent Families vol. II, p. 104-108 (McGregor and Finer).
10. *Cf*. Cohen, S., *Folk Devils and Moral Panics*. London, Eng.: McGibbon and Kee, 1972.
11. Report from the Select Committee on Violence In Marriage 1974-5 H.C. 553-i, para. 5.
12. The most useful are Gelles, Richard J., *The Violent Home: A Study of Physical Aggression Between Husbands & Wives*. Beverly Hills, California: Sage, 1974 and Dobash, R. and R., *Violence Against Wives: A Case Against the Patriarchy*. New

York, New York: Free Press, 1978 (forthcoming). Other research of note is referred to in the course of this chapter.

13. *Cf.* Kitsuse and Cicourel (1963), 11 *Social Problems* 131.
14. The annual Home Office publication, *Criminal Statistics: England and Wales* published by H.M.S.O. is singularly unhelpful on such questions.
15. *The Nature and Extent of Violence In Marriage in Scotland,* Scottish Council of Social Service, 1976.
16. See Biderman "When Does Interpersonal Violence Become Crime?", paper delivered to International Sociological Association Conference, Cambridge 1973, and Block (1974), 11 *Criminology* 555.
17. See Rubington E., and Weinberg, M., *Deviance — The Interactionist Perspective.* New York, New York: MacMillan, 1973, p. 31.
18. A good illustration of this is to be found in the initial reactions of the wife in Yarrow *et al.,* "The psychological Meaning of Mental Illness in the Family" (1955), 11 *Journal of Social Issues* 12.
19. See, for example, Samson *et al.,* "Family Processes and Becoming a Mental Patient" (1962), 68 *American Journal of Sociology* 88.
20. See Gelles, *op. cit.* note 12, p. 58ff and Jackson, "The Adjustment of the Family to the Crisis of Alcoholism" (1954), 15 *Quarterly Journal of Studies on Alcohol* 564.
21. See Parnas (1967), *Wisconsin L.R.* 914.
22. H.C. Debates, vol. 895, col. 982.
23. *New Society,* 8 May 1975, p. 333.
24. Gibson and Klein, *Murder 1957 to 1968.* H.M.S.O.
25. See Amir, *Patterns of Forcible Rape.* Chicago, Illinois: University of Chicago Press, 1971.
26. See Mulhill, Tumin and Curtis in *Crimes of Violence:* Staff Report to National Commission on Causes and Prevention of Violence, vol. 11 1969.
27. McClintock, F., *Crimes of Violence,* Macmillan 1963.
28. Boudouris, Detroit (1971), 33 *Journal of Marriage and the Family* 667; Voss and Hepburn, Chicago (1968), 59 *Journal of Criminal Law, Criminology and Police Science* 499; Willie, Michigan (1970), 4 *Revista inter-American de Psicologia* 131; Wolfgang, *Patterns in Criminal Homicide.* New York, New York: John Wiley, 1958; and (1969) 3 *Psychology Today* 54, 72. See also *ante,* chapter 2.
29. Maldonado (1968), 23 *Boletim da Administracao Penitenciaria e dos Institutos de Criminologia* 5.
30. Siciliano (1968), 7 *Annals Internationales de Criminologie* 403.
31. McCarthy in De Wit and Hartup (eds.), *Determinant and Origins of Aggressive Behaviour.* De Mouton, The Hague 1974. See Lystad (1975), 45 *American Journal of Orthopsychiatry* 328.
32. "Cruelty in English Divorce: Some Empirical Findings" (1972), 34 *Journal of Marriage and the Family* 706.
33. "Violence in Divorce Prone Families" (1971), 33 *Journal of Marriage and the Family* 692; also in Steinmetz and Straus *op. cit.,* note 8.
34. "Sources of Marital Dissatisfaction among Applicants for Divorce" (1966), 36 American Journal of Orthopsychiatry 803 (reprinted in Steinmetz and Straus, *op. cit.,* note 8 and Glasser and Glasser, *Families in Crisis.* New York, New York: Harper and Row, 1970.
35. Gelles found violence in 37 percent of his control group *(The Violent Home* p. 49); Straus, "Leveling, Civility and Violence in the Family" 36: *Journal of Marriage and the Family* 15 found that college students reported that 16 percent of their parents used physical violence against one another in the previous year; the Western Michigan School of Social Work, *Spouse Assault: its Dimensions and Characteristics in Kalamazoo County* (1975) estimate 10 percent in that county.
36. "Force and Violence in the Family" (1971), 33 *Journal of Marriage and the Family* 624.
37. *Op. cit.,* note 8, pp. 6-17.

38. *Cf.* Box, S., *Deviance, Reality and Society.* New York, New York: Holt, Rinehart and Winston, 1971, chapter 1.
39. Good illustrations of this are to be found in Cohen, *Images of Deviance.* Harmondsworth, Middlesex: Penguin Books, 1971, particularly the chapters on industrial sabotage, blackmail and football hooliganism.
40. *Op. cit.,* note 3, *passim.*
41. "Violence Begins at Home", *The Spectator,* 23 November 1974.
42. See also her evidence to the House of Commons Select Committee, (1974-5) Minutes of Evidence, p. 2.
43. *Idem,* p. 43.
44. *Br. Med. J.* (25 January 1975) 194
45. *Cf.* Kittrie, N., *The Right to Be Different,* Baltimore, Maryland: Johns Hopkins Press, 1971.
46. A point made cogently by Martin, *Battered Wives.* San Francisco, California: Glide, 1976. Good examples are Gayford's work (*op. cit.* note 44), Snell *et al.* "The Wifebeater's Wife", *Archives of General Psychiatry* (1964) 11: 107 and, to a lesser extent, Gelles, *op. cit.,* note 35. Positivistic criminology explained only 'official' deviants: most of this research concentrates on the victims of 'official' batterers.
47. It is, of course, more difficult to interview the husbands.
48. Durkheim, Emile, *The Division of Labour In Society.* New York, New York: Free Press, 1964; Durkheim, Emile, *Suicide.* New York, New York: Free Press, 1951.
49. "Social Structure and Anomie" (1938) 3 *Amer. Sociological Review* 672 and in Merton, *Social Theory and Social Structure.* New York, New York: Free Press, 1968. See also Horton J., "Order and Conflict Theories of Social Problems as Competing Ideologies" (1966), 71 *American J. of Soc.* 701.
50. Discussion Document on BASW Working Party on Home Violence (1975), 6 *Social Work Today* 409.
51. "Violence between Men and Women within the Family Setting", paper presented to VIII World Congress of Sociology, Toronto, Canada, August 1974.
52. *Op. cit.,* note 35, p. 185.
53. *Cf.* Bottomley, *Decisions in the Penal Process.* South Hackensack, New Jersey: Rothman, 1973.
54. *Op. cit.,* note 36, p. 628.
55. *Idem.*
56. *Op. cit.,* note 33.
57. Is this why their plight also came to public attention in the latter part of the nineteenth century? It is a plausible part-explanation.
58. In Mayo, (ed.) *Women in the Community.* Boston, Mass.: Routledge and Kegan Paul, 1977, ch. 11, p. 119.
59. Millett, Kate, *Sexual Politics.* New York, New York: Hart Davis, 1969, particularly pp. 43-46 and in her critique of Henry Miller, ch. 6 and comparison of Ruskin and Mill (pp. 99ff).
60. "Violence in Husband-Wife Interaction" in Steinmetz and Straus, *Violence In the Family, op. cit.,* note 8, pp. 75, 80.
61. *Idem,* p. 81.
62. "Violence and the Social Control of Women", paper presented to British Sociological Association Annual Meeting, Sheffield, Eng., March 1977.
63. *Idem,* p. 18.
64. *Idem,* p. 19.
65. Minutes, p. 190. Of course, if she succeeds in obtaining an injunction that will probably happen.
66. In a piece specially written for the Steinmetz and Straus collection *op. cit* note 8, p. 315.
67. See Delmer "Looking Again at Engel's Origin of the Family, Private Property and the State" in Oakley and Mitchell (eds.), *The Rights and Wrongs of Women.* Harmondsworth, Middlesex: Penguin Books, 1976, p. 271.

103 The Phenomenon of Marital Violence

68. *Op. cit.* note 62, p. 10.
69. *Idem,* p. 24.
70. Graphically described in volume 1 of Blackstone, Sir William, *Commentaries on the Law of England.* (4 volumes) Folkestone, Kent: Dawsons Pall Mall, 1966. See also, de Crow, Karen, *Sexist Justice.* New York, New York: Random, 1974.
71. *Per* O.R. McGregor quoted in Fletcher, *The Family and Marriage in Britain.* Harmondsworth, Middlesex: Penguin, 1973, p. 103.
72. Because of the cohabitation rule.
73. The expression is Savigny's (*System of Modern Roman Law* 1840).
74. See Dror, "Law and Social Change" (1959), 33 *Tulane L.R. 787;* Massell (1967), 2 *Law and Society Review* 179; Aubert (1966), 10 *Acta Sociologica 99; in Aubert, Sociology of Law.* Harmondsworth, Middlesex: Penguin 1969, p. 116. See generally Freeman, *The Legal Structure,* Harlow, Essex: Longman, 1974, ch. 3.
75. *Cf.* Eekelaar, *Family Security and Family Breakdown.* Harmondsworth, Middlesex: Penguin, 1971, p. 44.
76. 1 Hawkins P.C. 130.
77. Quoted in Blackstone, *op. cit.,* note 70.
78. 1 Commentaries 445.
79. Per Graveson, in Graveson and Crane, *A Century of Family Law:* London, Eng.: Sweet & Maxwell, 1957, p. 16.
80. [1891] 1 Q.B. 671, 682.
81. *Idem,* p. 679.
82. *Cochrane's Case* 8 Dowl. 630. Coleridge J. said there was "no doubt of the general dominion which the law of England attributed to a husband over his wife".
83. [7146] P. 216.
84. *McKenzie v. McKenzie, The Times,* 5 June 1959, commented on in Biggs, *The Concept of Matrimonial Cruelty.* London, Eng.: Athlone Press, 1962, p. 147.
85. See "No Comment" in *Ms,* August 1975.
86. *Cf.* Pizzey, *op. cit.,* note 3, p. 33.
87. *Op. cit.,* note 35, p. 59.
88. *Op. cit.,* note 21, p. 952.
89. See *The Daily Mirror,* 16 April 1974.
90. *Idem,* 18 February 1974.
91. *R. v. Clarke* [1949] 2 All E.R. 448.
92. *R. v. O'Brien* [1974] 3 All E.R. 663.
93. *R. v. Miller* [1954] 2 Q.B. 282.
94. *R. v. Reid* [1972] 2 All E.R. 1350.
95. *Holborn v. Holborn* [1947] 1 All E.R. 32.
96. *Foster v. Foster* [1921] P. 438.
97. Livneh, "On Rape and the Sanctity of Marriage" (1967), 2 *Israel L.R.* 415.
98. During the committee stage in the House of Commons of the Sexual Offences (Amendment) Bill (now Act), 1976.
99. Galsworthy, J., *Forsyte Saga.* London, Eng.: Heinmann, 1967. [quotes 1922 edition, pp. 245-6]
100. See Greenwood and Young, "Notes on the Theory of Rape and its Policy Implications", Paper presented to London Group on Deviancy, 1975.
101. "Rape: The All-American Crime" (Sept., 1971) *Ramparts* p. 28.
102. "Sexual Assaults in the Philadelphia Prison System" in Gagnon and Simon (eds.), *The Sexual Scene.* Chicago, Illinois: Aldine, 1970.
103. "Rape Myths", *Crime and Social Justice* (1974) 1: 18.
104. This comes out acutely in Eldridge Cleaver's description of his rape of white women as 'insurrectionary' (*Soul on Ice.* New York, New York: Dell, 1968.) See generally, J & H Schwendinger, "Review of Rape Literature" (1976), 6 *Crime and Social Justice* 79.
105. Under s. 47 of the Offences Against the Person Act 1861.
106. See *DPP v. Smith* [1961] A.C. 290, 334 and Smith and Hogan, *Criminal Law* (3rd ed, 1973), p. 297.

107. In *R. v. Miller* [1954] 2 Q.B. 282, 292.
108. Interpreted broadly to include pestering (*Vaughan v. Vaughan* [1973] 3 All E.R. 449).
109. *Viz.,* wounding and grievous bodily harm under sections 18 and 20 of the 1861 Act.
110. *R. v. Verolla* [1963] 1 Q.B. 285; *R. v. Lapworth* [1931] 1 K.B. 117. Nokes has commented that decisions to the contrary would have constituted "a charter for wife-beaters": Graveson and Crane, *op. cit.,* note 79, p. 148. These cases have recently been overruled. See *Huskyn v. Commr. of Police for the Metropolis* [1978] 2 AII E.R. 136.
111. Homicide Act 1957 s. 3.
112. A good example (though it does not involve an offence against a wife) is that of the Indian hot-dog salesman in McCabe and Purves, *The Jury at Work* (Oxford Penal Research Unit 1972). Osney Mead, Oxford: Blackwell, 1975.
113. See Kalven and Zeisel, *The American Jury.* Boston, Mass.: Little Brown & Co., 1966.
114. Reiss, *The Police and the Public.* New Haven, Conn.: Yale U. Press, (1971).
115. *The Times,* 28 April 1977.
116. *The Times,* 27 April 1977.
117. Discussed in Truninger, "Marital Violence — The Legal Solutions", (1971), 23 *Hastings L.J.* 259 and Martin, *Battered Wives.* San Francisco, California: Glide, 1976, p. 100-101.
118. 88 Cal. App. 2d 867 (1948).
119. *Per* Martin, *Battered Wives* p. 100.
120. Quoted from San Jose *Mercury,* 5 November 1975 by Martin, *idem* pp. 100-101.
121. *Idem,* p. 101.
122. See Annual Report of C.I.C.B. 1975-6 Cmnd. 6656 (12th report).
123. Reproduced in the Annual Reports. The scheme is still not statutory.
124. A good illustration is in the 10th Report (Cmnd 5791), pp. 10-11. The origins of the exclusion are found in Cmnd 1406 para. 38.
125. *R. v. C.I.C.B. ex parte Staten, The Times,* February 3, 1972. See also [1972] 1 All E.R. 1034.
126. *Cf. Hopes v. Hopes* [1949] p. 227, *Mouncer v. Mouncer* [1972] 1 All E.R. 289, *Fuller v. Fuller* [1973] 2 All E.R. 650.
127. See *Jones v. Jones* [1975] 2 All E.R. 12.
128. See 43 *S. Calif. L. Rev.* 85.
129. Carlin and Howard, *UCLA Law Rec.* 12: 381.
130. Marx, *The Social Context of Violent Behaviour,* Boston, Mass.: Routledge and Kegan Paul, 1976.
131. *Idem,* p. 18.
132. *Op cit.,* note 62, p. 18.
133. H.C. vol. 858, Written Answers, cols 149-50 *per* Mr. M. Carlisle.
134. *Nicholson v. Booth* (1888) 52 J.P. 662.
135. *Pickering v. Willoughby* [1907] 2 K.B. 296.
136. On their reluctance to intervene see (1974-5) House of Commons, Minutes of Evidence pp. 361-391, and Dow in Borland (ed.), *Violence In the Family.* Manchester, Eng.: Manchester U. Press, 1976, p. 129.
137. Minutes of Evidence, p. 366.
138. *Ibid.,* p. 369.
139. (1971), 36 *Law and Contemporary Problems* 539, 542.
140. (1967) *Wisconsin L.R.* 914, 920.
141. *Idem,* p. 920.
142. *Idem,* p. 921.
143. P. 376, Minutes of Evidence.
144. *Per* Field and Field "Marital Violence and the Criminal Process: Neither Justice Nor Peace" in (1973), 47 *Social Service Review* 221, 227.
145. See (1967), *Wisconsin L.R.* 914.
146. See Banton, *The Policeman in the Community.* Kennebunkport, Maine: Tavistock, 1964.
147. See Punch and Naylor, *New Society,* 17 May 1973, p. 358.

148. See Belson, *The Police and the Public*. New York, New York: Harper and Row, 1975.
149. Skolnick, *Justice Without Trial*. New York, New York: John Wiley, 1967, pp. 171-172.
150. (1975) Memoandum to Select Committee, House of Commons, Minutes of Evidence p. 367.
151. See (1967) *Wisconsin L.R.* 914 and 36 *Law and Contemporary Problems* 539
152. See the *Wisconsin L.R.* article at p. 922ff.
153. (1965), 12 *Social Problems* 276.
154. See the *Wisconsin L.R.* article at pp. 922, 929.
155. *Cf.* Pizzey, *op. cit.,* note 3 at p. 30.
156. See Bard and Berkowitz, "Training Police as Specialists in Family Crisis Intervention: A Community Psychology Program" (1967), 3 *Community Mental Health Journal* 315 and Bard in Steinmetz and Straus, *op. cit.,* note 8, p. 152.
157. *Cf.* Parnas, 36 *Law and Contemporary Problems* 539, 551, and Field and Field, *op. cit.,* note 144, pp. 237-8.
158. Memorandum to Select Committee, para. 44.
159. As reported in *The Daily Telegraph,* 28 February 1976.
160. Bedfordshire Police, Report on Acts of Domestic Violence Committed in the County between 1st February 1976 and 31st July 1976.
161. Cautioning is a variable practice, common in rural areas but less so in the metropolitan and urban areas.
162. Pizzey, E., *Scream Quietly or the Neighbours Will Hear.* Harmondsworth, Middlesex: Penquin, 1974, p. 129.
163. *Idem,* p. 120.
164. *Op. cit.,* note 144, p. 227.
165. Discussed by Parnas, 54 *Minnesota L.R.* 585 and by Maidment in (1977), 26 *Int'l & Comp. Law Quarterly* 403 and see ch. 6.
166. *Cf.* Freeman, *The Legal Structure.* Harlow, Essex: Longman, 1974 p. 38.
167. *Cf.* Kahn-Freund, (1969), 22 *Current Legal Problems* 1: 24-25.
168. On which see Eckhoff (1966), 10 *Acta Sociologica 158-66, in Aubert, Sociology of Law.* Harmondsworth, Middlesex: Penguin, 1969, p. 171.
169. *Idem* in Aubert at p. 175.
170. See Aubert (1963), 7 *Journal of Conflict Resolution* 26-42; (1967), 11 *Journal of Conflict Resolution* 40-50.
171. Also critical is Martin, *Battered Wives*. San Francisco, California; Glide, 1976, pp. 103-104.
172. The law was changed by the Law Reform (Husband and Wife) Act 1962.
173. *Cf.* McCurdy (1959), 4 *Villanova L.R.* 303.
174. *Per* McCardie J. in *Gottliffe v. Edelston* [1930] 2 K.B. 378, 392.
175. 24 *Mod. L.R.* 101.
176. This causes difficulties, for how does one quantify benefit? *Cf.* Street, *The Law of Torts.* London Eng.: Butterworths, 1976, pp. 468-9.
177. *Per* Larson, 4 *Wisconsin L.R.* 467, 499.
178. *Cf. per* Sir George Baker, H.C. Select Committee Minutes p. 468.
179. See Ploscowe, Foster and Freed, *Family Law: Cases and Materials.* Boston, Mass.: Little Brown, 1972, pp. 852-4.
180. 376 P 2d. 65.
181. *Per* Law Commission, Law Com. (20 October 1976) 77: para. 3, p. 15.
182. *Dodd v. Dodd* [1906] P. 189; *Harriman v. Harriman* [1909] p. 123. Even if the clause was inserted without the applicant's consent: *Mackenzie v. Mackenzie* [1940] P. 81.
183. *Corton v. Corton* [1965] P. 1, *Jolliffe v. Jolliffe* [1965] P. 6.
184. (1970), 33 *Mod. L.R.* 63.
185. *Idem,* p. 65.
186. On which see SHAC, *Violence in Marriage,* 1976; Grant, *Local Authority Housing: Law, Policy and Practice in Hampshire,* 1976, ch. 5; Nat. Women's Aid Federation (NWAF), *And Still You've Done Nothing,* 1976.

187. *Op. cit.,* note 181, para. 3, p. 40.
188. See McGregor *et al., Separated Spouses.* London, Eng.: Duckworth, 1970.
189. Supplementary Benefits Act 1976, Schedule 1, para. 3.
190. *Per* McGregor, in Proceedings from Conference on Matrimonial Jurisdiction of Magistrates, Institute of Judicial Administration, Birmingham 1973, quoted in Seago and Bissett-Johnson, *Cases and Materials on Family Law.* London, Eng.: Sweet & Maxwell, 1976, p. 104-105.
191. *Op. cit.,* note 195, *passim.*
192. Marsden, *Mothers Alone.* Harmondsworth, Middlesex: Penguin, 1973, ch. 10.
193. *Report of Committee on One-Parent Families* (1974) Cmnd. 5029, s.5-11.
194. *Ibid.* s. 13 and s. 14.
195. H.C. Debates vol. 898, cols. 51-60. See also H.L. Debates vol. 366, cols. 1560 — 1 *per* Lord Chancellor.
196. See criticisms of this by Maidment, 7 *Family Law* 50, 52.
197. See Law Com No. 77 pt. III.
198. This Bill is likely to be enacted in the course of 1978.
199. *Viz.,* the Domestic Violence and Matrimonial Proceedings Act 1976 s.1 (2), discussed in section 10 below. See *Davis v. Johnson, The Times,* 10 March, 1978.
200. *Op. cit.,* note 181, para. 3.12.
201. See also *The Times,* 27 May, 1977, for similar suggestion of Brian Harris.
202. For example, California, Australia.
203. The Law Commission thought the proposals of *Putting Asunder* which would have left the question at large impracticable. See discussion of this in Freeman (1971), 178 *Current Legal Problems* 183-5.
204. In s. 1 (2)(b) of the Matrimonial Causes Act 1973 (henceforth, M.C.A.).
205. *Per* Bagnall J. in *Ash v. Ash* [1972] 1 All E.R. 582, 585.
206. *Idem,* p. 585.
207. *Idem,* p. 585-6. This should not be taken too literally: each could be granted a decree.
208. *Ash v. Ash, op. cit.,* note 211 and *Bradley v. Bradley* [1973] 3 All E.R. 750, are but two reported examples.
209. [1973] 3 All E.R. 750.
210. *Idem,* p. 752.
211. Matrimonial Causes Act (M.C.A.) 1973 s. 3(1).
212. M.C.A. 1973 s.3(2).
213. See Royal Commission on Marriage and Divorce (Morton Commission) Cmnd. 9678, ch. 5. (1956); *Putting Asunder,* S.P.C.K. 1966, para. 78; Law Commission, *Field of Choice,* Cmnd. 3123, para. 19.
214. See Hayes, 4 *Family Law* 103; Miller, 4 *Anglo-American Law Review* 163, Mortlock, *The Inside of Divorce.* London, Eng.: Constable 1972, pp. 11-15.
215. See *Bowman v. Bowman* [1949] P. 353; 356-7, *per* Denning L.J.
216. See *Hillier v. Hillier* [1958] P. 186.
217. *McGibbon v. McGibbon* [1973] Fam. 170. *McCleod v. McCleod* (1973), 117 Sol. Jol. 679 is sometimes cited as an authority to the contrary, but there the *wife* was the *tenant.*
218. As from 1 April 1977. It is still available to seek an injunction. On the withdrawal see Freeman, 6 *Fam. Law* 255, and Davis and Murch 7 *Fam. Law* 71.
219. H.L. Debates vol. 373, col. 1438. See also H.C. vol. 905, col. 858 *per* Miss J. Richardson.
220. *Per* Truninger (1971), 23 *Hastings L.J.* 259, 260.
221. *Per* Pizzey, *Scream Quietly or the Neighbours Will Hear.* Harmondsworth, Middlesex: Penguin, 1974, p. 41.
222. See LAG Bulletin, June 1976, p. 125.
223. H.L. Debates vol. 373, col. 1441.
224. *Des Salles d'Epinoix v. Des Salles d'Epinoix* [1967] 2 All E.R. 539.
225. *Montgomery v. Montgomery* [1965] p. 46.
226. *Jones v. Jones* [1971] 2 All E.R. 737.
227. *Robinson v. Robinson* [1965] p. 39; *Brent v. Brent* [1974] 2 All E.R. 1211.

228. *Hall v. Hall* [1971] 1 All E.R. 762.
229. (1974), 4 *Fam. Law* 87.
230. A digest of recent cases is in LAG Bulletin, June 1976 p. 137.
231. [1975] Fam. 76, discussed below. See now also *Walker v. Walker, The Times,* 19 December 1977.
232. On the Act see Freeman 127 *New L.J.* 159, and "Man's Inhumanity to Wife" in *Mod. L.R.* (1978, forthcoming). There is also a detailed legal commentary by Freeman in *Current Law Statutes Annotated.* London, Eng.: Sweet & Maxwell, 1976. See also Masson, 7 *Fam. Law* 29; Maidment 7 *Fam Law* 50.
233. *Davis v. Johnson, The Times,* March 10, 1978.
234 See *Ruddell v. Ruddell* (1967) III S.J. 497.
235. See *Phillips v. Phillips* [1973] 2 All E.R. 423.
236. See *Stewart v. Stewart* [1973] 1 All E.R. 31; *Phillips v. Phillips* [1973] 2 All E.R. 423.
237. See *Adams v. Adams* (1965) 109 S.J. 899.
238. *Pinckney v. Pinckney,* [1966] 1 All E.R. 121.
239. *Idem* and *Jones v. Jones* [1971] 2 All E.R. 737. See also *Bowens v. Bowens, The Guardian,* 10 August 1973.
240. The Law Commission has rejected community of property, though it is currently considering the conveyancing complications of what it calls 'a matrimonial home trust'. See Law Com. No. 52.
241. See *W. v. W.* [1951] 2 T.L.R. 1135 in the light of *Pettitt v. Pettitt* [1970] A.C. 777.
242. *Cf.* the facts of *Nanda v. Nanda* [1968] P. 351.
243. H.C. vol. 905 col. 859.
244. *Bassett v. Bassett* [1975] Fam 76.
245. *Idem,* p. 82.
246. *Idem,* p. 84.
247. [1975] 5 Fam. Law 21.
148. *Cf.* 125 *N.L.J.* 493.
249. Even outside cases of violence. See *Browne v. Pritchard* [1975] 3 All E.R. 23, *Williams v. Williams* [1977] 1 All E.R. 28, *Martin v. Martin* 7 Fam Law 80.
250. *The Times,* 19 December 1977.
251. *Rennick v. Rennick* [1977] 1 WLR. 1455.
252. See, generally, Pizzey, *op. cit.,* note 221, Tracey, *Battered Wives.* London, Eng.: Bow Group 1974; Women's Aid, *Battered Wives,* June 1973.
253. See *op. cit.,* note 221.
254. LAG Bulletin, June 1976, p. 125.
255. Minutes of Evidence, p. 463. The 'record' is apparently 4½ hours.
256. See 'The Saga of Mrs D' in H.O.C. Minutes p. 62.
257. See s. 2. But on judges' unwillingness to attach a power of arrest see LAG Bulletin, December 1977, p. 274.
258. *Op. cit.,* note 221, p. 119.
259. *Idem,* p. 118.
260. In Borland, (ed.) *Violence in the Family.* Manchester, Eng.: Manchester University Press, 1976, p. 117.
261. P. 378.
262. H.L. Debates vol. 373, col. 1443.
263. Most domestic violence takes place at weekends. Friday nights is very common. Are the police then to release the man on Saturday evening? The alternative is for duty judges to operate a weekend roter. This has been promised. See Shaw, *The Daily Telegraph,* June 1, 1977.
264. In striking contrast to the Bail Act 1976 which has created a statutory presumption in favor of bail.
265. A point made by Mr. I. Percival, H.C. Debates vol. 905, col. 879.
266. Discussed in R. Bailey, *The Squatters.* Harmondsworth, Middlesex: Penguin, 1973.
267. Particularly in the confrontation over the King Hill Hostel in Birmingham.
268. See National Assistance Act 1948 s. 21.

269. Circular 18/74, para. 24.
270. National Women's Aid Federation (NWAF), *And Still You've Done Nothing,* 1976, p. 2.
271. *Idem.*
272. *Idem.*
273. See s. 2 and Code of Guidance A.10.
274. See Shelter Housing Aid Corporation (SHAC), *Violence in Marriage;* Grant, *Local Authority Housing;* NWAF *op. cit.,* note 272.
275. *Op. cit.,* note 270, p. 4.
276. See SHAC report, *op. cit.,* note 274.
277. *Idem.*
278. *Op. cit.,* note 270, p. 9.
279. See SHAC report, *op. cit.,* note 274. It is less common in Hampshire; see Grant, *op. cit.,* note 274.
280. See SHAC report, *op. cit.,* note 274.
281. See *Thompson v. Thompson* [1975] 2 All E.R. 208; *Regan v. Regan* [1977] 1 All E.R. 428.
282. *L.B. of Southwark v. Williams* [1971] Ch. 734.
283. *McPhail v. Persons Unknown* [1973] 3 All E.R. 393.
284. Criminal Law Act 1977. See sections 6, 7, 8 and 10 and Tarlin 1977 LAG Bulletin 285.
285. Under s. 1 of Children Act 1948. The play "Cathy Come Home" stirred up national conscience on this issue.
286. Under s. 1 of Children and Young Persons Act 1963.
287. See Heywood and Allen, *Financial Help in Social Work.* Manchester, Eng.: Manchester U. Press, 1971, and Emmett, *Under the Safety Net* (1976), Child Poverty Action Group.
288. See *Roberts v. Dorset CC., The Times* 30 July 1976. See also House of Commons Report, para. 26.
289. See Martin, *Battered Wives.* San Francisco, California: Glide, 1976, p. 197.
290. A detailed source of reference is Martin, *idem* ch. 10. A useful article is Marcovitch, *Social Work Today* No. 2 p. 34.
291. (1975) House of Commons Select Committee Report, para. 29.
292. *Idem.*
293. *Op. cit.,* note 270, pp. 13-14.
294. See its Observations on the Select Committee Report, Cmnd. 6690, para. 35, and *The Times,* 10 December 1976.
295. *Op. cit.,* note 291, para. 30.
296. See Minutes of Select Committee, pp. 67-68.
297. See NWAF Report *op. cit.,* note 270, p. 15.
298. See *op. cit.,* note 294, para. 4.
299. See *Simmons v. Pizzey,* [1977] 2 All E.R. 432.
300. *Cf.* Harper, 127 *New Law Journal* 479, 503.
301. *Per* Pizzey, *op. cit.,* note 221, p. 28.
302. House of Commons Select Committee Report, para. 20.
303. *Idem.*
304. Finer Report, p. 289*ff.,* on which see Eekelaar, Public Law 64 (1976).
305. *Op. cit.,* note 274.
306. The whole question of violence in the family is considered further in Freeman, *Violence In The Family.* London, Eng.: Saxon House, 1978.

Chapter 6

The Law's Response To Marital Violence: A Comparison Between England and the U.S.A.*

Susan Maidment†

It has been universally assumed that society must offer various services to the perpetrators and victims of marital violence[1] in order to ameliorate their condition and re-educate them. Such services must include medical and psychiatric help, marriage guidance,[2] social work, housing advice, women's refuges and crisis centers,[3] and the importance of collaboration between these services has been stressed.[4] The two services of specific interest to the lawyer are those offered by the police and the law. The police, indeed, may have a special role to play in this area, as they are not only very often the first to be called in to the scene of the violence, but as a result of this immediate participation are also eminently in a position to act as a referral agency to the other available services.[5] The law, on the other hand, must be seen as just one of these other available services. It is a mistake to see resort to the law as a panacea. One does not have to accept the ultra-cynical view of Bankowski and Mungham[6] that lawyers have an 'interest' in defining events as 'legal problems' to realize that the legal remedy is just one of a number of ways of providing a solution for preventing intrafamily violence. It is for the victim and non-legal experts to decide when and whether the legal solution is appropriate to prevent the recurrence of violence. The lawyers would do well to heed the warnings of those who write with real experience of the problem, for example, Erin Pizzey of Chiswick Women's Aid, who in her evidence to the House of Commons Select Committee on Violence in Marriage suggested very emphatically that in this area the law was not worth the paper it was written on[7]: "The pot of black pepper I have in my bag is greater protection to me than a High Court injunction" (p. 4), and that essentially wife-battering was a medical problem (p. 4).[8] Dr. Gayford, who studied 100 cases of wife-battering mainly from the Chiswick Women's Aid Hostel, agreed with her that in particular legal proceedings were impossible as long as the woman was still living with her husband (pp. 4 and 37). The Select Committee itself ultimately recognized that "no laws, however well enforced can prevent marital assaults" (p. xvi). The Cobden Trust do-it-yourself booklet says: "At its best, the law is a cumbersome,

---

* The content of this chapter appears, in modified form, under the title "The Law's Response to Marital Violence in England and the U.S.A." in (1977), 26 *Int. and Comp. L.Q.* 403.

† Department of Law, University of Keele, England.

long-winded and inappropriate means of dealing with a failure in human communication" (p. 1).[9]

The problem which they have all highlighted is that a legal solution, however good its theoretical framework, may in some cases simply not be an appropriate or effective way of preventing future violence. Legal compulsion, through court orders or prison sentences, will not solve the problem which has caused the violence in the first place, nor may it even prevent further manifestations of the violence. Indeed it may in fact, as has been amply documented, only exacerbate the woman's situation and lead to further violence against her for having sought legal help, a factor which may explain only too well her reluctance to pursue a legal remedy which she has already initiated. At the most the law may be effective as an interim measure, *e.g.,* to stop the violence until and so that further treatment can take place. The limitations of the legal resource available to battered women must therefore always be borne in mind. Nevertheless the legal resource itself must be the best that can be devised so that when it is used it provides a satisfactory service to the user. The main point of this chapter then is to investigate the adequacy of the legal provisions to which the battered women may look for help. The focus here must be not only on the legal provisions themselves, but also on the way those legal rules actually operate or are operated. Current comment on the law for battered women reflect these two concerns. There are those who have criticized the law, *e.g.,* that non-molestation injunctions should be available without the necessity of instituting divorce proceedings, and imply that if the law was so changed all would be well.[10] On the other hand there are those who say the law is basically fine if only lawyers knew how to use it effectively.[11] It is submitted that it is of the first importance that the legal remedies available to battered women should be the best possible, not only in theory but also in their practical application. This may have serious implications for the administration of the legal rules. For if a resource is to be available to the battered woman, it must be adequate to the job, not only in terms of her human expectations when she chooses to use the legal remedy, but also for the respect and self-esteem of the law and the legal profession.

The range of possible legal provisions and ways in which they can be implemented can best be seen by comparing different jurisdictions. This chapter will compare the legal response to marital violence in England with some developments in the United States.

1. England and Wales : An Overview[12]

Criminal Proceedings

There is no doubt that the criminal law contains adequate provision for dealing with violence between any two persons, including husband and wife. Depending on the degree of severity of the violence, there is at the most serious murder or manslaughter, including attempts, descending through the assault offences in the Offences against the Person Act 1861,[13] down to the power of the justices to bind over to keep the peace.

While the law is clearly adequate, there has been considerable dissatisfaction with its operation. The Select Committee concluded: "If the criminal law of assault could be more uniformly applied to domestic assaults there seems little doubt that it would give some protection to the battered wife" (p. xvi). The Metropolitan Police in its evidence admitted that:

[W]hereas it is a general principle of police practice not to intervene in a situation . . . between a husband and wife in the course of which the wife had suffered some personal attack, any assault upon a wife by her husband, which amounted to physical injury of a serious nature is a criminal offence which it is the duty of the police to follow up and prosecute. Police will take positive action in every case of serious assault and will prosecute where there is sufficient evidence (pp. 375-376).

In contrast to this is the typical complaint by battered wives of police reluctance to intervene and inactivity,[14] and this despite the severity of their injuries which they describe.[15] One must not ignore the fact that the police may actually fear getting involved because of their personal safety. In the U.S.A. it has been said that "40 percent of injuries to police occur while intervening in family disputes."[16] A particular complaint is that the police refuse to arrest even in serious cases, though the Select Committee thought that practice on this varied between different police forces (p. 430). The source of one of the conflicts here must be the police assessment of what actually amounts to 'serious injury'. Police discretion to prosecute is absolute (though the Select Committee commented on the double standard which operates for strangers and for husband and wife (p. 430) and on their very different attitude towards offences against children (p. 433)). But this does not preclude a revision of the use of its discretion, *i.e.,* how the police define serious injury and on what principles they decide to arrest and prosecute in this context. For example it has been suggested that the police should take seriously "instances which fall short of the criminal process but where attendant circumstances give rise to a suspicion of future anti-social behaviour" (Select Committee, p. 369), and that early detection of and action on violence can prevent some murders or their attempt.[17] At present it seems the police do tend to regard most marital violence as minor.[18] This is illustrated by the Metropolitan Police survey already referred to in which out of 89 reported cases of husband and wife assault, only 24 were considered by the police to be anything more than common assault.[19]

The second explanation for police non-involvement in marital violence is the oft-quoted argument that women are "reluctant to take their husbands to court; they may fear reprisals, the family unit could be broken; and financial hardship could result should he be sent to prison" (Select Committee, pp. 376, 377).[20] Thus in the Metropolitan Police survey, of the 24 serious cases, in 12 the wife refused to make a statement, or continue with the complaint, or withdrew a statement already made, or failed to prosecute at court. This reluctance to prosecute is an undeniable fact, but more importantly quite understandable to the sympathetic observer. The difficulties of wives who take legal action and who must return home where their husbands are still living, and must suffer whatever reaction the husband displays, *e.g.,* further attacks, withholding of money and emotional stress, have been amply described.[21] In addition it is quite common for wives to feel that they do not want to be the cause of their husband's imprisonment.[22] It must be accepted that wives can still love their husbands and hope that the marriage can be saved despite his past actions towards her. They may also fear the publicity incurred as a result of criminal proceedings.[23] No doubt the police can understand all these feelings and motives, yet from a professional point of view these wives are wasting their time. Police effectiveness and competence depend on the number of offences 'cleared up' in the sense of satisfactory prosecution. This militates against the police reporting of marital offences in the first place,[24] so that at present we cannot even know how many calls are made to the police for help; and it equally militates against the arrest of a husband even on a serious assault charge when it is believed that the wife will subsequently play the 'reluctant victim'.[25]

It is for these reasons that it appears to be police policy[26] to advise the wife to initiate her own proceedings for common assault. In fact under s. 42 of the Offences Against the Person Act 1861 only the person assaulted can lay an information, unless he or she is "so feeble, old and infirm as to be incapable of instituting proceedings and is not a free agent but under the control of the person committing the assault."[27] It has been suggested that a wife is under the control of her husband and thus not a free agent, and that therefore the police should act for her.[28] This point is not really as frivolous as it might appear, for it takes account of the pressure and fear under which a wife may be when contemplating acting on her own to bring criminal proceedings. In addition she suffers from the fact that legal aid is not available for private prosecutions.[29] There would appear to be no reason why the police could not initiate criminal proceedings for aggravated assault occasioning actual bodily harm under s. 47 of the 1861 Act,[30] even where the injury is not that serious. Certainly the penalties imposed in the Metropolitan Police survey for offences under s. 47 do not indicate the more serious nature of these offences as opposed to common assault, e.g., husband bound over for 12 months, conditional discharge, £25 fine, three months' imprisonment suspended for 12 months.[31]

It has actually been reported[32] that some magistrates have taken a poor view of the police advice to a woman to apply for a summons. Where the magistrates consider that the complaint contains evidence of unlawful wounding or causing actual grievous bodily harm, and that therefore a summons is inappropriate because of the delay before the hearing and the possibility of further violence in the meantime, the magistrates may refer the matter back to the police for further investigation with a view to an application for an arrest warrant. In London it is said that the police will thereafter cooperate. The advantage to the wife is that bail from arrest until the actual trial may not be granted depending on the real danger of further violence. It is also possible to grant bail subject to conditions, e.g., that the husband must not enter the matrimonial home, or in any way interfere with the wife or children. Breach of such conditions would clearly warrant immediate arrest by the police and detention in custody. This procedure clearly depends on the magistrates' initiative and may not be representative of the country.[33] And the Select Committee concluded categorically: "Chief Constables should review their policies about the police approach to domestic violence" (p.xvii).

Fundamental to the whole discussion so far however, is the role of the police. There can, though need not be, a dichotomy between the role of the police as law enforcers and their role as a social service. Certainly some police officers can accept both.[34] Others will see the number of successful prosecutions as a measure of their efficiency, and view mediation and advice in husband and wife disputes "very time-consuming and a distraction to overall police effort" (Select Committee, p. 377). Yet criminal proceedings may not be appropriate in a marital dispute. The initial call to the police for help may not be a request for criminal action at all. For, as has been well pointed out, the police "are the sole agency available 24 hours a day, seven days a week, to enter into any situation, garbed with the cloak of authority, to sift and assess the gravity of each occurrence."[35] In addition there is "the importance to any effective violence prevention program of utilizing the vast amount of knowledge which the operational police officer carries around in his head."[36] The role for the police should therefore be to consider all possible solutions, including simple advice or mediation, and clearly also prosecution depending on the gravity of the injuries. Barring that, their role must be one of referral to other available social services (including the civil law). This role has already been accepted in the areas of juvenile offenders and child abuse, but not in the field of marital violence. Thus liaison with other bodies, regarded as the most effective tool of all in so many areas, does not officially exist[37] and does not appear to be particularly welcomed, by some policemen at least.[38] Others believe in the benefits of mutual trust and cooperation and collaboration.[39] The problem has been well put:

Before the policeman is prepared to act as "the eyes and ears" of such agencies and adopt an even broader service role, however, he will need to be convinced, and no doubt rightly so, that they have an effective contribution to make and that their approach can achieve more than the one he is accustomed to adopting.[40]

The Select Committee touched on this (at p. xvii of their Report) when recommending special instruction to new recruits on the question of domestic violence, the need to arrest the husband until his appearance in court, or to escort the woman and child to a refuge or other safe place:

It may well be that given this initial protection and if referred to a solicitor, the woman will prefer to pursue a civil remedy rather than a criminal one or there may be a reconciliation. Neither should be seen as proof that the initial police action was a mistake. Rather the reverse. This is not the kind of case where the conviction rate can be a justification of the initial action.

That the police can fulfil a role other than their traditional one of control and repression as law enforcers has been illustrated by experiments in the U.S.A. Bard has reported[41] on a program in police family crisis intervention in New York City (which has now been copied in other places) based on special selection and an intensive training program, with the goal of both "crime detection and preventive mental health." The overall purpose was to train police officers to render an interpersonal service (which overall is estimated to take up as much as 90 percent of their working time) with "skill and compassion". Bard concluded that:

. . . the experiment in family crisis intervention shows promise of demonstrating that policemen provided with skills appropriate to the complexities of today's social existence succeed in minimizing violence which might otherwise be exacerbated by their well-meant but inept performance.[42]

Parnas[43] describes mediation and referral as the two common police diversionary responses, but sees them as short-term adjustment. He has reported on police attempts to provide a follow-up service with a "social work, non-crisis, specialist approach", with possible referral on to a proper social service agency, in Winston-Salem, North Carolina, and in Berkeley, California. The justification for this approach is that:

. . . domestic problems can be deemed to be significantly diverted from the criminal process only when the result of a police service call is not only restoration of order but activation of a process which at least has the potential to resolve the source of the conflict.[44]

Parnas has also reported on a joint police-prosecutor screening structure in Detroit for diversion of domestic complaints away from the criminal courts.[45]

The effective diversion of marital violence away from the criminal process must largely depend on police action and innovation, since they will inevitably receive the first request for help in many cases, especially from among the poorer, less-educated sections of the community.[46] Underlying and concluding this discussion on the relevance of criminal procedure to marital violence must then be the sentiment that often "the criminal process is not a particularly appropriate or effective means for dealing with the problem."[47] This was, it is submitted, the fatal flaw in Jack Ashley's private member's Battered Wives (Right to Possession of Matrimonial Home) Bill (which was talked out in the House of Commons in 1975), which would have required the courts to make an order giving the wife of a man who had been convicted of an act of violence against her the complete right of possession of the matrimonial home if she applied for such an order. Its emphasis on the criminal process alone, and thus the encouragement to use it, was completely misguided.[48]

Civil Proceedings

(i) Divorce Court Injunctions

Perhaps the most important civil remedy available to a battered wife is the injunction. Matrimonial injunctions, available in the High Court[49] and county court,[50] are of two kinds. The non-molestation injunction, *i.e.,* an order to the offender not to molest, assault, pester or interfere in any way with the spouse (it thus covers lesser to graver situations including cases where there is not actually any physical violence), and the injunction to vacate the matrimonial home. The court may, instead of granting an injunction, accept an undertaking by the offender not to molest. Breach of the injunction or an undertaking is a contempt of court, for which the penalty can be imprisonment. The contempt can be purged, *i.e.,* a release from prison, by a promise of good behavior in the future.

Procedurally, injunctions are very flexible, indeed this is their greatest advantage. Normally two days' notice of the hearing to the offender is required to give him a chance to be heard in his own defence,[51] and a full hearing is normally held seven days after the complaint. But in a case of emergency, an *ex parte* application can be made and an interim injunction granted in the absence of the offender. Solicitors have vied with each other in the race to see who can get the quickest injunction. One report claimed a record injunction to vacate served on the husband within four-and-a-half hours of having received the initial complaint from the wife (the speed was aided by the prior existence of an emergency legal aid application, and by not submitting written evidence to the court).[52] It has been reported however that the President of the Family Division thinks that too many *ex parte* injunctions have been granted to wives, and that solicitors should be encouraged to give two days' notice to the husbands.[53] The effect of this comment is not known.[54]

The availability of injunctions is now helped by the judges in some areas, in particular London, being on a rota duty in the evenings and on weekends in case emergency injunctions are needed, and in other areas a judge will be contacted by a court officer by telephone where necessary.[55] As a result of these new arrangements, injunction hearings can be held even at a judge's home, and on Sundays (even though as a general rule at common law judicial acts may not be done on a Sunday).[56] The Lord Chancellor's Office conducted a small survey on *ex parte* applications for injunctions. In four weeks there were 252 applications, 75 percent of them in large cities.

One application only was made outside normal working hours. 84 percent of the applicants obtained an interim injunction, although 20 cases were stood over to allow the respondent to attend. 88 percent of the orders were made within a day of the application and 58 percent within an hour. Problems of getting a judge were most severe in the North East, the Lakes and the Isle of Wight. The order has to be settled and signed before it can be served. These formalities were completed within three hours of the judgment in all but one case, and most within one hour.[57]

There is no doubt therefore that in cases of real urgency, emergency *ex parte* injunctions are available.

Another advantage of the injunction is that the court can attach various subsidiary orders to it, *e.g.,* an interim custody order to the wife or an order to the husband to return the child to the wife; an order that the husband be responsible for all outgoings; an order restraining the husband from parting with possession of the matrimonial home or its contents or damaging them, or interfering with the wife's rights of occupation; and an order for costs to be awarded against the respondent.[58]

While the injunction as described would appear to be a most powerful remedy, in particular the speed with which it can be obtained and the ultimate penalty of imprisonment, the limitations and technicalities which have until 1977 surrounded it were quite restricting. Firstly the injunction was seen as an ancillary remedy, *i.e.,* that there had to be a substantive cause of action already before the court out of which the need for an injunction arose. In practice this meant that a battered wife had to commence divorce (or judicial separation) proceedings to get an injunction. This ancillary nature of the injunction was seen as its most serious flaw, in particular that it forced a confused woman into legal action of a kind which she may not have wanted.[59] The Domestic Violence and Matrimonial Proceedings Act 1976, which came into force on June 1, 1977, has now remedied the position. Section 1(a) provides that in the county courts non-molestation injunctions and injunctions to vacate the matrimonial home will be available "whether or not any other relief is sought in the proceedings."

In the High Court, a change in the High Court Rules has been made by the High Court Rules Committee to allow the wife to take out an originating summons for an injunction (as with wardship or under the Matrimonial Homes Act 1967).

The second major problem with the law on injunctions is uncertainty over their availability after the divorce beyond the decree absolute, and over the principles on which injunctions to vacate will be granted. It would appear to be the law that a non-molestation injunction is available for the physical protection of the wife and children at any time before or after the divorce. Injunctions to vacate the matrimonial home are equally available before and after the divorce, so long as some substantive issue, *e.g.,* financial provision or custody, still exists.[60] They are also available, it seems, even when all issues are settled where necessary to protect the interests of children,[61] or where it was "imperative and necessary . . . for the protection of the health, physical or mental, of the wife or child."[62]

The difficulty with injunctions to vacate is the courts' traditional protection of property rights, which makes them reluctant to order a property-owning spouse out of his or her own home. This applies whether he is sole or joint owner. Before the divorce the power under the Matrimonial Homes Act 1967, s. 1(2) to protect the wife's right of occupation in the matrimonial home during the marriage does not by judicial interpretation extend to excluding the property-owning spouse, as the husband usually will be, either solely or jointly.[63] The Select Committee recommended that this interpretation be amended accordingly,[64] and the Domestic Violence and Matrimonial Proceedings Act, s. 3, overrules the House of Lords, decision in *Tarr v. Tarr,* and thus amends the Matrimonial Homes Act 1976, s. 1 (2). The effect is that when protecting the wife's rights of occupation of the matrimonial home, the court may now 'prohibit, suspend or restrict' instead of simply 'regulate' the rights of occupation of the owner or tenant-spouse. Section 4 makes a similar provision in relation to spouses who are joint owners or joint tenants.

The conflict between emphasis on the need for protection and on property rights becomes most apparent in this area. But it is thought that, ultimately, the courts will protect the wife. The Lord Chancellor's Office gave evidence to the Select Committee (p. 393) to the effect that:

[Injunctions] are made sparingly where the husband is the owner or tenant of the home but without hesitation if he is so violent that it is impossible for the spouses to live together.

This statement is in line with the most recent leading case on the question of whether and in what circumstances the court will grant injunctions to vacate. In *Bassett v. Bassett*[65] the Court of Appeal held that while it may be a drastic step to order a husband out of the matrimonial home, its refusal might also have drastic effects on the wife and children. Both wife and children must be protected both physically and psychologically, and "the protection of children from the psychological stress of parental breakup is at least as important as protection of the parent seeking relief". Ultimately the choice for the court is a balance of hardship, *i.e.,* protection of the wife by excluding the husband as against hardship to the husband in finding somewhere else to live.

The third major problem in injunction law is its enforcement.[66] The problem is one of preventing violence before the injunction is obtained, and after, and between breach and committal to prison. An injunction is an order from a civil court, breach of which is a civil contempt, so that its enforcement is undertaken by the civil law enforcers. Nevertheless one of the most common complaints from battered wives is that they find it too difficult to enforce their injunctions.

Section 2 of the Domestic Violence and Matrimonial Proceedings Act now provides that a judge may "if he is satisfied that the other party has caused actual bodily harm . . . and considers that he is likely to do so again, attach a power of arrest to the injunction". The police power of arrest will thus only arise after what has already been fairly serious violence, where the injunction was initially granted on the basis that actual bodily harm had occurred, not where such actual bodily harm occurs merely on breach of the injunction. This limitation ignores the evidence which suggests that an escalation of violence is common, and the problem of the different interpretations placed on the term 'actual bodily harm' by the judges and the police. In addition the husband, who may as a result now be arrested without warrant, must be brought before a judge within 24 hours. According to the Court of Appeal in *Lewis v. Lewis* [67] there is a lacuna in the law here in that there is no authority to hold him in custody any longer than 24 hours if for any reason he cannot be brought before a judge within that time. In addition the granting of the power to arrest lies in the discretion of the judge. It may be that the initiative will have to come from the woman herself or her solicitor. Can it be assumed that solicitors will see the need for a power of arrest in appropriate cases? The Court of Appeal has also said that in any case the power of arrest can only be granted as an exceptional remedy. Finally it is not clear whether the suggestion made by the Select Committee (para. 45) that injunctions should be registered with the police so that they may easily check on its existence has been accepted or will be implemented.

(ii) Magistrates' Courts Domestic Proceedings

The general problems to which domestic proceedings give rise are well known, *i.e.,* the outdated law based on the matrimonial offence, their criminal atmosphere and formal setting, *etc.,*[68] and need not be repeated here. The law which at present operates in the magistrates' court will not much help the battered wife who makes a complaint of persistent cruelty. First, there is the delay before the hearing, reported to be as much as six months in busy courts,[69] which is of critical importance to the battered wife. Secondly, the court can only make a separation or non-cohabitation order, which it appears has only recently been discovered is unenforceable and merely relieves the spouses of their duty to cohabit.[70] Thirdly, there are technical problems, *e.g.,* the absolute bar of adultery, which will deny the wife her remedy for a reason totally extraneous to the violence which brought her to the court. Although replacement of the magistrates' courts by a unified family court is not realistically expected, reform of magistrates' court law has been promised in the near future, and the ground of persistent cruelty will be replaced by the 'unreasonable behavior' ground for divorce and the bars to relief will disappear.

The Law Commission's proposals for dealing with marital violence are that the magistrates will be given a new power to make a personal protection order in favor of the wife or children in a case of actual or threatened violent behavior.[71] They will be able to make an exclusion order where there is a danger of physical injury to the wife or children and:

(i) the husband has used violence against the wife or children; or
(ii) the husband has threatened violence against the wife or children, and has used violence against another person; or
(iii) the husband has disobeyed a personal protection order by threatening violence. In order to prevent physical injury the personal protection order (but not an exclusion order) may be expedited, even by a single justice, with a date for a full hearing to be set with a minimum of delay. The general powers of the magistrates will thus be somewhat similar to those of the High Court and County Courts in granting injunctions.[72]

The Select Committee had also suggested that whereas magistrates should have the power to exclude the husband from occupation of the matrimonial home, which they cannot do at present, and even where he is the sole owner or tenant of it, they should not have power to transfer the tenancy to the wife under the Matrimonial Homes Act 1967.[73] The Law Commission agreed with this (para. 3.27).

The recommendations of the Law Commission have been incorporated in the Domestic Proceedings and Magistrates' Court's Bill 1978 and when it is enacted the magistrates' court will become a far more important source of help for the battered wife. At present its role is minimal.

(iii) County Court Injunctions for Unmarried Women[74]

Divorce Court injunctions until the present time were only available to married women, dependent as they were on the activation of matrimonial proceedings. Now that the law has been reformed as indicated above, injunctions by way of originating summons will be available to a woman regardless of her marital status. Certainly till now the only way a woman could protect herself against the man with whom she was living was by criminal prosecution, or by bringing a claim for damages in tort (for assault or battery, or trespass to person or land) to which an application for an injunction could be ancillary. This method was the one advocated by women's groups.[75] Yet Sir George Baker told the Select Committee (p. 468): "It is a very simple procedure in the county court, but nobody will ever use it. I do not know why".

There is one possible legal problem arising out of county court injunctions: there is a strong principle that the claim for damages must be the substantial claim for damage done, and the injunction only ancillary to that. The battered cohabitee would have to admit that the injunction is her main remedy, and her claim for damages merely the vehicle for getting that.[76] This is another grey area of law which will disappear now that the law on injunctions has been reformed. The Domestic Violence and Matrimonial Proceedings Act, s. 1(2), now states that the county court injunction allowed by s. 1(1) will be available "to a man and a woman who are living with each other in the same household as husband and wife." Similarly, s. 2(2) referring to the police power to arrest for breach of such an injunction. Nice questions have already arisen as to the interpretation of these subsections. In *Davis v. Johnson*[77] the House of Lords held that the Act's protection was available to a cohabitee against the sole or joint owner/tenant of the home.

2. Towards a New Approach

It would probably be fair to say that there is wide agreement that if only the police would cooperate more in prosecuting violent husbands, and if the various technical changes discussed above were made in magistrates' court law and injunctions, then the legal provisions for battered wives would be beyond criticism.[78] It is submitted, however, that the system, even if so reformed, would in a number of basic ways be inadequate as a fair and effective protection.

At this point it is necessary to consider what is the fundamental purpose of a law for the protection of battered women, *i.e.*, what exactly it is intended to regulate and how. Social science research has told us that intrafamily violence occurs widely, though its extent may not be accurately known. It has also suggested various reasons why this may be so, *e.g.*, learned behavior by children from their parents, the release of frustrations and aggressions caused by poor economic and social conditions.[79] There is however disagreement over whether the expression of violence is beneficial. Thus the psychoanalysts believe in a cathartic theory, *i.e.*, that the release of normal violence reduces the chance of serious violence caused by an accumulation of tension.[80] This disagreement is very important for the lawmakers, since the fundamental question for them is whether and to what extent family violence is to be regarded as legitimate violence in our society, as is fighting wars and imposing punishment on offenders, *etc*. There are those who take the view that no violence is to be tolerated, *e.g.*, those who argue nowadays that children should have a legal right not to be smacked, *etc.*, by their parents. Others will say that some degree of physical aggression is socially accepted, by children, wives, men involved in a pub brawl, *etc.*, as well as by the police (in their decision not to prosecute) or by the judges (in their refusal to convict or grant injunctions, or when they impose derisory penalties).[81] What is clear in Great Britain at least is that the degree of tolerated violence differs between wives and the police. Is it possible then to define violence in such a way as to set a standard for official involvement? Steinmetz and Straus defined violence as "the intentional use of physical force on another person".[82] Dr. Gayford defined a battered wife as "a woman who had received deliberate, severe and repeated demonstrable physical injury from her husband. Thus, the minimal injury was severe bruising".[83]

Perhaps a definition is not really important, since the limits of unacceptable violence, at least among adults, can define itself. A call for help by a wife to any outside body should be taken as unassailable evidence that the violence suffered was unacceptable to that wife, and therefore to society at large.[84] The difficulty with this approach of course is that the initiative for action and also for the change in societal attitudes towards violence depends on the woman, and her inferior role and oppression by and fear of her husband may prevent her from making that call for help.[85] Both the raising of her consciousness and the need for a change in male attitudes towards their partners will therefore depend on education and official pronouncements deploring family violence, *e.g.,* the imposition of adequate penalties where necessary. Thus the plea that, if the police will not prosecute, the least they can do is tell the husband that he has no right to assault his wife.[86]

The aim of the law must therefore be to provide protection against physical violence, whenever the victim wants it. This very limited goal does not pretend that the prevention of violence will in any way solve the problems which give rise to the violence,[87] but the amelioration of poor economic and social conditions is obviously beyond the scope of this particular study. In any case, while emphasis on the immediate problem must not blind us to the more fundamental situation, neither must appreciation of the wider issues divert attention from dealing with the more limited question. It would be a social feat of great value if the idea took hold that whatever the argument or provocation, a husband did not have the right to hit his wife, that he should control his aggressive instincts, and as one U.S. judge was heard to repeat to every defendant before him, "Just walk away from it!"

Accepting then the limited aim of the law as being to prevent unacceptable physical violence between husband and wife, it is necessary to consider what criteria are relevant to formulate a law that is both 'good' and effective in achieving this aim.

(a) Equality Before the Law[88]

It is a requirement of formal justice that the law be available and accessible to all who need its protection. In this context it requires that the law is available all the time, not just when lawyers are at work, that it is geared to emergency action, not just when it is convenient for lawyers, and that it is used sympathetically and expertly, so that the victim can rely on good advice, action and representation. On this criterion the present law in England and Wales fails. First, the fact is that many women do not use their legal remedies, either out of ignorance or out of the psychological blockage about going to solicitors.[89] Secondly, legal aid is not available to many middle-class women who require a remedy but are prevented from getting it because of the cost.[90] Thirdly, "there is often a total lack of communication between solicitor and client".[91] And finally there is the difficulty of finding a solicitor who is willing to take on this kind of matrimonial work.[92] The Select Committee responded to this with the suggestion of adequate and widely distributed referral lists of solicitors willing to deal with such matters in the locality (pp. xx, 77, 394, 399-400, 404) and it is now reported from the Law Society that a national computerized referral list is available. In a sense all of these problems are just particular applications of the general problems which exist in relation to access to the law. But in this context the most constant and damning criticism of the present system is that solicitors simply do not know or know how to use the law.[93] Thus Erin Pizzey accused solicitors of giving bad legal advice, and of not "knowing their business".[94] Marion Cutting said: "Many solicitors do not have the knowledge or the imagination to see what is required".[95] The problem arises particularly in the area of emergency action. Though denied by the Lord Chancellor's Office evidence to the Select Committee (p. 394), Erin Pizzey said:

From a solicitor's point of view, battered wives are not good business. The work is often urgent and it takes up a lot of time. A complicated injunction can mean three appearances in court during one week, getting a man committed to prison for breaking an injunction can take four whole days. The fees are small compared with what can be got for commercial work.[96]

Evidence was given to the Select Committee of delays of between seven to 14 days before even an *ex parte* injunction is brought before a court by solicitors out of London, and the accusation was made that solicitors simply do not know the procedures (p. 76). On the other hand, the Select Committee was told (pp. 77, 81):

[I]f you have an efficient solicitor who knows the ropes, as it were, and knows how to get legal aid in London certainly there seems to be no difficulty to act quickly.[97]

The common sentiment that "properly used (the mechanism) does provide effective safeguards" (Select Committee, p. 81) in effect begs the issue for the crucial question is whether the private practice solicitor system is capable of providing an efficient service in this area. Reference was made in the Select Committee to the neighbourhood law centers (of which very few exist outside of London, and even in London only serve a few limited areas),[98] being more geared to getting injunctions and referring women on to sympathetic solicitors, and the National Council for Civil Liberties evidence suggested a national network of neighborhood law centres (p. 94). Erin Pizzey took a somewhat less enthusiastic view in 1974 when she reported that some neighborhood law centers were refusing to take on any kind of matrimonial work, either because it was too time-consuming compared to other work or because it was "social work anyway". She said:

If solicitors at law centers won't help these people, who will? The law centers' present policy is an eternal discredit to them. It must be reversed.[99]

It is thought that her criticisms are in fact somewhat out of date now,[100] but the Select Committee still felt justified in recommending "that more law centers take on this type work, if thought advisable transferring cases once the immediate emergency had been dealt with to local solicitors" (p. xxi). And the Select Committee certainly took the point (p. xxi) about the inadequacy of private solicitors:

We consider that law centers are potentially admirably suited to deal with the emergency situation caused by domestic violence, being situated in the community with links with other agencies and flexible working hours.

The argument has so far progressed from enforcement of the law by private solicitors to a public legal service, *i.e.,* salaried lawyers working in a law center. That law centers are more likely to be sympathetic, expert, flexible in terms of hours, and not constantly considering the financial reward is not denied, and is indeed their great advantage. But it is submitted that the emphasis on law centers is perhaps misplaced. First, family law is only one of their areas of activity — thus their expertise is inevitably diluted. Secondly, it ignores what is considered to be the very important principle already discussed, *i.e.,* that the legal remedy must always be seen as just one of a number of alternatives. A law center will tend to specialize in the legal remedy even where social or community workers are attached to it. It is thought that the Select Committee's idea of a public agency, a Family Crisis Center, providing a 24-hour emergency advisory service would be more suitable.[101] There is no reason why salaried lawyers, authorized to take legal action on behalf of battered wives, could not be employed by such centers. In consultation with colleagues in the center the decision could then be taken as to whether legal action was appropriate, necessary, or whether it would be counter-productive in terms of further violence, *etc.*[102] These lawyers could make the professional decision between a civil remedy or to recommend to the police that they pursue a criminal prosecution.

(b) Unbiased Judges and Interpretation

A second formal requirement of justice is that the lawyers and the judges are unbiased. In this context all that it is necessary to point out is that a certain kind of 'sexism'[103] must not be allowed to creep into either the legal advice to take or not to take action, or into the judicial decision to grant whatever remedy is sought. In other words the feeling that a certain amount of wife-beating is legitimate, or that it is legitimate among certain groups of society,[104] or that 'the wife asked for it'[105] must not be allowed to enter into the decision. The aim of the law is to prevent physical violence for whatever reason it occurred. The arbiter of its legitimacy is, as already explained, the victim.

In particular the law must be interpreted sympathetically by the judges.[106] The aims of the law must be made clear, and the judges who operate it must be understanding of and sympathetic to the spirit of the law. It may well be that just as magistrates are to be chosen specially for the matrimonial bench, so should judges. It is not so much their training which counts, but their human qualities of being able to listen to, understand and show concern for the problems. It is basic sympathy for human problems which is needed, not a dogmatic legalistic approach which may be appropriate in other areas of the law. There is an argument to be made for lay assessors to provide the social context for the legal decision,[107] as in, *e.g.,* race relations cases, but it is submitted here that nothing is more important than a sympathetic and understanding judge. The under-representation of women on the bench is at least one area for improvement.

(c) A Fair Hearing

A third formal requirement is that a fair hearing be provided to both sides. Legal representation must be available to the husband, *e.g.,* if he is not otherwise represented through a duty solicitor scheme in the magistrates' court, and also at the county court (this is possible at present under the Legal Advice Scheme under s. 2(4) of the Legal Aid Act 1974). Where an emergency injunction is required, there would appear to be no objection in principle to an *ex parte* interim injunction being granted until a proper hearing can be held. The potential gravity of the wife's situation must temporarily take precedence over the husband's right to be heard. But the importance of a proper hearing for the husband is vital, because while a truism, it still takes two to have a fight, and the husband may have many complaints against his wife. While this does not justify his violence, it may explain it, and may help the court to remove the labels of offender and victim, in the sense of total guilt and total innocence. Hearing the husband may also uncover for the court, but especially for the husband himself, the underlying social causes of his aggression.

(d) The Criminal or Civil Process?

There is a fundamental point of substance which needs to be considered, *i.e.,* whether the criminal or the civil process is suitable as a mode of legal regulation of family violence, and who should make the choice of process.

There is no doubt that certain degrees of violence must be dealt with as a criminal offence. Where it is fatal, charges of murder or manslaughter must clearly be brought. In cases of extreme violence, Erin Pizzey wrote:

I think the most practical use of the law is for it to ensure that in every case of extreme violence the man is shut off from further contact with his wife and children.[108]

Parnas has also pointed out:

Generally, the more serious the injury, the easier the intervention decision, although the situational nature of the family offence nonetheless makes the disposition decision, at best, difficult.[109]

But more common in practice are those grey areas where the lesser injuries to the wife must be balanced against the psychological injury and possible counter-productiveness of labelling a man a criminal.[110] Serious consideration must be given to whether prosecuting a husband for a criminal offence, even if it is only common assault, will achieve anything in terms of improving the marital relationship, the mutual respect which husband and wife should have for each other, or the husband's ability to understand and control his aggressions. The problem has been well expressed by Subin:

[Of] all of the areas in which an alternative to criminal treatment seems justified, the area of marital disputes is the most obvious. This is not to say that violence, theft or neglect between spouses should be ignored, but it does appear that these cases deserve different treatment than they are now given. Whether prosecution is decided upon or not, it would seem that beyond the point of immediate police response to danger, the criminal process is largely irrelevant in these cases. If anything, its very invocation may exacerbate poverty-related and/or psychological problems. The summary, rather shallow treatment given these complainants does not answer the need that they have expressed for help.[111]

Use of the criminal process should therefore be restricted to occasions when the need is present for coercive prevention of violence in view of the physical danger to the wife. In England the decision to invoke the criminal process lies partly in the hands of the wife, *i.e.,* in her choice of agency to which she goes for help, *e.g.,* police or solicitor, but partly also in the hands of the police in their decision to prosecute. Police discretion in refusing may have a desired effect in general, though in specific cases the evidence of battered wives certainly suggests that police discretion is used too restrictively. But the desired effect in general may not come about for the right reasons. Their reluctance to get involved in domestic disputes is for reasons relating to their perceived role for the police, not because they have decided in principle that the civil law is a more appropriate remedy.

The decision-maker holds a crucial position and, it is submitted, ought to be a professional person trained to make a principled choice. The public lawyer in a Family Crisis Center could make the choice ideally in consultation with the complainant. There are however two other models for decision-making which will be discussed more fully later which operate in the U.S.A. and which are worth considering, *i.e.,* the court itself in New York, and the U.S. Attorney (public prosecutor) in consultation with the Corporation Counsel (equivalent to local English government lawyers) in Washington D.C.

(c) The Powers of the Court

Another issue of substantive justice is the powers of the courts when dealing with problems of family violence. Assuming that in the near future the magistrates' courts and county courts will continue to exist, though with a concurrent jurisdiction in this field, they will still be left with only the strictly legal remedy. And just as legal action is only one alternative to be considered in the attempt to stop the violence, so at the other end the strictly legal remedy is only one of a number of possible remedies which the courts could impose. It is time that the courts in England and Wales were given the power to consider social work support, *e.g.,* marriage guidance counseling, or psychiatric treatment (*e.g.,* for alcoholism) as complimentary orders to the legal one.[112] It may be that the American experience described below could be followed.

For it is so easy in the traditional court context of adversary proceedings to forget that the offender may need help as much as the complainer, though of a different kind. She needs her protection, but (so the Select Committee was told: p. xv) he needs:

> . . . to be treated considerately. . . . In some cases alcoholism or mental illness may require treatment; in others considerate advice and discussion may bring him to realize what caused the violence so that it is not repeated and he becomes a more successful person when his wife returns, or is able to form a lasting and happy relationship with a new partner.

125   The Law's Response To Marital Violence

Thus the National Council for Civil Liberties recommendation to the Select Committee (p. 92) was that:

[A] welfare service should be provided at the court for men and women involved in these cases. Men excluded from the home should be helped to find alternative accommodation.

It has also been recommended that the courts have power to order medical and psychiatric reports on the husband before deciding what steps to take.[113]

3. The United States Experience[114]

Many attempts have been made in the U.S.A. to adapt the traditional criminal process to take account of the special nature of intrafamily violence.[115] The Chicago Court of Domestic Relations has a jurisdiction roughly equivalent to the English magistrates' court jurisdiction in domestic proceedings concerning maintenance, affiliation, and children in need of care. It does not deal with felonies, juvenile offences, nor separation, divorce, or adoption. There is a social service department of the court which provides counseling, and can refer persons to other community resources both before and, at the request of a judge, after the court hearing. It also provides a continuing casework service in some areas. The court can also refer persons appearing before it to the court psychiatric institute. The powers of the court in dealing with offenders are varied but traditional, but the most interesting development which is used predominantly in the area of intrafamily violence is the 'peace bond' equivalent to the English binding over to keep the peace, but which, on the admission of the judges, is legally unenforceable, though they believe it to be psychologically beneficial.[116] It is in effect a warning 'not to do it again', because, if breached, the offender will be charged with a substantive offence. Its significance is, however, that no conviction is recorded nor is any record kept of the bond. In other words, it is an attempt by the court to decriminalize the situation. In Detroit the Police Department has set up a Misdemeanor Complaint Bureau which acts as a 'preliminary *quasi*-judicial forum' to screen cases which would otherwise be resolved in court. The police who do the screening also use the entirely illegal and unenforceable 'peace bond' as a warning. In the Milwaukee Misdemeanor Court a criminal judge instituted a three-day cooling-off period between the spouse's complaint and the issuance of a warrant, a pre-trial conference in intrafamily assault cases, and adjournment of the case for a period (either unsupervised or with a referral to the probation department) at the end of which no conviction is recorded if he has been of good behavior. These are all interesting and innovative examples of criminal courts attempting to decriminalize intrafamily assaults.

However, in two jurisdictions, New York City and Washington D.C., there have been attempts to create a truly radical alternative to the criminal process. The 'civil protection order' is in essence very similar to the matrimonial injunction. Yet in the way it operates it satisfies so many more of the objectives, already described, of a 'good' system of legal regulation.

In New York City[117] a family court was set up in 1962 with jurisdiction over all family matters, including intrafamily assaults, except separation, annulment and divorce. The purpose of the family offences proceedings is actually written into the Family Court Act itself, s. 811 of which states:

In the past, wives and other members of the family who suffered from disorderly conduct or assaults by other members of the family or household were compelled to bring a 'criminal charge' to invoke the jurisdiction of the court. Their purpose, with few exceptions, was not to secure a criminal conviction and punishment, but practical help.

The family court is better equipped to render such help, and the purpose of this article is to create a civil proceeding for dealing with such instances of disorderly conduct and assaults. It authorizes the family court to enter orders of protection and support and contemplates conciliation proceedings. If the family court concludes that these processes are inappropriate in a particular case, it is authorized to transfer the proceeding to an appropriate criminal court.

The court has jurisdiction over disorderly conduct or assaults[118] between spouses, parent and child, or members of the same family or household (s. 812).[119] Proceedings for family offences in the family court can be brought by the victim, authorized agencies, the police or other person with the court's permission (s. 822). All family offences must be brought before the family court, if necessary being transferred from a criminal court, and the court itself decides whether to proceed to a civil protection order (or conciliation order)[120] or to transfer the case to a criminal court. The decision to use the criminal process thus lies squarely in the hands of the judges. It is possible though that the case will never get to court, since the probation service has the power to attempt preliminary 'informal adjustment' of suitable cases (*e.g.*, counseling by the probation service, or by one of the voluntary marital counseling agencies on the premises, or by reference to the court's mental health service (s. 823)); but the probation service cannot compel this nor prevent a petition being filed if the party so wishes. On filing of the petition by the petitioner (*i.e.*, there is no 'prosecutor') the court may either issue a summons or an arrest warrant, *e.g.*, where "the safety of the petitioner is endangered" (s. 827).[121]

The Act (s. 141) warns the judges of their personal responsibilities in this area.

[T]he court is given a wide range of powers for dealing with the complexities of family life so that its action may fit the particular needs of those before it. The judges of the court are thus given a wide discretion and grave responsibilities. . . . Judges of the family court should . . . be familiar with areas of learning and practice that often are not supplied by the practice of law.

And in New York City judges are appointed "who are especially qualified for the court's work by reason of their character, personality, tact, patience and common sense" (s. 124).

The powers of the court are to dismiss the petition, suspend judgment for six months, order one year's probation, or make a civil protection order (s. 841).[122] The civil protection order is the most commonly used method of disposition. The court may order 'reasonable conditions of behavior' to be observed by the petitioner or respondent, or both, for a maximum of one year, and in particular may order a party

(a) to stay away from the home, the other spouse or the child;

(b) to permit a parent to visit the child at stated periods;

(c) to abstain from offensive conduct against the child or against the other parent or against any person to whom custody of the child is awarded;

(d) to give proper attention to the care of the home;

(e) to refrain from acts of commission or omission that tend to make the home not a proper place for the child;

(f) to notify the court or probation service immediately of any change of residence or employment;

(g) to cooperate in seeking and accepting medical and/or psychiatric diagnosis and treatment, including family casework or child guidance for himself, his family or child.

The court may also award custody of the child during the term of the order of protection to either parent, or to an appropriate relative within the second degree. Nothing in this section gives the court power to place or board out any child or to commit a child to an institution or agency (s. 842).

An order under (g) is clearly only available where the parties are willing, but it is of the greatest importance that the court has this power to use when appropriate.

Once the order is made a copy of it is given to the parties, and presentation of this certificate to the police authorizes them to "bring the person charged with violating the order before the court" (s. 168).[123] The penalty for contempt of the order is a maximum of six months' imprisonment, though it may be suspended, or with conditions, *e.g.,* for treatment, or to be served on specific days.

The Washington D.C. scheme,[124] introduced in 1971, based as it was on the New York legislation, is essentially similar, but differs in a number of important respects. An intrafamily offence is defined as an act which could be punished as a criminal offence, but is committed by one spouse against the other, by a parent against a child, or by any person against another "with whom he shares a mutual residence and is in close relationship" (D.C. Code, c. 16 s. 1001(1)).[125] All complaints of criminal conduct come initially before the U.S. Attorney, *i.e.,* the chief prosecutor for D.C. The U.S. Attorney's office decides whether to pursue a criminal prosecution, but in all cases of intrafamily offences it must notify the Director of Social Services, whose office is part of the D.C. Superior Court organization, and the Director through one of his social workers may make recommendations to the U.S. Attorney, *e.g.,* about conditions of release taking into account the intrafamily nature of the offence. Alternatively, the U.S. Attorney may decide, after mandatory consultation with the Director of Social Services about the appropriateness of the referral, that a civil action is more appropriate. The matter will then be referred to the Corporation Counsel (*i.e.,* city attorneys, equivalent to English local government lawyers, though they also prosecute in juvenile cases) to petition the Family Division of the Superior Court for a civil protection order.[126] Once evidence in the civil process has begun to be taken, criminal proceedings based on that offence are not allowed. In theory then the U.S. Attorney (*i.e.,* the prosecutor), in consultation with the Director of Social Services (*i.e.,* a social worker), decides whether to pursue the criminal or civil remedy, though in practice the Corporation Counsel often make the decision (they are all situated in the same building) and can refuse to take a case referred by the U.S. Attorney. For example, some Corporation Counsel will refuse to take proceedings in respect of acts which are criminal felonies.[127]

Once the Corporation Counsel has decided to pursue a civil remedy, though the legislation does not provide for this, he may attempt an informal resolution of the matter, *e.g.*, by a letter to the respondent warning him that a complaint has been made, or by conducting an informal hearing himself, though these practices depend very much on the particular attorney involved. More commonly the Corporation Counsel will file a petition for a civil protection order. In the case of emergency,[128] *i.e.*, where "the safety or welfare of a family member is immediately endangered by the respondent", the Corporation Counsel can ask the judge in chambers for an *ex parte* temporary civil protection order which is effective for 10 days, provided that it is served personally on the respondent within five days and there is a full hearing within the 10-day period. It is thought that such *ex parte* applications are not denied, but in the fiscal year 1975, only 16 temporary civil protection orders were issued as against 366 full orders.

The filing of a complaint is of course no protection against further violence, and from complaint to trial can take from about four to eight weeks.[129] The judge has power, as in New York as well, to issue a bench warrant for the respondent's arrest, though in Washington D.C. the appropriate step, if there is a danger of further serious violence, is a temporary civil protection order. One of the most difficult problems in practice is getting the respondent to court. Often he is not actually served with the summons (this must be done in person by a U.S. marshal) or else he fails to attend the hearing. In the latter case, a bench warrant may be issued. It is estimated that in about a quarter of all cases the complainant herself fails to appear, and in about half of the rest (75 percent) the respondent fails to appear. Should the hearing actually take place (in open court, unless the judge closes it as he or she has the discretion to do so — in New York it is closed) with both parties present, in about 50 percent of cases the respondent admits the allegations[130] (though it has been observed that in many more cases he will admit the facts but dispute the reasons or add to the surrounding circumstances).

On proof of the complaint, for which the standard is "good cause to believe the respondent has committed or is threatening an intrafamily offence", the court may issue a civil protection order for a period of up to one year. The standard civil protection order provides for an order that the respondent:

(a) shall not molest, assault, or in any manner threaten or physically abuse [the complainant]
(b) [or] the child[ren] of [the complainant];
(c) shall completely avoid [the presence] [the residence] [the place of employment] of [the complainant][131]
(d) not carry any dangerous weapon, including licensed firearms.

The court may further order that the respondent or complainant or both:

(a) shall participate in psychiatric or medical treatment or appropriate counseling programs, as may be established by the Director of Social Services;
(b) shall participate in a program of family counseling as may be established by the Director of Social Services;
(c) shall participate in a program of alcoholic rehabilitation, as may be established by the Director of Social Services.

Other special conditions may be attached.

Breach of the order is contempt for which the respondent can be imprisoned for up to six months, though this is often suspended, possibly with conditions, over and above those in the civil protection order. Fines are also often imposed. In the fiscal year 1975, there were some 1,400 complaints, 366 civil protection orders, 16 temporary orders, and 62 motions for contempt (in two-thirds of these a contempt was found).

Some judges apparently issued mutual civil protection orders. This may be realistic in the sense that although one is the complainant, the judge decides that both are to blame for the violence, but the legality of such orders in the context of the D.C. law has been questioned. The restraining clauses of the civil protection order are by law directed against the respondent, while the partici-pating clauses may be directed against both. Difficult questions could arise where the respondent claimed a breach of the civil protection order by the complainant, since the Corporation Counsel brings the proceedings but the respondent is not his client. The respondent could have a private lawyer to represent him, but the proceedings are intended to be a public action.

The counseling clauses are used to differing degrees by different judges. The willingness of both parties is clearly a prerequisite, but a sympathetic judge can sometimes elicit a degree of goodwill that is left in the relationship and put it to good use. Unlike the New York law there is no provision in Washington D.C. for a custody order, and this must be a vital omission, since early determination of custody can only be for the benefit of the children involved.

These experiments in the U.S.A. appear to have been universally welcomed. Parnas has written of the New York family court:

Besides being a clear diversion out of the criminal process, the family court utiilizes problem-solving professionals and techniques necessary to have a reasonable chance at preventing repeated or increased violence within the police, prosecutor's and criminal court's jurisdiction. . . . In domestic disputes, underlying causes are sometimes deep and subject to continual eruption because of the close emotional contact of the parties. They need the intensive treatment of the social services which the adjunct agencies of a family court can at least begin to give.[132]

In a New York case, the judge said:

This innovation . . . has proved one of the most imaginative and progressive methods of avoiding the crime and punishment and substituting prevention and treatment if appropriate via a non-criminal ambience — the family court.[133]

And in Washington D.C. a judge said publicly:

The people who came before this [court] will be, if they are offenders, civil offenders. . . . We do not wish to stigmatize them. We want them to keep their earning capacity and also the possibility of self respect, and their connection with the family.[134]

A Washington D.C. lawyer has commented:

The legalization is sound. Many cases involve people who yearn for professional help in a sincere effort to salvage their marriages. They seek solutions from the court such as marriage counseling, alcoholic and drug rehabilitation, psychiatric assistance, and sometimes a declaration from the court that marriage is not a license to commit mayhem.[135]

The conclusion must be that judged by the stated criteria of a 'good' and effective law for the prevention of family violence, the American examples come out better in many ways than the English law. In the first place, the legal system is more available and accessible. In Washington D.C. the system has been put clearly in the public sector. All complaints are made to a centrally located, clearly identifiable, Citizen's Complaint Center, situated near the court complex. It is open from 9 a.m. to 10 p.m., five days a week. The staff in the center, prosecuting attorneys from the U.S. Attorney's office, social workers from the Director of Social Services' office, and Corporation Counsel all cooperate in achieving a considered solution to the problem. Physical proximity at least allows the opportunity for liaison and collaboration. The staff, though not solely devoted to intrafamily offence work, are quite heavily committed to it, and thus become expert and, one hopes, sympathetic if only through the experience. The Corporation Counsel in particular are expert at the legal procedures and geared to take emergency action where necessary.

Secondly, as has been seen, in New York the judges are (at least in theory) chosen for their particular personal aptitude for family work, and recognition is given to the need for understanding of extra-legal subjects. In Washington D.C., though there are no comparable provisions, many of the judges observed showed a concern and interest in the problem. One judge sighed with frustration at the end of a long morning hearing petitions for civil protection orders that this was just the tip of an iceberg and recognized his own limited role in the prevention of violence. Another judge, a young attractive woman, gave a sympathetic talk to all the parties present in court for the morning's cases, explaining to them the purpose of the hearing — that it was to help them, not punish them; that the possibility of counseling that existed, and her aim was to keep the family unit together but that if that was not possible, they could at least live separately in peace. She then closed the court and heard each case in private. Unbiased but sympathetic interpretation by the judges then is a pre-requisite for an effective system.

Thirdly, in Washington D.C. no proceedings were allowed to continue against a man unless he had first been advised of his right to a lawyer. In civil cases he may represent himself if he so wishes, and most respondents in civil protection cases are not in fact represented. In contempt hearings however it is thought that he must have a lawyer on constitutional grounds, because of the possibility of imprisonment. Even without representation, the importance of the husband being heard cannot be exaggerated. The other side of the story so often changes the whole context of the violence, in particular in explaining provocation or exposing violence on the part of the wife. This would explain the need for mutual civil protection orders in some cases.

Fourthly, it is quite clear that the importance of decriminalizing family violence is taken very seriously in the U.S. Only professionals can take this decision: in Washington D.C. the U.S. Attorney in consultation with the Director of Social Services, and the family court judge in New York City. It is said that the New York system is more flexible in that the judge who makes the initial decision can at any time during the civil proceedings transfer the case to a criminal court.

Fifthly, the powers of the courts in disposing of the case in the U.S. are so much more enlightened. In addition to the traditional powers of the English injunction (though perhaps with greater emphasis on the protection of the children in New York through a custody order), the courts have the very important role of calling upon medical, psychiatric and counseling services, most of which are provided by the court structure itself, or by outside agencies otherwise. The judge himself or herself is therefore bound to consider remedies other than the strictly legal one both for the respondent and for the complainant, or both. The success of such provisions is not known, but the need for their availability cannot be disputed. Some parties may be already well on the way to divorce or separation; others may welcome an official invitation to saving their marriage. And a sympathetic judge can help immensely in the willingness of both parties to agree to treatment or counseling. Most important of all, no system in this context can be fair unless there is consideration for the 'offender' and possibilities for help to be given to him.

Finally, the power of the police to arrest for breach of the order, as in New York, must be noted.

4. Conclusions

It is to be regretted that the House of Commons Select Committee was not more inventive and innovative in its recommendations regarding the law available to battered women. It recognized that the private sector of the legal profession was unlikely to be able to operate the legal provisions adequately and so recommended an increased role for the neighborhood law centers. Reasons have already been advanced against this proposal even assuming that neighborhood law centers could ever exist in every neighborhood in every town or part of the country. The Washington D.C. system of a public agency dealing with intrafamily offences in a non-criminal setting with non-legal services at hand appears a more attractive model. The nearest equivalent to the D.C. system in England would be a local government office, somewhat akin to a local government consumer or housing advice center or Trading Standards Department, staffed by local government lawyers who would bring actions on behalf of complainants in the local courts. Alternatively one could envisage a local office of a central agency similar to, for example, the now obsolete conciliation committee of the Race Relations Board. The idea of such bodies 'prosecuting' actions on behalf of members of the public is not so extraordinary, for the Trading Standards Department can bring prosecutions; what is more important in this context, the Race Relations Board could bring civil actions under the Race Relations Acts 1965-68. What is urged here is a far more innovative role for the family crisis centers proposed by the Select Committee. Public salaried lawyers as professionals, expert and sympathetic to the persons and their problems, could make the vital decision to advise the woman to take criminal or civil proceedings. It may be difficult to give them the right to prosecute, since the police are the traditional prosecutors in England, though there is a precedent in the right of the local authority to initiate care proceedings in the juvenile courts in respect of criminal offences. There is also the possiblility of a system of public prosecutors, akin to the U.S. or Scottish systems, to whom the family crisis center lawyer could leave the decision. Whatever the prosecution system however, if prosecution is not undertaken, it would be left to the family crisis center lawyer to take the civil action. This action could be brought by the lawyer either as representative of the client, *i.e.,* as a private lawyer-client relationship, or on behalf of the public agency.[136]

Family crisis centers would be ideally placed to provide the battered woman with accessible legal services. They would be open all day, every day, staffed by experts, with access to all the various services which might need to be called upon, including temporary refuges, marriage counseling, psychiatric and medical services, and housing advice, in addition to the legal remedies.

As far as the law itself is concerned, the changes now brought about by the Domestic Violence and Matrimonial Proceedings Act, 1976, making injunctions available in the county courts independently of matrimonial proceedings and regardless of marital status, and giving the police power to arrest for breach, are certainly necessary. But the whole question of what powers the courts should have when granting an injunction has been ignored. A power to encourage the parties to undergo counseling or treatment, and order them to do so if they are at all willing, is essential.

[The courts] are ill-suited to the task of permanently resolving such [domestic] disputes, and they know it. Furthermore, their traditional role offers scant room for improvement. The most successful response they can make is to insure that the disputes resulting in judicial attention are securely placed in the hands of resources capable of solving the problem.[137]

Thus all along the line the law is seen as only one alternative method of dealing with the problem. It is important not to forget the psychological effect of an official invitation to attempt to save a marriage and/or to behave better.[138]

The final comment that needs to be made is a plea for realism. The law is a limited resource. Its effectiveness must not be over-estimated:

Legal reforms cannot solve the problem of battered women, they can only alleviate it. No matter what legal changes are made, men will continue to batter women until there are profound changes in the structure of our society. In the meantime, the establishment of women's aid centers in every neighborhood would provide a refuge and a source of moral support and practical assistance.[139]

In some cases the law may serve an important function. In others it will be useless:

I don't believe that the court is the proper place to resolve the problems of battered wives.

133   **The Law's Response To Marital Violence**

Their husbands are outside the law: they have been imprinted with violence since childhood, so that violence is part of their normal behavior. All the legislating and punishment in the world will not change their methods of expressing their frustrations.[140]

In each case the professionals involved must make judgments about the efficacy of the various available courses of action. At least a 'good' law can make a contribution.

NOTES

1. See generally: Steinmetz S.K., and Straus, M.A. (eds.), *Violence in the Family*. New York, New York: Dodd, Mead, 1974; Brandon, S., "Physical Violence in the Family: An over-view," in Borland, M. (ed.), *Violence in the Family*. Manchester, Eng.: Manchester University Press, 1976; Report from the Select Committee on Violence in Marriage, H.C. 553-i, and Minutes of Evidence, H.C. 533-ii, 1974-75, hereafter referred to as the Select Committee. The Report had not, at the date of writing, been debated in the House of Commons; Gelles, R.J., *The Violent Home: A Study of Physical Aggression between Husbands and Wives*. Beverley Hills, Calif.: Sage Publications, 1972; Parnas, R.I., "Prosecutorial and Judicial Handling of Family Violence" (1973), 9 *Criminal Law Bulletin;* R.I. Parnas, "Judicial Response to Intra-Family Violence" (1970), 54 *Minnesota Law Review* 585; R.I. Parnas, "Police Discretion and Diversion of Incidents of Intrafamily Violence" (1971), 36 *Law and Contemporary Problems* 539; Marsden, D. and Owens, D., "The Jekyll and Hyde Marriages" *New Society,* May 8, 1975, p. 333; Gayford, J.J., "Battered Wives" (1975), 15 *Medicine, Science and the Law* 237; Gayford, J.J., "Wife Battering: A Preliminary Survey of 100 Cases" (1975) *British Medical Journal* 194; Tidmarsh, M., "Violence in Marriage" (1976), 7 *Social Work Today* 3; Jobling, M., "Battered Wives: A Survey" (1974), 47 *Social Services Quarterly* 142; BASW Working Party discussion document "Home violence — is there an Answer?" (1975) BASW News 409; Owens, D., "Battered Wives: Some Social and Legal Problems" (1975), 2 *British Journal of Law and Society* 201.
2. See Steinmetz and Straus, *op. cit.,* chap. 3.
3. See Select Committee, *passim.*
4. See Borland, *op. cit.,* chap. 8.
5. *Ibid.,* chap. 7. See also Parnas, *Law and Contemporary Problems, passim;* Steinmetz and Straus, *op. cit.,* chap. 14.
6. Bankowski, Z., and Mungham, G., *Images of Law*. Boston, Mass.: Routledge Kegan and Paul, 1976, chap. 2, especially p. 40.
7. Select Committee, p. xviii.
8. See also Pizzey, E., *Scream Quietly or the Neighbours Will Hear*. Harmondsworth, Middlesex: Penguin, 1974, pp. 116, 120, 129.
9. Gill, T., and Coote, A., *Battered Women — How to Use the Law*. London, Eng.: Cobden Trust, 1975.
10. Raisbeck, B.L., "The Legal Framework," in Borland, *op. cit.,* p. 102; Mostyn, F.E., *Marriage and the Law*. London, Eng.: Oyez, 1976, p. 127.
11. Pizzey, *op. cit.,* chap. 6, especially p. 116; Cutting, M., "Some legal Problems of Women on the break-up of Marriage" (1973) Legal Action Group Bulletin 165. Owens, D., *op. cit.,* p. 202 suggests a third view that whatever the legal provisions "the battered wife may find a major obstacle in the stereotypical ideas of marriage, of appropriate behavior within marriage, and of marital violence which are held by law officials with whom she must deal."
12. See chap. 5 for a more detailed account of the English provisions.

13. *I.e.,* actual bodily harm (s. 47), unlawful wounding (s. 20), grievous bodily harm with intent (s.18). See Memo. of Association of Chief Police Officers, Select Committee, p. 366; Metropolitan Police Memo., Select Committee, p. 379; Home Office Memo., Select Committee, pp. 406-407.
14. *E.g.,* Jobling, *op. cit.,* p. 144; Russell, M., gave evidence to the Select Committee, p. 79, that the police turn their backs on crimes of a serious nature; Select Committee, pp. xvii, 96, 97. In particular it is alleged that the police are reluctant to arrest: Gill and Coote, *op. cit.,* p. 16; similarly in the U.S.A.: Parnas, *Law and Contemporary Problems,* p. 543.
15. See, *e.g.,* Select Committee, pp. vii-viii; Gregory, *op. cit.,* pp. 117-119.
16. Bard, M., "The Study and Modification of Intra-Familial Violence," in Steinmetz and Straus, *op. cit.,* chap. 14, at p. 134. See also Parnas, *Law and Contemporary Problems,* pp. 542-543; Russell, M., told Select Committee, p. 79 of a policeman stabbed while intervening between husband and wife.
17. Scott, P.D., "Battered Wives" (1974), 125 British Journal of Psychiatry 433, discussed in Gregory, *op. cit.,* pp. 110-111.
18. Gregory, *op. cit.,* p. 117; Pizzey, *op. cit.,* p. 98. Dow, M., "Police Involvement" in Borland, *op. cit.,* p. 129 at p. 133 suggests that it is the reporting by victims or friends which underestimates the seriousness of the violence.
19. *E.g.,* assault occasioning actual bodily harm (s. 47, Offences against the Person Act 1861). According to Dow, *op. cit.,* p. 132, common assault is appropriate where there is no direct evidence of injury, *i.e.,* no obvious sign of injury to the wife.
20. See also Dow, *op. cit.,* p. 132; Gregory, *op. cit.,* p. 118; Chatterton, *op. cit.,* p. 41.
21. Gregory, *op. cit.,* pp. 117-119, 125; Gayford, Select Committee, pp. 4, 37.
22. Gayford, *British Medical Journal,* p. 196; Marcovitch, A., "Refuges for Battered Women" (1976), 7 *Social Work Today* p. 34, at p. 35. Gregory, *op. cit.,* p. 117 says wives often feel that he needs "help, not punishment."
23. Thus it has been suggested that it might be possible to deal with husband and wife assaults in closed court as domestic proceedings: (1974) Legal Action Group Bulletin 66; Memo. of Association of Chief Police Officers, Select Committee, p. 368.
24. Chatterton, *op. cit.,* pp. 38-45. See also Parnas, *Law and Contemporary Problems,* pp. 545-548: he calls this police diversion or "screening". On the other hand, *cf.* Home Office Memo., to Select Committee, p. 409: "Any assault which is reported to the police will be investigated."
25. Chatterton, *op. cit.,* p. 40. Unless of course there is a danger of medical complications or fatality. Dow, *op. cit.,* p. 134 discusses the possibility of compelling a wife to give evidence, as a hostile witness if necessary. Home Office Memo. to Select Committee, p. 407 says that the main common law exception to the rule that an accused's wife is incompetent to give evidence for the prosecution is in cases of personal violence against her. Thus while she is competent and compellable, she is unwilling.
26. Memo. of Association of Chief Police Officers, Select Committee, p. 368.
27. Select Committee, p. 376 citing *Pickering v. Willoughby* [1907] 2 K.B. 296. The reason given is to not encourage civil and criminal proceedings for the same assault (Home Office Memo., Select Committee, p. 407). It is also said that there is no power of arrest unless it is committed in view of the police (Select Committee, p. 375).
28. Dow, *op. cit.,* p. 132.
29. But it has been suggested that legal advice is available under the £25 scheme for the preliminary work (*e.g.,* by a duty solicitor scheme) and even for representation. Quaere, is it also available to the defendant? ((1974) Legal Action Group Bulletin, pp. 66-94). Pizzey, *op. cit.,* suggests that the probation service will help the wife through her case in court p. 109), but also refers to the difficulties of wives acting for themselves (p. 117).
30. See generally Smith, J.C., and Hogan, B., *Criminal Law* (3rd ed.) London, Eng.: Butterworths, 1973, p. 281. The maximum penalty in a summary trial is six months or £100 fine, compared to two months or £50 for common assault.
31. Select Committee, p. 377. See Pizzey, *op. cit.,* pp. 116-117 for comment on derisory

sentences. Gregory, *op. cit.,* pp. 117, 125 comments on the lighter sentences than for assaults between strangers. On the other hand it could be argued that the sentences reflect a judicial concern for diversion from criminality. Parnas, *Law and Contemporary Problems,* pp. 543-544 says: "judges hesitate to incarcerate or even fine such defendants. They fear that the results of the sanction — loss of employment, reduction of the family's already tight budget by imposition of a fine, relegation of the family to welfare, removal of the children's father figure, or exacerbation of already existing tension — may have more severe consequences for the family unit than did the crime." Similarly Parnas, *Minnesota Law Review,* pp. 610-611.

32. (1973) Legal Action Group Bulletin 277.
33. (1974) Legal Action Group Bulletin 66.
34. Dow, *op. cit., passim,* and especially p. 129. And see discussion in Steinmetz and Straus, *op. cit.,* p. 130.
35. Dow, *op. cit.,* p. 133. And see Bard, *op. cit.,* p. 136: "Appeals to the police are in the nature of requests for authority and objectivity in the resolution of conflict — not for enforcement of law."
36. Chatterton, *op. cit.,* p. 46.
37. Memo. of Association of Chief Police Officers, Select Committee, p. 368; Metropolitan Police Memo., Select Committee, p. 376.
38. *Ibid.* The need for "facilities to monitor domestic situations" after proceedings is recognized (p. 368), as is the need for the police to inform Social Services. But comment is also made on the delicate issues raised by referral (p. 269).
39. Dow, *op. cit.,* pp. 130, 135; Chatterton, *op. cit.,* pp. 46-47; Tomlinson, T., "Inter-agency Collaboration: Issues and Problems" in Borland, *op. cit.,* chap. 8.
40. Chatterton, *op. cit.,* p. 47.
41. Bard, *op. cit., passim.*
42. *Ibid.,* p. 130. Also pp. 134-135.
42. Parnas, *Law and Contemporary Problems,* passim.
44. *Ibid.,* p. 551. See also Bard, *op. cit.,* p. 136: referrals by ordinary police were 95 per cent to the Family Court, by the specially trained police only 45 percent. He also says at p. 138: "The policeman in the family unit have little doubt that they are policemen — they do not regard themselves as psychologists or social workers, nor do they perform as such. They restore the peace and maintain order, but it is 'how' they do it is the measure of their success."
45. Parnas, *Law and Contemporary Problems* pp. 558-559. He also discusses diversion by prosecutors (in their discretion not to prosecute or informal hearings by prosecutors), by arbitration, and by the courts (through the peace bond, or by the New York Family Court) in the Criminal Law Bulletin.
46. Select Committee, p. vii; Parnas, *Law and Contemporary Problems,* p. 564; Parnas *Minnesota Law Review,* p. 641.
47. Parnas, *Law and Contemporary Problems,* p. 539. See also Gayford, *British Medical Journal,* p. 196; BASW Working Party, op. cit., p. 413.
48. For other objections to the Bill e.g., distinction between the duty or power of the court, inadequacy of definitions, limited scope, see second reading debate, 895 H.C. Debs. cols. 982-1010.
49. Supreme Court of Judicature (Consolidation) Act, 1925, s. 45, and R.S.C., Ord. 29, r. 1.
50. County Courts Act 1959, s. 74. In both courts proceedings are now closed, though the judge has a discretion to open them: [1974] 2 All E.R. 1119. See comment in (1974) *New Law Journal* 629 against unnecessary secrecy.
51. *Practice Direction,* [1972] 2 All E.R. 1360. It is said that a hearing can take up to 14 days, but Sir George Baker said in evidence to the Select Committee, p. 463, that these cases are given "absolute priority."
52. (1973) Legal Action Group Bulletin 230. See Select Committee, p. 76, for difficulties in getting emergency legal aid.
53. *Ibid.,* p. 277. For an account of the procedure generally see *ibid.,* pp. 175-176, and do-

it-yourself kits mentioned in note 67. But see comments of Russell, M.: "You have actually got to present [the judges] with a near corpse before they will take emergency action" (Select Committee, p. 79).

54. And see now *Ansah v. Ansah,* [1977] 2 All E.R. 638 for a decision disapproving of the granting of an *ex parte* injunction in circumstances which are not considered by the Court of Appeal to have been an emergency.

55. (1975) Legal Action Group Bulletin 200. The best organized rota is in the South-East circuit (*i.e.,* the London area), and 90 percent of all urgent applications are made there. In other areas arrangements are made to contact a judge by telephone where necessary. See Appendix 13 to Select Committee, Memo. by Lord Chancellor's Office: Procedure for dealing with urgent business in the courts.

56. Select Committee, p. 403. But the procedure can only be used by counsel or a solicitor, not the woman herself. See later for problem of finding a sympathetic solicitor.

57. (1976) Legal Action Group Bulletin 125. On the basis of these figures, it is estimated that there would be about 3,000 applications a year (ibid., p. 137).

58. Kemp, Knightly and Norton, op. cit., pp. 14-15.

59. (1973) Legal Action Group Bulletin, pp. 174, 203, 277; Gill and Coote, *op. cit.,* p. 17; Kemp, Knightly and Norton, *op. cit.,* p. 5; Raisbeck, *op. cit.,* p. 100; Jo Richardson in second reading debate on Domestic Violence and Matrimonial Proceedings Bill, 905 H.C. Debs. col. 858 (February 13, 1976).

60. *Stewart v. Stewart* [1973] 1 All E.R. 31.

61. *Ibid.*

62. *Phillips v. Phillips* [1973] 2 All E.R. 423.

63. *Tarr v. Tarr* [1973] A.C. 254.

64. Select Committee, pp. xviii-xix. See also Irvine, Select Committee, p. 65.

65. [1975] 1 All E.R. 513. The decision was supported emphatically by the Select Committee, p. xix. There is no mention in the case at at all of who owned the property, thus indicating its insignificance.

66. See generally Russell, M., and Gill, T., Select Committee, pp. 92-93; joint memo. by Home Office and Lord Chancellor's Office, Select Committee, pp. 395-398, and discussion, pp. 400-403.

67. *The Times,* October 31, 1977.

68. McGregor, D.; Blom-Cooper L.; and Gibson, C., *Separated Spouses.* London, Eng.: Duckworth, 1970.

69. *Ibid.*

70. Law Commission Published Working Paper, No. 53, Matrimonial Proceedings in Magistrates' Courts (1973), p. 46.

71. Law Commission No. 77, Report on Matrimonial Proceedings in Magistrates' Courts, October 1976, pp. 22-32, and cl. 13 of draft Bill.

72. See *infra,* on injunctions. For critical comment on the Law Commission's proposals, see this author (1977), 7 *Family Law* 50.

73. The magistrates' court order would be complementary to a county court order under the Matrimonial Homes Act 1967 (overruling *Tarr v. Tarr* [1973] A.C. 254). See evidence of Irvine, M., Barrister, Select Committee, pp. 63-65. See also Select Committee, pp. xviii-xix, xx. The Solicitor-General gave evidence against the power of magistrates to exclude the husband from the matrimonial home, and against the power of magistrates to commit for breach of the non-molestation order (Select Committee, p. 398).

74. This procedure is equally available to a married woman : Law Reform (Husband and Wife) Act 1962, whereby husband and wife can sue each other in tort.

75. Gill and Coote, *op. cit.,* pp. 9-12; Coote, A., and Gill, T., *Women's Rights: A Practical Guide.* Harmondsworth, Middlesex: Penguin, 1974, pp. 163-164.

76. It has been suggested that legal aid would not be made available to the cohabitee in these circumstances, and that effectively denies her a remedy.

77. *The Times,* March 10, 1978.

78. Select Committee, p. xx; Pizzey, *op. cit.,* p. 128: "It's a matter of enforcing the law rather than substantially changing it."
79. Steinmetz and Straus, *op. cit., passim;* Gelles, *op. cit.,* especially chaps. 6 and 7.
80. *Ibid.,* pp. 14-16 and chaps. 34 and 35.
81. *Ibid.,* p. 4, note 1. They suggest that spanking a child is legitimate but spanking a wife is illegitimate violence in contemporary society.
82. *Ibid.,* p. 4.
83. Gayford, *British Medical Journal,* p. 194. It is a more sophisticated version of the Royal College of Psychiatrists' one (Select Committee, p. vi). And see Chatterton, *op. cit.,* pp. 26-32, for a discussion of the definitions of violence.
84. This approach differs from the one currently adopted in divorce law, *i.e.,* the objective test used to prove the "ground" of "unreasonable behavior."
85. Owens, *op. cit.,* pp. 208-209; Gill and Coote, *op. cit.,* p. 1; Gregory, *op. cit.,* p. 122.
86. Gregory, *op. cit.,* p. 119; Brixton Women's Aid letter to Home Secretary, quoted in A. Coote, "Police, the Law and Battered Wives," *The Guardian,* May 23, 1974.
87. Gelles, *op. cit.,* chap. 7, talks of a social structural theory of violence; Steinmetz and Straus, *op. cit.,* pp. 9-10: violence can be used "to compensate for lack of such other resources as money, knowledge, and respect," or "as a normal response to frustration (in) familial and occupational roles." The limited aim of protection is very important: see Marsden and Owens, *op. cit.,* p. 335 "for rather than total escape, many of these wives wished only to eliminate the darker side of their Jekyll and Hyde relationships with their husbands."
88. See generally memo. from Lord Chancellor's Office, Select Committee, p. 394;
89. See *e.g.,* Select Committee, pp. xxiii (re Scotland) and 75.
90. Select Committee, p. 75. It is thought that while the violence is classless, it is the poorer who get more involved in the criminal process: Parnas, *Law and Contemporary Problems,* p. 564; Memo. of Association of Chief Police Officers, Select Committee, p. 366.
91. Cutting, *op. cit.,* p. 167.
92. Kemp, Knightly and Norton, *op. cit.,* pp. 24-26; Pizzey, *op. cit.,* p. 114.
93. Cutting, *op. cit.,* pp. 165-167 (in general context of divorce work); Pizzey, *op. cit.,* p. 112, Cook, Cp. M.J., "Battered Wives and the Law", *Law Society's Gazette,* Feb. 11, 1976.
94. Pizzey, *op. cit.,* pp. 112-113.
95. Cutting, *op. cit.,* p. 167. Similarly Gill and Coote, *op. cit.,* p. 1.
96. Pizzey, *op. cit.,* p. 114.
97. This ties up with Sir George Baker's observation of an increase in injunctions in London but not elsewhere (Select Committee, p. 462). See comments by Dunwoody, G., Select Committee, pp. 462-463.
98. Select Committee, p. 77. At the latest count there were 28 neighborhood law centers. T. Harper, *New Society,* Feb. 17, 1977.
99. Pizzey, *op. cit.,* p. 115. Similarly Coote, *op. cit.:* "The 9 existing Law Centers tend to steer clear of wife-battering cases"; Gill and Coote, *op. cit.,* pp. 17-18.
100. Coote, A., said: "The point is they are too busy. They have not the time. Some of them have to decide on specific priorities" (Select Committee, p. 97). McBain, P., said that they do do emergency matrimonial work (Select Committee, p. 97).
101. Select Committee, p.x. 3 primary roles were suggested (1) an emergency service (2) co-ordination of local arrangements (3) specialist advisory services, education and publicity programs, group support. *Cf.* Owens, *op. cit.,* p. 210 refers to a similar center for child abuse in Colorado, U.S.A. He suggests that the center could be run on the lines of the Samaritans. Marsden and Owens, *op. cit.,* p. 355 say: "There is . . . an unmet need for more accessible and effective counseling services."
102. Pizzey, *op. cit.,* p. 129.
103. Cp. A. Sachs, *Sexism and the Law.* London, Eng.: Martin Robertson, 1977; Gill and Coote, *op. cit.,* pp. 1, 17.
104. Select Committee, p. 94, quoting a judge who is supposed to have said: "If he had

been a miner I might have overlooked (the wife beating) but he was a cultured gentleman living in a respected part of the community."

105. Gelles, *op. cit.*, chap. 5.
106. Cutting, *op. cit.*, p. 166 says: "The courts themselves, as well as solicitors approached, are not always sensitive enough to the issues involved."
107. Select Committee, p. 94: apparently the Police Superintendents' Association are in favor of informal tribunals for lesser assaults (*i.e.*, domestic disputes) with magistrates as chairmen and social workers as assessors.
108. Pizzey, *op, cit.*, p. 129.
109. Parnas, *Criminal Law Bulletin*, p. 734.
110. Though it is believed that lesser injuries became greater in many cases (Parnas, *Minnesota Law Review*, p. 585). Thus in terms of prevention, all assaults should be taken seriously.
111. Subin, H., *Criminal Justice in a Metropolitan Court* (1966), pp. 56-57. And see Parnas, *Law and Contemporary Problems*, p. 542: "Absent serious threats or injury or repeated minor incidents, it is arguable that the closer the relationship, the less anti-social is the violent behaviour. . . . Thus even if the problem is regarded criminal in nature, invocation of criminal processes may damage the interdependent relationship of the offender and victim as well as cause distress for children or other family members. Physical and emotional problems may ensue not only at the time the process commences, but after it is completed."
112. Kemp, Knightly and Norton, *op. cit.*, p. 21.
113. Gill and Coote, *op. cit.*, p. 18; Kemp, Knightly and Norton, *op. cit.*, p. 31.
114. It is interesting that a comparative approach is almost entirely lacking in British writing on the subject (except for the U.S. model for Family Crisis Centres) especially in the Select Committee's report.
115. See generally Parnas, *Minnesota Law Review*.
116. *Ibid.*, pp. 602-603. He compares it to the magistrates' power to bind over not just the defendant but also or alternatively the informant.
117. *Ibid.*, pp. 621-641 for full details of the procedure. Also Parnas, *Criminal Law Bulletin*, pp. 750-753. A similar system is said to exist in Hawaii, but information has not been found.
118. This is interpreted not to include felonies because of the lack of constitutional safeguards against detention without indictment (note to s. 813, McKinney's *Consolidated Laws of New York*, Annotated. Book 29 (A)).
119. Problems arise where a member of the family is not in the same household, and vice versa. *Cf. People v. Allen* (1970), 313 N.Y. S. 2d 719 held that even though living in the same household a couple not amounting to a common law marriage could not invoke the jurisdiction, *i.e.*, the two conditions must both be satisfied. See criticism by Parnas, *Criminal Law Bulletin*, note 34.
120. The court may at the party's request make use of conciliation procedure provided by the court conciliation service (Family Court Act, 1962, Art. 9).
121. Parnas, *Minnesota Law Review*, p. 636, says that while this depends on the judge, a very small percentage get transferred from the Family Court. In fiscal year 1966-1967 it was 2 percent. Once the civil protection order is made, no criminal proceedings are possible (s. 845).
122. *Ibid.*, p. 637. In fiscal year 1966-1967, 28 percent were withdrawn or dismissed, 2 per cent put on probation, and the vast majority were granted C.P.O.s.
123. This is said to give the police the protection they like. They are reluctant otherwise to arrest unless there is clear evidence of wrong. See *supra* for power in this country to back the injunction with police power of arrest.
124. The information here is based mainly on personal observation of the system Figures were given by the Corporation Counsel. The procedure was intended to provide "an informal and civil proceeding for dealing with criminal offences committed between members of a family unit which at present are often left unresolved or otherwise fall within the jurisdiction of the criminal court, both being unsatisfactory solutions."

(D.C. Code Encyclopedia. Legislative and Administrative Service, 1970. Court Reform Act 1970, p. 456).

125. The requirement of a mutual residence makes it clearer than the New York law. Thus it has been held that the law does not apply to an aunt and niece who do not share a mutual residence: *U.S. v. Harrison,* 149 U.S. App.D.C. 123 (1972). But equally there must be a close relationship, thus it would not cover room-mates, but it is thought that homosexual partners could come under the provisions. It has been defined unofficially as a "family-like relationship." Quaere: does it cover a common-law marriage, a boy-friend/girl-friend relationship, or either of these where the parties have now separated?

126. The statute provides for other persons or agencies to apply to the Corporation Counsel to file a petition for a C.P.O., but in practice this does not seem to happen.

127. Others will take felonies, depending on the appropriateness of the remedy. The Corporation Counsel can refer the case back to the U.S. Attorney in which case they can get into a running battle. The U.S. Attorney tends not to like these cases (for the same reasons as the police) partly in order to keep down the crime statistics, partly because they see family problems as not really serious.

128. Emergency provisions in New York are not known, except the bench warrant issued by the family court judge.

129. It is thought that more complaints and respondents would turn up for the hearing if it was quicker.

130. *Cf.* Select Committee, p. 432: 90 percent of husbands in this country admit to assaulting their wives. The same point was observed by Parnas, *Minnesota Law Review,* p. 642, that the facts are not seriously disputed.

131. This is not the same as an injunction to vacate: Corporation Counsel made a strong point that under U.S. law an injunction ordering a husband out of his own property is unconstitutional because of the lack of due process. Nevertheless it was thought that some judges do so order, but that the point would fail on appeal — though appeals never occur (and are not apparently provided for in the statute). The court can order a husband out under the contempt power *e.g.,* by attaching a condition to that effect to a suspended sentence.

132. Parnas, *Law and Contemporary Problems,* p. 562.

133. Quoted in *U.S. v. Harrison* (note 125).

134. *Ibid.*

135. Paper given to American Bar Association, Annual Meeting, 1972, Family Law Section, by Samuel Green, Attorney, p. 9.

136. Raisbeck, *op. cit.,* p. 105, makes the good point that the woman needs protection in her situation which requires that action can be taken on her behalf, rather than by her through a representative.

137. Parnas, *Minnesota Law Review,* pp. 643-644. Under the new Family Law Act 1975 in Australia, s. 14(4), the court has power to direct or advise either or both parties to a marriage counselor.

138. *N.B.* Use of conciliation procedures, as in New York. *Cf.* Parnas, *Criminal Law Bulletin,* p. 757.

139. Gill and Coote, *op. cit.,* p. 19.

140. Pizzey, *op. cit.,* p. 129.

Chapter 7

La violence au sein du couple: ébauches de réponses juridiques en droit continental*

M.T. Meulders†

1. Introduction

(a) Ignorance du problème

Si le problème des enfants maltraités commence à être mieux connu, sans être pour autant résolu, celui des violences entre époux apparaît au départ si ignoré, si complexe et si fondamental qu'il semble tout à la fois désespérant et urgent de s'y attaquer.

Peu de pays jusqu'à ce jour ont pris conscience de l'existence de ce phénomène et le considèrent comme un réel problème. Certes de nombreuses personnes (médecins, avocats, magistrats, travailleurs sociaux) et services privés ou publics (hôpitaux, homes, services sociaux), confrontés quotidiennement avec ces situations conflictuelles, en ont connaissance. Mais, outre le fait que beaucoup de ces situations ne sont jamais révélées par honte, par crainte ou par ignorance, les données qui pourraient être disponibles restent éparses et ne sont pas parvenues jusqu'ici au niveau d'une coordination objective et scientifique susceptible de déboucher sur une action de type législatif ou social.

* Nous tenons à exprimer ici notre reconnaissance à M. H. Vanderpoorten, ancien Ministre de la Justice et à Madame S. Ochinsky, Directeur de l'Office national de Protection de la Jeunesse qui nous ont aidé à obtenir des renseignements de la part des différents Départements de la Justice des pays d'Europe occidentale; Monsieur V. Van Honste, Procureur général près la Cour d'appel de Bruxelles; M. J.M. Piret, Procureur du Roi et M. Van de Walle, 1er Substitut au Parquet de Bruxelles qui ont grandement facilité nos recherches, ainsi qu'à MM. et Melles M. Straetmans Ph. Richir, M. Collard, A. Declerc, M.C. Minguet, N. de Vroede et Ch. Van Audenarde, sans la contribution active desquels cette recherche n'aurait pu s'appuyer sur une étude concrète du problème des violences entre époux en Belgique. Nos remerciements vont également à l'Association belge des Femmes juristes qui nous a aidé à entamer une enquête sur ce sujet auprès des avocats, à M. Jacques Verhaegen, Professeur de Droit pénal à l'Université catholique de Louvain et M. Guy Laffineur, Chercheur au F.N.F.C. et auteur d'une monographie relative aux statuts et missions des différentes polices en Belgique.
† Centre de Droit de la Famille, Université Catholique de Louvain, Belgium.

Cette attitude générale d'ignorance, que nous avons nous-même rencontrée en Belgique en abordant le thème de ce rapport, ressort clairement des réponses remarquablement concordantes qui nous ont été fournies par les différents Départements de la Justice des pays d'Europe que nous avons consultés: la France, la Grande-Bretagne, les Pays-Bas, l'Allemagne fédérale, la Suisse et l'Italie. Il n'existe nulle part de statistiques criminelles susceptibles d'apporter une vision quantitative ou qualitative du problème de la violence conjugale, pas même en Grande-Bretagne [1] qui, la première en Europe a pris conscience du problème et y fait actuellement figure de pionnier avec le Domestic Violence and Matrimonial Proceedings Act 1976[2]. Quant à la Belgique, les seules données statistiques dont nous disposons sont le fruit d'une enquête limitée au ressort du tribunal de première instance de Bruxelles que nous avons nous-même menée avec un groupe d'étudiants de la Faculté de Droit de Louvain et la collaboration des membres du Parquet[3].

La cause invoquée pour justifier cette ignorance est, dans tous les pays indiqués l'absence d'incrimination spéciale pour les délits et les crimes commis entre époux, à l'exception de l'Autriche[4]. Mais la raison véritable semble plus profonde, car il serait relativement aisé d'établir des statistiques sélectives, malgré l'absence d'incrimination spéciale[5]. Elle réside dans une attitude culturelle inconsciemment enracinée dans les mentalités: bien qu'il n'existe plus dans nos systèmes juridiques de "droit de châtiment" du mari sur sa femme comme dans nos anciens droits coutumiers[6] ou en Common Law[7] ni même de puissance maritale[8], il semble implicitement admis que l'homme exerce son autorité et affirme sa virilité au besoin par la force, que ce qui se passe au foyer mérite un autre traitement que ce qui se passe dans la rue, que la part des torts respectifs et la preuve des infractions conjugales soit si difficile à faire qu'elle permette de jeter un voile pudique sur elles, et que ce voile soit même considéré comme bénéfique pour la sauvegard de la "paix des familles" et la stabilité du mariage.

Culturellement donc, le phénomène de la violence au sein du couple, sa fréquence dans toutes les couches de la société[9] et son caractère déviant ne semblent pas avoir accédé au niveau de la prise de conscience collective dans les pays continentaux, en sorte que l'un des facteurs même de cette violence pourrait bien être la tolérance tacite dont elle jouit. Le premier remède à suggérer serait donc sans doute qu'un effort concerté de dépistage et d'analyse statistique et scientifique soit entrepris au plus tôt par tous les services et organismes privés et publics concernés pour mieux cerner le problème afin d'y rechercher les réponses appropriées.

(b) Importance du problème

Le problème en effet paraît fondamental, tant pour la protection des personnes que des institutions familiales ou sociales.

Il est étrange, à ce propos, de constater que la plupart des législations se soucient de la protection de la famille en tant que cellule sociale de base, du mariage en tant qu'institution d'ordre public, de la moralité et des bonnes moeurs, en incriminant certains actes tels que la bigamie, l'adultère, les délits sexuels ou les outrages aux moeurs; qu'elles se penchent, depuis une époque relativement récente, avec une sollicitude croissante sur la protection des enfants et des adolescents, soit par souci effectif de leur vulnérabilité plus grande, soit parce qu'ils sont porteurs de l'avenir d'une nation; et que l'on oublie dans le même temps de protéger les membres de la famille les plus proches: les époux, et en particulier la femme qui, par la force des choses, se trouve dans une situation d'inégalité sur le plan de la force physique et trop souvent encore de dépendance économique, alors que les violences sont destructrices du foyer et susceptibles de perturber gravement l'équilibre physique et mental des enfants qui en sont témoins, même lorsqu'ils n'en sont pas les victimes directes. Comment dès lors ignorer ce problème? Et quels remèdes y apporter?

(c) Remarques liminaires

Avant d'essayer de répondre à cette question, plusieurs remarques doivent être faites.

(1) Le problème ne peut être abordé que sur un pied de stricte égalité entre l'homme et la femme. La violence pouvant provenir de l'un ou de l'autre[10], il ne saurait être question de surprotéger la femme par des dispositions particulières, et les remèdes à envisager sont "sexuellement neutres". Aucune violence, quelle qu'en soit la victime, ne devrait être tolérée.

Statistiquement cependant, les violences entre époux semblent bien être le plus souvent exercées sur la femme, du moins en ce qui concerne les violences physiques ou sexuelles[11].

La situation présente en outre ceci de particulier que la victime a légalement le devoir de cohabiter avec son agresseur dans un domicile réputé sanctuaire inviolable de la vie privée, et que, nonobstant des lois de plus en plus libérales en matière de divorce, la dépendance ou l'infériorité économique de la femme, son absence de refuge où trouver abri avec ses enfants et son souci de conserver un foyer à ceux-ci l'empêchent, bien plus que les obstacles légaux, d'échapper à des sévices parfois extrêmement graves et souvent répétés[12]. On ne s'étonnera donc pas que les remèdes envisagés soient souvent dictés par cette donnée de fait qui vaut également, bien que dans des termes juridiques différents, pour la concubine: comment protéger la femme et les enfants?

(2) Quant aux violences elles-mêmes? Il est bien clair qu'il en est de différente nature, physiques ou mentales, sur la typologie desquelles il appartient aux spécialistes de s'attarder davantage[13]. Précisons simplement que des remèdes doivent être recherchés à toute forme de violence et que bien souvent sans doute la cruauté mentale précède et *provoque* la violence physique ou l'accompagne[14]. Mais la subtilité et la difficulté de preuve en sont telles que, dans la plupart des cas, force est de se limiter à la partie visible de l'iceberg: les violences d'ordre physique ou sexuel caractérisées par *l'usage volontaire et malveillant de la force brutale sur la personne du partenaire.*

Parmi ces violences physiques, il faut en outre souligner, et cela nous paraît important à propos des solutions à rechercher, qu'il y a une *gradation* dans l'importance des mauvais traitements et sévices, qui s'étalent de la gifle accidentelle aux blessures graves et à l'homicide[15]. Nous ne pensons pas qu'il faille sous-estimer l'importance psychologique de voies de fait mineures, car elles révèlent une faille sous-jacente et probablement une crise latente, mais il est évident que leur traitement doit être différent de celui des violences qui mettent en danger la vie et la santé physique ou mentale de l'un des conjoints—et éventuellement celle des enfants—dont le nombre, mal connu, est certainement plus élevé qu'on ne le soupçonne généralement. Dans l'enquête que nous avons nous-mêmes menée à Bruxelles, 20% des dossiers (soit par extrapolation près de 350 cas pour l'année 1975) concernaient des brutalités et sévices graves ou répétés), et le "chiffre noir" est certainement beaucoup plus élevé.

Il faut donc pouvoir disposer, comme le soulignent certains experts consultés par le Select Committee on Violence in Marriage anglais, d'une gamme de solutions permettant de trouver des mesures adaptées ("tailored") à chaque cas[16]. Encore faut-il pour cela *attacher une importance réelle à chaque cas signalé.* C'est là une seconde ligne de réforme à mettre en relief dès le départ.

(3) En ce qui concerne la gamme des *remèdes* enfin, plusieurs observations de base doivent encore être formulées. Il convient par exemple de distinguer clairement les *moyens de protection à court ou moyen terme,* qui consistent à combattre les *symptômes* de la maladie, des remèdes proprement dits, qui s'attaquent aux *causes* même de celle-ci. Combattre la fièvre n'est pas nécessairement guérir le malade. A ce titre, l'emprisonnement du mari ou le divorce ne sont pas des remèdes, mais tout au plus des solutions. La loi elle-même ne saurait apporter à elle seule le véritable remède, qui se trouve essentiellement au niveau du changement des mentalités et des moeurs, du moins lorsqu'il ne s'agit pas de cas pathologiques.
Pourtant il serait faux de prétendre que la loi est totalement impuissante en ce domaine. Elle est au contraire indispensable pour organiser un réseau suffisamment dense de moyens de protection et de prévention, dans une approche compréhensive et globale du problème, et même pour "changer les mentalités".

Nous essaierons donc d'envisager les différentes mesures et solutions légales que l'on peut songer à mettre en oeuvre en les abordant sucessivement sous l'angle *pénal, civil* et *social.* Beaucoup d'entre elles existent déjà, mais sont mal ou trop peu exploitées. D'autres sont à créer ou à renforcer.

Il va de soi que nous n'avons pu établir pour cela un inventaire exhaustif des différents moyens juridiques disponibles ou susceptibles de l'être dans le droit des pays continentaux, les dispositions nationales étant trop particulières, par exemple en ce qui concerne l'organisation des polices ou des juridictions, les règles de compétence ou de procédure pénale et civile, ou encore les régimes de sécurité sociale. Nous nous contenterons donc de baliser les grandes artères, et de nous référer pour les exemples principalement à la législation belge ou française, en les comparant, le cas échéant, au droit anglais tel qu'il vient d'être modifié par le Domestic Violence and Matrimonial Proceedings Act 1976.

Ce faisant, l'accent nous paraît devoir être porté sur quatre points fondamentaux:

— la *nécessité d'agir* d'abord, donc de sortir de la passivité;
— la *coordination maximale* de l'information et des moyens d'action des différents services publics et privés concernés, ensuite;
— la *rapidité* de l'intervention:
— et enfin la *souplesse* et la *diversité* des modes de protection et de prévention.

2. Les mesures de protection pénales

Les mesures de protection pénales, auxquelles on songe en premier lieu, sont-elles pertinentes en matière de violence intra-familiale, et si oui, comment les employer le plus judicieusement?

Par définition, les mesures répressives constituent une arme à laquelle il n'est souhaitable de recourir que dans les cas extrêmes contre les atteintes les plus graves à l'ordre social ou à la sécurité des personnes. L'opportunité et l'efficacité elle-même du droit pénal en matière de prévention, sanction et amendement est aujourd'hui amplement controversée. A fortiori son immixtion dans la vie familiale fait-elle l'objet de nombreuses réticences au niveau de la politique criminelle, que ce soit dans les pays continentaux ou anglo-américains. Outre le *respect de la vie privée,* différents arguments militent en ce sens, parmi lesquels:

— la *difficulté de la preuve;*
— l'*inopportunité d'investigations et de sanctions* susceptibles de compromettre définitivement l'équilibre familial plus que de le rétablir
— les *réticences* de la victime elle-même.

Tels sont en règle générale les motifs indiqués pour justifier les hésitations de la police et des autorités judiciaires à intervenir dans le domaine des violences entre époux[17].

Dans la mesure cependant où ces actes de violence sont constitués d'atteintes à l'intégrité physique rentrant dans la catégorie de délits et de crimes qui, pratiqués sur des tiers, seraient certainement poursuivis et sanctionnés, et dans la mesure aussi où ces actes mettent parfois directement la vie ou la santé de l'un des conjoints en danger et risquent de compromettre gravement l'équilibre des enfants et de la famille, il convient cependant d'examiner plus attentivement la question.

(a) Faut'il envisager une incrimination spéciale pour les sévices entre époux ou renforcer les sanctions?

La plupart des pays occidentaux ne prévoient aucune incrimination spéciale pour les mauvais traitements et sévices entre époux et n'envisagent pas de le faire[18]. A part les articles 413 et 419 du Code pénal autrichien, qui cesseront du reste d'être en vigueur le 31 décembre 1977, nous n'avons pas trouvé, dans les codes pénaux européens, de disposition réprimant spécialement les atteintes à la vie ou à l'intégrité physique *entre époux*[19]. Ce type de comportement rentre dans le *droit commun* des infractions contre les personnes — lésions corporelles, coups et blessures volontaires — assorties de différentes gradations dans l'échelle des peines délictuelles ou criminelles suivant:

— la gravité des faits (emploi d'une arme ou non);
— l'importance du dommage occasionné (coups et blessures simples, coups et blessures avec incapacité de travail temporaire ou permanente, perte d'un organe ou décès;
— ou encore l'absence ou la présence de préméditation.

La plupart du temps les *menaces verbales* ne constituent *pas un délit.* Tel est le cas notamment en droit belge (art. 398 à 415 C. pén.)[20] et en droit français (art. 309 à 312 C. pén. fr.)[21] En *Belgique,* seul le fait que les coups et blessures[22] ont été infligés par un descendant à ses père ou mère légitime, naturel ou adoptif ou à un ascendant légitime, ou encore par les père ou mère légitimes, naturels ou adoptifs[23] à un enfant de moins de 16 ans[24] constitue une circonstance aggravante attachée au lien de parenté unissant l'auteur et la victime (art. 410 C. pén.)[25].

Y subsiste au contraire une cause *d'excuse* archaïque pour l'homicide et les coups et blessures volontaires perpétrés par l'un des époux sur l'autre en cas de *flagrant délit d'adultère* (art. 413 C. pén.)[26]. D'autre part, la *provocation* par "violences graves" (physiques ou morales) constitue une *cause générale d'excuse* — différente des circonstances atténuantes — applicable à l'homicide et aux coups et blessures en général (art. 411 C. pén.) et entraînant une réduction de la peine (art. 414 C. pén.)[27]. Elle ne s'applique pas si le coupable a commis le crime ou le délit envers ses père, mère ou autres ascendants légitimes, ou envers ses père et mère naturels (art. 415 C. pén.) mais elle *joue entre époux*[28].

En matière sexuelle, la doctrine et la jurisprudence belge et française considèrent par ailleurs qu'à défaut de disposition expresse, il ne saurait y avoir de *viol* entre époux, le devoir conjugal, exercé par la force et la contrainte, ne pouvant constituer un acte illicite[29], mais éventuellement un acte de violence s'il est accompagné de coups et blessures volontaires[30]. Il est surprenant de constater à ce propos que les législations américaines relatives aux délits sexuels, bien que massivement réformées depuis 1974-1975, conservent la plupart une "exception conjugale" en ce qui concerne le viol[31]. En revanche, les *attentats à la pudeur* avec violence ou menaces entre époux sont sanctionnés, dans la mesure où il ne s'agit pas d'actes "conformes aux fins légitimes du mariage"[32].

Enfin, il faut souligner qu'en droit français comme en droit belge, les *menaces verbales* ne constituent pas un délit lorsqu'elles ne sont pas assorties *d'ordre ou de condition*[33]. La plupart du temps les plaintes de femmes menacées ne sont pas prises au sérieux et il arrive que l'on constate, trop tard, que ces menaces, mises à exécution, ont abouti au décès de la victime ou à des blessures graves[34].

Convient-il alors de revoir nos législations et d'y inclure une incrimination spéciale pour les atteinte à la vie ou à l'intégrité physique entre conjoints ou de faire de cette qualité une circonstance aggravante? On pourrait à ce propos se demander pourquoi la qualité d'ascendant ou de descendant peut constituer une circonstance aggravante et non la qualité d'époux. Dans un cas comme dans l'autre le lien de parenté ou d'affection et les devoirs réciproques qui en découlent confèrent une qualité particulière à la victime et à l'auteur, et le fait de devoir vivre sous le même toit rend en outre la situation des époux particulièrement dangereuse en cas de conflit. Supprimant toute distinction, le *Code pénal polonais* (art. 184) prévoit ainsi dans une disposition unique l'infraction commise par celui qui "maltraite physiquement ou moralement un membre de sa famille", et la frappe d'une peine de 6 mois à 5 ans de prison. La disposition est intéressante dans la mesure où elle englobe *tous* les membres de la famille et attire l'attention sur le fait qu'ils méritent une protection particulière. A ce titre, sa valeur est essentiellement de nature *exhortative*, mais son intérêt dépend, en fin de compte, de la question plus fondamentale de l'efficacité des mesures pénales dans les matières familiales.

Avec ou sans incrimination spéciale, on doit donc se demander si une application plus attentive, ou éventuellement rénovée, par la police et les autorités judiciaires, des mesures disponibles sur le plan pénal serait susceptible de remédier au moins en partie aux dangers dénoncés. Il faut à ce propos distinguer les mesures de protection immédiate des mesures de sanction, de traitement et de prévention.

(b) Le rôle de la police et les mesures de protection immédiate

Les études effectuées récemment aux Etats-Unis[35] et les témoignages d'experts recueillis par le Select Committee on Violence in Marriage[36] soulignent très clairement à quel point la police est le premier service public confronté avec le problème des violences intra-familiales et l'importance du nombre d'appels et de plaintes, parfois extrêmement graves, qu'elle reçoit couramment. D'après l'enquête que nous avons nous-même effectuée, 85% des cas de coups et blessures entre époux qui ont donné lieu à l'ouverture d'un dossier au Parquet de Bruxelles en 1975 avaient été dénoncés par une plainte au bureau de police ou de gendarmerie, et 15% environ avaient donné lieu à un appel suivi d'une plainte[37]. Très peu avaient fait l'objet d'une plainte adressée directement au Parquet[38]. Comme la police est aussi le seul service à pouvoir utiliser la force et la contrainte pour intervenir, et qu'elle seule est disponible de jour et de nuit, son rôle paraît prépondérant en la matière.

Il est évidemment impossible de rentrer ici dans le détail de l'organisation et des compétences des polices dans les différents pays continentaux, car celle-ci est infiniment trop complexe. En Belgique par exemple, trois corps de police, la police communale[39], la police judiciaire[40] et la gendarmerie, corps militaire institué pour assurer la police du territoire[41] collaborent étroitement et de manière extrêmement complexe à la protection de l'ordre et des citoyens, et aux actes de police judiciaire[42]. La question est de savoir si les pouvoirs dont ces polices disposent sont suffisants ou non pour intervenir efficacement dans les problèmes de violences familiales et quel rôle de protection et de prévention elles peuvent ou pourraient jouer. Nous partirons de l'exemple belge pour fournir les principaux éléments de réponse.

(i) Visites domiciliaires[43]

En cas d'appel émanant de la victime ou d'un tiers (enfant, ami ou parent, voisin), la police *doit-elle intervenir* et *peut-elle pénétrer dans une habitation privée* sans commettre de violation de domicile prohibée par l'art. 10 de la Constitution belge[44] et sanctionnée par l'art. 148 C. pénal?[45] *La réponse est formellement affirmative.* D'une manière générale, les officiers de police judiciaire, éventuellement accompagnés d'agents de police judiciaire[46], peuvent effectuer des visites domiciliaires dans une habitation privée dans les cas suivants:

— *de jour ou de nuit,* pour *constater un crime ou un délit flagrant* (art. 32 et 49 Code d'Instruction criminelle; art. 1, 2° de la loi du 7 juin 1969 sur les perquisitions nocturnes), sur *appel de n'importe quel particulier*[47].
— *de jour ou de nuit,* sur réquisition du *"chef de la maison",* pour constater un crime ou un délit *même non flagrant* commis dans cette maison (art. 46 et 49 C. d'instr. criminelle), ou avec le consentement de la personne qui a la jouissance effective du lieu (art. 1, 3° de la loi du 7 juin 1969)[48].
— *de jour ou de nuit,* sur *appel au secours venant de l'intérieur* (art. 1, 4° de la loi du 7 juin 1969)[49].
— *après 5 heures du matin et avant 9 heures du soir* seulement, en cas de mandat de perquisition domiciliaire (art. 1 de la loi du 7 juin 1969)[50].

Les officiers et agents de police ou de gendarmerie ont en outre *l'obligation de porter assistance à toute personne en danger* (voy. notamment l'art. 17 de la loi sur la gendarmerie du 2 décembre 1957) et cette obligation est telle qu'elle pourrait être sanctionnée pour *omission de porter secours* au cas où la personne en danger subirait un dommage grave par suite de non-assistance injustifiée (art. 422 bis C. pénal)[51].

La police a donc le pouvoir et le devoir de pénétrer dans un domicile privé dès l'instant où il y a appel au secours de l'intérieur, ou même appel ou dénonciation venant de l'extérieur, lorsqu'un crime ou un délit est en train ou vient de se commettre. Elle peut le faire aussi, même lorsqu'il n'y a plus flagrant délit, pour constater l'infraction, sur demande du chef de maison ou de l'habitant. Ce sont là des points essentiels.

En règle générale, il semble qu'en Belgique la police réponde assez promptement aux appels pour lesquels elle dispose de numéros téléphoniques spéciaux (901 et 906) quel que soit ensuite son mode d'intervention[52].

(ii) Arrestations

La question de savoir si la police peut procéder à une *arrestation sans mandat* est plus délicate. Hors le cas de flagrant délit, une telle arrestation constitue en effet une atteinte, pénalement sanctionnée, à la liberté individuelle garantie par l'art. 7 de la Constitution belge[53]. En Belgique, l'art. 106 du Code d'Instruction criminelle énonce que tout dépositaire de la force publique — et même tout particulier — est tenu de saisir une personne surprise en état de *"flagrant délit"* et de la conduire devant le Procureur du Roi, sans mandat d'amener, si l'infraction est punissable d'une *peine criminelle.*

Les art. 40, 49 et 50 du Code d'Instruction criminelle donnent le même pouvoir au

Procureur du Roi et à ses auxiliaires officiers de police judiciaire en cas de *flagrant crime*[52]. Mais la jurisprudence de la Cour de cassation a élargi la notion de flagrant délit et admis que les officiers et agents, agissant dans le cadre de leur mission de police judiciaire, peuvent arrêter provisoirement toute personne fortement soupçonnée d'avoir commis un *crime ou un délit,* et cela même hors du *flagrant délit, lorsqu'il existe des indices* sérieux de culpabilité à sa charge[55]. Il faut cependant souligner qu'une telle arrestation n'a pas pour but de mettre l'individu en état de détention pour l'empêcher de nuire, mais seulement de le conduire devant le magistrat compétent pour l'interroger et décerner éventuellement contre lui un mandat d'arrêt dans le cadre de la loi sur la détention préventive[56]. Cet interrogatoire doit avoir lieu dans les 24 heures de l'arrestation, au terme desquelles la personne arrêtée doit être libérée si aucun mandat d'arrêt n'a été décerné contre elle. Quant à la détention préventive elle-même, elle n'est qu'une mesure de garde exceptionnelle justifiée par l'intérêt de la sécurité publique dans des circonstances particulièrement graves[57].

Il est donc certain que ni l'arrestation provisoire de 24 heures maximum, ni la détention préventive, n'ont pour but d'assurer la sécurité de la femme ou des enfants battus. Pareilles arrestations sont du reste inexistantes en cette matière, en dehors des cas d'homicide. Et s'il arrive que la police locale, dans le cadre de mesures de *police administrative* (maintien de l'ordre) et non judiciaire[58] garde pendant quelques heures au dépôt un mari pris de boisson en attendant qu'il se calme[59] pareille mesure ne permet pas non plus de protéger sa famille de manière prolongée.

Comme en outre la violation des mesures de protection civile (v. infra) ne constitue pas, comme en droit anglo-américain, un délit de "contempt of court" susceptible de donner lieu à une incarcération[60] et que les *avertissements* donnés par le Ministère public (v. infra) ne constituent qu'une menace de poursuites pour une infraction déjà commise, en cas de récidive[61], sans comporter de pouvoir d'arrestation immédiat, il faut bien avouer que la police et les autorités judiciaires elles-mêmes se trouvent relativement démunies sur ce point. Seule une réforme législative pourrait, semble-t-il, combler cette lacune, en instaurant un système de protection spécial pour les cas de violences familiales.

En l'absence d'un tel système, il est clair que le salut immédiat se trouve le plus souvent dans sa fuite. D'où la nécessité de créer des maisons d'accueil permettant de mettre la femme et les enfants en sécurité en attendant de trouver une solution plus adéquate.

(iii) Enregistrement et transmission des plaintes et dénonciations

D'une manière générale, la police a, dans le cadre de ses attributions de police judiciaire, le devoir de rechercher et de constater les infractions, de recevoir les plaintes et les dénonciations[62]. Il lui incombe ensuite de transmettre les procès-verbaux aux Ministère public (droit continental) ou de poursuivre elle-même (droit anglo-américain)[63]. Elle collabore par ailleurs à tous les actes d'information nécessaires, sur réquisition du Ministère public ou du juge d'instruction[64], ou plus simplement dans le cadre du droit général d'information administrative que la jurisprudence lui a reconnu indépendamment même de l'action publique[65].

Il est malaisé de savoir si, dans la pratique, toutes les plaintes sont enregistrées ou si les polices locales se contentent d'acter celles qu'elles considèrent comme "sérieuses". Dans ce cas il sera difficile à la victime de violences conjugales de prouver ultérieurement qu'elle s'était déjà plainte une ou plusieurs fois auparavant. Mais il arrive aussi fréquemment que la femme viennent retirer elle-même sa déposition et demander qu'aucune poursuite ne soit introduite contre son mari, une fois la tempête passée[66]. La police, en principe, n'a pas à tenir compte de ce revirement et *doit* transmettre la plainte au Procureur (art. 29 du C. d'instr. criminelle). Mais en pratique, il se peut qu'elle omette de le faire, ou, si elle transmet, c'est en actant la volonté de la femme dont le Procureur tiendra le plus généralement compte pour classer le dossier sans suite.

Quoiqu'il en soit, c'est à l'occasion de l'enregistrement des appels et des plaintes que la police pourrait et devrait jouer, outre sa mission de protection, son rôle le plus important, car c'est à ce moment qu'elle peut:

— dépister les cas dangereux;
— centraliser les informations;
— informer la victime des possibilités de secours ou de recours dont elle dispose;
— faire comprendre à l'agresseur le caractère inadmissible de son comportement;
— tenter une médiation entre les époux;
— les orienter vers les services médicaux et sociaux susceptibles de les aider;
— attirer l'attention du Parquet (correctionnel ou de la jeunesse) sur la gravité du cas.

Si toutes ces tâches étaient remplies avec la conscience aiguë que les violences entre époux constituent un délit *aussi grave, sinon plus,* que les autres, les services de police pourraient devenir la première plaque tournante d'un réseau de dépistage, de coordination et d'aide sociale qui constituerait un progrès important, et les améliorations que l'on peut suggérer en ce sens seraient les suivantes:

— une meilleure *formation des policiers en matière sociale et familiale* et l'élaboration de directives précises d'intervention et d'action (médiation entre les époux, protection, accompagnement, information des victimes) en cas de conflits[67];
— la *création de brigades spécialisées "famille-jeunesse"* dans toutes les agglomérations[68] et de postes d'*agent de quartier,* plus proches de la population;
— l'*enrôlement d'agents féminins,* plus accessibles aux aspects psychologiques et humains des conflits familiaux[69];
— l'amélioration du système local d'*enregistrement* des appels et des plaintes pour violences conjugales ou familiales et la *centralisation* de ces données au niveau local, régional ou national, aux fins d'analyse statistique[70]. Les *statistiques judiciaires* elles-mêmes devraient clairement distinguer les affaires de coups et blessures courantes des affaires spécifiquement familiales. Il y a sur ce point une *lacune majeure;*
— la *coordination entre la police,* premier service social local, *et les autres services médicaux, sociaux, administratifs et judiciaires.* La police jouerait ainsi le rôle de première "plaque tournante" (v. infra).

Telles sont aussi, dans leurs grandes lignes, les recommandations du Select Committee on Violence in Marriage.

(c) L'application de la loi

(i) Les poursuites

L'enregistrement d'une plainte constitue la première démarche. Le déclenchement des poursuites est normalement la seconde. En réalité, si le nombre des plaintes pour violences entre époux est relativement élevé, le nombre des poursuites est anormalement bas: 7 dossiers sur 155, dans notre enquête, furent l'objet soit d'une citation directe, soit d'une mise à l'instruction. 148, soit 95,5% furent "classés sans suite". Le même phénomène se produit, semble-t-il, dans tous les pays et les raisons en sont sensiblement les mêmes.

(a) Lorsque l'initiative des poursuites appartient à la *police,* celle-ci se trouve doublement freinée par deux sortes de considérations: son attitude générale de non-intervention et de temporisation en matière domestique; et surtout la difficulté de rapporter la preuve, lorsque la femme, après s'être plainte pour obtenir une protection plutôt que des poursuites, se refuse à témoigner contre son mari, soit parce qu'elle s'est réconciliée avec lui, soit qu'elle craigne des représailles plus grandes encore, soit qu'elle ne veuille pas ruiner définitivement son ménage et se retrouver, ainsi que ses enfants, privée de toit et de ressources. C'est là un des arguments majeurs invoqués par les experts policiers anglais consultés par le Select Committee, et il paraît difficilement surmontable[71]. Par ailleurs, lorsque la police ne veut ou ne peut poursuivre, mais conseille à la femme d'agir elle-même, celle-ci a si peu de chances de voir aboutir son action à une condamnation qu'elle y renonce généralement.

Bien que différente en droit continental, et notamment en droit belge, où l'initiative des poursuites revient principalement au Ministère public[72] auquel il appartient d'effectuer d'abord une information préalable pour vérifier s'il y a lieu de poursuivre, la situation n'est pas sans analogie. Cette première information en effet peut se clôturer de deux manières: soit par la mise en mouvement de l'action publique, soit au contraire par un classement sans suite dont les motifs sont éventuellement la simple "inopportunité des poursuites", même si les charges sont suffisantes[73]. Ce droit d'apprécier l'opportunité des poursuites, qui ne repose sur aucun texte légal[74], mais sur la considération qu'une poursuite pénale pourrait causer un dommage plus grand que celui de l'infraction elle-même, confère au Ministère public un rôle de "filtre" que corrige partiellement seulement le droit de la partie lésée de se constituer partie civile devant le juge d'instruction, ou de procéder par voie de citation directe devant le tribunal répressif (art. 145 et 182 du Code d'instr. criminelle). Le Ministère public use fréquemment de ce droit, ainsi qu'en témoignent les chiffres.

Ainsi, en 1971, le Parquet de Bruxelles a traité 127.092 affaires, dont 83.849 furent classées sans suite, soit 66%, parmi lesquelles: 19.543 pour infraction non établie, 28.544 pour auteur inconnu, 27.648 pour absence d'infraction, 26.239 pour *inopportunité des poursuites,* 1.695 parce que l'auteur était en fuite et 195 pour d'autres motifs[75].

Il semble donc qu'en matière de coups et blessures entre époux, le classement sans suite soit la règle, et l'inopportunité des poursuites l'argument le plus fréquemment invoqué.

(b) Le second argument avancé pour justifier la rareté des poursuites est la *difficulté de la preuve:* outre le fait déjà signalé que, bien souvent, la femme elle-même ne veut plus de poursuites et refuse alors sa collaboration, le défendeur lui-même nie, dans la majorité des cas (66% dans notre enquête) les faits, en tout (34%) ou en partie (30%), ou invoque la provocation. L'absence de témoins rend la preuve difficile, et la preuve par témoignages est elle-même incertaine. Quant aux certificats médicaux, produits dans 47% des cas dans notre enquête, ils ne peuvent attester que des traces, mais non de l'origine des coups[76].

(c) Entre en jeu également la *surcharge du Parquet* (en 1975, 139.831 affaires ont été traitées au Parquet de Bruxelles par 60 magistrats), et sans doute aussi, bien que plus ou moins inconsciente, une attitude culturelle latente tendant à considérer les coups entre époux comme faisant partie du tout-venant matrimonial. Signalons qu'en revanche un nombre impressionnant de condamnation pour adultère — plus de 5.000 en 1975 — sont prononcées chaque année en vue de servir de base et de preuve dans une action en divorce[77]. Une dépénalisation de l'adultère permettrait de désencombrer utilement les tribunaux correctionnels et d'éviter ce détournement de la justice à des fins radicalement opposées au but de l'incrimination[78]. Plus d'attention pourrait alors être accordée aux violences. A l'heure actuelle, on ne poursuit donc à Bruxelles, pour coups et blessures entre époux, que lorsqu'il y a attaque avec une arme dangereuse, incapacité de travail d'au moins 10 jours (cas rares) ou récidives nombreuses.

Il serait injuste cependant d'en conclure que le Ministère public demeure totalement passif ou indifférent. Il lui arrive assez souvent de faire prendre des informations supplémentaires par la police locale et d'ordonner, le cas échéant, de surveiller temporairement le cas mais beaucoup plus rarement de faire procéder à une enquête sociale[79] ou d'adresser un avertissement ou une admonestation à l'intéressé, soit par la police, soit en le convoquant au Parquet. Le classement sans suite, du reste, n'est pas un classement définitif et le dossier peut être rouvert en cas de récidive de fait, sauf lorsque la prescription est intervenue entretemps. Dans ce sens, cette suspension prétorienne des poursuites pourrait avoir une fonction probatoire si elle était assortie de conditions à respecter et de mesures de surveillance et de guidance. Telle fut d'ailleurs, juqu'à la loi du 29 juin 1964, la seule forme de probation en Belgique[80]. La loi du 29 juin 1964, instaurant la probation légale[81] n'a en principe pas supprimé cette probation prétorienne[82], qui, dans le cas des violences familiales, pourrait garder une certaine utilité dans la mesure où elle permet d'éviter l'ouverture de l'action publique tout en assurant une certaine guidance[83]. Mais elle semble en avoir restreint considérablement l'application, sans que la probation légale elle-même trouve l'occasion de s'appliquer, en cas de classement sans suite. C'est une lacune extrêmement regrettable.

Lorsqu'il existe des *enfants mineurs,* il est d'usage aussi qu'une copie du dossier soit adressée par la Section du Parquet correctionnel chargée des délits contre les personnes, à la Section du Parquet affectée aux affaires "famille-jeunesse" auprès de la chambre civile des divorces et du tribunal de la jeunesse, afin que des mesures de surveillanc et de sauvegarde puissent être éventuellement prises à

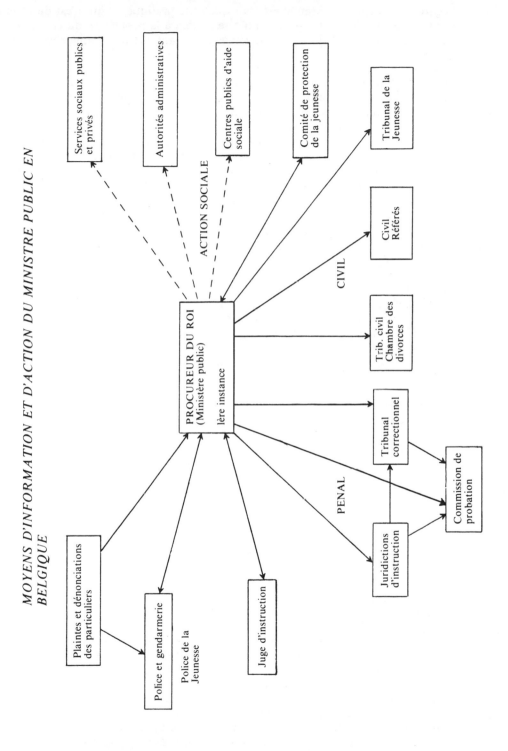

MOYENS D'INFORMATION ET D'ACTION DU MINISTRE PUBLIC EN BELGIQUE

Services sociaux publics et privés

Autorités administratives

Centres publics d'aide sociale

Comité de protection de la jeunesse

Tribunal de la Jeunesse

ACTION SOCIALE

Civil Référés

CIVIL

PROCUREUR DU ROI
(Ministère public)
1ère instance

Trib. civil Chambre des divorces

Tribunal correctionnel

Commission de probation

PENAL

Juridictions d'instruction

Plaintes et dénonciations des particuliers

Police et gendarmerie

Police de la Jeunesse

Juge d'instruction

153   La violence au sein du couple

l'égard de ces enfants. Mais il est clair que cette pratique — qui n'est du reste pas suivie dans tous les cas[84] — ne contribue en rien à la protection du *conjoint* victime de sévices, le tribunal de la jeunesse n'ayant aucune compétence en la matière.

Dans l'ensemble, on peut dire que le Parquet, par la position centrale (Figure 1) qu'il occupe entre les juridictions répressives et civiles d'une part, et les organismes extérieurs (polices, services administratifs et sociaux) dont il collecte les informations et auxquels il donne ou transmet des ordres d'autre part, constitue une véritable "plaque tournante" dans les pays continentaux. *De lege lata,* cette position-clé pourrait être utilement revalorisée si elle était systématiquement exploitée, alors qu'une politique de classement sans suite non probatoire a pour conséquence de *minimiser dangereusement* la gravité de comportements qui, en d'autres circonstances, seraient jugés intolérables.

(ii) Les mesures

Faut-il pour autant prôner l'application systématique de *sanctions pénales* dans les affaires de coups et blessures entre époux? Et lesquelles? Hors les cas les plus graves ou de récidive, on peut en douter. L'emprisonnement aurait sans doute pour effet de mettre temporairement la famille à l'abri, mais ruinerait ses moyens de subsistance (sauf peut-être en cas d'arrêts de fin de semaine ou de semi-liberté). Quant aux peines d'amende, elles seraient nécessairement prélevées sur le budget familial.

En revanche, les *mesures de sûreté,* de *traitement et d'assistance,* ordonnées après enquête sociale et si besoin en est examen médico-psychologique, doivent retenir l'attention car elles permettraient sans doute de mieux cerner chaque cas d'espèce et d'assurer de manière plus efficace la protection de la famille elle-même et le traitement du délinquant, lui-même souvent victime de troubles dont il n'est pas toujours responsable (troubles psychologiques ou sexuels, alcoolisme, reproduction du cycle de la violence . . .)[85].

A l'heure actuelle en Belgique les mesures de sûreté et de traitement ne trouve d'application qu'au travers de deux lois: la loi de *défense sociale* à l'égard des anormaux et des délinquants d'habitude du 1er juillet 1964[86] et la loi du 29 juin 1964 sur la *suspension, le sursis et la probation*[87]. Quant à la loi du 8 avril 1965 sur la protection de la jeunesse, elle ne permet pas d'imposer des mesures de traitement aux parents eux-mêmes, dans le cadre des mesures d'assistance éducative ou de la déchéance de la puissance paternelle[88].

L'application de la loi sur la défense sociale postule que l'inculpé soit en état de *démence,* ou dans un *état grave de déséquilibre mental,* ou de *débilité mentale le rendant incapable du contrôle de ses actions.* Elle entraîne l'internement, à durée indéterminée, de l'inculpe[89]. Eu égard à ces conditions et à la gravité d'une mesure telle que l'internement, la loi de défense sociale, telle qu'elle est actuellement appliquée, paraît trop peu souple pour les cas intermédiaires de déséquilibre ou de troubles pathologiques dont relèvent peut-être certaines formes de sévices et elle semble totalement inutilisée en matière de violences entre époux.

C'est donc plutôt vers la loi sur la *suspension, le sursis et la probation* qu'il faut se tourner. Judicieusement appliquée, celle-ci devrait permettre: une étude sérieuse de chaque cas par voie d'enquête sociale ou d'examen médico-psychologique, l'application de mesures de surveillance et d'assistance adéquates, et la discrétion souhaitable dans la mesure où elle autorise la suspension de la condamnation et évite toute mention au casier judiciaire lorsqu'elle n'est pas révoquée (art. 3, al. 5)[90].

Encore faut-il, pour que la *suspension probatoire* soit applicable, (a) que la prévention soit établie, (b) que l'inculpé n'ait pas encouru de condamnation antérieures à une peine criminelle ou à un emprisonnement correctionnel principal de plus d'un mois, même avec sursis, (c) que la condamnation à prononcer ne soit pas de nature à entraîner aux yeux du juge une peine supérieure à un emprisonnement correctionnel de 2 ans ou une peine plus grave, et que l'inculpé lui-même soit d'accord sur la suspension et les conditions de probation (art. 3).

Ces conditions sont considérées aujourd'hui comme *trop restrictives*[91]. De plus, tout comme l'application correcte de la loi sur la protection de la jeunesse est enrayée par le manque de délégués et d'assistants sociaux[92], le manque d'assistants de probation empêche le bon fonctionnement de la loi et l'extension de son application[93]. Tous les cas, il est vrai, ne se prêtent pas à la probation[94]. Mais en matière familiale, il semble qu'elle soit particulièrement peu employée. L'une des raisons en est peut-être que l'application elle-même de la probation légale suppose que l'action publique soit engagée et que les juridictions répressives d'instruction[95] ou de jugement aient été saisies par le Parquet. Celui-ci redoute en général d'engager une famille dans ce processus et préfère classer sans suite.

On en arrive ainsi à poser non plus une question de sanction ou de traitement mais une question de *juridiction* la plus apte pour rechercher et appliquer une solution adéquate, dans un cadre qui ne soit pas nécessairement répressif.

(iii) Les juridictions compétentes

L'un des problèmes les plus ardus en cette matière réside actuellement dans le cloisonnement rigide des compétences d'attribution en matière civile et pénale dans les pays continentaux, même là où l'expérience des 'tribunaux de la famille' a déjà été amorcée. En France, notamment, où certaines 'chambres de la famille' se sont attribué prétoriennement des compétences en matière pénale[96], l'expérience fait l'objet de réticences[97] et n'a pas été généralisée jusqu'ici. Mais en fait la question est moins de savoir s'il faut attribuer des compétences pénales aux juridictions familiales que de rechercher la manière de 'décriminaliser' au moins en partie, le traitement de certaines infractions, notamment lorsquelles sont commises entre membres d'une même famille.

Jusqu'ici en Belgique, ce processus de *'décriminalisation'* n'a reçu d'ébauche consistante qu'en matière de protection de la jeunesse. La délinquance juvénile y relève, jusqu'à l'âge de 18 ans, des juridictions non-répressives que sont les tribunaux de la jeunesse — lesquels exercent aussi des attributions en matière civile[98] — et les mesures qui lui sont applicables sont des mesures de garde, de préservation et d'éducation. Toutefois, l'art. 38 de la loi du 8 avril 1965 prévoit que le tribunal de la jeunesse peut *renvoyer* devant le tribunal correctionnel — juridiction répressive — le mineur de plus de 16 ans pour lequel une telle mesure est jugée inadéquate ou insuffisante.

On peut donc see demander si certaines infractions familiales ne pourraient être orientées d'abord vers une juridiction de type familial dont les compétences et les moyens de traitement, d'assistance et de guidance seraient considérablement élargis, avec possibilité de renvoi des affaires les plus graves ou autrement insolubles vers les juridictions répressives, si besoin en est.

Pareille réforme touchant à la fois aux règles d'organisation judiciaire et aux règles de compétence d'attribution[99], relèverait cependant d'une réforme législative, élargissant à tout le champ familial la réforme inachevée de la protection de la jeunesse, sans pour autant exclure l'application de sanctions répressives là où elles s'avèrent positivement nécessaires. Elle permettrait en outre de jeter un pont entre les mesures de protection civile et de protection sociale qui nous restent encore à examiner.

3. Les mesures de protection civile

S'il existe une analogie entre la politique de non-intervention dans les affaires familiales des pays anglo-américains et des pays continentaux en matière pénale, il n'en va pas de même en matière civile.

Une ligne de clivage nette sépare en effet à ce niveau l'attitude protectionniste de certains pays continentaux tels que la Belgique et la France, qui n'hésitent pas à intervenir lorsque 'l'intérêt du ménage' ou de la famille est en cause, même lorsque le ménage vit encore ensemble[100], et le parti-pris de non-ingérance des pays de Common Law dans la vie privée d'une famille, du moins aussi longtemps que les époux ne sont pas séparés ou en instance de divorce[101]. Ce clivage se manifeste à deux points de vue: d'une part la recevabilité des actions entre époux n'a jamais véritablement été contestée dans les pays continentaux, comme elle l'a été jusque très récemment dans les pays de Common Law au nom du principe d'unité des époux[102]; d'autre part il n'a jamais été entendu dans nos pays qu'en matière civile une telle action serait nécessairement soumise à la condition préalable de la séparation des époux ou de l'introduction d'une instance en divorce[103]. Cette politique non-interventionniste, apparemment dictée par le souci de la 'paix des familles' et le respect de la 'vie privée' nous paraît avoir été à la source des principales difficultés rencontrées par la Grande-Bretagne en matière de violences conjugales, difficultés auxquelles le Domestic Violence and Matrimonial Proceedings Act 1976 tente d'apporter des solutions inédites en ouvrant une brèche assez remarquable dans le système traditionnel, puisqu'il renonce expressément au caractère 'ancillaire' des injonctions matrimoniales (Section 1, sous section 1).

Il est clair que le problème se pose en d'autres termes dans les pays continentaux et que ceux-ci paraissent relativement mieux armés pour organiser une ligne de premier secours en matière civile, sous forme d'un régime de crise applicable *avant* et *indépendamment* de toute action en séparation de corps ou en divorce. Ce dernier reste bien entendu la solution la plus radicale, mais aussi la plus simpliste, et il ne résout du reste pas toutes les questions.

C'est pourquoi nous nous attacherons plus spécialement à l'étude des mesures de protection civile dites 'urgentes et provisoires' durant le mariage et à la recherche des améliorations possibles à ce niveau.

(a) Les mesures urgentes et provisoires durant le mariage

En cas de menaces, de cruautés ou de sévices de la part de l'un des conjoints, l'objectif à atteindre en ordre principal est d'assurer la *sécurité* de la ou des victimes (dispense de cohabitation, garde des enfants), et, en ordre subsidiaire, leur logement, leur subsistance et la protection des biens du ménage. Est donc requis un dispositif permettant d'aménager rapidement la situation globale de la famille et susceptible d'exécution forcée ou, le cas échéant, de sanction. A ce niveau, les qualités requises sont la *rapidité,* la *simplicité* et l'*efficacité.*

La Belgique possède un dispositif de ce genre, relativement simple et complet. C'est pourquoi nous le choisissons comme exemple. Néanmoins il n'est pas sans lacunes, et ce d'autant plus que s'il a bien été conçu pour protéger la famille contre les abus, il n'a pas été *spécialement* aménagé pour répondre aux problèmes des violences familiales. Il ne constitue donc qu'une base susceptible d'améliorations.

Ce dispositif s'insère dans ce qu'il est convenu d'appeler désormais "le régime matrimonial primaire", c'est-a-dire la charte impérative des droits et devoirs réciproques des époux, auxquels il ne leur est pas permis de déroger conventionnellement, quel que soit leur régime matrimonial[104], régime récemment modifié et renforcé par la loi du 14 juillet 1976 portant réforme des régimes matrimoniaux. La disposition — clé en est l'article 223 C. civil, complété par les art. 215 et 221 du même Code et les art. 1253 bis à octies nouveaux du Code judiciaire.

Il convient d'y ajouter le régime de droit commun de la procédure en *référé* qui donne au Président du tribunal de 1ère instance de chaque arrondissement compétence pour statuer *d'urgence* dans toutes les matières qui relèvent du pouvoir judiciaire (art. 584 et 1035 à 1041 du Code judiciaire). En cas d'instance en divorce ou en séparation de corps, c'est dans le cadre de cette procédure que doivent être réglées toutes les mesures provisoires à prendre durant la procédure (art. 1280 C. jud.). Celles-ci prennent alors le relais des mesures prises *avant* le début de l'instance dans le cadre du dispositif ici étudie[105].

Concrètement, la disposition-clé de l'art. 223 C. civ. prévoit que: *"Si l'un des époux manque gravement à ses droits, le juge de paix* (magistrat cantonal) *ordonne, à la demande du conjoint, les mesures urgentes et provisoires relatives à la personne et aux biens des époux et des enfants. Il en va de même, à la demand d'un des époux, si l'entente entre eux est sérieusement perturbée"*[106]. Il s'agit donc d'une *clause générale,* dont les conditions d'application sont soit une *faute grave* de l'un des conjoints, soit même, et ceci constitue une innovation, la preuve d'une *mésentente sérieuse* du ménage, quel qu'en soit le responsable, pour autant qu'il s'avère que des mesures urgentes doivent être prises dans l'intérêt du ménage, de l'autre conjoint ou des enfants. La preuve de l'urgence se déduit de l'utilité qu'il y a à prendre immédiatement des mesures susceptibles de prévenir ou de remédier à un dommage grave. Elle est laissée à la libre appréciation du juge[107].

Semblable clause pourrait se retrouver en *droit français* dans l'article 220-1 du Code civil, à vrai dire moins clairement formulé, si la jurisprudence française avait voulu interpréter l'alinéa 1er de cet article comme applicable à toutes les mesures d'ordre extra-patrimonial ou patrimonial dictées par l'intérêt de la famille. Mais il semble qu'elle se soit bornée jusqu'ici à des mesures d'ordre patrimonial, en sorte que la France ne dispose pas d'un 'régime de crise' aussi souple que la Belgique[108]. Cela se ressent notamment en matière de dispense de cohabitation[109]. En *Suisse,* les articles 169 à 172 du Code civil semblent répondre à des préoccupations analogues à celles du système belge[110].

Dans la pratique, quels sont les problèmes auxquels le dispositif belge permet de donner une solution en cas de sévices ou de menances de violences de la part de l'un des conjoints?

(i) Dispense de cohabitation

Il importe de distinguer la notion d'autorisation de résidence séparée et celle de dispense de cohabitation, les deux notions étant différentes dans leurs causes et dans leurs conséquences[111]. La première permet à l'un des époux de ne pas habiter avec l'autre parce que la résidence elle-même présente des inconvénients pour lui ou par la famille[112]. La seconde ne met pas le choix de la résidence en cause, mais le principe même de la cohabitation. C'est donc bien la dispense de cohabiter qui nous concerne dans le cas des violences.

Il faut remarquer à ce propos que, même en l'absence de texte légal, la jurisprudence belge et française ont toujours admis que la femme pouvait résider ailleurs qu'au domicile du mari, même sans autorisation judiciaire, lorsque celui-ci ne lui fournissait pas de conditions de logement et de sécurité suffisantes en contrepartie du devoir qu'elle avait de le suivre où bon lui semblerait (art. 215 ancien), ou ne remplissait pas correctement ses devoirs[113], notamment en cas de mauvais traitements[114]. Une femme "battue" peut donc quitter la résidence conjugale sans autorisation préalable, sans se rendre coupable d'abandon injurieux, mais à charge de prouver le cas échéant qu'elle avait des motifs valables de le faire. En cas d'urgence, cette solution s'impose.

Néanmoins, il est plus intéressant pour elle d'obtenir une dispense judiciaire de cohabitation, assortie de ses effets juridiques propres permettant d'organiser, temporairement, sa situation juridique et matérielle et celle de ses enfants. La jurisprudence française n'a pas étendu l'art. 220-1 C. civ. à cette fin. La Belgique utilise l'art. 223. Ce dernier permet au juge d'accorder, à titre premier, l'autorisation de quitter la résidence conjugale. Mais il permet d'aller au-delà.

(ii) L'attribution exclusive du droit d'occuper la résidence conjugale

Traditionnellement, on a cru faire beaucoup en autorisant la femme à quitter le domicile conjugal pour aller s'installer ailleurs, éventuellement en emmenant ses enfants. Mais dans le cas où c'est le mari qui commet les sévices et met la famille en danger, cette solution est à la fois injuste et déraisonnable. Il est injuste que l'auteur du danger demeure installé à la résidence conjugale. Et il est déraisonnable d'obliger la femme et les enfants à chercher refuge ailleurs, leur occasionnant ainsi des frais plus lourds et un traumatisme supplémentaire. La solution qui s'impose est donc l'exclusion — momentanée à tout le moins — de l'auteur du danger.

L'article 223 permet d'obtenir ce résultat[115] et d'ordonner au mari non seulement de quitter le logement familial mais de ne pas y importuner sa femme, bien qu'il semble relativement peu appliqué en ce sens, sans doute par traditionnalisme. L'effet d'une telle décision est d'accorder à la femme la jouissance exclusive du logement[116] — celui-ci fût-il un bien propre du mari — et d'en faire une résidence privative, en telle manière que si le mari s'efforçait de s'y introduire contre son gré, elle puisse faire appel à la force publique (police) pour l'en expulser, et qu'au cas où il s'y introduirait par menace, ruse ou violence, il se rende coupable d'une violation de domicile pénalement sanctionnée (art. 438 C. pénal).

Concrètement, il est donc possible d'assurer de la sorte non seulement un toit, mais le toit familial lui-même à la femme et aux enfants. Il est clair que si par hasard les violences émanaient de la femme, le mari pourrait jouir de la même faculté. En revanche, l'art. 223 n'est jamais applicable entre concubins[117].

(iii) La garde des enfants

La même disposition permet au juge de paix d'attribuer, à titre provisoire, la garde des enfants à l'époux victime de mauvais traitements, pour autant que cette solution soit conforme à leur intérêt. A vrai dire, elle ne serait pas indispensable, car l'art. 373 al. 2 du Code civil, modifié par la loi du 1er juillet 1974, confère d'office l'exercise exclusif de l'autorité parentale sur la personne et les biens des enfants mineurs à celui des parents qui exerce sur eux la garde matérielle de fait ou de droit[118]. Mais il est clair qu'il est préférable d'asseoir cette garde matérielle sur une décision judiciaire. Il faut souligner à ce propos, tout l'intérêt qu'il y a pour la femme, à conserver la disposition de la résidence conjugale, car trop souvent lorsqu'elle est obligée de fuir, la réaction ultérieure des juges de la jeunesse, avertis du danger encouru par les enfants, sera de "placer" ceux-ci en institution ou en famille d'accueil, autrement dit de les séparer de leur mère, au risque de les traumatiser davantage encore[119].

Quant au droit de visite du père, il est parfaitement possible de le lui refuser provisoirement, pour éviter tout risque de nouvelles violences et ne pas favoriser un enlèvement, qui reste, hélas, toujours possible. Complémentairement, il faut mentionner enfin la possibilité d'obtenir une *déchéance* de la puissance paternelle, conformément aux dispositions des art. 33 et s. de la loi du 8 avril 1965 sur la protection de la jeunesse. Mais celle-ci relève du juge de la jeunesse, et les délais en sont longs. De plus, la pratique démontre que les juges répugnent à la prononcer[120].

(iv) L'entretien financier

Avec le logement, le problème des moyens de subsistance constitue un point vital. C'est faute de ressources économiques que beaucoup de femmes hésitent à se plaindre ou à quitter leur mari. Normalement, le *droit au secours entre époux* (art. 213 C. civ.) s'exerce en nature à la résidence conjugale. En cas de séparation, il ne peut être revendiqué que par celui auquel la rupture de la vie commune ne peut être imputée[121]. Quant au *droit des enfants à l'entretien* (art. 203 C. civ.), il peut être invoqué en toutes circonstances par celui qui en a la garde.

On ne peut donc douter que l'époux contraint de quitter le logis familial par les agissements de l'autre conserve son droit de demander un secours alimentaire pour lui-même et pour les enfants, et même la contribution aux charges du ménage (art. 221 C. civ.). Le juge compétent en cette matière est également le juge de paix, entre les mains duquel se trouve donc actuellement regroupées toutes les mesures constituant la ligne de premier secours. Ce magistrat dispose en outre de moyens d'investigation spéciaux pour connaître les ressources du défendeur[122] et peut autoriser le créancier d'aliments à se faire payer directement par les débiteurs de son mari[123]. La délégation de somme ainsi accordée est opposable à tous les débiteurs actuels ou futurs du mari (ou de la femme) sur simple notification[124] et jout d'une priorité de rang par rapport aux autres créanciers du débiteur alimentaire[125], du moins lorsque le conjoint débiteur est appointé ou salarié, c'est une arme appréciable. Dans la pratique cependant, il arrivera souvent que l'époux démuni de ressources doive se tourner vers un organisme public ou privé pour obtenir un secours matériel immédiat.

(v) La protection des biens

L'art. 223 C. civil permet encore d'obtenir toutes les mesures nécessaires à la protection des biens du ménage, mobiliers ou immobiliers, contre tout acte de disposition ou de détournement, et même de déplacement en ce qui concerne les meubles, ou au contraire l'autorisation d'emporter certains meubles nécessaires à une installation temporaire. Une procédure d'*extrême urgence* est même prévue pour éviter les actes d'aliénation et de détournement[126] et la sanction prévue pour les actes passés en violation d'une telle mesure est l'annulation[127]. Il va de soi que ces dispositions s'appliquent au premier chef au logement familial et aux meubles qui le garnissent. Mais celui-ci est soumis en outre à une protection particulière dans le nouveau régime primaire.

(vi) La protection speciale du logement familial (art. 215 C. civ., § 1 et 2)

Il est frappant de constater que dans toutes les législations récentes le logement destiné à abriter la vie de la famille bénéficie d'une protection spéciale en raison même de son affectation[128]. Tel est le cas en *droit francais* depuis la loi du 13 juillet 1966[129] et en droit belge depuis celle du 14 juillet 1976[130]. En *Belgique,* cette protection porte tant sur les droits réels (propriété, usufruit, usage, habitation) que personnels (bail) relatifs à l'habitation principale du ménage. Même lorsque celle-ci constitue un bien propre ou personnel à l'un des époux, et quel que soit le régime matrimonial, elle la préserve de tout acte de disposition entre vifs, à titre onéreux ou gratuit, entendu au sens large — c'est-à-dire tout acte qui aboutirait à priver la famille de la continuité de jouissance du logement — passé sans l'accord de l'autre conjoint[131]. Quant au droit au bail, il est considérée comme appartenant d'office aux deux époux, durant le mariage, même si à l'origine un seul d'entre eux était preneur[132].

La même disposition interdit tout acte de disposition entre vifs, à titre onéreux ou gratuit, ou la mise en gage des *meubles* garnissant le logement principal, sans l'accord du conjoint[133]. La sanction de cette double protection est l'annulation de l'acte irrégulièrement passé[134].

Une difficulté particulière pourrait surgir, bien sûr, quant à la notion de "logement familial" lorsque précisément la cellule familiale s'est dissociée et qu'il y a séparation de fait. La doctrine belge et française s'accordent cependant pour maintenir la protection dans ce cas, aussi longtemps que le logis est susceptible de conserver sa 'vocation initiale', c'est-à-dire jusqu'au moment du divorce[135].

Mais il faut souligner, et c'est un point important, qu'en droit belge la question de l'attribution préférentielle du logement familial, en propriété ou en usufruit, ou du droit au bail, *après dissolution du mariage par divorce* n'a pas été résolue aussi clairement que dans d'autres législations[136] et laisse place à des sources d'insatisfaction ou d'incertitude[137].

(vii) Durée des mesures de sauvegarde

Par définition, les mesures 'urgentes et provisoires' n'ont pour effet et pour but que de remédier à une situation temporaire, et non d'organiser une séparation de fait à durée illimitée. Pourtant rien n'impose au juge de fixer une durée déterminée aux mesures qu'il ordonne, celles-ci pouvant toujours être modifiées ou révoquées en cas de changement de la situation[138] et c'est parfois 'jouer la carte du mariage' que d'autoriser les époux à prendre une certaine distance. Il faut ajouter que ces mesures ne cessent pas de plein droit lors d'une reprise de la vie commune[139]. La plupart du temps cependant, ces mesures de sauvegarde ne sont que le prélude à un divorce. Dans ce cas, le relais est pris par les mesures provisoires pendant l'instance, pour lesquelles compétence générale est donnée au président du tribunal saisi de la demande en divorce et statuant en référé[140].

Dans des circonstances de crise aiguë, la rapidité et la simplicité des procédures et leur coût peu élevé font eux aussi partie des moyens de secours souhaitables. La complexité et la lenteur des démarches judiciaires désespèrent généralement les justiciables. En matière familiale, ce problème revêt un aspect particulièrement grave et désolant.

Les règles de procédure belges applicables en matière de mesures urgentes et provisoires échappent *partiellement* à ces défauts. Non seulement le magistrat y est facilement accessible — le juge de paix[141], est le plus proche du justiciable, géographiquement et même psychologiquement, du moins dans les cantons ruraux et les petites agglomérations — mais la procédure est simple et peu coûteuse: la demande se fait par *requête écrite ou verbale, sans que le secours de l'avocat soit nécessaire*: le juge convoque les parties, tente de les concilier, et s'il ne peut parvenir à un accord, doit rendre son ordonnance dans les 15 jours. Bien que susceptible de voies de recours, l'ordonnance est exécutoire par provision, c'est-à-dire immédiatement. Sans doute le délai de 15 jours peut-il être considéré comme relativement long, mais il est indispensable pour pouvoir convoquer le défendeur et procéder à un minimum d'investigations. Le cas échéant, il peut être écourté: 8 jours minimum. Mais pour les cas paroxystiques et d'une gravité exceptionnelle, il reste un autre recours: celui du référé[142] et notamment du *'référé d'hôtel'* qui permet de saisir le Président du tribunal de 1ère instance, éventuellement à son propre domicile par simple requête, et d'obtenir qu'il statue sur le champ[143]. Sa compétence générale, fondée sur l'urgence, lui permet de prendre "toutes mesures nécessaires à la sauvegarde des droits de ceux qui ne peuvent y pourvoir"[144] et ses décisions sont exécutoires, par provisions[145].

Des recours relativement rapides, simples et peu coûteux existent donc, permettant d'aménager une situation de crise au moins de manière provisoire.[146] La plupart du temps malheureusement, les justiciables en ignorent l'existence. De plus, il faut bien reconnaître que, n'ayant pas été spécifiquement prévues pour les cas de violences, ces mesures comportent des lacunes dont certaines pourraient être comblées par une utilisation plus judicieuse des moyens existants, mais d'autres requerraient un appoint législatif.

(b) Les lacunes du dispositif de protection civile

(i) Insuffisance de mesures de protection immédiate

Il faut d'abord souligner qu'en matière de protection immédiate, les personnes semblent être moins bien protégées que les biens. Alors que les art. 223 C. civ. et 1253 septies du C. jud. belge, combinés, organisent une procédure d'extrême urgence permettant de faire échec à toute aliénation de biens meubles et immeubles, ni le juge de paix, ni le président du tribunal civil statuant en référé, ni aucun juge civil ne peuvent délivrer une ordonnance enjoignant à la police locale d'exercer immédiatement une protection spéciale — sous forme d'une surveillance renforcée — à titre intérimaire ou durable, sur une famille menacée de violences ou en danger de nouvelle agression. Ils n'ont aucune compétence pour cela. A l'heure actuelle, seul le Ministère public, saisi d'une plainte ou d'une dénonciation peut ordonner de surveiller le cas, sans qu'il s'agisse vraiment d'un ordre de protection[147]. D'autre part, jamais la police locale n'est informée des mesures urgentes et provisoires relatives à la protection d'un conjoint et des enfants, même lorsqu'elles sont justifiées par des actes de violence. Il n'appartient pas au juge civil de les lui notifier, bien que le soin d'assurer l'exécution des décisions judiciaires incombe, notamment, à la force publique. Rien n'empêche évidemment les avocats ou les parties d'avertir la police des décisions obtenues, mais il ne semble pas que cette pratique soit utilisée. Inversément, le juge de paix, qui doit statuer dans les 15 jours ne dispose jamais à temps des informations recueillies par la police[148]. Dépourvu de service social et même de Ministère public pour, parfaire ses informations, il ne dispose pratiquement que des dires des parties.

On conviendra donc au total que la protection des familles en danger est relativement mal assurée en raison du *clivage des compétences civiles et pénales, du manque de coordination des informations et de l'absence de disposition permettant d'obtenir dans un minimum de temps une ordonnance de protection durable.* Ce sont des lacunes auxquelles il y aurait lieu de remédier par voie législative ou par voie de règlements et directives. D'autre part, il ne semble pas que les ordonnances de dispense de cohabitation et d'attribution de la jouissance exclusive du logement familial à l'un des conjoints soient jamais assorties d'une interdiction de venir importuner, menacer ou aggresser l'autre époux et les enfants aux abords de ce logement, de l'école des enfants, ou du lieu de travail de l'époux demandeur. Bien que le texte de l'art. 223 soit suffisamment souple pour ne pas exclure expressément, pareille interdiction de séjour paraît difficilement compatible avec le caractère civil de la mesure et le respect des libertés individuelles. Si l'utilité en est néanmoins reconnue, il serait souhaitable de l'insérer dans un texte législatif, à l'instar du Domestic Violence and Matrimonial Proceedings Act 1976 (Sect. 1 (1)(c)). Mais le problème à ce niveau est plus encore celui de l'exécution forcée et de la sanction.

(ii) Insuffisance des moyens d'exécution forcée

L'exécution des décisions judiciaires, plus particulièrement dans cette matière, est le point névralgique par excellence. Il n'existe pas, en droit continental, de délit de 'contempt of court' et nous avons déjà dit nos réticences à ce sujet. En cas de violation ou d'inexécution d'une mesure civile urgente et provisoire, les moyens de contrainte ou de sanction sont donc ceux du *droit commun* (ex. expulsion du logement ou reprise des enfants par huissier ou par la force publique, ou éventuellement des sanctions pénales fondées sur une *incrimination spéciale* telle que la violation de domicile (art. 438 C. pén.), l'enlèvement d'enfant (art. 369 bis C. pén.), ou l'abandon de famille pour non paiement volontaire d'une pension alimentaire (art. 391 bis). Mais comment empêcher un mari de rôder autour de la résidence ou du lieu de travail de sa femme, ou de l'école des enfants, de les menacer ou de les agresser?

Le Domestic Violence and Matrimonial Proceedings Act apporte à ce problème une réponse originale dans la mesure où il autorise les juges civils des County Courts[149] à délivrer une injonction de "non molestation" ou d'"exclusion" du logement ou d'une zone de protection déterminée assortie d'un pouvoir d'*arrestation sans mandat* en cas de violation, s'il constate la perpétration de blessures (actual bodily harm) et craint une récidive. Le fait d'user de violence ou simplement de pénétrer dans les lieux interdits permet dès lors à la police — sans toutefois l'y obliger — de procéder à une arrestation, avec mission de déférer l'inculpé dans les 24 heures à la juridiction qui a rendu l'injonction (Sect. 2)[150]. Celle-ci pourra alors appliquer la sanction qu'elle jugera adéquate au 'contempt of court' que constitue la violation de l'injonction[151].

Pareille solution semble difficilement transposable en droit continental à moins d'ériger en infraction pénale, passible d'arrestation immédiate et de sanction, la violation d'une ordonnance du juge de paix ou du juge des référés, ou d'un avertissement du Ministère public. Mais quelle sanction?

En revanche, l'obligation de délivrer une copie de l'ordonnance rendue à la police du lieu de résidence du demandeur[152] paraît intéressante car, indépendamment du pouvoir d'arrestation qui y est attaché, elle attire nécessairement l'attention de celle-ci sur le danger existant et l'incitera à agir avec plus de diligence. Ce système devrait être étendu à tous les cas où une ordonnance de sauvegarde est rendue par un magistrat dans un cas de conflit avec violences ou menaces de violences[153].

(iii) Absence de mesures d'assistance, de traitement et de guidance

Enfin, aucune juridiction civile n'a compétence jusqu'à ce jour en Belgique pour décider d'une mesure quelconque d'assistance, de traitement ou de guidance à l'égard d'adultes. Le tribunal de la jeunesse lui-même peut *conseiller* de telles mesures aux parents (ex. cure de désintoxication éthylique) dans le cadre de mesures d'assistance éducative ou de déchéance; il ne peut en décider. Et de toutes manières, il n'est pas compétent lorsqu'il n'est pas saisi d'un problème relatif aux enfants. Ainsi se trouve soulevé à nouveau le problème des juridictions spécialisées en matière familiale.

(c) Les juridictions compétentes

A vrai dire, la question de la création de juridictions spécialisées en matière familiale trouve son fondement dans plusieurs problèmes. Le premier est le nécessaire *regroupement des compétences* actuellement dispersées, source de complications, de lenteurs et de frais inutiles pour les justiciables déjà aux prises avec des difficultés personnelles souvent dramatiques. Le problème semble être le même dans tous les pays.[154]

Le second est la nécessité de mieux en mieux perçue de *traiter les problèmes familiaux de manière spécifique,* d'humaniser la procédure et de rechercher les solutions légales les plus adéquates. Le dialogue et la négociation sont à la base d'une telle humanisation. D'autre part, la recherche de solutions adaptées aux besoins ne s'accommode plus de la traditionnelle dichotomie entre le civil et le pénal. La plupart du temps, les mesures à prendre relèveront plutôt d'une justice 'sociale'. Le traitement des violences intra-familiales illustre cette nécessaire et croissante compénétration du civil, du pénal et du social. De là la création de 'juridictions familiales' dans un nombre croissant de pays. Quelles que soient les aménagements techniques préconisés — juridictions autonomes à compétences intégrales[155] ou sections spécialisées des tribunaux de 1ère instance, à compétence plus ou moins étendues[156] les idées de base sont les mêmes et gravitent autour de la recherche d'une approche globale des difficultés familiales et de solutions alternatives.

On ne peut qu'acquiescer à cette nouvelle étape qui complète logiquement la réforme inachevée de la protection de la jeunesse, à condition pourtant d'en mesurer les implications, les dangers et les limites. Au niveau des *implications,* il est d'ores et déjà démontré que les meilleures lois ne donnent pas les résultats espérés ou sont insuffisamment exploitées lorsqu'elles ne sont pas dotées des moyens de leur politique. Ainsi, en Belgique, des lois de protection de la jeunesse[157] et de probation[158]. Des juridictions de la famille ne peuvent être utiles que si elles sont pourvues en nombre suffisant de magistrats spécialement motivés et formés, assistés d'équipes pluridisciplinaires et de travailleurs sociaux directement impliqués dans le diagnostic, la concentration, la négociation des décisions et leur application, de concert avec les intéressés[159].

Mais l'Etat ne semble pas avoir encore compris que l'investissement le plus économique pour lui et le plus bénéfique pour les individus et leur famille serait un équipement convenable en matière de prévention et de guidance, bien que la preuve expérimentale en ait déjà été faite[160].

Au niveau des *dangers,* ceux de l'inquisitorialité, du paternalisme et de la 'morale du juge' sont les plus connus; celui de la médicalisation outrancière et le risque d'amenuisement des garanties offertes par les règles de procédure pénale ou civile traditionnelles le sont peut-être moins. Il faut y être attentif[161].

Quant aux *limites,* elle sont diverses. En matière de violence, plus spécialement, il n'est pas certain que tous les actes de violence conjugale ou familiale relèvent d'un traitement psycho-social ou médical. Ceux-ci du reste peuvent difficilement être *imposés* à des adultes, qui doivent conserver le droit d'assumer leur responsabilité devant une juridiction pénale. Certains actes, d'autre part, sont si graves, qu'ils doivent être jugés par une juridiction répressive. Une solution possible serait alors d'interposer la juridiction familiale en manière de filtre afin de pouvoir traiter par l'assistance et la guidance *consentis*[162] le maximum de cas possibles et de ne renvoyer au répressif que les cas graves autrement insolubles[163]. Mais cet effort de 'décriminalisation' serait vain, s'il n'était accompagné d'un effort complémentaire et préalable de 'déjudiciarisation' au sens de limitation maximale de toute intervention judiciaire dans la vie familiale par la mise en oeuvre de voies d'action novatrices au niveau des collectivités locales[164] en matière de prévention, de médiation et de conciliation[165].

4. Les mesures de protection sociale

Ici encore, il faut distinguer — à propos du problème spécifique de la violence familiale la ligne de premier secours et les moyens de protection à moyen et long terme. On classera parmi les mécanismes de protection immédiats la création de refuges ou foyers d'accueil, l'amélioration de l'assistance judiciaire et la meilleure coordination des services administratifs et sociaux locaux. A moyen terme on rangera: la politique de sécurité sociale, du logement, de l'emploi et de la garde des enfants, et pour terminer la politique de prévention au niveau éducatif.

(a) Les mesures de protection immédiates

(i) *La création de refuges ou foyer d'accueil*

La pratique démontre que, face à la lenteur ou à l'impuissance des moyens de protection judiciaires, le salut réside souvent dans la fuite. Seul le bon sens des femmes a répondu à cette question par la méthode la plus directe: la création de centres de crise, ou de premier accueil permettant aux victimes de violences familiales de trouver un refuge immédiat et si possible secret. L'a b c du premier secours se trouve là, hors de toute discussion possible.

Mais la discussion surgit au niveau du choix entre les formules: le *refuge autonome* et peut-être sauvage, et le *foyer d'accueil institutionnalisé.* Tout le problème se trouve résumé dans les difficultés rencontrées en Angleterre par E. Pizzey au Chiswick Women's Aid[166], et en Belgique, par les mouvements féminins soucieux d'obtenir une aide matérielle sous forme de locaux et de subsides tout en conservant une certaine ou totale autonomie.

La création de refuges autonomes s'inscrit dans le contexte de voies d'action sociales novatrices, porteuses d'un dynamisme propre[167] les méritent à ce titre l'appui financier et la collaboration des services administratifs et sociaux locaux, sans qu'une fonctionnarisation excessive risque d'étouffer leur richesse innovatrice et expérimentale. La promiscuité elle-même possède une vertu cathartique en cas de crise aiguë, pour autant qu'elle ne se prolonge pas outre mesure. Intéressante aussi est la création de refuges pour "hommes violents" imaginée par le Chiswick Women's Aid.

S'en tenir là, en revanche, reviendrait à considérer que le problème peut être traité par des moyens de fortune. Il revient donc aux pouvoirs locaux et régionaux de créer de leur côté des maisons d'accueil qui ne soient pas nécessairement réservées à des femmes et des enfants maltraités. Toute commune de quelque importance devrait disposer d'un centre de ce genre, accessible 24 heures sur 24 à toute personne en détresse[168].

(ii) *La coordination des moyens d'information et d'aide ou d'action sociale*[169]

Outre l'absence de refuge et de foyer d'accueil, l'un des maux actuels les plus graves réside sans doute dans la dispersion chaotique des informations et des moyens d'aide sociale tant au niveau local que régional et national. Devant la prolifération anarchique de services publics et privés, souvent subsidiés mais relativement peu centralisés et coordonnés, il est pratiquement impossible de savoir qui fait quoi au bon moment.

Nous avons déjà souligné plus haut le rôle que la *police* pourrait jouer comme service de protection et de médiation et comme première plaque d'orientation vers les différents services administratifs, sociaux et médicaux locaux. Il faut rappeler ici la nécessaire liaison qui devrait être établie à ce niveau et le changement de mentalité qu'elle implique.

Le second organisme majeur, au niveau local, devrait être un *organisme public* suffisamment décentralisé pour demeurer proche de la population, et doté d'une mission de liaison suffisamment souple et efficace pour ne pas étouffer les autres initiatives tout en conjuguant leurs efforts.

En Belgique, cet organisme pourrait et devrait être, au niveau communal, le Centre Public D'Aide Sociale, qui a remplacé, depuis la loi du 8 juillet 1976, les anciennes Commissions d'assistance publique[170]. En effet, non seulement la philosophie de cette loi a substitué à l'antique notion de 'bienfaisance' un droit subjectif de tout citoyen à l'aide de la collectivité[171], mais, parmi les missions nouvelles des C.P.A.S. figurent la *collaboration* et la *concertation* avec les personnes, institutions et services déployant une activité sociale dans le même ressort[172]. Pareille coordination est indispensable non seulement parce que les C.P.A.S. des petites communes ne disposent pas des moyens suffisants pour remplir toutes les missions qui leur sont désormais imparties, mais parce qu'elle permettrait la concentration des informations et des moyens d'action en matière sociale, dans un centre 'visible' pour la population tout en favorisant le 'libre choix' des usagers, voulu par la loi[173]. Peu de C.P.A.S. semblent avoir pris conscience à ce jour de la force que pourrait représenter cette concertation dans la diversification des actions. A défaut de quoi, ce sont des organismes privés ou semi-publics[174] qui, ici ou là, entreprennent de manière sporadique et nécessairement insuffisante d'informer le public de ses droits et des possibilités d'aide existantes.

Parmi ces moyens, l'aide judiciaire et juridique devrait, en principe, occuper un rang prioritaire. Tel n'est cependant pas le cas.

(iii) L'aide juridique, judiciaire et extra-judiciaire

Assez curieusement en effet le droit à l'aide médicale et à l'aide sociale se sont développés bien avant que n'émerge la notion de *droit à l'aide juridique*. Dans la plupart des pays, ce volet social essentiel demeure aujourd'hui encore confiné à la notion d'assistance aux indigents et de charité exercée principalement par les auxiliaires de justice, spécialement les plus jeunes[175]. D'autre part, même dans les pays où l'aide judiciaire a été modernisée par des lois récentes, celle-ci demeure généralement limitée à une assistance dans les procédures introduites devant les tribunaux et se trouve beaucoup plus rarement étendue à une assistance juridique extra-judiciaire sous forme de bureaux d'information et de consultation[176], et plus largement encore, d'une éducation du public[177]. A fortiori n'existe-t-il pas de service public appointant des juristes dont la fonction serait de conseiller et représenter les personnes démunies en justice[178]. Les expériences réalisées en *Suède*[179], en *Angleterre*[180] et en *Allemagne*[181] démontrent cependant que cette aide judiciaire et extra-judiciaire constitue une forme d'aide sociale fondamentale, principalement en matière de logement et de sécurité sociale et surtout en matière familiale, où elle constitue le complément nécessaire à la consultation psychologique, médicale et sociale. Il n'est pas impossible que la notion de "combat judiciaire", base du principe accusatoire, et les privilèges des auxiliaires de justice soient à la base de ce retard. La recherche d'une solution équilibrée en cette matière constitue certainement un problème extrêmement délicat, mais impérieux[182].

En *France,* les conditions d'aide judiciaire ont été modifiées par la loi du 3 janvier 1972. Celle-ci a permis l'attribution de l'aide judiciaire selon des critères plus objectifs et réduit la part d'arbitraire des bureaux d'aide judiciaire. L'aide comporte la remise des frais dus au Trésor, la dispense de l'avance ou de la consignation des autres frais et la gratuité du ministère des auxiliaires de justice (avocats, officiers publics et ministériels, avec possibilité de libre choix). Elle s'étend de plein droit à la défense aux recours exercés contre une décision profitant au bénéficiaire et aux procédures et actes d'exécution. L'aide judiciaire *partielle* est désormais possible. Mais le 'service social d'aide juridique' extra-judiciaire n'a pas été inclus dans cette réforme, pas plus que la prise en charge, par l'aide judiciaire, de consultations auprès de praticiens du droit. C'est, a-t-on dit, une réforme manquée[183].

En *Belgique*[184], la réforme de l'assistance judiciaire semble encore plus en retard. *L'assistance gratuite,* ou à frais réduits, d'un avocat est entièrement laissée à charge de l'Ordre des avocats qui "pourvoit à l'assistance des personnes dont les revenus sont insuffisants par l'établissement d'un Bureau de consultation et de défense, selon les modalités qu'il détermine" (art. 455 C. jud.). Ce sont les avocats stagiaires qui assurent cette assistance, pratiquement sans rémunération[185], et, par la force des choses, sans l'expérience et l'autorité nécessaires.

Quant à *l'assistance judiciaire proprement dite,* minutieusement rélementée par les art. 664 à 669 du Code judiciaire, elle ne porte que sur les *frais de procédure —* en ce compris les honoraires des officiers publics et ministériels — mais elle n'assure pas la gratuité définitive de celle-ci dans la mesure où elle ne fait que dispenser le bénéficiaire de l'avance des frais de justice qui pourront être éventuellement récupérés à sa charge[186] ou à celle de la partie adverse. Elle ne s'étend pas aux voies de recours pour lesquels une nouvelle demande devra être faite. Les conditions de ressources ne sont pas précisées par la loi sous forme de plafonds, comme dans la loi française, mais laissées à l'appréciation du Bureau d'assistance judiciaire du tribunal compétent, sur base des pièces justificatives d'indigence qui doivent être présentées en même temps que la requête[187]. *L'assistance partielle* est possible[188]. En matière de divorce, il a été jugé que l'assistance judiciaire peut être accordée uniquement pour le dépôt de la requête et les mesures provisoires, une provision "ad litem" pouvant être obtenue de la part du conjoint, au niveau des référés[189]. Enfin, l'assistance judiciaire n'est accordée que si la prétention *paraît juste* (autrement dit plausible) et, en principe, après une tentative de *conciliation* destinée à obtenir un accord éventuel des parties[190]. Dans la pratique, même si cette formalité n'est pas respectée, la longueur des délais constitue à elle seule une entrave à l'accès à la justice[191].

Si l'on y ajoute que le législateur a refusé d'étendre aux missions des Centres publics d'aide sociale celle d'organiser un bureau de consultation juridiques gratuites[192] et que, si les Centres de consultation conjugale agréés[193] et certains organismes d'action sociale privés ou semi-publics sont admis à avoir un conseiller juridique, celui-ci n'a jamais le droit de plaider pour les consultants, on conviendra qu'il existe dans notre pays une carence majeure au niveau de l'accès du public, et particulièrement des personnes démunies, à l'information juridique et à la justice. Cette carence s'ajoute encore à l'impuissance des victimes de violences familiales.

(b) Les moyens de protection à moyen et long terme

De toutes les solutions que l'on peut envisager en matière de violences conjugales, le *divorce* est la plus radicale, mais il est loin de tout résoudre.

Dans le contexte de l'évolution actuelle des législations, la simplification croissante des conditions d'obtention du divorce est sans doute de nature à apporter une réponse définitive au problème du conjoint maltraité et à soulager le fardeau de la preuve, autrefois exigeante en matière de cruauté et de sévices[194]. Mais cet avantage se trouve contrebalancé par l'adoption du système de divorce 'sans faute' qui pourrait bien aboutir, dans les systèmes les plus avancés, à des solutions particulièrement injustes, dans la mesure où il s'accompagne d'une *absence de réparation du préjudice causé* et même de la *suppression de tout devoir alimentaire postérieur à la dissolution du mariage*[195]. Pour la femme, dépendante économiquement lorsqu'elle est sans profession et sans fortune, ou lorsque son salaire est trop bas pour assurer sa subsistance et celle de ses enfants, les répercussions de cette évolution et de l'insuffisance actuelle des moyens de protection des 'familles à parent seul' est particulièrement grave. C'est pour elle que se pose de la manière la plus aiguë la question du 'maintien des revenus', doublée de problèmes connexes tels que le logement, le travail et la garde des enfants[196]. On ne saurait donc omettre d'énumérer rapidement les pistes de réforme à aménager dans ce secteur, au titre de moyens de protection à moyen et long terme.

(i) *Le recouvrement des pensions alimentaires et les avances sur prestation d'entretien*

Là où elle subsistent, les obligations alimentaires légales l'emportent généralement sur les lois d'assistance[197]. Le principe paraît sain. Les obligations d'entretien à charge des enfants et la pension après divorce rentrent dans ce cadre.

Il est cependant bien connu que le recouvrement de ces pensions ne se fait, dans la majorité des cas, que de manière irrégulière ou pas du tout[198]. C'est l'un des problèmes majeurs des femmes seules avec enfants à charge, et la sanction pénale de l'abandon de famille n'a qu'une valeur comminatoire très relative. Des lois telles que la loi française du 3 janvier 1972 sur le *recouvrement direct des pensions alimentaires*[199] ou du 11 juillet 1975, sur le *recouvrement par le Trésor public*[200] semblent remédier à cet état de choses de manière assez satisfaisante. Pour les cas résiduaires, on pourrait songer à créer un Office national des créances alimentaires, chargé d'avancer les fonds aux ayants droit et de les récupérer ensuite à charge du débiteur. Pareil système existe dans les pays scandinaves, mais il s'avère qu'en pratique les fonds avancés sont rarement récupérés[201]. Il est donc très coûteux pour la collectivité, à laquelle il finit par transférer les responsabilités individuelles. A moins d'opter pour ce transfert, le système français paraît donc préférable, au moins à titre principal[202]. Il n'a cependant pas été suivi jusqu'ici en Belgique, ou le paiement direct demeure lié à certaines créances alimentaires particulières[203] et où une proposition de loi récente tend au contraire à introduire un système généralisé de recouvrement des créances alimentaires par un Office national spécialisé[204].

(ii) Les prestations de sécurité sociale et les lois d'assistance

Les prestations de sécurité sociale constituent une garantie contre certains risque sociaux (maladie, invalidité, accidents de travail, chômage, vieillesse, décès) et un complément de moyens de subsistance dans certains autres cas (prestations familiales). Pour les "familles à parents seuls", elles sont un rempart essentiel[205].

Il saute aux yeux cependant que cette protection est beaucoup moins bien assurée pour la femme et les enfants dans un système de sécurité sociale à *base professionnelle* que dans un système à *base universaliste*. Dans la mesure en effet où les droits de la femme mariée qui n'exerce pas de profession dérivent, au titre de 'personne à charge' de l'assujettissement du mari, la couverture ainsi assurée dépend elle-même de la stabilité du lien conjugal[206]. Tel est le case en Belgique où la femme non active doit, en cas de divorce, recourir à l'assurance volontaire pour soins de santé, au titre de 'personne non encore protégée' ou cotiser pour continuer à s'assurer une pension de vieillesse. Il en va de même pour les allocations familiales, dans le cas, par exemple, où la mère est sans profession et où le père s'abstient de travailler ou de payer une cotisation de travailleur indépendant[207].

D'autre part, il est certain que le divorce lui-même n'est pas, jusqu'à ce jour, considéré comme un risque social dont la charge devrait être assumée par la collectivité dans la majorité des pays continentaux[208].

A défaut d'autres ressources, seules les *prestations non contributives* fournies à titre résiduaire par les lois d'assistance permettent à l'heure actuelle de combler partiellement la perte de ressources liée au divorce. Mais elles ne concernent que les personnes véritablement indigentes et n'offrent que des subsides tout à fait insuffisants. Tel est le cas en Belgique de la *loi sur le minimum de moyens d'existence,* du 7 août 1974[209]. Seules des réformes profondes du système de sécurité sociale pourraient, semble-t-il, remédier partiellement à cet état de choses.

(iii) Politique de l'emploi, de la garde des enfants et du logement

Mais le meilleure garantie des moyens d'existence consiste certainement à permettre à la femme de trouver ou de retrouver un emploi le plus rapidement possible. Dans la mesure où cet emploi n'est pas un emploi de routine ou de seconde zone, c'est aussi le moyen de l'aider à recouvrer son équilibre et d'assurer le mieux-être matériel et psychologique des enfants, pour autant que le problème de leur garde soit correctement résolu.

La *réinsertion professionnelle* de la femme dans le monde du travail n'est cependant pas sans poser elle-même des problèmes parfois insolubles[210], lorsqu'en raison du nombre d'années d'interruption de carrière la femme a perdu toute qualification professionnelle, ou qu'elle n'en a jamais eu parce qu'elle s'est mariée et s'est entièrement consacrée à son ménage. De plus, en période de crise, c'est sur la une main-d'oeuvre féminine que se répercute d'abord le chômage[211]. Enfin, même en cas d'emploi, il est connu que les salaires féminins demeurent, inexplicablement, inférieurs aux salaires masculins pour un travail égal, nonobstant les lois et conventions prévoyant l'égalité des rémunérations[212]. Les obstacles à ce niveau semblent se situer plus encore dans les faits que dans les lois.

La loi cependant peut apporter un secours précieux dans la mesure, par exemple, où elle subordonne la cessation d'une pension alimentaire après divorce à la réinsertion effective de la femme dans un emploi compatible avec sa qualification et avec sa condition sociale antérieure. La *loi allemande du 14 juin 1976* constitue un modèle en ce genre[213]. De plus il faut signaler que la politique sociale des Etats peut avoir un impact considérable en cette matière[214]. Celle de la République fédérale d'Allemagne paraît particulièrement intéressante par le programme de formation de base, de perfectionnement et de recyclage qu'elle a introduit dans la loi de 1969 sur la promotion de l'emploi, l'organisation spéciale des cours et horaires, et les allocations d'encouragement qu'elle fournit.[215]. Une politique du même type est pratiquée en Suède et au Danemark. On ne saurait en dire autant en Belgique, où la *loi sur les 'crédits d'heure'* destinée au perfectionnement professionnel n'est ouverte qu'aux travailleurs en activité[216], et où les lois relatives au chômage cessent de s'appliquer après un arrêt de travail de plus de trois ans postérieurement à la naissance du dernier enfant[217]. Corollairement les cycles de formation professionnelle organisés par l'Office national de l'Emploi ne sont pas accessibles aux non-chômeurs[218]. Toute la politique de la réinsertion professionnelle de la femme ménagère dans le marché de l'emploi reste donc à faire.

Parallèlement, il faut évoquer encore les difficultés rencontrées en matière de garde des enfants et du logement[219]. Que les femmes soient seules ou non, le problème de la *garde des enfants* est à l'heure actuelle un problème majeur pour toutes celles qui exercent une activité professionnelle. Même dans les pays qui pratiqueent une politique active dans ce secteur, les équipements collectifs sont insuffisants, et insuffisamment diversifiés[220]. Il n'en va pas autrement en Belgique ou l'équipement en crèches et prégardiennats est nettement insuffisant[221]. Une formule intéressante est le gardiennant familial. En Belgique il est supervisé par l'Oeuvre nationale de l'Enfance pour les enfants de moins de 7 ans.

Quant au *logement,* il pose des problèmes ardus, surtout dans les pays où règne encore une crise du logement[222]. Mais même là où ils sont suffisants, comme en Belgique, les loyers sont élevés. La création de logements sociaux, spécialement équipés, est une solution à développer, de même que l'attribution d'allocations-logement. La politique belge en matière de logement social paraît très peu cohérente[223]. L'intérêt de pouvior se faire attribuer préférentiellement la résidence conjugale aprés divorce parâit d'autant plus évident. Le code civil belge contient encore une lacune sur ce point.

Il est clair çependant que, de tous les modes d'action qui viennent d'être énumérés, bien peu peuvent être considérés comme de véritables remèdes, au sens préventif ou curatif du terme, et que les vrais remèdes ne se trouvent pas dans la loi. C'est aux *causes* de la violence elle-même qu'il faut s'attaquer.

Indépendamment des troubles psycho-pathologiques ou autres, auxquels la médecine peut éventuellement remédier, la violence est un mal culturel, né d'une longue tradition et renforcé de manière insidieuse par les conditions de vie des sociétés post-industrielles, dites sociétés de bien-être. Car il serait faux de croire que la violence est le seul fruit de la misère. Ses véritables causes plongent leurs racines dans la frustration permanente d'individus enfermés dans une civilisation uniquement axée sur la consommation et la compétition, l'inhumanité d'une foule solitaire, la violence distillée de jour et de nuit dans et par les mass-media, l'illusion tragique d'une libération sexuelle délibérément asservie à des fins politiques ou commerciales, et la quête insatiable d'un bonheur de plus en plus insaisissable.

Le projet de résolution du Conseil de l'Europe du 9 novembre 1976, relatif à la protection des enfants contre les mauvais traitements, invite les Etats membres, "à combattre les attitudes culturelles génératrices de violences, sous une forme ou sous une autre". Peut-être devrions-nous aussi tourner nos regard de ce côté, et conclure en disant que le seul véritable remède à la violence se trouve, sans doute, dans le long et patient apprentissage de la tendresse et de la chaleur humaine.

RÉFERENCES

1. Sauf en ce qui concerne les homicides. *Cf.* Select Committee, Minutes of Evidence, 1974-1975, Evidence taken from the Home Office, 248-xiii, sp. p. 408 in fine.
2. *Cf.* Report from the Select Committee on Violence in Marriage, H.C. 553-i sp. p. Vi et Minutes of Evidence, H.C. 553-ii, 1974-1975.
3. L'enquête a porté sur un échantillon de 500 dossiers prélevés sur le nombre total de dossiers ouverts en 1975 au Parquet de Bruxelles sous la rubrique "Coups et blessures volontaires" (+ 6000 dossiers). Ces dossiers ont été prélevés sur 9 communes bruxelloises représentant des types de population allant des quartiers à population essentiellement ouvrière et étrangère (nord-africains) aux quartiers résidentiels. 155 dossiers sur 500 (soit 35%) concernaient des plaintes pour coups et blessures entre époux (plus rarement, concubins). Par extrapolation, on pourrait considérer qu'il y a eu, pour l'année 1975, près de 1800 dossiers ouverts pour coups et blessures entre époux dans le ressort du tribunal de Bruxelles. Compte tenu du fait que les plaintes en ce domaine sont nettement plus rares que pour les autres infractions, on peut supposer que le "chiffre noir" est en réalité beaucoup plus élevé et que ces 35% ne représentent qu'une fraction de la réalité. Ce pourcentage est relativement plus élevé que celui qui a été évalué en Angleterre (25 à 30% des plaintes) par certains experts des corps de police consultés par le Select Committee on Violence in Marriage (Minutes of Evidence, 1974-1975, sp. p. 366-367).
4. V. *infra,* note 19.

5. Il suffirait d'ajouter un indice spécial aux dossiers concernant des affaires de violences entre époux (ou membres d'une entité familiale), par exemple.

6. Voy. par exemple le *droit coutumier de Bruges* (XIVe s.): "le mari peut battre et blesser sa femme, la taillader de bas en haut et se chauffer les pieds dans son sang, il ne commet pas d'infraction s'il la recoud et qu'elle survit", cité dans la préface de l'ouvrage Pizzey, Erin,: *Crie moins fort, les voisins vont t'entendre*; v. aussi Chauveau-Helie, *Théorie du Code pénal*, 1892, chap. XLV, Des coups et blessures volontaires, sp. no. 2584.

7. V. Bromley, *Family Law*, 5th ed., p. 109.

8. En *Belgique*, la *puissance maritale* (autorité sur la personne de la femme) a été abrogée par la loi du 30 avril 1958 en même temps que l'incapacité de la femme mariée. La première étape avait été marquée par la loi du 20 juillet 1932. *Cf.* à ce sujet, De Page, Traité élémentaire de droit belge, 1962, t. I, no. 709; Baeteman, G. et Lauwers, J.P., *Droits et devoirs des époux*, Bruxelles, Bruylant, 1960. En *France*, les lois du 18 février 1938 et du 22 septembre 1942 ont supprimé le devoir d'obéissance de la femme et la notion de puissance maritale, Celle-ci ne comportait cependant plus, dans le régime du Code Napoléon, le droit du mari de *châtier* sa femme Marty V., et Raynaud, *Droit civil*, 1976, Les personnes, no. 199; Baeteman et Lauwers, *op. cit.*, no. 18.

9. Dans l'enquête effectuée à Bruxelles, la situation économique des couples concernés était la suivante: 2, 3% manquaient du nécessaire — 38% vivaient modestement — 51,7% vivaient dans l'aisance — 8% dans le luxe. Les mauvaises conditions économiques, de logement ou de travail ou le chômage, n'apparaissent donc pas comme des facteurs déterminants de la violence familiale en Belgique. Quant à la typologie des violences exercées, il semble que les sévices soient plus raffinés, mais non moins cruels dans les couches les plus élevées de la sociétés.

10. Dans notre enquête la plainte était déposée: dans 71,5% des cas contre l'homme, dans 7,1% des cas contre la femme et dans 21, 4% réciproquement.

11. V. note précédente. D'autre part, sauf lorsqu'elle attaque avec une arme (cas rare), les voies de fait exercées par la femme sont généralement plus bénignes (gifles, morsures, par ex.). En revanche, il est impossible de se faire une idée exacte des *violences verbales* ou autres formes de *cruauté morale* qui peuvent avoir provoqué l'agression physique brutale de l'homme.

12. Comp. Select Committee, Minutes of Evidence, 1974-1975, Evidence taken from Police Organizations, sp. p. 368 et 377; Gelles, R., *Abused wives: Why Do They Stay?*, Doc. ronéotypé, 1975.

13. Dans notre enquête, les sévices pour lesquels la plainte avait été déposée se répartissaient comme suit: 96,8% coups et blessures volontaires, 1,3% sévices sexuels et 1,9% séquestration.

14. Dans les dossiers étudiés des violences morales accompagnant les violences physiques étaient dénoncées dans un cas sur quatre (25,7% des cas au total, soit: 10,6% injures verbales, 8,8% menaces contre les biens ou la personne, avec ou sans conditions et 6,2% menaces de mort). On peut estimer que ces chiffres ne correspondent pas à la réalité, les violences physiques s'accompagnant généralement d'injures et de violences verbales.

15. Parmi les violences physiques relevées: — 44,3% concernaient des voies de fait relativement légères (gifles) —32,2% des brutalités plus graves (coups de pieds ou de poings) — 19,3% des sévices graves ou très graves (avec ou sans arme) ou répétés.

16. *Cf.* Select Committee, Minutes of Evidence, 1974-1975, Evidence taken from Police Organizations, sp. p. 366.

17. Comp. Select Committee, Minutes of Evidence taken from Police Organizations, 1974-1975, p. 366 et 369. Des réponses analogues nous ont été fournies par différents Départements de la Justice et par des magistrats. La crainte de compromettre définitivement la cohésion du groupe familial semble prépondérante. Voy. aussi Parnas, R.I., "Police Discretion and Diversion of Incidents of Intrafamily Violence" (1971) *Law and Contemporary Problems* 539 et s., sp. p. 542.

18. Réponses fournies notamment par le Département de la Justice des *Pays-Bas, d'Italie,* d'*Allemagne fédérale* et de *France.* En *Belgique* aucune modification n'est envisagée pour le moment. En *Suisse,* la Commission d'experts pour la révision du Code pénal propose simplement d'élargir l'actuel article 134 C. pén. suisse (mauvais traitements et négligences envers les enfants) à la protection des *faibles* en général. Voy. notamment: *art. 123 de l'avant-projet de révision du Code pénal.* "1. Celui qui intentionnellement, aura fait subir à une personne une (autre) atteinte à l'intégrité corporelle ou à la santé, sera, sur plainte, puni de l'emprisonnement. 2. La peine sera l'emprisonnement et la poursuite aura lieu d'*office* . . . si le délinquant s'en est prix à une personne qui était hors d'état de se défendre, ou *dont il avait la garde,* ou sur laquelle il avait le *devoir de* veiller". La question est de savoir si le devoir de secours et d'assistance entre époux permettrait de faire rentrer ceux-ci dans cette dernière catégorie . . . L'*article 126 al. 2 de l'avant-projet* prévoit également la poursuite d'office de celui qui se sera livré à "des voies de fait n'entraînant ni lésion corporelles ni atteinte à la santé", "de manière réitérée sur une personne dont il avait la garde ou sur laquelle il avait le devoir de veiller".

19. Aux termes de l'*article 413 du Code pénal autrichien,* le droit de correction domestiqué ("hausliche Zucht"), ne permettait pas d'user de mauvais traitements susceptibles d'entraîner des lésions corporelles. Cet article s'étendait explicitement aux mauvais traitements infligés par l'un des époux à l'autre. En cas de violation de l'art. 413, l'art. 419 prévoyait comme sanction un blâme sévère, ou le cas échéant une arrestation d'une semaine à 3 mois, susceptible d'être aggravée en cas de récidive. En 1973, les statistiques criminelles autrichiennes révèlent 1199 condamnations pour mauvais traitements entre époux, dont 1072 contre un homme et 127 contre une femme (en 1974: 1145 condamnations dont 1016 contre un homme et 129 contre une femme). Les *articles 92 et 93 du nouveau C. pén. autrichien,* en vigueur depuis le 1er janvier 1975, ne sanctionnement plus que les mauvais traitements (physiques ou moraux, négligences ou sévices) infligés aux enfants de moins de 18 ans ou aux personnes *faibles* et *sans défense* (malades, etc. .)

20. Nypels et Servais, *Code pénal interpréte,* Bruxelles, 1899, t. III, art. 398 et s.; Pandectes belges, Vo. Coups et blessures; *Répert. prat. dr. belge,* t. III, Vo. Coups et blessures; Marchal et Jaspar, *Droit criminel, Traité théorique et pratique,* t. I, 1975, p. 434 et s.

21. Chauveau et Helie, *Théorie du Code pénal,* Ed. belge, 1892, chap. XVI, Des coups et blessures volontaires; Garçon, Traité de Droit pénal, *Encyclopédie Dalloz,* Répertoire de droit criminel et mise à jour, Vo. Coups et blessures; *Jurisclasseur pénal,* vol. II, Vo. Blessures et coups volontaires non qualifiés de meurtres, art. 309 à 312; Lambert, L., *Traité de droit pénal spécial,* Paris, Ed. Police-Revue, 1968 et mise à jour 1971, p. 92-149.

22. On distingue les *coups et blessures simples* des *coups et blessures* avec *circonstances aggravantes, objectives* (liées à la gravité du résultat) ou *subjectives* (liées à la préméditation ou à la qualité de l'agent). On entend par "coups" les violences physiques qui ne laissent pas de traces, par opposition aux "blessures". Il est admis en jurisprudence qu'*un seul coup suffit* pour constituer l'élément matériel de l'infraction (Cass. 7 janvier 1957, Pas. 1957, I, 497; Marchal et Jaspar, 1975, t. I, no. 1174; R.P.D.B., Vo. cité, no. 16 et 17). En ce qui concerne l'échelle des peines, correctionnelles ou criminelles correspondant à ces différentes infractions, voy. les art. 398 à 405 et 410 à 415 du Code pénal belge.

23. Ou tout autre personne ayant autorité sur l'enfant ou en ayant la garde.

24. Mais le *droit de correction,* attribut de l'autorité parentale, exclut cette incrimination pour les châtiments corporels modérés infligés sans méchanceté et sans excès, par les parents à leurs enfants mineurs (*Rép. prat. dr. belge,* Vo. Coups et blessures, no. 21; Marchal et Jaspar, *op. cit.,* no. 1176). Cette distinction n'a jamais été applicable aux époux, même à l'époque où existait la puissance maritale (Chauveau et Helie, *op. cit.,* no. 2584-2585; Cass. fr. 9 avril 1825, Sir. 1826, 1, 254; 7 mai 1851, Dall. 1852, 5, 564). Pour la *France,* voy. l'art. 312 C. pén. fr.

25. L'article 410 al. 2 C. pén. étend cette circonstance aggravante aux coups et blessures

infligés à une *personne de n'importe quel âge dont l'état physique ou mental ne lui permet pas de subvenir elle-même à son entretien,* par ses père et mère légitimes, naturels ou adoptifs ou tout autre personne ayant autorité sur l'*incapable* ou en *ayant la garde.*

26. *Rép. prat. dr. belge,* Vo. Coups et blessures, no. 77-78; *Les Novelles,* Droit pénal, t. I, vol. 1, no. 2997-3002. En *France,* cette cause d'excuse atténuante au meurtre du conjoint trouvé en flagrant délit d'adultère (art. 324 al. 2 C. pén.) a été abrogée en même temps que l'incrimination de l'adultère lui-même par la loi no. 75-617 du 11 juillet 1975.

27. *Rép. prat. dr. belge,* Vo. Coups et blessures, no. 67-74, Les *Novelles,* Droit pénal, t. I, vol. 1, no. 2973-2985. En *Belgique,* il est admis que l'excuse de provocation tirée des "violences graves" exercées envers les personnes peut résulter de violences *physiques* aussi bien que *morales* (R.P.D.B., Vo. cité, no. 68; *Les Novelles, op. cit.,* no. 2974-2975) Des outrages par paroles, actes ou gestes, ou des menaces verbales *graves,* peuvent donc servir de cause d'excuse à des coups et blessures ou à un homicide. En *France,* seules les violences *physiques* semblent être admises comme excuse de provocation (art. 321 C. pen. fr.; Lambert, L., *op. cit.,* p. 138-145, sp. p. 140; Cass. 9 février 1923, D.P., 1924, 1, 114, considérant comme illégale l'excuse admise à propos des voies de fait commises par un mari sur la personne de sa femme en réponse à des injures verbales de celle-ci).

28. En *France,* l'excuse de provocation par violences n'est pas applicable au meurtre entre époux (art. 324 C. pén.), mais elle peut l'être aux coups et blessures volontaires au conjoint, ou même à un ascendant (Lambert, L. *op. cit.,* p. 144-145).

29. *Cf.* pour la *Belgique, Rép. prat. dr. belge,* t. Ier et complément t. I, Vo. Attentat à la pudeur et viol, sp. no. 37-38; Rigaux et Trousse, *Crimes et délits du Code pénal,* Bruxelles, Bruylant, 1968, t. V, art. 375-378 C. pén., sp. p. 333; Biltris, "L'attentat à la pudeur et le viol. (1925) *Rev. dr. pén.* 1002-1046 et 1161-1199, sp. no. 54 et s. En *France, Jurisclasseur pénal,* t. II, V Attentats aux moeurs, no. 105; Garraud, *Traité théorique et pratique de droit pénal français,* t. V, 2084; Garçon, Code pénal annoté, art. 331 à 333, no. 21 et s.

30. Alger, 28 avril 1887, Sir. 1888, 2, 114; Chauveau et Helie, *Théorie du Code pénal,* no. 2819-2821; Nypels et Servais, *Code pénal interprété,* t. II, art. 373, no. 5, p. 489. En *Allemagne* et en *Suisse,* l'acte de violence par lequel un mari contraint sa femme à avoir des relations avec lui n'est pas constitutif de viol, mais l'auteur peut être puni du chef de *contrainte* (voy. notamment art. 181 C. pén. suisse). La Commission d'experts pour la révision du Code pénal suisse suggère de modifier l'art. 187 C. pénal et d'étendre la répression, *sur plainte,* au viol entre époux, ceci essentiellement pour tenir compte de la situation d'époux séparés, mais non encore divorcés.

31. Voy. Bienen, L., "Rape II" (1977) *Women's Rights Law Reporter* 90 et s.

32. Cass. fr. 21 novembre 1839, Sir. 1839, 1, 817; Cass. fr., 18 mai 1854, D.P. 1854, 1, 262; Cass. belge, 20 janvier 1975 (1974-1975) *Rev. dr. pén.* 555-556; Chauveau et Helie, Théorie du Code pénal, éd. belge. no. 2819-2821; Nypels et Servais, t. II, Code pénal interprété, art. 373, no . 5, p. 489; Rigaux et Trousse, Crimes et délits du Code pénal, t. V, art. 372 à 374 et 376 à 378, sp. p. 297; *Rép. prat. dr. belge,* V Attentat à la pudeur et viol, no. 14; *Jurisclasseur pénal,* t. II, Vo. Attentats aux moeurs, no. 135.

33. En ce qui concerne les *menaces,* voy. art. 327 à 331 C. pénal belge, art. 305 à 308 C. pénal français; Rigaux et Trousse, *Crimes et délits du Code pénal,* t. V, art. 327 à 331, p. 25 et s., sp. p. 32-36; *Rép. prat. dr. belge,* Vo. Menaces; Lambert, L., *Traité de droit pénal spécial,* p. 157 et s., sp. p. 159-160. En outre, en *Belgique,* seule la menace d'un fait criminel (et non délictuel, par exemple des coups et blessures) peut constituer un délit. En *France,* la menace de coups et blessures, assortie d'ordre ou de condition est incriminée par l'art. 308 C. pénal.

34. En *Suisse,* il semble que certains règlements de police cantonaux ou communaux permettent à la femme *menacée* par son mari, d'obtenir une *carte de protection* lui donnant la possibilité de recevoir un secours rapide de la police. Cette pratique pourrait être intéressante à développer.

35. Voy. notamment Eisenberg, S.E., et Micklow, P., "The Assaulted Wife: 'Catch 22'

Revisited" (1977) *Women's Rights Law Reporter* 138 et s.; Steinmetz, S., et Straus, M., *Violence in the Family,* New York, New York: Dodd, Mead and Co., 1974; Parnas, R.I., "The Police Response to the Domestic Disturbance" (1967) *Wisconsin Law Review* 914-960; Parnas, R.I., "Police Discretion and Diversion of Incidents of Intrafamily Violence" (1971) *Law and Contemporary Problems* 539.

36. Select Committee, Minutes of Evidence, Evidence taken from Police Organizations, p. 361-391.

37. Dans 82% des cas, la plainte émanait de la femme, 8% de l'homme, 4,5% des deux époux. Dans 5% des cas environ, la dénonciation provenait d'un tiers (voisin, membre de la famille, médecin, enfant).

38. Dans 96,8% des cas la plainte avait été déposée directement au Commissariat de police ou à la brigade de gendarmerie. Dans 3,2% des cas seulement elle avait été adressée directement au Parquet.

39. Hoeffler, J., *Traité de l'instruction préparatoire en matière pénale,* Courtrai, U.G.A., 1956, no. 51-52. Chaque commune de 5.000 habitants dispose d'une *police communale.* Celle-ci exerce à la fois des fonctions de *police administrative* (maintien de l'ordre), prévention des infractions (police préventive), sous l'autorité du bourgmestre, et des missions de *police judiciaire* (recherche et constatation des infractions, recherche et constatation des preuves et des auteurs des infractions (police répressive) — art. 8 du Code d'instr. criminelle) sous l'autorité du commissaire de police, lui-même auxiliaire du Procureur du Roi. Les polices communales comptent environ 14.000 membres en Belgique, et n'ont en général compétence que sur le territoire de leur propre commune.

40. Hoeffler, J., *op. cit.,* no. 45-50. La *police judiciaire des Parquets,* créée par la *loi du 7 avril 1913,* est rattachée à chaque Parquet et dirigée par le Procureur du Roi, sous le contrôle des Procureurs généraux. Uniquement chargée de missions de police judiciaire, elle est spécialisée dans les affaires criminelles complexes qui exigent des investigations sur l'étendue de tout le territoire belge. Elle compte environ 1.000 membres, officiers judiciaires ou agents judiciaires, répartis en sections spécialisées, y compris des membres féminins depuis 1948. Depuis la *loi du 21 août 1948,* complétant l'article 8 de la loi du 7 avril 1913, il existe des officiers et agents de police judiciaire *féminins* auprès des Parquets, spécialement chargés, outre leurs attributions générales, de la recherches des infractions contraires aux moeurs, dont des femmes ou des enfants sont victimes ou témoins.

41. Hoeffler, J., *op. cit.,* no. 53. Force armée, la gendarmerie dépend à la fois du *Ministre de la Défense nationale* (pour son organisation), du *Ministre de l'Intérieur,* pour ses missions de *police administrative* (maintien de l'ordre public) et du *Ministre de la Justice,* par l'intermédiaire des procureurs généraux, pour l'exercice de missions de *police judiciaire* (recherche et constatation des crimes et délits et arrestation de leurs auteurs) et de la police des étrangers (loi du 2 décembre 1957 sur la gendarmerie). Compétente sur l'ensemble du territoire, elle comprenait en 1977 environ 18.600 membres.

42. En ce qui concerne l'organisation et les fonctions de la police judiciaire en *Belgique,* voy. notamment Braas, *Précis d'Instruction Criminelle et de Procédure pénale,* Bruxelles, Bruylant, 1950, t. I, no. 321-383; Caron, La police judiciaire, Les Novelles, Procédure pénale, t. I, vol. 1, Larcier, 1946; Hoeffler, J., *op. cit.,* no. 44-61 et 65-94. Pour la *France,* Stefani, G., et Levasseur, G., Précis Dalloz, Droit pénal général et procédure pénale, 1970, p. 205 et s.; *Jurisclasseur de procédure pénale,* tome I, Police judiciaire.

43. Art. 32, 36, 46 du Code d'instr. criminelle et loi du 7 juin 1969. Braas, *op. cit.,* no. 380-383; Hoeffler, J., *op. cit.,* no. 235-250.

44. Voy. aussi la loi du *7 juin 1969* sur les perquisitions et visites domiciliaires; Wailliez, G., "La loi du 7 juin 1969 et les perquisition nocturnes." (1970) *Journ. Trib.* 165-166.

45. En ce qui concerne le délit de violation de domicile commis par un agent de l'autorité (art. 148 C. pén.), voy. Marchal et Jaspar, *Droit criminel, Traité théorique et pratique,* 1975, t. I, no. 223 à 262.

46. Sur la distinction, qui ne se retrouve pas en droit anglais entre les fonctions et compétences respectives des *officiers* et *agents* de police judiciaire voy. Hoeffler, J., *op. cit.*, sp. no. 69-75, et, en ce qui concerne les perquisitions et visites domiciliaires, no. 235-250.

47. Selon l'article 41 du Code d'Instruction criminelle, il y a *délit flagrant* lorsque le délit *se commet actuellement* ou *vient de se commettre*; lorsque l'inculpé est *poursuivi par la clameur publique,* ou lorsqu'il est trouvé saisi d'effets, armes, instruments ou papiers faisant présumer qu'il est auteur ou complice, pourvu que ce soit dans un temps voisin du délit.

48. Depuis la loi du 30 avril 1958, chacun des époux a la qualité de "chef de la maison" dans la maison conjugale (Cass. 29 octobre 1962, Pas. 1963, 283).

49. Dans ce cas, et dans celui du consentement formel de l'habitant, les simples *agents* de police sont autorisés à pénétrer dans une habitation, sans la présence d'un officier de police judiciaire.

50. Le mandat de perquisition ne peut être délivré aux officiers de police judiciaire que par le *juge d'instruction* régulièrement saisi par réquisition du Procureur du Roi ou constitution de partie civile. Voy. Hoeffler, *op. cit.*, no. 242.

51. En ce qui concerne le délit d'omission de porter secours, voy. notamment Constant, J., "La répression des abstentions coupables — Loi du 6 janvier 1961" (1961-1962) *Rev. dr. pén.* 31 et. s.; Tillerkaerts, Commentaire de l'art. 422 bis du Code pénal, in L'officier de police, 1964, no. 5, 6 et 7.

52. Dans notre enquête, la police s'était rendue sur place dans 18, 7% des cas, ce qui correspond plus ou moins aux 15% d'appels enregistrés, plus les cas où la police a raccompagné à son domicile la femme venue se plaindre ou se réfugier au bureau de police.

53. Voy. art. 147, 155, 156, 157 du Code pénal sanctionnant les arrestations et détentions illégales et arbitraires; Marchal et Jaspar, *op. cit.,* t. I, 1975, p. 68 et s.; Braas, *op. cit.,* t. I, no. 513.

54. Braas, *op. cit.,* no. 514, 517 et 517 bis.

55. Cass. 21 octobre 1901, Pas 1902, I, 15; Cass. 23 janvier 1934, Pas. 1934, I, 142. Jurisprudence critiquée. En ce qui concerne le pouvoir d'arrestation et de garde à vue en France, voy. Stefani, G., et Levasseur, G., *op. cit.,* t. II, no. 265 et 266, 276 et 277.

56. Braas, *op. cit.,* no. 514 et 517.

57. *Loi du 20 avril 1874,* relative à la *détention préventive,* modifiée par la loi du *13 mars 1973.* Après l'interrogatoire, le juge d'instruction pourra décerner un mandat d'arrêt lorsque le fait est de nature à entraîner un emprisonnement correctionnel de 3 mois ou une peine plus grave, et seulement dans des circonstances graves et exceptionnelles, si cette mesure est réclamée *dans l'intérêt de la sécurité publique,* lorsque l'inculpé à sa résidence en Belgique (art. 1). Ce mandat d'arrêt ne sera pas maintenu s'il n'est pas confirmé dans les 5 jours par la Chambre du conseil (art. 4). Celle-ci devra ensuite confirmer le maintien en détention de mois en mois, si elle n'a pas statué sur la prévention et seulement pour les mêmes motifs exceptionnels (art. 5).

58. Braas, *op. cit.,* no. 515.

59. 8, 3% des cas dans notre enquête.

60. L'incarcération pour "mépris de cour" nous paraît impensable en raison du caractère indéterminé de la peine et du risque d'arbitraire qu'elle comporte. Ce système, qui n'a pas pour but spécifique d'assurer la protection des familles en droit anglo-américain, ne semble du reste pas apporter aux femmes anglaises et américaines la sécurité qu'elles espèrent. Voy. Pizzey, E., *op. cit.*, sp. p. 181 et s.; Eisenberg, S., et Micklov, P., "The Assaulted Wife. 'Catch 22' Revisited" (1977) *Women's Rights Law Reporter* sp. 153-154.

61. Il n'existe pas non plus, en droit continental, de "peace bond" (engagement de garder la paix, éventuellement assorti de caution) utilisable en cas de *simples menaces.* Cette pratique para-légale utilisée dans certains Etats américains semble n'offrir d'intérêt que lorsqu'elle est elle-même assortie de possibilités de poursuites et de sanction. Voy. sur ce point, Bannon, J., "Law enforcement problems with Intrafamily Violence",

Communication présentée à l'American Bar Association Convention, Août 1975; Parnas, R., "Judicial Response to Intrafamily Violence" (1970) *Minn. L. Rev* 538 et s., sp. p. 600; Truninger, "Marital Violence: the Legal Solutions (1971) *Hastings L.J.* 259 et s., sp. p. 266; Eisenberg, S., et Micklov, P., *op. cit.,* sp. p. 150-151.

62. Art. 8 et 29 du Code d'Instr. criminelle belge. Les *officiers* de police judiciaire sont tenus de dresser *procès-verbal* chaque fois qu'ils constatent une infraction ou reçoivent une dénonciation ou une plainte, ou sur rapport des agents de police qui leur sont soumis, et de transmettre ce procès-verbal sur le champ au Procureur du Roi. Les *agents* de police peuvent seulement faire rapport à leurs supérieurs. Les procès-verbaux dressés ainsi par les officiers de police valent à titre de simples renseignements. Très souvent ils sont accompagnés d'un *bulletin de renseignements* complémentaire dressé après enquête préalable faite à l'initiative de la police elle-même sur la famille et le milieu concerné.

63. Art. 29 du Code d'Instr. criminelle. Pour une comparaison de la procédure pénale continentale et de la procédure pénale anglaise, voy. Hoeffler, J., *op. cit.*, p. 7-11; Hoeffler, J., *Notions sommaires de procédure anglo-saxonne,* Larcier, 1952; Les *Novelles,* Procédure pénale, t. II, p. 387 et s.

64. Sur le devoir d'information de la police judiciaire, voy. Hoeffler, J., *Traité,* p. 99 et s.

65. Sur le droit d'information de la police judiciaire en Belgique, voy. Hoeffler, J., *Traité,* p. 89 et s.

66. Voy. dans le même sens, Select Committee, Minutes of Evidence, Session 1974-1975, Evidence taken from Police Organizations, p. 363 et 376-377.

67. Voy. Bannon, J., *op. cit.*, note 61; Bard, M., "Family Intervention Police Teams as a Community Mental Health Resource" (1969b) *J. of Crim. Law, Criminology and Police Science* 247-250; Bard, M., *Training Police as Specialists in Family Crisis Intervention: Final Report,* Washington D.C.: U.S. Government Printing Office, 1970a; Select Committee, Report, 1974-1975, H.C. 553-i, sp. p. xvii. A l'heure actuelle cette formation semble insuffisante, sinon inexistante, en Belgique comme en de nombreux pays qui n'ont pas encore été sensibilisés au problème. La gendarmerie reçoit une formation militaire. En ce qui concerne les polices communales, la formation et le recrutement varient de commune à commune. Il n'existe pas d'Ecole de Police nationale.

68. Il en existe déjà dans les polices communales de certaines grandes agglomérations. Le diplôme d'assistant social est exigé pour les assistant (e)s de police (Circ. Min. Intérieur du 1er avril 1974). D'autre part, la loi de protection de la Jeunesse du 8 avril 1965 a créé des Unités de Police de la Jeunesse auprès des Parquets de chaque arrondissement. D'une manière générale le nombre des effectifs est insuffisant.

69. Des membres féminins existent actuellement dans la Police des Parquets (depuis 1948), la gendarmerie (depuis 1975), certaines polices de la Jeunesse. Mais leurs attributions sont souvent différentes de la police familiale et leur nombre est minoritaire.

70. La centralisation nationale pourrait être envisagée au niveau du *Ministère de la Santé publique.* Tous les médecins et services médicaux et sociaux devraient également y faire converger les informations dont ils disposent, tout en respectant le secret professionnel.

71. Select Committee, Minutes of Evidence taken from the Police Organizations, p. 375-377; Report from the Select Committee, 1974-1975, H.C. 553-ii, p. XVii.

72. Pour la *Belgique,* Rép. prat. dr. belge, Vo. Action publique, no. 7 et s.; Vo. Ministère public, no. 351 et s. Pour la *France,* Pradel, J., Droit pénal, t. II, Procédure pénale, Paris, Cujas, 1976, sp. p. 8, 115-116, 281 et s.; Soyer, J. Cl., *Droit pénal et procédure pénale,* Paris, L.G.D.J., 1976, p. 228-229; Stefani et Levasseur, *op. cit.,* t. II, Procédure pénale, no. 106 et s., 402 et s.; Jurisclasseur Procédure pénale, T. I., art. 39 à 44 C.P.P.; Vo. Procureur de la République, no. 54 et s.

73. Voy. Glesener, A., "Le classement sans suite et l'opportunité des poursuites", (1972-1973) *Rev. dr. pen.* 353-362; De Nauw, A., "La décision de poursuivre. Instruments et mesures" (1976-1977) *Rev. dr. pén.* 449; Rolland, M., Le Ministère public, agent non

seulement de répression mais de prévention (1957) J.C.P. 1342; *Jurisclasseur Procédure pénale*, art. 39-44; Vo." Procureur de la République", no. 56-64; Pradel, J., *op. cit.*, p. 281 et s.

74. Il s'agirait d'un principe de droit coutumier l'emportant sur celui de la légalité des poursuites. Glesener, A., *op. cit.*, p. 354.

75. Glesener, A., *op. cit.*, p. 353.

76. Indépendamment de ce fait, la plupart des médecins, selon les renseignements qui nous ont été fournis, ne semblent pas prendre véritablement au sérieux les cas de sévices entre époux et n'en avertissent pratiquement jamais la police (0, 8%) des cas dans notre enquête, bien qu'ils puissent le faire pour protéger leur patient(e) (voy. notamment l'art. 20 de l'A.R. du 31 mai 1885) et que le secret médical puisse être levé par le patient lui-même. Sur le secret médical en Belgique, voy. Rijckmans, X., et Meert-van de Put, R., *Les droits et les obligations des médecins*, Bruxelles, Larcier, 1972, t. I, no. 161 et s.; Marechal, A., "Le secret professionnel médical" (1955-56) *Rev. dr. pén.*, 59 et s., spéc. p. 77-78; Legros R., "Considérations sur le secret médical" 1957-58 *Rev. dr. pén* 859 et s.; R.P.D.B., Vo. Secret professionnel. Comparer, en *France*, la rédaction de l'art. *378 C. pén.* notamment en ce qui concerne l'obligation ou la faculté de dénoncer certaines infractions.

77. Trousse, P.E., Les sanctions pénales du droit de la famille in *Famille, Droit et changement social dans les sociétés contemporaines*, Actes des VIIIes Journées d'Etudes juridiques Jean Dabin, Bruxelles, Bruylant, 1978.

78. En *France* l'adultère a été dépénalisé par la loi du 11 juillet 1975 portant réforme du divorce. Il en va de même au *Grand-Duché de Luxembourg* (loi du 11 novembre 1974). En *Belgique*, la loi du 28 octobre 1974 a maintenu la pénalisation de l'adultère tout en l'adaptant au principe d'égalité des époux, uniquement en vue de faciliter le divorce. Voy. Spreutels, J.P., "Les récentes modifications législatives en matière d'adultère en Belgique et au Grand-Duché de Luxembourg" (1974-1975) *Rev. dr. pén.* 796; Vilain, F., "Vers une dépénalisation de l'adultère", (1974-1975) *Rev. dr. pén.* 390.

79. Dans le cadre de son pouvoir général d'information, pour autant qu'il ne soit pas fait usage de la contrainte. Voy. Hoeffler, J., *op. cit.*, p. 89 et s. Voy. aussi art. 2 de la loi du 29 juin 1964 sur la suspension, le sursis et la probation.

80. Charles, R., Réflexions sur dix ans de probation prétorienne, (1961) *Journ. trib.*, 457 et s.; Charles, R., La loi du 29 juin 1964 concernant la suspension, le sursis et la probation 1964 *Ann. Droit et Sc. Pol.*, 196 et s., sp. p. 230 et s.

81. La probation légale peut désormais accompagner soit la *suspension du prononcé de la condamnation* par les juridictions d'instruction ou de jugement (art. 3 à 7 de la loi), soit la *condamnation avec sursis* à l'exécution des peines (art. 8). Sur les modalités de la probation, voy. art. 9 et s. de la loi et sur son application, Dautricourt, J.Y., "Le rôle de la probation dans le traitement des délinquants en Belgique" (1969-1970) *Rev. dr. pén.* 521 et s.; Dautricourt, J. Y., "Le traitement probatoire" (1971-1972) *Rev. dr. pén.* 3 et s.; Dautricourt, J. Y., "Le rôle de la défense dans l'application de la loi du 29 juin 1964, concernant la suspension, le sursis et la probation" (1966) *Journ. Trib.* 217-224; Versele, S.C., "L'intégration de la probation dans le monde judiciaire belge" (1969), *Rev. Inst. Sociologie U.L.B.* 611-654; Somers-Demanck J., et Versele, S.C., "Contribution à la recherche des facteurs de réussite et d'échec en matière de probation", (1969-1970) *Rev. dr. pén.* 575-611; R.P.D.B., Complément t. III, Vo. Suspension, sursis, probation.

82. Charles, R., *op. cit.*, (1964) *Ann. Dr. et Sc. Pol.*, sp. p. 231 et les travaux parlementaires cités.

83. On a essentiellement reproché à la probation prétorienne le risque de discrimination découlant du préjugé favorable accordé aux possibilités éducatives de certains milieux économiquement plus favorisés, et le manque de moyens effectifs d'assurer un accompagnement valable du probationnaire. Voy. notamment Somers-Demanck, J., et Versele, S.C., *op. cit.*, p. 581, note 8. En revanche, la probation prétorienne est plus discrète et plus souple que la probation légale. Voy. Charles, R., *op. cit.* (1964) *Ann. Dr. et Sc. Pol.*, sp. p. 232 et 233.

84. Notamment lorsque le cas ne paraît pas suffisamment grave.

85. Voy. The Select Committee Report, H.C. 553-i, p. viii et ix, et le cycle de la violence décrit par Pizzey, E., *op. cit.,* chap. 4.

86. Remplaçant les dispositions de la loi du 9 avril 1930, Voy. au sujet de cette loi, Mathijs, J., "La loi de défense sociale à l'égard des anormaux. Evolution des conceptions" (1964-1965) *Rev. dr. pén.* 399-495 et la bibliographie; Fettweis, A., et Van Den Boncke, J., "L'évolution récente de la législation belge de défense sociale" (1967-1968) *Rev. dr. pen.* 133-144; Constant, J., "Traité élémentaire de droit pénal", t. I, no 319-444.

87. Voy. à propos de cette loi les références citées *supra,* note 81.

88. Art. 30, 31, 32 et 33 de la loi du 8 avril 1965. Les Comités de protection de la jeunesse, dans le cadre de leur action sociale préventive, pourraient éventuellement obtenir des parents qu'ils se soumettent à un traitement médico-psychologique ou à une cure de désintoxication, mais uniquement avec leur accord (art. 2). Voy. Piret, J.M., "Les mesures à l'égard des parents" (1966) *Ann. Dr.* numéro spécial sur la protection de la jeunesse, p. 141 et s.; Verboven, E., et Piret, J.M., "Les mesures prévues à l'égard des parents" (1971) *Ann. Dr.,* premier bilan de la loi du 8 avril 1965, p. 89 et s.

89. Eventuellement un régime de semi-liberté (art. 15 de la loi).

90. Voy. Charles, R., *op. cit.,* (1964) *Ann. Dr. et Sc. Pol.,* sp. p. 206-207.

91. Dautricourt, J.Y., *op. cit.* (1969-1970) *Rev. dr. pén.,* sp. p. 551-552.

92. Sept assistants de probation seulement pour tout l'arrondissement de Bruxelles, c'est-à-dire, le plus important du Royaume. Sur les lacunes du cadre et de l'équipement de la probation, voy. Dautricourt, J.Y., *op. cit.* (1969-1970) *Rev. dr. pén.; op. cit.,* sp. p. 558 et s.

93. L'*enquête sociale* n'étant *pas obligatoire,* n'est pas suffisamment ordonnée (44% seulement des cas de probation, terminés à Bruxelles entre 1964 et 1969). Les examens *médico-psychologiques* encore moins (14% des cas). Voy. Versele, S.C., *op. cit.* (1969-1970) *Rev. dr. pén.,* sp. p. 586 et s. La probation elle-même n'est pas systématiquement exploitée là où elle pourrait l'être. Certains arrondissements l'ignorent totalement. Voy. Versele, S.C., *op. cit.* (1969) *Rev. Inst. Sociologie U.L.B.*

94. Sur les *"indications"* de la probation, voy. Dautricourt, J.Y., *op. cit.* (1969-1970) *Rev. dr. pén.,* sp. p. 548 et s.

95. En principe les juridictions d'*instruction* ne peuvent prononcer la *suspension probatoire* qu'à titre exceptionnel lorsqu'elles estiment que "la publicité des débats pourrait provoquer le déclassement de l'inculpé ou compromettre son reclassement" (art. 3, al. 2).

96. Voy. en ce qui concerne les expériences faites par les chambres françaises de Metz, Bordeaux, Lyon et Lille, Volff, J., La chambre de la famille de Metz, Gaz. Pal., 1973, 304; Aldebert, La chambre de la famille de Lyon en février 1972, C.F.R.E.S., Vaucresson; Allaer, C., et Martaguet, M., La pratique des juridictions familiales in Les juridictions familiales au service de l'enfant, Libr. Techniques, Paris, 1966; Allaer, C., "L'expérience lilloise" (1971) *Journ. Trib.* 194 et s.; Colloque du Centre de formation et de recherche de l'éducation surveillée, Vaucresson (1973) *Rev. Rééducation,* no. 255-260.

97. Notamment parce que ce justiciable accepte mal d'être toujours confronté au même juge, Voy. Poelman, F., "Une expérience française: la chambre de la famille" (1976) *Journ. Trib.* 1-7, sp. p. 2.

98. A la différence de la France où les Tribunaux pour enfants n'ont pas d'attributions en matière civile, le tribunal de la jeunesse belge regroupe pratiquement toutes les compétences en matière d'exercice de l'autorité parentale sauf durant l'instance en divorce. Voy. Kebers, A., "Les dispositions de droit civil relatives aux mineurs" (1966) *Ann. Dr.* 85 et s.

99. En *France,* l'expérience des chambres de la famille s'est effectuée de manière prétorienne. En conséquence, le problème des compétences en matière pénale semble s'être résolu non en modifiant les règles de compétence d'attribution, mais en désignant les magistrats des chambres de la famille pour siéger dans les chambres

correctionnelles dans les affaires pénales consécutives à des mesures ordonnées par eux. Ce qui est très différent et n'apporte en soi aucune modification à la procédure suivie en matière pénale. Voy. Poelman, F., *op. cit.* (1976) *Journ. Trib.*, sp. p. 2; Voy. aussi Solus et Perrot, Sirey, 1973, Droit judiciaire privé, t. II, La compétence, no. 29 et 30.

100. Voy. not. Aulagnon, L., "L'intervention du juge à propos de l'exercice du droit des époux" (1956) Mélanges Ripert, p. 39 et s.; Rouast, A., "Le juge et la vie familiale en droit français", in (1963) Mélanges Dabin, t. II, 865; Labrusse, C., "Les actions en justice intentées par un époux contre son conjoint" (1967) *Rev. int. dr. comp.* 431-456; Thery, R., "L'intérêt de la famille," (1972) J.C.P., 2485; Rigaux, F., Précis de Droit des personnes, t. I, Les relations familiales, Bruxelles, Larcier, 1970, sp. p. 118-119; Meulders-Klein, M.T., Famille, Droit et changement social dans les sociétés contemporaines, Rapport de synthèse, Actes des VIIIes Journées d'Etudes juridiques Jean Dabin, Bruxelles, Bruylant, 1978.

101. Voy. sp. Glendon, M.A., "Power and Authority in the Family: New Legal Patterns as Reflections on Changing Ideologies" (1975) *Am. J. Comp. Law* 1-33; Labrusse, C., *op. cit.*

102. Labrusse, C., *op. cit.*, sp. p. 436-444.

103. Select Committee. Evidence given by Sir George Baker, President of the Family Division, 2dd July 1975. Report, H.C. 533-i, sp. no. 47-48, xviii; "Battered women and the Law," Inter-action advisory Service, Handbook 3, 1975, p. 6-7.

104. Voy. au sujet de l'apparition progressive de ce régime primaire en droit anglo-américain et en droit continental, Caparros, E., *Les lignes de force de l'évolution des régimes matrimoniaux en droit comparé et québecois*, Presses Universitaires de Montréal, 1975, sp. p. 82 et s.; en droit belge, Renard, C., *Le régime matrimonial de droit commun*, Bruxelles, Bruylant, 1960, p. 42 et s.; en France, Cornu, G., (1966) J.C.P., I, 1968.

105. Voy. Rigaux, F., *Précis de droit des personnes*, p. 525-536.

106. Avant la loi du 14 juillet 1976, la compétence appartenait au Président du tribunal de 1ère instance (art. 214 j de la loi du 20 juillet 1932; art. 221, loi du 30 avril 1958). Désormais le magistrat compétent est le plus proche du justiciable (Comp. les Magistrates Courts en Grande-Bretagne).

107. Voy. De Gavre, J., et Lampe, M. F., Le régime primaire ou les droits et devoirs respectifs des époux, in La réforme des droits et devoirs respectifs des époux et des régimes matrimoniaux. Loi du 14 juillet 1976, Ed. Jeune Barreau, Bruxelles, 1977, p. 80-194, sp. p. 167 et s.

108. Voy. Foulon-Piganiol, C.I., Les premiéres orientations jurisprudentielles de l'art. 220-1 C. civ., Dall., 1967, chr. XXIII.

109. Voy. Toulouse, 30 janvier 1961, Dall. 1961, p. 324, note Rolland, H., Cass. lère, 1er juillet 1969, J.C.P. 1969, II, 15056, conclusions Lindon; Dall. 1970, p. 148, note Le Calondec; R.T.D.C., 1970, p. 156, obs. Nerson; Foulon-Piganiol, C.I, Le droit de ne pas demander le divorce, Dall. Sir. 1970, Chr. p. 140; Nancy, 12 décembre 1968, Dall. Sir. 1969, p. 300, note Foulon-Piganiol, C.I.; Cass. Civ. lère 14 mars 1973, J.C.P. 1973, II, 17430, note Lindon; Cass. Civ. lère, 24 octobre 1973, J.C.P. 1975, II, 17991; Dall. Sir., 1975, 724, note Benabent; Nerson, R., Obs. R.T.D.C., 1975, p. 301-304; Marty et Raynaud, Droit civil, 1976, no. 195 et 209.

110. Lemp, P., Das Eherecht, Berner Kommentar, 1968, 1. Abteilung, 2. Teilband, Art. 169-172, p. 105 et s.

111. Voy. Nerson, R., Rev. trimestrielle dr. civil, 1975, p. 299, no. 2.

112. Voy. l'art 214 C. civ. belge et l'art. 215, al. 3 C. civ. fr., avant la modification apportée par la loi du 11 juillet 1975.

113. Marty et Raynaud, *op. cit.*, no. 195 et les références.

114. Voy. not. Cass. fr. Req., 27 janvier 1908, Dall. 1908, 1, 154.

115. Les pouvoirs du juge sont *discrétionnaires*. Voy. Baeteman et Lauwers, *Devoirs et droits des époux*, Bruxelles, Bruylant, 1960, sp. p. 338-340; De Gavre, J., et Lampe, M.F., *op. cit.*, sp. p. 168-169.

116. Au plus tard jusqu'à la dissolution du mariage. A défaut de réglementation relative à

l'attribution préférentielle du logement familial après divorce (sauf moyennant remboursement de la valeur excédentaire après liquidation et partage du régime matrimonial (art. 1446 C. civ.) le juge n'est plus compétent pour statuer sur celle-ci.

117. Comp. le Domestic Violence and Matrimonial Proceedings Act 1976, Section I, sous-section 2.

118. Voy. Vieujean, E., De la puissance paternelle à la puissance parentale (1976) *Ann. dr.* 7-41, sp. p. 23-30. L'autre parent conserve cependant un droit de *contrôle* et de *recours* devant le tribunal de la jeunessse, dans l'intérêt de l'enfant, et un droit de *visite*.

119. Voy. également en ce sens les remarques de Pizzey, E. *op. cit.*

120. *En 1970,* 86 déchéances totales et 31 déchéances partielles (soit 188) ont été prononcées par le Tribunal de la jeunesse de Bruxelles. *En 1975,* 72 déchéances totales et 15 déchéances partielles (soit 87).

121. Rigaux, F., Précis de Droit des personnes, no. 1591-1610; 1991-1709.

122. Voy. art. 1253 quinquies du Code judiciaire.

123. Voy. art. 221, al. 2 du Code civil.

124. Art. 221, al. 3 du Code civil; Voy. De Gavre J., et Lampe, M.F., *op. cit.,* p. 161-164.

125. Art. 1412 du Code judiciaire.

126. Art. 1253 septies du Code judiciaire.

127. Art. 224 du Code civil; Voy. De Gavre, J., et Lampe, M.F., *op. cit.,* p. 177 et s.

128. Voy. notamment en droit comparé Caparros, E., *op. cit.,* p. 111-141 et les références.

129. Art. 215 C. civ. fr. Voy. Guyon, Y., Le statut du logement familial en droit civil, (1966) J.C.P. 2041; Chartier, Y., "Domicile conjugal et vie familiale" (1971) *Rev. trim. dr. civ.* 510 et s.; Mayer-Jack, A., "Singularités du domicile conjugal et avènement du domicile conjugal" (1972) *Rev. trim. dr. civ.* 1 et s.; Nerson, R., Obs., (1975) *Rev. trim. dr. civ.* 292-299.

130. Art. 215 nouv. C. civ. belge; De Gavre, J., et Lampe, M.F., *op. cit.,* p. 101-127; De Cock, Y., et De Lat, J., *De bescherming van de gezinswoning,* Jura Falconis, 1977, p. 355-387.

131. Art. 215 s. 1 C. civ.

132. Art. 215 s. 2 C. civ.

133. Art. 215 s. 1, al. 2 C. civ.

134. Art. 224 C. civ.

135. Colmar, 11 juin 1974, Gaz. Pal., 4-5 décembre 1974, note Viatte; De Cock, Y.; et De Lat, J., *op. cit.* sp. no. 9; Nerson, R., Obs. (1975) *Rev. trim. dr. civ.* 292 et s.; De Gavre, J., et Lampe, M.F., *op. cit.,* sp. p. 119-123.

136. Comp. les art. 1446, 1447 du C. civil belge et l'art. 285-1 C. civ. français; Lindon, R., "La nouvelle législation sur le divorce et le recouvrement public des pensions alimentaires (1975) *J.C.P.,* 2728.

137. De Cock, Y., et De Lat, J., *op. cit.,* sp. p. 385-387.

138. Baeteman et Lauwers, *op. cit.,* p. 334-337; Jottrand, J., L'ordre des familles et l'art. 223 nouv. du Code civil (1977) *Journ. Trib.* 705-706.

139. Comp. à propos des Magistrates' Courts Matrimonial Orders, Bromley, *Family Law,* 5th éd. 1976, p. 232.

140. Art. 1280 C. jud.

141. Art. 1253 bis à quater C. jud.; Voy. Panier, Ch., "Le régime primaire, Aspects judiciaires" (1977) *Ann. dr.* 70-91.

142. Délai de citation de 2 jours. Art. 1035 C. jud.

143. Art. 1036 C. jud.

144. Art. 584-3° C. jud.

145. Art. 1039 C. jud.

146. A l'inverse, les procédures en divorce ou en séparation de corps sont longues, coûteuses et relativement compliquées (art. 1254 à 1275 C. jud.).

147. Cependant, rien ne s'opposerait semble-t-il à ce que le Procureur du Roi saisi d'une plainte ou d'une dénonciation, use méthodiquement de son droit d'information pour requérir la police locale ou la gendarmerie d'exercer une mission de surveillance plus intensive sur les familles "en danger". Ordonnée rapidement et exercée avec l'accord

du conjoint menacé, cette forme de surveillance pourrait constituer une protection appréciable.

148. L'expédition de la plainte ou de la dénonciation enregistrée par la police ne peut lui être fournie que par l'intermédiaire du Parquet, sur demande de la partie demanderesse (art. 125 Tarif criminel). Le délai d'obtention de cette copie est généralement beaucoup trop long.

149. Mais non des Magistrates Courts (équivalents de nos justices de paix). Voy. cependant les recommandations de la Law Commission (Law Comm. no. 77, p. 22-32) citées par Maidment, S., "Laws for Battered Women. Are They an Improvement?" (1977) *Fam. Law* 50-52.

150. Mais il faut pour cela que des blessures aient déjà été infligées *antérieurement*. De plus, la faculté d'attacher un pouvoir d'arrestation sans mandat est laissée à la discrétion du juge, de même que celle de procéder à une arrestation est laissée à la discrétion de la police. Voy. à ce sujet, Maidment, S., *op. cit.*, p. 51.

151. Voy. Masson, J.M., "Domestic Violence and Matrimonial Proceedings Act 1976" (1977) *Fam. Law* 29-31.

152. Home Office Circular, no. 68/1977 of the 6th May 1977.

153. Voy. dans le même sens la *carte de protection* utilisée dans certains cantons suisses.

154. Voy outre les références citées à la note 96, Hirsch, J.L., "Pour un tribunal de la famille" (1971) *Journ. Trib.* 211-213; Mathijs, J., "Le tribunal de la famille, Essai d'une expérience judiciaire" (1974) *Journ. Trib.* 381-394, sp. no. 12-13; Giesen, D., *Zur Problematik der Einfuhrung einer Familiengerichtbarkeit in der Bundesrepublik Deutschland*, Görresgesellschaft, Neue Folge, Heft 171, Schöning Verlag, Paderborn, 1975; Dyson, E.D., et Dyson, R.B., "Family Courts in the United States" (1968) *J. Fam. Law* 507-586, sp. p. 515-516 et 1969-1970, p. 1-100; Commission de la réforme du droit du Canada, Doc. de travail no. 1, Le tribunal de la famille, janvier 1974, sp. p. 7-14; Eekelaar, J., *Family Security and Family Breakdown*, Harmondsworth, Eng.: Penguin Books, 1971, sp. chap. 11.

155. Voy. en Belgique, propositions de loi no. 616/1 et 733/1 déposées à la Chambre le 14 juin 1973 et le 5 décembre 1975; Rouard, P., "La proposition de loi créant les tribunaux de la famille" (1973) *Journ. Trib.* 701-710; Rouard, P., "La nouvelle proposition de loi créant des juridictions de la famille" (1976) *Journ. Trib.* 473-479.

156. Voy. en ce sens les expériences françaises et, en Belgique, Mathijs, J., *op. cit.*, sp. no. 17 et s.; Kebers, A., La spécialisation du juge en matière familiale, in Famille, Droit et changement social dans les sociétés contemporaines, Actes des VIIIes Journées d'Etudes Juridiques Jean Dabin, p. 614-632.

157. Voy. Hirsch, J.L., "La grande misère de la protection de la jeunesse" (1970) *Journ. Trib.*, no. 4693; Blondeel, G., "Dix ans de protection de la jeunesse" (1976) *Journ. Trib.*, p. 749 et s.

158. Voy. Dautricourt, J.Y., *op. cit.* Le problème est encore plus grave en matière de défense sociale.

159. A la limite on pourrait imaginer qu'à l'instar de certaines cours de la famille américaines ou canadiennes, ce soit des services de conciliation qui soient chargés d'étudier avec les intéressés les accords qu'ils n'auraient plus qu'à soumettre ensuite à l'entérinement du juge.

160. En Belgique, deux expériences récentes effectuées de 1972 à 1975 dans les villes de Mons et Termonde, à l'initiative du Ministère de la Justice, ont démontré qu'un renforcement du personnel des services sociaux de protection de la jeunesse avait non seulement pu éviter un nombre considérables de placements d'enfants en homes et institutions (103 sur 126 enfants en danger à Termonde, et 95 sur 177 à Mons) tout en réalisant des économies substantielles par rapport au coût des placements (25 millions de francs belges à Termonde et 17 millions à Mons). Renseignements communiqués par l'Office de Protection de la Jeunesse. Cette expérience doit être étendue actuellement aux principales grandes villes de Belgique. En ce qui concerne le coût de l'emprisonnement, voy. Dautricourt, J.Y., *op. cit.* (1969-1970) *Rev. dr. pén.*, sp. p. 536 et s.

161. Voy. à ce sujet, Poelman, F., *op. cit.* (1976) *Journ. Trib.*, sp. p. 2-3.

162. Voy. dans le même sens, Etudes sur la déjudiciarisation, Commission de réforme du droit du Canada, Projet de réforme du droit pénal, 1975, Document de travail, sp. p. 18 et s.

163. *Id.* Le tribunal de la famille, Commission de réforme du Canada, Document de travail no. 1, 1974, sp. p. 26.

164. Ex.: Centres d'information et de consultation locaux et comités de quartier, interventions médiatrices de la police, centres de désintoxication ou de réadaptation, etc. . . .

165. Nous employons ici le terme de "déjudiciarisation" dans un sens différent de clui de la Commission de Réforme du droit du Canada qui y voit essentiellement un effort de limitation du contact avec les juridictions pénales. Il s'agit selon nous de tenter d'éviter au maximum *toute intervention judiciaire,* quelle qu'elle soit, dans la vie familiale, pour laquelle elle ne peut et doit être qu'un ultime et dernier recours.

166. Sur la prolifération de ces centres en Angleterre et aux Etats-Unis, voy. Pizzey, E., *op. cit.* et la liste d'adresses donnée par Warrior, Betsy, *Working on Wife Abuse,* Cambridge, Mass., 1976.

168. Voy. les recommandations du Select Committee on Violence in Marriage, Report, H.C. 533-i, sp. p. X et s.

169. Sur la distinction entre 'aide sociale' et 'action sociale', voy. Alfandari, E., Aide sociale, action sociale, Précis Dalloz, 1974, sp. p. 94 et s.; Voy. aussi Lory, B., *La politique d'action sociale,* Toulouse, Privat, 1975.

170. Voy. au sujet de cette loi, Huvelle, P., "La loi organique des centres publics d'aide sociale" (1977) *Journ. Trib.* 449-454; Senaeve, P., De organieke wet van 8 juli 1976 betreffende de openbare centra voor maatschappelijk welzijn, Recht. Weekbl., 1976-1977, col. 1180. Les centres publics d'aide sociale, Doc. du Centre d'études politiques, économiques et sociales (C.E.P.E.S.), 1976, no. 4; Centres publics d'aide sociale, année O, Union des Villes et Communes belges, Section Aide sociale, 1976.

171. Art. 1 de la loi. Huvelle, P., *op. cit.,* sp. p. 14-17 et les références aux travaux parlementaires.

172. Art. 61 et 62 de la loi. Voy. à ce sujet Huvelle, P., *op. cit.,* sp. no. 25-30.

173. Art. 59 et 60 de la loi.

174. Services sociaux locaux, centres de consultation conjugale et prématrimoniale, associations féminines, etc.

175. Voy. Alfandari, E., *op. cit.,* spra, p. 597 et s.

176. Voy. en Angleterre le réseau de "Bureaux de consultation pour les citoyens" (Citizen's Advice Bureaux) et sur le rôle de ceux-ci Lewis, P.S.C., L'assistance juridique à l'intention des personnes démunies du Royaume-Uni; Actes du 6e Colloque de droit européen, Leiden, 1976, sp. p. 85 et 88.

177. Voy. à ce sujet, L'assistance juridique à l'intention des personnes démunies, notamment dans les zones urbaines, Actes du 6e Colloque de droit européen, Leiden, 11-13 mai 1976, Doc. Cons. Europe, 45.705-05.3; Oppetit, B., L'aide judiciaire, D. 1972, chr. 41.

178. Voy. en Angleterre les "centres juridiques" créés dans les zones peu prospères, dépourvues d'avoués, Lewis, P.S.C., *op. cit.,* sp. p. 89-92.

179. Voy. Hellners, H.T., "L'assistance juridique à l'intention des personnes démunies en Suede", Actes du 6e Colloque de droit europeen. p. 71-82.

180. Lewis, P.S.C. *op. cit.,* p. 83-97.

181. Baumgartel, M.G., "L'assistance juridique à l'intention des personnes démunies en République fédérale d'Allemagne", Actes du 6e Colloque de droit européen, p. 43-54, avec annexes relatives à l'aide juridique en Suisse et en Autriche.

182. Voy. Alfandari, E., *op. cit.,* p. 597-624.

183. Alfandari, E., *op. cit.,* sp. p. 607.

184. Rep. prat. dr. belge, Voy. Assistance judiciaire; Fettweis, A., Droit judiciaire privé, Presses Universitaires de Liège, 1976, p. 481 et s.

185. Selon les revenus indiqués par la partie, le Bureau peut décider d'accorder l'assistance complète, ou déterminer un montant à verser soit à titre de provision préalable, soit à titre d'honoraires (art. 455, al. 4 C. jud.).

186. "S'il est établi qu'une modification de son patrimoine, de ses revenus ou de ses charges est intervenue depuis la décision lui accordant le bénéfice de l'assistance judiciaire, et qu'il est dès lors en état de payer" (art. 693 C. jud.). En outre, si l'indigent succombe, il est condamné aux dépens et l'adversaire peut poursuivre le remboursement de ses frais contre l'assisté, s'il est en état de payer Fettweis, A., *op. cit.*, p. 492, no. 505.

187. L'art. 667 C. jud. parle de "l'insuffisance des revenus". Cette notion est plus étroite que celle de "ressources" en ce qu'elle exclut les avoirs en capital (Fettweis, A., *op. cit.*, p. 481, note 4). Il s'agit des revenus de l'année *antérieure* à l'année de la demande, mais l'appréciation se fait compte tenu des charges et des modifications survenues entretemps (art. 676 C. jud.).

188. Art. 669 C. jud.

189. Cass. 26 mars 1971, Pas. 1971, 689.

190. Art. 667 et 678 C. jud.

191. Une procédure d'urgence est cependant prévue à l'art. 673 C. jud.

192. Rapport au Sénat, Doc. parl., 1974-1975, no. 581/2, p. 113; Huvelle, P., *op. cit.*, no. 23.

193. A.R. du 3 avril 1970, modifié par les A.R. du 28 juin 1972, 11 mars 1974, et 8 février 1977, réglant l'agréation de Centres de consultations prématrimoniales, matrimoniales et familiales. La mission de ces centres ne comporte normalement pas la diffusion de conseils juridiques.

194. Sur l'évolution des législations en matière de divorce, voy. en particulier Ancel, M., *Le divorce à l'étranger, La Documentation française*, Paris, 1975; Ancel, M., *Le divorce en Europe, La documentation française*, Paris, 1975.

195. Voy. Renchon, J.L., Les séquelles alimentaires du divorce en droit civil belge et en droit comparé, in Famille, droit et changement social dans les sociétés contemporaines, Actes des VIIIes Journées d'Etudes juridiques Jean Dabin, Bruxelles, 1978, p. 324-367; Meulders-Klein, M.T., Famille, droit et changement social dans les sociétés contemporaines, Rapport général de synthèse, p. 685-751, sp. p. 717-722. Schwartz, V.E., "The Serious Marital Offender: Tort Law as a Solution" (1972) *Fam. Law Quarterly* 219-232.

196. Voy. sur ce problème des familles à parent seul *Finer Report* on One Parent Families, London, H.M.S.O. Cmnd. 5629 et 5629-1. Voy. aussi "Maintien du revenu des familles ayant un seul parent" (1975) *Rev. int. séc. soc.* 3-73; Parents seuls avec enfants à charge, Rapport établi à l'intention de la XIIe Conférence des Ministres européens chargés des questions familiales, Stockholm, 1971, Doc. jur. Cons. Eur. 22360, 03.2, ainsi que le rapport du Conseil de l'Europe, Coopération sociale en Europe: "Action sociale préventive de la désintégration familiale, de l'abandon de l'enfant et de la délinquance juvénile", Strasbourg, 1972. Sur l'ensemble du problème de la désolidarisation du couple et de ses répercussions, voy. Meulders-Klein, M.T., Rapport général de synthèse, Actes des VIIIes Journées d'Etudes juridiques Jean Dabin, p. 691-751.

197. Voy. Pelissier, J., Les obligations alimentaires, Unité ou diversité, Paris, L.G.D.J., 1961, sp. p. 223 et s.

198. Pour une approche comparative de ce problème, voy. Conseil de l'Europe, Aperçu des législations des Etats membres en matière de paiement des pensions alimentaires entre conjoints divorcés, Strasbourg, février 1974. En France, avant la loi de 1972, 20% seulement des pensions auraient été payées régulièrement, 32%, de manière aléatoire et 48%, totalement impayées.

199. *Loi no. 73-5 du 2 janvier 1973* sur le paiement direct des pensions alimentaires et décrets du 1er mars 1973, no. 73-216 et 73-217 sur les modalités d'exécution. Voy. à ce sujet Gebler, M.J., Le paiement direct des pensions alimentaires, Dall. Sirey, 1973, chr. XIV, p. 107-112; Viatte, J., Le paiement direct des pensions alimentaires (1973) *Rec. gén. Lois et Jur.* 425 et s.

200. *Loi no. 75-618 du 11 juillet 1975* relative au recouvrement public des pensions alimentaires. Voy. à ce sujet Lindon, R., La loi nouvelle sur le divorce et le recouvrement public des pensions alimentaires (1976) *J.C.P.* Chr. 2728, no. 220-268; Lindon R., et Bertin, Ph., Divorce 1976, Paris, Libraires Techniques, 1976, p. 70-82.

201. V. Maintien du revenu des familles ayant un parent seul (1975) *Rev. int. séc. soc.*, sp. p. 42-46. Dans les pays scandinaves, la restitution effective des fonds publics avancés serait d'environ un tiers à la moitié.

202. L'efficacité de la loi du 3 janvier 1972, modifée par celle du 11 juillet 1975, devrait assurer le recouvrement des pensions dans 85 à 90% des cas. Le recouvrement par le Trésor public n'interviendrait qu'à titre résiduaire (Lindon, R., *op. cit., J.C.P.* 2728, no. 268).

203. Notamment la contribution aux charges du ménage (art. 221 C. civ.) et, depuis la loi du 9 juillet 1975, la pension alimentaire après divorce (art. 301 bis C. civ.).

204. Proposition Hanquet, Doc. parl. Session 1974-1975, no. 433, actuellement en voie d'être redéposée après caducité. Une autre proposition de loi tendant à généraliser le paiement des pensions alimentaires par prélèvement direct chez l'employeur ou les débiteurs du débirentier, selon le modèle français, n'a pas été relevée de caducité. (Doc. parl. Sénat, 1972-1973, no. 310).

205. Voy. notamment Maintien du revenu des familles ayant un parent seul, précité.

206. Sur l'ensemble du problème, voy. Denis, P., "Les conséquences du divorce dans le droit de la sécurité sociale belge"; Vogel-Polsky, E., "Les conséquences du divorce dans quelques systèmes de sécurité sociale en Europe"; et Meulders-Klein, M.T., Rapport général de synthèse, in Famille, droit et changement social dans les sociétés contemporaines, précité, sp. p. 368-392; 393-420; et 718-728. Vogel-Polsky, E., La sécurité sociale de la femme non employée dans les pays membres du Conseil de l'Europe, Rapport préparé pour le Comité d'experts en matière de sécurité sociale du Conseil de l'Europe (EXP/SS (1973) 12; Grounin, M., Les questions de sécurité sociale concernant les femmes, Doc. B.I.T., C.S.S.E./D3, 1975, Genève. Voy. aussi Giesen, D., "Divorce Reform in Germany" (1973) *Fam. Law Quart.*, sp. p. 368 et s. et les références.

207. Denis, P., *op. cit.*; Lonfils, E., "Situation de l'épouse séparée et divorcée en matière de sécurité sociale" (1976) *Rev. belge de séc. soc.* 158-170; Smeesters B., et de Viron, G., "Les incidences du divorce et de la séparation de fait en matière de sécurité sociale" (1976) *Journ. trib. Trav.* 77-83. Depuis la loi du 20 juillet 1971, la Belgique possède un régime d'*allocations familiales garanties* en faveur des enfants qui ne sont protégés par aucun autre régime, mais elle est soumise à un plafond de ressources extrêmement bas.

208. Voy. les références citées à la note 207.

209. Voy. De Busschere, J., "L'institution du droit à un minimum de moyens d'existence" (1974) *Rev. belge séc. soc.* 1051-1060; Mayer, A. La loi du 7 août 1974 instituant le droit à un minimum de moyens d'existence (1976) *Journ. Trib.* 225-231; Senaeve, P., "Recension des dispositions 'marginales' du droit de la sécurité sociale et d'autres branches du droit" (1975) *Rev. belge séc. soc.* 590; Le droit à un minimum de moyens d'existence, Cahiers du C.E.P.E.S.S., 1974, no. 2. Au 1er janvier 1976, le montant annuel accordé était de 80.000 F belges pour un couple marié vivant ensemble et 57.000 F pour une personne isolée, montant rattaché à l'indice des prix à la consommation, mais diminué du montant des ressources indiquées à l'art. 5 de la loi. Ces sommes sont versées par les Centres publics d'aide sociale, qui peuvent y ajouter *facultativement* des secours en argent ou en nature dans le cadre des missions de la loi du 8 juillet 1976.

210. Sur l'ensemble du problème, voy. Sullerot, E., "L'emploi des femmes et ses problèmes dans les Etats membres de la Communauté économique européenne", 1970; Vogel-Polsky, E., "Le retour des femmes sur le marché du travail" (1975) *Rev. Trav.* 627 et s.; O.C.D.E., "Re-entry of Women on the Labour Market After an Interruption, in (1971) *Employment*; Meulders-Klein, M.T., *op. cit.*, Actes des VIIIes Journées d'Etudes Juridiques Jean Dabin, sp. p. 728-735.

211. O.C.D.E., Le rôle des femmes dans l'économie, 1975, sp. p. 38-41. Il y avait en Belgique, en janvier 1976, 230.000 chômeurs, soit 14% de la main-d'oeuvre féminine et 6% de la main-d'oeuvre masculine.

212. O.C.D.E., Le rôle des femmes dans l'économie, 1975, sp. p. 61-70.

213. Erstes Gesetz zur Reform des Ehe-und Familienrechts, vom 14 Juni 1976, s. 1569-1586b BGB, sp. s. 1573-1575.

214. Conseil de l'Europe, Parents seuls avec enfants à charge, précité, sp. p. 51-57; Maintien du revenu des familles ayant un parent seul, précité, p. 47 et s.

215. Maintien du revenu des familles ayant un parent seul, précité, sp. p. 52-54.

216. Voy. la loi du 10 avril 1973 accordant des crédits d'heure aux travailleurs en vue de leur promotion sociale. L'application de cette loi est en outre soumise à une condition d'âge de moins de 40 ans.

217. A.R. du 20 décembre 1963 relatif à l'emploi et au chômage, art. 118 complété par l'A.R. du 14 mars 1975.

218. A.R. du 20 décembre 1963 relatif à l'emploi et au chômage, art. 83; Babilas, L., "L'O.N.E.M. et la formation professionnelle" (sept., 1975) *Rev. Trav.* 579.

219. Conseil de l'Europe, Parents seuls avec enfants à charge, précité, sp. p. 39-51.

220. Maintien du revenu des familles ayant un parent seul, précité, sp. p. 60-65.

221. Steels, "Perspectives de nouvelles prestations familiales" (1972) *Rev. belge de séc. soc.* 1410-1413; Presvelou, Cl., Les crèches, les prégardiennats en Belgique. Etude des équipements et des utilisateurs, Centre d'Etudes de la population et de la famille, Bruxelles, Ministère de la Santé publique, 1976.

222. Conseil de l'Europe, Parents seuls avec enfants à charge, précité, p. 39-45; Maintien du revenu des familles ayant un parent seul, précité, p. 55-60.

223. La difficulté provient notamment du fait que les habitation sociales dépendant de différents organismes, notamment les communes, les centres publics d'aide sociale et les société immobilières agréées par la Société nationale du logement. Voy. A.R. du 1er décembre 1970 portant Code du logement; A.R. du 2 juillet 1973 sur le régime des loyers des habitations appartenant aux sociétés agréées par la S.N.L., sp. art. 6 à 8; A.R. du 16 décembre 1975 déterminant l'attribution prioritaire de logements sociaux à certaines catégories de personnes défavorisées. Celle des familles à parent seul n'y apparaît pas spécifiquement.

Chapter 8

The Relevance of Criminal Law To Inter-Spousal Violence

Raymond I. Parnas*

The title of this chapter may seem a curious one. Clearly the issue raising word is intended to be 'inter-spousal'. If it were omitted the only possibly arguable question implied in the issue of 'the relevance of criminal law to violence' would be whether the existence or operation of the criminal law itself contributed adversely in some manner to the violence it was created to control. In fact however, the question of the law as a negative, counterproductive or, at best, ineffectual force rather than a positive, ameliorating entity, despite the frequently overlooked status of such a query, should be a fundamental issue for every new legislative, judicial or executive fiat or procedure regardless of the area of law concerned. Whereas there appears to be little argument with the basic proposition that the criminal law is relevant to acts of violence, the definition of violence, the kinds of violent acts to be prohibited or regulated, and the official manner of handling such acts are all questions which immediately follow and are frequently difficult to resolve adequately.

Inter-spousal violence in the United States has traditionally been prohibited by general provisions of the penal codes dealing with disorderly conduct, assault, battery and homicide with occasional statutes specifically directed at wife-beating. In practice, however, the phenomenon, at least at the lower levels of violence, has been viewed as *sui generis,* both because of the internal family nature of the dispute itself as well as the complications to the legal process caused by allegations and evidence of victim precipitation, victim attempts to withdraw complaints and to refuse to testify, and the problem of support provision for the family of the alleged offender. Thus inter-spousal violence has been handled over the years by a refusal to respond or prosecute, temporary quelling of the violence by presence of authority or forced momentary separation, on-the-spot counseling, prosecutorial mediation, threat inspired cooling-off periods and peace bonds as well as the full range of more generally applicable police, prosecution and judicial processes and sanctions.

In the last ten years recognition of the peace-keeping role of the police and the exorbitant amount of criminal justice agency time spent on relatively minor family disputes has led to systematic attempts to deal with this problem. The efforts have

---

* School of Law, University of California, Davis, U.S.A.

primarily concentrated on crisis intervention training and techniques for the police, mediation centers, procedures for the prosecution and family court jurdisdiction by the judiciary.[1] The compassion and humanity of the social services has been increasingly interjected to effect more organized and 'knowledge-able' efforts at diversion, counseling, referral, mediation and treatment in much the same way that juveniles received the 'benefit' of such progressive thought by the creation of the *quasi*-criminal juvenile courts and their behavioralist adjuncts at the turn of the century. In both input and output the same rehabilitative ideal basic to the juvenile court caused a considerable change in adult processing. Most jurisdictions adopted an indeterminate sentence law for adults based on the treatment model. Probation and parole burgeoned in the 20th century and diversion programs for young adult offenders became the fad of the 1960's. The trouble with such a trend for inter-spousal violence *now* is that the juvenile and adult processes, in the United States at least, confronted with intolerable rates of delinquency and criminality, have recently been discarding and rethinking the commendable, but still unproven, facets of models based on sickness, treatment and rehabilitation, and have been returning to the known entities of personal public accountability for bad acts, with appropriate and acknowledged punishment, enlightened and softened somewhat by prior experience with the social services.[2]

At present, however, inter-spousal violence remains in that marginal area termed by Frank Allen as "the borderland of the criminal law" subject to "problems of 'socializing' criminal justice." In his classic essay, Allen asked:[3] "What may we properly demand of a system of criminal justice? What functions may it properly serve? What are the obstacles and problems that must be confronted and overcome if a system of criminal justice is to be permitted to serve its proper ends?"[4] In partial answer to his own questions he said: "Whenever penal sanctions are employed to deal with problems of social service, two things are almost certain to happen and a third result may often occur. First, the social services will not be effectively rendered. Second, the diversion of personnel, resources, and energy required in the effort will adversely affect the ability of a system of criminal justice to fulfill those functions that it can perform. Finally, the effort may sometimes result in the corruption and demoralization of the agencies of criminal justice."[5] As to his first point, Allen asserts that: "When penal treatment is employed to perform the functions of social services, selection of those eligible for penal treatment proceeds on inadmissible criteria . . . by reference to their poverty or their helplessness."[6] In such instances, he says, neither effective social services nor equity prevail. With regard to his second point, Allen recognizes that if the resources expended produced constructive results then, despite the cost, it might be worth it.[7] Finally, he states that forcing incompatible obligations on law enforcement agencies sometimes leads to job demoralization and the corruption of improper and illegal procedures and sanctions.[8]

On one level Allen was disturbed by the inclusion of "certain types of conduct that might better be left to the exclusive concern of medicine, psychiatry or the general moral sense of the community."[9] These included consensual sex acts between adults, intoxication (whether by alcohol or other drugs), gambling and any behavior involving the so-called willing victim. (Inter-spousal violence would hardly fall into this category except in the most masochistic sense.) Even on this level, however, where Allen's predisposition is clearly towards decriminalization, he asks "why . . . fundamental reform of the system of criminal justice has been delayed so long"[10] and points out that, though the familiar scapegoats of lack of public interest and financial support are real enough, they do not provide the most fundamental explanation. "We should not overlook the fact that, in many areas, our basic difficulties still lie in our ignorance of human behavior in its infinite complexities . . . [and the lack of] reasonably reliable, inexpensive, and expeditious therapy."[11] Next, Allen asks "what peculiar danger and perils lurk in the path of such fundamental reform of the system of criminal justice."[12] Here, like Nick Kittrie in his later work, *The Right to be Different,*[13] Allen is concerned about the absence of adequate checks on error in those coercive processes which have been removed from or have developed independent of the constitutional guarantees of the criminal process in the name of treatment and therapy such as the juvenile court and mental health procedures. He points out, as many have before him, that the "beginning of wisdom is the consciousness of ignorance."[14] Coercive processes based on faulty assumptions about deviancy causation and our ability to diagnose, treat and cure, may not only be ineffective but dangerous to the individual being treated and the public being protected. "Ignorance, of itself," Allen says, "is disgraceful only so far as it is avoidable. But when, in our eagerness to find 'better ways' of handling old problems, we rush to measures affecting human liberty and human personality on the assumption that we have the knowledge which, in fact, we do not possess, then the problem of ignorance takes on a more sinister hue."[15]

Incidents of inter-spousal violence, no matter how minimal, must remain subject to police intervention. For years a disproportionate number of disturbances, assaults, batteries, uses of deadly weapons, mayhems, and homicides have involved family members. Despite the resources necessary and the danger inherent in responding to such calls, no entity other than a police agency has the authority and ability to cope with such volatile situations. Central to the function of the police and the criminal law is the protection of life and limb.

The basic question is: what response, if any, should the legal system make after the dispute has been halted by police intervention? This is a crucial stage for another reason. It is at this point that an offender and a victim in a continuing volatile situation have been identified. All of the data showing the extent of inter-spousal violence and the experience of escalation from minimal to aggravated injury indicate that it would be irresponsible governmental action to drop the matter at this point. In fact, however, what we have been doing is to ignore the extremely important preventative, corrective, retributive, incapacitative, and deterrent implications of this early official knowledge of subsequent potential violence. At the very least, an adequate record keeping procedure must be implemented so that all those responding to subsequent incidents will know of the disputants' prior history so that an appropriate relevant additional response can be made. But even more important than our criminal law's traditional escalation of meaningless slaps on the wrist until too late, is recognition of the need for a breakthrough at the outset to the consciousness of the disputants as to the seriousness of their behavior and not later than the second time around at most.

In my judgment, only the coercive, authoritative harshness of the criminal process can do this. Efforts at therapy can, and I suppose should, be included in the process but should not be given undue emphasis, for there is simply no evidence that we know how to diagnose, much less treat, disputants' problems in a manner that will prevent repetition. Simply put, we must go with what we know. And we know that we cannot ignore or condone acts or threats of imminent violence. We know that the police are best equipped to protect others and themselves. We know how to punish, whether by fine, incapacitation, other denials of full liberty, embarrassment, inconvenience, *etc.* And we know punishment is a clear statement of the personal responsibility of the offender and the condemnation and retribution of society. We also know that where punishment is to be imposed, the criminal process provides the best safeguards that such punishment is imposed on the appropriate person under the most adequate circumstances. We know that incapacitation prevents repetition during the period of incarceration. Finally I submit that we are increasingly coming to believe that punishment, quickly, fairly, proportionately and appropriately imposed, may deter or reduce the quality and quantity of some kinds of bad conduct at least as well, if not better, than attempts at speculative therapy, and thus may serve the rehabilitation function even better from the perspective of non-repetition.

Some will argue that increased criminal processing of family disputants will reduce the calls for governmental intervention, on the one hand, and increase subsequent violence by the processed offender, on the other, as well as increase divorce and welfare rolls. In some specific instances these allegations may be true. Nonetheless I submit that when a person is seriously threatened with harm, she will usually call for help wherever she can get it, her first concern being for personal protection regardless of any tangential consequences. In fact, more rather than less governmental sanctions might return a greater number of victims to public attention than increased processing would lose because of the current disenchantment of many with a system which does little, if anything, to protect. As to the threat of increased violence upon the return of an offender who has been fined, jailed or otherwise sanctioned rather than merely counseled and released as in the past, I can only point out once again that such leniency has not seemed to work to prevent repetition and increased injury and therefore we seem to have nothing to lose by returning to the traditional concepts of the criminal law. In addition, the excellent current trend towards crisis shelters for battered spouses should help to alleviate this problem. With regard to increasing divorce, it is difficult to conceive of any more of that than is currently the case, but since the trend of the law presently is to make that process an easy one for everyone, it is difficult to understand why greater attempts should be made to hold violent relationships together. Concerns about divorce rates and welfare rolls, as important as these problems are, simply cannot be significant where protection from violence is the dominant purpose to be served.

Thus the criminal law, the police, the prosecutor and the courts should not only continue to respond to incidents of inter-spousal violence, but should emphasize the importance of the traditional response of arrest, prosecution and sanction as a sign of public disapprobation and protection, not only at the upper levels of violence, but also at the first minimal signs of trouble. Most related existing social services and therapeutic techniques could be retained and new ideas continue to be fostered. For example, arbitration and lay neighborhood courts of one's peers exerting the most immediate and influential of pressures may have considerable merit. But all extant and new methods should be clearly placed in the context of experimental adjuncts to the dominant criminal process and its goals, with offenders and victims (the public too) under the criminal law's protective mantle. In the words of Professor Allen: "Our great problem today and for the future is to domesticate scientific knack and technique so that they may operate compatibly with the values and assumptions of a legal order and, at the same time, make their important contributions to our needs."[16]

NOTES

1. For descriptions of the problem of inter-spousal violence and responses thereto in the United States, see this author's other articles on the subject: "The Police Response to the Domestic Disturbance" (1967) *Wisconsin Law Review* 914-960; "The Response of Some Relevant Community Resources to Intrafamily Violence" (1969), 44 *Indiana Law Journal* 159-181, "Judicial Response to Intrafamily Violence" (1970), 54 *Minnesota Law Review* 585-644, "Police Discretion and Diversion of Family Violence Incidents" (1971), 36 *Journal of Law and Contemporary Problems* 539-565, "Prosecutorial & Judicial Handling of Family Violence" (1973), 9 *Criminal Law Bulletin* 733-769.

2. For example, the indeterminate sentence has recently been replaced by fixed sentence legislation in California, Maine and Indiana, with efforts at such change afoot in many other states including Illinois, Minnesota and Florida. Maine abolished parole periods, Illinois recommended such a change, and California greatly limited parole terms. The implications of such changes for diversion and probation are apparent. Changes in the juvenile process, in addition to the procedural ones wrought by the Supreme Court in the last 10 years beginning with *In re Gault,* include efforts at using advisory juries, increased disclosure of offender names, and recent California legislation reducing the jurisdiction of the Juvenile Court over violent offenders.

3. Allen, Francis A., "The Borderland of the Criminal Law: Problems of 'Socializing' Criminal Justice," reprinted in *The Borderland of Criminal Justice.* Chicago, Illinois: University of Chicago Press, 1964.

4. *Id.* at p. 4.

5. *Id.* at p. 5.

6. *Id.* at p. 7.

7. *Id.* at p. 8.

8. *Id.* at p. 9.

9. *Id.*

10. *Id.* at p. 11.

11. *Id.* at p. 13.

12. *Id.* at p. 11.

13. Kittrie, Nick, *The Right to be Different.* Baltimore, Maryland: John Hopkins, 1971.

14. See Allen, note 3, *supra,* at p. 15.

15. *Id.* at p. 13.

16. *Id.* at p. 23.

Chapter 9

Inter-Spousal Rape: The Need For Law Reform

*Joanna McFadyen**

This analysis of the law relating to inter-spousal rape is set primarily within the context of the reform of the criminal law in Canada. Reform of the criminal law should be based on a consistent philosophy of what the aims and purposes of the criminal law are. The Law Reform Commission of Canada, in its Report to Parliament entitled *Our Criminal Law,* suggests that one of the functions of the criminal law are to reaffirm fundamental values and to denounce acts considered wrong. The criminal law is seen as having, in conjunction with its other functions, a moral, educative role whereby it acts as a socializing agent which reinforces attitudes necessary in a free and just society. In considering the reform of the criminal law, therefore, the first question necessary to ask is: 'Are the values expressed in the present law consistent with the values of modern Canadian society?' To answer this question, we must first determine the values of present law and of modern Canadian society.

1. The Law of Inter-Spousal Rape

The legal position in Canada in regard to inter-spousal rape is very straight-forward. Although it is a serious crime for a man to have sexual intercourse with a woman without her consent, it is no crime whatsoever when the victim of the rape is the man's wife. In Canada the marital exception to the crime of rape renders rape automatically legal when it occurs between spouses.[1]

The English courts have developed certain qualifications to the marital exception to rape. A wife who has obtained certain forms of legal recognition of marriage breakdown such as, for example, a separation order, may charge her husband with rape in the event of sexual intercourse without her consent.[2] Canadian jurisprudence does not admit the same qualifications. It would seem that a rape charge between a husband and a wife will not lie until such times as a decree absolute of divorce is obtained.[3]

The origin of the marital exception to the crime of rape may be traced at least as far back as statements made by Sir Matthew Hale, a seventeenth century British

* Research Consultant, Law Reform Commission of Canada.

jurist. Hale contended that the marriage contract contained an implied, non-retractable consent on the part of the wife to sexual intercourse with her husband.[4] At the time in which Hale lived, women were regarded as the property of their husbands, with little or no free will of their own. This perception of women was applied to virtually every aspect of life, including sexuality. The proposition that women forfeit their right to exercise free will in relation to sexual interaction by virtue of a term implicit in the marriage contract is seen by many as discriminatory in relation to women as wives, subjecting them to an unequal and subordinate position in relation to their husbands. Sir Matthew Hale's reasoning clearly reflected attitudes towards women prevalent three hundred years ago. Attitudes about women have changed drastically in the last decade, so much so that the values embodied in Hale's statements can no longer be regarded as sufficient justification for the continued sexual oppression of women in marriage. Nor, I would further suggest, is there any other reason sufficient to justify the prolongation of the spousal exception to rape.

Many commentators, from John Stuart Mill[5] and Friedrich Engels[6] to Susan Brownmiller[7] and other members of the feminist movement, have stated with grave concern that the subordination of women as wives to their husbands' sexual demands is a perpetuation of sex-role dependency relationships. This encourages and supports the inaccurate and damaging myth that women 'desire' to be dominated and that men have a right to be sexually aggressive. It has been repeatedly demonstrated that perceptions of males as dominant and females as submissive have their roots in the socialization of children and the continued social pressures placed on both sexes to fulfil sex-role stereotypes. These stereotypes may be seen as being destructive not only to women but to men as well, in that they inhibit human beings from inter-relating through their full potential. They promote interaction based on predetermined attitudes and capacities which may in fact bear little relation to the needs and capabilities of many, if not most, people.

Through its failure to recognize the right of married women to exercise free will in relation to sexual activity, the present law of rape in Canada not only places women in positions of subordination to their husbands, it also affirms perceptions of women as sexually submissive and lacking in the need, capacity or right to exercise free will. In addition, the law treats married women differently from their unmarried counterparts, who enjoy the fullest protection offered by law against the crime of rape. This sexist, prejudicial perspective of women is no longer acceptable in a society which is undergoing a major revolution respecting the roles of women in the family and in society. Although some people may contend that attitudes about women have not as yet changed sufficiently to warrant an alteration in the present law, such an approach is, at best, shortsighted. The question whether law reform should precede, coincide with or follow societal value changes is perplexing and without a simple answer. Changes in values and changes in laws are inextricably bound together. There is no single formula which operates to dictate in what order they should occur. Given that there is a general recognition of the need to transform our attitudes about women in order to treat them equally and fairly, a change in the criminal law removing the spousal exemption now seems appropriate. Such a reform would replace an anachronism with a policy which more accurately reflects current attitudes to women in Canadian society.

2. Reform of the Law of Rape

The offence of rape should be removed from the Canadian Criminal Code and replaced by a new offence of sexual assault. This new offence should apply to all forms of unwanted sexual contact involving victims and aggressors of both sexes and to married and unmarried men and women alike. A number of commentators have suggested that the offence of rape should be re-conceptualized as an assault, so as to focus attention on unwanted sexual intercourse as a violation of the integrity of the person. This change in emphasis reflects the opinion, that rape is an aggressive, violent act in which sex is merely an ingredient, rather than an unnatural sexual act based on perverse sexual drives. In addition, the new offence would be distinctly different from the present offences of rape and indecent assault, which it would subsume, in that it would apply to all unwanted sexual contact and penetration involving males and females as both victim and aggressor. This would represent a movement away from the traditional sex-role stereotyping of males as aggressors and females as victims.

No discussion of the rape/sexual assault re-conceptualization would be complete without mentioning that one of the broader positive effects anticipated as a result of the reform is a gradual lessening of the negative stigma which presently attaches to a rape victim. Through the change of emphasis from one of role stereotyping and the shift from the sexual aspect of the crime to its assaultive nature it is possible that the folklore which presently exists about men, women and rape, which inevitably reflects unfavorable perceptions of both men and women, will diminish and eventually disappear. The re-conceptualization of unwanted sexual intercourse as assault will also be helpful in emphasizing that the inter-spousal rape is a part of the larger question of violence in the family. Any policy developed to cope with or to confront violence in the family should apply to sexual assault between spouses, as it is merely another expression of family disharmony manifested in aggressive activity.

3. Use of the Criminal Law

Even though we may agree that the values contained in the law of inter-spousal rape are no longer acceptable, such an agreement does not exhaust the questions which must be confronted by those seeking law reform. Given that we see the present law as unacceptable, we must be sure not to create a new law which is equally if not more problematic. It is necessary to consider whether the criminal law is the best mechanism to deal with the harm of unwanted sexual intercourse between spouses, and to assess any possible negative effects which such a reform may have. Among those raised most frequently are the undermining of the family unit through unnecessary legal intervention, abuse of the law by vindictive spouses and fostering of disrespect for the law by creating a law which will present critical problems of enforcement and proof.

As for undermining the family unit, it is difficult to see that the availability of a sexual assault charge to spouses would disrupt constructive family relationships, as a healthy family will not be the situs for sexual assault. Even in those families experiencing some difficulty, it is unlikely that a spouse will resort to a sexual assault charge without first seeking other, more supportive and less traumatic intervention. A marriage will not stand or fall on the availability of a sexual assault charge, but rather the stability of a marriage depends upon a positive relationship between spouses. Violence in the form of sexual assault is an indicator that the family unit may need intervention. A sexual assault charge would not be used every time such activity occurred, just as assault and battery charges do not result from every family brawl. The charge is likely to be used only where the relationship is so destructive as to force the victim to seek extreme legal intervention. In these cases we should offer the individual members the full protection of the law.

The suggestion that sexual assault charges will be laid falsely by vindictive spouses is grounded in negative folklore about rape victims. There is no empirical data to support such an assumption and it will only be by providing access to the judicial process for all that it can be discovered whether the law would be abused. In addition, the criminal justice system has evolved to include a series of checks and balances created to ferret out the innocent and to punish only the guilty. In a system somewhat renowned for letting ten guilty people go free so as not to convict one innocent person, unjustified charges should not be a serious problem.

It is possible that there will be problems in the enforcement of the sexual assault provision when it is applied to spouses, just as there are presently problems of enforcement in relation to existing assault and battery laws. The police are, understandably, hesitant to interfere in family life, and are aware that they run a high risk of injury when they do so. However, problems of enforcement must not be permitted to supercede fundamental values and the protection of spouses from family violence. These problems should be confronted by those responsible for the administration of justice and efforts should be made to change attitudes and improve procedures for family intervention.

The same points may be made in regard to the obvious problems of proof which would arise in sexual assault charges between spouses. The present rape law is notorious for the evidentiary problems which arise at trial, yet few, if any, would argue that we should remove the offence for that reason and give no protection to potential victims. Difficulties of proof have never deterred the legislature or the courts from enacting or implementing laws which address the preferred shared values in our society. In addition, until we have seen the law in action, we are hard pressed to determine whether difficulties of proof will be prohibitive. It would be erroneous and unfortunate, particularly from the perspective of women in Canadian society, to defer law reform based on well-founded principle simply due to apprehended procedural difficulty. We must be careful not to fall into the trap of regarding legal systems, in both their substantive and procedural content, as static and unchangeable. They must continually be modified and adapted in response to evolving societal perceptions.

Change, whether it be legal change or, on a broader scale, social change, does not come in tidy, pre-measured instant packages which solve all problems simultaneously and provide easy answers and smooth roads. Therefore the preferred order of priorities, at least within the law reform context, should be, first to change the law so that it reflects the principle and value of equality in marriage; then to observe the law in operation and determine what, if any, further changes are necessary.

4. Alternative Forms of Intervention

Although this chapter argues for the criminalization of inter-spousal sexual assault, I am by no means suggesting the application of the full force of the criminal law in every case. The criminal law is not the most appropriate tool for intervention into most families. Criminalizing inter-spousal sexual assault will symbolically affirm the equality of women in marriage. It will provide spouses with the opportunity to seek police intervention should it be needed and it may have some deterrent value. It should not, however, preclude the options available at civil law and it need not mean that the traditional criminal justice system will be unleashed in its full force in response to a criminal charge between spouses.

The civil law provides several courses of action which may be pursued by an abused spouse. Among these are actions in tort for injury, restraining orders for injunctions, separation orders and divorce actions. Each of these actions could be reformed so as to provide more appropriate and effective remedies for inter-spousal assaults. For those spouses who do not find civil remedies adequate and who wish to pursue the criminal law, it is possible to conceive of modified uses of the criminal law in relation to violence in the family, which would provide less destructive alternatives than the traditional criminal process of arrest, trial and imprisonment. For example, it may be preferable to designate the family court as the court of first instance in cases of violence in the family, including inter-spousal sexual assault. This alternative becomes particularly attractive when one considers the possibility of creating family courts which emphasize conciliation and support services as well as sentencing alternatives to imprisonment. Unfortunately, such courts as presently exist in Canada are only experimental.

Within the alternative of designating the family court as the court of first instance in cases of intrafamilial violence, there are several options. The judge could have the discretion to transfer the case to criminal court, with or without the consent of one or both of the parties. Conversely, the court of first instance could be the criminal court, with discretion in the judge to transfer the case to family court with or without the consent of one or both of the parties. Each of these alternatives has advantages and drawbacks, but each one would be, in most cases, preferable to resorting to the full weight of the criminal justice system. It is far better that a husband and wife between whom a sexual assault has occurred should have an opportunity to receive counseling or, alternatively, to agree to separate, than to bring the offending spouse before the criminal court for a determination of guilt or innocence. The latter will have little if anything to do with the relationship between the spouses within the family unit and may result in further unnecessary disruption of the family unit. However, the choice of which alternative to pursue must ultimately be left to the victim and the accused person's right to jury trial must not be infringed without his or her consent.

There are thus several possible alternative courses of action which may be taken in relation to inter-spousal sexual assault. Among the alternatives are determination and eradication of the primary causes of intrafamilial violence; increased public dialogue and education about violence in the family in order to change attitudes about it so that it is increasingly discouraged; increased supportive/preventive services of families experiencing problems; use of the civil law as a source of protection and redress and, finally, use of the criminal law in a modified form to provide symbolic value statements, intervention, supportive services and various sanctions.

Removal of the inter-spousal exception to rape and consequently to sexual assault may result in an increased use of some or all of these resources. These must be improved in quality and availability in order that the criminal law, although available to those who feel that it is necessary, be regarded as a last resort on a continuum of resources focused on the increased well-being of the family unit and each of its members.

NOTES

1. Criminal Code, R.S.C. 1970, c.c-34, s. 143: "A male person commits rape when he has sexual intercourse with a female person *who is not his wife* (a) without her consent, or (b) by her consent if the consent (i) is extorted by threats or fear of bodily harm, (ii) is obtained by personating her husband, or (iii) is obtained by false and fraudulent representations as to the nature and quality of the act." (Emphasis supplied).
2. *R. v. Clarke,* [1949] 2 All E.R. 448; *R. v. Miller,* [1954] 2 Q.B. 282; *R. v. O'Brien,* [1974] 3 All E.R. 663.
3. The total absence of reported Canadian cases concerning a charge of rape brought by a wife against her husband suggests that the language in section 143 has been given a strict interpretation by prosecutors.
4. This justification of the inter-spousal rape exception may also be found in *R. v. Miller* (above, note 2).
5. Mill, John Stuart, "The Subjection of Women", reprinted in Rossi, Alice S. (ed.), *Essays on Sex Equality by John Stuart Mill and Harriet Taylor Mill.* Chicago, Illinois: University of Chicago Press, 1970.
6. Engels, Friedrich, *The Origin of the Family, Private Property and the State.* Reprinted, New York, New York: Int'l Publishers, 1942.
7. Brownmiller, Susan, *Against Our Will: Men, Women and Rape.* New York, New York: Simon & Shuster, 1975.

Chapter 10

Spousal Abuse in the United States: The Attorney's Role

*James B. Boskey**

In evaluating the attorney's role in situations of spousal abuse the first question is whether there is in fact any such role, or, if there is, whether that role is in any way different from the general role of advisor and counselor that is the primary function of any attorney in a family law matter of any kind. The assumption has been made in the United States in recent years that the law is able to provide a solution to all kinds of social problems, and this attitude has been encouraged by the partial success of the law in dealing with problems such as child abuse,[1] discrimination on the basis of race[2] and similar matters.

In the case of inter-spousal violence, however, it appears that the law may have met its match. A problem has come to the fore to which the law, as practiced by private counsel, can provide no answer. This is not to say that there is not a role for private counsel in attempting to ameliorate the situation of a wife or husband who has been subjected to unreasonable physical or emotional violence. It is rather a recognition that the role of the attorney in such matters is not distinguishable from the usual practice of family related law, and that the attorney, in cooperation with other professionals and advocates, should therefore seek law reform to ease the difficulties of those who are caught in such violence.

In order to understand the reason that the attorney's role is so limited, it is necessary to examine the traditional responses of the law to inter-spousal violence. While such violence has only recently been recognized by the 'helping professions' as endemic,[3] the law has recognized it for many years. Any attorney whose practice has included matrimonial matters has heard time and time again the allegation that a particular spouse was physically abused by his or her husband or wife, and indeed in England the phrase, 'he beat me on and about the head' became a legal synonym for a trite pleading, so commonly did it appear in the allegations of those seeking divorce or other matrimonial remedies.

Over the years the law has developed a series of responses to such intrafamilial violence. Prior to the development of modern divorce laws, an action would sound in equity to bar the continuation of violence that threatened the life or health of a spouse,[4] and it was recognized, even in the canon law, with its extreme

* Seton Hall Law School, U.S.A.

respect for the sanctity of the matrimonial home, that the spouse who was the subject of physical violence had a right to leave the marital home and to receive suitable compensation in the form of support on undertaking such a departure. With the development of modern divorce laws, an even clearer remedy for such violence was provided.[5] A spouse who was subjected to physical cruelty was, in most jurisdictions, provided the opportunity to escape from his or her marriage and to receive payment of support and the expenses of divorce where that remedy was sought.[6] It should be noted that this remedy was, until recently, usually restricted to the wife, but the justification for this, appropriate to the time in which it arose, was that the husband was far more likely to be able to support himself than was the wife after a termination of their marriage.

In addition to these civil remedies, the law provided a number of criminal remedies which could be invoked against the violent spouse. While the crime of rape was not recognized between husband and wife,[7] most of the other offenses of violence were not formally so limited, and a spouse who caused injury to his or her mate could be prosecuted criminally for the commission of such violence.

The objection must now be raised that, although all of these laws are on the books, they do not provide a truly adequate remedy in many cases of inter-spousal violence. The criminal penalties exist, but they are difficult to enforce as both the police and prosecuting authorities (where the two are separate entities) are reluctant to intervene and even where one party to the violence actively attempts to have a prosecution brought, he or she may be deterred by the barriers erected by such officials.[8] In addition to the reluctance to bring such actions, the effect of these actions being brought is often harmful rather than helpful to the abused spouse. He or she may be subjected to further violence in response to having brought and prosecuted the criminal complaint, and, even where that does not occur, the loss of income suffered by the violent spouse (either in paying a fine for the offense or from loss of time at work during imprisonment) may mean that there is even less money available to meet the needs of the victim. Further, it should be pointed out that the criminal penalties for non-homicidal assaults are relatively light and the protection the victim receives by virtue of the isolation of the offender in prison will be short-lived.[9]

As for the civil remedies, these may be even less effective for the complaining spouse. In many cases the spouse is not seeking to terminate the marriage, and these remedies are frequently available today only in the context of an action for divorce.[10] Even if the spouse is willing to go to this extreme, the civil remedies pose additional difficulties which may prevent their use.

In the first place, the civil action does not provide immediate relief to the petitioner. If the spouse-victim lacks funds for his or her support during the pendency of the action, even the relatively short delay before an order for temporary support can issue may be fatal to the opportunity to bring the action. In many cases the victim of spousal abuse is an isolated individual who may not have family or friends to tide them over the period of economic difficulty, and even when this is not the case, the victim may be too embarrassed by his or her situation to be willing to seek or accept such support from those who might offer it.

Even if an order for support issues rapidly, the enforcement of such orders is a somewhat chancy matter. Recent studies have indicated that of all support orders issued only a nominal number continue to be met seven years after their establishment, but in many cases even obtaining the first payment under the order may be a matter of substantial difficulty. The expense and time involved in regular prosecution for failure to meet a support order is such that counsel may be reluctant to undertake a matter in which such intransigence is likely, and even if it is undertaken, the expense may consume much of the monies recovered.

Even assuming that financial barriers to such an action do not exist or can be overcome, other problems remain with respect to the civil action as a solution in these cases. The only remedies against continued spousal violence which the civil law provides are the above-mentioned equitable restraining order and its cousin, the temporary restraining order (or, as it is commonly known, TRO). The effect of either of these orders is to direct the offending spouse not to undertake any action which might interfere with the rights of the petitioner. The order may be restricted to prevent only specific types of activities or may be sufficiently extensive to direct that the offending spouse shall not physically approach the petitioner at any time. Could such an order be directly enforced, it seems likely that it might provide a solution to the problem of continued violence after the separation of the parties, but, in general, the only form of enforcement which is available is the issuance of a contempt citation which can be done only after the offense has occurred.

Nor is the threat of a contempt citation likely to put fear in the heart of a person who seriously intends to injure his or her spouse. A violation of the order can, in extreme cases, lead to imprisonment, but the more usual sanction is a fine or, still more likely, a direction from the court to the offender not to repeat the offense. There are many examples of repeated contemnors who have never been subject to any sanction more serious than an occasional lecture on their midconduct from the bench.[11] Thus the abused spouse who attempts to make use of his or her civil remedies is likely to find that the only effect that this has is to increase the degree of risk to which he or she is subject without providing any assurance of a better life situation.

The existence of these lacunae in the enforcement of the law would seem to suggest that the attorney does in fact have a substantial role to play in dealing with the problems of spousal abuse. Traditionally, in areas where the law has been weak, it has been individual counsel, representing a particular client, who has, through creative litigation, been able to bring the majesty of the law to bear on the resolution of such social problems. Even more, where litigation has failed, it has been the attorney who has led in the search for legislative reform to create new judicial remedies that would resolve the difficulties that his or her client faced.

Unfortunately the problem of spousal abuse is a peculiarly difficult one for the courts to resolve. If they could be enforced, existing legal remedies would suffice to resolve this problem in most cases, but the reasons for their non-enforcement rest, not so much with defects in the nature of the remedies or unwillingness of the courts to act, as with very real social forces which appear to require that they should not be used to the full. The sources of these difficulties become apparent when we compare the nature of legislative response to the problem of child abuse to the attempts at providing remedies for abused spouses.

The first question which is always asked by one unfamiliar with the problem of spousal abuse on being made aware of its existence is 'why didn't the abused husband (or wife) simply leave his (or her) spouse?' On its face this question is a perfectly reasonable one, and some commentators have suggested that this is indeed the only proper response for one who has been subjected to serious violence in the course of a marriage. From the viewpoint of the abused spouse, however, the question may be a far more difficult one. Most people feel that when they marry they have a substantial investment in the continuance of the marital relationship. Despite the current high statistical probability of divorce resulting from any marriage, the ideal typical marriage is seen as one that lasts for the lifetime of the spouses. This view is encouraged by the religious doctrine of most, if not all, religions and even by the words of the model marriage ceremony: 'till death do us part'. The extent of this investment is no less for a person who enters into a marriage with a person who turns out to be physically or emotionally abusive.[12]

The same ideal-typical lifelong relationship exists in the parent-child relationship, but from the viewpoint of legal doctrine, the state, as a third party, has a far more serious interest in this relationship. While the state has a formal interest in every marriage, the extent of that interest has usually been seen as limited to a desire that the relationship, whatever its nature, is as permanent a one as possible, and it has usually been felt that the only time that the state should be permitted to intervene between husband and wife is at the time of formation or termination of that relationship.

With regard to the parental relationship, however, the state has always been far more ready to intervene. The state's position as *parens patriae* to all children has long been seen as giving it the right to intervene in the manner in which a child was raised, at least in extreme circumstances. A major part of the rationale for this power was the fact that the child did not have the ability, either physically or legally, to protect itself in a situation of danger. Also important is the fact that it could be assumed that the child would not be able to make a mature decision as to its own needs, and that that very immaturity entitled the state to substitute its decision for that of the child. Thus, under modern law, when a child is abused it is assumed that the state has the power to intervene to remove the child from its home or to otherwise assure that the source of the danger to it is removed, by treatment of the parent or otherwise. It is worth noting, as has been frequently stated in the literature, that in many cases even the most severely abused child would, if consulted, oppose the action of the state in removing it from the only home which it has ever known.[13]

In dealing with inter-spousal violence, however, the basis for state intervention is far more tenuous. Despite Tolstoy's statement that "(h)appy families are all alike; every unhappy family is unhappy in its own way,"[14] it is clear that every married couple makes its own accommodations to the stresses of matrimony and long-term cohabitation. Unless the form of this accommodation is such as to be a substantial disturbance to the way of life or mores of the surrounding community, it seems inappropriate for the state to intervene to regulate it.

In the child abuse model, however, this is exactly what the state would be required to attempt. Certainly some forms of spousal abuse are so extreme that they cannot be tolerated by the surrounding community (*i.e.,* homicide), but in many cases the fact that there is violence between the spouses in a marriage may be, for that couple, an appropriate means of dealing with the strains of daily living. If the state were to attempt to regulate such forms of interaction, the only effect that would be likely would be to drive the problem even further underground and to make it still more difficult for a spouse to escape from an undesired form of violence.

Thus, it is apparent that the prime reason for the success of the law in dealing with child abuse is the fact that there is an appropriate philosophical basis for bringing the force of the law to bear on the problem. Counsel can operate in the system, as there is clearly, in the view of the public or the state, a person who is in need of protection and the law can intervene to protect the person who has no option to protect him or herself. In spousal abuse this pattern does not apply. It is unacceptable to intervene to protect an adult who does not request this protection, and counsel is therefore limited to acting on the request of the victim. This means that there can be little serious attempt, through the law, to treat the problem generically, and the most that can be done is to provide those who wish a way out of their dilemma with services.

This becomes increasingly clear in an examination of the range of alternatives which have been used for the treatment of child abuse. I do not mean to suggest by this that such an evaluation would exhaust the intervention alternatives for dealing with inter-spousal violence, but merely that such analysis is revealing of the types of problems that would likely result from an attempt at comprehensive treatment. The ultimate treatment option in child abuse is removal of the victim from the home.[15] The reasons that this is unacceptable in spousal abuse situations have already been indicated. However, one additional factor should be pointed out. When a child is removed from its home, it is presumed that the child will be placed in a setting that will supply the things that were lacking in its home environment. No model has yet been proposed for a facility which could provide these same needs for an abused spouse. Even the 'in home' treatment modalities for child abuse provide no greater likelihood of success when applied in the arena of spousal violence. Two basic treatment styles exist, but each of them fails in substantial degree to be useful in dealing with spousal abuse.

The first major treatment model is that of counseling. Such counseling may range from intensive psychiatric care to the provision of behavior modification techniques such as alternative foci for the anger that gives rise to abuse or facilities which can be used to give temporary protection when violence is likely to occur. Although each of these techniques has had some degree of success in the treatment of child abuse, and each has its advocates, none of them has been shown to be consistently effective. When these techniques are applied to the spousal violence situation, the likelihood of their success is slight. Both psychiatric and other forms of counseling are successful only when there is a strong motivation for the participant to cooperate fully. In child abuse that motivation can be provided by the threat of removal of the child, but no such pressure can be brought to gain cooperation in spouse abuse cases.

The second model, education, fails for similar reasons. Again, motivation plays a major role in its success with child abuse, and the same impulse is lacking here. Further, this model has been most successful in child neglect cases where the problems arose from lack of knowledge, while in spousal abuse the role played by lack of knowledge is more limited and the kind of information on establishing a suitable relationship is far more difficult to convey. Thus, the implications of the failure of the child abuse model for the role of the private attorney in the generic treatment of spousal violence should be clear. We have already noted the various types of services that it is possible for an attorney to render to a person seeking a way out of such a situation, but it is now appropriate to re-examine them in the light of this evaluation.

The classic area of participation of private counsel is the civil courts, and it is therefore appropriate to examine this first. As already noted, divorce may be an appropriate remedy in cases of spousal abuse, and here the attorney can be of help to the victim. The nature of the attorney's assistance is not, however, substantially distinct from the services that he or she might render in a divorce action which did not involve such abuse. True, it is possible for the attorney to obtain a temporary restraining order (TRO), but, for reasons we shall examine in a moment, this is not a particularly useful remedy. It may also be possible for the attorney to move rapidly to obtain support for the victim, but this is his or her role regardless of existence of abuse, and, in fact, it seems likely that the case will not be handled substantially differently than any other case of termination of marriage.

The prime apparent differences between the divorce case which involves spousal abuse and that which does not is the obtaining of the restraining order. Such an order is not likely to have any substantial effect in reducing the amount of post separation violence.[16] It has already been pointed out that the prime enforcement mechanism for such orders, contempt, is applicable only after the fact of their violation. The reason that the contempt citation, even where used, has been such an inadequate protection rests in the lack of sanctions that are normally imposed for its violation.

There are, however, good reasons for the court's general refusal to impose serious sanctions for violation of the TRO. It is a generally accepted tradition in western law (and almost always elsewhere as well) that divorce is undesirable. The effect of a non-molestation order is to prevent the parties who are seeking the divorce from meeting, and thus substantially to reduce any possibility of reconciliation. Statistics in this area are very weak, but it is an article of faith in the courts that reconciliation after the commencement of a divorce action is a real possibility. Thus the court is usually reluctant to issue a TRO in the first place as it will limit the possibility of reconciliation and is unwilling to give it too stringent enforcement for fear that in doing so it will eliminate any such possibility in the future.

A further factor in discouraging the use of the TRO as an effective means of limiting post-separation violence is the difficulty the court faces in knowing the reality of the threat which it is claimed is posed to the victim. Even in jurisdictions which have, in theory, eliminated fault as a factor in the awarding of support, many judges continue to consider it, *sub silentio,* in the awarding of alimony and the fixing of property settlements. Thus it is not uncommon for a TRO to be sought as a device to help establish in the court's mind the justifiable position of the alleged victim.

Similarly a TRO may be sought as a matter of spite by a spouse who, at the time of divorce, is bitter about the breakdown of the marital relationship. Its use in such cases can be to create inconveniences for the other spouse in the enforcement of his or her rights in the divorce action. With the strong likelihood of such ignoble motives in mind, the court is generally unwilling to use the full scope of its enforcement powers to support the TRO. It is only in the rare case where the court can be sure that protection is seriously needed that the court will be willing to bring its full force to bear, and this can usually occur only after serious harm has already occurred to the petitioner. While it might, in theory, be possible to avoid these problems by requiring substantial proofs to be entered in support of a request for a TRO, this would in fact be self-defeating as this would delay the issuance of the order, and, in many cases make the expense of obtaining it prohibitive.

It thus seems appropriate to discard the civil arena as a likely area for increasing the effectiveness of the courts in providing assistance to the victim of inter-spousal violence. What then of the criminal case as a means of attempting to solve the problem?

The first observation to be made is that the criminal courts have rarely proved a suitable arena for the adjustment of social problems. The reasons for this are too well known to bear repeating here, but most of them apply with equal vigor to this area. The basic function which the criminal law could serve in this area is the protection of the victim from further harm. In order to serve this purpose it would be necessary either for the risk of punishment to serve as a deterrent to abusive action or for the abuser to be locked away from the victim, presumably by being jailed. Neither of these is likely to occur as a result of criminal prosecution.

The likelihood of arrest for intrafamilial violence is extremely low for several reasons. In the first place, the victim may well be reluctant to bring the force of the criminal law to bear on the abuser, either because of current or residual affection for the abuser or for fear that, on release, the abuser will be more violent as a result of the victim's conduct. Even once the victim calls upon the forces of the law, however, there are substantial factors which inhibit the use of criminal process.[17] (These are discussed in Chapters 5 and 6) It is, of course, possible for the experienced attorney to intervene to encourage the making of an arrest in such situations, but it is rare that the opportunity is presented. Intra-family battles do not usually occur in the attorney's office, and it would be highly unusual for the attorney to be present at the time that they do occur. Thus, it would generally be unrealistic to expect attorney intervention at this level.

Even in the absence of an arrest it is possible to proceed with a criminal prosecution, but many of the same problems surrounding arrest interpose themselves at this time. Most of the family cases in which a complaint is filed are dropped for lack of prosecution by the complaining witness, and it is very difficult for even the most experienced prosecutor to determine which complaints are likely to lead to trial. In addition, evidence of the assault is usually circumstantial at best, and the problems of proving a case of spousal abuse are such as to discourage their active pursuit.[18] As stated earlier, even a successful prosecution is not likely to lend substantial protection to the victim of abuse. Sentences are seldom severe, but even if they are, they could do more harm than good if there is any chance at continuing the marital relationship.

However, the situation for the abused spouse need not be so bleak as it may appear from the foregoing. While no substantial aid for the victim of abuse is to be found in legal remedies, other approaches to the problem are more hopeful. For the victim who wishes to escape from the abusive marriage, the legal mechanisms exist to make this possible. When these are combined with the provision of shelters for abused spouses and their children which are now coming into existence throughout the world, the opportunity to escape becomes a more realistic one.

For the victim who hopes to improve his or her situation without terminating the marriage relationship, the prospects are bleaker, but not totally lacking. It appears that in many cases counseling can be effective to stop abuse and, while there are no effective legal sanctions to bring the abuser to accepting such counseling, a variety of social institutions exist that can aid in bringing pressure to bear on the abusive spouse to accept treatment. In many cases, of course, such treatment may be unavailing, but the opportunity to try to ameliorate the situation is there.

NOTES

1. See generally Kempe, H.C. and Helfer, R., *Helping the Battered Child and His Family.* New York, New York: Lippincott, 1972.
2. *Brown v. Board of Education,* 347 U.S. 483 (1954). For the partial nature of the success, see Graglia, L.A., *Disaster By Decree* (1976).
3. Martin, D., *Battered Wives.* San Francisco, California: Glide, 1976, chap. 2.
4. deFuniak, W.R., *Handbook of Modern Equity.* Boston, Mass.: Little Brown & Co., 1956, p. 127.
5. Physical cruelty was one of the first grounds of divorce to receive near universal recognition.
6. See generally Talley-Morris, N.B., *Family Law Practice and Procedure Handbook.* Englewood Cliffs, New Jersey: Prentice Hall, 1973.
7. *State v. Smith,* 100 N.J.L.J. 489 (Essex Cty. Ct. 1977).
8. Langley, R. and Levy, R., *Wife Beating.* New York, New York: E.P. Dutton, 1977, chap. 10.
9. Martin, *supra* note 3, chap. 5.
10. Langley, *supra* note 9, chap. 5.
11. Martin, *supra* note 3, chap. 5.
12. Krause, H., *Family Law.* St. Paul. Minnesota: West Publ. Co., 1976, pp. 575-583.
13. See generally Kempe, *supra* note 1.

14. Tolstoy, L., *Anna Karenina,* p. 1.
15. Kempe, *supra* note 1.
16. Martin, *supra* note 3, 101-108.
17. Truninger, E., "Marital Violence: The Legal Solutions" (1971), 21 *Hastings L.J.* 259, 271-5.
18. See Parnas, "The Police Response to the Domestic Disturbance", (1967) *Wisc. L.R.* 914.

Chapter 11

Inter-Spousal Violence: Discovery and Reporting

*Garry L. Bell**

The objective of this chapter is to discuss some of the methods which will assist us to increase the percentage of reported cases of inter-spousal violence and simultaneously to apply innovative approaches to meeting the problem. By 'reporting' I refer to the processes of making contact between the service system and the people involved in inter-spousal violence. It has been stated that any comprehensive theory on the causation of inter-spousal violence "must take into account factors at several levels, placing individual functioning within the social group and within the cultural norms by which the group operates."[1] Similarly any examination of factors inhibiting people from reporting such behavior must account for an equally diverse variation in the source of such inhibitions.

From a statistical and academic frame of reference reporting is an end in itself. From a humanistic, legalistic, or service point of view reporting is merely the point of entry. The primary goals in relation to inter-spousal violence may be stated as follows:

(1) To provide immediate assistance to those individuals currently victimized by or victimizing a spouse through violent behavior.
(2) To identify and alter those societal norms and socializing patterns deemed to sanction the use of violence as a coping mechanism.

Discovery (that is, the gathering and tabulation of data) and reporting are precursors to any meaningful action in achieving these goals. Reporting refers to the crucial question of 'case finding'. We rely on two sources to discover any instance of domestic violence, either self-report or third party complaint. The number of inhibiting factors surrounding both these sources means that we have very crude estimates of the extent of inter-spousal violence. Statistics that we do have are seldom codified to give meaningful answers to this specific topic. Reporting is needed to discover the nature of the problem. Our understanding is minimal; we must have more information.

---

* Youth Services, Royal Canadian Mounted Police.

At present the most obvious sources of information are police reports, court rosters and files of hospital emergency departments. Police do not report on all domestic complaint calls, and reports that are made are generally filed as assault, aggravated assault, homicide, or special. Information specific to marital violence cannot easily be culled out of these records. Hospital records are invalid because a large percentage of people requiring emergency medical care deny the source of their injuries out of embarrassment, fear or for other reasons.[2] In spite of these shortcomings, a great many domestic violence cases come to the attention of the authorities. Del Martin reports some American police departments as having greater than 50 percent of all calls recorded as domestic disputes.[3] One hospital in 1974 reported that 70 percent of the assault cases they handled were women assaulted in their own homes.[4]

Sixty percent of the women receiving service from Interval House in Toronto report having been beaten.[5] In Transition House Regina, 60 percent of their clients were there for that reason.[6] The raw numbers of domestic complaints alone make it obvious that family violence is a pervasive problem. The U.S. Federal Bureau of Investigation has estimated in 1973 that the "unreported figure for rape is ten times the reported incidence" and further that "wife abuse is more under-reported than rape."[7] If such estimates have any validity then the incidence of this problem is staggering. Either way, we are challenged to turn silence and inactivity into righteous indignation and action.

My experience in the Youth Services of the Royal Canadian Mounted Police at Regina, Saskatchewan, has centered on efforts to translate the first of the primary goals stated earlier. That is, provision of immediate assistance from an abstract goal into programs with more specific objectives. Out of this experience I have identified five basic processes which seem to recur and have particular relevance to the question of 'reporting'. I propose first to introduce and describe briefly the five processes. The remainder of the chapter will be devoted to discussing the processes as they apply to three specific programs with which I have had the opportunity to be associated. First let me describe the processes:

1. Recognition of the Problem

If I am not aware that I have a problem, do I have a problem? This seemingly redundant question has special significance to the reporting of inter-spousal violence. For example, if you beat me I obviously feel the pain and discomfort. If however I believe that you have been assigned the right to do it, or that I need it, or that I have no opportunity to escape, I will tell no one. Consider that parents, or anyone acting *in loco parentis,* have the right under English common law to discipline a child with force or violence. Consider the norm suggested by the Chinese proverb that says "A woman married is like a pony bought — to be ridden or whipped at the master's pleasure."[8]

Because we are "culture bound" with a horrendous history of family violence," it is significant for us to recognize that we are no longer to tolerate such behavior."[9] New standards based on the ideal that non-accidental injury perpetrated by one spouse on the other is beyond acceptable limits are needed.

Interveners must be culturally sensitive to their proposed target populations. Both aggressors and victims need to be taught the new norms. Old stereotypes, clichés or traditional forms of interaction sanctioning violence towards one's spouse must be replaced. The style and emphasis of the program must be geared to the readiness of the target population to support the new standards. For example, it may be inappropriate to recommend criminal proceedings and stronger sentences in areas with traditional cultures. Public education may in these areas take priority over legal action.

2. Decision to Act

As was stated earlier, my present concern is with programs oriented toward more immediate or short range change. Translation of theory into practice requires the selection of specific objectives. It requires the selection of a small nucleus of people capable of spearheading such projects. It requires most specifically the acceptance of responsibility to do something about the problem. Action is required at all levels from the individual, public and private sectors, local, provincial and federal jurisdictions; human services, law enforcers, legislators and judiciary alike. All of them must collaboratively endorse their responsibility before action will ensue.

3. Creation of a Climate Favorable to Reporting

This process refers to the methodology of public education. The messages, and the methods used to convey them, are to some extent situation specific. Each of the sub-populations in a given target area can be reached through its own formal and informal network of communication.

In regard to the second primary goal of altering societal conditions giving rise to violent behavior, this process may represent a goal in itself. In fact the processes of public awareness and community participation may be the beginnings of a cultural revolution which will ultimately deal with the primary causes of this problem. In relation to the first goal, getting people to more immediate help can only enhance the number of reported cases.

4. A Reporting Channel

Whether this channel be a crisis hot line, a rape center, a police department or a legal aid center it must meet certain criteria in order to increase the rate of reporting. These are:
Credibility — it must be accepted by the population as a helpful place to call. Past performance counts a great deal in the informal communication network of the target population. Such things as maintaining confidentiality prevent the drying up of reporting sources and help the creation of new ones.
Visibility — the service must be highly publicized and widely known in the target area.

Accessibility — this refers both to being available at the time of need (*i.e.,* 24 hour service 7 days a week) and also to location of premises or ideally a mobile (service goes to client) operation.

Immediacy — this means no waiting list; in crisis terms it means mobile service. If your reporting channel satisfies these criteria the rate of reporting will obviously increase.

5. Evaluation and Data Collection

Hunches, notions, estimates and speculation based on dramatic examples are poor arguments in the eyes of the program funder or the serious student. Gropper and Marvin draw attention to the lack of any reliable national statistics on family violence.[10] At the local level we must begin to gather and codify information on all aspects of family violence. We will never know the actual incidence of such abuse but we can at least know the numbers seeking help.

These five processes alone will not ensure the success of any program designed to provide short term assistance to battered adults. However, not accounting for these processes will ensure less than maximum efficiency in terms of discovery and reporting. These processes can be better understood in application to the three programs which will now be discussed.

(A) Training Police In Crisis Intervention

Policemen play a pivotal role in the reporting of domestic violence. First, they are the only group in society trained to cope with violence. Secondly, they are generally the only universally available 24 hour source of assistance. Lastly, they have greater mobile capacity than other agencies and are regarded as the most logical source of help in regard to violence. Factors like these make the 'police channel' the most crucial link we have to the reporting and management of domestic crises.

One of the most practical steps which has been taken to come to grips with the pervasive problems of family violence is the training of police officers in crisis theory and conflict management techniques. The original impetus for such training arose from the discovery of alarming rates of death and injury to police officers as a result of intervention in domestic disputes.[11] Deeper understanding of the causes of such disputes coupled with more effective use of defusion and de-escalation techniques pays off immediately in increased safety for police.[12] A closer look at this situation reveals a host of potential benefits in a number of areas. Some of the benefits accrue to the client or victim directly, others to the police force as a whole and still others to the public or society generally.

Informed and effective police intervention has the potential to make a major impact on the discovery and reporting of incidents of inter-spousal violence. As with any service delivery system, the role of the 'first contact agent' between service giver and receiver is critical in determining outcome.[13] Apart from the obvious benefits of preventing more serious injury, or property damage, or simply preventing violence and restoring calm, there are more subtle and long range influences. Changing an unknowledgeable and uncertain police intervener into a more confident, assured and receptive source of assistance is an objective of crisis training. Police departments, through unbiased and effective case management, will cease to be viewed as a 'deaf' or 'chauvinistic' ear of an unconcerned society. The more knowledgeable the policeman is about family violence the more confident he will be. Increased confidence means increased willingness and receptivity. In areas where police are accused of giving a 'low profile' to domestic disturbance, knowledge and training have proved to be useful first steps in overcoming these internal sources of resistance.[14]

One of our primary goals in dealing with inter-spousal violence was the provision of immediate assistance. Clearly this goal cannot be achieved without an enlightened and cooperative approach from police departments everywhere. In areas where these programs have begun, the results have been most encouraging. Recipients of service report positive changes in police behavior towards them.[15] Increased rates of referral to social agencies and continued requests for more training from policemen themselves are some indicators of the success of these programs. In my opinion the task is clearly to train all policemen to understand domestic violence and to manage it effectively. To the extent that this task is accomplished, the public view the police as a viable, accessible first step in contending with inter-spousal violence.

(B) Mobile Family Service Society

In 1972, a small group of people in Regina, Saskatchewan, created the Mobile Family Service Society. At the time of implementation, Regina had a multitude of service agencies that were providing a less than adequate service to people with critical family problems after hours and on weekends. The purpose of Mobile was to provide 24 hour crisis intervention services to the city of Regina, regardless of who was experiencing the crisis, what the crisis was and regardless of what agency was mandated to provide the follow-up service. In addition Mobile was responsible for an effective referral for follow-up services.

Mobile Family is operated by a corporate board. In 1976-77 twenty-six human service agencies in the city were represented on this board. This cooperative endeavor to deliver service has done more to operationalize the lofty notions of communication, coordination and integration than I have seen in dozens of committees established for those very purposes.

In terms of accessibility, Mobile communicates with the public in several ways. By telephone they are reached through a mobile family service society number, crisis lines, police department switchboard, department of social services emergency number and a child abuse line. Walk-in clients have increased in frequency each year. Over 60 percent of their contacts are face to face.[16] In terms of the criterion of immediacy, response time per call for 1976-1977 dropped to seven minutes from a previous years average of 14 minutes.[17]

It was suggested earlier that the rate of reporting was closely allied to the degree of 'visibility' of the program. My assumption is that Mobile Family in three years has become as well known to the public as most social service agencies which have existed for twenty years or more. This assumption is supported by the evidence that the rate of self-referral has increased to a remarkable 42 percent.[18] Police referrals have dropped to 27 percent, suggesting that many people who previously came via the police are now making direct contact. The increase in second party complaints may also support the notion of a generally higher level of visibility to the public. If we assume that the overall usage of a service by the public is a measure of the relevance and credibility of the service, then Mobile Family is being successful in creating a favorable climate for reporting. This statement is based on the fact that Mobile has tripled itself in demands for service over three years.[19]

As was mentioned earlier, data collection regarding inter-spousal violence is almost non-existent. In 1976-77 Mobile Family switched its data collection format to a computer based system which will allow for a much more precise breakdown of information. At the moment we know that eleven percent of the work-load deals with marital discord. By the end of next year we will have specific information pertaining to the use of violence in the family.

The existence of Mobile Family came about as an indirect by-product of the training of the police in crisis intervention. It is ironic and encouraging that a number of recruits in training at Police Depot Division in Regina now spend time working with the staff at Mobile Family. This integration and cross-fertilization of roles and functions at the training level will have significant impact on police community relations in years ahead.

(C) Regina Transition House

This third program on which I would like to comment relates more exclusively to the problem of inter-spousal violence than either of the two previous programs. It originated from the insights and efforts of two of the original staff of crisis workers in the Mobile Family Program. Having identified the need from their first hand experience at Mobile, Lisa Brownstone and Karen Perrin spearheaded the creation of Regina Transition Women's Society in September of 1975. Their purpose was to establish a house which would provide safe, temporary housing and support counseling to women and children leaving their homes in crisis situations.[20]

A house was purchased, and opened its doors, in January 1976. The facility has a capacity for six families with each family having their own private room. Communal cooking, dining and living is carried out on the main floor. In the first year a total of 108 families (353 people) stayed an average of sixteen days per family unit.[21] Almost 70 percent of the women came because of marital breakdown. Alcohol use contributed to 94 percent of these breakdowns. Sixty percent of the women and seven percent of the children who came had been physically abused.[22] In this facility, as in virtually every one of its kind,[23] overcrowding and waiting lists give evidence that the demand outstrips the supply of this service. Interestingly, Mobile Family Services are the largest single referring source to Transition House, accounting for 41 percent of their intake.

As a result of data collected on women leaving the facility, another support program has been created in the community. Thirty percent of the women went through conciliation and returned to their husbands. The remaining 70 percent seem to find difficulty learning to cope with the community on their own.[24] To this end Transition House has aided in the creation of a 'Self-Help Club' that meets monthly to support one another throughout the final stage of their transition to single parent families.

Each of the programs discussed in this chapter are cited as examples of actions taken to confront particular aspects of the problem of inter-spousal violence. Each program separately would be less effective than the interdependent coalition of all of them. Police trained in conflict management rely on the back-up counseling and referral skills of Mobile Family's crisis staff. Mobile Family relies on the existence of Transition House to provide the service. Transition House relies on Mobile Family for referrals and on the police to ensure the safety of their residents. The total impact of this network of services on the community is the creation of visible, credible, and accessible sources of assistance. The problem as stated was to find ways to increase the rate of reporting and discovery of inter-spousal violence. The effective implementation of such crisis management programs as have been discussed here give us, as a society, a potential to respond without which reporting would be senseless. This potential, coupled with a massive education program, represent the key elements in increasing report rates and ultimately in dealing with the causes of inter-spousal violence.

NOTES

1. Hanemann Lystad, Mary, "Violence at Home: A Review of the Literature" (April, 1975), 45 *American Journal of Orthopsychiatry* no. 3, 328.
2. Martin, Del, *Battered Wives.* San Francisco, California: Glide Publications, 1976, p. 11.
3. *Ibid,* p. 12.
4. *Op. cit.,* p. 12.
5. Gropper, Arlene, and Marvin, Joyce, "Violence Begins At Home" (Toronto: Canadian Magazine, November 20, 1976), p. 4.
6. Annual Report, Regina Transition Women's Society (unpublished 1976), p. 8.
7. Martin, Del, *Battered Wives,* p. 12.
8. Gropper, Arlene, and Marvin, Joyce, "Violence Begins at Home", p. 4.
9. de Mause, Lloyd, (ed.), *History of Childhood.* New York, New York: Psychohistory Press, 1974, p. 1.
10. Gropper, Arlene, and Marvin, Joyce, *op. cit.,* p. 4.
11. New York City Police Study, Crisis Intervention: *Training Police as Specialists in Family Crisis Intervention* (Washington: U.S. Government Printing Office, 1970), p. 3.
12. *Ibid,* p. 35.
13. Martin, Del, *op. cit.,* p. 135.

14. Reitz, Willard E., *Evaluation of Police Family Crisis Training and Consultation* (Department of Psychology, University of Western Ontario. London, Ontario: Research Bulletin #289, July 1975), p. 7.
15. *Ibid,* p. 7.
16. Annual Report, Mobile Family Services Society (unpublished 1976), p. 2.
17. *Ibid,* p. 2.
18. *Ibid,* p. 2.
19. *Ibid,* p. 1.
20. Annual Report, Regina Transition Women's Society (unpublished 1976), President's Report, p. 1.
21. Annual Report, Regina Transition Women's Society (unpublished 1976), Executive Director's Report, p. 3.
22. *Ibid.,* p. 8.
23. Martin, Del, *op. cit.,* p. 196.
24. Annual Report, Regina Transition Women's Society (unpublished 1976), p. 8.

Chapter 12

The Family Consultant Service With the London (Ontario) Police Force

*Peter Jaffe and Judy Thompson**

The idea for a Family Consultant Service with the London (Ontario) Police Force was born out of discussions in late 1970 between the present Chief of Police, Walter T. Johnson and Willard E. Reitz, formerly Director of Clinical Psychology Training at the University of Western Ontario. These discussions were stimulated by local newspaper accounts of the alarming number of police calls to handle family conflicts without the needed professional back up. In fact, family crises accounted for four percent to five percent of the police department's dispatched calls, or approximately 4,000 per year. Most of these calls originate in the evening or on weekends between 8 p.m. and 1 a.m. At these times, community social service agencies are not open, with the exception of hospital emergency departments. Police officers feel they neither have the time, competence nor societal mandate to deal with such problems. In addition to this, domestic disputes are amongst the most dangerous calls that police make.

1. The Police Training Program

A solution that seemed the most feasible and also coincided with the possibilities that the Police Force had explored was a training program on family crisis intervention. Funds received from private foundations were utilized to set up such a training program for police officers in 1972. Half the force was trained in the first two months of 1972 (the experimental group) and the other half was trained in the last two months of the year (the control group).

The police training program was broken down into two major components. The first component consisted of the traditional lecture method and covered topics relevant to family crises. Lawyers, social workers, officials of social agencies and hospitals were invited to lecture on their particular areas of expertise. The second component was more experiential in nature. It consisted of role playing wherein officers intervened and handled crisis situations presented to them by actors.

---

* Psychology Department, University of Western Ontario, Canada.

A partial evaluation of this program was performed by Reitz (1975). By interviewing families that had experienced a single intervention with a trained or untrained officer, he found that out of 22 questions that were asked about police services, 14 of the means favored the trained group. The questions 'How satisfied were you with police handling of the problem for which you called them?' and 'How did the London Police act toward you?' yielded statistical significance in favour of the trained group. Reitz also found that the number of spontaneous commendatory letters rose by 75 percent from 1971 for the experimental group and only by 31 percent for the control.

Further evaluation of the training manipulation yielded the following results:

(1) Referrals are an important aspect of a crisis solution. That is, if a family is referred to an agency and receives professional help, it is more likely that the family will seek appropriate assistance rather than call the police when future difficulties arise. This leads to a reduction in domestic disturbance calls to the police department. Our findings indicate that trained officers made significantly more referrals than did untrained officers.
(2) During training, officers were made aware of the large number of specialized agencies within the city. Trained officers made referrals to 37.5 percent of the 40 available agencies while untrained officers made referrals to less than 18 percent of them. Hence, the trained officers used the information given at the training to make a referral to the most appropriate source.
(3) If a family is already involved with a particular agency, officers will often call the agency and relate relevant information concerning the intervention. Trained officers significantly more frequently contacted a previously involved agency than did the untrained officers.
(4) If a family is referred to an appropriate agency or the crisis is dealt with effectively by an officer, the chances of a repeat call should be minimized. For chronic families (defined as families with five or more police interventions) it was found that more untrained officers were attending the first call when compared to all other calls (suggesting unsuccessful crisis resolution). In contrast, more trained officers handled the last call compared to all other calls for chronic families, which indicates successful crisis resolution.
(5) The training manipulation should have no effect on the length of time spent on a case. This hypothesis was confirmed. Thus, the training program produced an increase in effectiveness without a loss of efficiency.

Finally, with regard to the training program, the overall evaluation of the training by officers was clearly favorable with less than five percent giving overall ratings that dropped into the unfavorable range.

2. The Family Consultant Service

The Family Consultant service was planned for 1973, following the training program, and was designed to provide 'around-the-clock' mental health consultation for officers. The consultants became a specialized civilian branch of the force geared to assist officers in providing the best possible service to families and individuals in times of crisis.

Private funding dwindled in the spring of 1974. The Solicitor General's Department at the Federal and Provincial levels, recognizing the value of continuing the project as a possible model for police forces across the country, invested funds for a two year period to maintain and foster the development of the program. The number of Family Consultants expanded to five in 1975 and the service has remained an active and integral part of the London Police Force. As of April, 1976, the Family Consultant service has been solely funded at the municipal level, although research funds are still provided by the Solicitor General of Canada. As a result of this ongoing municipal backing, a more permanent structure was adopted. Basically, the structure consists of:

a) A Management Committee (responsible to the Police Commission) which oversees the activities of the Family Consultant (FC) service and makes recommendations regarding program and personnel policies;
b) A Professional Advisory Council which provides professional consultation and acts as liaison with social service agencies;
c) The Family Consultant service, itself, consisting of a service co-ordinator, four Family Consultants who are responsible for the ongoing functioning of the service, and
d) A Research Co-ordinator who is responsible for collection, evaluation and reporting of data regarding the FC service.

The philosophy and goals of the FC service are:

(1) To assist officers by providing immediate assessment of and intervention in crisis situations and supplying information about or arranging referrals to appropriate community resources,
(2) To aid in the prevention of serious social and/or emotional dysfunctions through early detection and intervention,
(3) To facilitate increased understanding and co-operation between mental health and law enforcement professionals,
(4) To increase community awareness of the social role of the police force,
(5) To provide a model of human services to other communities through careful documentation and evaluation, and
(6) To provide informal in-service and field training for police officers in the area of crisis intervention.

The service operates directly out of the headquarters of the London police department and provides service from 9 a.m. to 4 a.m. weekdays and noon to 4 a.m. on weekends. This seven day a week schedule optimizes service availability and program costs vis-a-vis community and police needs. The consultants, who are in constant radio contact with the communications center for the police, are mobile and can therefore provide immediate assistance to police crisis calls. Approximately 10 percent of all the calls received by the police relate to matters within the domain of the FCs (*e.g.,* domestic disputes, juvenile trouble, suicides, *etc.*). Of these, about one quarter result in an officer's request for assistance from the FC service.

3. Activities of Family Consultants in 1976

The Family Consultants intervened in 1,418 crises with 1,096 families in 1976. Approximately 80 percent of these cases were new cases in 1976 and the remaining families/individuals were from previous years. Seventy-two percent were in response to uniformed officers, six percent from officers in the criminal investigation division and nine percent from other police personnel. Thus, over 85 percent of the calls represent direct assistance to the police, with the rest accounted for by a variety of sources such as agency requests or client initiated calls.

The most frequent types of cases handled by Family Consultants involve either some type of 'family or marital dispute' (32.8 percent) involving physical or verbal conflict, or 'problems with juveniles' (29.4 percent) such as runaways or behavioral management difficulties. Other types of cases include emotional problems (7.2 percent), depression (3.3 percent), alcohol/drug abuse (5.6 percent), need of food or shelter (3.6 percent) and suicidal threats (5.3 percent). As might be expected, the underlying issues leading to a call to the police department are complex. A review of Family Consultant cases in 1976 revealed that 'fear of violence' is one of the most prevalent issues (35.5 percent). In fact, in one-fifth of all interventions, an assault between family members had taken place, with a husband on wife assault being most common. Other issues leading to the crisis are 'separation problems and/or custody rights' (22.9 percent), 'money problems' (22.9 percent), 'child demands greater freedom' (21.5 percent), psychological dysfunctioning' (19.5 percent) and a variety of other, less frequently occurring issues. Further, it appears that alcohol abuse exacerbated the problem in more than one-third of the disputes. This is important as the incidence of family assaults is significantly related to the presence of alcohol in such cases.

For the most part, a uniformed officer will attend a call first and do whatever he feels is necessary to restore the peace and eliminate any possible danger to the individual or family. At this point each officer makes a decision as to whether to call in an FC. There are no hard and fast guidelines set down as to the conditions under which the assistance of a consultant is requested. The usual criteria is that the family or individual benefits from a therapeutic intervention and is willing to utilize this service. The latter criterion may not be observed if an FC intervention is required for individuals whom the officer feels may be a danger to themselves or others.

The FC responds to an officer's call as quickly as possible. In 92 percent of the calls, the interval from the time the call was received until the intervention was less than one hour. Upon arriving at the scene of the call, the officer gives the FC all relevant information pertaining to the crisis and introduces the individual or family to the FC. The officer is then free to leave unless in his judgment a reoccurrence of violence is likely, or he feels he has something to contribute to or learn from the crisis intervention. The FC role at this point is to assess the situation and provide as much counseling as is considered necessary to bring the family or individual through the immediate crisis.

The Family Consultants implement six courses of action in resolving the crisis encountered. The forms of crisis resolution are as follows:

(a) Family Consultant Mediation Alone

In 30.7 percent of the cases the consultant provides immediate counseling at the time of the crisis and feels the family/individual is able to cope with the situation without further intervention by other community resources. The intervention process involved here includes calming the clients, fact-finding and assessment of the problem, deciding upon and pursuing a resolution with the family and, when appropriate, attempting to marshall social network resources such as family and neighbors.

(b) Referral to an Agency

The Family Consultant refers an individual or family to appropriate agencies in those cases (16.3 percent) where the family/individual needs and is willing to seek further assistance for the problems that led up to the crisis. A referral is made to an agency if there is no agency presently involved. The consultant contacts the agency to relay information about the family and to share observations and concerns that arose from the crisis.

(c) Recontact of Agency

When the individual or family is already involved with an agency, the Family Consultant contacts the worker and informs him/her of the crisis as soon as possible. Furthermore, the consultant gives the worker his/her own impressions of the family and makes recommendations regarding treatment. The agency worker usually furnishes background information about the case and, in many instances, the Family Consultant and the agency worker jointly plan a tentative course of action in the event that the consultant intervenes again. An agency is recontacted by an FC in 29.8 percent of the cases.

(d) Assessment at the Emergency Department of a Hospital

The Family Consultant recommends immediate psychiatric assessment for individuals at one of the local hospitals. The consultant usually attends at the hospital to offer support to the person and his family and to inform the hospital staff of the presenting problem and any relevant background information. This form of resolution occurs in approximately one-tenth of the cases.

(e) Physician, Lawyer, Clergy or Justice of the Peace Contacted

In 7.1 percent of the cases, the Family Consultant contacts the doctor, lawyer, *etc.,* to inform him of the crisis situation and to share his/her impressions of the family. Sometimes, the consultant assists in making an early appointment for the family or individual.

(f) No Meaningful Intervention Provided

In 4.8 percent of the cases, the individual or family appear unmotivated or do not want to attempt any suggested changes in their lives at that time.

4. Program Evaluation

Since the inception of the FC program, evaluation has been a major goal and a characteristic interest of those involved in the evolution of the service. The initial evaluation concerns involve a few basic issues: (i) When do family crises occur and does the FC program provide a service which does not overlap with other community agencies? (ii) Is there a therapeutic and cost advantage to immediate or early intervention as the literature suggests? (iii) Is the program effective in preventing future family crises? (iv) Do the police and social agencies evaluate the service positively? and (v) Does the FC program increase cooperation between mental health and law enforcement professionals?

With respect to the first concern it is clear that the FC program provides crisis services at times when other agencies cannot. This, together with the immediacy of the FC intervention, increases the likelihood that adaptive changes will result from the crisis intervention. The majority of family crises occur when existing social agencies are closed. The most likely times are weekends and after 8 p.m. A more detailed breakdown reveals that 88 percent of the disturbances occur at times other than the traditional 9 a.m. to 5 p.m., Monday to Friday working hours of most social service agencies. Thus, before the advent of the FC service, police officers were left to their own resources to resolve most crises.

The next question concerns the advantages of early intervention; one of the defining characteristics of the FC approach, of course, is the ability to intervene immediately following the 'cooling' of the crisis by the police officer, and often during the actual crisis period. The only data we have been able to gather to date concerns the immediate post-crisis period. Our data indicates a relationship between the immediacy of agency contact following a crisis and the acceptance of appointments. Eighty-five percent of the families/individuals referred to agencies by Family Consultants accepted appointments if the contact was 24 hours or less following the FC intervention. In contrast, approximately 30 percent of the families did not accept appointments with agencies if the time lapse between the crisis intervention and the agency contact was more than 24 hours. This finding emphasizes the importance of immediate contact by agencies in assisting individuals or families in time of crisis. In this capacity, the FC program plays a critical role. The importance of this role is highlighted by preliminary data we have gathered showing that unresolved family crises, as reflected in multiple call families, significantly increases the probability that physical violence will occur in future family disputes.

This brings up the question of prevention. Does the FC service prevent the occurrence of future family crises? To evaluate this we examined the extent to which both one contact and multiple contact ('repeat callers') families were reduced following introduction of the FC program. The importance of looking at multiple contact families as a distinct group lies in the higher cost of treatment associated with such families, who often (about 25 percent) are involved with three or more social agencies within a single year. Characteristic of these chronic call families is their resistence to treatment and their poor response to most therapeutic interventions offered by social service agencies. Referral feedback information received from agencies indicated that 45 percent of those referred did not accept appointments. Of those accepting appointments, contact was only continued in a minimum of cases. These multiple call families over-utilize either the services of the police or other agencies in proportion to their numbers and frequently resist treatment or are given a poor prognosis for treatment by social service agencies. A major thrust of the project is to utilize police as early warning indicators to get people more immediate assistance, thus reducing the probability of them becoming repeat callers. It seems, therefore, that the FC program has been considerably effective in its preventative role.

Another concern in our initial evaluation was the acceptance and evaluation of the FC program by the police officers. A preliminary survey conducted by Reitz (1975) revealed an overwhelming and positive evaluation of the service by the police. An expanded version of the survey was conducted again in 1976 to determine whether such initially favorable views mellowed in the three years of police-consultant activities. However, again the general response of police personnel towards the Family Consultant program was very positive. Over 90 percent of the police officers had a good understanding of the role of the Family Consultant. Furthermore, most officers viewed the consultants as cooperative (99.3 percent), competent (98.4 percent) and having a good understanding of the police role (94.5 percent).

Finally, this evaluation concerns itself with the acceptance of the program by community social service agencies. In late 1976, a questionnaire surveying opinions regarding the Family Consultant service was distributed to social service agencies who accept referrals from the FC service. There was an impressive agency return rate of 74 percent with 68 staff members from 23 different agencies responding. All levels of staff were surveyed and 68.7 percent of the respondents had over five contacts with the FCs in the past year. Almost 90 percent of the respondents indicated that they were satisfied with the 'accuracy of assessment' made by FCs, felt that the FCs were cooperative in the handling of referrals, and indicated that the FCs had an adequate to outstanding 'knowledge of the agency worker's role'. The vast majority of respondents (95.2 percent) acknowledged that the FC service facilitated increased cooperation between law enforcement and mental health professionals. In addition to these more structured responses, there were spontaneous positive comments from one-third of those agency staff sampled which further indicates the widespread acceptance and support of the FC service by community agencies.

A major reason for this strong support is the effectiveness of the service as a liaison between community agencies and the police officers. Before the introduction of the Family Consultant service, only 27.5 percent of the officers utilized the services provided by social service agencies. Presently, however, 88 percent regularly refer cases to the Family Consultants. Social service agency personnel are rarely available at times when crises arise and officers' shifts are such that a considerable amount of time elapses before a referral can be made. Family Consultants can become immediately aware of the crisis and make an appointment with the appropriate agency the following morning. Two-thirds of the FC cases are brought to the attention of community and social service agencies. More meaningful rapport with agencies is possible by means of five Family Consultants than through three hundred officers. In this respect, the Family Consultants are promoting increased cooperation between mental health and law enforcement professionals and, in so doing, ensuring that individuals and families are receiving assistance in times of crisis.

In sum, the evidence appears to support a favorable outcome for the five initial evaluation concerns of the FC program postulated at the beginning of this section. Admittedly, some of this evidence is problematic or only indirectly bears upon these issues, *e.g.,* advantages of early intervention. However, the purpose of this initial evaluation is to establish the basic utility of the program and the merits of further development and evaluation. Current evaluation research is intended to further substantiate the validity of the program.

REFERENCE

Reitz, W., *Evaluation of Police Family Crisis Training and Consultation,* University of Western Ontario Research Bulletin 289, 1975.

Chapter 13

Rapid Intervention With Families in Crisis in a Court Setting

*Barbara Cohn Schlachet**

1. The Rapid Intervention Project

In New York City the Family Court is the legal agency which has authority in all problems and disputes involving members of a family, as well as all matters involving juveniles, defined as all persons under sixteen years of age. Thus, such disparate problems as custody disputes, foster care decisions, abuse of a child or a spouse, support disputes, juvenile delinquency offenses and persons in need of supervision fall under the aegis of the Family Court. Divorce and legal separation are handled by other courts, but issues arising out of a divorce or separation often find their way back into the Family Court.

Until March 1972, the mental health services of the Family Court operated solely in the traditional way that court mental health services have operated in New York City; that is, a staff of mental health experts, housed in one centrally located court building, scheduled evaluations with court-referred clients in order to make recommendations around questions raised by the court. They then submitted a written report to the court, describing the results of their evaluation. The period of time involved from the initial court referral to the time that the judge received the report was approximately two months, and resulted in the case being postponed for that period of time. If a case came before a judge that involved a crisis, one where immediate action had to be taken to prevent harm coming to a person or persons (*i.e.,* suicide, violence, and the like), the judge most often would have to remand the person to a hospital for evaluation. This resulted in many unnecessary hospitalizations, involving considerable cost to the client, both emotionally and physically, as well as to the city. If the judge happened to be housed in the same building as the mental health service, an informal crisis intervention service was devised, whereby the judge could send the person or persons up to the mental health service immediately, have them evaluated by a psychologist or psychiatrist, who would then come directly back to the courtroom and give a verbal report to the judge. The mental health expert could then discuss

---

* (Formerly) Psychologist with the Family Court, New York City, U.S.A.

his/her recommendations with the judge, who could then take them into account in making a disposition. While the judges reported that this was a most valuable contribution of the mental health services, it was not available to most of them, as the Family Court is housed in all boroughs of New York City, and mental health services was only in one courthouse in Manhattan. Also, since the same staff that performed crisis evaluations was also scheduled for appointments in advance, they were only available for a limited number of crisis evaluations. It also became clear that the professional staff who were utilized for these crisis evaluations had to be highly trained, extremely experienced professionals who could operate under stress, often in high-risk situations, and who could conceptualize and present their recommendations under a great deal of time pressure.

This crisis evaluation provided the germ for the Rapid Intervention Project (or RIP, as it came to be known), which was funded by the Law Enforcement Assistance Administration in 1972. RIP was designed to operate, and, indeed, became the 'emergency room' of the Family Court. A separate staff of highly qualified and carefully screened psychologists and psychiatrists, as well as a staff of social workers and community health workers, were hired and housed in court buildings in four boroughs of New York City. These were to operate as teams, to provide not only crisis evaluation, but also follow-up cases that were referred to RIP. No appointments in advance were scheduled for this staff; cases that were not urgent continued to be referred to the traditional court mental health services. Thus, the RIP staff was always suitable for 'on the spot' crisis intervention as soon as the need for it occurred in the court or in the department of probation.

Cases were referred to RIP either by the Court itself, or by Intake Probation, the agency mandated to screen cases before they are assigned to a court for hearing. Cases referred by Intake Probation were often referred for the purpose of diverting the case from the court; e.g., when a case involved a family problem that did not appropriately belong in the court system, but which arrived there because a desperate family had no knowledge of any agency other than the court to which to turn for help. In such cases, RIP was often the means by which the family could be referred to an appropriate social agency, rather than get caught in an endless legal process that would have little to offer them in the end, and often served to exacerbate the problems that brought the family to the court in the first place. Cases were referred directly from the Court for many reasons. A person or persons involved in an action before the Family Court may have exhibited 'bizarre' behavior in the courtroom, or his offense may have been exceptionally violent or strange; a judge may have had a question regarding the need for an immediate disposition, such as whether a person needed to be hospitalized, whether a child could be sent home with his/her parents, or whether immediate placement was indicated. Such cases would be seen immediately by a RIP psychologist or psychiatrist, in conjunction with a community mental health worker, about whom more will be said later. The RIP team, consisting of the psychologist or psychiatrist, social worker, and community mental health worker would then confer to formulate the best recommendation and plan for the people involved. At this point the mental health professional assigned to the case returned to the court to give an oral presentation of the evaluation of the problem, to discuss the judge's questions, and to outline the recommendations jointly agreed upon by the team. The mental health expert was also available for examination by any and all attorneys involved in the case. The RIP staff was available for consultation with all court personnel; probation, representatives of court-related agencies, law guardians, and the like. This brief description describes only the 'bare bones' of RIP. Much could be said about the crucial role of the community mental health workers, the importance of the project's emphasis on outreach into the community and the enlistment of community agencies, the dedication of the staff to both the court and the community that it served, the importance to judges of having an expert who is known and trusted with whom to discuss dispositions involving mental health issues. However, our topic here is how crisis intervention operated in situations of family violence, and what follows is confined to the particular issues and problems that arose in coping with these kinds of cases.

2. RIP and Family Violence

As can be imagined, a fairly large percentage of crisis cases did involve incidents of intrafamilial violence. RIP's orientation was particularly well suited to working with these cases, as it was geared toward seeing a family as an interactional unit, rather than as petitioners and respondents. Thus, where it could be helped, no one member of a family was seen, but, rather, as many members of the family as possible were evaluated before a recommendation was made. It was felt that a family is a unit in which the actions of one person affect all persons, and that frequently the actions of any individual are the result of the interactions between him/herself and other members of the family.

The RIP staff was also sensitized to the culture in which the family exists, both the culture at large, and the sub-cultures to which the family court clients belonged. This becomes an important isue because various sub-cultures have different traditions pertaining to family violence, and what is 'bizarre' in one culture may be acceptable, and even traditional in another. While this may seem to be a shocking statement, let us pause, and consider it for a moment. In almost all Western cultures (I am not familiar with others) some form of intrafamilial violence is condoned, and even encouraged. "Spare the rod, and spoil the child", we say, or we shake our head at the parent who is patiently trying to explain to a child why he should not hurl a toy at the head of his playmate for the third time. "What that child needs", we say, "is a good spanking". Nobody looks askance at the parent who is slapping a child's hand as he reaches toward an empty light socket, or a flame on the kitchen stove, or at the parent who plants a firm slap on the bottom of a child who has just been grabbed out of the path of an oncoming car. Similarly, we have a tradition of accepting violence on the part of husbands towards wives. Shakespeare's *Taming of the Shrew* details the reasons for and methods to insure that a wife knows and is kept in her place. Police and courts are reluctant to intervene in family disputes, even though they may involve violence that, if perpetrated by one stranger on another, might result in a jail sentence. In many civilized cultures, crimes of passion go unpunished or lightly punished, because we can understand the anger that a husband might feel when he discovers that his wife has been having an extra-marital affair, or has even neglected home and hearth for non-sexual outside activities. "A man's home is his castle", we say, and we are reluctant to intervene in the internal workings of that castle, much as we hesitate to intervene in another country's internal strife. Thus, we must be clear when we talk about violence in the family that we are, essentially, talking about the *degree* of violence as a problem, not it's existence.

In this light, it becomes clear that the first task of a court crisis intervention unit is to evaluate whether the violent act that has occurred is one that warrants court intervention, or, for that matter, any intervention. Where do we cross the line between socially sanctioned violence, and violence punishable by law, or requiring intervention? This is not an easily answered question. If a father beats up his adolescent daughter because he finds out that she has been sexually promiscuous, it is a rare court that would prosecute. If he beats up his daughter's girlfriend for the same reason, he is not protected by the umbrella of patriarchal right, and is open to an assault charge. It should be noted, in this context, that family violence is sanctioned according to the power structure of the family. Those who are in a position of power, and presumably responsible for those with less power, are permitted certain kinds of physically and emotionally violent behavior. Those in a family who are bigger, stronger, and more economically powerful are accorded the right to punish, deprive, and verbally abuse those who are smaller, weaker, and economically dependent, within ill-defined limits. Thus, it is usually parents who can be violent towards children, and husbands who can be violent towards wives. It is not unheard of for a parent, on hearing of a teacher's complaint about his/her child's behavior in school, to turn around and, in front of the teacher, slap the child's face. Without other evidence of abuse, such an act would never be brought to the attention of the authorities, or thought to require intervention. Yet, imagine for a moment, the reaction that would take place if the action were reversed; if the child were to slap the parent, or verbally abuse the parent in front of the teacher. This would be a real problem indeed. The problem, however, would not be the violent action; it would be that the lines of power were being crossed.

In determining what consitutes a violent act that requires intervention many issues come into play, not the least important of which is what the evaluators consider to be appropriate violence, based on their own cultural values, and what they consider to be inappropriate violence. Obviously, there are clear-cut cases, such as those where injuries are sustained that require medical or hospital treatment. Many cases are less clear cut. A case in point: during a family interview that I conducted at the court, it emerged that parents were punishing a ten year old child by making her kneel on pebbles for several hours. This seemed like a cruel and bizzare kind of punishment to me; one that I had never heard of before, and that alerted me to the possibility of severe disturbance in the family. Fortunately, the community health worker who was conducting the interview with me came from the same ethnic and cultural sub-group as the clients, and informed me that this was a common form of punishment within this group, and that she, herself, has been subjected to the same kind of punishment as a child, and, even as a child, did not consider it an unusual form of punishment, as her friends were disciplined in the same way. I am not proposing this as an optimum form of discipline, but presenting it to illustrate how seeing the context in which the violent action takes place determines the kind of intervention that takes place. In such a case, rather than having to undertake any sort of drastic action, it was sufficient for the mental health worker to intervene with the parents in an educative fashion, pointing out the deleterious effect of such a punishment on the child, and alternate ways of achieving the same disciplinary end. It should be mentioned here how important it was that the mental health worker did come from the same background as the clients, as for me to try to achieve the same ends would have been received by the family as hostile intervention from an outsider who had no knowledge or appreciation of the sub-group's traditions.

To sum up what has been said so far; the first task of the crisis intervention team (and no easy task at that) is to evaluate whether the violence that has occurred is beyond that socially accepted norm. The next task is to try to understand the factors contributing to the violence, in order to arrive at some appropriate means of intervention. The unique advantage for the mental health team working under the auspices of the court is that the court is immediately available if some drastic action must be taken to insure the safety of one or more of the parties, such as removal from the home. This is an advantage that the private practitioner, or mental health professional in some other clinical setting does not have. However, even this advantage has it's limits. Where children are the victims of violence, a removal from the home, if it is indicated, can be legally effected rather simply. When it is an adult, most often a wife, who is the victim, court intervention is often a meaningless, and sometimes inflammatory gesture. A wife can be given an order of protection, which means that the next time the husband assaults her she can call the police and have him arrested by showing them her order of protection. Husbands have become so enraged by this that they have initiated particularly severe assaults following orders of protection, police have been reluctant to act upon them, and the wife is most often in the position of being economically and emotionally dependent on the person whom she has just turned over to the police and the court, and of having no choice but to resume living with a person who is even angrier than before as a result of her actions. It is rather like the position of someone who has informed on a person who has committed a crime, and pressed charges, then having to live with and be dependent on that person.

Returning to our evaluation of the causes of the violence; perhaps the most important aspect of this is the determination as to whether the family can, in fact, be worked with as a unit without a danger to the victim or victims of violence, or whether someone must be removed from the home. If, for example, the violence is severe and uncontrollable, as with a psychiatric parent, it may become necessary to effect that person's removal from the home (perhaps to a hospital) and recommend treatment for that person outside of the family setting, while the rest of the family is referred elsewhere for help with handling the problems that both contributed to and result from the family violence and disruption that has occurred. Sometimes the violence can be handled by crisis intervention modes geared toward the intact family, as, for example, in cases where the family is under the kind of extreme pressure where their controls and limits are being severely tried. In one such case, involving what the court calls 'neglect' rather than 'abuse' (that is, the children were considered to be endangered by the parents' lack of action, rather than action), evaluation, including a home visit by a team of mental health workers, indicated a family that was completely overwhelmed by illness, poverty, and cultural change. The family, consisting of parents and five small children, had recently come from a rural area in Puerto Rico to New York City. They had arrived in winter, were unprepared for cold weather and urban living, had no financial resources, spoke no English, had no knowledge of how to contact or make their way in the bureaucracy of helping agencies, or obtain medical care. To boot, the father was severely ill with tuberculosis, and was unable to work or obtain proper medical care. The family was brought to court by the Bureau of Child Welfare because the children had not been in school. The welfare workers had become even more alarmed because, on visiting the home, they observed toddlers on the floor, playing with nails and rusty objects that they could put in their mouths and swallow. Intervention here involved contacting the appropriate social agencies, helping the family obtain welfare funds and proper housing, effecting medical hospitalization for the father and medical treatment for the rest of the family, and obtaining homemaker services for the mother to help her function and learn the ways of a culture with which she was not familiar. Follow-up visits were instituted by mental health workers to ascertain how the family was doing, and in the end the family was able to be helped to stay together, although the wish of some of the agencies involved was, initially, to place the children in foster homes.

Although the removal of a child or children from the home is often a necessary action to insure the safety of a child (as was mentioned earlier, it is much more difficult to order an adult from the home and insure that he or she really does stay away from the child; also, the adult who is abusive is often the same adult who is the only caretaker of the child), the child's removal from the home is often perceived by the child to be a punishment to him or herself. Thus, removal can be experienced as the victim of the violence being punished, rather than the perpetrator of the violence. This is particularly so when the children are victims of sexual abuse by a parent or family member. It becomes all too easy, when most children feel guilty and complicitous in such an action in any case, for them to perceive themselves as being punished for their part in an incestuous relationship. It is crucial, when it is necessary for such a child to be removed from the home, for follow-up treatment to be instituted to help the child work through feelings about what has happened.

3. The Termination of RIP

Although judges, probation officers, and other court-related agencies were unstinting in their praise of RIP, and an independent evaluation of RIP prepared for the Appelate Division, First and Second Judicial Departments of the State of New York in 1974 stated that" . . . for the Family Court, RIP is the most important addition, the *only* substantial positive event since it's creation", the Rapid Intervention Project was dropped from the Family Court budget in July of 1975, ostensibly because of lack of funds. However, it had become abundantly clear by that time that the very things that were so unique about RIP also contained within them the seeds of RIP's destruction. Designed to offer recommendations to judges in a legal system based on adversary action, RIP, more often than not, was instrumental in moving the action out of the adversary area, giving rise to complaints from a new court administration that the Family Court was being cast in the role of a social agency, rather than a court of law. The crucial difficulty here, it would seem, is that family disputes and cases involving the welfare of a child or children are handled under the law by the same procedures and rules as are criminal and other cases. The issues are those of guilt and innocence, good versus bad parents, and ultimately, winners and losers. The problem is that, unlike what happens in most other legal situations, these winners and losers often have to co-exist to one degree or another after litigation is completed. Viewing litigants as a unit, gearing evidence to the understanding of that unit, and decisions towards the welfare of that unit are not a part of our legal system, which has its basis in adversary action. Although it was not designed to do so, RIP engendered a different model of dealing with such cases. In having an essentially neutral team evaluate the parties in a family dispute the issues became those of the well-being of the unit, rather than the guilt or innocence, goodness or badness of any party. From a strictly legal standpoint, problems arose. Legally, it may well have been that some rights were violated. Home visits were made by mental health workers before a fact-finding hearing was held. Families were seen, and information was shared with judges without counsel being necessarily present. It is certain that legal experts could take issue with these and other matters in the handling of cases. Yet, one must wonder if the legal model is appropriate to many cases involving family disputes, or whether they are, in fact, social agency problems, with the Family Court being the socio-legal agency mandated to deal with them.

In point of fact, we are not at all clear where we stand with regard to the handling of family abuse cases under the law. We insist on their being dealt with in the same legal framework as any other abuse case (a hearing, adherence to rules of evidence, *etc.*), but once a fact-finding is held, and a verdict reached, we are reluctant to deal with them as we do with cases between strangers. We have no reluctance to impose a jail sentence on a husband who assaults someone else's wife, even though it disrupts his own family. Yet, if it is his own wife that he assaults, we become highly concerned about the impact on his family of punishment by imprisonment. We have not yet been able to resolve whether we will treat these cases as we would any other case involving the same physical abuse under the law, or make special legal provisions which run all the way through the handling of these cases.

Another issue that arose, and may have been one of the factors that eventuated in the dissolution of RIP, was the fear that the mental health experts had the potential for usurping the judicial function; that the court will and has relied too heavily on expert recommendations. This, it would seem, is equivalent to claiming that the Secretary of Agriculture of the United States Government is usurping the Presidential function in government. Just as Executive decisions are made after consideration of information given by expert cabinet members, judicial decisions should be in no way undermined when supported by information gleaned from mental health and other experts. It would seem ideal if a judge were to have a 'cabinet' at his or her disposal in such cases; a panel of relevant experts with whom he or she could discuss the issues involved, and whose information and recommendations could then be considered and weighed in arriving at a disposition.

Be that as it may, this unique crisis intervention service is no longer a part of the New York City Family Court system. It is the hope of many of us who were involved with the development and functioning of the Rapid Intervention Project during its period of tenure at the Family Court that some of the orientation and techniques that were special to the project will prove useful to those involved with helping families in crisis who do become involved with the courts.

Chapter 14

Professional Education and the Violent Family

Paul L. Havemann*

The literature and research on the problems of violence in the family are not much concerned with the education and training of professionals coping with this multi-disciplinary problem. This chapter embraces both the areas of inter-spousal violence and child abuse. In it I shall, 1) examine the problems of curriculum evaluation in professional schools; 2) paint a picture of possible components for curricula; 3) outline the existing state of curricula at professional schools.

1. Definitions

(A) 'Education' and 'Training'

It is impossible to make a rigid division between education and training, but for these purposes 'education' consists of tuition of an academic nature provided at University or other institutions of higher learning, whilst 'training' consists of in-service, continuing post-qualification tuition (often of short duration) provided by a professional body for its members or an agency for its employees. This chapter is largely restricted to the law school, medical school, social work school, para-medical school and police college stage of professional education. The reasons for this are that in-service training is very difficult to evaluate, is frequently a response to inadequate professional education and that it would seem appropriate to expect high quality, relevant basic education to be provided by educational institutions rather than the professions or agencies themselves. Educational institutions also have the resources and relative leisure to design appropriate curricula. Finally, the educational stage of professional learning is usually the longest and can be a most formative influence upon the professional before entry into the real world of practice.

---

* Human Justices Services Program, University of Regina, Canada.

(B) 'Professional' and 'Professionalism'

The 'professional' is difficult to describe. So, rather than see him as the possessor of a specialist qualification and an integral part of the rational bureaucracy, as Weber[1] did, or as the custodian and fount of a new moral order, as Durkheim[2] and Halmos[3] have done, I will concentrate on that attribute of the professional to which education must substantially contribute and by which I seek to evaluate professional education. This is the ability to contribute specialist expertise in a collaborative and consultative capacity to multi-disciplinary problem solving (perhaps better called 'problem alleviation'). This ability is relevant to all professionals coping with violence in the family. Is it something that ought to be left to the haphazard stage in the learning process when the neophyte professional is 'sitting next to Nelly', namely, during the apprenticeship stage?

2. Evaluation of Curriculum Content of Professional Education

The research, such as it is, on this subject has not by and large been concerned with curriculum content. There are endless articles about methods of assessment, student recruitment and so on. In the United Kingdom,[4] such interest as Government has taken in professional education has been largely devoted to the process of education in terms of timing and qualifications for entry rather than curriculum content. This is not surprising as most of the professions concerned are characterized by collegiate control. In Johnson's typology of occupational control this means: "the producer defines the needs of the consumer and the manner these needs are catered for . . . collegiate control is exemplified by the emergence of autonomous occupational associations."[5]

An approach to the evaluation of curricula now widely[6] accepted is the aims and objectives analysis whereby the learning process can be classified in terms of the fulfillment of objectives,[7] the development of skills and the informing of attitudes. Thus the learning process can be divided into the cognitive domain (knowledge and skill areas) and the affective domain (attitudinal area). In professional education we are concerned with the optimum combination of these domains. It is in the combination of these which converts the mode of operation from the technical to the professional as judged by the ability "to contribute specialist expertise in a collaborative and consultative capacity to multi-disciplinary problem alleviation."

3. Inter-Professional Relationships — The Role of Education?

(A) The Context

The re-discovery[8] of family violence is a relatively recent phenomenon. Family violence makes some of the most acute demands upon inter-professional co-ordination and communication. It frequently highlights quite glaringly the rudimentary state of multi-disciplinary problem-alleviation. Professor Olive Stevenson stated at the Royal Society of Health conference in Eastbourne (1977) that it was no exaggeration to say that the life of a child might depend to a considerable extent on the over-coming of inter-professional tension and rivalries. Likewise Erin Pizzey[9], commenting on the professions' response to the problem of the battered wife said, "It would probably take a Charles Dickens to do full justice to the labyrinth of indifference, red-tape callousness and simple incompetence that exists between people in need and so many of the agencies that are meant to help them."

In the United Kingdom the problem of family violence has not gone unnoticed. There has been a series of *quasi*-judicial reviews[10] of child abuse incidents and Select Committees of the House of Commons on Violence in the Marriage (1974-75) and on Violence in the Family (1975-77). The result has been a very detailed scrutiny of the legislation and services relevant to the victims and perpetrators of violence in the family. Memoranda were received from no less than 50 bodies and several hundred individuals gave oral evidence concerning child abuse and wife beating. These bodies included the N.S.P.C.C., Chiswick Women's Aid, the President of the Family Division of the High Court and the Government Departments concerned with major aspects of the problem. The Select Committee on Violence in Marriage made some scathing criticisms[11] about the government departments concerned. In all the evidence — time and time again — there are recommendations for more research, legislative reform and improved inter-professional communication, collaboration and co-ordination.

The different sets of beliefs and assumptions held by each profession constitute a major obstacle in securing this communication between them. Admirable diagramatic representation of the complex and apparently irreconcilable differences of professional values and obligations are to be found in Jan Carter's book, *The Maltreated Child. (Tables 1 and 2).*

One would have thought with all this that professional education would have featured in the United Kingdom debate on research and remedies for family violence. Somewhat surprisingly the educators by professions in the universities and polytechnics are only represented by one contribution to the Select Committee. The Open University's Post-experience Courses Unit indicated that it was at a developmental stage with Newcastle Polytechnic in the preparation self-instruction materials for the in-service training of professionals under the title 'Abused Children'.[12] Further bibliographies on violence in the family reveal no published work on this subject other than five very brief prescriptive papers about what should be learnt presented at the Tunbridge Wells Study Group Conference, 1974.[13] Typical of the references to the state of professional education made to the Select committee were those from the Department of Health and Social Security (DHSS)[14] and the British Association of Social Workers.[15]

The DHSS Memorandum observed:

Although the helping professions have some basic education about emotional development there seems to be some indication that many professionals feel inadequate when dealing with family and marital problems especially where there is violence. There is a need for the professions concerned to build up a body of knowledge as a source of reference.

Seminars short conferences can help to disseminate experience and information more widely, till the stage is reached when it can be more effectively embodied in the professions' normal educational . . . processes.

Table 1*

MAJOR SYSTEMS OF BELIEF AFFECTING CHILD ABUSE

	Penal	Medical	Social Welfare	
Framework	Legal	Scientific	Humanistic	
Presuppostion	Individual has free will	Behavior is determined	Behavior is determined	
Attitude to deviance	Punitive	Neutral	(a) *Traditional* Compassionate	(b) *Radical* Relativistic
Social rationale	Justice	Cure	Social control by adjustment	Social liberation via reorganization
Some practising groups	Police, judiciary, criminal courts	Doctors, some psychiatrists some psychologists	Social workers, some doctors, probation officers	Some social workers, sociologists
Focus of attention	Act of abuse	Disease processes	The person	Social processes
Tools	Legal code	Medical technology	Counseling relationships	Social change
Conceptions of parent	Responsible	←— Nil (derived —→ from other systems)	Psychologically inadequate	Socially victimized
Stated purpose of intervention	Punishment of guilt	Treatment of physical dysfunction	Personal rehabilitation	Social redistribution

* From Carter, Jan, "Problems of Professional Belief" in Carter, J. (ed.), *The Maltreated Child.* Sussex, Eng.: Priory Press, 1974, p. 52.

Table 2†

	Doctors (Hospital)	Medical social workers	Social workers in the social service dept.	Police
Domain	parts of the body	←————————→	the whole person	the community
Basis of authority	professional	←————————→	professional and statutory	legal
Organizational control	clinical autonomy	←————————→	some autonomy in a bureaucratic setting	bureaucratic
To whom accountable	the patient	←————————→	the patient and the community	the community
Therapeutic failure	tolerated (on grounds of clinical autonomy	←————————→	argued on grounds of clinical autonomy but less often acceptable	not tolerated

* From Armstrong, D., "Problems of Boundary" in Carter, J, (ed.), *The Maltreated Child.* Sussex, Eng.: Priory Press, 1974, p. 12.

It would be foolish to pretend that multi-disciplinary, high quality professional education is a panacea. Nevertheless, as Oppé says, violence in the family:

. . . presents problems of recognition, judgement (decision-making) an action, which involve concurrently and sequentially workers in a number of disciplines and several professions.

It is likely that the outcome in a particular case depends upon the communicating and co-ordinating skills of the workers as much as the technical expertise.[16]

The British Association of Social Workers[17] commented that "more inter-disciplinary training will enable the different professions to be aware of each others responsibilities, contributions and potential", and the Select Committee gave prescriptions for curricula only to medical schools and nursing colleges.[18]

(B) The State of Professional Education in the United Kingdom

A glance at the statement of aims and objectives for the professions by Royal Commissions and Government give educators considerable[19] encouragement to develop multi-disciplinary programs of the kind which should turn out professionals with "the ability to contribute specialist expertise in a collaborative and consultative capacity to multi-disciplinary problem-alleviation." In some instances the professional bodies themselves have also made imaginative prescriptions for curriculum designers.[20] A particularly useful attempt to do this was made by the Central Council for Education and Training in Social Work.[21] It identified seven major functions which any qualified social worker ought to have been educated to perform. These include one skill area involving multi-disciplinary education. It is the:

. . . ability to:
— facilitate communication and trust between professions and workers.
— draw on the knowledge base of other professions and workers.
— identify changes, common elements and differences in practice and skills.
— elucidate commonality and differences in values, priorities and accountability.
— clarify for others the essentials, strengths and weaknesses of social work practice.

(C) Curriculum Needs and Curriculum Content

Training in respect of child abuse is now widespread largely due to the work of the N.S.P.C.C.[22] and the DHSS. Training of personnel working with the inter-spousal violence has largely been provided by neighborhood law centers[23] and on a remarkably extensive scale by the National Women's Aid Federation which has addressed no less than fifteen institutions of higher education over the past year. Most of these exercises are remedial — or up-dating. They also tend to be specific to a particular aspect of the problem, for instance the diagnostic or the legal. Professional education on the other hand should provide a multi-disciplinary foundation for the worker coping with violence in the family.

Curricula directed at attitude-informing in professional schools would seem to involve classes or instruction of some sort in respect of the aetiology of child abuse and the social dynamics of family life, including the physical and psychiatric correlates of marital disharmony. Both *knowledge* and *attitudes* could also be developed through access to information and discussion of the modules covering the administrative and bureaucratic procedures and framework relevant to the management of child abuse cases and by modules relating to the existing state of social policy and services in respect of inter-spousal violence. Such themes would provide an opportunity for discussion of inter-professional relationships and differing professional outlooks and roles.

In the cognitive domain, the degree of skill and knowledge will differ for each professional school, though I would maintain that a common grounding in the diagnosis of child abuse and the law and procedure relevant to child abuse and the inter-spousal violence was relevant to all of them. These themes may provide a convenient indication of the core of subject matter required in the educational courses in which child abuse and inter-spousal violence might be expected to appear.[24]

Once having been so bold as to stipulate curricula needs, the writer sent questionnaires to professional schools and the police colleges, to find out to what extent these institutions dealt with the problems of family violence and whether they did so in a multi-disciplinary way by a combination of the modules previously mentioned. The results of this fact finding project do not present a comprehensive picture of this aspect of professional education. I will present a resumé of them for what it is worth.

(a) Medical, Nursing and Police Schools

A common response to the questionnaire from the sample medical schools, nursing and police colleges who replied indicates that 'violence in the family' is not a subject receiving specific focus. The treatment of this subject is, in other words, diffused and not coordinated, possibly being mentioned at various junctures under different topics in their curricula.

(b) Social Work Schools

Social work schools indicated a multi-disciplinary approach in which violence in the family did receive fairly coordinated treatment.

(c) Law Schools

An analysis of law school replies showed that only a minority adopted a contextual or multi-disciplinary approach. In addition, 45 percent of respondents did not teach the relevant child protection law and 28 percent did not teach the relevant law in respect of inter-spousal violence. Most respondents regretted that their coverage was largely legal, due to the limitation of time. There seems to be little contact between one professional school and another in the same university.

Only one law teacher reported teaching at a medical school, though 45 percent reported teaching in social work schools.

One hesitates to conclude too much from such a crude exercise, but curricula seems to neglect a multi-disciplinary approach and there seems to be little cross-fertilization from one school to another or indeed from the outside world.

In both the social work and law school replies there was a limited number of very good programs. There was also a widespread interest among many of the law school respondents who indicated that their courses were moving towards a more multi-disciplinary approach — or that they were planning to introduce these subjects in the ensuing academic year. Only one or two rejected the multi-disciplinary approach outright. There is therefore, some room for hope. Though let it be said that this can only be said about the schools who did reply. 'Adverse inferences' might be drawn about those who did not.

NOTES

1. Max, Weber *From Max Weber: Essays in Sociology.* Gerth, H., and Wright Mills, C., (transl.) New York, New York: Oxford University Press, 1946.
2. Durkheim, E., *Professional Ethics and Civic Morals.* London, Eng.: Routledge, 1957.
3. Halmos, P., *The Personal Service Society.* New York, New York: Schocken, 1970. See generally Johnson, T.J., *Professions and Power.* London, Eng.: Macmillan, 1972.
4. Royal Commission on Medical Education. 1965-8 Cmnd. 3569 HMSO (For an exception) (Todd Report) Report of the Committee on Legal Education, 1971 Cmnd. 4595 HMSO Report of the Committee on Nursing, 1972. Cmnd. 5115 Briggs Report.
5. Johnson, T.J. *supra.*
6. Beard, R., *Teaching and Learning in Higher Education.* 1972. Bligh, D., *What's the Use of Lectures.* 1971.
7. Bloom, B.S., *Taxonomy of Educational Objectives, I: Cognitive Domain.* Harlow, Essex: Longman, 1956. Krathwoh, D.; Bloom, B.S.; Masia, B., *Taxonomy of Educational Objectives, II: Affective Domain.* Harlow, Essex: Longman, 1965. For some application see: Simpson, M.A., *Medical Education A Critical Approach.* London, Eng.: Butterworths, 1972. Central Council for Education and Training in Social Work Paper 10 — *Education and Training for Social Work,* 1975.
8. Kempe and Silverman, "The Battered Child Syndrome" (1962) *J.A. Med. Assoc.,* 1968, Battered Child Res. Department N.S.P.C.C. (UK) set up, 1974, Chiswick Womens Aid —first battered wives refuge in the United Kingdom. Gelles, Richard, *The Violent. Home.* Beverley Hills, California: Sage, 1974, page 20. ". . . in the entire index of the Journal of Marriage and the Family (U.S.A.) from its inception in 1939 through 1969 there is not one article that contains the word violence in its title . . . ".
9. Pizzey, Erin, *Scream Quietly or the Neighbors will Hear.* Harmondsworth, Middlesex: Penguin, 1974.
10. DHSS: Report of Committee of Inquiry into the care and supervision provided in relation to Maria Colwell: 1974. DHSS: Report of Committee of Inquiry into the provision and care of the Family of John George Aukland, 1975. Norfolk County Council and Area Health Authority: Report of the Review Body Appointed to inquire into the case of Steven Meurs, 1976.
11. Select Committee on Violence in Marriage (1974-75) Volume I, Report para. 5. "A general impression must be recorded at the outset. We have been disappointed and alarmed by the ignorance and apparent apathy of some Government Departments and

individual ministers. Hardly any worthwhile research into either causes or remedies has been financed. . . . Reponsibility is diversified. . . . No fewer than 7 (departments) are concerned. Only in a very few does the problem . . . receive anything other than a very low priority in terms of manpower or financial resources."

12. Select Committee: Violence in Marriage Volume III, Appendix 44, paras. 110-160.
13. Franklin, A.W., (ed.): Proceedings of Tunbridge Wells Study Group Conference: *Concerning Child Abuse.* London, Eng.: Livingstone Churchill 1974, chap. 5.
14. Select Committee: Violence in the Marriage, Volume II DHSS Memorandum: Page 112, paragraph 72.
15. Select Committee: Violence in the Marriage, Volume II British Association of Social Workers Memorandum, p. 535, para. 514.
16. Oppé, Thomas, "Problems of Communication and Coordination," Franklin, A.W., (ed.), *Concerning Child Abuse.* London, Eng.: Livingstone Churchill, 1974, p. 161.
17. H.C. Select Committee Violence in Marriage, Volume II, page 335, para. 514.
18. Select Committee on Violence in Marriage, Volume I. Recommendation 13 "Medical Schools and Nursing Colleges should give special attention to the social dynamics of family life and to the Medical (both physical and psychiatric) correlates of marital disharmony."
19. Royal Commission on Medical Education, 1965-68. *op. cit.* p. 86, (Todd Report) "We take the view, therefore, that the aim of medical education should be to produce, at graduation, a person with two essential qualifications . . ., first, a knowledge of the medical and *behavioral* sciences." Report of the Committee on Legal Education, 1971. *op. cit.* p. 44 (Ormrod Report) *"Scope and Purpose of the academic stage".* Every effort, . . ., should be made at this stage to develop the students analytical ability and to introduce him, however, superficially to the knowledge and Methods of other diciplines which later on may have a divert bearing on his work as a professional lawyer. . . . *Nature and Functions of Vocational Courses,* p. 62 ". . . points of principle. 6. Cooperation with other disciplines such as . . . psychology, psychiatry, sociology and forensic medicine should be vigorously encouraged."
20. Central Council for the Education and Training of Health Visitors — prescribed Syllabus for Examination for Health Visitors in the United Kingdom — includes Section IV Social Aspects of Health and Disease — The importance of effective coordination and collaboration within the Health and Social Services.
21. CCETSW Paper 10 Education and Training for Social Work: 1975, p. 29. Law Society and Council for Legal Education have not, nor have they lived up to the Ormrod Report recommendations.
22. Vortex: Voluntary Organizations Register of Training Exercises, 1977-78.
23. Camden Law Center — London. Paddington Law Center — London.
24. In Medical Schools, Nursing Colleges, Social Work Schools, Law Schools and Police Colleges.

PART THREE

VIOLENCE AGAINST CHILDREN:
WHAT AND WHY

Parts III and IV treat specifically of that violence in the family which is directed against children. This area of family violence — child abuse — has been the focus of much of legal, medical and psychological research during the last decades.[1] Most recently, discussion of the research into child abuse on a world-wide basis was held in the 1976 Geneva Conference on Child Abuse and Neglect. The presentations at that conference have been published in the 1977 issues of *The International Journal of Child Abuse and Neglect* (Oxford, England: Pergamon Press).

In Chapter 15, Dr. Albert J. Solnit, co-author of the popular *Beyond the Best Interests of the Child,* deals with child abuse as a psychoanalytic problem. Traditionally the aggressive and sexual drives are viewed as inseparable, with the helpless child a magnet for nurture and love while at the same time, since it is a painful reminder of one's own fear of helplessness, as a magnet for attack. The child cannot survive if the adult in charge is not active enough in protecting and nurturing him or if on the other hand the adult's aggression is transformed into violence. When parents are depressed or suffer from the effects of their own deprived childhood, they may lack the ability to love and nurture. They transmit to their child the effects of their own childhood sufferings, and these hurtful effects may be passed on from generation to generation. Moreover, the nuclear family itself is undergoing a stressful period, as witness the tremendous increase in divorce, the number of 'single parents', and the very high percentage of working mothers. Dr. Solnit raises the question of how much responsibility for child abuse to attribute to these changes. The problem is further complicated by the interaction of the individual child with the individual parent, and by the effects, if any, of violence in the media.

The reporting laws that swept through the 50 states in the U.S. during the late 50's and 60's were at first hailed as a real breakthrough in the field. It was hoped that by identifying the victims a first long step had been taken toward eliminating the evil itself. But the negative effects of the reporting laws were soon apparent: the invasion of family privacy often on the basis of false reports, of unpopular life styles, or of prejudice against minorities and the poor. Emotional neglect was a still more tenuous concept to apply accusatively. Nor have many thousands of reports even when justified been matched by anything like the appropriate services to help the child and the family, since resources continue to be limited. The net result is sometimes greater danger than ever for the child. The family or parent who has been accused, angered by the coercive and sometimes contemptuous treatment of agents of the state, turns its frustration and violated emotions into even worse violence against the child.

In Chapter 19, J. Vesterdal writes about what sort of people become child abusers. Although mothers appear more often in this role, particularly in cases of mental abuse, the other parent knows about the abuse and acts as tacit accessory; the profile therefore is applicable to either parent. Only a few of these people have manifest psychoses, and no single psychiatric diagnosis is possible. Vesterdal treats child abuse as a disorder of the parent-child relationship which can exist in combination with practically any other psychological state. He points out that the relationship requires reciprocity — a symbiosis between mother and child. The mother may react inadequately because of her own birth experience; the child may be unwanted; the mother may have false expectations about the happiness and comfort the child will bring her. The mother's violent behavior may be only occasional and triggered by a particular stress. The fact remains, however, that the temperament of the child is of equal importance to the symbiotic relationship, and may in itself be the trigger for the mother's violence. The child may be difficult, restless, may cry frequently without apparent cause, may not respond to the mother's affection: in other words, may not play its role well.

Vesterdal believes that bad social conditions are in themselves a frequent matrix for child abuse and that the risk is greater among the poor than in upper levels of society. He cites the predictive studies by Gray *et al.* as one possible amelioration of child abuse, the importance and possibility of identifying, through pre- and neonatal experiments and treatment, the factors that lead to abuse. While it appears that risk mothers may to some extent be identified and successfully treated, there still remain important legal and policy issues that must be considered in these experiments.

One of the knotted problems in dealing with child abuse is the assessment of the effects of abuse on the development of the victimized child. Using her own clinical and research experiences at the Park Hospital in Oxford, England, in Chapter 17 Dr. Lynch concludes that small compehensive studies are of major importance in determining the key questions on which future large-scale projects will be based, with the proviso that small samples should not be used to make sweeping statements about whole populations.

It is a melancholy fact known to all the helping services that many abused children and their families need assistance for years after the initial identification. The difficulties of such backup aid begin from the widely differing uses of the term itself, 'abuse', which range from multiple skeletal injuries to any inflicted hurt, however mild. The problem of matched controls in follow-up studies is also approached in several ways, including the use of families with 'perfect child rearing techniques'. Dr. Lynch's ideal would be a longitudinal study of abused children over the same time period as a large-scale population study, but data collection would necessarily and unfortunately be limited by the available time, money and expertise. Questionnaires have their own pitfalls and are unlikely to be completed unless they are short and specific, and even then personal collection is almost a necessity, with tactful explanation of the purposes of the study.

It is not simple in a follow-up to interpret mortality and re-injury rates, since these may be unrelated to original abuse. And it is extremely difficult even to locate and evaluate the members of the original sample. An alarming number of children are not available for follow-up assessment — their whereabouts may be unknown, they may be dead, or their parents, adoptive parents or the institutions in which they have been placed may be unwilling to cooperate. Nevertheless, with the small samples she suggests and with the aid of the therapy which she is convinced is a necessary component of such research, Dr. Lynch believes that follow-up research and therapy can help abused children grow into healthy adults and non-abusing parents.

Chapters 16 and 18 are concerned with child abuse in cultures remote from contemporary Western society. In "Paternal Power and Child Abuse: An Historical and Cross-Cultural Study", M.C.J. Olmesdahl describes Roman law and African customary law as illustrated in the Zulu culture. He raises the question of how far we have advanced since the Roman patriarch had power of life and death over his wife and children.

The *patria potestas,* which extended over twelve centuries, was the central institution of law relating to the Roman family, and left children absolutely subject to their fathers and with absolutely no legal redress. The patriarchal image was aimed at carrying on both the purity of the family and the transmission of family property. Throughout the history of Rome there are examples of the father's power of death for criminal acts of wife or child, as well as for reprehensible conduct threatening family reputation. Nevertheless, by degrees this absolutism became legally regulated, until by 560 A.D. it had dwindled to a right of reasonable chastisement and included duties — of educating and maintaining — as well as powers.

Olmesdahl finds similarities to the Roman in African customary law and today's Bantu law. Zulu society was strongly patriarchal as well as polygamous. The father's absolute control over property was bolstered by an ancestor worship mystique of axiomatic reverence from sons and wives and by a dominating military system. The father had unchallenged monopolistic legal control both within the family and in the family's relations with other groups. He could and did administer physical and mental torture, mutilation and killing of wife and child; he could in effect outlaw and disinherit a son. Yet the father had always to be wary of public disgrace, and he was expected to exercise his supreme power within the limits of customary law. Today tribal culture is no longer coherent; individuals may operate according to tribal or western values, and although most legal relationships may come under Bantu law, the ordinary courts of the land have modified the duties and rights of the parent-child relationship.

Both in Rome and Zululand the child existed in a legal vacuum. It is apparent, Olmesdahl is convinced, that in a legalistic society insistence on legal rights is the only road to protection. The child must be under the full umbrella of the criminal law. He must have freedom from corporal punishment within and outside the home, and realistically early emancipation from a family relationship that has broken down, with an implicit right to his own counsel.

In the last chapter of Part III, Tahir Mahmood, compares Indian and Arab legal responses to child abuse with those in the United States and Great Britain. In

Indian and Arab societies he finds adolescents victimized more often than young children and mental rather than physical cruelty more prevalent, citing the special cruelty of stepmothers, of mothers-in-law toward child brides, still common in India despite the laws, and the abuse of illegitimates both within and without the family. In the affluent West he believes child abuse stems from psychiatric disorders; in India from poverty; and in Arab countries, which he describes as economically on a par with the United States, from a long misreading and misapplication of the Scriptures. He writes of Indian families with often as many as fifteen children, impoverished, with the youngest children committed under common law to arduous household duties or to earning minute sums in the market place and subject to extreme violence if they fail to meet parental standards. In the upper classes the victims are older children and adolescents. Parents in these countries may react to the 'generation gap' with ferocity; the child may be denied his daily bread, may be starved, beaten and insulted unless he returns to the traditional mores of his family. Nevertheless, Mahmood contends that the impact of child abuse is lessoned by the prevalence of the extended family and the continuous presence of the non-working mother.

The Children Act of 1960 in India provides for the care, education and rehabilitation of neglected and delinquent children and mandates a penalty for physical or mental abuse of a fine and/or six months imprisonment; but no complaint can be made without the sanction of the highest executive authority in a state. In the Arab countries action against a parent or guardian can be initiated only on the complaint of the 'aggrieved party', the abused child itself, a manifest absurdity in the case of young children. No provision exists in any of these countries for effective reporting of abuse or neglect. Nor is there recognition of the concept of adoption, which might ameliorate the lot of the abused child. No Arab country except Tunisia has legalized adoption; and in India, the law of adoption is applicable only to Hindus and of those only to persons who have no natural child, grandchild, or great-grandchild.

Mahmood feels that India and the Arab countries can profit by the Western experience. The problem must be attacked at its base, with widespread education for planned parenthood, drastic reform of laws, and effective machinery to implement the new laws. Above all there must be mandated reporting laws, and in this connection he believes the girl guides in Egypt, the judicial officers found in Arab countries, and the house-visitors working in India can be of vital importance.

NOTES

1. For a comprehensive review of the research see: Friedman, Robert M., "Child Abuse: A Review of the Psycho-Social Research"; Helfer, Ray E., "Medical Aspects of Child Abuse and Neglect: A Review of the Research Literature"; Katz, Sanford N., "The Laws on Child Abuse and Neglect: A Review of the Research"; Polansky, Norman A., "Analysis of Research on Child Neglect: The Social Work Viewpoint" in *Four Perspectives on the Status of Child Abuse And Neglect Research* March, 1976, (Accession No. PB250852, available at the National Technical Information Service, U.S. Department of Commerce, Washington, D.C.) For an analysis of all American laws on child abuse and neglect, see: Katz, S., McGrath, M., and Howe, R. *Child Neglect Laws in America* (American Bar Association: 1976).

Chapter 15

Child Abuse: The Problem

Albert J. Solnit, M.D.*

1. Introduction

There are two major roots of violence in human behavior: that which is the
outcome of the aggressive drives from within, and that which stems from the
child's indentification with a violent, behavior-shaping, important adult. We have
the dilemma of not knowing which root of violent behavior should be
emphasized; *i.e.,* on which one should we focus?

The definition of aggressive behavior is a controversial one. Many prefer to define
it as action that is damaging, injurious and destructive. This definition overlaps
with the accepted definition of violent behavior.

In this discussion aggressive behavior has no constructive or destructive
implication in itself. Its constructive or destructive meaning is determined by the
psychological motivation it represents and the meaning it has for the actor and by
its impact on the person, object, or environment it affects. In this frame of
reference, the psychoanalytic concept of the aggressive, instinctual drive is viewed
as one of two basic drives, sexual and aggressive, which for all intents and
purposes do not exist separately from each other.

The psychological and biological roots of instinctual drives, as differentiated from
the child's regulatory, mediating capacities, the ego, are best understood in terms
of the human infant's helplessness at birth. Helplessness is a magnet for nurture,
for attention and for action; it also is a painful reminder of one's own fear of
helplessness and can be a magnet for attack (violence). The protracted
helplessness and dependency of the young child dictate a biological and
psychological requirement for survival; they also represent, inevitably, the needs of
the helpless child to be acted upon by the adult. Therefore, newborns may not
survive if adults are not aggressive and loving enough, that is, if the adult is not
active enough in protecting and nurturing the child; or infants may not survive if
the adult's aggression becomes transformed into violent behavior. Such destructive

---

* Sterling Professor of Pediatrics and Psychiatry, Director, Child Study Center, Yale
University, U.S.A.

effects may be evoked either by the adult's incapacity to invest the child with affectionate care and expectations or because the adult loses control and becomes violent and assaultive; for example, such loss of control may be a repetition and have its origin in the past when the adult as a child was the object of violent destructive assaults by his or her own parent or parents.

Beyond survival these close biological and psychosocial ties become the basis for the individuated development of each child. The parent-child relationship is the matrix for the child's emerging socialization as a member of a family, the community and a society of children and adults which starts with each newborn being helpless at birth.

The child mediates as he is able the outside pressures to produce or conform, and his own inner pressures and tensions. Before the young child can fully mediate these competing, interacting demands, the adult, the parent, is the mediator. Thus, the adult protects the child from too much or too many environmental stimuli or demands and at the same time the parent-regulator soothes, satisfies and helps the child to reduce inner tensions and demands. In psychoanalytic terms the parent is an auxiliary ego for the young child. Among the child's most dynamic sources of power are his impulses, his drives and his unfolding capacity to become a unique person who has borrowed attitudes and behaviors from many models and yet retains his own individuality, whether dramatic, ordinary or uncommon. As he expresses his inner resources and responds to the pressures of the social environment, the child helps to change and form the emotional climate of his own world.

Sylvia Ashton-Warner (1959) in her book, *Spinster,* describes her sense of the child's inner world as she views the child's capacity to learn how to read. She implies what may underlie the child's repertoire of creative learning and violent behaviors.

What a dangerous activity reading is; teaching is. All this plastering on of foreign stuff. Why plaster on at all when there is so much inside already? So much locked in? If only I could get it out and use it as working material. And not dried out either. If I had a light enough touch it would just come out under its own volcanic power. And psychic power, I *read in bed* this morning, is greater than any other power in the world. What an exciting and frightening business it would be: even that which squeezes through now is amazing enough. In the safety of the world behind my eyes, where the inspector shade cannot see, I picture the infant room as one widening crater, loud with the sound of erupting creativity. Every subject somehow in a creative vent. What wonderful design of movement and mood! What lovely behavior of silk-sack clouds!

An organic design. A growing living changing design. The normal and healthful design. Unsentimental and merciless and shockingly beautiful.[1]

Can violence be beautiful — or only when the basic stuff, potentially violent, is transformed into constructive, creative expressiveness?

2. Responses of the Young Child

The young child is eruptible and direct in showing his colorful, pathetic and humorous side. He also caves in more suddenly than an older child when caught between the pressure of his own drives and intense feelings and the demand that he become a member of a civilized group of peers and take up the tools of communication, symbolic expression and mental reflection. In the midst of this crucial transformation of volcanic energies, the young child may experience romantic love or fearful hatred for his teachers and others who constitute his new community. Many of us will remember the passionate daydreams of those early days of kindergarten and the first and second grades. "If only she will wait until I grow up, we could get married," said one little boy about his teacher. Of such romantic love, displaced from the home, is the stuff of which passionate education is formed. It helps to provide an environment that enables the child to socialize and to become increasingly self-understanding — or to be battered and to help create for the next generation an environment in which battering is a prominent characteristic.

3. How the Older Child Reacts

The older child, with increasingly independent ways of acquiring basic skills and knowledge and the growing importance of his peer group, is not nearly so vulnerable to his own impulsive reactions and energies, or so evocative of violence in the adults. Though he may yield to and depend upon the pressures of his peer group, his own conscience is relatively well developed even if unstable and often too strict.

Clinically it is well known that aggressive behavior can be, and often is, constructive. When it is constructive, it is associated with a capacity for play, work, persistence and problem-solving. Aggression can be expressed, channeled and transformed constructively in the context of predominantly loving attachments to persons with whom there are sustained bonds and common experiences, as well as mutual expectations.

When aggressive drives are not modified by libidinal attachments, they are more likely to be associated with injury, damage and various kinds of destructive intents and impacts. Since human survival, as well as healthy maturation and development, requires at least one nurturing adult to care for, protect, stimulate and guide the young child, it is useful to assume that all aggressive behavior implies varying degrees of fusion of libidinal and aggressive drive energies. Another way of formulating this presumption is to speak of how the child's behavior is derivative of inner impulsive energies interacting with the demands and channeling impact of the social environment, established largely for the young children by their parents and siblings.

From a psychoanalytic and child development point of view, violent behavior, or violence, of the individual represents a social derivative of biological, psychological and cultural interaction. However, it will be necessary to clarify the difference between subjective and objective aspects of violent feelings, thoughts, phantasies, motives and behavior. The significance of violence that is not expressed as behavior or is not perceived as behavior tends to create theoretical disagreements because attitudes, mental activities and affectual states that are characterized as violent are difficult to pin down; *i.e.,* to get agreement about. Indeed, a common indicator used to document and characterize violence was that of police arrests for violent behavior. Perhaps one major reason for our concern is the felt awareness of increases in violent behavior in the western world. Conversely, is there more violence in the mental activities of our citizenry now than in earlier years?

The Canadian Commission on Violence on Television in its Interim Report (1976)[2] has called our attention to another facet of violence. In understanding the impact of violence on television on its viewers, the question arises, which theory is most useful? That of the vicarious safety valves experience? That which presumes the evocation of violence behavior? Or, are we mostly confronted by the issues of poor taste and seduction to passive gratifications? (See Appendix to this chapter.)

Thus, aggression is a deep-seated universal drive in human beings. Overt fighting in other mammals only seems to occur when population numbers have outstripped the environment's resources with associated overcrowding. Man is different from other mammals. According to Carthy and Ebling (1964) it has been estimated that 59 million human beings were killed by other human beings in wars and other murderous quarrels between 1820 and 1945.[3] Is human aggression innate? The current psychiatric evidence seems almost unequivocal; aggression is not merely a response to frustration, it is a deepseated, universal drive. However, aggression as a drive can be channeled into peaceful activities, into construction, work and play that are civilized and humane.

According to David Gil (1970), child abuse is ". . . the intentional, non-accidental use of physical force, or intentional, non-accidental acts of omission, on the part of a parent or other caretaker interacting with a child in his or her care, aimed at hurting, injuring or destroying that child."[4]

The nuclear family is changing in its structure and functions though it is still the mainstay of social organization and support for children and adults. Certain social indicators characterize some of the main changes, especially the divorce rate, the number of children raised in single parent families and those raised in families in which both parents work. For example, in the U.S.A. 45 percent of the mothers of children aged three to six years of age and more than one-third of the mothers of children under the age of three worked in 1975, and most worked full time (Kamerman and Kahn, 1976).[5] Are these indicators associated with child abuse?

As much as adults need and cherish children, they also resent and fear them as competitors, replacements and consumers of the limited resources of affection, energy, privacy, space, food and valued materials. There are few if any exceptions to this assumed formulation.

For example, the child abuse reporting laws that were passed in all of the 50 states of the U.S.A. in the 1950s and 1960s in record time were not intended and probably have contributed little to protecting children. They were intended mainly to safeguard the conscience and legal vulnerability of our adult society and those adults who were instructed that they must report suspected cases of abuse since the reporting laws provided them with immunity against legal risk. The laws rarely, if ever, provided more preventive, therapeutic or protective resources for children and their families.

Child rearing can be viewed largely as a matter of parents' dosing the nurturance, the stimulation, and the frustration that their children receive. A closer consideration of the meaning of nurturance indicates its importance at every phase of development. The human child is born helpless and perishes if he or she is not nourished, protected, soothed, and stimulated by an older person capable of providing such care on a continuing basis. What begins as biological helplessness leads to social and psychological attachment as a result of the interaction of the infant and maternal person or persons. The infant progresses from biological dependency to psychological and social attachment in which the child craves affection, approval, and predictable, dependable responses from the caretaking adults. This craving, or 'social addiction', is the 'stuff' out of which social development emerges as a result of positive or negative identifications. Through these close relationships, the child acquires and internalizes parental attitudes and expectations. These identifications are the core of the unique personality of each child.

In a sense we are endowed and plagued by this psychological and 'social addiction' for the rest of our lives. The gradual transformation of the addiction leads to the need for social closeness, friendship, companionship, and eventually to the re-establishment of another family group. It also is the source of a need for privacy and independence. As with many of the lines of development, passive experiences, *e.g.,* being fed or bathed, become the basis for actively taking care of oneself and later of others. Many of our neurotic and developmental deviations stem from the failure to turn passive experiences into active, self-initiating capacities, unique to the individual, but influenced to a significant extent by how the child indentifies with her parents and older siblings.

As we have already seen, these indentificatory processes may entrap the child in conflict or may be her pathway to a unique and well functioning personality. How the parents nurture and how they serve as advocates in regard to health care, schooling, and participation in the life of the community all are vital influences on the developing child's personality and sense of self. Probably the nurturance is more crucial for healthy development than the advocacy, although to separate them is somewhat artificial. The content and style of child rearing usually reflects the substance and style of the parents' nurturing and advocacy functions.

When parents are depressed or suffer from the long-term effects of deprivation in their own childhood, they may lack the capacity to stimulate, nurture, protect, guide, and support their children. They transmit to their children what they themselves had suffered. In this way, certain deficits and deviations may be transmitted from one generation to the next through the dynamics of the family interactions.

On the other hand, in healthy development, these identifying processes proceed from imitative behavior to the internalization of parental attitudes and expectations. Gradually, this enables the child to separate and individuate as the attachment to the dependable, guiding parental persons matures. Now the child is prepared to have short separations from the parents because her mental and emotional capacity has enabled her to have the parents with her psychologically when the child and her parents are physically separated. Children can go to a nursery school or play group. With the psychological presence of the parents, they are able to form attachments to teachers, peers, and others as their progressive development enables them to socialize, learn, play and move along through the toddler, latency, and adolescent phases. The styles of child rearing offer many options, so long as they are not the object of prejudice in the community. However, child rearing starts with nurturance in the home and becomes child advocacy when the child has needs (*e.g.,* for education or health care) that the parent makes available to the child from sources outside the home.

Throughout development, the need for continuity with the same primary love objects is crucial as the child defines herself against parents, siblings, and later on peers, teachers, and others. Each young child attributes to the primary or psychological parents the omnipotence and omniscience that early on become the basis for feeling secure with and later awed by these parents in the family setting. As maturation and development proceed, these attitudes and expectations undergo gradual change. The child's sense of herself becomes more clear and confident as she perceives reality more accurately and with the capacity to think logically.

Gradually, then, children undergo a disillusionment about their parents, who not only lose their mantle of omniscience and omnipotence but also 'reveal' their human imperfections. Normatively, as the disillusionment is worked through, children perceive their parents more realistically. This enables children and parents to move toward greater closeness as friends and companions after the rebelliousness of adolescence. Throughout, the child and adolescent are storing up their future adult capacities to nurture, guide, rear, and be the advocates for their own children. If children lose their primary parents or have multiple and changing parents, there is the risk that these children will persist in relating to parental figures at an immature level. They may be fixated at the level of infantile 'magic' thinking, in which adults in authority are viewed as omnipotent and omniscient. Often they are poorly equipped to become parents themselves.

Our knowledge about children's developmental needs converges with the judgment that the family unit should be supported and strengthened in a society where value preferences include the child's interests as paramount and state intrusion as minimal. This convergence is a substratum for optimal child rearing in which parents are the most important hope that child advocacy can and will be effective. Thus, it is crucial in assuring parents of support for their nurturing and advocating functions to respect the intimacy and privacy of the family. The dividing line between respecting and intruding into family privacy is child abuse, not child neglect. That is, there is little or no useful agreement on what constitutes emotional and psychological violence or neglect, we have agreement about physical injury, abuse and life-threatening injuries.

Our psychological understanding clearly states that one may and should think, feel, and phantasize in any way that appeals to him. It is the vital difference between behavior and the activities of the mind that is crucial, as well as how they influence each other.

To complicate further the meaning of violence, we can understand that the behavior of a child may be experienced by one adult as violent, another as playful, and by yet another as conforming social behavior. *E.g.,* in the young child, crying in association with paroxysmal fussiness:

(1) One parent or set of parents may experience that behavior as normative; they will rock, soothe and stay with the child patiently;

(2) Another parent may experience that behavior as illness in the child and call the pediatrician or discuss it with the visiting nurse;

(3) Yet another parent or set of parents may experience that behavior as violent and react in a way they feel is impelled by their need to survive — not to allow the violent baby to destroy them.

Obviously, in the case of younger children the chemistry of violence is one that incorporates the behavior of the child and the human environment's tolerances of and reactions to the child's behavior.

In another instance, an autistic psychotic child, age six, engaged in violent self-mutilating behavior and at other times in attacks upon household materials and occasionally on his parents and siblings. The parents understood this as the behavior of a sick child. They tried to curb it through a well-structured and simplified environment, through the elimination of environmental hazards and through the use of psychological and pharmacological treatment. They were able to mitigate all but the violent self-destructive behavior in which the child cut himself with any piece of glass he could find and break to form a sharp or pointed edge when it was too smooth. In this instance the mother described how the child could detect pieces of glass in the yard that had been overlooked by the family's extensive effort to eliminate the hazard. He could detect it by his extraordinary sensitivity to bright, flickering lights which such pieces of glass exhibited when the sun was out.

In this instance, the parents finally utilized the guidance of the National Society for Autistic Children in their paper* on behavior modification, which carefully delineates the way in which to use painful aversive conditioning as a teaching method — not a treatment — to rapidly bring under control behavior that ". . . threatens the child's safety or his survival in an optimum environment. Such aversive conditioning may involve spanking and electric shock."[6] The question of physical abuse in childhood can be seen as a relative one that requires an awareness of the complexity involved.

Finally, in describing the relativistic frame of reference in regard to violent behavior, the effect to use a non-violent strategy in coping with a threatening, violent human environment deserves careful study. This strategy was demonstrated by many youths who were involved in the Voter Registration Drive in Mississippi in the middle 1960s. It was also demonstrated by Yale students in the 1970 May Day Black Panther Rally in New Haven. The Student Council decided, with the support of the faculty and administration, to open the residential colleges to those who came to the rally, rather than to close them down and protect them against the risk of violence that the rally threatened.

Non-violence as a strategy was practiced. In order to do that in Mississippi and in

---

* "White Paper on Behavior Modification with Autistic Children." Revision by Clara and David Park and members of Professional Advisory Board, NSAC, of a statement drawn up by Creighton Newsome.

New Haven, the youths practiced in dramatic rehearsals being confronted by violent behavior so they could learn to control their responses and to protect themselves. This practicing tended to reduce the amount of tension and apprehension in confrontations, which empirically decreased the risk that violent feelings and motives would be translated into violent behavior. Students in those two settings were impressive in their courage, in their altruism and in their capacity to resist the invitation of certain adults to provoke them into violent behavior. They were greatly helped by a philosophy (for some) or a strategy (for others) that tended to reduce the social tension. Social tension is often a trigger that sets off violent behavior which all human beings are capable of expressing in their behavior. It is also very clear that violent feelings, thoughts and impulses are characteristic of the mental activities of all human beings.

These observations are illustrative of the crucial and differing meanings of violence and of the complexity of what constitutes the chemistry of violent behavior in the 1970s. With this as background, I want to sketch in the implications of this formulation for understanding the very real problem of the abused and battered child and our national response to these phenomena.

After World War II the condition of the battered child was first called to our attention by a pediatric radiologist, Professor John Caffey (1946, 1950, and 1957) of Columbia University P. & S.[7] As the awareness spread like a delayed virus, the studies revealed what appeared to be a large number of undetected cases of abused children. Some workers perceived or interpreted these findings to represent an epidemic of violent injuries and destruction of young children by their parents. The theory of delayed virus infection, as in multiple sclerosis, is heuristically useful. That is, parents who, as children were deprived, abused and battered, carry a 'virus' that may be activated as a pathogenic virus — or may produce an antibody — when those individuals have their own children. If it is activated by the child's particular pattern of behavior and development, then there is a high risk of the parent's past experience being repeated, but now with the child as the object of the adult's violent behavior. Conversely, the child's behavior and the parent's reaction to having been violently abused as a child may ward off the risk of battering, or physical abuse being transmitted from one generation to the next.

In the 1950s and 60s, laws to protect those who reported child abuse against legal risk and to require such reporting swept through 50 states faster than any state-by-state national legislation has ever been passed in the U.S.A. Our indignation translated into such action was a mixed blessing. The positive aspects of it were that we all became more aware of it. We planned to develop an orderly way of reporting child abuse, and we could begin to institute protective, educational and rehabilitative services. However, violence can beget chaos.

The negative aspects have been that family privacy has frequently been coercively invaded on the basis of false reports, on the basis of life style differences, and on the basis of prejudice against minorities, single-parent families, and low-income families. Also, the concept of emotional neglect has been used as a basis for coercive inquiry when there is no consensus of how to define emotional neglect operationally so we can distinguish emotional disturbance from emotional neglect. Finally, the eidemic of reporting has not been matched by proportionate, appropriate services to help the child and family; instead, we often permit the state to point the finger of suspicion or accusation when the state does not have adequate resources to help the child and his or her family. This lack of services has often left the child in greater danger than before the reporting of suspected abuse was carried out.

We have learned that inquiry and identification is a threat and a promise — and if the promise cannot be carried out, there is a threat of greater or more risk of violence to the vulnerable child. Our search for the roots of violence in the individual person is wryly, ironically and reflectively referred to by Walt Kelly, creator of Pogo, who said:

There is no need to sally forth, for it remains true that those things which make us human are, curiously enough, always close at hand. Resolve, then, that on this very ground, with small flags waving, and tiny blasts of tinny trumpets, we have met the enemy, and not only may he be ours, he may be us.

Appendix

The Canadian Commission on Violence on Television in its Interim Report points out the following:

In the first ten years of life, a child could have viewed 1300 violent deaths on television. The Report provides the following definition of violence and a range of implications:

Violence is action which intrudes painfully or harmfully into the physical, psychological or social well-being of persons or groups.
Violence or its effect may range from trivial to catastrophic.
Violence may be obvious or subtle.
It may arise naturally or by human design.
Violence may take place against persons or against property.
It may be justified or unjustified, or justified by some standards and not by others.
It may be real or symbolic.
Violence may be sudden or gradual.

Furthermore, the Report raises questions about the nature of media violence:

Violence depicted in film, television, sound, print or live performance is not necessarily the same as violence in real life.
Things not violent in reality may be violent in their portrayal.
Violence presented in the media may reach large numbers of people, whereas real violence may not.
The media may use many artificial devices to lessen or to amplify its emotional and social effects.
Violence depicted may do harm the original violence may not have done — or it may have no impact at all.

NOTES

1. Ashton-Warner, Sylvia, *Spinster.* New York, New York: Simon & Schuster, 1959.
2. *Interim Report,* Royal Commission on Violence in the Communications Industry, Government of Canada, Toronto and Ontario, 1976.
3. Carthy, J.D., and Ebling, F.J., *The Natural History of Aggression, Prologue and Epilogue.* New York, New York: Academic Press, 1964.
4. Gil, David G., *Violence Against Children.* Cambridge, Mass.: Harvard Univ. Press, 1970.
5. Kanerman, S.B., and Kahn, A.J., "European Family Policy Currents: The Question of Families with Very Young Children" (1976), (preliminary draft of a working paper, Columbia University).
6. See "White Paper on Behavior Modification with Austistic Children", by Park, Clara, and Park, David, revising a statement by Newsome, Creighton, in cooperation with the Professional Advisory Board, NSAC.
7. See Caffey, J., "Multiple Fractures in the Long Bones of Infants Suffering from Chronic Subdural Hematoma" (1946), 56 *American Journal Orentgenol* 163; Caffey, J., *Journal of Pediatric X-ray Diagnosis* (2nd ed., 1950), p. 684; and Caffy, J., "Some Traumatic Lesions in Growing Bones Other Than Fractures and Dislocations: Clinical and Radiological Features" (1957), 30 *British Journal Radiology* 225.

Chapter 16

Paternal Power and Child Abuse: An Historical and Cross-Cultural Study

*M.C.J. Olmesdahl**

Family relations in so far as they are regulated by legal rules and are thereby invested with the character of legal relations, are relations of power. Their effect is to subordinate one person within limits, to the arbitrary authority of another person, *i.e.,* to an authority founded on private law. The Right of Control based on family law produces subordination, not a mere obligation. It represents a power over free persons and a power which curtails the freedom of those subject to it, because the person in whom power vests is entitled to exercise it, up to a certain point, in his own interests alone, to exercise it, in a word, as he chooses.

Sohm[1]

The perspective of this chapter is governed by the belief that child abuse is inherent in the discretion that legal rules confer on parents. What can be seen as sick and deviant is not necessarily qualitatively different from what many cultures have accepted as normal. Child abuse is one end of a continuum starting with the legitimate exercise of parental authority. There is no clear cut point along it where the quantity and quality of physical force used becomes legally impermissible.[2]

The Roman patriach's power of 'life and death' over wife and children sounds dramatic and seems excessive. The question is: how far have we advanced since then? To obtain deeper cultural insights into the problem of child abuse, I will examine the position first in Roman Law and then in African customary law as exemplified among the Zulu. Finally I will reflect on the extent to which vestiges of extreme paternal authority can still be found in a modern, 'western', legal system, that of South Africa. The legal rules are not examined in isolation, but in the social context in which they operated and operate. Only in this way can a picture be obtained of what the rules actually mean in practice.

1. Roman Law

In the words of Lord Bruce:

There is not a problem of jurisprudence that it does not touch.

---

* Faculty of Law, University of Natal, South Africa.

The developments in Roman law were spread over 12 centuries, from 750 B.C. to 560 A.D. The provisions of the XII Tables (450 B.C.) are often presented as if they were still existent at the time of Justinian (527-565 A.D.). Although Roman society may initially have been an egalitarian one, it was soon marred by the division between patricians and plebians. Throughout its development the detailed rules perpetuated vast differences in social and legal power. Such rules as were enshrined in the law were relevant to the values of the ruling groups, and one cannot automatically presume them to be relevant to the lives and habits of the masses.

The extended agnatic family was the basic unit of social organization. It formed a monocratic legal unit[3] with the oldest male ancestor (the *paterfamilias*) at its head. The household was an aggregate of those bound together and subject to his extensive power, *patria postestas*. The family was largely autonomous and the instrument of that autonomy was the *paterfamilias*. Family life was governed by the traditions and customs[4] of the household as interpreted and applied by the *paterfamilias*. The intensity of this power and its lifelong duration was seen as unique to Romans.[5] With minimal 'government' the capacity to intervene in the family was limited — '*My home is my castle.*'[6] The *patria potestas* was the central institution of law concerning parents and children, and seems almost entirely to have absorbed the capacity for rights of the children subject to it. Legal relations between parent and children were hardly developed.[7]

This authority and the patriachal image, were created and sustained by various rituals of avoidance[8] — '*Sons grown to manhood do not bathe along with their fathers.*' [9] The father was to be revered by his children almost like a god.[10] This respect and veneration gave strength and force to the *patria potestas*. As head of the household, he was responsible for the preservation of the ancestral cult. The religious '*sacra*' could only be performed by him.[11] The importance of the family '*sacra*' necessitated the arrangement of marriages to provide descendants to carry on the family cult. The insistence on the fidelity of the wife was to ensure legitimate sons to perpetuate the personality of the ancestors. One must not forget that the Roman *paterfamilias* was a peasant. Like peasants of all ages he was full of superstition and hence the great importance of preserving good understanding with the gods.

The joint undivided family was also an economic unit. Control and ownership of all family property was vested in the *paterfamilias*. The concrete economic system created by the development of wealth necessitated a unilateral power to act, which vested in the *paterfamilias*. Acquisitions by members of the family vested in the family unit. The *paterfamilias* was seen as safeguarding the family patrimony and hence securing a material basis for the perpetuation of the family. He was liable for obligations of an economic and delictual nature connected therewith and there was vested in him the juridical power to act for the family, both externally and internally. The *paterfamilias* must be seen as a domestic judge, exercising supreme judicial power, and not simply arbitrary personal rule. He often acted with the advice of a family '*consilium*'[12] consisting of the older members of the family.

The *paterfamilias,* like his counterparts in the rest of the Aryan world, had the power to decide whether a newborn child should be brought up or exposed.[13] In militaristic Rome (as in Sparta) a deformed child had to be killed after it had been shown to five neighbours.[14] A deformed child was seen as a sign of divine wrath.[15]

A father shall immediately put to death a son recently born who is a monster, or has a form different from that of members of the human race.[16]

When a child was born, it was laid at the *paterfamilias'* feet. If he lifted it up he admitted it into the family: *'tollere libere'* (raised up the child).[17] This arbitrary power was tied to a recognition of paternity and that the child legitimately belonged to the family and was entitled to participate in the family cult.[18] It was to ensure that the blood of the family was kept pure, for alien blood would endanger the ancestral cult.[19] Thus manifest infidelity of a wife was traditionally one of the reasons for exposure.[20] The power was intimately tied to his religious authority and power to decide who was to be initiated into the family *sacra.* It was also connected with his economic control of the family, enabling him to preserve the family property by preventing division of the patrimony.

In Classical law (A.D. 150-250) exposure was not forbidden but there was legislation dealing with the rights of persons rescuing the child.[21] To avoid children being killed, Constantine (330 A.D.) allowed parents in cases of dire extremity to sell their child.[22] Exposure was prohibited by Valentinian III (434-450 A.D.) on pain of criminal penalties and Justinian (560 A.D.)[23] provided that the parents of a child who had been found and raised forfeited any right to the child's property.

The Power of Life and Death

A father shall have the right of life and death over his sons born in lawful marriage.[24]

Dionysius describes more dramatically this power enshrined in the XII Tables:

But the lawgiver of the Romans gave virtually full power to the father over his son, even during his whole life, whether he thought proper to imprison him, to scourge him, to put him in chains, keep him at work in the fields or put him to death.

It is significant that in other systems there were early limitations on the father's powers. The code of Hammurabi required judicial sanction for disinherision:[25] Jewish law[26] required punishments to be sanctioned by the elders of the city. But throughout the history of Rome we find recorded examples of the exercise of the power of death. Junius Brutus put his son to death[27] (509 B.C.); Fluvius was executed for his part in the Catilinarian conspiracy[28] (63 B.C.); Augustus banished Julia for immorality[29] (14 A.D.). It seems that the *paterfamilias'* power was not limited to 'criminal' acts, but extended to morally reprehensible conduct and that threatening the reputation of the family. Indeed his punishment might be heavier than the legal penalty. Yet this power was not totally arbitrary and unlimited. The father was seen to be acting in judicial capacity, bound by ancestral legal traditions.[30] The nature of this power is better illustrated by understanding its dual character as 'the power of life and death.' Yaron[31] argues that the first part, 'the power to keep alive', meant that the father 'was entitled to prefer mercy to strict justice, to grant a pardon if he so pleases'. He keeps alive an offender who has committed a capital 'crime', and pardons a person guilty of a crime. While the growing state power might allow the father to pass and execute sentence, it was more jealous of the power of remitting punishment for serious crime. Hence by the time of the written Roman sources, only the power of death is explained. The head of the family was not entitled to kill persons in his *potestas* on the basis of any sovereign power. He was not possessed of a proprietary *ius abutendi* (the right to destroy a chattel). He would require *iusta causa*[32] to put his son to death.

Admittedly, in early Roman society, adequate safeguards to control the exercise of power might not have existed. Nevertheless, the power of death was not arbitrary but a legally regulated exercise of power.[33] In earliest times, in addition to spiritual sanctions, arbitrariness would be met with moral disapproval and collective popular disapproval would result in *'infamia'*—a certain social stigma. Later the *'censors',* who regulated the morals of the people,[34] would take note of excessive punishment by putting a black mark (*nota censoria)* against the *paterfamilias'* name in the lists.[35] This entailed certain public law disabilities. In grave cases it was customary for the head to consult the family *consilium* (council) who would exercise some influence over him. In later times he was bound by the verdict of the *consilium.*[36] Tacitus[37] relates how Aulus Plautus, acting with the family council, held 'trial over his wife's life and reputation and declared her not guilty.' Finally, as the ancestor cult decayed and abuses increased, imperial legislation intervened.This also reflected the growth of the power of the state with which the *paterfamilias'* autonomous power was inconsistent. Hadrian[38] (117-138 A.D.) banished a father for misusing his power. Trajan[39] (98-117 A.D.) compelled a cruel father to emancipate his son. Constantine included the killing of a son in parricide.[40] These limitations on *patria potestas* required the father to invoke the assistance of the magistrate when imposing a penalty. Initially[41] the father could prescribe the penalty to the magistrates, later[42] full power was transferred to the magistrate to decide and punish. The other powers of the *paterfamilias* over persons in his *potestas* showed a similar decline. He loses his right to sell them into slavery across the Tiber or to pledge them as civil slaves in Rome.[43] His power to give them in noxal surrender rather than pay damges for their civil wrongs became obsolete.[44] His power to arrange and terminate their marriages fell away.[45] As Horace[46] shows:

Father blazes with wrath when his son mad on some tart refuses to wed a wife with a huge dowry.

Although the *patria potestas* has no application to public law[47] and was mitigated by the sons's increasing proprietary capacity,[48] one is still surprised, not at its original extent, but at its duration. Daube offers the explanation that the Roman upper classes preserved the rules because they expressed their innate superiority.[49] The better citizens were proud of their grotesque family structure and were prepared to endure it for the sake of status. 'We have to do with self-imposed discipline of an elite, rules, the orginal purpose of which is gone, but which are retained religiously for the sake of their present, almost more important function, to symbolize and strengthen the select and noble over against the common.'[50]

Nevertheless, by the time of Justinian (560 A.D.), the *patria potestas* has dwindled to a right of reasonable chastisement.

We grant the power of punishing minors to their elder relatives, according to the nature of the offence which they have committed, in order that the remedy of such discipline may exert its influence over those whom a praise-worthy example at home has not induced to lead an honourable life.

We, however, are not willing that the right to inflict extremely severe castigation for the faults of minors should be conferred, but that the exercise of paternal authority may correct the errors of youth, and repress them by private chastisement. If, however, the enormity of the deed should exceed the limits of domestic correction, we decree that those guilty of atrocious crime shall be brought before the courts of justice.[51]

The killing of children is punished by the penalty for parricide, which provided that the offender:

. . . shall neither be put to death by sword, nor by fire, nor by any other ordinary method, but shall be sewed up in a sack with a dog, a cock, a viper, and a monkey, and, enclosed with these wild animals and associated with serpents, he shall be thrown into the sea . . .[52]

In addition the duties of parents to educate and maintain their children are recognized.[53]

Thus in Roman Law it can be observed that *patria potestas* almost entirely obliterates any capacity of children subject to it to have rights. The concept of the legal unity of the family,[54] like that of husband and wife, operates to protect the father. Initially no action lay in contract or delict (tort) between them. Children wronged by the father had no legal redress for personal injuries[55] nor for mismanagement of property which would pass on succession. Later the child could sue but had to obtain the *praetor's* (judicial officer) consent to an action brought against his parents or guardian.[56]

The absolute propertylessness of the son introduced some element of violence into the family. Sons would wish their fathers dead and often the wish was father to the deed.[57] There are numerous references in the literature to this.[58] Cicero's first criminal trial is in defence of a man accused of murdering his father.[59] Hence the severe penalties for parricide. A son's zest for high living would lead him into the hands of the moneylender. Hence the *Senatus Consulta Macedonianum* (Senate legislation 1st century A.D.) which prevented the creditor ever reclaiming money lent to a son under the *potestas* of his father.[60]

In dealing with the position in African customary law, one is faced with a paucity of materials. Not only are the societies often pre-literate, but also by the very nature of customary family law, numerous rules of behavior are largely unwritten. To obtain a picture comparable to the Rome of the XII Tables (450 A.D.) one must attempt description at the stage of early contact with whites. The nature of the colonial administration was such as rapidly to supercede any African 'criminal' jurisdiction, although 'civil' law customs were generally left undisturbed.[61] Customary law was shorn of its coercive power.

The early first-hand accounts of travellers and missionaries are generally too unsystematic for legal analysis. Often there is a disproportionate emphasis and Victorian-type 'horror' of the sexual mores.[62] The anthropological writings contain certain ideological distortions. First there is the fiery dispute between Maine[63] and the supporters of the patriachal theory as against McLellan[64] and his adherents. Secondly the later more detailed writings are of course bounded within the authority and power of the colonial administration.

The field itself is also marked by lack of uniformity and by tribal variations, some societies having a strong central political authority and others only rudimentary political arrangements.[65] Nor are all the societies patrilineal. Matrilineal societies predominate in mid-Africa.[66] I propose therefore to concentrate on the Nguni speaking tribes living in Natal/Cape, with particular emphasis on the Zulu in Natal, relying on similar rules among Nguni for additional support. Examples are also taken from other African tribes.

Today a fair amount of legal materials exist in the form of text book writings and judicial decisions. However, this is descriptive of the law as presently applied by the courts and reflects the law at a later stage of development. I will therefore use the term 'African customary law' to describe early law and 'Bantu law' to describe the law as administered today.

Zulu society (like other Nguni tribes) was strongly patriarchal. Descent was patrilineal, marriage was patrilocal, inheritance and succession passed in the male line and family authority was patripotestal.[67] The normal Zulu family consisted of the family father, the Kraalhead, and a couple of wives with their sons and daughters of various ages. This household was not an amorphous mass but was segmented into houses, each wife with her children, all united by their allegiance to a common father into an integral unit.[68] On the death of the Kraalhead, the houses would emerge as independent units each under the control of the senior male child in that house. Each kraal was run on a system of patriarchal power, a mystique calling for axiomatic reverence from sons and wives. The division of labor and code of etiquette of kinship avoidance reinforced a dignified father image:[69] *'The ox is manlier than the bull'.*

The existence of a polygamous household meant that, although the relationship to the father implied respect and even fear, the father himself could not and did not concern himself much with the day-to-day discipline of his children. He was their instructor. *'When you follow behind your father you learn to walk like him.'* The wife did most of the beating of the younger children.[70]

A child which is to turn out any good is not reared entirely on a beautiful mat.[71]

The basic unit of food consumption and production was the polygamous family. The father had the custody and control of the family wealth. There could be no slaughter or sale of family livestock without his consent.[72] What members acquired vested in the Kraalhead. *'The hand catches for the master.'* [73] Individual interests were vested in the community. The father's control over property gave him the say in the selection of his sons' wives — there was a moral obligation on him to provide cattle (*lobola*) for the son's bride. The payment of *lobola* placed children of that wife in the father's lineage group. The prosperity and the welfare of the living depended on the spirits of the family's ancestors, who in turn depended on the living for sacrifices, for without them *'the ancestors' spirits would have to eat grasshoppers on the mountain side.'* The Kraalhead (father) was the vital link to the world of shades, acting as the ritual intermediary[74] in officiating at sacrifices. As he was the direct representative on earth of the ancestors, there was a supernatural backing to his authority in the family.

Zulu society was also moulded and determined by the military system which influenced and dominated every phase of life.[75] Three years after puberty the men would be formed into military regiments, which acted as a state army and 'police force'. At the age of about 40 they would be released by the Chief and given permission to marry and establish their kraals. The father's authority was then also part of the discipline inherent in the system.

The father was also master of the kraal. He had an unchallenged monopolistic control of legal relations both within the household to maintain order and settle quarrels between members of the family and to represent the family in its relations with other groups. He was responsible for every wrong committed by members of the family, and he would initiate redress for wrongs committed against the members of his family. The Kraalhead was then the person will full legal capacity.

Exposure of Newborn Infants

Various writers show that this practice did exist:

Whenever an obvious monstrosity was born, or a child, who through some deformity, proved after a year or two of trial incapable of ever becoming a normal human being, perhaps through inability to stand or walk, a cow was first of all slaughtered for the ancestral spirits, after which a goat was taken and tethered near some local forest with the child comfortably laid down beside it to be devoured by any passing wild beast.[76]

However, it is not clear if the exposure was obligatory or not, or if the motives behind it were in fact of a military nature. In respect of twins, there were religious motives in the killing of the lastborn twin and various sacrifices to the spirits were performed. As childbirth was the concern of the women alone, one of them would arrange the killing.[77]

As regards the legitimacy of the child, this might be shown by whether the mother gave birth at her husband's home or went back to her family to give birth.[78] It is not clear whether the father had a right to expose the child when born at his kraal when he suspected infidelity. After birth, the mother and child were isolated for several days and the father before entering the hut would acknowledge the child as his.[79] The effects of non-acknowledgement are unclear.

Disciplinary Powers of Kraalhead

Bryant[80] states that customary law conferred on a father similar drastic powers to those held by the Roman *paterfamilias*.

He could and did, though instances were very rare, administer physical and mental torture by thrashing, binding, starving, confining, bodily mutilating and even killing either wife, grown-up or daughter or child. For instance, an irate husband might emasculate a paramour and kill the adulterous wife caught in *flagrante delicto* or impale a night prowler (suspected witch) or mortally wound a dangerously aggressive son,

and

As absolute submission to the authority of the Kraalhead was the supreme rule of life within the family, so absolute loyalty to the chief was the supreme rule of life within the clan. The crimes therefore above all others most heinous were such as directed against the person or authority of the head of the family or chief of the clan and if the magnitude of the offence justified it, both possessed the right of inflicting capital punishment, a right rarely exercised by a father, though very frequently by the chief.[81]

Another method of discipline was corporal punishment. Cetywayo, the Zulu king, in giving evidence before the 1883 Commission, was asked:

Then the punishment is thrashing by the father?
Cetywayo: It is not done in all cases, but that is the way they punish them.[82]

In addition the father could expel an offending party from the home. This was in effect an outlawing and disinheriting of the son and would normally be done in a public meeting before relatives to give the accused a chance of defence before he was repudiated.[83] For continuous misbehavior the father could refuse to provide *lobola* for the son's first wife.

Although the father's power was supreme he was expected to exercise it within the limits of customary law. He always had to be wary of public disgrace to which most Zulu men were rather sensitive. For flagrant abuse he might be arraigned before the Chief.[84] Persons were considered the property of the Chief. Fines imposed for acts of violence committed against the person (cases of blood) were accordingly claimed by the chief. *'No man can cut his own blood.'* The fine for serious assaults varied from 1 to 5 head of cattle.

In addition, although the Kraalhead's right to beat his wife or her children was recognized, in cases of abuse she might appeal to the protection of her own kin group. Often they would extract a fine before allowing her or the children to return.[85] This feature may have provided more protection to the child than in monogamous Rome. This was then the position in African Customary Law. Under the colonial administration the criminal jurisdiction was removed, the extreme rights of parents were limited, exposing a child and excessive punishments became criminal offences[86] and the infliction of punishment was limited to reasonable chastisement.[87] The colonists declared their law to be the law of the land, with limited recognition of customary law in disputes between Africans.

In Natal, customary law was codified. Inmates of the kraal fall under control of the Kraalhead;[88] the father is recognized as the natural guardian of his legitimate offspring;[89] the Kraalhead is the owner of all property in the kraal[90] and is entitled to the earnings of all kraal inmates;[91] he has the power to disinherit his sons;[92] he is liable delictually for wrongs committed by inmates[93] and cannot be sued by inmates for wrongs committed by him.[94] Females are perpetual minors.[95]

Unfortunately this freezing of the law into the rules as understood then, was applicable to a society at a particular stage of development from which some Africans were already escaping. Dramatic social, economic and political changes have occurred since then. Separate courts were created to settle disputes between Africans and were given a discretion to apply customary law where appropriate.[96] However, the predominant approach was one of utilizing a theoretical idea of 'pure African law', not merely a recognition of custom as then applied but often a resuscitation of earlier customs. There was not much of the innovative role played by the *praetor* (Roman judicial officer) in adapting the administration of justice to the needs of a changing society. As the courts were separated by colour and culture there was never the possibility of the court fulfilling roles analogous to that performed in traditional African society.[97] There was and is little evidence of attempts to establish whether the parties before the court are still tribal or detribalized or whether pure customary law is the proper law for the settlement of the dispute or not. Indeed, tribal culture no longer exhibits a coherent set of values or institutions. Individuals are eclectic, operating according to tribal or western values depending on the needs of the situation. With justification, there is little African support for the continued duality in the legal system. In addition, governmental policy is such that there is a migratory system which causes severe dislocation in normal family life. Bantu law is not equipped to deal with family disorganization of the scale of today. Vast increases in the number of illegitimate births (60 percent)[98] and the resultant stress on mothers places the child in an exposed and vulnerable positon. Although most of the parties' legal relationships *inter se* may fall to be decided under Bantu law, in certain areas the ordinary courts of the land have in fact extended or modified the duties and rights in respect of parent/child relationships.

The duty of the father to maintain his children has consistently been decided under the more onerous civil law.[99] Normally the payment of *lobola* means that the father is the natural guardian of the child and thus entitled to custody on dissolution of the marriage. This rule is not applied where the parties have married by Christian/civil rites,[100] but is where it is a 'customary union'. There are also a few scattered cases where the father has abused or maltreated the child and his rights to custody have been refused.[101] Generally, however, matters of family relations are decided according to Bantu law.

3. Synthesis

Although, there are no figures regarding the extent of child abuse in Rome or in Zululand, one can safely infer from the social structure and legal rules, with their emphasis on paternal rights, that the child was in a legally exposed and vulnerable position. The child existed in a legal vacuum. Such laws as did provide some protection was minimal. He was largely an object over which others had legal rights. Generally improvements in women's rights, such as their right to bodily integrity free from the husband's right to moderate chastisement, have followed the establishment of their proprietary rights. Certainly the limitations on the father's authority in Roman Law followed the recognition of the son's right to *peculium* (property and booty acquired on military service).[102] In Bantu Law, the husband retains the right to moderate chastisement of his wife/wives.[103] Is this a reflection of her proprietary incapacity? She has no rights of succession in Bantu Law and even where she is married under civil law, her separate estate, if any, is administered by the husband. This may mean that until the child's proprietary capacity is freely recognized and his right to work, to own and administer his estate separate from parental control is acknowledged, dramatic improvements will not occur.

4. Modern Law

Historically, the emphasis has been on parental rights. It is time that the problem of child abuse is approached from the perspective of children's rights.[104] It is necessary to advocate insistence on legal rights because in a legalistic society this is the only way to protect the child's humanity.

First the child has a right to the full protection of the criminal law. The criminal law may be a clumsy instrument and inherently unsuited to the protection of the child.[105] It is a slow and time consuming process. Convictions in the circumstances of a child abuse may be difficult to obtain. It may not deter or rehabilitate the offender. It is clear, however, that there are cases where it must be utilized. To refuse to do so would be a failure to recognize the humanity of the child, to relegate him to the status of a 'lesser breed without the law.'

There is no need to introduce new crimes. The criminal law is quite adequate for any purpose it may serve in this area.[106] To create new statutory offences would undermine the moral obloquy in which society views child abuse, given the generally permissive attitude of the public to statutory crimes. This does not mean that one cannot express concern with those cases in which the court is reluctant to apply normal criminal law principles when the violence is inflicted by parents on children.

In *R. v. Marais*[107] a 5 month old baby had been badly burnt by being placed in a hot bath. Defence counsel argued that the statutory regulations directed against the evils of 'baby-farming' did not apply to natural parents. Thankfully the court rejected the argument and convicted the parent. *R. v. Jacobs*[108] was a case where a 5 year old child was held down on a bed and his genitals were burnt with a red hot screwdriver. The trial Court convicted the custodian of 'assault with the intent to inflict grievous bodily harm.' On appeal the verdict was reduced to 'common assault' since the intent to inflict grievous bodily harm was not shown. With respect, the nature of the weapon and the place of injury hardly left room for doubt as to the intention. A recent, particularly gruesome case, was *S. v. Mostert and Rogers.*[109] Here the mother and her boyfriend had persistently, over a fairly long period, beaten her 3 year old child with a pick handle and eventually caused his death. A verdict of culpable homicide (manslaughter) was returned. This finding seems inexplicable in view of the definition of the intent required for murder.[110]

The South African figures for child abuse as quoted by the Minister of Police in parliament show the following:[111]

	Number of Reported Assaults on Infants	Number of Prosecutions	Number of Convictions
Year 1973/4	68	44	29
Year 1974/5	83	54	35
Year 1975/6	119	74	41

The alarming annual increases emphasize the need to utilize the criminal law in respect of a child's right to be protected.

Secondly, the child has a right to bodily integrity within and without the home. South African law, built as it is on a Roman and Roman-Dutch foundation, recognizes the rights of parents and schoolteachers to apply corporal punishment to those in their charge. The courts generally grant a distressingly wide latitude:

Courts of law should not lightly interfere with the discretion of schoolmasters in the punishment of their pupils.[112]

Where a parent or teacher, who are after all the best judges of the necessity of corporal punishment, uses a cane, a court of law will not lightly interfere, but will only do so when it is made manifest that the use of the cane was unreasonable and unduly severe.[113]

Sometimes there is a welcome questioning of its use:

Methods of violence and force may create fear and hatred, but hardly ever respect or affection. The old saying 'spare the rod and spoil the child' has long been abandoned by educationalists. Our increased knowledge of the operation of the mind has revealed the incontestible fact that in the upbuilding of character the rod should be sparingly, if ever, used.[114]

There is a need for society and law to reject unequivocally the use of physical violence as a means of rearing children. Gil's[115] figures show that a majority of child abuse cases resulted from disciplinary measures. Often abuse is the exaggerated manifestation of culturally and legally approved behavior. A start towards its total abolition can be made by outlawing corporal punishment in schools, correctional institutions and other child care facilities.

Thirdly, a child has a right to be emancipated from a relationship that has broken down. One must be realistic in respect of the recidivism rate amongst battering parents.[116] Society is not entitled to replace the child in the home where he suffered abuse in order to preserve the family. In the words of Polansky:

> Because of their dedication to the notion of 'the family', or their zeal about 'rehabilitation', the formal policies of social agencies in this field are sanguine to the point of being fatuous regarding the potentiality for change in a large proportion of the parents involved. The fact is that most hard-headed observers report little success with the methods of aggressive casework (or unaggressive psychiatry) now being practiced. This is true even when an adequate attempt at treatment is made, something which is possible in only a few areas of the country.[117]

The law must recognize the limited success of rehabilitation attempts, and this recognition must condition the approach of the courts in civil hearings, (the care proceedings). The court must be prepared to intervene decisively and terminate parental rights to the child and declare him eligible for adoption. Where there has been a conviction arising from child abuse, this deprivation of parental rights should be automatic unless the child himself wishes otherwise. Unfortunately the South African legislation[118] places severe limits on the courts' use of such powers. A child in need of care may be removed from the home but the termination of parental power can be granted only in narrowly defined circumstances. It is in society's best interest to make the child's need paramount. *"Every time the cycle of grossly inadequate parent-child relationship is broken society stands to gain a person capable of becoming an adequate parent for children of the future."*[119] All such action in civil hearings should be based on the child's need for 'continuity of relationships' and the 'child's sense of time'. All deliberate speed must be used to facilitate the establishment of new and permanent relationships.[120]

Fourthly, the child has a right to counsel. It is also suggested that a copy of the initial report of child abuse should go to a lawyer, whose function from then on through subsequent hearings will be to represent the child's interest.[121] His function would be to ensure that placement hearings take place quickly, that the child is not being used as a pawn to hold the family together and to argue, where necessary, for the child to be made available for adoption. He would also investigate the desirability and feasibility of a delictual (tort) action against the abusing custodian.[122]

As children before school age seem to be at greatest risk,[123] there is the desirability of widening the ambit of child abuse reporting laws. As many societies provide child support payments, the possibility exists of requiring the child to be presented for checking/examination when the custodian collects the payment. Obviously this would necessitate some training to spot indications of child abuse.

One is left with the sobering thought that probably we have advanced little since Justinian. Parents's rights are still given largely untrammelled sway. Children's rights are now just emerging, but it is questionable whether we have the social commitment and economic structure to transform those rights into reality.

NOTES

1. Ledlie, J.C., *Sohm's Institutes of Roman Law* (1907) 449.
2. Gil, D.G., *Violence Against Children*. Cambridge, Mass.: Harvard University Press, 1970, p. 133.
3. Kaser, M., *Roman Private Law* (1965) 60.
4. Digest 1.6.8.
5. Just. Inst. 1.9.2; Gaius, Inst. 1.55.
6. Cicero, *In Vatinium* 9.22 *'domus exsilium est'*.
7. Schultz, F., *Roman Classical Law* (1951) 112.
8. Mayer, G., "Patriachal Image" (1975), 34 *African Studies*.
9. Cicero, *De Officis* Bk. 1.35.128.
10. Cicero, *Pro Plancio* 12.29. "His father whom he reveres as divine, and indeed a parent is little short of that in his children's eyes." Cicero, *Cato Major* 9.37 "The slaves feared him, the children honoured him, he was dear to all".
11. Westrup, C.W., *Introduction to Early Roman Law* Vol. III (1939), p. 255.
12. Cicero. *de Leg.* 3.8.
13. Westrup, *op. cit.* 249.
14. Dionysius A.R. 2.8.8. A.R. 2.15.2.
15. Suet. Cal. 5.5; Livy 27. 37.5.
16. Table III — XII Tables, Scott's translation (1932) vol. 1.
17. The *patria potestas* arose by birth *in justum matrimonium:* D. 1.9.3. D. 40. 4.29. The *tollere liberum* did not have legal significance. Further see Watson, A., *Law of Persons in Later Roman Republic*. New York, New York: Oxford University Press, 1967, 72*ff*.
18. Plato, *Theat C.* 15; Ody 29.401.
19. Livy 1.4.6.
20. Sueton. *Caesar* 27.
21. Cod. 8.52.2.
22. Cod. 4.43.2.
23. Cod. 8.52.3.
24. XII Tables, Scott, *op. cit.,* vol. 1, p. 64.
25. Yaron, R., "Vitae Necisque Potestas" (1962), 30 *Tijdschrift voor Rechtsgeschiedenis* 213.
26. *Deuteronomy* 21:18.
27. Leage, R.W., *Roman Private Law* (1920) 78.
28. Sallust, *Cat.* 39.5.
29. Leage, *op. cit.* 78.
30. Westrup, *op. cit.* 186.
31. Yaron, *op. cit.* 248.
32. Westrup, *op. cit.* 159. Kunkell (1966), 83 *Zeitschrift der Savigny-Stiftung* 219*ff*.
33. Westrup, *op. cit.* 180.
34. Cicero, *de Leg* 3.3.7.
35. Sometimes the censor might also act arbitrarily. Cato, as censor expelled a man from the Senate because he had embraced his wife in front of his daughter. Plutarch, *Cato Major* 1.7.7.
36. Suet., *de clem.* 1.15.2; Val Max 5.9.1. Gai. Aug. 85, Crook, *Law and Life of Rome* (1970) 107.
37. Tacitus, *Annals* 13.32.2.

38. D.48.9.5.
39. D.37.12.5.
40. D.48.9.1. *Lex Pompeia de parricide* omits sons; In Cod. 9.17.1 son is included.
41. D.49.16.13.6; D.48.8.2.
42. Cod. 9.15.1 Cod. 8.47.3.
43. Dion. *Halicarnassus* 2.98; Cod. 4.43.1; Cod. 4.43.2; Nov. 134.7; Watson, A. (ed.), *Daube Noster.* Hackensack, New Jersey: Rothman, 1974, 183-5.
44. Gaius, *Inst.* 4.75.i. D.9.4.2; D.12.2; Just., *Inst.* 4.8.7. Holmes, O.W., *The Common Law* (1923) 8-15.
45. D.23.1.13.
46. Horace, *Satires* 1.4.48-50.
47. D.1.12.4.
48. Buckland, W.W., *A Textbook of Roman Law.* Cambridge, Eng.: Cambridge University Press, 1950; Codish, M.I., "The Roman Law of Persons" (1974), *Am J of Jurisprudence,* 112.
49. Daube, D., *Roman Law.* Chicago, Illinois: Aldine, 1969, p. 85; Gaius, *Inst.* 1.55.
50. Daube, D., *ibid.,* p. 80.
51. Cod. 9.15.1; see also D. 48.19.16.2.
52. Cod. 9.17.1.
53. Cod. 8.47.9; D.25.3.5.
54. Cod. 6.26. *in fin.*
55. Leage, R.W., *Roman Private Law* (1920), 80.
56. D.2.4.4; D.2.4.6; Cicero, *de off.* 1.17.54.
57. Daube, *op. cit.* 88-91.
58. Terence, *Phormio* 302*ff.*
59. Cicero, *Pro Roscio Amerino,* 14.39 and 24.68*ff.*
60. Buckland, W.W., *supra.*
61. The Natal Code was first enacted in 1875. Reissued in proclamation R 195/1967.
62. Evans-Pritchard, E.E., *Essays in Social Anthropology.* London, Eng.: Faber, 1962 ch. 1.
63. Maine, H., *Ancient Law.* London, Eng.: Dent, 1973; Maine H., *Early Law and Custom* (1891) chs. 7 & 8.
64. McLellan, J.F., *The Patriachal Theory* (1885); Tylor, E.B., "The Matriac Family System" (1896) *Nineteenth Century.*
65. Fortes, M., and Evans-Pritchard, E.E., *African Political Systems.* Oxford, Eng.: Oxford University Press, 1961, p. 5.
66. Matrilineal societies — see Phillips, A., (ed.), *Survey of African Marriage and Family Life* (1953) ch. 4.
67. Brown, Radcliffe, *Structure and Function in Primitive Society* (1952) 22.
68. Bryant, A.T., *The Zulu People* (1949) 437; Tooke, W. Hammond, *Bhaca Society* (1962) 37.
69. Mayer, G., "Patriachal Image" (1975), 34 *African Studies.*
70. Goldin, B., and Gelfand, M., *African Customary Law in Rhodesia* (1975) 38-79.
71. Rattray, R.S., "African Child in Proverb, Folklore and Fact" (1933) *Africa* 456.
72. Hollemans, J.F., *Inheemse Regsgemeenskappe by die Zulu* (1938) 48.
73. *Mtungata v. Qemba,* 4 NAC 104.
74. Krige, E.J., *The Social System of the Zulus* (1936), ch. 13.
75. Bryant, *op. cit.,* 188; Krige, *op. cit.,* 261. See also Bryant, *op. cit.,* 639.
76. Ludlow, *Zululand and Cetewayo* (1882) 65.
77. Bryant, *ibid.,* 613; Krige, *op. cit.,* 68.
78. There is not the same concern regarding the 'purity of the blood'. The father's right to his wife's child bearing capacity turns on whether *lobola* has been paid. *Mdinda v. Pahlane,* 1917 NHC 56.
79. Krige, *op. cit.,* 69.
80. Bryant, *op. cit.*

81. Bryant, A., *Bantu Law and Ethics* (1923). Unpublished manuscript — Killie Campbell Africana Library, Durban. Bryant, *op. cit.* 185 — open revolt might easily have terminated in death of the transgressor.
82. Cetewayo's evidence before 1883 Commission, *Report and Proceedings of Native Laws and Customs.*
83. Hollemans, J.F., *Shona Customary Law.* Manchester, Eng.: Manchester University Press 1952, p. 519-50; Bryant, *op. cit.* 441, *Lobisini v. Ngakumbi,* 1941 NAC (C & O) 1.
84. Col. McLean, *Compendium of Kaffir Law and Customs* (1906) 78. An action for personal injury vested in the Chief: *Nkungana v. Dunke,* 1937 NAC (C & O) 68.
85. Phillips, A., *Survey of African Marriage and Family Life* (1953) 17.
86. Transkei Penal Code. 24/1886, s. 176; Natal Code s. 41, s. 54.
87. Transkei Penal Code, s. 75; s. 76; Murder s. 146; Assault s. 156/164.
88. Natal Code s. 38. *Mbata v. Mbata,* 1937 NAC (N & T) 75: S.M. Seymour, *Bantu Law in South Africa* (1970).
89. *Ibid.,* s. 44(1) and s. 82; *Ndlovu v. Ndlovu,* 1946 NAC (N & T) 13.
90. *Ibid.,* s. 36; *Mzimela v. Mzimela,* 1941 NAC (N & T) 8.
91. *Ibid.,* s. 35(1); *Zakaza v. Mkize,* 1947 NAC (N & T) 85.
92. *Ibid.,* s. 118; *Tiba v. Soviya,* 1944 NAC (C & O) 90.
93. *Ibid.,* s. 141; *Tusini v. Ngubane,* 1948 NAC (T & N) 17.
94. *Ibid.,* s. 142; *Molife v. Molife,* 1934 NAC (N & T) 49.
95. *Ibid.,* s. 27; s. 28 provides process for emancipation; Seymour, *op. cit.,* ch. 7.
96. Bantu Administration Act 38/1927, s. 11.
97. Suttner, R.S., "African Family Law and Research in South Africa today", paper presented Sept 30, 1970 — Afrika Studiecentrum, Leyden.
98. Krige, E.J., "Changing Conditions in Marital Relations and Parental Duties among Urbanized Natives" (1936), 9 *Africa* 1; Shropshire, D.W.T., *Primitive Marriage and European Law.* London, Eng.: Frank Cass & Co., 1970.
99. Hahlo, H.R., "Natives' Liability to Maintain Illegitimate Child" 71 *SALJ* 119 and cases cited therein.
100. *Nombida v. Flaman,* 1956 NAC 108(5).
101. *Tshabala v. Tshabala,* 1944(2) PH R47; *Munemo v. Mandiyera,* 1943 S.N.R. 12.
102. Buckland, W.W., *A Textbook of Roman Law,* (2nd. ed., 1950) 280-1; Kaser, M., *Roman Private Law* (1965) 259-261.
103. Natal Code of Bantu Law. Proclamation R 195/1967, s. 54.
104. See the growing literature on children's rights: Holt, J., *Escape from Childhood.* New York, New York: Ballantine, 1974; Wilkerson, A.E., (ed.), *The Rights of Children.* Phil., Pennyslvania: Temple Univ. Press, 1973; Foster, H.II., *A Bill of Rights for Children.* Springfield, Illinois: C.C. Thomas, 1974; Adams, P., *et al, Children's Rights.* New York, New York: Praeger, 1971.
105. Helfer, R., and Kempe, C.H., *The Battered Child.* Chicago, Illinois: University of Chicago Press, 1968 p. 176; Grumet, B.R., "The Plaintive Plaintiffs" (1970) *Fam. L.Q.* 296.
106. The Children's Act 33/1960, s. 18(1) provides that "any parent or guardian of a child or any person having the custody of a child who ill-treats, neglects or abandons that child or allows it to be ill-treated, shall be guilty of an offence".
107. 1910 C.P.D. 542.
108. 1954 (1) PH 59; *cf. R. v Thaling,* 1942 O.P.D. 264.
109. *Natal Witness,* April 28, 1977.
110. Hunt, P.M.A., *South African Criminal Law and Procedure,* vol. 2 (1970) 324; E. Burchell, vol. 1, 119-123.
111. *Daily News,* May 21, 1977.
112. *Queen v. Soga Mgikela* 10 S.C. 240.
113. *R. v. Schoombee,* 1924 T.P.D. 481.
114. *R. v. Theron,* 1936 O.P.D. 166 at 172.

115. Gil, D.G., *Violence against Children*. Cambridge, Mass.: Harvard University Press, 1970, p. 126. In 63 percent of the cases of abuse, it was as a result of disciplinary action taken by the parent, and in 73 percent an over-reaction to real or perceived misconduct by the child.

116. Gil, *ibid.,* 114. 31 percent of mothers and 39 percent of fathers had been perpetrators of abuse previously. Terr and Watson, "The Battered Child Rebrutalized" (1968) *Amer. J. Psychiatry* 1432.

117. Gil, *ibid.* 43-45. *Cf.* Glazier, A. (ed.), *Child Abuse: Community Challenge*. East Aurora, New York: Stewart Henry Inc., 1971 for a social work approach and the importance of preserving the family.

118. Children's Act 33/1960, ss. 59-60 and 71-73.

119. Goldstein, J.; Freud, A., and Solnit, A.J., *Beyond the Best Interests of the Child*. New York, New York: Free Press, 1973, p. 7. See also Grument, *loc. cit.* 309.

120. *Ibid.,* 42.

121. Grumet, *loc. cit.* (note 105) 314.

122. Gil, *op. cit.,* 53 percent of cases concerned children under 6.

123. Forer, "Rights of Children" (1969), 55 *ABAJ* 1155. The consent of the court is not necessary to sue parents (*Mare v. Mare,* 1910 C.P.D. 437) and there is no parental immunity in South African law: *Pinchin v. Santam Insurance,* 1963(2) S.A. 254.

Chapter 17

The Follow-Up of Abused Children — A Researcher's Nightmare*

Margaret Lynch†

My own work with abusing families in recent years has made me very aware of the many problems encountered when trying to plan research into any aspect of child abuse. Index cases for my research studies have been drawn from among the abused children and their families referred to the Park Hospital for Children, Oxford, England. This is a National Health Service Hospital with 30 beds, providing in-patient and out-patient services for children with neurological, psychiatric and developmental disorders. In 1964 a unit with accommodation for three families was built in the hospital grounds (Lynch et al., 1975). It was originally intended to provide residential therapy for families with handicapped children. As the number of referrals of abused children increased, it was adapted to provide residential assessment and treatment for the abused child and his family (Lynch and Ounsted, 1976). In the last five years, there have been 81 families admitted to the unit for actual or threatened abuse. Not all the abusing families referred to the hospital are admitted to the family unit. Some referrals are managed as outpatients or by admitting the child alone. Over 300 abused children have been known to the hospital. The staff at the hospital belong to a wide variety of disciplines and their expertise is available to all the families. On discharge, the family's follow-up and continuing therapy is shared between the hospital and community staff. I myself worked as a member of the assessment and treatment team for two and one-half years before commencing my research studies. A social worker, Jacquie Roberts, works with me full-time. We maintain strong links with the service staff and with many of the families I have treated.

We are able when necessary to use the hospital facilities and have received much help and encouragement from our colleagues. Jacquie Roberts is seconded by the local social service department. This link is valuable because many of our families are well-known to that agency. We are currently completing a very detailed follow-up study of 42 physically abused children and their families.

* I thank Jacquie Roberts for her help in preparing this chapter. The research described was funded by the Oxford University Medical Reseach Fund.
† Human Development Research Unit, Park Hospital for Children, Oxford, England.

Presumably the purpose of any systematic long-term follow-up study of abused children and their families is to help us understand the full implications of 'child abuse'. Our clinical experience has already shown us that many abused children and their families still need help years after the initial identification. By studying their later development we hope to learn how best to provide both immediate and long-term services. Follow-up studies of the whole family are needed to help us assess the effectiveness of initial intervention and subsequent treatment. I believe that at the present time, with our still limited understanding of child abuse, we are going to learn most from small comprehensive studies. The results of these studies may well help us to determine the key questions that should be asked in future large scale projects. However, the great danger of using small samples is that people will use the results to make sweeping statements about whole populations. For example, it was unfortunate that five children who died in Preston, Lancashire, in the years 1970-72 (Hall, 1975), led to the emotive, much-quoted and misleading statement that two children are battered to death by their parents each day in the U.K. (Howells, 1974; Sunday Times, 1977).

1. Sample Identification

The sample identified for inclusion in a study will depend on the definition of abuse used and the population available for study. As child abuse can take many forms. The researcher must be able to define clearly the criteria for inclusion of cases in his study. The literature reveals that the criteria for inclusion of children for follow-up study are almost as numerous as the studies themselves. For example, Elmer and Gregg's (1967) initial sample of 50 children all had multiple skeletal injuries. Other writers such as Martin (1974) include all inflicted injuries, however mild. Other researchers include cases of poisoning, hypothermia (McRae and Ferguson, 1973), neglect (Morse et al., 1970) (Birrell and Birrell, 1968) and failure to thrive (McRae and Ferguson, 1973). We restricted our own follow-up studies to children who had actually been physically abused. Our definition of actual physical abuse is as follows:

Injuries known to be inflicted. Either such abuse is admitted by the parents or an explanation of injury is not consistent with medical evidence. This category also includes attempted suffocation, strangulation, drowning and poisoning. Injuries may range from minor soft tissue damage to injuries endangering life.

The common factor in all studies is that some professional, somewhere, recorded that the child has, in his considered opinion, been abused. It is important to remember that the location of the sample of abused children may well limit the type of abuse considered. For example, cases identified in an accident and emergency department will inevitably include more examples of life-threatening injury. It is possible that the characteristics of the population from which the sample is drawn may have more influence on research results than will the actual abuse. For example, Elmer (1976) followed up a group of 'traumatized' infants referred to the Children's Hospital in Pittsburg. She compared them eight years later with controls matched for age, race, sex and socio-economic status. She looked at multiple variables and found few differences. One interpretation of her findings is that the underlying problems confronting all the families due to their severe poverty state overpowered any specific effect of the abuse *per se*. At the Park Hospital in Oxford we may well have a more varied sample of abused children than are included in many other studies. We have referrals both from the acute paediatric service and directly from the community. We serve rural and urban areas and see families from all social and economic groups. In the area as a whole housing is good, the unemployment rate is low and industrial wages are high. See for example the following table of social class distribution.

Fig. 1

SOCIAL CLASS — 42 children

Registrar General's Classification of Occupations

1 & 11	12%	Services	12%
111	21%	Unemployed	5%
1V	24%	In gaol	2%
V	7%	Unsupported mothers	17%

Code

1 & 11	Professional and managerial positions
111	White collar workers and skilled craftsmen
1V	Semi-skilled workers
V	Unskilled workers

2. Use of Control Groups

As the factors associated with child abuse are so complex, it is a matter of great debate how one can obtain meaningfully matched controls. For example, it could be argued that in Elmer's study (1976) the controls matched so exactly her index group that no differences emerged. Could they have even been abused and not identified? In direct contrast to this, others advocate seeking controls from among those with 'perfect child rearing techniques'. It could be questioned whether anyone is in the position to identify such 'super parents'. In the absence of controls many studies rely on using tests with well established norms, which at least provide a background of data against which results can be interpreted. The ideal would be a longitudinal study of the development of abused children run over the same time period as a large scale population study.

In our research we will again be making sib to sib comparisons (Lynch 1975) to see if any factors can be identified that distinguish the 'recognized as abused' child from siblings living in the same environment.

3. Data Collection

The amount of data gathered is in reality going to be limited by the time, money and expertise available. It is likely that the larger the number of cases followed up, the less comprehensive the assessment becomes and the more dependent the researcher is on distant and often unknown data collectors. Follow-up studies published so far have ranged from those collecting mortality and re-injury rates (*e.g.,* NSPCC, 1969, 1972, 1975) to those that try and provide detailed and comprehensive assessment of the child and his family (*e.g.,* Elmer, 1967; Martin, 1974, 1976). Other investigators have chosen to research in depth one aspect of the child's development. For example, Green *et al.* (1974) explored the impact of abuse on the ego function and behavior of school-age children. It is my impression that the more impersonal the study becomes, the less reliable are the results likely to be. For example, any large or detailed research project may well need to collect information by questionnaires sent out to professionals involved with the families. Unless these are short and explicit they are very unlikely to be filled in accurately if at all (Freeman, 1977).

The natural response to receiving a complicated and long questionnaire through the post is either to put it straight into the garbage can or to leave it at the bottom of the in-tray. In contrast to this we have recently been able to obtain 100 percent completion rate of the school questionnaires for children in our sample. This was achieved by arranging to collect the questionnaires personally.

When collecting information, especially on cases still receiving professional help, one is inevitably dependent on the cooperation of the individuals who are providing services. It is necessary therefore to consider the attitude these professionals might have towards one's research. Service personnel who see themselves as hardworking and underpaid often, not unnaturally, resent the researcher. From the outside, his life seems relaxed, far away from the constant demands of clients with the occasional extra bonus of a trip abroad to deliver a paper. Therefore it is vital that time is spent explaining the purpose of the research and its implications to those expected to deliver services to the families. The cooperation of a professional involved with a family is invaluable when one is trying to gain access. If the family has established a trusting and open relationship with the worker and that worker feels positively towards the research team, it is likely that the parents will agree to be seen or to allow information to be passed on. If one does not have the backing of such professionals one is liable to receive a letter that reads — "I explained your project to Mr and Mrs X. Their initial reaction was to agree to participate, but after discussing it with me, decided it would not be in their best interests". We must also remember that many professional workers are not comfortable when dealing with cases of child abuse. Their aversion to the problem may result in denial. If they cannot believe that a certain child was ever abused, they will not want to participate in a long-term follow-up of the consequences of that abuse. The management of child abuse is a sensitive area; because of recent public enquiries it is possible that social workers in particular will be anxious of being found lacking in the way they are handling a case. On top of all this there is the professional's suspicion of any project that might be interpreted as 'monitoring his professional practice.' Throughout our research studies we have made a point of always trying to meet any professional working closely with a family. This has entailed a lot of time and travel but the enthusiasm with which many have been prepared to help us has made it very worthwhile.

Because of the limitations on our project we decided to carry out a personal detailed study of a relatively small number of families. They had all spent some time in the family unit at the Park Hospital. Base line data was available therefore in the hospital records. For many, assessments have been carried out at intervals throughout the follow-up period. Thus for example, it will be possible to study most of the children's growth patterns after the abuse. The actual research assessment on the children includes a physical and detailed neurological examination carried out in all cases by myself. All the children under five years have a developmental assessment using the Mary Sheridan test (Sheridan, 1975). I did this, together with an occupational therapist skilled in developmental testing. This same therapist adds her observations to mine on the neurological status of the older children. We also observe all the children in a period of free play. All the children over two and one-half years are seen by a psychologist and verbal and non-verbal IQ scores obtained. The length of the assessment means that all the families spend at least one afternoon with us at the hospital. We try to make the experience as much fun as possible and ensure each child receives an explanation of the assessment appropriate to his age and circumstances. The parents have varied greatly in their ability to prepare the children for the visit.

Following the assessments, Jacquie Roberts visits the family at home and tape records a structured interview with the parents. This takes up to two hours. A questionnaire is then filled in from listening to the tape. When we were planning the interview and designing the questionnaire we asked the advice of several parents (abusing and not). This proved to be very valuable. It is all too easy to apply middle class values. For children not living with their natural parents we have tried to interview both the caretaker and the parents. Information about the uses the family has made of medical and social services is obtained from the parents, and with their permission, checked out against relevant records. Only legal orders and prosecutions concerning the children are checked against official sources. We rely on the parents (and the occasional press report!) to tell us of their other conflicts with the law.

Brief questionnaires are being sent to social workers and family doctors to obtain a few well defined facts and, if they wish to give it, their current opinion of the family. The teachers of the children in school have been seen and filled in a questionnaire about the child's behavior. Nursery schools, playgroups and residential homes have also been visited.

When all the families have been evaluated we will end up with some well standardized data, a lot of facts and numerous impressions. Our close personal involvement with the families will be criticized by some. It has however, given us privileged glimpses of life in families where a child has been diagnosed as abused. Some of the emotions the families have revealed to us could never be measured or punched on to a computer card. How does one code the anguish of a competent and intelligent housewife watching her two children play? One, a three and one-half year-old, is well grown and bright — the other, an eight year-old, is neurologically, visually and intellectually handicapped, the result of injuries inflicted by the same mother when she was only 17 and living in a very different world.

4. Interpreting Results

There are problems even in interpreting what appears to be straightforward mortality rates and re-injury rates. Mortality rates will include death from re-injury, the long-term consequences of abuse and deaths from apparently unrelated causes. Re-injury rates could easily be misinterpreted, especially when relating them to the effects of intervention. Reporting re-abuse rates without considering the severity of injury will give a depressing and false picture of the effect of the intervention. Even very mild inflicted injury will be reported in children of families who continue to receive treatment. In contrast, those children who are not known to therapists will only be identified if the abuse requires medical attention. Rates of subsequent injury in any case should never be the only criteria used for judging the quality of the child's life or the effectiveness of treatment. Even when subsequent injury does not occur we know that a child may still suffer from other forms of abuse and deprivation (Jones, 1976).

It must be remembered that whatever form our follow-up study takes we are never merely assessing the long term results of abuse. It is only one of the many factors that can influence the developing child's biography. Even for the child with severe brain damage known to be the result of an isolated abuse incident, subsequent development will be greatly influenced by the environment in which he lives. However, it is likely that most children from abusing homes will be exposed to similar detrimental influences; as many abusing parents, regardless of social or ethnic group, have certain characteristics in common. In particular, there are typical attitudes towards child rearing. These parents are rigid and intolerant with unrealistic expectations of their children's development and behavior. They demand much from their children emotionally but give little in return.

The results finally presented will be based on data collected only on those members of the original sample who can be located and evaluated. When reviewing the literature we were alarmed by the number of children who were not available for assessment. Martin *et al.* (1974), in their much quoted study, originally ascertained 159 abused children referred to Denver hospitals. The minumum follow-up period was one year. 25 percent of the sample were completely lost and a further 40 percent were not assessed for a variety of reasons *(See Fig. 2)*.

Fig.2   *The Original Sample*

Children evaluated	58
Unable to locate — whereabouts unknown	40
Located but parents uncooperative	20
Distance from Denver prohibitively excessive	26
Adopted but unable to obtain names of adoptive parents	8
Deceased	2
Institutionalized	1
Not evaluated for other reasons	4
TOTAL	159

From Martin *et al.,* "The Development of Abused Children" (1974), 21 *Advances in Pediatrics.*

He finally saw only 58 (36 percent). Martin's experience is not exceptional — other researchers have found similar problems. In Australia, Birrell and Birrell

(1968) were unable to locate 33 percent of their sample of 42 children after two years. In Rochester, New York, Friedman and Morse (1974) were unable in a five year follow-up to trace 25 percent of a group of 54 injured children (both accident and abuse cases.) In Winnipeg, McRae *et al.* (1973) attempted to follow up 88 abused children, 1-13 years after the injury. They located and examined 34 (39 percent). Of the others 16 were completely lost, eight dead, four in institutions and a further 26 either refused to come, lived too far away or failed to attend the arranged appointment. In Pittsburg, Elmer and Gregg (1967) were able to locate the whereabouts of all the 50 children in their sample, but 19 (28 percent) were considered not to be available for evaluation. All the reasons for non-evaluation given by Martin and others effect the interpretation of results. I shall consider each in some detail and describe how we ourselves avoided the whittling away of our sample.

(a) Not Located

We can never know if the characteristics of lost families are similar to the ones easily located. Among the lost families will be those who intend to lose themselves because of criminal offences, non payment of debt, *etc.* These are also the ones likely to have several aliases. Others become lost merely because of their disorganized way of life. They fail to keep appointments, to inform the social service department when they move, or in the U.K., to register with a new family doctor. Another group of families that could be hard to trace are those who do well and after discharge from clinical follow-up merely move to another part of the country. Some of the lost children could be dead. No follow-up study as far as I know has checked to see whether there are death certificates for children not located. The official policy of some agencies does not make the task of the researcher trying to trace families any easier. It is not unknown for social service departments to solve the problem of increasing case-loads by insisting that a worker must drop a child from his or her case-load every time a new one is allocated. The only purpose served by this ridiculous approach is to keep statistics from looking any worse then they already are. One social service department known to me keeps their child abuse index at a constant figure by this method. A family dropped in such a way may well move and prove difficult for another interested agency to trace. Indeed, the Denver team (Martin, 1976) found that one large Colorado child welfare department had lost track of one of their legal dependents, a child in their custody. They did not know where he had been for over a year. If even children on legal orders can be lost, it is not surprising that many families over which there is no legal hold are simply allowed to disappear.

In the U.K. long-term follow-up studies on subjects other than child abuse have used the subjects' National Health Service Number to trace them (Newhouse and Williams, 1974 and personal communications). Unfortunately, this can only provide a current address if the subject is registered with a family doctor in the area in which they live.

When considering the large number of lost children in research samples one is forced to ask the question — are these families receiving appropriate services and treatment? To ensure that health services reach all children in the U.K. the Court

Report (1976) recommends that "an effective system should be devised of recording 'transfers in' (*i.e.,* families moving into the neighborhood) and of 'transfers out' and for passing such information to receiving health authorities." The Report suggests that family allowance records could be used for this purpose. Since April 1977, child benefit is payable for all children. Thus, provided parents claim, all children would be traceable. I believe that is already possible for authorized personnel concerned about the safety of a child, to trace the whereabouts of the family if they are in receipt of certain locally paid social security (welfare) benefits, for example supplementary benefits. Indeed, theoretically, in any western country there can be very few families who would be impossible to trace if one were to use the records of local and central government agencies. Only those who pay no taxes, receive no welfare benefits and who are not known to the law enforcement agency would go untraced. Whether such powers should ever be invoked is worthy of debate.

When we embarked on our own follow-up study we were naturally apprehensive about the number of families we would be able to locate, as over 10 years had elapsed since some of the families had been discharged from the inpatient service. However, it is not the policy of the Park Hospital to terminate formally its contact with any family. Thus, a number of the families are still in regular clinical follow-up (nine of them with me). Others had maintained a more informal link with the hospital. Our task was further facilitated by our close links with medical and social services. Twenty-nine cases were still open social work cases. At the time of writing, only two index children remain untraced. Both of these were USAF families who returned with their mothers alone to the States. The mother of another child has not been traced. The child herself was located in a children's residential home in another area. At least a year of this child's biography is still unaccounted for.

(b) Uncooperative Parents

The success of any follow-up project which involves direct assessment of children and families must have the cooperation of those caring for the child. The hostile and resentful attitudes of many abusing parents towards authority makes refusal to participate in any project likely. Others can refuse because of continuing denial of the abuse or a genuine wish to forget the past. It is interesting that the families who refused to participate in Elmer's study came from the upper social classes (Elmer, 1967). It is unlikely that refusal necessarily means that things are going badly for the family. Some of the better functioning families in our sample subjected us to the most vigorous questioning before they were willing to participate. Twenty-nine of our children were living with their natural parents. These parents were given a full explanation of what the assessment entailed. This was usually done by one or both of us visiting the home. On the day of the assessment, transport to the hospital or travelling expenses were provided by us. We encouraged both parents to attend and if necessary we refunded lost wages. For the children living outside the parental home, permission was obtained from the local authority holding parental rights. The only index child to whom we have been denied access is in the care of a local authority and has been placed for adoption.

How much information it is ethical to gather without parental knowledge must be the concern of the individual researcher.

Another dilemma is how much of the child's and family's previous history should the researcher make available to current workers from whom the diagnosis of child abuse may have been concealed. I believe that in all cases the child's interest must come first and decisions should be made accordingly.

(c) Distance From Research Center

Excluding children and families who live at a distance from the research center which is described as 'prohibitively excessive' may well bias the sample. For instance, Martin, by restricting his follow-up to children living in the metropolitan Denver area, has excluded those from rural communities. The decision to restrict the follow-up is very understandable. By the time we have seen and gathered information on 37 index children still living in the U.K., some 8000 miles will have been travelled by us or the families. We have been impressed by the distance some parents have travelled to see us. One mother brought her three boisterous sons on buses and trains from the other side of central London.

(d) Adopted Children

Children who have been adopted or placed for adoption are frequently excluded from follow-up studies. Martin was unable to obtain the names of adoptive parents for eight of his sample. Unfortunately, we too were unable to see the index child who had been placed for adoption in our sample. As there is a present trend to encourage adoption of handicapped and older children, there is likely to be an increase in the number of abused children who are placed for adoption. In the U.K. the numbers are likely to increase further following the implementation of the 1975 Children's Act and the 1976 Adoption Act. The development of these children should be followed up especially as some would consider them a high risk group for adoption breakdown (Ounsted, 1971).

(e) The Dead

Of course dead children themselves cannot be followed up, though the cause of death should be accurately ascertained. Studies like ours looking at the whole family should include siblings and parents of dead children. All too often after death, a child's family disappears and neither siblings nor parents receive appropriate help.

277   The Follow-Up of Abused Children—A Researcher's Nightmare

(f) The Institutionalized

I am puzzled and saddened by the habit of not evaluating children in institutions. All too frequently they are dismissed together with the dead. We should not be allowed to forget that this group is likely to be the most severely handicapped in the sample, and that child abuse can result in a child having to live out its life in and institution for the mentally handicapped (Eppler and Brown, 1976; Buchanan and Oliver, 1977).

In our study we started our with 42 probands and 47 sibs or half sibs. If all goes according to plan and we have no last minute drop-outs, we will have a thorough assessment on 39 of these probands and 41 of the siblings/half siblings.

The reasons children in our sample are unavailable for assessment are shown in *Fig. 3* and the placements of those being seen in *Fig. 4.*

Fig. 3

Reasons children are unavailable

	Index n=3	Sibling n=6
Not traced	1	—
Adopted	1	1 (may yet be traced)
Dead	1	—
Refusals	—	5 (3 families)

Fig. 4

Placements of children being seen

	Index n=39	Sibling n=41
Both natural parents	21	32
One natural parent	9	8
Foster parents (all long term)	4	—
Children's Home	4	1
Institutions	1	—

5. What Our Data Will Show

The data collected on these children and their families has not yet been fully analyzed. It is however evident that the focus of attention in follow up must move from detection of subsequent injuries to concern over the emotional wellbeing of all children in the family. Ninety-one percent of the children we saw were growing satisfactorily at follow up. While 41 percent of them showed some neurological deficiency, for 60 percent of these it was very mild and only picked up on detailed examination. Developmental assessment of the under fives revealed only 52 percent to be completely developmentally normal (Lynch *et al.,* in preparation). The area of development most likely to be delayed was speech. This trend was also reflected in the differences between verbal and non verbal IQ scores for the older children. Despite this, the IQ results were encouraging, showing 67 percent of the school age children to be of average or above average intelligence. The most perturbing feature of the follow up was the extent of emotional and behavioral problems found. Forty-nine percent of the children were judged to be deviant in the class room with aggressive and hostile maladjustment predominating in girls and boys alike (Roberts *et.al.*, 1978).

It is hoped that when all the data is available that it might be possible to relate early events to outcome. It is already evident that within our sample we have a small group of delightful children who are developing normally and living with their natural parents in happy united homes. This outcome is certainly not related to the severity of the original abuse. It is possible that the biographies of these children will teach us something we would not learn from anguishing over all too frequent disaster stories.

6. Links Between Research and Practice

Without our close association with the diagnostic and therapeutic services of the Park Hospital our research would have been impossible. Our previous experiences of working with abusing families undoubtedly influenced the research design and our method of approaching the families. It is difficult to know how we would have coped without this experience. Families in crisis, and some abusing families always seem to be in one, are not going to distinguish between researchers and therapists. If such a family asks for help one must at least make sure they get it. It is unethical to make one's observations and disappear. Such action will simply confirm the families' feelings of distrust and resentment towards 'authority'. Back up clinical facilities are always required by researchers actually intending to see and evaluate abusing families. Any medical developmental or emotional problem revealed in the course of the investigation must be referred for assessment and treatment.

The aims of research and therapy must be the same to help abused children become happy adults who, if they choose to have children of their own, will not abuse them.

REFERENCES

Birrell, R.G. and Birrell, J.H.W., "The Maltreatment Syndrome in Children: A Hospital Survey" (1968), 2 *Med. J. Aust.* 1023-1029.

Buchanan, A. and Oliver, J.E., "Abuse and Neglect as a Cause of Mental Retardation", a Study of 140 children admitted to Subnormality Hospitals in Wiltshire (1977), 131 *J. Psychiat.* 458-467.

Court, S.D.M. (Chairman), Report of the Committee on Child Health Services "Fit for the Future", HMSO London, 1976.

Elmer, E., *Children in Jeopardy.* Pittsburg, Pennyslvania: Univ. of Pittsburg Press, 1967.

Elmer, E., "Follow-up Study of Traumatised Children", paper presented at the 1976 International Congress on Child Abuse and Neglect, Geneva.

Elmer, E., and Gregg, G.S., "Developmental Characteristics of Abused Children" (1967), 40 Paediatrics 596-602.

Eppler, M. and Brown G., "Child Abuse and Neglect: Preventable causes of Mental Retardation", paper presented at the 1976 International Congress on Child Abuse and Neglect, Geneva.

Freeman, R., "The Questionnaire as a Research Tool", ch. 6 in Franklin, A.W. (ed.), *Child Abuse: Prediction, Prevention and Follow-up*. London, Eng.: Livingstone Churchill, 1977.

Friedman, S.B., and Morse, C.W., "Child Abuse: A Five-Year Follow-up of Early Case Finding in the Emergency Department", (1974), 54 *Paediatrics* 404-410.

Green, A.H., Gaines, R.W. and Sandgrund, A., "Psychological Sequelae of Child Abuse and Neglect", paper presented at Annual Meeting of American Psychiatric Association (1974), Michigan.

Hall, M.H., "A View from the Emergency and Accident Department", ch. 2 in *Concerning Child Abuse, op. cit.*

Howells, J.G., "The Mystical Bond", ch. 3 in *Remember Maria*. London, Eng.: Butterworths, 1974.

Jones, C., "The Fate of Abused Children", paper presented at the 1976 Symposium on Child Abuse, Royal Society of Medicine, London.

Lynch, M.A., "Ill-health and Child Abuse" (1975), 2 *Lancet* 317-319.

Lynch, M.A. and Ounsted, C., "A Place of Safety", in Helfer, R.C., and Kemp, C.H. (eds.), *Child Abuse and Neglect: The Family and the Community*. Cambridge, Mass.: Ballinger, 1976.

Lynch, M.A., Steinberg, D., and Ounsted, C., "A Family Unit in a Children's Psychiatric Hospital" (1975), 2 *Brit, Med. J.* 127-129.

Lynch, M.A.; Learners; and Roberts, J., in preparation, the developmental progress of young children from abusing families.

Martin, H.P. (ed.), *The Abused Child: Multidisciplinary Approach to Developmental Issues and Treatment*. Cambridge, Mass.: Ballinger, 1976.

Martin, H.P.; Beezley, P.; Conway, E.S.; and Kempe, C.H., "The Development of Abused Children" (1974), 21 *Advances in Paediatrics* 25-73. (Chicago, Illinois: Year Book Medical Publishers.)

Morse, C.W.; Sahler, O.J.; and Friedman, S.B., "A Three year Follow-up Study of Abused and Neglected Children" (1970), 120 *Amer. J. Dis. Child* 439-446.

McRae, K.N.; Ferguson, C.A.; and Lederman, R.S., "The Battered Child Syndrome" (1973), 108 *C.M.A. Journal* 859-866.

NSPCC Studies (1969) Skinner, A.E., and Castle, R.L., "78 Battered Children: A Retrospective Study".

NSPCC Studies (1972) Castle, R.L., and Kerr, A.M., "A Study of Suspected Child Abuse".

NSPCC Studies (1975) "Registers of Suspected Non-Accidental Injury", a report on registers maintained in Leeds and Manchester by NSPCC Special Units.

Newhouse, M.L., and Williams, J.M., "Techniques for Tracing Past Employees. An Example from an Asbestos Factory" (1967), 21 *Brit, J. Prev. Soc. Med.* 35-39.

Ounsted, C., "The Dark Side of Adoption" (1971), 63 *Child Adoption* 23-36.

Roberts, J.; Lynch, M.A., and Duff, P., "Abused Children and Their Siblings — A Teacher's View" (1978), 6 *Therapeutic Education* no. 1.

Sheridan, M.D., *Children's Developmental Progress From Birth to Five Years: the Stycar Sequences*. Windsor, Eng.: N.F.E.R. Publishing Company, 1975.

Sunday Times Magazine 1977, 1 May, p. 33.

Chapter 18

Child Abuse in Arabia, India and the West — Comparative Legal Aspects

Tahir Mahmood[*]

1. Introduction

Absolute parental authority, unfettered guardianship rights and family privacy are some of those global traditions which have in recent times been upset almost everywhere by the forces of socio-legal change. These traditions, equally shared by the East[1] and the West,[2] generated the problem of child abuse which till the middle of this century lay eclipsed by a well-established world-wide presumption that parents could never ill-treat their children. With the growing awakening of social and legal reformers all over the world, the traditionally unbelievable existence of the victims of parental abuse came to the limelight. Efforts have therefore been made, of late, in various countries to rescue children suffering maltreatment at the hands of their parents, guardians and custodians. Among the ways and means adopted for this purpose to varying extent in different parts of the globe, there have been drastic reforms of many private and public laws. Moreover, in some parts of the world special child-abuse laws have been promulgated.

This chapter briefly analyzes various aspects of the problem of child abuse and evaluates legal responses thereto in some Arab states and in India, in comparison with parallels in Britain and the United States. The study is confined to the issue of ill-treatment of children within the family and does not touch upon the wider context of extra-familial child abuse.

2. Different Perspectives

In Britain and the United States social and legal reformers have, it seems, been concerned more about the problem of battered infants than that of the ill-treated adolescent. In both countries researchers have made extensive studies in parental

---

[*] University of Delhi, India, Honorary Legal Adviser, Indian Council for Child Welfare.

cruelty to infants. In the United States, while the federal Children's Bureau and other allied agencies have been extraordinarily active, nearly all state legislatures have enforced during the course of the last fifteen years special laws intended to prevent child abuse. Though most of the state laws mention sixteen or eighteen years as the upper age limit regarding the children subject to this protection, their provisions have been mostly invoked to save infants and toddlers from parental cruelty. This is well evidenced by the suggestions made for a better handling of the reported cases of child abuse in juvenile courts.[3] Moreover, though malnutrition, starvation and 'injuries caused by neglect' are required to be reported in a few states, generally the laws lay emphasis on physical injuries.

In Indian and Arab societies, cases of victimization of adolescents inside the family greatly outnumber those of parental cruelty to infants and toddlers. Or, at least, sufferings of grown up children are more conspicuous. In India, the expression 'child' in the context of the rights of parents and guardians generally means a minor up to the age of eighteen years, as laid down under the Majority Act of 1875.[4] Under the family law enactments of various Arab countries the range of childhood is fifteen to twenty years.[5] Thus, grown-up children, toddlers and new-borns are all subjected alike to the rights and privileges of parents and guardians, which include power to inflict physical correction and chastisement whenever 'necessary'. Further, ill-treatment of children in India and Arabia is not always physical. In numerous cases children are subjected to prolonged mental torture, emotional injury and wilful neglect causing severe disabilities. However, cases of physical abuse are not by any standards negligible.

3. Outmoded Concepts of Parental Authority

Neither the religions of Indian origin nor Islam conferred on parents and guardians arbitrary powers in regard to the person of the child. Nevertheless, the traditional family laws claimed to have been derived from these religions did not adequately protect the children against misuse of the parental position. Islamic religious treatises, for instance, directed people to be extremely kind to children. The Qur'an asked parents to treat them with kindness (*fadl*) and affection (*mawaddat*); and the Prophet described parents as 'herdsmen' (*ra'i*) for their children, who will be questioned about their 'herd' on the Day of Judgment. Strangely, however, the classical Islamic and Indian family laws clothed parents and guardians with absolute paramountcy in regard to children and wards. This is how these laws were, at least, interpreted.

In India, British rulers had enacted in 1890 a Guardians and Wards Act drawn mainly from the provisions of the then English Guardianship of Infants Act, 1886. Unamended for more than nine decades except in regard to certain technicalities, this old law still remains applicable. To the Hindus and Muslims it is available as an alternative to their respective personal laws, and when invoked it overrides those laws. Indian judges have, in compliance with the constitutional mandate regarding the protection of children,[6] tried to interpret the Act in the light of modern child-welfare theories. The other statutory law of guardianship, enacted after independence,[7] is naturally far better in its outlook than the old law of 1890. In several Arab countries, notably in Sudan, the traditional laws of guardianship have been drastically amended in recent years in order to transform absolute parental 'rights' and 'privileges' into protective obligations and responsibilities.[8]

Neither the courts nor the legislatures have, however, succeeded in wholly changing the traditional concepts of parental authority. In practice parents and guardians still enjoy the authority to 'deal' with their children and wards in any way they like. Any interference in the parent-child relationships by outsiders, which term includes juvenile courts and child welfare agencies, is frowned upon. The scope of and the reasons for child abuse in India and the Arab states are different from those that prevail in Britain and United States.

4. Scope of Child Abuse

The West has greatly aggravated the propensity for child abuse and enhanced its scope by adopting the nuclear family norm. On the contrary, in eastern countries extended families are still the order of the day. Though Islam has no joint family system in the context of property, in the Indian subcontinent Muslims and Hindus equally share the custom of living jointly generation after generation, not as 'tenants-in-common', but as a matter of habit and convenience. As regards joint families, sharing property under the present law of succession[9] has given it a severe blow even among the Hindus. However, multi-unit families still exist, more particularly in rural and semi-urban areas. Among the Muslims, whether in Arabia or India, the Islamic law of succession does not help the emergence of nuclear families. Thus, people in these countries generally live with their children, grandchildren, nephews, nieces and other descendants, all under the same roof. In such extended families there are, naturally, lesser chances of child abuse than in nuclear families. Since parent-child relations are watched by other members of the family — elders and collaterals — parents are not so 'free' to ill-treat the children. Moreover, availability of a grandmother or an aunt to look after the child keeps the temper of the working mother low. In the highly industrialized western societies both parents are busy outside the home for most of the day, and this prejudicially affects the children. In Arabia and India few mothers work, and where they do, other family members take charge of the children. Irritation resulting from day-long work, which in the West often leads to child abuse, is thus not generally allowed to play havoc with children in the extended families of the East. Incidents of child abuse, however, do take place, though these are not as numerous as, for instance, in the United States.

The sufferings of stepchildren, children of divorcees and illegitimates are, as in many other parts of the world, much higher also in India and Arabia. There the population of such children is quite numerous due to the prevailing concepts and principles of family law. In the Arab countries, in spite of the recent reforms,[10] polygamy and extrajudicial divorce are of common occurrence. Among the Indian Muslims, who have not so far allowed the state to introduce any change in these matters,[11] though polygamy is generally not adhered to, the divorce rate has not been especially low. As regards other Indians, while law has abolished bigamy and controls divorce,[12] in practice the frequency of either is not less than among Muslims. Bigamous marriages as well as remarriage of divorcees create the problem of stepchildren. The 'step' relation is generally 'intolerable' and one hardly hears of a case in which a stepchild has been amicably absorbed in the newly created family. This author has personally witnessed in several homes stepmothers brutally torturing the children.

Another avenue of child abuse, not known to the West, is the practice of child-marriage. Though in India the law penalizes such a marriage,[13] and most of the Arab countries marriage-age has been considerably raised,[14] nowhere are child marriages void *ipso facto*. In rural areas child-marriages still freely take place.[15] Child brides, wherever they exist, frequently suffer ill-treatment from their in-laws.

Illegitimacy being a curse in Indian and Arab societies, children having this stigma cannot escape abuse, and they invariably suffer mental torture, besides physical injury. In Arab countries modern legislation recognizes the traditional principle under which a minimum of six months' gestation during lawful wedlock is required in order to confer on the child the status of legitimacy.[16] In India this principle of the Muslim law, as also the parallel rule of Hindu religious law, stand superceded by the provision of the Evidence Act 1872, under which a child born to its lawfully wedded parents at any time after the date of marriage is presumed to be legitimate. However, in practice people have not abandoned the traditional law on the subject.[17] Therefore, children who are illegitimate (at law in Arabia and by custom in India) by reason of being born within the first few months of their parents' marriage often suffer abuse and cruelty.

The foremost reason which widens the scope of child abuse even by natural parents is the numerousness of children in every Arab and Indian home. Ideals of planned parenthood and family planning are far from being popularly accepted. Though the Qur'an recommends a small-family norm and permits birth control,[18] it is generally believed that Islam does not favor family planning. Everywhere the Muslims generally take pride in being *kathir al-ayal* (possessor of large family). In no other aspect of life are the Muslims so ignorant of their religion as in the matter of planned parenthood; and not much has been done anywhere to bridge this wide gulf between doctrine and practice. Very few states have adopted family planning programs,[19] since most of them economically do not need it. In India generally neither the Muslims nor others like to 'change the course of destiny' by interfering with the actions of God to whom traditionally belongs the jurisdiction of deciding the number of everybody's children. Here, though the administrative agencies of the previous government did attempt to enforce birth control by coercive methods, the legislature has so far done nothing beyond legalizing abortion.[20] Consequently in various Arab states and in India the number of children in each home generally ranges from five to fifteen, though exceptions are found on either side of the range.

Plurality of children leads to child abuse in more than one way. Quite naturally, parents have no special love and affection for any particular child when they have too many. Some researches in Egypt and India have shown that parents with fewer children behave with them in a much more considerate and affectionate manner than those with large families.[21] Moreover, large numbers of children often impoverish families with limited resources, especially in India, and on account of this parents suffer from frustration and irritation which spill over into child abuse.

5. Reasons

Among the poor, children suffer parental abuse mostly on account of poverty and illiteracy. Malnutrition, which in some American states is considered abuse under law, is the inevitable fate of millions of Indian children. While in the affluent Western countries psychiatric disorder in parents has been found to be a common reason of child abuse, in India poverty is the most frequent cause. In numerous homes children are abused for want of bare necessities of life. Moreover, boys and girls of tender age are required to earn for themselves and in many cases also for the family. In the cities there are 'dustchildren', 'washerchildren' and even child-beggars; in villages, children work as cultivators and tillers. Earnings of the child legally belong to the parent, and for this purpose children stand to parents in a master-servant relationship.[22] Any default or neglect by the child in the performance of his duties arouses parents' displeasure and provokes them to violence. Dismissed by his master for a petty fault like having broken a tumbler or for failing to come on time, the child is rebuked by the parents and often turned out to look for an alternative assignment.[23]

As under the common law, in India as well as in the Arab countries, parents and guardians have a right to enjoy domestic services of the children. Where anybody interferes with this right by disabling a child from rendering such services, there arises a cause of action.[24] In extended families, nephews, nieces and grandchildren of tender age (and in villages also child-brides) are required to cook meals, clean the house and do other extensive household work. Negligence in doing this work to the satisfaction of the elders leads to violence and ill-treatment.

Child abuse is not, however, a 'monopoly' of the poor, as poverty is most certainly not its only reason. Stories of child abuse are frequently reported also from the middle and upper class families; and here the victims are mostly older children and adolescents, while the reason leading to violent ill-treatment is often the 'generation gap'. Parents' displeasure befalls those children who cannot agree with the former's attitude to life. Deviation on the part of the children from the family's religious beliefs and practices provokes parents to inflict various kinds of punishment. While in England a father can lawfully veto the issue of a passport to his child,[25] in Indian and Arab societies parents can freely veto the issue of daily bread to the 'delinquent' children till they return to the faith and observe its practices. Failing to offer prayers, being profane and irreligious, having a friend of a lower status, not showing enough respect to an older member or friend of the family, growing hair and expressing curiosity about sex have been reported in innumerable cases as 'faults' for which children have been subjected to violent admonition. They are, as punishment, slapped, beaten, starved and insulted in many ways.

6. Protective Legislation

In England, parents neglecting their children can be prosecuted under various statutes. Parallel (and in some cases better) legal provisions do exist in certain Arab states and in India. In Libya, for instance, under the Penal Code of 1953 there are special provisions for the protection of children against violence both in and outside the family. Punishments are laid down for infanticide, foetus-killing, unauthorized abortion, causing injury to a child, failure to offer physical protection where necessary and abandonment of a child.[26] It is specifically provided that any parent, guardian or custodian of a child who causes injury to the child by exceeding his powers of correction (*islah*) and upbringing (*tarbiva*) will be guilty of an offence under the Code.[27] Also parents who fail to perform any of their legal obligations in regard to children will be punished.[28] Similar provisions are found also in the penal codes of Egypt, Syria and Tunisia.

In India the Penal Code of 1861 lays down penalties for infanticide and for 'exposure and abandonment' of a child by its parents or custodians.[29] In addition, an important piece of legislation relating to child abuse promulgated recently is the Children Act 1960 which provides for "care, protection, maintenance, welfare, training, education and rehabilitation of neglected and delinquent children" in the Union Territories.[30] In this Act it is laid down:

Whoever having the actual charge of, or control of, a child, assaults, abandons, exposes or wilfully neglects the child or causes or procures it to be assaulted, abandoned, exposed or neglected, in a manner likely to cause to such child unnecessary mental and physical suffering, shall be punishable with imprisonment for a term which may extend to six months or with fine or with both.[31]

The central Children Act, 1960 has been adopted or substituted by similar local laws by several state legislatures.

The Arab and Indian laws for the protection of children from parental abuse have, however, no comparison with the massive child abuse legislation of the United States. There do not seem to be any child abuse reporting laws anywhere in the Arab states or in India. On the contrary, under the penal codes of the Arab countries, action against a parent or guardian in respect of any of the offences against children, referred to above, can be initiated only on the complaint of the 'aggrieved party' (*al-tarf al-mudarrar*). This will mean the ill-treated child itself; and so it makes the provisions of the penal codes quite ineffective at least in the cases where the victim of parental abuse is an infant or a very young child. Under the Indian Children Act of 1960, prosecution of a guilty parent or guardian is to be based on a complaint; and no complaint can be made without the prior sanction of the highest executive authority in a state[32] or of an officer authorized by him in that behalf.[33]

Child welfare services do exist in most Arab countries, and in some of these they operate under statute law. In Tunisia, for instance, a law enacted in 1967 provides for foster-care in specially chosen families for abandoned and unprotected children.[34] The expenditure incurred by a foster-family so selected is to be reimbursed by the state.[35] An earlier law encouraged assumption of 'unofficial guardianship' of neglected children by individuals and also made provisions for institutional care.[36] In India agencies like the Indian Council for Child Welfare and the Children's SOS have been privately doing commendable work; but neither any of the guardianship laws of 1890 and 1956 nor the Children Act of 1960 provides for an effective reporting of child abuse to juvenile courts or to other state agencies. No such provisions are found in the Arab and Indian penal codes either.

Non-recognition of the concept of adoption in the traditional Islamic law adds much, in many cases, to the miseries of ill-treated children. No Arab country, except Tunisia,[37] has so far legalized adoption. In India, while the Muslims have succeeded in vetoing the enactment of the Adoption Bill 1972,[38] the only law of adoption now existing[39] is applicable only to Hindus, and under its provisions only those persons can adopt a child who have no natural child, grandchild and, in most cases, also no great-grandchildren.[40] It thus hardly helps those children who need new homes in order to be protected from ill-treatment meted out by natural parents or other 'lawful' guardians. Even an affectionate grandparent, uncle or aunt, of an abused child in India and Arabia cannot rescue it, as they have no *locus standi* under the guardianship laws and no rights under the laws of adoption. Nor can they report the case for action to any state agency: only in India can they file a complaint for which they require prior consent of the governor,[41] whom few can approach.

7. Need for Reform

There is no denying the fact that India and the Arab countries are lagging far behind the United States in providing legal protection against child abuse. Although India can to some extent plead want of resources, most of the Arab countries — no less affluent than the United States — have no justifiable reason for dragging their reformist feet. Unlike divorce law reform, here there is not an iota of conflict between scriptural principles and the required reform. In India, too, within the limits of available resources, the prevailing situation can certainly be redressed at least in part. Carelessness of the custodians of social reform, and not paucity of resources, is the real reason for legislative backwardness in the area under review.

Indians and Arabs have to adopt planned parenthood in order to provide for their children a more congenial, safe and protective domestic environment. The laws of guardianship, custody and adoption, the penal codes and the specific child legislation, now in force, are in need of drastic reforms. Machinery needs to be set up to enforce and implement these laws. The traditional concepts of parental authority and filial submission have to be effectively changed through a process of education preceding or accompanying the legislative process.

More particularly, emphasis is to be laid on the reporting of child abuse. While India and Arabia can learn much in this respect from the American experience, they can also fruitfully press into service the local agencies already doing other useful social work. The *raidat* (girl guides) who are quite active in Egypt, the *cadis* (judicial officers) found in almost all Arab countries, and the house-visitors working in India under the schemes like malaria-eradication and 'grow more food', can be extremely useful in reporting cases of child abuse. They only need legislative license. As regards immunity against action in tort, in the peculiar circumstances prevailing in these parts of the globe, what is more necessary than such an immunity is an assurance of strict secrecy on the reporters' identity. Here taking revenge on a private level is easier and more common than an action in tort; and the reporters of child abuse must be protected against it.

The working of juvenile courts in India needs a thorough revision. The statistical data show that these courts have been concerned only in punishing ill-treatment of children outside the family. Parental abuse has not been attended to by them in any sizable number of cases. Special principles of procedure are required to enable these courts to check child abuse by elders in the family. These may be enacted as a supplement to the new Criminal Procedure Code (1973) which at present only empowers the courts to secure maintenance for a neglected child. Besides juvenile courts, the village judicial bodies (*panchayats*) can play an effective role in restraining parents and guardians from ill-treating their children.

The Arab and Indian societies, too, are rapidly advancing toward industrialization. In big cities traditions of domestic life have already changed considerably. Soon a time will come when children in these societies will also need a wider and more effective protection of the law. The inadequacy of the existing laws is being already felt. The law-makers must begin amending them with an eye to future social conditions and in so doing they can gain considerably from the experience of those nations where the problem of child abuse has, by now, become quite acute and where solutions have, therefore, been sought. These preparatory steps will, besides taking care of the ill-treated child of today, avert to a great extent the danger that the Arab and Indian children of tomorrow will have to face even wider abuse and ill-treatment.

NOTES

1. See, generally, Yusuf, M., *Mahomedan Law relating to Marriage, Dower, Divorce, Legitimacy and Guardianship of Minors,* Vol. III (Calcutta, 1898); Fyzee, Asaf A.A., *Outlines of Muhammadan Law* (4th ed., 1974), chap. 6; Diwan, P., *Law of Parental Control, Guardianship and Custody of Children* (Lucknow, 1973).
2. See, generally, Macpherson, W., *A Treatise on the Law relating to Infants* (England, 1842); Simpson, A.H., *A Treatise on the Law and Practice relating to Infants* (England, 1926); Pettit, P.H., in (eds.) Graveson and Crane, *A Century of Family Law* (England, 1957) chap. 4.
3. See, for instance, Hansen, R.H., "Suggested Guidelines for Child Abuse Laws" (1967), 7 *Family Law Journal* 61-65.
4. The same upper age limit has been adopted under the Hindu Marriage Act, 1955. Under the Special Marriage Act of 1954 it is, however, twenty one years.
5. Under some family codes the age of majority for men and women is:

	Men	*Women*
Egypt	18	16
Iraq	18	18
Jordan, Lebanon & Syria	18	17
Morocco	18	15
Tunisia	20	20

See for details Mahmood, T., *Family Law Reform in the Muslim World* (Bombay, 1972) at 273-274.

6. Constitution of India, art. 39 (f), directs the state to secure that childhood is "protected against exploitation and against moral and material abandonment".
7. The Hindu Minority and Guardianship Act, 1956 applicable to Hindus, Buddhists, Sikhs and Jains.
8. See for details this author's work, *supra* note 5 at 273-4.
9. Contained in the Hindu Succession Act, 1956.
10. Only in Tunisia have polygamy and extrajudicial divorce been completely abolished; in many other Arab states they have only been subjected to judicial control which is not very effective. See for details this author's work, *supra,* note 5.
11. See, generally, Mahmood, T., *Muslim Personal Law: Role of the State in the Indian Subcontinent* (Delhi, 1977) chap. 7.
12. See the Hindu Marriage Act, 1955.
13. *Ibid.,* ss. 5 & 18. Also see Child Marriage Restraint Act, 1929.
14. *Supra,* note 5.
15. Till March, 1978 the two Acts referred to in notes 12-13 themselves permit marriage of a girl at fifteen. This age has now been raised to eighteen.
16. In Egypt, Sudan, Syria, Tunisia and Morocco, the law so provides. See for details, *supra,* note 9 at pp. 286-87.
17. See Mahmood, T., "Presumption of Legitimacy under the Evidence Act: A Century of Action and Reaction" (1972), 73 *Journal of the Indian Law Institute* (Special Issue).
18. See Mahmood, T., *Family Planning: the Muslim Viewpoint* (Dalhi, 1977) chap. 1.
19. *Ibid.,* chap. 4.
20. *Ibid.,* chap. 6.
21. See, for example Ammar, Abbas, "Psychological and Social Aspects of Family Planning: A Muslim Arab Point of View", *Proceedings of the Second Regional Conference of IPPF* (The Hague 1960), 11-17.
22. Derret, J.D.M., *Introduction to Modern Hindu Law,* p. 44 (1963).
23. In India, of course, under the Children (Pledging of Labor) Act, 1933 parents and guardians agreeing to pledge the labor of a child commit an offence.
24. See the Indian case, *Babu v. Subanshi,* A.I.R. (1942) Nag. where a seducer who impregnated a girl was successfully sued by her father for depriving him of her services. *Cf.* the English Law Reform (Miscellaneous Provisions) Act, 1970, s. 5.
25. *Hewer v. Bryant,* [1970] 1 Q.B. 357.
26. See the Libyan Penal Code, 1953, arts. 373, 379, 390-398.
27. Art. 397.
28. Art. 396.
29. See the Indian Penal Code, 1861, ss. 312-318.
30. See the preamble to the Children Act, 1960.
31. S. 41 (1). See, for instance, the Libyan Penal Code, 1953, art. 398.
32. Governor, Commissioner or Administrator.
33. S. 41 (2).
34. Law. No. 67-47 of 21 November, 1967. For a detailed study of this law see Mahmood, T., "Law relating to Children: Recent Reforms in Tunisia" (1974), 1 *Supreme Court Journal* 23.
35. *Ibid.*
36. Law No. 58-27 of 4 March, 1958. For details see this author's work, *supra,* note 33.
37. *Ibid.*
38. The Bill sought to enact a secular law of adoption to be made available to all Indians alike. See for details Mahmood, T., *An Indian Civil Code and Islamic Law* (Bombay, 1976) chap. 9.
39. The Hindu Adoptions and Maintenance Act, 1956.
40. If a person wants to adopt a son he must not have a son, grandson or great-grandson — natural or adopted. Those who wish to adopt a girl must not have a daughter or son's daughter — natural or adopted.
41. *Supra,* note 31.

Chapter 19

Psychological Mechanisms in Child Abusing Parents

*J. Vesterdal**

This chapter considers rather briefly what sort of people child abusers are. What are the psychological mechanisms involved, how and when do these abnormal ways of thinking and feeling arise, and how early can we detect them? I must emphasize that the term 'child abuse' is used only for the sake of brevity, as we cannot clearly separate it from psychological maltreatment or neglect.

This topic is a rather new field of scientific investigation, and it is only in the last few years that we have gained some insight into the psychological disorders which cause these patterns of behavior. This is due to the work of Kempe, Helfer, Klaus, Franklin, Margaret Lynch, their co-workers, and others.

Who in the Family Maltreats the Child?

There are no good statistics about this; some of the published figures are based on court findings of guilt and this mainly represents cases of the most severe physical abuse. In a Swedish government report (*Barn som far illa* (1)) the mother alone was found guilty or suspect of physical injury in 30 percent of the cases, and it was the mother together with the father or stepfather in 11 percent. It was the biological father alone in 34 percent, and a stepfather in 11 percent. In other words: the mother was involved in 41 percent and the biological father in 40 percent of the cases. But that concerned only physical injury. When psychological maltreatment and neglect are included there is no doubt that the mother plays a predominant role.

In practical work with these cases it seems, however, more appropriate just to say that there is violence in the family making it dangerous for the child. It is less important to identify the offender, particularly because even if only one of the parents maltreats the child, the other one will know about it and will cover it up and thus acts as an accessory.

---

* Department of Pediatrics, Glostrup Hospital, Denmark.

Psychological Mechanisms in the Abusing Parents

Only a few of the abusers have a manifest psychosis, such as schizophrenia or depressive psychosis. Much more common are various types of psychoneurosis and character disorders. The abusing parents frequently have psychosomatic illnesses and very often a slight degree of depression. There is no single psychiatric diagnosis that is characteristic of child abusers, and we must say that child abuse is a disorder of the parent-child relationship which can exist in combination with practically any other psychological state (Lee (4)). Smith & al. (6) found that 76 percent of the mothers had an abnormal personality and 48 percent were neurotic. Their mean IQ was significantly lower than in a control group, and the same was true about the fathers. Among these, 29 percent had a criminal record, and one-third were psychopaths. But that a variety of other factors may be present is made clear by the description which follows of how disturbances might arise in the mother-child relationship.

In studies done in recent years of the psychological disorders that cause abnormal parent-child relationships, the interest has mainly been focused on the mothers because they are most often involved, and also because the symptoms of the disorders are more easily observed in the mothers than in the fathers. The following therefore mainly concerns the mothers, but it should be remembered that similar factors may play a role in the male.

The Mother-Child Symbiosis

It is now becoming clear that the ability of the female to act as a mother is something which is deeply influenced by the events around her own birth and of the way in which her own mother took care of her in infancy. This has been observed in both animal and human mothers, but I shall deal only with the latter.

If the start has been wrong, the ability of the female later in life to bond herself to her own child will be impaired, and she may not be able to live up to the task of taking care of her child in an appropriate way.

Normally the birth of the child will elicit a specific behavior in the mother, and this works with great force. We must remember, without being too lyrical, that the normal pattern of reactions of the mother is that she feels that her newborn baby is the most wonderful thing in the world, and she will love the baby to such an extent that she devotes her life completely to it. She takes care of it all around the clock, feeds it, shifts its diapers, strokes it, talks to it, soothes it and treats it with infinite tender loving care. As Klaus *et al.* (2) pointed out, when the mother sees the child for the first time immediately after its birth, she will react in a certain way. All normal mothers will look at the baby, touch it, stroke it, *etc.*, in practically the same way.

It must, however, be emphasized that in the normal relationship between mother and child there is a reciprocity such that the sequence of actions which the mother performs will influence the infant, generally so that it will be calmed and soothed, which in turn will have a satisfying effect on the mother. In other words, it is necessary for an optimal interaction that the infant also reacts in a certain way. Under normal circumstances the result is a development of a symbiosis between mother and child which is extremely important.

Under primitive conditions in developing countries this symbiosis is necessary simply for keeping the child alive. In developed countries it cannot be said to be absolutely necessary for the survival of the infant, although severe disturbances of it ultimately may result in the death of the child by maltreatment or neglect. This symbiosis is nevertheless very important for the happiness and thriving of the child, and also for the happiness of the mother. And it has a deep influence on the behavior of the child later in life, particularly on its ability to act as a parent when it grows up and becomes fertile.

Disturbances in the Mother-Child Relationship

This symbiosis between mother and infant can be disturbed or inhibited by inadequate reactions from both sides. *The mother* can react inadequately in several ways. First, it may happen that the mother does not like the newborn baby; she may even hate it from its birth or even from before its birth. She may not want the baby and may feel that the child has brought disaster into her life. Some of the mothers in Klaus' series did not like the look of the baby when it was shown to them by the nurse just after birth. They did not want to touch it and asked the nurse to take it away. Such an unwanted child will not be exposed to normal warm and gentle care, and as a result it may become an unhappy, unruly, crying baby, and this may again increase the mother's aversion against it, thus starting a vicious circle. Another inadequate reaction by the mother is caused by false expectations about the child. Perhaps because she is very young and inexperienced, she may not understand how little such a small infant can comprehend and do. If the baby cries, she will tell it to stop, and if it does not obey this order, she will interpret it as naughtiness and feel that the baby has deserved to be punished for this insubordination.

In some cases the mother has very much wanted to have a child, and she expects that it can bring her happiness and comfort. There is here an inversion of the parent-child roles in such a way that the mother, instead of devoting her life to the child, expects that the child should take care of her and her problems. When she feels tired, unhappy and lonely, she wants the baby to smile at her and comfort her and if the baby does not do that but cries, burps and soils its diapers, she will get disappointed and angry with it. This abnormality of the parent-child relationship is seen very frequently in families with child abuse and neglect. The origin of it apparently lies in the infancy of the mother. If she as an infant has been treated harshly by her mother instead of being comforted, she has not learned the normal parent-child relationship. The mother will then seek in her own child the comforting parent she did not know in her infancy. When the child grows up, it in turn will lack the ability to take adequate care of its own child and thus this disorder will 'infect' successive generations.

Normally the mother is the only, or at least the most important, person with whom the infant can find safety and protection. But if the mother is unkind to the baby every time it turns to her for comfort, this will of course have a very frustrating effect on the baby, and one consequence of this is that the child later in life will have great difficulty in trusting other persons and establishing durable friendships. The deleterious effect will be even worse if the mother is very inconsistent in the care of the child in such a way that she is sometimes kind, hugging and kissing the baby, and at other times treats it coldly and harshly.

These psychological disturbances in the mothers may of course appear in varying degrees of seriousness. There are mothers who are quite unable to take care of their children under any circumstances and there are others who can act reasonably well under optimal conditions, but who will prove inadequate under conditions that are less than optimal. Thus we may see that the abnormal behavior may be elicited under situations of stress such as unemployment, poverty, bad housing conditions, marital problems, or single parenthood.

The stress situation may also be caused by *the child*. This may happen if the child is a difficult baby. We must admit that babies are born with different temperaments. Some are placid and quiet, they cry only rarely and are easy to soothe. Others are restless and fidgety. They cry night and day and are difficult to handle. A child of the latter group does not respond well when the mother tries to calm and soothe it, and one may say that it does not play its role in the symbiosis well. Only a particularly patient mother can cope with such a baby. A somewhat inadequate mother may be able to take care of an easy child reasonably well, but it may be beyond her powers to handle a difficult child. This may in turn make the child still more difficult so that the problems will increase. If the child has congenital defects, such as malformation or mental deficiency, the result may be that the mother rejects the child, and she may feel frustrated or have a sense of guilt because she has not been able to give birth to a normal child.

Finally we come to a very important point: the mother-child interaction may be stopped at the very beginning by separation of the child from the mother. This will happen if the baby has to be taken to a special care unit of the hospital immediately after birth because of prematurity or some serious illness. Also in these cases the mother may feel disappointed with the baby or with herself, and there will of course be enormous difficulties in establishing contact between mother and child, with the result that she may feel alienated towards it and a normal bonding cannot develop. It is a general experience that there is a much higher proportion of prematurity and neonatal disease in abused children than in the normal population (5).

From all this it can be seen that factors both in the mother and in the child can have an adverse effect on the symbiosis between mother and child, and this effect may be enhanced by environmental factors. It is therefore easy to understand that under bad social conditions the risk of child abuse is much greater than in the upper levels of society. It is, however, well known that it also occurs there. There was a case in Denmark where the father was a psychiatrist, head of a hospital department, and the mother a nurse. They adopted 10 children, mainly from Korea and other places overseas, and maltreated six of them. Three children died, probably from maltreatment or neglect, but this was rather obscure because the father, being a doctor, wrote the death certificate himself.

Child abuse in the upper classes may in some cases be due to stress, perhaps financial or marital, but in other cases, where there apparently are no such problems, it may be due to religious or other strong moral convictions where the parents believe in very severe methods of upbringing to counteract the sinful tendencies of the child. Certain ethnic groups in our society may have similar customs.

The importance of identifying psychological factors tending to abuse is illustrated by the predictive and follow-up studies such as those of Margaret Lynch (see Chapter 17). Much work is currently in progress in this field. In the investigation by Gray *et al.* (2), which is still in progress at the time of writing this article, a large number of mothers were examined by interviews and questionnaires before the birth of the child and by observation during and after delivery, and a group of 100 mothers were identified as high risks for abnormal parenting practices. Fifty of these mothers were treated in the ordinary way and the other 50 were given special care, *e.g.*, by a health visitor or nurse in the home. During the first year after delivery child abuse occurred in both groups, but the number of severe cases was significantly lower in the group treated with special care. Thus it is to some extent possible to identify a risk group of mothers and to do something to prevent the maltreatment of the children, but the intensity at which such services can be offered depends on the resources available and the precision with which such identification can be made. The question how far intervention may be imposed on the basis of risk prediction also raises important legal and policy issues.

NOTES

1. *Barn som far illa. Nya Lagerblads Tryckeri AB,* Karlshamn, Sweden, 1975.
2. Gray, J.D.; Cutler, C.A.; Dean, J., and Kemps, C.H., "Prediction and Prevention of Child Abuse", trans. of 1st Int. Congr. of Child Abuse and Neglect, Geneva 1976, p. 15.
3. Kennel, J.; Voss, D., and Klaus, M., "Parent-infant Bonding", in Helfer, R.E., and Kempe, C.H., *Child Abuse and Neglect.* Cambridge, Mass.: Ballinger, 1976, p. 25-53.
4. Lee, H.S., "The Psychological Aspects of Abusing Parents," trans. of 1st Int. Congr. on Child Abuse and Neglect, Geneva 1976, p. 110.
5. Lynch, M., and Roberts, J., "Child Abuse — Early Identification in the Maternity Hospital," *ibid.,* p. 13.
6. Smith, S.M.; Hanson, R., and Noble, S., "Parents of Battered Children: a Controlled Study", in Franklin, A.W. (ed.), *Concering Child Abuse.* London, Eng.: Livingstone Churchill, 1974, p. 41-55.

PART FOUR
SOCIETAL RESPONSES TO VIOLENCE AGAINST CHILDREN

In Chapter 20, Drs. Newberger and Bourne write about medicine as an agency of social control which may label as sickness almost any form of deviant behavior and how law treads closely on the heels of medicalization. But there are conflicts between the two professions in the field of child abuse. Lawyers see the abuser's intention as vital; doctors find it less relevant and by no means clearly identifiable. Lawyers define the abuser as a wrongdoer; physicians may consider both abused and abuser as victims. Nevertheless, the trend in both law and medicine is toward a therapeutic rather than a punitive approach to the whole abusive situation. Yet the 'patient', the abusive parent, may view the therapy itself as punitive since it subjects him to interminable instruction, treatment and discrimination inflicted on him for his presumed benefit. The poor, so visible in city hospitals and wards, are of course the most frequent beneficiaries; and once the abuser label has been attached, it is very difficult ever to detach. Both law and medicine view abuse as the problem of the abuser, not of society. Drs. Newberger and Bourne find that treating abuse as a sickness has made it harder to 'cure', and that without addressing the issues of poverty and inequality, or of the lack of social and medical resources, the underlying factors are ignored and untreated.

In Chapter 21, Barbara Chisholm reports on the social aspects of child abuse in Canada. Throughout the Provinces there are differences in definition, reporting, procedures, and public education that make statistics on the nature and frequency of abuse unreliable, but available figures and reported experience suggest, as elsewhere in the world, that many cases of abuse are never recorded. What information there is tends to concentrate on young children. Abuse of adolescents may be masked under the label of generation gap or adolescent rebellion — adolescent suicide has increased sharply, and may well be connected with abuse. Treatment of the abuser also follows the pattern in Western attitudes which emphasize either punishment or cure of the maltreater.

Deterrent sentencing is still an old and honored approach in child-abuse cases and reflects the index of repugnance society attaches to the event: recently the Attorney-General of Ontario successfully appealed a child-abuse sentence and won a much longer one. But Chisholm is convinced that the bulk of the abusing group is not dangerous to the community of children at large, and that, with timely and skilled intervention by agents of the community, even removal of the child from the abuser may be necessary only briefly if at all. The majority of programs now operating in Canada are described as 'environmental manipulation', help with such externals of people's lives as decent housing, day care and homemaker services, and income improvement. These large goals require the kind of basic change in socio-economic structure urged by Drs. Newberger and Bourne; but achievement is presently small and partial, and any movement toward change is hindered by assumptions that families are still 'extended', and that a basic requirement of adulthood is self-help. Suspicion and hostility of the abuser toward any kind of 'treatment' and community lethargy, found in India, and Arabia, and Europe, and England, also have their counterparts in Canada.

A creative experiment to break the child abuse chain of violence and violation has been going on for several years in Amsterdam, Holland. In Chapter 22, Rob van Rees describes and comments on The Socio-Therapeutic Institute, The Triangel, which works with the whole family as a unit under the concept that child abuse is only an alarm signal of a family in distress. As many as twenty family groups at a time, whose stay at The Triangel may continue as long as six months, are attended continually by a team of four workers and one or two apprentices, and the placing agencies are closely involved in the treatment. In the first weeks the group workers largely take over the care of the children and routine household duties, but gradually many of the customary responsibilities are resumed. The object is to give the parents a chance to be relieved of some of the daily pressures and conflicts, and in the meantime they are living with other family groups and working with people outside the family. The Triangel's implicit purpose is to create a climate where choked family functions can be changed, and the new routines, the confrontation with others and the different life rhythm do often lead to a real awakening. Efforts are also brought to bear to change external circumstances, such as finding a new house, different employment for the parents and even retraining, stimulation of hobby membership in sports clubs, and education in budgeting. But the stay at The Triangel and its therapeutic effects is considered by the Institute only as a temporary 'thickening' of the line of help. After the family's departure two workers are assigned to accompany it for some time, and every effort is made to involve the original placing or some other agency in back-up services.

In Chapter 23, Bernard Dickens of Toronto discusses the necessity and the dangers of the law's intrusion in child neglect or abuse cases. To begin with, the legal definition itself may be either too comprehensive or too narrowly specific, ranging from battering to inadequate affection, and ignoring the bias of cultural and socio-economic norms, so that the cure may be worse than the trouble. Dickens quotes Sanford N. Katz's analysis of typical United States laws regarding children in need of judicial protection[1] and compares them with Canadian laws in order to demonstrate the wide spectrum covered by the legal concept of child abuse.

There are many variables also in reporting and in decision-making. While there are dangers in criminal sanctions for non-reporting, and numerous prosecutions might suggest that the law itself was ineffective in controlling omissions, the result of such laws, which Dickens feels should be mandatory only for a broad range of professionals, may best be educative, with an occasional symbolic prosecution to keep professionals alert to their responsibility. When injury or threat of injury to the child occurs and criminal prosecution may be used, the prosecutor must

---

* [1] Katz, Sanford N., *When Parents Fail*. Boston, Mass.: Beacon Press, 1971, p. 57 - 58.

determine whether there are alternative solutions for protecting the child or curbing the parents' violence; and when there is prosecution and conviction, the judge may have the choice between a custodial or non-custodial penalty. Although currently there is a strong movement in the United States back toward the concept of punishment, Dickens supports individualization as the modern ideal of penology, and certainly in the case of child abuse he makes a strong case against custodial penalties.

When he deals with evidentiary and procedural issues, Dickens quotes the Law Reform Commission in its widely held view that the adversary approach is unrealistic when applied to family problems, but he likewise finds highly unrealistic the idea that drastic applications to supervise a child in its home, remove it, or terminate parental rights can be resolved amicably or by a wise judge whose wisdom all parties will acclaim. It is generally accepted now that parents should be represented by counsel, and while less widespread, the concept of independent legal representation for the child is also gaining ground. Child's counsel may represent the child's best interests, in agreement or disagreement with the agency, rather than the child's wishes at the time; but the interesting question arises: at what age may the child be allowed the adult prerogative of making a mistake?

Finally, in a discussion of child abuse registers, now existing with special frequency in North America, Dickens, while recognizing their aim to protect the child by providing physicians and social workers with its possible past history of injury, points out the dangers inherent in such a system: the registering of an abuse report whether true or unfounded, the lack of provision for removal of records after a given period of inactivity, the problem of access and breach of confidentiality, the uneasy position of the social service agency between friendship with the family and 'betrayal' to the law.

In Chapter 24, Annemaree Lanteri and Susan Morgan describe the disparate laws and practices of three Australian states. The abused child in Victoria, for instance, may be treated exactly like a minor charged with a criminal offense; proceedings usually begin with police intervention and as a result the members of the helping professions are prevented from taking action when they suspect abuse but have no legal proof. South Australia has the most progressive statutes of the three, with separate processes for juvenile delinquency and child protection cases. Children in this state may be held in a hospital or institution for up to ninety-six hours if abuse has been suspected; there are mandatory provisions for reporting and protection for reporters; and emphasis is on supporting the family.

One of the troublesome areas discussed by Lanteri and Morgan is that of the power of entry, limited now to the police and authorized persons after they have obtained a warrant. The urgency of the danger may sometimes seem to require entry power without a warrant, but the balance between the protection of the child and the civil liberties of the parents is delicate, and certainly no private person should be given the power to enter a home where he believes a child is being abused without having obtained a warrant. There is the same dichotomy about reporting in Australia as in many other parts of the world: a desire to protect the child along with suspicion of the authorities and fear of involvement; and there are underlying societal assumptions: that intervention is bad for parents and as a result for children, that on the one hand battering parents should be subject to criminal prosecution and on the other that the family should be preserved.

Lanteri and Morgan place great emphasis on the need for further legislation to correct some fundamental weaknesses, chief of which is the delay in bringing the abused child into the system. They are convinced that there must be efficient preventive intervention and supportive rather than punitive treatment, and that those who exercise powers of disposition should not be limited to members of the legal profession but must include people with special expertise in the field of child health and welfare.

In France medical regulations and laws are well organized in theory to foresee and forestall child abuse, with twenty required and free health visits before the child is six — twenty opportunities to discover abuse or the risk of abuse, especially if the physician works in liaison with the social services. Practice falls short, as Mme. Gebler and Dr. Deschamps write in Chapter 25. On the day fixed for a visit the child may not present any disturbing symptoms — abuse may not yet have occurred or signs have disappeared. The doctor may not know the child or the family and may not recognize what signs do exist. The biggest loophole of all is that the child may not even be brought in, since with only three of the examinations does failure to appear carry some risk for the parents, and that risk merely involves the loss of state grant payments. Health supervision is accompanied by social supervision, and social service workers may visit the home at any time and without advance notice. Again in theory it should be difficult to conceal child abuse. But some families refuse to admit the social workers, either in to the home itself or at least to the child's room, and caseloads are too heavy for full efficacy. In spite of all these hurdles and hazards, there is a real value in the complementing of medical and social supervision, and many victims or potential victims of abuse are discovered, treated and saved.

Penalties for child abuse in France are heavy, heavier than in common law. They may include termination of civic, civil and parental rights and, for even involuntary neglect, one year in jail. But courts have been reluctant to apply these sanctions, and the laws have not acted as deterrents. There is always the dilemma of protecting the child by punishing the parent and thus ruining the child's future. It may be immediately imperative to remove the child from danger, but this need not always necessitate removal from his family. By convincing the parent that the child needs more intensive care, parental consent to hospitalization might be one solution, or in less dangerous cases the child may be left at home with social worker aid. It is interesting to note that these workers often have great influence and prestige among French families. Finally, the judge may place the child under protection while leaving him at home, and the Damoclean sword of the child's removal may restrain the parent from further violence.

The child's physical wounds may disappear; the child is healed; the family is not. The roots of the family disturbance and the available resources to help must be evaluated, and the courts and the agencies must make a plan for the child's future with a real chance of success, whether this will be support and retraining of the family, temporary foster care for the child, or termination of all parental rights and a permanent placement. Legislation exists. What are lacking are rapid action by the courts and agencies, more and more intensively trained personnel, and coordination between all the helping services.

In West Germany even the laws are not helpful. There are no reporting laws, no systematic registration of child abuse cases, no real public involvement, no recognition of psychological damage to the child, and scarcely any scientific studies in the field. Nor has child abuse been recognized as an obvious link in the chain of individual and societal failure. Nevertheless, Dr. Gisela Zenz points out in Chapter 26 that foreign models can serve only as indications of how domestic resources might be utilized in the domestic legal and social environment.

One of these resources is the Custody Court, whose traditional responsibility is to 'help to solve problems', to protect the child from family dangers and the family from government intrusion; whose procedure is informal, whose standards for intervention are broadly defined, and whose decisions are not bound by the decisions of other courts. This is the ideal. In reality the investigations and decisions of the Custody Court and the criminal court which tries child abuse cases are almost invariably identical; the Custody Court has even openly postponed its proceedings until the criminal case was decided. In addition to the damaging delays this will cause in deciding the child's future, the whole tone of the testimony in a child protection proceeding is, or should be different or heard in a different context from that in a criminal case.

The other dependency of the Custody Court is upon the Youth Office, which regularly initiates the proceedings and provides all information on the case, information generally accepted by the Custody judge without further investigation. Of course the Youth Office has the advantage of the trained competence of its social workers, but the child and the parents may suffer from the self-interest common to bureaucracies. The Youth Office itself tries to avoid involving the Custody Court, when it considers a child endangered but the evidence insufficient to satisfy the court, by pressuring the parents to agree to a 'voluntary' placement in order to escape court proceedings.

The Custody judge by law may take the 'necessary measures' to protect the child, but practically speaking his powers are almost entirely limited to the alternatives of outside placement or leaving the child with its family. Such precautions as a change of housing, improvement in the financial situation of the family or a special school for the child, on the pattern of The Triangel in Holland, are outside the power of the judge and the social and economic actualities in West Germany.

The role of the police in child abuse cases, discussed less frequently than those of the social worker, the judge and the lawyer, and often pejoratively, is treated from two Canadian viewpoints in the last part of part four. In Chapter 27, Sergeant Holmes, of the Royal Canadian Mounted Police of Ottawa, writes of disparities between rural areas, where the population is spread over thousands of miles and people are accustomed to calling the police for help in almost any difficult situation, and the urban centers, where there are now specialists in medicine, psychology, social work and law to treat different aspects of each problem. In thinly settled sections of the country the well-being and even the life of a child may depend directly on the police.

From an array of charges specified in the laws of the country and from the Child Welfare Acts of all the provinces, it would seem that every Canadian child is fully protected, but there is overwhelming evidence that the vast majority of child abuse cases go unreported. Holmes sees as the first priority the establishment of a reliable reporting system. He feels that the public at large, in which he includes all the professions in contact with children, must learn that without their active participation few crimes of any kind would be solved or even come to the attention of the police. Most citizens will call the police when they witness a robbery, a street fight or an adult being beaten (although in this connection one remembers the murder of a woman in the parking lot of her New York apartment building, where dozens of people heard her scream but took no action because they thought it was a mere case of wife-battering). But the same adults, probably for long-rooted sociological reasons, will very seldom report even a severe assault of a parent on his child. In the past the police, themselves reflecting the social values of the community, were apathetic about intervening and when they did so, long before there were agencies, they often had to act as untrained social workers. Today, with the increase in specialized professions and agencies of the government, the problem for the police is to develop and professionalize its part in child abuse cases, to unlearn its bias against social workers, and to cooperate closely and immediately with all who can help children.

In Chapter 28, Chief of Police Walter Johnson of the London, Ontario Police Force, and Judy Thompson, a Consultant in that same body, describe an original approach to the police role in child abuse cases. It has been traditionally been assumed in Canada that the police emphasis is on punishment, and that of the children's agencies on therapy. Now, recognizing family problems as potential indicators of abuse, the London, Ontario Police Force is operating a program which may well attack the problem at its root: the Family Consultant Service.

The Consultant Service is a specialized civilian branch of the force, designed to offer around-the-clock mental health consultation for police officers and is geared to help officers provide the best possible service to families in times of crisis. The Consultants are in constant radio contact with the police communications center, are mobile, and can therefore give instant attention to police crisis calls. Their goals are to assist officers by providing immediate assessment and intervention, to prevent serious family dysfunctions through early detection, to promote increased cooperation between mental health and law enforcement professionals, and to offer field training for the police in crisis intervention. The Consultants guide officers through example to be non-judgmental, to understand that abuse is most often a by-product of family stress and that criminal sanctions are frequently counter-productive. Most importantly, the Consultant Service is basically a tool for liaison, as indicated by the fact that only a small percentage of cases was resolved solely by its mediation, and that one of its primary goals and successes has been to facilitate increased cooperation between the police and community services.

Chapter 20

The Medicalization and Legalization of Child Abuse*

*Eli H. Newberger,† and Richard Bourne***

Child abuse has emerged in the last fifteen years as a visible and important social problem. Although a humane approach to 'help' both victims of child abuse and their families has developed (and in fact is predominantly expressed in the title of one or more influential books on the subject, *Helping the Battered Child and His Family*),[1] a theoretical framework to integrate the diverse origins and expressions of violence toward children and to inform a rational clinical practice does not exist. Furthermore, so inadequate are the 'helping' services in most communities, so low the standard of professional action, and so distressing the consequences of incompetent intervention for the family that we and others have speculated that punishment is being inflicted in the guise of help.[2]

What factors encourage theoretical confusion and clinical inadequacy? We propose that these consequences result, in part, from medical and legal ambiguity concerning child abuse and from two fundamental, and in some ways irreconcilable, dilemmas about social policy and the human and technical response toward families in crisis. We call these dilemmas *Family Autonomy versus Coercive Intervention* and *Compassion versus Control.*

We integrate in this paper a discussion of these dilemmas with a critical sociological perspective on child abuse management. Through the cognitive lens of social labeling theory, we see symptoms of family crisis, and certain manifestations of childhood injury, 'medicalized' and 'legalized', and called 'child abuse', to be diagnosed, reported, treated, and adjudicated by doctors and lawyers, their constituent institutions, and the professionals who depend on them for their social legitimacy and support.

* Supported in part by a grant from the Office of Child Development, U.S. Department of Health, Education, and Welfare (Project OCD-CB-141)
© E.H. Newberger and R. Bourne, 1978. To be published in *Critical Perspectives on Child Abuse,* Lexington Books, D.C. Heath Co., Lexington, Mass., 1978.
† Director, Family Development Study, Children's Hospital Medical Center, Boston., Assistant Professor of Pediatrics, Harvard Medical School, Boston, U.S.A.
** Assistant Professor of Sociology, Northeastern University, Boston, U.S.A.

We are mindful, as practitioners, of the need for prompt, effective, and creative professional responses to child abuse. Our critical analysis of the relationship of professional work to the societal context in which it is embedded is meant to stimulate attention to issues which professionals ignore to their and their clients' ultimate disadvantage. We mean not to disparage necessary efforts to help and protect children and their families.

How children's rights — as opposed to parents' rights — may be defined and protected is currently the subject of vigorous, and occasionally rancorous, debate.

The *Family Autonomy v. Coercive Intervention* dilemma defines the conflict central to our ambiguity about *whether* society should intervene in situations of risk to children. The traditional autonomy of the family in rearing its offspring was cited by the majority of the U.S. Supreme Court in its ruling against the severely beaten appellants in the controversial 'corporal punishment' case (*Ingraham v. Wright, et al.*).[3] The schools, serving *in loco parentis,* are not, in effect, constrained constitutionally from any punishment, however cruel.

Yet in California, a physician seeing buttock bruises of the kind legally inflicted by the teacher in the Miami public schools risks malpractice action if he fails to report his observations as symptoms of child abuse (*Landeros v. Flood*).[4] He and his hospital are potentially liable for the cost of the child's subsequent injury and handicap if they do not initiate protective measures.[5]

The dilemma *Family Autonomy v. Coercive Intervention* is highlighted by the recently promulgated draft statute of the American Bar Association's Juvenile Justice Standards Project which, citing the low prevailing quality of protective child welfare services in the U.S., would sharply *restrict* access to such services.[6] The Commission would, for example, make the reporting of child neglect discretionary rather than mandatory, and would narrowly define the bases for court jurisdiction to situations where there is clear harm to a child.

Our interpretation of this standard is that it would make matters worse, not better, for children and their families.[7] So long as we are deeply conflicted about the relation of children to the State as well as to the family, and whether children have rights independent of their parents', we shall never be able to articulate with clarity *how* to enforce them.

The dilemma *Compassion v. Control* has been postulated and reviewed in a previous paper,[8] which discusses the conceptual and practical problems implicit in the expansion of the clinical and legal definitions of child abuse to include practically every physical and emotional risk to children. The dilemma addresses a conflict central to the present ambiguity about *how* to protect the children from their parents.

Parental behavior which might be characterized as destructive or criminal were it directed towards an adult has come to be seen and interpreted by those involved in its identification and treatment in terms of the psycho-social economy of the family. Embracive definitions reflect a change in the orientation of professional practice. To the extent to which we understand abusing parents as sad, deprived, needy human beings (rather than as cold, cruel murderers) we can sympathize with their plight and compassionately proffer supports and services to aid them in their struggle. Only with dread may we contemplate strong intervention (such as court action) on the child's behalf, for want of alienating our clients.

Notwithstanding the humane philosophy of treatment, society cannot, or will not, commit resources nearly commensurate with the exponentially increasing number of case reports which have followed the promulgation of the expanded definitions. The helping language betrays a deep conflict and even ill will toward children and parents in trouble, whom society and professionals might sooner punish and control.

We are forced frequently in practice to identify and choose the 'least detrimental alternative' for the child[9] because the family supports which make it safe to keep children in their homes (homemakers, child care, psychiatric and medical services) are never available in sufficient amounts and quality.

That we should guide our work by a management concept named 'least detrimental alternative' for children suggests at least a skepticism about the utility of these supports, just as the rational foundation for child welfare work is called into question by the title of the influential book from which the concept comes, *Beyond the Best Interests of the Child*. More profoundly, the concept taps a vein of emotional confusion about our progeny, whom we both love and to whom we express kindness with hurt.

Mounting attention to the developmental sequelae of child abuse[10] stimulates an extra urgency not only to insure the physical safety of the identified victims but also to enable their adequate psychological development. The dangers of child abuse, Schmitt and Kempe assert in the latest edition of the Nelson Textbook of Pediatrics,[11] extend beyond harm to the victim:

If the child who has been physically abused is returned to his parents without intervention, 5 percent are killed and 35 percent are seriously reinjured. Moreover, the untreated families tend to produce children who grow up to be juvenile delinquents and murderers, as well as the child batterers of the next generation.

Despite the speculative nature of such conclusions about the developmental sequelae of child abuse,[12] such warnings support a practice of separating children from their natural homes in the interest of their and society's protection. They focus professional concern and public wrath on 'the untreated families' and may justify punitive action to save us from their children.

This professional response of control rather than of compassion furthermore generalizes mainly to poor and socially marginal families, for it is they who seem preferentially to attract the labels 'abuse' and 'neglect' to their problems in the public setting where they go for most health and social services. Affluent families' childhood injuries appear more likely to be termed 'accidents' by the private practitioners who offer them their services. The conceptual model of cause and effect implicit in the name 'accident' is benign: an isolated, random event rather than a consequence of parental commission or omission.[13]

Table One:

DILEMMAS OF SOCIAL POLICY AND PROFESSIONAL RESPONSE

Response	FAMILY AUTONOMY	*Versus*	COERCIVE INTERVENTION
Compassion ('support')	1 Voluntary child development services 2 Guaranteed family supports: *e.g.,* income, housing, health services		1 Case reporting of family crisis and mandated family intervention 2 Court-ordered delivery of services
Versus			
Control ('punishment')	1 "Laissez-faire": No assured services or supports 2 Retributive response to family crisis		1 Court action to separate child from family 2 Criminal prosecution of parents

Table One presents a graphic display of the two dilemmas of social policy (*Family Autonomy versus Coercive Intervention*) and professional response (*Compassion versus Control*). The four-fold table illustrates possible action responses. For purposes of this discussion, it is well to think of 'compassion' as signifying responses of support, such as provision of voluntary counseling and child care services, and 'control' as signifying such punitive responses as 'blaming the victim' for his/her reaction to social realities and as the criminal prosecution of abusing parents.

The Relationship Between Child Abuse and the Professions of Medicine and Law

The importance of a technical discipline's conceptual structure in defining how it approaches a problem is clearly stated by Mercer:[14]

Each discipline is organized around a core of basic concepts and assumptions which form the frame of reference from which persons trained in that discipline view the world and set about solving problems in their field. The concepts and assumptions which make up the perspective of each discipline give each its distinctive character and are the intellectual tools used by its practitioners. These tools are incorporated in action and problem solving and appear self-evident to persons socialized in the discipline. As a result, little consideration is likely to be given to the social consequence of applying a particular conceptual framework to problem solving.

When the issues to be resolved are clearly in the area of competence of a single discipline, the automatic application of its conceptual tools is likely to go unchallenged. However, when the problems under consideration lie in the interstices between disciplines, the disciplines concerned are likely to define the situation differently and may arrive at differing conclusions which have dissimilar implications for social action.

What we do when children are injured in family crises is shaped also by how our professions respond to the interstitial area called 'child abuse.'

Though cruelty to children has occurred since documentary records of mankind have been kept,[15] it became a salient social problem only after the publication by Kempe and his colleagues describing the 'battered child syndrome'.[16] In the four-year period after this medical article appeared, the legislatures of all fifty states, stimulated partly by a model law developed under the aegis of the Children's Bureau of the U.S. Department of Health, Education, and Welfare, passed statutes mandating the identification and reporting of suspected victims of abuse.

Once the specific diagnostic category 'battered child syndrome' was applied to integrate a set of medical symptoms and laws were passed making the syndrome reportable, the problem was made a proper and legitimate concern for the medical profession. Conrad has discussed cogently how 'hyperactivity' came officially to be known and how it became 'medicalized'.[17] Medicalization is defined in this paper as the perception of behavior as a medical problem or illness and the mandating or licensing of the medical profession to provide some type of treatment for it.

Pfohl associates the publicity surrounding the battered child syndrome report with a phenomenon of 'discovery' of child abuse. For radiologists, the potential for increased prestige, role expansion, and coalition formation (with psychodynamic psychiatry and pediatrics) may have encouraged identification and intervention in child abuse. Furthermore,

. . . [T]he discovery of abuse as a new 'illness' reduced drastically the intraorganizational constraints on doctors' 'seeing' abuse. . . . Problems associated with perceiving parents as patients whose confidentiality must be protected were reconstructed by typifying them as patients who needed help. . . . The maintenance of professional autonomy was assured by pairing deviance with sickness. . .[18]

In some ways, medicine's 'discovery' of abuse has benefited individual physicians and the profession. "One of the greatest ambitions of the physician is to discover or describe a 'new' disease or syndrome."[19] By such involvement the doctor becomes a moral entrepreneur defining what is normal, proper, or desirable: he becomes charged 'with inquisitorial powers to discover certain wrongs to be righted."[20] New opportunities for the application of traditional methods are also found as, for example, the systematic screening of suspected victims with a skeletal X-ray survey to detect previous fractures and the recent report in the neurology literature suggesting the utility of diphenylhydantoin* treatment for child abusing parents.[21]

Pfohl's provocative analysis also takes note of some of the normative and structural elements within the medical profession which appear to have reinforced a *reluctance* on the part of some physicians to become involved: the norm of confidentiality between doctor and patient and the goal of professional autonomy.[22]

---

* Dilantin, a commonly-used seizure suppressant

For many physicians child abuse is a subject to avoid.[23] *First,* it is difficult to distinguish, on a theoretical level, corporal punishment that is 'acceptable' from that which is 'illegitimate'. Abuse may be defined variably even by specialists, the definitions ranging from serious physical injury to non-fulfillment of a child's developmental needs.[24] *Second,* it is frequently hard to diagnose child abuse clinically. What appears on casual physical examination as bruising, for example, may turn out to be a skin manifestation of an organic blood dysfunction, or what appear to be cigarette burns may in reality be infected mosquito bites. A diagnosis of abuse may require social and psychological information about the family, the acquisition and interpretation of which may be beyond the average clinician's expertise.

It may be easier to characterize the clinical complaint in terms of the child's medical symptom rather than in terms of the social, familial, and psychological forces associated with its etiology. We see daily situations where the exclusive choice of medical taxonomy actively obscures the causes of the child's symptom and restricts the range of possible interventions: examples are 'subdural hematoma' which frequently occurs with severe trauma to babies' heads (the medical name means collection of blood under the *dura mater* of the brain) and 'enuresis' or 'encopresis' in child victims of sexual assault (the medical names mean incontinence of urine or feces).

Third, child abuse arouses strong emotions. To concentrate on the narrow medical issue (the broken bone) instead of the larger familial problem (the etiology of the injury) not only allows one to avoid facing the limits of one's technical adequacy, but to shield oneself from painful feelings of sadness and anger. One can thus maintain professional detachment and avert unpleasant confrontations. The potentially alienating nature of the physician-patient interaction when the diagnosis of child abuse is made may also have a negative economic impact on the doctor, especially the physician in private practice.

'Legalization' and Its Problems

The legal response to child abuse was triggered by its medicalization. Child abuse reporting statutes codified a medical diagnosis into a legal framework which in many states defined official functions for courts. Immunity from civil liability was given to mandated reporters so long as reports were made in good faith, monetary penalties for failure to report were established, and familial and professional-client confidentiality privileges, except those involving attorneys, were abrogated.

Professional autonomy for lawyers was established, and status and power accrued to legal institutions. For example, the growth in the number of Care and Protection cases* before the Boston Juvenile Court "has been phenomenal in recent years . . . four cases in 1968 and 99 in 1974, involving 175 different children."[25] Though these cases have burdened court dockets and personnel, they

---

* Care and Protection cases are those juvenile or family court actions which potentially transfer, on a temporary or permanent basis, legal and/or physical custody of a child from his biological parents to the state.

have also led to acknowledgement of the important work of the court. The need for this institution is enhanced because of its recognized expertise in handling special matters. Care and Protection cases are cited in response to recommendations by a prestigious commission charged with proposing reform and consolidation of the courts in Massachusetts. Child protection work in our own institution would proceed only with difficulty if access to the court were legally or procedurally constrained. Just as for the medical profession, however, there were normative and structural elements within law which urged restraint. Most important among them were the traditional presumptions and practices favoring family autonomy.

If individual lawyers might financially benefit from representing clients in matters pertaining to child abuse, they — like their physician counterparts — were personally uncertain whether or how to become involved.

Public concern over the scope and significance of the problem of the battered child is a comparatively new phenomenon. Participation by counsel in any significant numbers in child abuse cases in juvenile or family courts is of even more recent origin. It is small wonder that the lawyer approaches participation in these cases with trepidation.[26]

Lawyers, too, feel handicapped by a need to rely on concepts from social work and psychiatry and data from outside the traditional domain of legal knowledge and expertise. As counsel to parents, lawyers can be torn between advocacy of their clients' positions and that which advances the 'best interest' of their clients' children. As counsel to the petitioner, a lawyer may have to present a case buttressed by little tangible evidence. Risk to a child is often difficult to characterize and impossible to prove.

Further problems for lawyers concerned with child abuse involve the context of intervention: whether courts or legislatures should play the major role in shaping practice and allocating resources; how much formality is desirable in legal proceedings; and the propriety of negotiation as opposed to adversary confrontation when cases come to court.

Conflicts Between Medical and Legal Perspectives

Despite the common reasons for the 'medicalization' and the 'legalization' of child abuse, there are several areas where the two orientations conflict:

(1) The Seriousness of the Risk

To lawyers intervention might be warranted only when abuse results in serious harm to a child. To clinicians, however, *any* inflicted injury might justify a protective legal response, especially if the child is very young. "The trick is to prevent the abusive case from becoming the terminal case."[27] Early intervention may prevent the abuse from being repeated or from becoming more serious.

307   The Medicalization and Legalization of Child Abuse

(2) The Definition of the Abuser

To lawyers the abuser might be defined as a wrongdoer who has injured a child. To clinicians both the abuser and child might be perceived as victims influenced by sociological and psychological factors beyond their control.[28]

(3) The Importance of the Abuser's Mental State

To lawyers whether the abuser intentionally or accidentally inflicted injury on a child is a necessary condition of reporting or judicial action. So-called 'accidents' are less likely to trigger intervention. To clinicians, however, mental state may be less relevant, for it requires a diagnostic formulation frequently difficult or impossible to make on the basis of available data. The family dynamics which are associated with 'accidents' in some children (*e.g.* stress, marital conflict and parental inattention) often resemble those linked with inflicted injury in others. They are addressed with variable clinical sensitivity and precision.

(4) The Role of Law

Attorneys are proudly unwilling to accept conclusions or impressions lacking empirical corroboration. To lawyers the law and legal institutions become involved in child abuse when certain facts fit a standard of review. To clinicians, the law may be seen as an instrument to achieve a particular therapeutic or dispositional objective (*e.g.,* the triggering of services or of social welfare involvement) even if, as is most often the case, the data to legally support such objectives are missing or ambiguous. The clinician's approach to the abuse issue is frequently subjective or intuitive (*e.g.,* a *feeling* that a family is under stress or needs help, or that a child is 'at risk') while the lawyer demands evidence.

Doctoring and Lawyering the Disease

These potential or actual differences in orientation notwithstanding, both medicine and law have accepted in principle the therapeutic approach to child abuse.

To physicians, defining abuse as a disease or medical syndrome makes natural the treatment alternative, since both injured child and abuser are viewed as 'sick' — the one, physically, the other psychologically or socially. Therapy may, however, have retributive aspects, as pointed out with characteristic pungency by Illich:

The medical label may protect the patient from punishment only to submit him to interminable instruction, treatment, and discrimination, which are inflicted on him for his professional presumed benefit.[29]

Lawyers adopt a therapeutic perspective for the following reasons:

(1) The rehabilitative ideal remains in ascendance in criminal law, especially in the juvenile and family courts which handle most child abuse cases.[30]

(2) The criminal or punitive model may not protect the child. Parents may hesitate to seek help if they are fearful of prosecution. Evidence of abuse is often insufficient to satisfy the standard of conviction beyond a 'reasonable doubt' in criminal proceedings. If an alleged abuser is threatened with punishment and then found not guilty, he/she may feel vindicated, reinforcing the pattern of abuse. In fact, they may well be legally freed from any scrutiny, and badly needed social services will not be able to be provided. Even if found guilty, the perpetrator of abuse is usually given only mild punishment, such as a short jail term or probation. It the abuser is incarcerated, the other family members may equally suffer as, for example, the relationship between spouses is undercut and child-rearing falls on one parent, or children are placed in foster home care or with relatives. Upon release from jail, the abuser may be no less violent and even more aggressive and vindictive toward the objects of abuse.

(3) The fact that child abuse was 'discovered' by physicians influenced the model adopted by other professionals. As Friedson notes: "Medical definitions of deviance have come to be adopted even where there is no reliable evidence that biophysical variables 'cause' the deviance or that medical treatment is any more efficacious than any other kind of management."[31] Weber, in addition, contends that 'status' groups (*e.g.*, physicians) generally determine the content of law.[32]

The Selective Implementation of Treatment

Medical intervention is generally encouraged by the Hippocratic ideology of treatment, or the ethic that help, not harm, is given by practitioners, and by what Scheff calls the medical decision rule: it is better to wrongly diagnose illness and 'miss' health than it is to wrongly diagnose health and 'miss' illness.[33]

Physicians, in defining aberrant behavior as a medical problem and in providing treatment, become what sociologists call agents of social control. Though the technical enterprise of the physician claims value-free power, socially marginal individuals are more likely to be defined as deviant than are others.

Characteristics frequently identified with the 'battered child syndrome', such as social isolation, alcoholism, unemployment, childhood handicap, large family size, low level of parental educational achievement, and acceptance of severe physical punishment as a childhood socializing technique, are associated with social marginality and poverty.

Physicians in public settings seem from child abuse reporting statistics to be more likely to see and report child abuse than are those in private practice. As poor people are more likely to frequent hospital emergency wards and clinics, they have much greater social visibility where child abuse is concerned than people of means.

The fact that child abuse in neither theoretically nor clinically well defined increases the likelihood of subjective professional evaluation. In labeling theory it is axiomatic that the greater the social distance between the typer and the person singled out for typing, the broader the type and the more quickly it may be applied.[34]

In the doctor-patient relationship, the physician is always in a superordinate position because of his/her expertise; social distance is inherent to the relationship. This distance necessarily increases once the label of abuser has been applied. Importantly, the label is less likely to be fixed if the diagnostician and possible abuser share similar characteristics, expecially socioeconomic status. If the injury is serious or manifestly a consequence of maltreatment, however, the less likely would social class influence the labeling process.

Once the label 'abuser' has attached, it is very difficult to remove, so even innocent behavior of a custodian may be viewed with suspicion. The tenacity of a label increases as does the official processing. At our own institution, until quite recently, a red star was stamped on the permanent medical record of any child who might have been abused, a process which encouraged professionals to suspect child abuse (and to act on that assumption) at any future time that the child would present with a medical problem.

Professionals thus engage in an intricate process of selection, finding facts which fit the label which has been applied, responding to a few deviant details set within a panoply of entirely acceptable conduct. (Schur calls this phenomenon 'retrospective reinterpretation'.)[35] In any pathological model "persons are likely to be studied in terms of what is 'wrong' with them", there being a "decided emphasis on identifying the characteristics of abnormality"; in child abuse it may be administratively impossible to return to health, as is shown by the extra-ordinary durability of case reports in state central registers.

The response of the patient to the agent of social control affects the perceptions and behavior of the controller. If, for example, a child has been injured and the alleged perpetrator is repentant, a consensus can develop between abuser and labeller that a norm has been violated. In this situation, the label of 'abuser' may be less firmly applied than if the abuser defends his/her behavior as proper. Support for this formulation is found in studies by Gusfield,[36] who noted different reactions to repentant, sick and enemy deviants, and by Piliavin and Briar,[37] who showed that juveniles apprehended by the police receive more lenient treatment if they appear contrite and remorseful about their violations.

The Consequences of Treatment for the Abuser

Once abuse is defined as a sickness, it becomes a condition construed to be beyond the actor's control.[38] Though treatment, not punishment, is warranted, the *type* of treatment depends on whether or not the abuser is 'curable', 'improvable' or 'incurable' and on the speed with which such a state can be achieved.[39]

To help the abuser is generally seen as a less important goal than is the need to protect the child. If the abusive behavior cannot quickly be altered, and the child remains 'at risk', the type of intervention will differ accordingly (*e.g.,* the child may be more likely to be placed in a foster home). The less 'curable' is the abuser, the less treatment will be offered and the more punitive will society's response appear. Ironically, even the removal of a child from his parents, a move nearly always perceived as punitive by parents, is often portrayed as helpful by the professionals doing the removing ('It will give you a chance to resolve your own problems', *etc.*). Whatever the treatment, there are predictable consequences for those labelled 'abusers'.

Prior to diagnosis, parents may be afraid of 'getting caught' because of punishment and social stigma. On being told of clinicians' concerns, they may express hostility because of implicit or explicit criticism made of them and their childrearing practices yet feel relief because they love their children and want help in stopping their destructive behavior. The fact that they see themselves as 'sick' may increase their willingness to seek help. This attitude is at least in part due to the lesser social stigma attached to the 'sick', as opposed to the 'criminal', label.

Socially marginal individuals are likely to accept whatever definition more powerful labellers apply. This definition, of course, has already been accepted by much of the larger community because of the definers' power. As Davis writes:

The chance that a group will get community support for its definition of unacceptable deviance depends on its relative power position. The greater the group's size, resources, efficiency, unity, articulateness, prestige, coordination with other groups, and access to the mass media and to decision-makers, the more likely it is to get its preferred norms legitimated.[40]

Acceptance of definition by the child abusers, however, is not based alone on the power of the labellers. Though some would consider the process 'political castration',[41] in fact as long as he is defined as 'ill' and takes on the sick role the abuser is achieving a more satisfactory label and role. Though afflicted with a stigmatized illness (and thus "gaining few if any privileges and taking on some especially handicapping new obligations")[42] he at least is sick rather than sinful or criminal.

Effective social typing flows down rather than up the social structure. For example, when both parents induct one of their children into the family scapegoat role, this is an effective social typing because the child is unable not to take their definition of him into account even if he so wishes.[43] Sometimes it is difficult to know whether an abusive parent has actually accepted the definition or is merely 'role playing' in order to please the definer. If a person receives conflicting messages from the same control agent (*e.g.,* 'you are sick and criminal') or from different control agents in the treatment network (*e.g.,* from doctors who use the sick label, while lawyers use the criminal), confusion and upset predictably result.[44]

As an example of how social definitions are accepted by the group being defined, it is interesting to examine the basic tenets of Parents Anonymous, which began as a self-help group for abusive mothers:

A destructive, *disturbed* mother can, and often does, produce through her actions a physically or emotionally abused, or battered child. Present available *help* is limited and/or expensive, usually with a long waiting list before the person requesting help can actually receive *treatment* . . . We must understand that a problem as involved as this cannot be *cured* immediately . . . the problem is *within us* as a parent. . .[45]

To Parents Anonymous child abuse appears to be a medical problem, and abusers are sick persons who must be treated.

The Consequences of Treatment for the Social System

The individual and the social system are interrelated; each influences the other. Thus, if society defines abusive parents as sick there will be few criminal prosecutions for abuse; reports will generally be sent to welfare, as opposed to police departments.

Since victims of child abuse are frequently treated in hospitals, medical personnel become brokers for adult services and definers of children's rights. Once abuse is defined, that is, people may get services (such as counseling, child care, and homemaker services) which would be otherwise unavailable to them, and children might get care and protection impossible without institutional intervention.

If, as is customary, however, resources are in short supply, the preferred treatment of a case may not be feasible. Under this condition, less adequate treatment stratagems, or even clearly punitive alternatives, may be implemented. If day care and competent counseling are unavailable, court action and foster placement can become the only options. As Stoll observes, "(T)he best therapeutic intentions may be led astray when opportunities to implement theoretical guidelines are not available."[46]

Treating child abuse as a sickness has, ironically, made it more difficult to 'cure'. There are not enough therapists to handle all of the diagnosed cases. Nor do most abusive parents have the time, money or disposition for long-term therapeutic involvement. Many, moreover, lack the introspective and conceptual abilities required for successful psychological therapy.

As Parents Anonymous emphasizes, abuse is the *abuser's* problem. Its causes and solutions are widely understood to reside in individuals rather than in the social system.[47] Indeed the strong emphasis on child abuse as an individual problem means that other equally severe problems of childhood can be ignored, and the unequal distribution of social and economic resources in society can be masked.[48] The child abuse phenomenon itself may also increase as parents and professionals are obliged to 'package' their problems and diagnoses in a competitive market where services are in short supply.

As Tannenbaum observed in 1938:

Societal reactions to deviance can be characterized as a kind of 'dramatization of evil' such that a person's deviance is made a public issue. The stronger the reaction to the evil, the more it seems to grow. The reaction itself seems to generate the very thing it sought to eliminate.[49]

Conclusion: Dispelling the Myth of Child Abuse

As clinicians, we are convinced that with intelligence, humanity, and the application of appropriate interventions, we can help families in crisis. We believe, however, that short of coming to terms with — and changing — certain social, political, and economic aspects of our society, we will never be able adequately to understand and address the origins of child abuse and neglect. Nor will the issues of labeling be adequately resolved unless we deal straightforwardly with the potentially abusive power of the helping professions. If we can bring ourselves to ask such questions as 'Can we legislate child abuse out of existence?' and 'Who benefits from child abuse?' then perhaps we can more rationally choose among the action alternatives displayed in the conceptual model (*Table One*).

Although we would prefer to avoid coercion and punishment, and to keep families autonomous and services voluntary, we must acknowledge the realities of family life and posit some state role to assure the wellbeing of children. In making explicit the assumptions and values underpinning our professional actions, perhaps we can promote a more informed and humane practice.

Because it is likely that clinical interventions will continue to be class and culture-based, we propose the following five guidelines to minimize the abuse of power of the definer.

(1) Give Physicians, Social Workers, Lawyers and other Intervention Agents Social Science Perspectives and Skills

Critical intellectual tools should help clinicians to understand the implications of their work, and, especially, the functional meaning of the labels they apply in their practices.

Physicians need to be more aware of the complexity of human life, especially its social and psychological dimensions. The 'medical model' is not of itself inappropriate; rather, the conceptual bases of medical practice need to be broadened, and the intellectual and scientific repertory of the practitioner expanded.[50] Diagnostic formulation is an active process and it carries implicitly an anticipation of intervention and outcome. The simple elegance of concepts like 'child abuse' and 'child neglect' militate for simple and radical treatments.

Lawyers might be helped to learn that in child custody cases they are not merely advocates of a particular position. Only the child should 'win' a custody case, where, for example, allegations of 'abuse' or 'neglect', skillfully marshalled, may support the position of the more effectively represented parent, guardian, or social worker.

(2) Acknowledge and Change the Prestige Hierarchy of Helping Professions

The workers who seem best to be able to conceptualize the familial and social context of problems of violence are social workers and nurses. They are least paid, most overworked, and have as a rule minimal access to the decision prerogatives of medicine and law. We would add that social work and nursing are professions largely of and by women, and we believe we must objectively come to terms with the many realities — including sexual dominance and subservience — which make these professions unable to carry forth with appropriate respect and support. (We have made a modest effort in this direction at our own institution, where our interdisciplinary child abuse consultation program is organized under the aegis of the administration rather than of a medical clinical department. This is to foster to the extent possible colleagial status and communication on a coequal footing among the disciplines represented in the Trauma X Group (social work, nursing, law, medicine, and psychiatry).)

(3) Build Theory

We need urgently a commonly understandable dictionary of concepts which will guide and inform a rational practice. A more adequate theory base would include a more etiologic (or causal) classification scheme for children's injuries which would acknowledge and integrate diverse origins and expressions of social, familial, child developmental, and environmental phenomena. It would conceptualize strength in families and children as well as pathology. It would orient intervenors to the promotion of health rather than to the treatment of pathology.

A unified theory would permit coming to terms with the universe of need. At present, socially marginal and poor children are virtually the only ones susceptible to being diagnosed as victims of abuse and neglect. More affluent families' off-spring, whose injuries are called 'accidents' and who are often unprotected, are not included in 'risk' populations. We have seen examples of court defense where it was argued (successfully) that because the family was not poor, they did not fit the classic archetypes of abuse or neglect.

The needs and rights of all children need legally to be spelled out in relation to the responsibilities of parents and the state. This is easier said than done. It shall require not only a formidable effort at communication across disciplinary lines but a serious coming to terms with social and political values and realities.

(4) Change Social Inequality

We share Gil's[51] view that inequality is the basic problem underlying the labeling of 'abusive families' and its consequences. Just as children without defined rights are *ipso facto* vulnerable, so too, does unequal access to the resources and goods of society shape a class hierarchy which leads to the individualization of social problems. Broadly-focused efforts for social change should accompany a critical review of the ethical foundations for professional practice. As part of his/her formation as doctor, lawyer, social worker, or police officer, there could be developed for the professional a notion of public service and responsibility. This would enable individuals to see themselves as participants in a social process and to perceive the problems which they address in their work at the social as well as the individual level of action.

(5) Assure Adequate Representation of Class and Ethnic Groups in Decision-Making Forums

Since judgments about family competency can be affected by class and ethnic biases, they should be made in settings where prejudices can be checked and controlled. Culture-bound value judgments in child protection work are not infrequent, and a sufficient participation in case management conferences of professionals of equal rank and status and diverse ethnicity can assure both a more appropriate context for decision making and better decisions for children and their families.

NOTES

1. Kempe, Henry C., and Helfer, Ray E. (eds.), *Helping the Battered Child and His Family*. Phil., Pennsylvania: Lippincott, 1972.
2. Bourne, Richard, and Newberger, Eli H., "'Family Autonomy' or 'Coercive Intervention'? Ambiguity and Conflict in a Proposed Juvenile Justice Standard in Child Protection" (1977), 57 *Boston University Law Review* No. 4, 670-706. See also Juvenile Justice Standards Project (1977), *Standards Relating to Abuse and Neglect*.
3. *Ingraham v. Wright*, 45LW 4364 U.S. Supreme Court, 1977.
4. *Landeros v. Flood*, 131 Calif. RPtr 69, 1976.
5. Curran, William J., "Failure to Diagnose Battered Child Syndrome" (1977), 296 *New England Journal of Medicine* 795-796.
6. Juvenile Justice Standards Project (1977), *Standards Relating to Abuse and Neglect*.
7. Bourne, Richard and Newberger, Eli H., *op. cit., note 2*.
8. Rosenfeld, Alvin A., and Newberger, Eli H., "Compassion Versus Control: Conceptual and Practical Pitfalls in the Broadened Definition of Child Abuse" 237 *Journal of the American Medical Association* No. 19, 2086-2088.
9. Goldstein, Joseph R.; Freud, A.; and Solnit, A., *Beyond the Best Interests of the Child*. New York, New York: Free Press, 1973.
10. Galdston, Richard, "Violence Begins at Home" (1971), 10 *Journal of the American Academy of Child Psychiatry* No. 2, 336-350. See also, Martin, Harold P. (ed.). *The Abused Child: A Multidisciplinary Approach to Developmental Issues and Treatment* (1976).
11. Schmitt, B.D., and Kempe, C.H., "Neglect and Abuse of Children", in Vaughan, V.D., and McKay, R.J. (eds.), *Nelson Textbook of Pediatrics* (10th ed.), Phil., Pennsylvania: Saunders, 1975, pp. 107-111.
12. Elmer, Elizabeth, "A Follow-up Study of Traumatized Children" (1977), 59 *Pediatrics* No. 2, 273-279; and Elmer, Elizabeth, *Fragile Families, Troubled Children* (1977).
13. Newberger, Eli H., and Daniel, Jessica, "Knowledge and Epidemiology of Child Abuse: A Critical Review of Concepts" (1976), 5 *Pediatrics Annals* No. 3, 140-144; and Newberger, Eli H.; Reed, R.B.; Daniel, Jessica; Hyde, James N.; and Kotelchuck, M., "Pediatrics Social Illness: Toward an Etiolog Classification" (1977), 60 *Pediatrics* 178-185.

14. Mercer, Jane R., "Who is Normal? Two Perspectives on Mild Mental Retardation", in Jaco, E.G. (ed.), *Patients, Physicians and Illness* (2nd ed.), New York, New York: Free Press, 1972.
15. de Mause, Lloyd (ed.), *The History of Childhood.* New York, New York: Psycho-history Press, 1974.
16. Kempe, C. Henry, *et.al.,* "The Battered Child Syndrome" (July 7, 1962), 181 *Journal of the American Medical Association* 17-24.
17. Conrad, P., "The Discovery of Hyperkinesis: Notes on the Medicalization of Deviant Behavior" (Oct., 1975), 23 *Social Problems* 12-21.
18. Pfohl, Stephen J., "The 'Discovery' of Child Abuse" (1977), 24 *Social Problems* No. 2, 310-323.
19. Illich, Ivan, Medical Nemesis: *The Expropriation of Health* (1976).
20. *Ibid.*
21. Rosenblatt, S.; Schaeffer, D.; and Rosenthal, J.S., "Effects of Diphenylhydantoin on Child-Abusing Parents: A Preliminary Report" (1976), 19 *Current Therapeutic Research* 332-336.
22. *Op. cit.,* note 18.
23. Sanders, R.W., "Resistance to Dealing With Parents of Battered Children" (1972), 50 *Pediatrics* No. 6, 853-857.
24. *Op. cit.,* note 16., see also Fontana, Vincent J., *The Maltreated Child: the Maltreatment Syndrome in Children* (2nd. ed.) Springfield, Illinois: C.C. Thomas, 1974., Gil, David G., "Unravelling Child Abuse" (1975), 45 *American Journal of Orthopsychiatry* 346-356.
25. Poitrast, Francis G., "The Judicial Dilemma in Child Abuse Cases" (1976), 13 *Psychiatric Opinion* 22-28.
26. Isaacs, Jacob L., "The Role of the Lawyer in Child Abuse Cases", in Helfer, R.E., and Kempe, C.H. (eds.), *Helping the Battered Child and His Family.* Phil., Pennsylvania: Lippincott, 1972.
27. *Op. cit.,* note 6.
28. Gelles, Richard J., "Child Abuse as Psychopathology: A Sociological Critique and Reformulation" (1973), 43 *American Journal of Orthopsychiatry* 611-621; see also Newberger, Eli H., "The Myth of the Battered Child Syndrome" (1973), 30 *Current Medical Dialog.* 327-334. Reprinted in, Chess, S., and Thomas A. (eds.) *Annual Progress in Child Psychiatry and Child Development.* New York, New York: Brunner Mazel, 1974.
29. Illich, Ivan, Medical Nemesis: *The Expropriation of Health* (1976).
30. Allen, Francis A., *The Borderland of Criminal Justice.* Chicago, Illinois: University of Chicago Press, 1964.
31. Freidson, Eliot, *Profession of Medicine: A Study of the Sociology of Applied Knowledge.* New York, New York: Dodd Mead, 1970.
32. Rheinstein, Max (ed.), *Max Weber on Law in Economy and Society.* Cambridge, Mass.: Harvard University Press, 1954.
33. Scheff, Thomas J., "Decision Rules, Types of Error, and Their Consequences in Medical Diagnosis", in Freidson, E,. and Lorber, J. (eds.), *Medical Men and Their Work.* Chicago, Illinois: Aldine, 1972.
34. Rubington, Earl and Weinberg, Martin S., *Deviance: The Interactionist Perspective.* New York, New York: Macmillan, 1973.
35. Schur, Edwin, *Labeling Deviant Behavior.* New York, New York: Harper & Row, 1971.
36. Gusfield, Joseph R., "Moral Passage: the Symbolic Process in Public Designations of Deviance" (Fall, 1967), 15 *Social Problems* 175-188.
37. Piliavin, Irving and Briar, Scott, "Police Encounters With Juveniles" (1964), 70 *American Journal of Sociology* No. 9, 206-214.
38. Parsons, Talcott, *The Social System.* New York, New York: Free Press, 1951.
39. *Op. cit.,* note 31.

40. Davis, F. James, "Beliefs, Values, Power and Public Definitions of Deviance", in Davis, F. James and Stivers, R. (ed.), *The Collective Definition of Deviance*. New York, New York: Free Press, 1975.
41. Pitts, Jesse R., "Social Control: the Concept", in *The International Encyclopedia of the Social Sciences,* Vol. 14. New York, New York: Macmillan, 1968, p. 391.
42. *Op. cit.,* note 31.
43. *Op. cit.,* note 34.
44. Stoll, Clarice S., "Images of Man and Social Control" (1968), 47 *Social Forces* No. 12, 119-127.
45. *Op. cit.,* note 1.
46. *Op. cit.,* note 44.
47. Gelles, Richard J., *op. cit.,* note 28; see also Conrad, P., *op. cit.,* note 17.
48. Gil, David G., *Violence Against Children*. Cambridge, Mass.: Harvard University Press, 1970.
49. Tannenbaum, Frank, *Crime and the Community*. New York, New York: Columbia University Press, 1938.
50. Engel, George L., "The Need for a New Medical Model: A Challenge For Biomedicine" (1977), 196 *Science* 129-136.
51. *Op. cit.,* note 48.

REFERENCES

Becker, Howard S., *Outsiders: Studies in the Sociology of Deviance*. New York, New York: Free Press, 1963.

Chambliss, William J., "A Sociological Analysis of the Law of Vagrancy" (Fall, 1964), 12 *Social Problems* 67-77.

Cupoli, Michael, J., and Newberger, Eli H., "Optimism or Pessimism for the Victim of Child Abuse?" (1977), 59 *Pediatrics* 311-314.

Fraser, Brian, in Kempe, C.H., and Helfer, R. (eds.), *Child Abuse and Neglect: The Family and the Community*. Cambridge, Mass.: Ballinger, 1976.

Gelles, Richard J., "Violence Towards Children in the United States", paper presented at the annual meeting of the American Association for the Advancement of Science, Denver, Feb., 1977.

Hyde, James N., "Uses and Abuses of Information in Protective Services Contexts", *Fifth National Symposium on Child Abuse and Neglect,* Denver, 1974, pp. 56-62.

Joint Commission on the Mental Health of Children (1970), *Crisis in Child Mental Health.*

Kittrie, Nicholas, *The Right to Be Different*. Baltimore, Maryland: John Hopkins, 1971.

Newberger, Eli H.; Newberger, Carolyn; and Richmond, Julius, "Child Health in America: Toward a Rational Public Policy" (1976), 54 *Milbank Memorial Fund Quarterly/Health and Society* No. 3, 249-298.

Paulsen, Monrad, "Juvenile Courts, Family Courts, and the Poor Man" (1966), 54 *California Law Review* 694-716.

Ryan, W., *Blaming the Victim*. New York, New York: Random, 1972.

Scheff, Thomas J., *Being Mentally Ill: A Sociological Theory*. Chicago, Illinois: Aldine, 1966.

Schrag, Peter and Divoky, Diane, *The Myth of the Hyperactive Child*. New York, New York: Pantheon, 1975.

Whiting, Leila, "The Central Registry for Child Abuse Cases: Rethinking Basic Assumptions" (1977), 56 *Child Welfare* No. 1, 761-767.

Chapter 21

Questions of Social Policy — A Canadian Perspective

*Barbara A. Chisholm**

1. Introduction — Statistics

There are no accurate figures on the incidence of child abuse in Canada. Reasons for this include:

(1) lack of a standard, useable definition of child abuse;
(2) variation in reporting systems;
(3) lack of consistent procedures in dealing with child abuse;
(4) failure to recognize (or perhaps to acknowledge) child abuse, which thus leads to non-reporting; and
(5) problems of professional and public education.

The types of injuries identified as child abuse vary from province to province. Some provinces provide information on the source of the original complaint report.[1] Some provinces identify emotional and physical neglect, others spell out physical abuse only and still others provide for identification of abuse or neglect without a physical injury. At present, nine of the twelve provincial or territorial jurisdictions in Canada have legislation making reporting of abuse or ill-treatment of children mandatory.[2] (The three provinces without such reporting are initiating systematic monitoring programs.) But even within those nine statutes requiring reporting of child abuse, four contain no penalties for failing to report; two have 'general penalties'; one has a penalty which has not yet been proclaimed; and only two provinces have a specific penalty for such failure.[3]

Of the nine jurisdictions in Canada (exclusive of the federal one), only four provinces — Alberta, Manitoba, Quebec, and the Yukon — extend the age of statutory protection against neglect and abuse to the age of majority in that province. This raises a query about adolescent abuse. So much attention is (properly) being directed at infant, toddler and young-child abuse that we may be neglecting another aspect of the problem, but one that is no less urgent. Adolescent suicide is now so serious[4] as to require investigation on its own. Is

* Canadian Council on Children and Youth, Toronto, Canada.

there a connection? We may be (and probably are) missing many instances of adolescent abuse because it is disguised as teenage behavioral problems or generational conflicts. And, where does the adolescent victim of abuse or incest turn for help and action? The helplessness of the adolescent is just as critical an issue for us.

Many attempts have been made to predict the actual and antipated incidence of child abuse in Canada,[5] as elsewhere. But we do not yet have consistency in reporting, and therefore, depending upon who is discussing the situation, we may get quite varying pictures. *Table 1* illustrates the point regarding the province of Ontario:[6]

Table 1

Number of Deaths in Ontario
Caused by Child Abuse, 1970-1975

Chief Coroner's Office Statistics	Central Registry Statistics
50	23

Whatever the actual incidence figures, it seems fair to suggest that more physical, sexual, and psychological abuse of minors goes on than is noted and counted and that we appear to tolerate a considerable amount of abuse of children and youth in our society.

2. Punishment and Treatment

Whatever the problems of establishing the incidence, we have the other problems related to response or 'management'. These problems grow out of a significant difference of opinion about the appropriate approach for society and for professionals to take to battering or abusing parents or other adults. Examination of the literature of the past decade[7] reflects the difference of opinion, which in a somewhat over-simplified way may be expressed thus:

a) the 'punish them' approach, with deterrent sentencing as a characteristic; and
b) the 'treat them' approach, which relies on a medical-model.

Polarization to either position is surely not useful. Each merits consideration.

The Punishment Approach: The Adult Removed From the Child

The use of deterrent sentencing is an old and still (in some circles) honored approach to the problem of serious anti-social behavior. The degree of severity of the punishment is a form of 'weighting', a kind of index of the 'degree of repugnance' society attaches to the event. Thus the Attorney-General of Ontario recently successfully appealed the sentence meted out in a child abuse case, and won a much longer one.

The deterrent point of view may be supported, at least partially, by observing the reality of present society. There *are* adults who are dangerous. We know that. We recognize too, other adults' rights to physical safety and to walk about the city free from fear and potential assault. Therefore, we incarcerate those acknowledged or convicted offenders designated as 'dangerous'. Do we not need to acknowledge that the same situation may pertain to children — that there are adults in their environment who are dangerous to them (or if a child is already dead, potentially dangerous to other children)? Should we retreat from facing the potential necessity of removing from society those adults established as dangerous to children, even if they are their biological parents? Do minors have less defendable rights to physical safety than adults?

Table 2[8]

Number of Child Abuse Reports, Charges Laid, and Convictions, in Ontario, 1970-1975

Number of Reports	Charges Laid	Convictions Obtained
3249	348	78

Table 2 shows the numbers of charges and convictions relative to reports of child abuse in Ontario 1970-1975. I am not here *advocating* punishment as the way to deal with abusing parents. Rather I am raising a question for consideration: that protection of citizens from dangerous persons may from time to time require that such persons be removed from active society, and this protection applies to children as well as to adults.

The Treatment Approach: The Child is Often Removed From the Adults

Not all adults who have abused a child are dangerous to the community of children at large. This probably constitutes the large bulk of the abusing group; they do not require punitive removal from the community. Indeed, if it is necessary to separate the abused child (or the child at risk of abuse) from the abusing or threatening parent, it is usual for the child to be removed.[9]

Intervention by agents of the community is essential in these instances, to 'catch' the behavior before it becomes even more abusive. Help which involves (or should involve) many years of caring support is indicated; incarceration is not necessary. The prognosis for some parents in this so-called 'treatment' group appears more encouraging than that of the dangerous adult group, largely because we do not seem to know what to do with the dangerous group except incarcerate them. But it seems inexact to suggest that the majority of programs presently in progress in Canada are providing 'treatment', in the narrow medical use of that word. They are, instead, a combination of services more appropriately related to a social work than to a medical model. They may be described as 'environmental manipulation' and 'the provision of support services'.

'Environmental manipulation' means help with the externals of people's lives: decent, spacious-enough housing, for example. A family under stress (indeed, any family) needs housing which provides clean and dry shelter, free of vermin and rodents. A family under stress also requires space sufficient to absorb the realities that come out of inter-personal physical closeness: in other words, a chance to 'get away from each other' from time to time, when pressures and tempers are high. It seems to me that the development of housing policies is one of the issues to which we have failed to pay significant enough attention in Canada. In urban and suburban society we have become a nation of apartment dwellers. Many young families occupy vertical rather than horizontal space. Because we (the planning, building, decision-making administrators of the country) may remember having back-yards and parks to play and roam in in our own childhood, we seem to believe that most young families today have the same opportunities. But this is not the case.[10] The present economy makes it impossible for most young families to consider a home like that. The result is that small children, busy toddlers, and active adolescents are cramped in conditions in which they cannot escape one another in moments of stress. Add to this one or two tired adults, and the spark of irritation may feed itself on counter-irritations, flare into out-of-control anger, and someone gets hurt.

Other external needs related to people's lives with which we should be concerned through 'environmental manipulation' in much fuller form than we are at present include:

— day care, and emergency day care services for working parents; sole-support parents; overwhelmed parents;
— homemaker services, short and long term;
— income improvement (basic) and income management assistance (debt counseling);
— help with fighting one's way through the bureaucratic red tape maze of various governmental 'helping' programs; and
— relief for a special child with special needs, at periods of crisis or stress in the family.

Our very hesitant move in the direction of this last item reflects, at least, two current characteristics in much of our thinking: one is the old belief that to help adults (*e.g.,* parents) weakens their capacity to help themselves, which is a preferred societal mode of parental (adult) behavior; and the other is that, in spite of all the evidence of the last two decades, somehow we do not quite believe that the so-called nuclear family is here. We still imagine family members aid one another. This serves to strengthen the anxiety about and resistance to government intervention in the family. While this is a matter of legitimate concern, I suggest that in this context, the state cannot choose to remain out.

'Provision of Support Systems' refers to the sort of practical and emotional assistance required to improve and sustain a person's (or a family's) capacity to deal with day-to-day problems, or with episodes of particular stress. Examples of such help, as related to the managing or prevention of child abuse, would include:

— parents anonymous groups (child battering or potential battering parents who come together for initial help and support, much on the Alcoholics Anonymous pattern);
— 24-hour distress 'hot lines', with well-publicized telephone numbers;
— volunteer befrienders, whose non-judgmental befriending reaches out to the parent(s) in difficulty;
— 'grandmothers-by-informal-adoption' programs; these were originally directed toward helping the separated child without a family but now are seen to be of value to the parent in need of parenting as well;
— self-help groups separate from Parents Anonymous, to assist with the 'post-partum blues', which try to involve husbands and fathers in the attempt to understand what's going on with a depressed new mother, reducing hopefully the buildup of stress which may lead to an assault on the infant, or serious neglect.

Use of the Term 'Treatment'

Intensive social work of one kind or another, then, appears to be the mainstay of our management and/or prevention of child abuse. Of course some parents are referred for treatment by a psychiatrist, and go voluntarily. Such treatment may exist by itself or in cooperation with social work assistance, or parallel to it. Psychiatric consultation can be of use also to social workers and non-professional helpers trying to help the abusing parent.

Common use of treatment terminology, however, instead of the language of 'management', may have harmed our attempts to involve the whole community in dealing with child abuse. Treatment is a process of skill, undertaken by experts, which leads to cure, or at least to a significant reduction in symptoms. Generalized and inexact use of the term, I believe, lulls both professionals and the general public into a feeling that; 1) there are methods more or less readily available to 'cure' the child abuser or significantly to reduce his/her behavior; 2) that if we could only undertake to employ these methods, child abusers could be cured or controlled; and 3) that the skills of such methods are special, and therefore not within the arsenal of tools available to the 'average' social worker or citizen. Such thinking eliminates or excludes the average citizen and may have something to do with the community lethargy reflected in lack of reporting of child abuse cases.

A precedent of a kind exists for this point of view. Insertion of the treatment concept into the area of juvenile delinquency has created a special problem: in trying to make a *quasi*-social agency out of juvenile court we have, in the opinion of some, compromised the court's capacity to be a court. In attempting to 'treat' the youthful offender, we have complicated his need (and some suggest his right) to experience clear and connected consequences to his behavior. In the same sense, I fear we may make the same mistake in child abuse. In focussing exclusively on the concept of treatment, at least in the *language* of our concern, we may (and do, I believe) compromise the functions and the problem. It is probable that some abusing parents (or indeed, other adults in a child's life) are emotionally seriously disturbed or damaged. Victims themselves of too many pathological experiences, they are in danger of failing in life as people, never mind as parents. *These persons are often emotionally sick, and do need treatment.* However, for other abusing or potentially abusing parents, it is possible that the orientation the word 'treatment' creates is a disservice. Not everyone who offends our social codes is 'sick'. Their treatment orientation could lead to these consequences:

a) we may rely on too narrow a conceptual base in our search for viable action-programs directed at child abuse. That is, we may rely too much on the scientific model for the design of programs governments will be willing to fund (*i.e.,* time-limited, research-oriented, control-group restricted projects). Also, our approach may be too 'professional' oriented; and

b) we may continue to exclude from our co-ordinated approach those very programs which are most directly related to 'environmental manipulation' and 'the provision of support systems' mentioned above. Thereby we risk focussing on one aspect (treatment) at the expense of another (those services which are particularly within the scope of social work), and short-circuit the results.

3. Questions of Prevention, Intervention, and Rights

The Government of Canada recently addressed itself to the problem of child abuse in Canada. The Report of the Standing Committee on Health, Welfare and Social Affairs of the Parliament of Canada entitled *Child Abuse and Neglect* was tabled in July 1976.[11] Its findings were many and varied, and a total of fifteen recommendations were made. A significant observation made by the Committee was that the Canadian pattern of response to social problems has been (and is) essentially that of 'waiting till the horse is stolen to lock the barn door'. We wait until a problem is visibly severe before we act; we are not strong on prevention. The Committee made the following statement about prevention:

The Committee, in noting the lack of support services to families with children, noted also that many services become available to a child once he has been removed from his own home because of family breakdown. The Committee recognizes that there are often no alternatives to the removal of the child. If appropriate support services had been available to the family from the time of the child's birth, it is possible that the child would have remained in his own home.

[The] Committee noted that expensive services are required for emotionally disturbed children, for battered children, for broken families but, unless preventive services are also provided, the cycle becomes self-perpetuating. Services which enable parents to care for their own children can often prevent the need for protection.[12]

Any suggestion of family support raises the spectre of intervention, and this in turn leads to the question of the rights of parents and the rights of children.

(a) *the rights of parents* to the full custody of their children is a traditional manner of thought which is so deeply ingrained in our society that questioning it in any form is guaranteed to raise cautious resistance if not actual hackles. We are reminded that the family is the Basic Unit in Society. As such, it enjoys, and should continue to, a basic right to function with minimum interference, especially from the state.

Of course, this is an over-simplification of the reality. The state is already deeply involved in the affairs and well-being of the family: income tax deduction provisions, the Family Allowance program, housing subsidy policies, education, public health programs, consumer protection legislation, medicare programs, public libraries, public transportation facilities — the list goes on. It is somewhat innocent to argue the case of Parents' Rights on the theme that 'the least government is the best government'. The government is already in.

Nevertheless, there is in our society a general expectation that parents raise their children by themselves. As noted by the Parliamentary Committee, we tend to withhold intervention until a serious problem of incapacity or refusal to parent has emerged. This attitude of public policy reinforces the ancient concept of the 'ownership' rights of parents. Our religious attitudes and our laws have reinforced this position. It has been assumed that the interests of parents and children always coincide, and that the decisions of parents regarding their children will always be made on behalf of the children. Our assumption that every child should be in his own home rationalizes resistance to removing a child or returning a child to his parents. In a large majority of cases that is the right conclusion. But there is another claim which cannot be ignored:

b) *the competing rights of children* to grow free from fear, capable of trusting others and thus themselves. Our theories of child development — physical, emotional, intellectual, psychological — still view the child as being essentially passive and dependent, however exciting and amusing. His role is to cooperate, obey, and go to school when he's old enough. Although affectionate, this attitude sees the child as having no role to play in adult decision-making about him. Perhaps innocently, but nevertheless effectively, this perception renders the child invisible. But the concept of Children's Rights shifts that perception, to recognition of the child *as a person who happens to be a child.*

This is not just an exercise in word games. If we change our perception of children from that of dependent incompetent possessions, to one of recognizing them as persons in their own right, who happen to be children who are also dependent and in need of protection, then we inevitably shift our weighting of parents' rights, and their burden of parental responsibility.

The Parliamentary Committee referred to earlier took note of this point.

Among the issues involved in providing preventive services to children and families, the question kept arising, 'What are the rights of the child?' and 'What are the rights of the parent?' It was made clear by a number of witnesses that by tradition and law the rights of the parent have always superceded those of the child unless or until the breakdown of the family necessitates the intervention of a public authority. For this reason, there is often a reluctance on the part of a citizen or even an official agency to intervene in family affairs even if there appears to be some cause for concern on the child's behalf. Established agencies do not usually take any initiative in helping and assisting parents to care for their children until the parent or child directly requests help or someone outside the family complains about the care the child is receiving and by that time it may be too late to help the family.

The Committee believes that it is possible to preserve the integrity, privacy and sanctity of the family and, at the same time offer support services to the family in the raising of their children.[13]

At present the rights of parents and the entitlements of children appear to be on a collision course. Perhaps it will be useful to acknowledge that the claims of parental 'ownership' are neither absolute nor permanent. The dependency of children and youth is reduced with time and maturation. But dependency is not to be equated with subjugation, en route. Perhaps the reluctance to intervene in cases of suspected child abuse reflects an unconscious agreement with the position that children are possessions of their parents. Such an assumption places parents' rights first, even while it may be articulated in phrases of concern for the child.

The philosophical underpinning that states that every child should be in his own family is right and proper, as far as it goes. We have few specific guidelines to assist judgment when situations arise which challenge this moral precept, except listed definitions of neglect which justify action in child welfare cases, or the 1909 White House Conference on Children Credo that no child should be removed from his own home for reasons of poverty alone. Perhaps the statement should now read: "Every child should be in his own home unless to remain there threatens his personal and/or civil rights."

In California recently[14] a Supreme Court decision (June 1975) has brought to the foreground in that state the rights of the child subjected to abuse. Discharge of a 'battered child' back to the battering parent(s) may now constitute malpractice. Thus the role of the professional and the judgments exercised by professionals are coming under scrutiny, with an extension of present accountability for failing to protect the rights of children against their parents.

4. Complicating Factors

Inter-Professional Difficulties

A special problem associated with the management and prevention of child abuse is that related to inter-professional cooperation (or lack of it). Particular attention to the issue is certainly indicated in any serious approach to child abuse. Inter-discipline and inter-agency tensions reduce the effectiveness of any 'team' approach and create resistances which direct the focus of attention away from the problem onto what might be termed 'upmanship' or 'games of control'. Many factors complicate this problem: pressure of work, lack of knowledge (and therefore understanding) of the training of other disciplines; thus a lack of understanding of both the extent and limitation of their skills; ignorance of how the individual agency 'helps'; lack of trust among professionals that the other service or agency will carry out its mandate, leading to the attitude that 'if it's going to get done I'd better do it myself'; lack of reliance on the judgment of other professionals; unresponsiveness of one service or agency to the requests of another for action on behalf of a child, and consequent exasperation and anger; and a simple lack of courtesy toward each other, in terms of information — sharing and joint planning. Medical personnel can inform the child-caring agency early about their concern for a child. Short notice, if avoidable, is a disservice to the child and hinders good planning.

Inter-disciplinary understanding can be fostered in at least two ways: (there are others, of course)

(1) through the development of committees (perhaps called Child Abuse Committees) whose members are professionals and non-professionals and part of whose function it would be to learn about each other and *then* to liaise with each other's organizations and with government; and
(2) through the development of continuing cross-professional education and study programs; some important initiatives have been made between social workers and lawyers, but there is a long way to go.

Corporal Punishment

Concern about the relationship between physical punishment and child abuse is becoming more and more evident. Physical punishment has long been tolerated. The Criminal Code of Canada still allows for it in section 43. Even the Parliamentary Committee Report referred to earlier dealt with the issue briefly:

Your Committee is pleased to note the reference in the Brief of the Department of Justice to the effect that the question of the necessity and/or desirability of introducing a 'cruelty to children' offense in the Criminal Code is under study by that Department.

Section 43 of the Criminal Code was discussed by several witnesses in the context of child rearing corporal punishment in the schools, and as a reflection of cultural values. The Committee is aware that some provincial legislation specifically forbids physical punishment of children.

It is felt by many who have experience with the care of children in groups and with the education and training of staff who provide group care, that the elimination of physical punishment encourages staff to develop more creative programs and more sensitive ways of encouraging positive acceptable behavior in children. The result is an improvement in the relations between staff and child.

The Committee considers that the relationship between parent and child needs to be considered separately from the relationship between a child and a teacher, nurse, child care worker or other person standing in the place of the parent.

The Committee recommends further consideration of section 43. . . .

The Committee suggests that alternatives to physical force as a means of discipline be encouraged through studies and programs of public education. . . .[15]

It is to be hoped that exploration of this subject will proceed. Is physical punishment of any constructive educational value? If so, what are its boundaries; if not, how can we replace it with more constructive measures? How should the Criminal Code view the question?

The Difficulties Inherent in Giving Service

Much has been written about the characteristics of abusive parents. This literature tends to focus on their dynamics, or how they became abusive. The literature deals also with another important characteristic, namely, the 'workability' of such adults. It is pointed out that not infrequently they have problems trusting others, and experience great difficulty reaching out for help and in making and sustaining relationships.

Thus, goals in working with abusive adults, or attempting to do so must be practical and realistic. The main responsibility is protection of the child or children, and if hard choices must be made about 'working with parents', the child's claims to emotional and physical integrity must come first. If this means placement, then that will have to be undertaken. If working with the family while the child remains with the parents at home is the undertaking, then very long-term service is subsequently implied. Supervision of a once-abused child in his own home is a very difficult undertaking; one cannot be there all the time. Even the team approach which provides a multiple-person involvement may meet problems of resistance, refusal of access to the home, and differences in judgment and perception about what is going on. The judgments that are demanded in this situation by social workers, public health nurses, physicians and volunteers are of critical importance, and are difficult. In our concern to help parents at risk we must not lose sight of this reality. Otherwise, there is a danger that in concentration on the parents the child may be overlooked.

NOTES

1. Alberta, Nova Scotia, and Ontario.
2. Jurisdictions which lack this specific legislation are New Brunswick, the Northwest Territories, and Prince Edward Island. These all have legislation, of course, in company with all other provinces, directed generally to the protection of dependent/neglected children.
3. (a) British Columbia, Manitoba, Ontario, Saskatchewan; (b) Nova Scotia, Quebec, (c) Alberta; (d) Newfoundland and the Yukon.
4. See: *Perspective Canada, A Compendium of Social Statistics,* Government of Canada, Ottawa.
5. See: Stolk, Mary Van, *The Battered Child in Canada* (1972).
6. Dawson, Ross, "Current Issues in Child Abuse in Ontario" (Nov., 1976), 9 *Journal of the Ontario Association of Children's Aid Societies* No. 19, 3.
7. See, for example: references contained in *Child Abuse — a Bibliography* by Bakan, Eisner, and Needham, pub. by Canadian Council on Children and Youth, 1976; and Jayaratne, S., "Child Abusers as Parents and Children: A Review" (Jan., 1977), 22

Social Work Journal of the National Association of Social Workers (U.S.) No. 1, 5-9.

8. See: Dawson, Ross, *supra*, p. 3.

9. This is a topic that requires further separate consideration: removal of children rather than that of the adult further 'victimizes the victim' removing him from siblings, the other parent, *etc.*

10. See for example: *Perspective Canada, supra,* chapter 10, p. 207.

11. *Child Abuse and Neglect* — Report to the House of Commons, Standing Committee on Health, Welfare and Social Affairs, First Session, Thirtieth Parliament, 1974-75-76. Ottawa. (Supply and Services Canada).

12. *Child Abuse and Neglect, supra,* p. 21.

13. *Ibid.,* pp. 20-21.

14. *Landeros v. Flood* (1975), 50 Cal. App. 3d. 189. See article on this case entitled "The Battered Child: A Doctor's Civil Liability for Failure to Diagnose and Report", by Clymer, J.N. (1977) 16 *Washburn Law Journal* 543.

15. "Child Abuse and Neglect", *supra,* pp. 18-19.

Chapter 22

Five Years of Child Abuse as a Symptom of Family Problems

Rob van Rees*

1. Introduction

Five years age we had to deal for the first time with abused children in practical
situations. Then, on January 1, 1972, the Socio-Therapeutic Institute, The
Triangel, was started in Amsterdam.[1] The general rise of interest in the
phenomenon of child abuse took place at the same time and we, of course,
participated in many discussions and publications about this subject, and we
closely cooperated with the Medical Referee for Child Abuse in Amsterdam.

Nevertheless, as a consequence of the more or less striking features of child abuse,
we at first underrated its complexity. Gradually, however, we realized that,
whenever we tried to gain a better insight in this phenomenon, we found ourselves
faced with the necessity to penetrate into the essence of the family situation as a
whole, just as this is the case with other serious signals indicating a disturbed
family pattern. In the Triangel we are in a position to work with complete families
and thus to discover — and influence — the causes which account for the
situation of 'the family as a patient' in a treatment unit.

To almost everyone, life in a family is a matter of course. We are born in a family
and we see families everywhere around us. We also speak about families as if we
all know exactly what a family is. But do we really know?

The more we study family dynamics, the more obscure is the outcome of a comparison
between the dynamics of a family and of other groups which we do not call a family — not
to mention that between various families. And the same applies to the structure. We can
never get beyond doubtful comparisons and generalizations.[2]

Many things have been written about the changing society and about the
problems families, and in particular families with growing children, have to cope
with as a result of this change.

---

* Socio-Therapeutisch Instituut De Triangel, Amsterdam, Netherlands.

In our opinion, the problems concerning the development of the family mainly have to do with two important functions of the family: the function to educate and the function to impart a capacity to enter into relations. For a proper understanding of the background of child abuse in a family, an historical review of these family functions — briefly summarized — is indispensable.

2. The Functions of the Family in an Historical Perspective

In a former study[3] we have explored the alterations in the educational and relational functions of a family from 1200 to the present. We came to the conclusion that the contents of these essential functions have changed to a considerable degree. An adequate fulfilment of both functions in the present society is a very comprehensive and complicated task.

After 1200, *education* in the western world developed from a rapid adaptation of the child to the life of the adults (which could hardly be called education), via a period in which the child was protected and educated in its own world ('the world of the child') to the era which we, following Lea Dasberg,[4] would call the period of pedagogic inconsistence. The present period seems to be a period of transition and a search for new forms. Needless to say, this transitional stage constitutes a heavy burden for the family. Education is poised between two concepts: the declining view emphasizing the isolated world of the child and the new approach of educating youth in and for a wider society. Families choosing the latter, progressive view of education are still confronted with many uncertainties.

Relationships within the family have also changed very much in the western world after 1200. In mediaeval society, the child — seen as a 'pocket size' adult — learnt from its youth to get along with a comparatively large group of family members. The positions of the head of the family, the mother, the child, the relatives, the apprentices, *etc.* were associated in very precisely defined relationships. In the later period when parents tried to act as protectors and guardians of an isolated world of the child, which had to be full of joy and free from care, the relationships were very different.

From the beginning of the 20th century a new development took place which was accelerated by the turbulent events after World War II. The communication media in this new world make it much easier to enter into more numerous, but also more superficial relations. As a result, intimate relationships within the immediate family or community are emphasized and subjected to more far-reaching demands. Five years of experience with problem families have taught us convincingly that child abuse is one of the most alarming — but by no means a unique — signal that the functions of education and practising relationships can no longer be fulfilled by a family and that it is, therefore, in urgent need of help.

3. The Triangel Procedure

Some Factual Data

— The total capacity of the Triangel is 30-35 families per annum.
— There are 6 living units; in each unit 2, 3 or 4 (complete or incomplete) families can be placed depending on the number of family members.
— The ultimate duration of the stay is 6 months.
— The living groups are attended to continually by members of a team of 4 group workers and 1 or 2 apprentices.
— The placing agencies stay involved in the treatment rather closely. Frequently, a framework for further care is built up together with them.
— We speak of 'socio-therapy' because, to families which are admitted to the Triangel, the social factors which disturb family life are of primary concern and demand a therapy which includes the family as a unity. The method is marked by cooperation, as intensive as possible, in which the boundaries between the family and the Institute sometimes almost completely fade away.

Application and Admission

Application for treatment of a family in the Triangel can be done by any social worker or any social service in the region of Amsterdam. In the past five years it has been done by almost every kind of social service, such as general social welfare centers, family doctors, crisis centers, day-care centers, child guidance clinics, councils for child protection, the medical referees for child abuse, local social service departments, university, and other institutes for social care. In a few cases families themselves applied. Applications should be made by letter. Moreover, a personal description and a very thorough history of the family as well as an outline of the purpose of the admission are essential. The applicant should also mention the possibility of prolonged assistance to the family after the stay in the Triangel. After this, an intake-discussion is held between the applying agency, the intake-staff of the Triangel, a representative of the (financial) local social service and other social services concerned.

The Orientation

During the application procedure the family in question is sometimes visited at its home, but in most cases it is also invited to pay an orientation visit to the Triangel. In this way, the motivation of the family for the Triangel can be tested, and the nature and limits of what can be offered are explained. The family can get an impression of the Triangel, look at the room where it will live, ask questions, share meals, *etc.* The impressions could lead to an abandoning of the request for treatment. If, however, the positive view dominates and the family dares to take the step, a date can be set for the arrival at the Triangel.

Many families who turn to the Triangel have been confronted with an overwhelming multiplicity of problems. They cannot see a way out of them. This may provide the explanation for their being able to take the rather drastic decision to leave home and settle in an institute like the Triangel with their entire family.

4. The Treatment

After five years of working, a more or less balanced treatment model has been established. This model is not rigid, but is developing. Its scientific basis and proof is a priority issue, for which the first steps already have been taken.

The Living Group

Each living group has at its disposal: a spacious living room, a kitchenette to make coffee, tea and cold meals, and several sleeping apartments. In this living group 3 or 4 families live together. As they arrive at different times, the composition of the group never remains the same for more than two or three months.

In the first weeks after the arrival of a family, the group workers to a large extent take care of the children, although the parents stay closely around. To be able to leave to others some apparently trivial tasks like taking the children to bed or to school, getting them dressed, keeping an eye upon them with meals, *etc.*, may relieve the parents and give them an opportunity to lift themselves out of the pressure of responsibilities and conflicts. This mainly applies to the first period of their stay.

Meanwhile, the husbands continue their work, and the children attend school (if possible, their own) and the small children go to an infant school or day-care center near the Triangel. The mothers are relieved of their routine household duties which in many cases were a stress factor. However, some contribution to the housework is required and the mothers may also participate in some non-obligatory tasks like cooking. On school and working days it is rather quiet in the Triangel. But in the afternoon, when everybody gets home, it becomes livelier. The rush hour is dinner time. The group workers, who collectively maintain a continuous service, take care of the functioning of the living group, together with the parents and older children. There are always two group workers present during rush hour.

The principal purpose of the group process is the creation of a climate for an unprejudiced acceptance of the 'self' and 'the other', an essential condition for a valuable relationship. By influencing and accompanying the individual clients in the totality of the group process, attempts are made to bring about conditions in which distorted family functions might be changed. It is highly desirable that all members of a family are present in the Triangel. During the stay, conflicts and stress tend to become less acute as a result of the fact that people from different families are present and participate in every day life. Moreover, working together with other people to achieve something may be an experience which opens new important perspectives to individuals and entire families.

The therapeutic measures can be distinguished into:

(a) Efforts to make alterations in *external circumstances:*
 — the search for a new house
 — assistance in finding suitable employment for the father/the mother, including re-training.
 — support in the finding of new or special schools for the children
 — stimulation of leisure time activities (membership of associations, sporting or hobby clubs)
 — advice in the solution of financial problems; family budgeting.
(b) Efforts to straighten out *the relations within the family:* Discussions are started, reaction de-conditioned, vicious circles broken. This may be done by
 — discussions in actual situations
 — examples by group workers and other group members how people react, for instance in playing with the children, dealing with aggression, *etc.*

The Triangel has a group of 22 *group workers* at its disposal. The principal selection criteria relate to personality and a high level of understanding, which are considered of greater importance than specific training or education. Many group workers, however, have a second vocation or even more. The Triangel itself provides an institution-directed in-service training.

The Psychological Department

The psychological department of the Triangel is also an instrument for influencing the family process. Besides testing the development levels of *the children,* the co-ordination of these levels in the actual constellations of their lives are examined. Children may also be prepared for new or difficult living conditions by intensive playing treatment or therapy. Parents may be kept informed, advised and guided by separate conversations about the development of their children and are sometimes taught how to play and get on with them. They may also have discussions about their own problems.

The psychological department also participates, together with the other members of the staff and the teams, in making a diagnosis of the situation of each family and advises about how to deal with them.

Conversational Contacts

Besides the conversations in the group there are the following opportunities for discussing problems with staff members:

333   Five Years of Child Abuse as a Symptom of Family Problems

a) Counseling Discussions

These are meant to keep a mirror to the client in order to enable him to recognize or to discover the source of his problems.

b) Couple Therapy

These are discussions between a couple and one, or usually two, therapists. The purpose may be the elucidation and improvement of the relationship. Sometimes elucidation may lead to the separation of the partners, in which cases they also receive help and guidance.

Movement Awareness Therapy

In the Triangel we have recently been using the movement awareness approach (boxing, symbolic-exercises, ball-games, balancing-exercises, *etc.*). In our opinion, this non-verbal way to come into contact with people is a valuable addition to the usual methods and in certain cases has favorable results. Clients asking for help are in most cases 'out of balance' in the widest possible sense. This condition has psychical, physical and social components and, therefore, adequate help has to focus on each of them. The principle that the client has to contribute in the determination of the treatment methods to be applied, also holds true for the movement area. In each situation and with each client the selection of the methods to be chosen will have to be made anew. In some cases — and here we think for instance of aggression therapy in cases of acute child abuse — movement awareness therapy, whether or not combined with other methods, may be an obvious course.

Activities and Recreation

Recreation by the members of the family is a part of our therapy too. Going to a movie, visiting a theater and taking a walk, have often been abandoned within their problems and misery. The same applies to visits to friends and relatives. In the Triangel there is a hobby cellar, where people may be at work on creative handicraft. This might be a springboard to more activities and contacts.

Medical Care and Massage

A team of family doctors deals with the medical aspects of the family during their stay in the Triangel. The family has a right to engage their own physician, but practical reasons often make this difficult or impossible. There also is a (part-time) masseur in the Triangel, to whom clients may appeal in cases of extreme tension or inability to relax.

Delegation of Care After Treatment in the Triangel

As a result of the intensive and specific concern with the families during their stay at the Triangel, the assignment of further care and support to other agencies has proved quite complex. It partly depends on whether the agency which made the application for admission of the family is in a position to take over again.

The Triangel considers its period of intramural treatment as a temporary 'thickening' of the usual lines of help, which, preferably, should not be interrupted. We, therefore, welcome the participation of the placing agencies in our discussions, and encourage them to continue their visits to the families during the stay at the Triangel. Some agencies, however, are not in a position to take over a family on discharge. For this reason, two of our workers are assigned to observe the families for some time after their departure from the Triangel. The duration of this period and the frequency of the contacts depend on the special needs of the families.

In this way the Triangel may remain present in the background and eventually come to help again. For the latter purpose we now use another building, in which families who are in need of a second — shorter and intensified — admission period can be helped in order to prevent their relapse into serious difficulties again.

To avoid misunderstanding, it should be noted that, in our treatment, we do not assume that a family should stay together under all circumstances. Diagnosis and treatment may lead to the conviction that a divorce or the housing of a child outside of the family should be recommended and carried out. Such a decision, however, should always be reached gradually and in close cooperation with the family members involved.

5. Some Specific Remarks on Child Abuse as a Symptom of Family Problems

We mentioned earlier that, in our opinion, child abuse
(i) is not a phenomenon by itself, but an alarming signal of a family in distress;
(ii) does not fill a special place among the problem syndromes indicating a disturbed family.

Consequently, the help given to child abuse families will have to follow the same lines and is subject to the same conditions as in other cases of family problems. In other words, we must not fight only the symptoms. It stands to reason that certain miserable circumstances call for an immediate and practical solution, but the background problems of family interaction are the heart of the matter.

Without derogating from this principle, we may offer some specific observations on child abuse based on our family treatment experience. The reason for doing so is that we feel that, among the signals through which families ask for help, child abuse is a very complicated as well as conspicuous one.

(1) In most cases child abuse is not the only symptom. It is accompanied by other signs of a family in distress, which may or may not be of an aggressive nature. As treatment progresses, the child abuse symptom generally disappears as other problems come to the fore.

(2) The opposite may also happen. Real threats of child abuse may be present although they had not as yet been carried out. These families would have been admitted to our institution for other reasons. Our experience is that this latent form of child abuse can also be treated effectively. This preventional aspect is quite important.

(3) In cases of child abuse especially, the obvious way to restore the balance in a family is often help of a practical kind. Bad housing conditions combined with problems such as unemployment, which result in the necessity to live together too closely with too few opportunities for individual activities or privacy may easily lead to explosions of violence towards family members. Concrete support by finding a job or a new house may be a very effective part of treatment.

(4) We have to consider the indignation and repugnance raised by child abuse which are very difficult to overcome. A family has to face these feelings in its everyday surroundings. We therefore consider it highly desirable to give a family which has committed child abuse in any acute form the opportunity to move to another neighborhood. Otherwise, a genuine new start is impossible.

(5) A reduction of the family's isolation may also constitute a distinct purpose of treatment. In our society the number of persons to whom feelings of love and affection may be directed is rather limited. This also applies to the range of people who may be the target for expressions of aggression and frustration. Efforts to increase the number of persons and objects to which family members may direct their feelings of affection, their interests or their attention, in short, the widening of their world may be an essential element of the aid to be rendered.

(6) The question whether in cases of child abuse it is better to treat the family at home or intramurally depends on which treatment would improve the family situation as a whole. In our experience, however, in cases of serious and repeated child abuse, intramural diagnosis of the situation has proved a necessity in order to gain a real insight into the interaction pattern within a family. In these cases the period of intramural treatment is only a more intensive phase of or, as we called it earlier, a 'thickening' in the line of help.

6. The Attitude of the Helper

In the help to be given, two aspects are of great importance:

In cases of child abuse especially, this fundamental condition is difficult to attain. In its shattered condition, the family has to deal with indignation and contempt from relatives, neighbors, school, *etc.* If agencies like the police, juvenile court, child protection services, *etc.* are involved, the sense of guilt and impotence will usually increase. These factors may tend to make the clients suspicious of helping people too. The helper will have to prepare himself for a laborious process during which the client has to be freed from his position of underdog. Only after this has happened will it be possible to enter into a relationship which is based on confidence and equality.

On the side of the helper this process requires insight and understanding, but no less willingness to make demands. The observance of a contract of aid has to be compelled like any other contract. The client should be held responsible whenever he does not keep appointments or other arrangements. In concrete terms, for the helper this means: Go to the client, phone him, shout at him if necessary, but let him hear something from you. In this way the idea of equality is put into words in a much more genuine form than is done by using the (benevolent but in essence rather aloof) phrase: You may at all times appeal to me again.

The Necessity to Work in a Multi-Disciplinary Team

In Holland, the Medical Referee for Child Abuse is a key figure in the process of help in cases of child abuse. After consulting him, people from the various disciplines involved should work together according to a plan. This necessity for integrated cooperation applies also to judicial authorities.

NOTES

1. Socio-Therapeutisch Instituut De Triangel, Lauriergracht 51-55, Amsterdam. Tel. 020 - 255363/64.
2. Laing, Ronald, *Family Patterns.* Boom: Meppel, 1972, p. 11.
3. Oudendijk, N.C., and van Rees, R., *The Family.* University of Utrecht, 1976.
4. Dasberg, Lea, *Bringing up by keeping down as a historical phenomenon.* (Transl. of Dutch title), Boom: Mepel, 1976.

Chapter 23

Legal Responses To Child Abuse*

Bernard M. Dickens†

1. Introduction

The lawyer's trained response to an incident of interpersonal violence is to isolate
its legally relevant elements and invoke the penal provisions of criminal law or the
compensatory machinery of civil litigation, or both. It is of no special significance
that assailant and victim are known to each other, nor that the victim is young.
It is not even of special note that the parties to the incident have shared a
continuing relationship, and while the victim's dependency upon the assailant may
serve to aggravate the enormity of the wrong, it does not change its legal
character. Assault of a child is in principle simply an assault; that is, a violation
of an individual's right to be left alone, to enjoy bodily integrity and appropriate
autonomy.

A parent's assault of his child, however, is different. Parents (and comparable
guardians)[1] are bound by positive duties actively to care for and to protect their
children, and the duty is greater the younger the child. They must make provision
for their safety and welfare, ensuring a secure physical, emotional and intellectual
environment in which their children can develop. Children are entitled to expect
such provision adequately to be made, and have an interest in preserving the
society of their parents and the instruction of their homes. Countervailing the
parent's duties are his rights.[2] He may impose reasonable discipline, including
corporal discipline, upon his child for the purpose of correction and training,[3] and
within broad limits compel compliance throughout the child's earlier formative
years with his philosophical, social, cultural and religious convictions. The law's
intrusion into this relation under the claim of protecting the child from the
parent may be at the cost of interests of both parent and child upon which society
places a high value.

Lawyers are accordingly inclined in general to be conservative, not necessarily in
the sense of being reactionary but in conserving the existing institution until its
unsuitability is adequately demonstrated. Courts usually guard against precipitate

---

* This article appeared in the Spring, 1978 issue of the *Family Law Quarterly*.
† Faculty of Law, University of Toronto, Canada.

intervention and inordinate responses, by themselves and by agencies committed to protecting children.

The problem of legal intervention is compounded by the child's continuing involvement with the parent and family. Traditional civil litigation may have little to offer to resolve improprieties, since to require a parent to transfer his money (should he have any) to the child by way of civil compensation for legal wrong may simply impoverish the family and secure no immediate restitution for the child. Damage awards for injuries inflicted upon children are usually tied into trusts by judicial order until the child's majority. Periodic payments during minority for medical treatment and, for instance, education, may be of advantage to the child, of course, but where a requirement of such payment is judicially imposed upon a parent, this may disproportionately favor the child in relation to other children in the same family, and disturb family cohesion no less than the family economy. Most jurisdictions in the United States respond to the disruptive or futile potential of such litigation by barring a child's right to civil action for compensation against his parent.[4] The British Law Commission has recommended application of the same policy to prenatal injury, except regarding motor vehicle accident claims, where money would come to the living child from a third party insurer.[5]

Similarly, criminal proceedings resulting in a fine will deplete family resources, depressing rather than enhancing the child victim's environment for desirable development within the family, and a custodial sentence, while possibly removing an immediate physical threat to the child, may damage his home-life and sense of emotional security with no less far-reaching consequences. The social effect of removing the parent from the child is, of course, to remove the child from the parent, and a judicial decision of the latter intention is considered to require the exercise of special sensitivities; their exercise is not part of the criminal sentencing process of an adult, however, even though ill-considered removal of the parent may make the child a double victim.

Nevertheless, the law may be obliged to intervene in a family upon evidence that the parent-child relation has become dysfunctional to the child's intolerable detriment or risk. Intervention may range from imposing supervision on parental management of the child in his home, through, for instance, a welfare agency or social worker, to terminating the legal and social bond between biological parent and child, opening the way to the child entering the charge of new 'parents', to become 'their' child. This chapter is designed to survey certain legal principles and problems that have been found to arise in structuring and operating such intervention, and to identify interests and values that will be affected, deliberately or otherwise, by legal determinations.

2. Defining Child Abuse

Attempts to tackle child abuse by legislation may be flawed by overambition. Outrage engendered by parental violence to children is hard to contain within a precise legal formula of assault, and flows over to condemn violence done to a child's reasonable expectations of care and to his need of a protective, nurturing and stimulating home-life. Legal definitions of child abuse and of children in need of care or protection have therefore gone beyond mere physical battery, and are inclined to include a guardian's physical neglect endangering a child's welfare. They also range from causing positive emotional damage, such as a depressed self-image and sense of worthlessness, to giving inadequate affection or attention, so as to induce emotional deprivation and lack of opportunity to develop relationships. The will to attack physical and emotional abuse of children at every point, both positive and negative, generates interlocked schemes of compulsory reporting, institutional or agency intervention to rescue children at risk, judicial proceedings to arrange a child's supervision in his home or outside, and proceedings permanently to sever the parent-child link. Each of these purposes may require a separate or limited definition of child abuse, and the tendency to make a single verbal formula serve this variety of purposes may result in legal or administrative frustration or overreaching.

A paradox of legal definition is that the more comprehensive it appears, the less it may actually permit to be achieved. All-embracing definition may decay into mere description. Courts, especially when asked to intervene in protected human relations such as exist between parents and child and in an individual's allegiance to his religion or philosophy, require precision. The precisely-sharpened legal scalpel may enter where the blunt-edged hatchet has no access, and the tendency to legislate a rude hatchet attack upon abusive parents may be self-defeating. Widely phrased formulae may become applicable to acts and persons they were not intended or expected to cover, but penal or deprivatory laws in particular should not cover less culpable behavior equally with the heinous conduct at which they are aimed.[6] A court may therefore treat a broad definition with caution, recognizing that indiscriminate words may not be sufficiently related to the specific incident or person charged. The court may refine distinctions to meet the legislature's supposed true intention. It is a long-standing canon of statutory construction that penal and deprivatory provisions are to be read restrictively, to impinge upon individual liberty of action only to a minimal degree consistent with the purpose and policy of the enactment. In addition, the court may be able to rule the enactment improperly vague, and decline to enforce it on that ground.[7]

The opposing risk to a court being too hard to persuade of legislation's applicability to a specific case or incident, namely that the court is too easily persuaded, is no more acceptable. Judicial overreaching can intervene in a child's home-life upon socially or developmentally inadequate indications, and protectively intended legislation can threaten the right to family security of no less children than it may rescue.

The danger of legislative excess becomes apparent when the cultural content of child abuse is recognized. In the absence of state-established standards for parenthood,[8] those who the influential bulk of a given society predetermines are unfit for the responsibilities of parenthood may procreate their kind. The conditions in which a child of such parents is situated may, however, be popularly (and judicially) comprehended by a crude stereotype or at best by a statistically composed profile or typology, rather than upon their individual merits.[9] Thus, the child-rearing patterns of an identifiable minority group within a defined society, perhaps promoting juvenile self-reliance at an earlier age or to a stricter level than in the prevailing, indulgent population, or permitting overt sexuality generally considered precocious, or denying opportunities for autonomy generally permitted, may lead to misguided and culturally insensitive interventions. Similarly, the accommodations the materially deprived must make to their poverty may deny their children what the wider community considers the minimum resources of childhood, and intervention may more easily take the form of removing particular children to a better material environment rather than of social resource reallocation to alleviate this effect of poverty while maintaining the home intact.

Almost invariably, reference is made in legislated definitions of an abused child, or a child in need of care or protection, to danger to his moral welfare. Tests of morality in western and westernized countries tend to center upon sexual activity, and exposure of young girls to the risk of pregnancy certainly gives this approach a relevant cutting edge, but use of the expression further shows how definitions of child abuse can drift into vagueness and subjectivity. It also opens the way to a general misconception of assessing the condition of the child upon the basis not of the child's formulating experiences but of what the parent has done. This incident-oriented basis for intervention in the parent-child relation may do grave injustice and injury to both, particularly when centered upon isolated occurrences, and become the instrument of censorious oppression that tolerates neither unorthodoxy nor lapse.[10]

Sexual abuse of children by their guardians is particularly difficult to approach dispassionately. Particular instances may so outrage normal sensibilities as to trigger public, institutional and judicial reactions of repugnance themselves bordering on violence. Police authorities in particular may be inclined to characterize sexual offences by guardians not as child abuse at all, in which child welfare agencies have a role to play in management and remedy, but as the very kind of viciously exploitive behavior that heavy punishment can deter. Nevertheless, distinctions may need to be drawn, for instance between behavior that abuses a child's body and that which abuses the child's affection in a way it may not perceive, such as indecent fondling. Incest is often included in the category of offences of violence,[11] and this may be appropriate in that a male parent's sexual use of an immature and dependent female does violence to our sense of propriety and care. Insofar as incest is consensual, however, as opposed to rape, it involves no use of force, and is an act of violence only by metaphor. Sexual offences against children are clearly forms of child abuse, but the tendency to treat them in a special category may be a projection of special public attitudes towards sexuality onto incidents that, from the child's perspective, may not have a violent quality nor create the psychological effects of violence. A number of such offences, although highlighted by penal laws as distinctive and heinous, may properly be left to the domestic or other civil management of child welfare agencies.

An analysis by Sanford Katz of typical United States laws on children in need of judicial protection reveals the various legislated tests combinations of which have been employed by the several states.[12] A child may be in need of protection:

(1) When the child lacks parental care because of its parent's fault or its parent's mental or physical disability.
(2) When a parent refuses or neglects to provide for a child's needs.

(3) When a parent has abandoned a child.

(4) When a child's home, by reason of neglect, cruelty or depravity of its parents, is unfit.

(5) When a parent refuses to provide for a child's moral needs.

(6) When a parent refuses to provide for a child's mental needs.

(7) When a child's best interests are not being met.[13]

(8) When a child's environment, behavior or associations are injurious to it.

(9) When a child begs, receives alms or sings in the street for money.

(10) When a child associates with disreputable or immoral people or lives in a house of ill repute.

(11) When a child is found or employed in a bar.

(12) When a child's occupation is dangerous or when it is working contrary to the child labor laws.

(13) When a child is living in an unlicensed foster home or has been placed by its parents in a way detrimental to it or contrary to law.

(14) When a child's conduct is delinquent as a result of parental neglect.

(15) When a child is in danger of being brought up to lead an idle, dissolute or immoral life.

(16) When a mother is unmarried and without adequate provision for the care and support of her child.

(17) When a parent, or another with the parent's consent, performs an immoral or illegal act before a child.

(18) When a parent habitually uses profane language in front of a child.

This list of typical statutory provisions demonstrates the breadth, subjectivity, cultural and aesthetic components of the legislated concept of child abuse. In Canada, for instance, Ontario's Child Welfare Act[14] defines a "child in need of protection" in section 20(1)(b) in eleven operative sub-clauses covered by typical provisions 2-6, 8-10 and 14 above. In addition, sub-clause (viii) of the Ontario enactment covers "a child whose parent is unable to control him", sub-clause (ix) refers to "a child who, without sufficient cause, habitually absents himself from his home or school", and sub-clause (xi) renders in need of protection "a child whose emotional or mental development is endangered because of emotional rejection or deprivation of affection by the person in whose charge he is".

In contrast, the Children and Young Persons Act 1969[15] relevant to England defines a child as liable to care proceedings, under section 1(2):

If the court before which a child or young person is brought under this section is of the opinion that any of the following conditions is satisfied with respect to him, that is to say —
(a) his proper development is being avoidably prevented or neglected or his health is being avoidably impaired or neglected or he is being ill-treated; or
(b) it is probable that the condition set out in the preceding paragraph will be satisfied in his case, having regard to the fact that the court or another court has found that that condition is or was satisfied in the case of another child or young person who is or was a member of the household to which he belongs; or
(c) he is exposed to moral danger; or
(d) he is beyond the control of his parent or guardian; or
(e) he is of compulsory school age within the meaning of the Education Act 1944 and is not receiving efficient full-time education suitable to his age, ability and aptitude; or
(f) he is guilty of an offence, excluding homicide, and also that he is in need of care or control which he is unlikely to receive unless the court makes an order under this section.

3. Identifying Child Abuse

Identification of child abuse is a function of its definition, of course, in that the broader the law tolerates its definition to be, the greater is the ease of identification. The negative side of a broad, legally effective definition, however, is that it creates ease of misidentification, and of possibly oppressive and destructive intrusive excesses. Law requires a high degree of normative definition and predictability, so that the rational individual can plan his conduct to fall within the meaning of its terms, ensuring that he does not offend standards the law requires him to maintain. Further, evenness in enforcement of the law is a precondition to its potential for achieving justice, in the sense of treating alike not only complainant and defendant, but also complainant and complainant and defendant and defendant. When intervention in the parent-child relation may be made upon amorphous indications, however, inconsistency and idiosyncrasy may be given too much play, and misguided and vexatious use of the law may become possible.

While the care and vigilance of relatives, neighbors and benign strangers have much to offer the cause of child protection, and are to be both encouraged and protected, it may appear that a systematic legal approach to child abuse cannot give primacy to reliance upon lay initiative. Child abuse must be rendered identifiable by tests that are meaningful to those with a trained competence in fields of child welfare and protection, and a professional or official duty of care.[16] Identification should be through the more objectively assessed condition and circumstances of each child, upon which professional disciplines permit practitioners a level of consensus, rather than through such incidents as parental performance of an illegal or immoral act,[17] or finding a child in a bar.[18]

Emotional abuse or mismanagement of a child, for instance, may have expression in the child's physiological failure to thrive, or in his psychological maladjustment. These pathologic conditions are capable of objective demonstration by reference to standards, and while parents or guardians will almost invariably lack the ability themselves to measure their child by these standards, they have access in most developed communities, by voluntary and involuntary means, to the specialists whose conclusions and recommendations their child's welfare requires them to heed. Parental refusal or failure to follow an advised remedial program may represent such a risk to the child's future as to justify legal intervention.[19]

Such professionals as physicians, nurses, social workers, day-care attendants and, regarding the older child, schoolteachers may be considered in the forefront of identification of child abuse. It is therefore realistic for legal schemes addressed to control of child abuse to gear their provisions to the skills and functions of such specialists, whether they operate in the private sector of social organization as independent practitioners or through private agencies or in the public sector, for example as public hospital employees or officers of governmental agencies concerned with, for instance, school health services or social welfare. Similarly, legal implementation of social policy may be designed to serve child protection through recourse to professional expertise. The French policy of making financial child-support grants to families, for instance, is implemented not by rendering payments automatically through postal or banking facilities but by channelling grants through child health clinics, to which children must be regularly presented for inspection as a precondition of child-support payment.

The timing of legal intervention in an abusive setting raises not just practical problems but also philosophical issues affecting the interaction of security and liberty. A child's security against abuse or neglect clearly requires a prompt response to an identified abusive condition, but may also justify earlier action by way of anticipation. A long-standing and praiseworthy judicial attitude is that "The courts are never called upon to wait until physical injuries have been received or minds unhinged. It is sufficient if there be a reasonable apprehension that such things will happen, and the courts should interfere before they have happened if that be possible".[20] Prospective or anticipatory intervention to protect a child may, however, unduly impinge upon the liberty of parents to maintain undisturbed the integrity of their home-life.

The law may, by recourse to its commonplace doctrine, achieve a compromise between violating the sanctity of a child's domestic environment in anticipation of abuse and standing passively by until a child has been adequately hurt to compel rescue or at least to make intervention clearly justifiable. Courts may identify the present fact of abuse or need of protection on the traditional civil standard of proof,[21] established on a balance of probability, but require a claim for anticipatory action to be made out to the higher standard of criminal proceedings, in which the initiating party must establish his case beyond reasonable doubt. Thus, when a child appears beyond reasonable doubt to be at risk of abuse, including neglect, judicial intervention may be permitted even when no identifiable harm has yet occurred. Relevant evidence may exist in the earlier judicial finding of abuse of another child of the household.[22]

4. Reporting Child Abuse

It is very widely, if not universally, agreed that all persons should be permitted to report in good faith their reasonable suspicions of child abuse to appropriate authorities and agencies, with protection against civil and criminal liability for non-malicious even if erroneous reporting. In 1977 the House of Lords, the highest English court, recognized this principle[23] when it declined on policy grounds to compel the National Society for the Prevention of Cruelty to Children to disclose to a potential plaintiff the name of its informant against whom defamation proceedings were intended to be brought. The 'good faith' qualification is not insignificant, however, since disturbed relationships may generate malicious allegations of abuse by one parent, marital partner or other child guardian or former child guardian against another.

Issues of legislative concern are whether reporting powers should be enacted into legal duties, who should be bound by any such duties, what should be reported and to whom, and what rights should be acknowledged for those reported.[24] The argument that every person has a civic and moral duty to disclose knowledge of crime is not adequately specific or enforceable to obviate the need for express child abuse reporting laws, and professional persons such as doctors and social workers may invoke ethical requirements of confidentiality to show a duty of non-disclosure.

Such professionals face a dilemma, however, since they may have independent legal obligations to children, and their failure adequately to respond to knowledge of children's danger may make them liable if predictable injury is subsequently suffered. The Californian case of *Landeros v. Flood*[25] was argued upon local statutes, but it contains illustration of basic Common law reasoning that shows a physician in particular to have a potential duty of care to a child-patient, and so to be potentially liable to the child whose risk of future injury he foresees,[26] but which, through non-reporting, he fails to act appropriately to prevent. The case of *Tarasoff v. Regents of the University of California* further confirms that a professional conflict between duties of confidentiality to a patient and of care to another identifiable (non-patient) party at risk of grave harm through the patient must be resolved in favor of the party at risk. The physician must therefore favor protection of a child over protection of confidentiality of a potential assailant of the child,[27] and may discharge his prior duty by appropriate reporting. Accordingly, reporting the risk to an agency appointed or equipped to receive such a report, whether under statute or otherwise, may protect the physician as well as the child.

Self-reporting has a role to play in child abuse, but to be feasible it requires the consequence to be non-penal, aimed at helping the self-reporting abusive guardian of a child to face his problem and distressing truths about himself, and for instance to undertake the program he is offered of sensitization to the child's needs and of education to meet those needs. If authorities are visibly poised to prosecute all cases indentified without discrimination, perhaps because of their sense of public pressure upon them to strike incisively at abusive parents as a class, or because of an internal dynamic fashioned by the experience of handling pathetic and damaged victims of abuse, they may deter self-reporting by guardians who gain insight into their terrible potential for violence or harmful neglect triggered by crises they know are likely to recur. Clearly, the legal liability of self-reporting abusive guardians is no less than that of guardians reported by others or otherwise detected, but an appeal for help may betoken a capacity for responding to professional attention that should not be frustrated or deterred.[28]

While self-reporting is to be promoted, the practical problem to be faced in legislation is whether to bind all persons to report child abuse, on a broad or restricted definition of abuse, or to select particular persons for legal duties, or, indeed, whether to bind no-one but simply to encourage everyone. The absence of a reporting law is not uncommon, although this position tends to exist by default rather than by deliberate legislative decision. There is no specific reporting law in the United Kingdom, for instance,[29] and at present, while Ontario's Child Welfare Act provides that "Every person having information of the abandonment, desertion, physical ill-treatment or need for protection of a child shall report the information to a children's aid society or Crown attorney",[30] and that "notwithstanding that the information is confidential or privileged . . . no action shall be instituted against the informant unless giving of the information is done maliciously or without reasonable and probably cause",[31] Ontario statutes contain no sanction for non-reporting.[32]

Sanctioning non-reporting compels determination of whether to bind everyone or only those, for instance, possessed of special skills, opportunities for detection or social responsibilities. It has been seen that professionals and others may be bound by existing duties under the general civil law,[33] and they may be liable to professional discipline for unethical or incompetent conduct, but a parallel system of legislated criminal sanctioning has a higher public profile and speaks more clearly of society's decision that child abuse is not a private or domestic peccadillo or perversion protected by principles of confidentiality but a grave matter calling for public scrutiny and perhaps for intervention by agencies of the state. It may be observed, however, that enacting criminal sanctions serves a more sophisticated criminological function than simply paving the way to prosecutions; indeed, a long-term sequence of prosecutions for non-reporting would suggest not that enactment of sanctions was sound policy, but rather that it was ineffective to control the conduct it was designed to limit. The purpose of such legislation may best be to educate, direct and to reinforce good intentions, subject perhaps to an occasional symbolic or admonitory prosecution to keep professionals alert to their responsibility. News of proceedings would be circulated in professional journals, and the requirement of the law would thereby be emphasized. Many professionals are lax about reporting, moreover, because they are reluctant to become involved in legal procedures. It is not cynical to convert this reluctance into a positive force by making personal involvement with the law appear more imminent and fearful for not reporting than for reporting.

The objection that compulsory reporting will deter guardians from presenting their injured children for medical attention and other help is more intuitive than empirical. The claim that compulsory reporting law would be counter-productive has never been proven by statistics in a field much given to statistical research, and anecdotal evidence tends to the contrary, although by definition non-presenting abusive guardians may not furnish materials for statistics or anecdote. Positive abuse of children tends to be triggered by crises, and when these have passed parents show concern to obtain treatment. The eminent authority, Monrad G. Paulsen, has observed that, "The number of parents who are willing to risk the life of their child by not seeking medical help is likely to be small. Many of those who inflict deliberate injury in moments of tension, high passion or psychological imbalance will respond to a child's obvious need in later, calmer times."[34] Some have even suggested, indeed, that "the fact that the physician is legally mandated to report a case of suspected child abuse should also remove, or at least reduce, the parent's resentment,"[35] and in any event it should remove or reduce the physician's embarrassment.

Regarding the ambit of the reporting duty, a requirement that 'any person' or 'every person' with knowledge of child abuse should so report may be opposed as diluting rather than accentuating the duty, permitting one individual to depend upon the duty and enterprise of another. A more specifically identified professional or officer may feel duly burdened in the absence of such relief, and come to consider that reporting is an attribute of his professional or official function. The range of obligated professionals has widened in the practice of many American states, and in recent years increasing numbers of non-health-care professionals have been mandated to report. Distilling this experience to formulate their Model Child Abuse and Neglect Reporting Law, Alan Sussman and Stephan J. Cohen proposed in s. 3 that:

Any physician, nurse, dentist, optometrist, medical examiner or coroner, or any other medical or mental health professional, Christian Science practitioner, religious healer, school teacher or counselor, social or public assistance worker, child care worker in any day care center or child caring institution, police or law enforcement officer having reasonable cause to suspect that a child coming before him in his official or professional capacity is abused shall be required to report.[36]

This degree of specification creates the danger of exonerating professionals not listed. Pharmacists, for instance, may be approached by abusive parents wanting something for their injured or distressed children. An alternative is to provide a formula for compulsory reporting, applicable for instance, to "every person gaining reasonable cause to suspect abuse of a child encountered in the course of professional or official activities." Some professionals and officers are clearly within this formula, and persons such as relatives and neighbors are clearly not. The position of marginal cases may be determined by judicial interpretation, statements of administrative policy (as judicially regulated) and the ethical rulings of professional organizations. There may be little practical disadvantage and no strong theoretical objection to leaving this area of obligation with a slightly indeterminate edge.

To require reporting of 'abuse' of a child may be unacceptably vague. While the concept of abuse may properly be reasonably accommodating for purposes of administrative and judicial intervention, it may have to be narrowed for the purpose of compulsory reporting. Despite the breadth of employed definitions indicated by Sanford Katz,[37] Sussman and Cohen's concern specifically with reporting led them to the restricted definitions that:[38]

An abused child shall mean a person under eighteen years of age who is suffering from serious physical harm, or sexual molestation, caused by those responsible for his care or others exercising temporary or permanent control over the child,

and that a neglected child shall mean one:

whose physical and mental condition is seriously impaired as a result of the failure of those responsible for his care or others exercising temporary or permanent control over the child to provide adequate food, shelter, clothing, physical protection or medical care necessary to sustain the life or health of the child.[39]

The objective components of these tests are particularly capable of assessment by medical personnel. It may be an unnecessary and limiting element of the definitions, however, that they go beyond the medically identifiable condition of the child and require conclusions of human causation, namely that the child's condition was caused by those responsible for his care. It may be adequate to require the fact of the child's endangered condition to be reported, leaving the authorities receiving the report to trace causation as part of their function of planning care and protection. It may be emphasized, however, that the report concerns the child's condition, and not simply and isolated event or incident, although a single incident of severe physical harm or sexual molestation may strongly indicate the presence of such a condition.

The agency to receive reports will be determined by a reporting law, but its selection is a matter of no legal significance, and is made as a matter of adminstrative management. Most juridictions employ child welfare agencies to receive and immediately respond to reports made, whether by telephone, such as by a 24 hour 'hot line', in writing or otherwise. Police authorities, to which lay people may be inclined to have resort, are only infrequently employed in legislation to receive reports, although the Ontario Child Welfare Act specifies that reports are to be made to a children's aid society or to a Crown attorney, who acts as the prosecuting branch of the police service. Since Crown attorneys have been shown to test evidence simply in terms of Criminal Code provisions, and to liaise poorly with children's aid societies in cases not to be prosecuted,[40] there is a case for confining the receipt of reports to such welfare and protection agencies.

Penalties for non-reporting may justifiably be relatively minor, since the fact that they exist may be expected to achieve the intended deterrent and educative effect upon the professionals and officials at whom they are directed rather than the fact that penalties are heavy. This may be socially objectionable, however, in seeming to trivialize the reporting duty as against other duties backed by sanctions, and may appear improperly to discriminate in favor of 'white collar' offenders, and afford greatest relief from liability to a heavy fine to those most able to bear the fine. Many jurisdictions make non-reporting simply a summary offence or a misdemeanour, the maximum punishment for which is governed by the general law without special regard to child abuse. In this way, punishment may include an imprisonment alternative to the ubiquitous fine, although on its own merits non-reporting of child abuse by professionals or officials may seem not to warrant this sanction.

Only fines can be applied where liability for failing to report attaches not just to individuals but also to institutions, such as hospitals or agencies. United States' laws often provide for institutions to be fined, which may influence private bodies run for profit and charities having to raise running costs by donations, but to fine public agencies appears a pointless sanction even without regard to statutory immunities for governmental institutions, since it may simply transfer public funds from one pocket to another.

5. Judicial Responses to Child Abuse

Penal Responses

Every criminal suspect and adequately demonstrated or self-confessed offender is at the disposal of a prosecutor as to whether or not a charge is brought, and the exercise of prosecutorial discretion is a growing theme in legal literature.[41] Similarly, institutionalization of the practice of non-prosecution in public policies of diversion of offenders from the criminal justice process is a developing trend.[42] Clearly, the more grave the offence, the less discretion the prosecutor has about declining to bring it to court. Murder, for instance, is almost invariably non-negotiable, whereas at the other end of the criminal spectrum a minor or technical assault would be almost pointless to pursue in itself, although prosecution and the threat of prosecution might be a strategy of managing a more complex situation; a leader of a politically-inspired incident may be charged on a technical count, for instance, such as common assault of a police officer. The varieties of child abuse often afford considerable choice not only regarding whether or not to charge, but also whether to characterize the circumstances in a grave light, fit for condign punishment, or as an isolated and inconsequential incident that can properly be the subject of no more than a formal or informal caution.[43]

The essence of the wrong of child abuse is its pervasive threat to the child's environment for healthy and secure development, in primarily physical, mental, educational, sexual and social regards. Accordingly, even when parental inadequacy does not express itself in an episode or incident adverse to any of the child's developmental interests, legal intervention in the child's unpromising circumstances may still be justifiable for protective purposes. Civil intervention, leading to civil judicial care or protection proceedings, serves this purpose. When a damaging or threatening episode or incident has occurred, however, the condition of criminal prosecution may be satisfied. Then, a prosecutor will have to determine whether alternative solutions exist for achieving the child's welfare or for curbing the child-guardian's harmful propensity. Voluntary parental agreement to place the child in care by civil process, for example, may meet the circumstances to his satisfaction, possibly reached in consultation with child welfare authorities, or parental submission to mental health care, on a voluntary or involuntary basis, may seem an appropriate remedy.

Where no alternative to prosecution exists, however, because of the enormity of the outrage upon the child or, for instance, the unavailability of suitable alternative regimes, due to the lack of informal corrective facilities or the dire extent of the parent's needs, conviction of the offender will present a judge with the issue of choice of sentence.[44]

A judge may have access to a range of pre-sentence reports, including psychiatric and social reports, although he cannot always be required to have resort to them, and only very rarely indeed can he be required to follow the direction in which they tend when he does decide to call for their assistance. At the point of sentence, furthermore, he usually has a much more narrow variety of disposals open to him than is available to a prosecutor in considering the alternatives for diversion from the path of prosecution. Although the way is being opened to enriching the range of judicial dispositions in general cases through the addition of, for instance, social service orders and week-end or spare time imprisonment, most often the basic choice will be between a custodial or non-custodial sentence, the latter often meaning a fine or an order for release subject to conditions by which the convicted offender agrees to abide for a time period up to a legislatively specified maximum.

The modern ideal of penology is individualization (or 'individuation') in the sense of concentrating primarily on the condition and needs of the offender; the need of a public example is acknowledged and protection of the public and, under more recent doctrine, the reasonable expectations of the victims are also taken into account, but the judge will determine the type and extent of sentence primarily by reference to the individual offender. Sentencing is not a mechanical process of applying the traditional tariff of punishment impersonally. A tariff may exist, and a judge may be expected to give specific reasons before he departs from its limits, but the utilitarian concept that the punishment should fit the crime is giving way to the realization that the subject of punishment is not a crime but a criminal, which brings out the human dimensions of the application of punishment.[45] The humane quality of criminal disposition consists in its rehabilitative component, although empirical evidence of the effects of particularly custodial dispositions has somewhat discredited the rehabilitative theory; some authorities, indeed, consider it a success if an offender emerges from a medium-term custodial experience no more anti-social than when he was committed to it.

Child abusers cannot be trained or conditioned while in penal custody to meet the demands of normal domestic life upon release, including the requirements of safe and responsible child-rearing, and time spent in the dependent and decision-free environment of custody does nothing to improve the offender's parenting skills. A judge imposing custodial sentence, unless realistically confident of its rehabilitative effects or the high quality of after-care upon release, may therefore purchase the child's security from the offender's immediate abuse at the cost of the child's longer-term interest in maintaining the offender as a member of the household and family. Depending upon the strength of the family's structure, the sacrifice of longer-term interests to the needs of immediate security may in particular cases be worthwhile, but a judge must see that in imposing a custodial sentence, he is achieving inescapable and not necessarily beneficial effects upon the offender's family. It does not follow that a parent guilty of an abusive incident, committed perhaps in a crisis or as a culmination of intolerable stress, is unsuitable to be in charge of the child, or that the child's welfare requires his separation from the parent. It cannot be guaranteed at sentence, however, that a judge will be adequately informed of or responsive to interests of members of the offender's family, since they are not before the court, except perhaps as victims, and their objectively assessed prospects and welfare needs may be no more influential upon him than their subjective preferences.

Custodial punishment of an abusive parent may therefore be at variance with promotion or preservation of important interests of others, including a victim, in a way to which a court cannot be compelled to attend. Obviously, situations arise in which abusive conduct warrants a severe judicial response without regard to its effects upon the offender's family cohesiveness, and not uncommonly criminal proceedings will generate parallel protection proceedings to monitor or sever the parent-child association.[46] Equally, however, punishment of offenders is not always compatible with victims' best interests where offender and victim share a continuing relationship, and there are criminally abusive circumstances in which the victim's needs have a claim to respect and even to priority over punishment of an adult offender. The dilemma of selecting between the competing demands of punishment offenders and protection of victims' general and long-term interests is acute, and experience shows it not always to be uniformly or satisfactorily resolved.

Protective Responses

Protection proceedings need not be contentious, since parents may concede their child to be in need of care or protection; indeed, in the context of the English Children and Young Persons Act, parents have been known to take the initiative to obtain a finding that their child is beyond control,[47] especially when an older female child persists in keeping company the parents disapprove of. The power of parents so to apply judicial control to their child is not necessarily always wisely used, and judges bear a responsibility in hearing such consensual cases to be vigilant of the child's interests. Since all adults concerned may have agreed in predetermining the issue, and require the court simply to set the seal of its formal approval upon the terms agreed, the only officer capable of protecting the unrepresented child's independent interests may be the judge. This is no less the case where, for instance, a child welfare agency has prevailed upon perhaps somewhat timorous parents, or a single parent, to accept the agency's assessment of the child's needs, and to concur in, or not to resist, an application for a care or protection order the agency decides to bring. A judge may be obliged, through recourse to such an officer as an Official Guardian, Official Solicitor or Law Guardian[48] to render more contentious any protection proceedings a child's parents bring, permit or otherwise fail to contest.

When a child is shown to be in need of care or protection, judicially ordered intervention may occur in principle at three levels; the general *status quo* may be preserved but fall under official supervision, the child may be temporarily removed from parental care and placed under supervision or, at the extreme, the parental tie may be severed and the child placed in the care and disposal, for instance by way of adoption, of an official agency. The Ontario Child Welfare Act[49] expresses the range in section 26, which provides that:

Where the [family court] judge finds the child to be a child in need of protection, he shall make an order,

(a) that the child be placed with or returned to his parent or other person subject to supervision by the children's aid society for a period of not less than six months and not more than twelve months . . .; or
(b) that the child be made a ward of and committed to the care and custody of the children's aid society . . . for such period, not exceeding twelve months, as in the circumstances of the case he considers advisable[50]; or
(c) that the child be made a ward of the Crown until the wardship is terminated . . . and that the child be committed to the care of the children's aid society . . .

It is important to distinguish the assessment of the abused child's circumstances from the availability of child welfare agency resources. A child is not shown in need of protection simply because an agency can satisfy a judge that it can offer the child preferable circumstances to those provided by the parents. Before the question of disposition can arise, a child must be shown to be in need of protection or care according to objective standards. Judicial recognition of the good intentions and sincere concern of welfare personnel and of their capacity to improve the child's material and other conditions of life is not in itself a sufficient basis for intervention between parent and child.

Dispositions of particular children will be sought by protective agencies according to their assessment of the requirements of the particular situation, and they will act according to their professional judgment rather than in accordance with any legally established prescription. The role of the law is really confined to testing the case argued and to ensuring observance of due process.[51] When parental default, for instance of physical control or of material provision for their child, appears capable of remedy within the home, such as by education and training, or medical or mental health care (of parent or child), an order for domestic supervision may be adequate for the child's protection and future welfare. A principle of minimal intervention may be preferred, since this preserves maximum integrity of the domestic environment and emphasizes parental duties of self-reliance and of responsibility for protection of their child.

Servicing a home supervision order may be very demanding, however, upon scarce agency funds and personnel, and an agency may find it more economic of resources to have the child removed from the home and placed in care of the agency, in its own residential facility or with trusted foster parents. This may not necessarily serve the child's interests, however, since a child needs some continuity and intimacy in adult relationships. The effects of maternal deprivation and under-stimulation in institutionalized children have been long observed,[52] for instance, and while institutions plan to counteract these effects in designing their programs, they may not necessarily present to a court considering disposition of a child the record of their success.

When it is proposed that a child be removed from his home for relocation in a setting of superior care, a court is entitled to an estimate of how much better that care is likely to prove in overall terms, bearing in mind the child's needs not only of the protection of a safe, abuse-free environment, but also of personally supportive, enriching and affectionate adult relationships. Stereotypes of abusive parents must be forsaken, since such parents do not necessarily fail to provide such relationships even when prone to occasional outbursts of intolerable violence; similarly, institutional homes do not invariably nurture each ward's individual personality, and not every child responds to, or can be lodged with, foster parents. There is a disturbingly high number of abusive incidents, moreover, attributable to foster parents, who respond to the same human pressures as natural parents.[53]

An application to sever the parent-child link requires the most scrupulous attention to both the substance and form of the proceedings, since they may so finally affect the interests of both parent and child. The urge to disqualify the adult from the rights of parenthood must be curbed by the duty not summarily to terminate the child's interests in affiliation. Too much can be made, and traditionally has been made by courts of law, of the dispositive influence of biology and genealogy,[54] but ties of social fact may exert a pressure in favor of continuity. Courts should therefore require exhaustion of all prospects of preserving social relationships of any depth of feeling or experience before they cast a child into a new and strange environment, and should not act upon nothing more than an institutionally borne and judicially shared hope that his future will be more favorable. The situation should be close to requiring rescue of the child before this step be taken unless, of course, the child has been abandoned in law or fact. In particular, no severance should be made in circumstances of abuse that can be relieved by institutional or state redeployment of resources, such as where the underlying problem of the family under consideration is poverty.[55]

While abuse may be better understood as a pervasive condition than as an isolated incident, courts of both criminal and protective jurisdiction are concerned with individual acts of violence whose legal attribution to parents conditions legal consequences. Many of such acts occur, however, in domestic or other private settings and are not independently witnessed. They may be seen by a spouse and by other children of the family but, depending on the nature of the act in question, a legal spouse may not be a competent witness in criminal proceedings, and the testimony of young children is not easily admitted in courts of law, and has decreasing cogency with passage of time since the events attested. Without regard to the desirability of compelling children to testify against their parents in penal proceedings, legal rules on receiving sworn and unsworn testimony from children can be complex, and requirements for corroboration introduce an element of both high legalism and uncertainty that may make a prosecutor and a protective agency reluctant to be dependent upon such testimony.

The disability of lawful spouses to testify against each other originated in interaction of the historic concept of unity of husband and wife and the individual privilege against self-incrimination, but it has evolved in recognition of the need of domestic cohesiveness. In principle, the bar is absolute, and excludes from testifying even the willing spouse. Where the family appears not to be cohesive, however, such as where one spouse is alleged to have assaulted the other or a child of the family, the testimonial barrier may be dysfunctional, and a number of legal systems permit, and no less a number may compel, one spouse to give evidence in such cases against the other.[56] Legal practice is not uniform, however, and in Canada, for instance, while a spouse can be compelled to testify regarding sexual offences against children by the other,[57] there is no comparable power regarding assault, even when it kills. Reform of this position has been recommended,[58] but not implemented to date.

In the absence of admissible evidence from witnesses of violence, those instigating legal proceedings may be driven to circumstantial evidence to show the non-accidental origin of a child's injury, and to defeat explanations a parent may offer. This in itself is not enough, however, since showing the injury was not accidental does not show on a balance of probability, and even less beyond reasonable doubt, that a particular adult caused it. Equally, theorizing as to how the suspect could have caused the injury does not adequately show that he did.

Evidentiary rules in both criminal and civil courts may preclude reference to a suspect's past convictions for violence, whether against children or otherwise, and statistical, sociological, psychological or psychiatric evidence of the suspect falling within the profile of a child-abuser are clearly inadmissible as being neither probative nor cogent. If the suspect, by way of defence, raises such issues to show the unlikelihood of his violence or to show another, notably the domestic partner, to be more liable to acts of violence, the prosecutor or applicant for a protective order may have recourse to comparable evidence in rebuttal, but normally such evidence cannot be used to demonstrate a person's liability for a specific act of violence. The effect of the need to rely upon circumstantial evidence is shown in a

1973 report on child abuse in the province of Ontario. Regarding 1,049 children hospitalized in the 1968-70 period, it noted that, 'Minimum use was made of the Courts in prosecuting child abusers. Charges were laid in the abuse of only 158 children. Convictions were obtained in almost half of the cases. Lack of substantiating evidence was the major reason for most of the dismissals or withdrawals of charges."[59]

A suspect may, of course, be innocent in fact as well as by legal inference of acquittal or judicial refusal of a protective order, but a high proportion of deaths from child abuse occurs in homes of which a child welfare agency already has evidence of a parent's abusive propensity.[60] A case may therefore be made for putting some burden upon parents in protection proceedings[61] to explain their conduct in the light of the adverse evidence, namely their child's non-accidental injury. This would have the effect of easing the burden of proof upon authorities initiating protection proceedings, but its function would be better to serve the needs of children who have actually been injured and who remain at apparent risk.

Some United States' courts accordingly require an applicant for a protection order to show only that a child has suffered serious injury while under parental custody, and the parent is then required satisfactorily to excuse or explain the injury.[62] In the absence of such excuse or explanation, a court has a discretion to find the child in need of protection by appropriate order. Other courts are more demanding in requiring initial evidence of serious injury and that it would not ordinarily be sustained without parental participation,[63] which imports the *res ipsa loquitur* concept from negligence law, reversing the normal burden of proof. The New York Family Court Act, for instance,[64] gives statutory expression to the presumption of culpability that may arise from injury to a child not otherwise explained. Further, the legislation provides that "proof of the abuse or neglect of one child shall be admissible on the issue of the abuse or neglect of any other child of, or the legal responsibility of, the respondent".[65]

6. Procedural Safeguards

The suitability of the traditional Common law adversarial system of trial procedure to resolve child protection applications has been doubted, not least because of the desirability, in a child's interests, of speedy disposition. This may be frustrated by full pre-trial confrontation of charge and response, pre-trial disclosure of documentation, including the making and exchange of medical, psychiatric, social and similar reports, the partisan atmosphere at trial, with examination and cross-examination of witnesses and expert witnesses to support one's own case and damage one's opponent's, emphasis on points of conflict and suppression of points agreed, and recourse to regional and national appellate tribunals to reverse an unfavorable result, or at least to set it aside in favor of a new trial. The Law Reform Commission of Canada expressed a widely held view in stating that, "in general the adversary approach promotes a ritualistic and unrealistic response to family problems"[66] and that, "considerable modification is needed, particularly where children are involved".[67]

Room for modification by simplification of form may well exist, but the belief that applications judicially to apply supervision of a child in his home, to remove a child from his home, or permanently to terminate parental association with a child can be resolved in amicable consensus, or that a benign inquisitor can speedily determine truth and apply wisdom that contending interests will acclaim, is itself unrealistic. Indeed, the Canadian Law Reform Commission pointed directly to the problem at issue when commenting on the experience of recently established informal family courts; it found that, "While there is a desirable de-emphasis on adversarial procedures, there is also a failure to provide adequate protection of the rights of individuals, particularly children".[68]

A trial at law that fails to protect individual rights is a paradox, if not an outrage. Procedural thinking on child protection is in conflict with itself in favoring both informality and rejection of strict legal forms, in order to loosen adversarial rigidity, while at the same time favoring better protection and representation of the interests of both parents and children that the adversarial system can offer. Child welfare officers' confidence in the merits of a case they bring is often founded on legally inadmissible evidence, and failure in court leaves them feeling humiliated, frustrated, and filled with foreboding for the future safety of the child they were unable to 'rescue'.[69] The court's acceptance of views such officers have rejected, advanced by or on behalf of parents they consider unworthy, they ascribe to the courts' defective procedures. Lawyers see the opportunity for open and full confrontation as essential to proper trial, however, and this is accepted no less by those trained in the inquisitorial procedural tradition of Continental Europe.

As evidenced by the spread of publicly financed legal aid schemes, the entitlement of parents to legal representation is increasingly recognized. Because of the differential incidence of child abuse, or more probably the selective presentation of protection applications,[70] a high percentage of parents involved in court proceedings are poor,[71] and without publicly provided lawyers would be unrepresented.[72] The thought that the children involved in proceedings should also have independent legal representation is too new to be widely accepted, but it is gaining ground, resisted decreasingly in principle and contested more upon pragmatic grounds, such as concern the availability and cost of suitable advocates.[73] The U.S. Supreme Court's decision *In re Gault,*[74] regarding juvenile delinquency proceedings, where a right to counsel was acknowledged, has inspired thinking along extended lines.

Beyond the question of supply of advocates for children, however, lies the question of their function. Contesting the case advanced by an agency seeking a care or protection order,[75] challenging arguments advanced by the parents, and monitoring the conduct of the court, meaning principally the judge, are expected and proper functions of a child's advocate, but a child is not a routine client. The language of the law is that the client 'instructs' his lawyer, but the capacity of a child to do this is clearly conditioned by age, intellignce and other obvious factors. It is unclear whether a child advocate's function is to represent his client, or his client's interests. Counsel's first duty is to the court and to the administration of justice rather than to his client's purposes,[76] but if he departs from his client's preference he is normally liable to dismissal. If he represents his child client's interests rather than the child's views, he may appear superfluous since child welfare agencies are usually mandated to achieve this purpose.[77] The detachment from the agency's policies and economic and other constraints that independent counsel can bring to this task is valuable, but, apart from the danger that his interpretation of his client's interests may be vigorously opposed by the client, such counsel may in practice be reliant upon social and other reports that will be parallel to those generated by the agency. A situation may result comparable to that now affecting psychiatric reports and testimony, where doctrinal adherence to different schools of thought may cause conflicting reports to negative or neutralize each other, and the court is aided only in the demonstration that evidence from which it might otherwise have taken direction is not necessarily reliable.

If the advocate is simply to express the child's views and preferences as to his placement before the court, the child must be of adequate age and maturity to formulate views worthy of serious consideration, and the advocate must be able to extract those views from his client. A lawyer's capacity to communicate with a young child and to interpret his direct and indirect intimations and responses is not specially trained, and he has no more skill than any other person who lacks understanding of child development and imagery. If the expressed preference appears to the advocate singularly ill-considered and lacking perspective, imagination and foresight, moreover, he may be tempted to conclude that his client is not really mature enough to have views capable of representation; that is, evidence that the child's views are adequately formulated may be their proximity to the representative's. The lawyer may not be able to counsel a child as he may an adult, moreover, since that may appear to be applying improper pressure to impose his views, and he may not be as free to withdraw from the case without prejudice to his client's interests.

Irrespective of whether the advocate for a child is a court officer, appointed to an agency independent of the court service or drawn from the ranks of private practitioners upon a duty counsel or *ad hoc* basis,[78] the function he is to discharge for his client requires considerable clarification. Further, society at large must determine at what age and under what conditions a minor's views ought to be taken into account, and when he may reach decisions determining his future, possibly to his detriment; that is, at what age he may be allowed to exercise the adult prerogative of making a mistake.

7. Administrative Responses

In order to maintain a record of abused children and abusive families, many jurisdictions, especially in North America, have established central child abuse registers. These detail incidents of abuse or alleged abuse, identifying victims, parents, addresses and follow-up information. Illinois was the first American state to institute a state-wide register in 1965, but by 1973 forty-six states had such registers, many large metropolitan areas had local registers and soon after 1973 a voluntary national register was established among twenty-five states.[79] Few registers accept reports directly from members of the public who, in conformity with legal duties or acting voluntarily, notify agencies or other authorities, such as the police, of a suspected incident. Generally, registers are maintained by a governmental welfare or social service department to receive reports from agencies, which have means to screen out misconceived and malicious allegations. Upon receipt of a report from an appropriate agency, the registrar consults the records to discover any past entries concerning the family, suspected assailant or child, and informs the agency so that it may measure the likely risk to the child, and decide upon and plan its remedial program.

Apart from providing data to determine the demographic incidence of child abuse for the purpose of policy planning, registers may also provide physicians and social workers with information of a child's history, which may disclose a sad sequence of beating or other abuse suggesting that a particular suspicion of abuse fits into an ominous pattern. The register also keeps track both of transient families (not just nomadic families, since even the executive cadre may be quite mobile today) in which abuse has been recorded, and of those who take their injured children to different doctors or hospitals, for instance in downtown or suburban areas. Further functions are to avoid duplication of effort where a family has caught the attention of different agencies or government departments, perhaps because of its multiple needs, and to assist agencies in management of their caseloads. An additional though longer-term effect of a register showing the progressive situation of an abuse victim may be to demonstrate the effectiveness of alternative dispositions in child care.

It cannot be pretended that these potential advantages of central registers are realized in practice, although this may be an argument for maintaining a more adequate, uniform and comprehensive register rather than for not maintaining one at all. There are more specific hazards in maintaining a register, however, than the prospect of its futility. The information recorded, perhaps under compulsory reporting laws, is of *bona fide* suspicions that may in fact prove to be unfounded. An operational distinction may therefore be attempted that treats the information regarding a child as disclosing abuse, but that treats that same information insofar as it concerns the guardians, as unestablished.

Even if true, the information must be guarded to protect privacy, of guardian and child, and in any event guardians must be informed of its registration and be given means of challenge and cancellation of registration. While administrative review may be favored to accommodate guardians' challenges, the machinery has the potential to become legalistic, not least since unjustified cancellation may harm interests of the child, so that an appeal may need to be accommodated on his behalf against such deregistration. A further dilemma concerns the length of time for which information is stored. The prognostic value of an incident fades unless those involved appear in subsequent entries, but very few of the registers in the United States provide for automatic removal of records after a given time of inactivity. Access to the register must be restricted to those with an authentic interest in using it, which may focus on professional and official personnel. This restriction may conflict, however, with evolving team approaches to helping abusive families, including, for instance, involvement of lay people from the community who possess limited training but are able to teach by example mothering and other parenting sensitivities and skills an abusive family or guardian lacks. The more closely an agency is integrated into its community, the more easily may breach of confidentiality occur.

The general role of public or *quasi*-public welfare agencies requires clarification, since their communal responsibilities may interact in child abuse cases with those of police services. The association of the police with prosecution and criminal sanctions may make recourse to their services dysfunctional in view of agencies' aims to collaborate with parents. If abuse recurs, however, or for instance an abused child eventually dies of injuries, police may intervene, and in any criminal proceedings a principal prosecution witness may be an agency welfare worker.[80] In some jurisdictions, such as Ontario, criminal proceedings can be taken, and in given circumstances may need to be, by the agency itself, when the welfare worker, admitted to the home as a helper, may seem cynically to betray the confidence the guardian reposed in him or her. A number of agencies are therefore anxious to shed their criminal law-enforcement associations, and be confined to a welfare role.

This may abate their difficulty but cannot remove it, since discharge of a welfare role will in a number of cases compel them to act to sever the parent-child link by instigating protection proceedings. These will no doubt appear penal to the parents, and principal witnesses against them will probably include the welfare worker who 'befriended' the family and offered 'help'. Some United States jurisdictions have tried to limit the harm of parents seeing social workers they admitted to their homes giving adverse reports and testimony in protection proceedings by excluding parents from the court. Apart from this being objectionable in principle, however, it serves little purpose when parents are legally represented, and is more oppressive when they are not. The solution to the dilemma may lie in training of agency workers, so that they can explain their obligatory function in the court while keeping open their access to the home. The agency and its personnel must accept, however, that, as a formal or informal branch of the administrative section of government, they have unavoidable obligations to the management of legal responses to child abuse.

NOTES

1. The expression 'parent' is used in a social rather than biological or legal sense, and includes a child's *de facto* general adult guardian. See generally Goldstein, J.; Freud, A.; and Solnit, A., *Beyond the Best Interests of the Child*. New York, New York: Free Press, 1973, p. 98 on the concept of the psychological parent.
2. See generally Eekelaar, "What Are Parental Rights?" (1973), 89 *Law Quarterly Review* 210.
3. The Canadian Criminal Code (R.S.C. 1970, c. C-34), for instance, in s. 43, provides that "Every schoolteacher, parent or person standing in the place of a parent is justified in using force by way of correction toward a pupil or child, as the case may be, who is under his care, if the force does not exceed what is reasonable under the circumstances".
4. It has been noted, however, that "In the U.S.A. .... opposition to such actions nowadays seeks support in the fear of collusion rather than disharmony", Fleming, J.G., *The Law of the Torts* (4th ed.) New York, New York: Oxford University Press, 1971, p. 597. In *Gelbman v. Gelbman* (1969) 245 N.E. 2d 192 for instance, intrafamilial immunity from tort proceedings was abolished in New York.

5. The Report on Injuries to Unborn Children Cmnd. 5709 (1974), noted that "We now recommend that, as a general rule, legislation should specifically exclude any right of action by a child against its own mother for prenatal injury" (para. 63), but "that legislation should provide an exception to the general rule namely, that where a mother causes pre-natal injury to her child by her negligent driving of a motor vehicle she should be liable to her child" (para. 64). See Congenital Disabilities (Civil Liability) Act 1976, U.K. Statutes 1976, C. 28.

6. In the Oregon case of *State v. McMaster* (Ore., 1971) 486 P. 2d 567 for instance, termination of parental rights was sought upon evidence that while in her parents' custody, a child was not allowed to "maximize her potential". The Supreme Court of Oregon declined to intervene, since "many thousands of children are being raised under basically the same circumstances as this child. The legislature had in mind conduct substantially departing from the norm and unfortunately for our children, the McMasters' conduct is not such a departure", at 573.

7. In *Baggett v. Bullit* (1964) 377 U.S. 360, 367 the United States Supreme Court observed that "a law forbidding or requiring conduct in terms so vague that men of common intelligence must necessarily guess at its meaning and differ as to its application violates due process of law".

8. But see *Buck v. Bell* (1927) 274 U.S. 200., *in re Sterilization of Morse* (1976) 221 S.E. 2d 307 and the survey in Shaw, "Legislative Naivete in Involuntary Sterilization Laws" (1976) 12 *Wake Forest L. R.* 1064. Contrast *In re D (a minor) (wardship: sterilization)* [1976] 1 All E.R. 236., and see generally Dickens, "Eugenic Recognition In Canadian Law" (1975) 13 *Osgoode Hall L. J.* 547.

9. Experience has suggested that "Perhaps the most prevalent characteristic of families charged with neglect is poverty; this raises the troubling possibility that class or cultural bias plays a significant role in decisions to label children neglected or abused": see Arren, "Intervention Between Parent and Child: A Reappraisel of the State's Role in Child Neglect and Abuse Cases" (1975) 63 *Georgetown L.J.* 887, 888, 889. For evidence that the incidence of child abuse occurs in families of all income levels, see Gil, D.G., *Violence Against Children*. Cambridge, Mass.: Harvard University Press, 1970, p. 112, table 22.

10. For admirable attempts to promote rational and restrained standards, see Wald, "State Intervention on Behalf of 'Neglected' Children: Standards for Removal of Children from Their Homes, Monitoring the Status of Children in Foster Care, and Termination of Parental Rights" (1976) 28 *Stanford L.J.* 623; and Ketchem, and Babcock, "Statutory Standards for the Involuntary Termination of Parental Rights" (1976) 29 *Rutgers L.R.* 530.

11. See the approach of, for instance, Walters, D.R., *Physical and Sexual Abuse of Children: Causes and Treatment*. Bloomington, Indiana: Indiana University Press, 1975.

12. See Katz, S., *When Parents Fail*. Boston, Mass.: Beacon Press, 1971.

13. But see note 6, *supra*.

14. R.S.O. 1970, c. 64.

15. U.K. Stats. 1969, c. 54.

16. This duty may not necessarily coincide with a legal duty of care owed to the child, but see *Landeros v. Flood* (1976), 13 *Cal. Rptr.* 69, where a physician's breach of duty regarding a child at risk of abuse was held legally actionable.

17. See Katz's category 17, *supra* note 12.

18. See Katz's category 11, *supra* note 12.

19. Ontario's Child Welfare Act (*supra* note 14) provides in sub-clause (x) of s. 20(1)(b) that a child in need of protection includes "a child where the person in whose charge he is neglects or refuses to provide or obtain proper medical, surgical or other recognized remedial care or treatment necessary for his health or well-being, or refuses to permit such care or treatment to be supplied to the child when it is recommended by a legally qualified medical practitioner. . . ."

20. *Per* Dennistoun, J.A. in *Newton v. Newton* [1924] 2 W.W.R. 840 (Manitoba C.A.).

21. For confirmation that protection proceedings are to be determined on a civil as opposed to a criminal standard of proof, see *Re B and Children's Aid Society of Winnipeg* (1976), 64 D.L.R. (3d) 517 (Manitoba C.A.).
22. See the Children and Young Persons Act 1969 (*supra* note 15) s. 1(2)(b) and the presumption under the New York Family Court Act, see *infra* note 65.
23. Reversing the Court of Appeal, which had ordered disclosure; see *D.* v. *N.S.P.C.C.* (1977), 2 W.L.R. 201 (H. of L.).
24. The question of rights of persons reported is considered *infra* note 27.
25. See *supra* note 16.
26. Or which he should foresee, acting within the range of professional competence; see *Tarasoff v. Regents of the University of California* (1976) 551 P. 2d 334.
27. Unless, of course, a statute gives a specific exemption from civil liability for non-reporting. Many public authorities enjoy general protection from civil suits.
28. On a systematic approach to prosecution alternatives, see Working Paper 7 *Diversion*, Law Reform Commission of Canada, 1975.
29. See Stark, Jean, "The Battered Child — Does Britain Need a Reporting Law:" (1969) *Public Law* 48.
30. R.S.O. 1970, c. 64 s. 41(1).
31. *Id.* s. 41(2).
32. See generally Dickens, Bernard M., *Legal Issues in Child Abuse*. Toronto, Canada: University of Toronto Criminology, 1976, chapter II.
33. See *supra* notes 16 and 27.
34. "The Law and Abused Children" in Helfer, R., Kempe, C., *The Battered Child*. Chicago, Illinois: University of Chicago Press, 1968, p. 185.
35. Committee on the Infant and Pre-School Child, American Academy of Pediatrics: see "Maltreatment of Children, the Physically Abused Child" (1966), 37 *Pediatrics* 377.
36. Sussman, Alan, and Cohen, Stephen, *Reporting Child Abuse and Neglect: Guidelines for Legislation*. Cambridge, Mass.: Ballinger, 1975, p. 418.
37. See *supra* note 12.
38. Age limits are not uniformly established; in Ontario, for instance, 'child' means a boy or girl actually or apparently under sixteen years of age, under s. 20(1)(a) of the Child Welfare Act.
39. See *supra* note 36 at 3, 14-18 (section 2 of the Model Reporting Law).
40. See generally Greenland, Cyril, *Child Abuse in Ontario: Research Report 3,* (Ontario Ministry of Community and Social Services, 1973).
41. See the seminal study Davis, K.C., *Discretionary Justice: A Preliminary Inquiry*. Baton Rouge, Louisiana: Louisiana State University Press; Muller, F., *Prosecution: The Decision to Charge a Suspect with a Crime*. Boston, Mass.: Little Brown & Co., 1969.
42. See *supra* note 28.
43. In England formal police cautions are enumerated in the annual Criminal Statistics.
44. On the general effectiveness of criminal sanctions, however, see Fraser, "A Pragmatic Alternative to Current Legislative Approaches to Child Abuse" (1974), 12 *Am. Crim. Law R.* 103, 119 *et seq.*
45. The human characteristics of the sentencing judge have also been recognized: see Hogarth, J., *Sentencing as a Human Process*. Toronto, Canada: University of Toronto Press, 1971.
46. Objection may be taken, however, to the recorded practice of some Massachusetts court clerks who require filing of a criminal charge before accepting a civil neglect petition: see "The Neglected Child" (1970), 4 *Suffolk L. R.* 631, 650.
47. U.K. Stats. 1969, c. 54 s. 1(2)(d).
48. See discussion of Procedural Safeguards.
49. R.S.O. 1970, c. 64.
50. *Id.* s. 31. An order may be renewed, but not to exceed a total of 24 months wardship.
51. See *supra* note 48.
52. See Bowlby, John, *Child Care and the Growth of Love* (2nd ed.), New York, New York: Penguin, 1965., and also: Goldfarb, "Effects of Psychological Deprivation in

Infancy and Subsequent Stimulation" (1945), 102 *American Journal of Psychiatry* 13.

53. See *supra* note 9. Gil has shown abusive parents to exist in all social strata and locations, and to be indistinguishable from other parents.

54. See, for instance, *In re Jewish Child Care Association* (1959) 156, N.E. 2d 700, where a five and a half year old child, living for four and a half years with the same devoted foster parents, who wanted to adopt her, was returned to her natural mother, who had not requested return and was unable to assume responsibility for her care and education. This case is discussed in full in Katz, S., *When Parents Fail, supra* note 12, pp. 96-106.

55. See Areen, *supra* note 9.

56. Making testifying compulsory rather than just voluntary relieves the spouse from the other's pressure not to testify, and from subsequent recrimination.

57. See Canada Evidence Act (R.S.C. 1970, c. E.-10), s. 4(2).

58. Section 57 of the proposed Canadian Evidence Code (Law Reform Commission Report Evidence (1977) renders a spouse competent and compellable, within the judge's discretion as directed by the section.

59. Greenland, *Child Abuse in Ontario, supra* note 26.

60. See Besharov, "Epilogue" in Fontana, V. (ed.), *Somewhere a Child is Crying: the Battered Child.* New York, New York: Macmillan, 1973, p. 251. For statistics showing that over half the children returned home after an incident of abuse will be injured again or killed. See Fontana, V., *The Maltreated Child: the Maltreatment Syndrome in Children* (2nd ed.), Springfield, Illinois: C.C. Thomas, 1974.

61. As opposed to proceedings to establish their criminal guilt.

62. See, for instance, *In re J.Z.* (North Dakota, 1971), 190 N.W. 2d 27, 35 and *In re Edwards* (1973), 335 N.Y.S. 2d 575, 578.

63. See *In re S.* (1965), 259 N.Y.S. 2d 164.

64. N.Y. Family Court Act. ch. 962, s. 1046 (a)(ii) (McKinney Supp. 1970). See also the Idaho Code s. 16-1602(a) (Supp. 1974). Idaho defines an abused child as one who:

". . . exhibits evidence of skin bruising, bleeding, malnutrition, sexual molestation, lumps, burns, fractures of any bone, subdural hematomas, soft tissue swelling, failure to thrive or death, and such condition or death is not justifiably explained, or where the history given concerning such condition or death is at variance with the degree or type of such condition or death, or the circumstances indicate that such condition or death may not be the product of an accidental occurrence".

65. *Id.* s. 1046(a)(i). *Cf.* the Children and Young Persons Act 1969. R.S.O. c. 64 s. 1(2)(b) (1970).

66. Working Paper I, *The Family Court* (1974) 11.

67. *Loc. cit.,* Law Reform Commission of Canada, Working Paper I.

68. *Id.* at 15.

69. The 'rescue' syndrome deeply affects attitudes of many social workers: see Platt, A., *The Child Savers* (2nd ed.), Chicago, Illinois: University of Chicago Press, 1977., Tamilia, "Neglect Proceedings and the Conflict Between Law and Society" (1971), 9 *Duquesne L.R.* 579, 585.

70. See Gil, D.G., *supra* note 9.

71. See Areen, *supra* note 9.

72. A study in New York found that where parents lacked counsel, 7.9 percent of neglect petitions were dismissed in court and 79.5 percent resulted in neglect findings. Where parents were represented, 25 percent were dismissed and 62.5 percent resulted in findings of neglect; see "Representation in Child Neglect Cases: Are Parents Neglected?" (1968), 4 *Colum. J. Law and Soc. Prob.* 230, 241.

73. Resistance to independent representation as such is based upon the more traditional ground that the child welfare agency instituting the protection proceedings is the representative of the child: see, for example, *Re Helmes,* (1977) 13 O.R. (2d) 4 (Ont. Div. Ct.).

74. (1967) 387 U.S. 1.
75. This function is overlooked in the approach adopted in such cases as in *Re Helmes, supra* note 73.
76. This classical ideal is expressed in *Rondel v. Worsley*, [1969] A.C. 191 (House of Lords).
77. In *Re Helmes, supra* note 73, where a family court judge's appointment of the Official Guardian to represent a child was quashed on appeal, it was ruled that "the Children's Aid Society is a society appointed by the community to act in matters to protect the interest of children," *per* Morand, J. at 5. The court permitted the Official Guardian himself to decide, however, whether he wanted to intervene.
78. See generally Dickens, Bernard M., "Representing The Child in the Courts" in Baxter and Eberts (eds.), *The Child and the Courts* (1978).
79. See *supra* note 36 at p. 165.
80. See *supra* note 60 on subsequently recorded injuries and death.

Chapter 24

Some Legal Aspects of Child Abuse in Australia

Annemaree Lanteri and Susan Morgan*

Non-accidental injuries and emotional deprivation and abuse suffered by children raise a variety of problems cutting across boundaries of professional expertise and responsibility. They involve moral and social issues which must be confronted and resolved by the whole community in accordance with its culture and goals. The breadth of issues which are involved in an attempt to confront and resolve the problem of child abuse in developed Western communities derives largely from the range of precipitating and causative factors giving rise to the phenomenon. The Report of the Community Welfare Advisory Committee on the Enquiry into Non-accidental Physical Injury to Children in South Australia 1976 (hereinafter referred to as the Murray Report) noted forty-six such factors and grouped them under listings relating to community attitudes, the family, the abusers and the child. The many possible legal responses to these types of problems should be regarded properly as an indication of prevailing societal attitudes. The law is after all a tool which can achieve only the goals inherent in its precise formulation. It is the identification of goals which is decisive. As a community's goals undergo changes with its growth and the passage of time, so will the legal tools useful towards their achievement require reform. Of course inadequate or incorrect identification may result in inappropriate and therefore limiting formulations of legal control tools.

State intervention in family relationships is usually rationalized on the basis that the community has an interest in the legally sanctioned family as the preferred unit of social and economic organization and that consequently it has an interest in intervention when the family unit breaks down. Perhaps overlying this and a certainly more frequently articulated justification is that the protection the state can provide for weaker and more vulnerable members of the community is in itself an adequate basis for intervention. However, despite these theoretical rationalizations, in Australia state intervention in family life, particularly with respect to child-parent relationships which involve violence, has historically been oriented towards *ex post facto* action. It has focussed on the punishment of parents and the placement of the child outside the family group. This pivots action on what is a presenting symptom of family dysfunction and delays intervention beyond the point of time when it might have optimal effect for all parties.

---

* Faculty of Law, University of Melbourne, Australia.

There has been little or no emphasis placed on positive supportive intervention. The approach has been one of the imposition of criminal responsibility and the consequential involvement of police, magistrates, courts and various punitive processes. This has led to the development of legal resources along the lines of courtroom procedures and disposition of the child outside the home, instead of notification procedures, provisions for holding orders, expanded descriptions of children who are in need of care to include emotional injuries and the imposition of legal duties on various departments to take positive steps to prevent the occurrence of child abuse.

Despite the fact that child abuse cannot be viewed in isolation from other aspects of family welfare and that a comprehensive and coordinated system of legislation and service delivery would be ideal, recent developments in Australia have tended to focus attention on certain relatively discrete issues of particularly legal significance. Since 1974 South Australia, Western Australia, Tasmania and New South Wales have legislated to modify their procedures for state intervention in parent-child relationships.[1] In Victoria some groundwork has been done towards legislative and administrative reform, and public debate has been stimulated by considerable media coverage given to the phenomenon of child battering and its associated problems. Issues which have emerged with both social and legal significance have been those relating to compulsory notification of incidents of child abuse to the police or some other central responsible body, the criminal prosecution of maltreating parents and procedures to allow for the holding of a child in hospital for assessment and treatment when parents are uncooperative. Arising out of these points some attention has been given to the powers of entry to private premises for the purpose of removing a child in immediate physical danger and the availability of appeals by both parents and state at several points during the process of intervention. In view of the fact that each of these matters involves consideration of legislative provisions and the criminal process it is worthwhile to compare a selection of those legal responses which have been made elsewhere in Australia and to consider their implications for proposed reforms in Victoria. Tasmania and South Australia provide examples of legislative intervention which have existed for some time and which can usefully be compared with the existing Victorian approach.

1. Victoria

In Victoria the apprehension of maltreated children is covered by the Social Welfare Act 1970. Their ultimate disposition is governed by the Children's Court Act 1973. The Social Welfare Act provides that a child who answers any one of a number of fairly specific descriptions shall be deemed to be a child "in need of care and protection".[2] Under s. 32 any member of the police force or authorized person[3] finding a child in the circumstances enumerated in s. 31 may immediately apprehend the child without warrant. However, a warrant is necessary before the police officer or authorized person may enter any house or building in order to apprehend the child. The member of the police force is then obliged immediately to make an application to the Children's Court[4] for an order deeming the child to be in need of care and protection. After apprehension and pending the application to the Children's Court the child may be released or may be taken to a reception center or, if over 15, to a remand center or be admitted to bail or placed with 'some respectable person' or in the home of the apprehending officer.[5] The child can in fact be dealt with in precisely the same way as a child charged with a criminal offence. Similar and apparently overlapping powers of apprehension of children are provided by s. 81 of the Social Welfare Act 1970 which makes child maltreatment a crime punishable by a fine of $1,000 or 12 months imprisonment.

It will be noted that there is at present no provision for any 'holding order' or interlocutory stage. The child must be declared 'in need of care and protection' by the Children's Court before there is any right in any person to detain the child against its parents' wishes for any length of time. There is no provision for the detention of a child in hospital in order that its injuries can be treated and its needs assessed even when presented there as a patient, if the parent or guardian is determined to remove it without a care and protection order being made. This situation can be criticized on numerous grounds. Police intervention is required in most cases. As the child can be detained only after a court order, the parents are stigmatized and may therefore feel resentful and fail to cooperate with supportive services. If the prosecution fails, the child may be at the risk of further neglect or ill treatment if the parents see it as the cause of unpleasant allegations against them. There is, in practice, little difference between the procedure faced by a juvenile charged with an offence and a child, who through no fault of its own, has been the subject of a care and protection application. Proceedings with respect to both are instigated, in most cases, by police intervention. Both are dealt with by the same Children's Court and are subject for the most part to similar dispositions usually involving institutionalization.

Perhaps more significantly it prevents psychiatrists, pediatricians or social workers from taking any action in situations where they suspect that the child has been abused, but feel unable to provide proof to the satisfaction of the court. Children must in such cases be returned to their parents with disastrous and sometimes fatal results.[6]

The existing Victorian legislation does not provide for any formal means of notification of known or suspected cases of child abuse nor does it provide any protection from civil liability arising from the notification for those members of the public who might inform the police or authorized officers of their suspicions that a particular child is being maltreated.

2. Tasmania

In Tasmania on the other hand, the present position is somewhat different. In 1974 the Child Protection Act was passed with the aims of overcoming the deficiencies of the existing legislation which were largely similar to that currently existing in Victoria. Before 1974 the law with respect to maltreated children in Tasmania was governed by the Child Welfare Act 1966, which set up machinery for dealing with 'neglected children'. In terms of definition, the procedures for bringing such children before the court and ultimate powers of disposition, the Tasmanian Act was virtually identical with the present Victorian legislation. As in Victoria, little distinction was made between neglected children and children charged with an offence and the same criticisms were made of that system as are now made of the Victorian system. The Child Protection Act 1974 removed jurisidiction over the maltreated child from the Children's Court and provided for an independent system for dealing with such cases. It also set up an apparently simple machinery for the notification of suspected cases of child maltreatment and the disposition of children found to be suffering from 'cruel treatment'.[7]

The Act establishes a Child Protection Board, the chairman of which must be a legal practitioner and the other members must include a pediatrician and a medical practitioner with special experience in relation to social work.[8] Power is given to appoint 'authorized officers'[9] and the Board has now established a network of authorized officers which includes Board members, social workers and probation officers.[10] The Act then provides that any person who suspects on reasonable grounds that a child who is apparently under 12 years has suffered cruel treatment is entitled to report the fact to an authorized officer.[11] Persons of specified classes must make such a report when circumstances warranting it come to their notice in the practice of their profession.[12] Provision is then made for the protection of any person making such a report from civil proceedings based on breach of professional ethics, defamation, malicious prosecution or conspiracy. The contents of such reports are not fully admissible in hearings and disclosure of related documents may not be compelled.[13] When authorized officers to whom the report is made consider that a child has suffered cruel treatment they may require the parent or the person apparently in charge of the child to take the child to hospital to be examined by a pediatrician and can take steps to ensure that treatment is carried out.[14] They are required to notify the Board of any measures they have taken.[15] The Board may apply to a magistrate for a 'child protection' order that the child be detained in a public hospital for a period of not more than 30 days.[16] A child who is subject to such an order cannot be removed from hospital by any person during the specified period and this period may be extended for another 30 days.[17]

In deciding an application by the Board for a child protection order the magistrate may also exercise the same powers that he would have if sitting at a children's court and the child were brought before him under the provisions of the Child Welfare Act 1960 (Tas.).[18] In general this gives the magistrate the power to make the child a ward of the State or to make a supervision order or to require the parent or guardian to enter into a recognizance to provide proper care and control of the child.[19] If the child is made a ward of the State the Board may request the Director of Social Welfare to deal with the child in a particular manner.[20] The Child Protection Act also gives justices of the peace power to issue a warrant to a police officer to enter premises in order to remove the child and take it to hospital.[21] The Act empowers the magistrate, upon application by a parent or person willing to care for the child, to revoke the child protection order if he is satisfied that the continuance of the order in force is no longer in the interests of the child.[22]

The Child Protection Act represents a significant departure from the pre-existing Tasmanian position and creates a system which is arguably preferable to the present Victorian one. The maltreated child is no longer dealt with in the same way as a child charged with an offence. The child protection order enables hospitals to detain children for long enough to ensure a thorough examination.

The power of the Board to issue directions to the Director of Social Welfare is a significant step towards ensuring that children who become wards of the State under the provisions of the Child Protection Act are not routinely dealt with in the same way as children convicted of offences and admitted to institutions. Steps can be taken to ensure that necessary treatment is provided in the context of a continuing relationship with its family. This provision, together with that providing for applications for the revocation of child protection orders, may ensure that children do not become 'lost' in the institutional system. However the same magistrates hear applications by the Board under the Act as deal with children brought before the Children's Court charged with an offence. Whilst the powers of magistrates when hearing applications with respect to maltreated children are now prescribed by the Child Protection Act and not by the Child Welfare Act, the final step of setting up completely separate and independent bodies has not been taken. It should also be noted that no penalty is provided for failure by persons in specified classes to notify authorized officers of suspected cases of child abuse.

The Act as its stands has been criticized and amendments have been proposed which aim to give the Board wider powers of control in the management, detection and prevention of the problem. The powers granted to order the child be detained in hospital for 30 days and then to extend the period are rarely used. More often an order is made to detain the child in hospital for three days, and if further legal protection is thought necessary, the magistrate will be asked to exercise his powers as if sitting as a children's court. The fact that the child may be the subject of an application by the Board to be declared a ward of the State does not necessarily evidence an intention on the part of the Board that he is to be removed permanently from his parents. However, the members of the Board believe that if there is a risk to the safety of the child in placing him with his parents then a change in legal status is a basic safeguard against such a placement being made without a serious reconsideration of all circumstances.[23]

3. South Australia

South Australia provides an example of a third approach to legislative control in this area. The relevant legislation is the Juvenile Courts Act 1971-1977 (S.A.) and the Community Welfare Act 1972-1976 (S.A.). Together they represent perhaps the most comprehensive method currently in effect in Australia, although some amendments are of such recent origin that sufficient data is not yet available to indicate practical effects reliably.

The system is designed to separate as far as possible the procedures for dealing with neglected or maltreated children from those involving juvenile offfenders. It also attempts to introduce a wider range of expertise into the decision making processes than characterizes a traditional adversary courtroom. Juvenile offenders under the age of 16 are dealt with in most cases by Juvenile Aid Panels made up of justices of the peace, police officers and representatives of the Department of Community Welfare.[24] These panels have power to warn and counsel children and their parents and to require undertakings from them with regard to future behavior, rehabilitation or training programs. They are also able to refer cases to a juvenile court where cooperation on the part of the child or parents is not forthcoming, or where the circumstances of the case generally seem to warrant it.[25]

The juvenile courts[26] deal with cases referred from the panels, charges of homicide and complaints alleging that a child is neglected.[27] Both the courts and the panels are under a positively expressed duty to consider the welfare of the child and the desirability of removing it from the family environment before making any determination as to how they are to be dealt with.[28] Maltreated children are the primary concern of regional panels established under the Community Welfare Act after amendments passed in 1976.[29] These amendments are contained in the Community Welfare Act Amendment Act 1976, assented to 16th December 1976. The Regional Panels are to consist of persons nominated by the Director-General of Community Welfare, the Mothers and Babies Health Association Incorporated, a child psychiatrist nominated by the Director-General of Medical Services, a nominee of the Commissioner of Police and a legally qualified medical practitioner. The amendments follow the recommendations of the Murray Report made in January 1976. The functions of the regional panels are *inter alia* to receive notifications of cases of maltreatment, to decide on the appropriate action to be taken in each case and to coordinate the relevant community services providing support and guidance for families in need.[30] These panels must be consulted before a prosecution for child maltreatment under the Community Welfare Act is launched[31] and it is envisaged that in practice the agreement of the regional panel should be a prerequisite to the determination of any care and guardianship application in respect of a maltreated child made by a juvenile court. The notification provisions[32] of the Community Welfare Act impose a duty to report cases of maltreatment to the panels on groups which have particular expertise or opportunity to observe children. They are medical practitioners, dentists, nurses, teachers, members of the police forces and employees of welfare agencies. Protection is provided in that no civil liability will attach to the informant from the making of a *bona fide* notification, whether the informant is within one of thse special groups or is a member of the general public. The need for the provision of a procedure allowing a child to be temporarily held for medical assessment despite opposition from parents or guardians is met by the enactment of s. 82f of that Act. Temporary detention of a child in a hospital or institution for periods of up to 96 hours will be lawful where the "person in charge of the hospital or institution . . . suspects upon reasonable grounds that an offence . . . has been committed in relation to the child."[33]

4. Notification

The arguments most frequently put against the imposition of a duty to report incidents of child abuse are that such a duty imposed on medical practitioners, especially those in private practice, would disrupt and undermine the confidentiality of the patient-doctor relationship to the detriment of the patient; that this would also affect the readiness of parents to seek medical care for children in need of it where there might be a diagnosis of child abuse; that the duty would be virtually unenforceable, bringing the law into disrepute and further adding to its ineffectiveness and that the provision of such duty does not of itself guarantee that simultaneous provision would be made for adequate support services.[34] It might also be argued that family privacy could be invaded on the basis of differences in life-style, racial prejudices, or prejudices against single parent families or low income groups especially where the definitions of neglect or maltreatment are vague and judgmental. These arguments are based on a number of assumptions which should be reviewed carefully. Most if not all of the specific reasons given for opposing compulsory notification can be traced to an underlying assumption that intervention will be bad for the parents and consequently also for the child. The attitude of the community towards intervention generally must be resolved before an informed decision can be made. The aim of providing formally for notification procedures should be primarily the protection of children and the mobilization of support services for the family involved. So long as the community's attention is focussed on child maltreatment as an example of criminal behavior in the parents, the provision of a duty to report or notify is unlikely to be effective. What public interest may exist in seeing justice done will be outweighed by disinclination to submit other people to a punitive criminal process, especially when it is directed against intrafamilial behavior. This is hardly surprising where the only receptors of reports are the police forces or groups such as the Children's Protection Society. Although reports to the latter do not necessarily lead to prosecution, there is a degree of uncertainty in the mind of the public about the rule of these types of societies which gives rise to inhibitions against involving them. Of course there is also a practical limiting factor, namely their availability to receive and respond to reports.

The possibility of prosecuting maltreating parents in the criminal courts is a real one in cases where the child is severely abused physically. Most jurisdictions provide for a specific offence[35] arising out of an act of child maltreatment which exists in addition to whatever provisions may be relevant in the general body of criminal law, such as assault or wounding. The attitude of the community at large towards proposals for the removal of the specific maltreatment offences from the law is usually one of opposition, despite the existence of those other equally available provisions for prosecution. There is deep opposition expressed to removing the possibility of criminally prosecuting parents for the maltreatment of their children. It is not difficult to understand or even to share this opposition although the emphasis on family support service is not totally consistent with this attitude. It does seem clear that few jurisdictions would be prepared to accept a situation where no prosecution could be launched at all, although it is possible to envisage a compromise to ensure selective prosecution. One method of achieving this would be to introduce a requirement that consultation with appropriately qualified experts be imposed on the police or the Crown Law Department before a prosecution can be made in these cases.[36] This should filter out from the criminal process those cases where less disruptive strategies can beneficially be invoked while retaining the possibility of penal sanctions operating in cases where community outrage cannot be assuaged and where there may be some justification for penal intervention on a deterrent basis.[37] The stigmatization which initially follows even an unsuccessful prosecution is counter-productive to an approach directed towards therapeutic intervention in individual cases and the whole process is at odds with any attempt to encourage notification as a step preparatory to mobilization of services.

Of course it is true to say that the passage of legislation providing for notification does not ensure provision of support services. Indeed even the passage of legislation providing for the establishment of those services does not ensure their physical existence and their real effectiveness. These are matters relating to administration and finance within the appropriate state government departments. However it is possible and necessary to consider compulsory notification as a separate phenomenon while recognizing that its purpose would be quite defeated should support services not be available.

More specific objections to compulsory notification relate particularly to the role of the medical doctor as reporter. An assumption is sometimes made that only doctors would be required to notify, although two of those states which have such a duty have imposed it upon a wider range of groups.[38] Thus the definition of persons on whom a duty to report is imposed, the definition of the basis upon which reporting should be made, the penalty for non-compliance and the protection from liability offered to reporters are all matters of significance in that they can affect the practicability and success of any such provisions.

The definitional issues raise broad questions of policy as well as drafting problems. Arguments in favor of imposing a duty to notify on the community as a whole can be based on the theory that the wider the responsibility the less significant are personal choices. This presumably would cut the ground from the reasons often raised by particular professional groups for opposing compulsion. This opposition arises from the fear that notification would interfere with doctor-patient relationships generally and perhaps result in a number of cases which need treatment not being presented. A universal duty would be supported by arguments related to the educative value of increasing public awareness in the area, resulting in increased vigilance generally towards protecting children. The arguments against a universal duty and in favor of only specific persons or groups nominated are related to the problem of defining appropriate cases for reporting. If special expertise or access is necessary to make a reasonable assessment of a child's situation then there is probably little to be gained by imposing a duty to notify on the general public. A class specific duty also reduces the likelihood of ill-founded reports, although the 'busy body' or spiteful report can be made whether or not there is a duty legally imposed on such people, and in fact its occurrence would seem to be largely unaffected by these issues. Those states where some form of compulsory duty has been imposed have not adopted the universal duty approach, but have indicated with varying degrees of comprehensiveness specific classes as being appropriate by reason of their skills and opportunities to observe children. These states however do formally invite notification from the whole community without the imposition of a duty to do so, and with some protection from civil liability.

The definition of grounds or situations where reporting or notification is required is of crucial importance both in crystallizing community attitudes to the responsibility of adults for children and in providing for realistic assessment under what must often be conditions adverse to a totally objective judgment. A comparison could be made between the definitions of 'cruel treatment' in Tasmania and 'neglect' in South Australia and the definition of a child 'in need of care and protection' under s. 31 of the Victorian Social Welfare Act.[39] The difficulty of drafting a suitably certain and specific list of criteria which at the same time avoids the dangers of excessive rigidity and the incorporation of moral judgments is not easily resolved. A phrase such as "shows evidence of suffering physical or emotional injury or neglect" may be too broad to be acceptable especially should the duty to notify be universal without the built-in limiting orientation of a professional expertise. Nevertheless it may be possible for an adjudicating body made up of experts in psychiatry, medicine, social work and law to apply and interpret such a broad definition in a satisfactory manner. This would retain the advantages of a broad definition whilst achieving an indication of boundaries for its application in specific cases.

The Murray Report in South Australia, however, noted as a possible factor in the poor response to reporting the requirement that the reports had to be made in a very wide variety of circumstances under the provisions of s. 82e of the Community Welfare Act 1972-1976.[40] The Committee considered it desirable that a more definite statement of circumstances should be made and suggested the following definition of a maltreated child for this purpose: ". . . a maltreated child is one who is less than 15 years of age, whose parents or other person inflicts or allows to be inflicted on the child physical injury by other than accidental means, which causes or creates a substantial risk of death or serious protracted disfigurement or protracted impairment to physical or emotional health or creates or allows to be created a substantial risk of such injury other than by accidental means, or commits or allows to be committed an act of sexual abuse against the child."[41]

That there should be a clear movement towards including non-physical abuse and towards situations which need not necessarily have arisen through any culpable action on the part of the parent or guardian is clear. This would be in line with the broad rationalization of the compulsion to notify being based on the need to support and protect children and families generally rather than to punish parents.

Perhaps the most difficult problem is to arrive at realistic enforcement and penalty procedures if notification is made compulsory. The detection of a failure to comply may prove difficult and it will surely only be easy when a child is presented with old injuries and when evidence exists of prior presentation to a person on whom the duty rests. Even then it might be possible to avoid liability if the basis for reporting is one of reasonable suspicion rather than the fact of injury. Of course it might be argued that it is only in fairly extreme cases such as this that prosecution for failure to notify should take place. Difficulty of enforcement or detection has not always been seen as an argument against the imposition of a legal duty in other areas. Medical practitioners are already under various similar duties imposed both by statute or common law. The duty to report cases of infectious diseases and the law relating to complicity and misprision of felony are two examples. The educative effect would not be lost even if the actual risk of prosecution was relatively slight. Of those States in Australia which have adopted compulsory notification, Tasmania and South Australia have not really faced this problem, choosing rather to adopt an approach where the duty is imposed but no penalties are expressly laid down for failing to comply. The New South Wales provisions differ in this respect.[42]

The desirability of providing for protection from civil liability of those who do in fact report is clear whether the report is compulsory or voluntary. It removes some of the inhibitions which would otherwise reduce the effectiveness of notification provisions. The formula used in legislation varies somewhat although all seem to have adopted the view that civil liability be removed from all *bona fide* reporters, whether acting under a duty or not.[43] The adoption of a simple general formula rather than an attempt to enumerate all possible actions would seem to be the simplest and easiest method of providing protection in these cases. Whether the body or person receiving the report should be protected against negligence actions arising out of their use or failure to use the information has not been fully considered. The question is different from that of protecting the informant against liability for defamation actions. However, if notification is to be encouraged it would seem desirable to extend the protection available to those who do notify to cover all civil liability and to rely on a sensible interpretation of what is *bona fide* to discourage hasty, ill-judged or spiteful reports.

5. Holding Orders

Criticisms of the Victorian status quo have already been made in relation to the absence of any summary procedure leading to a 'holding order'. This places those in a position to initiate immediate action either for the protection of the child or for treatment of its injuries in a dilemma. Medical personnel in the casualty departments of public hospitals have under the present legislation no power to detain children without the parents' consent. The legal basis for detaining a child before a care and protection order is made is clearly precarious. If legislation to remedy this deficiency is introduced it must provide for a procedure which can be instigated immediately without the necessity for following complicated procedural requirements. However, at the same time the tension between the child's immediate need for protection and the potential for misuse of power must be resolved. It must be admitted that the diagnosis of child abuse may be hasty and unfounded and for that reason alone some provision for the protection of parental rights must be made.[44] Legislation enabling the issue of a 'holding order' must ensure that the child be held long enough for a thorough examination to be made free from the threat that the parents may remove the child and disappear. It is this perhaps which most concerns those involved in emergency treatment of abused children.

Legislation should also provide a speedy and effective means of review so that a child is not held and separated from its family for an unduly lengthy period in circumstances where the necessarily hasty diagnosis of child abuse has proved to be incorrect. It is undesirable in cases where the child is to be held to suggest that it is being detained because of the fault of its parents. Any holding procedures adopted should resemble as closely as possible the normal procedure whereby a child with an illness or physical injury is admitted to hospital for observation.[45]

6. Powers of Entry

If comprehensive legislation to deal with the problems of child abuse is to be enacted in Victoria, consideration must also be given to the difficult issues which arise from the vesting of powers to enter premises in members of the police force and other persons. Under the existing legislation police officers and authorized persons may enter premises only after having obtained a warrant. The situation of the child is often desperate. The most dramatic example will illustrate the problem. A neighbour notifies a police officer or authorized person that a child is being physically abused. The officer or authorized person immediately responds to the call and satisfies herself that the plight of the child demands urgent action. It may easily be argued that such a situation requires a power to enter premises and remove the child against the wishes of the householder.[46] However, the issue of whether particular persons or classes of persons should have the power to enter private premises is fraught with difficulties and the need for maintaining a delicate balance between the interests of the child and the civil liberties of the parents arises. The issue becomes more serious when one considers that in extreme cases the possibility of criminal proceedings against the parents is a real one.

The Australian Law Reform Commission has recently made recommendations with respect to warrants.[47] The commission's attention was directed towards search warrants in relation to criminal proceedings but the same issues arise in this situation. Whilst a power to enter premises and to remove children is obviously vital it is clear that, as the commission pointed out, a power of entry is potentially destructive as far as rights to privacy and civil liberties are concerned. While there is no doubt that the welfare of the child should be the paramount concern of those drafting legislation, these issues should be born in mind. The commission was of the view that in general all searches without warrant should be unlawful. It was however mindful of the existence of emergency situations particularly, for example in relation to narcotics law enforcement. It recommended that searches without warrants be lawful only:

(a) in response to circumstances of such seriousness and urgency as to require and justify immediate action without the authority of such order or warrant,

(b) with the consent of the person occupying the premises, or

(c) pursuant to specifically designated statutory authority.

Some proponents of civil liberties may have reservations about vesting powers of entry without warrant in police officers. Such people will probably take the view that powers of entry should be granted only in the most urgent and exceptional cases. The difficulty is, of course, to make a prediction as to which cases are 'urgent and exceptional'. Powers of entry without a warrant should certainly not be vested in private citizens. If such people are to be given power to enter the homes of fellow citizens there is an even greater need to safeguard against the abuse of power. Rigid controls must be imposed. The requirement of a warrant would seem to be minimal.[48] How can this protection of civil liberties and rights to privacy be safeguarded whilst at the same time ensuring that the interests of the child are paramount? Legislative provision for an efficient system of telephone warrants could perhaps be considered. The system of telephone injunctions developed by the Family Court of Australia could perhaps be used as a precedent.

Consideration could also be given to providing a system whereby police officers and an expanded list of authorized persons have the power to enter premises without warrant in cases of extreme and perhaps life-threatening emergency but with an obligation to justify their actions before a justice or magistrate within a reasonably short period of time.

7. Conclusion

The breadth of issues raised by the problem of child abuse and neglect is such that any solution proposed must, to be effective, involve both legal and administrative action. It must be emphasized that legislation, however comprehensive and wisely drafted, cannot achieve results unless there is an associated provision for multidisciplinary coordination through adequate and responsive support services. This chapter has outlined some deficiencies in the law relating to child abuse in certain Australian jurisdictions. The most fundamental and common defect is that the point of time at which the child is inducted into the system established theoretically for its protection is too late to be optimally beneficial. The state intervenes only after physical maltreatment has occurred and usually then by means of a procedure which is essentially punitive and which often subjects the child to the same treatment as that meted out to a child charged with a criminal offence. A more positive approach would allow speedy and efficient intervention aimed at prevention and support rather than punishment. Such an approach should be designed to resolve the needs of the child and the family together rather than tending to isolate the child from the family as a solution in itself.

If the needs of both the child and family unit are to be met then the bodies with jurisdiction over them should be composed of a collection of people with a range of expertise, experience and qualifications and not of lawyers or police alone. The precise structure of authority and provision of support services should be tailored to the physical and administrative character of the jurisdiction. For example, a large state with widely separated population centres may be best served by a regionalized system. Any legislation with respect to the maltreated child should however be based upon the following principles:

(1) That the welfare of the child is the paramount consideration when a child has been abused and should outweigh the rights of the parent or guardian.

(2) An adequate system should be established whereby a child suspected of having been maltreated may be brought to the notice of appropriate persons and provision may be made for the assessment of its condition and needs. Such provision must provide that the body responsible for such assessment has the facilities at its command to make the proper assessment of the child and the treatment required for both the child and the family and can set in motion the appropriate supportive services.

If these considerations are to be paramount a problem of some complexity arises. The very definition of maltreatment presents the necessity for striking a delicate balance between conflicting interests. It should be wide enough to include both emotional and physical injury and acts of omission and commission. But on the other hand boundaries must be drawn to maintain a fair balance between the interests of the child at risk and the interests of the parent whose child is not at risk. Those of the latter require a definition which is sufficiently precise to exclude them from the ambit of the legislation. The rights of parents with respect to their children and their personal rights to privacy and their civil liberties must be respected. Legislation must, therefore provide a procedure that ensures swift, firm action in favor of the child and also protects the rights of parents.

It has already been suggested that an effective and speedy means of review of holding orders should be provided. This is particularly important when the holding order has the potential to remain in the force for a lengthy period. Where provision is for holding orders of a relatively short duration and the order is to be discharged if further proceedings are not taken within such a period, it is arguable that there is no necessity to provide for applications to review the order. If the initial diagnosis of abuse is found to be erroneous the child would be returned to the parent within a very brief period of time.

With regard to ultimate disposition orders, it is clearly essential that an appeal machinery be provided. The right to appeal should be granted not only to the child, but also to the parents. Provision should also be made to enable a child or perhaps a Children's Protection Society to appeal against an order dismissing an application to have the child declared in need of care and protection.

If Children's Courts have the power to commit children to institutions for an indefinite period which may not expire until they reach their majority, their progress should be automatically subject to review at regular intervals. In addition parents should have the right to apply for review of the child's position without being forced to lengthy and expensive procedures before superior courts.

In June 1975 a potentially significant step was taken in Victoria when a multidisciplinary workshop was set up under the auspices of the Department of Health. Members of the workshop included doctors, lawyers, social workers, teachers, sociologists, nurses, police, welfare officers, psychiatrists, nursery school teachers and representatives from parents self-help associations and from some interested government departments. The aims of the workshop were the development of a program to bring about attitudinal changes which would lead to appropriate approaches to the prevention of child maltreatment and the development of programs for treatment and management. Following the inaugural meeting of the Workshop, in June, 1975, six working groups were set up. Their tasks were:

Group 1: To examine professional and community attitudes to child maltreatment and to assess methods of achieving —
(i) professional understanding and expertise; and
(ii) community awareness and action.

Group 2 & 3: To determine the need for preventive services and how these may be developed.

Group 4: To examine and evaluate methods of assessment, management and treatment and to recommend alternative methods.

Group 5: To make a study of socio-cultural influences in relation to child maltreatment.

Group 6: To study the law in relation to child maltreatment and to make recommendations regarding its revision.

Participants selected the area in which they wished to work. Often they went to the group to which they had most to offer because of their professional expertise, but this was not always the case. Membership of the group considering legal issues included a family court judge, academic lawyers, a psychiatrist, a psychologist, social workers, an infant welfare sister, a police officer, several legal practitioners and a pediatrician.

The report of the workshop was released in May 1977.[49] Briefly, with regard to the legal aspects of the problem, the workshop was faced with several choices. While it was agreed that provision for holding orders was essential, the workshop was divided as to whether compulsory notification should be implemented. Ultimately a majority of the workshop voted against compulsory notification and in favor of a system of voluntary notification.[50] It was agreed unanimously that provision should be made to protect persons making such notification from civil liability. Two alternative pieces of legislation were drafted. One took the form of a draft bill following the Tasmanian model which provided for a system separate from the Children's Court to deal with child abuse. The other alternative dealt with most matters in need of reform but by means of amendment to the existing legislation. The workshop as a whole ultimately put forward thie amending bill as its recommendation. The main argument in favor of the draft bill was that it would permit experimental concepts to be introduced on a limited scale and avoid the necessity of integrating those provisions with existing machinery. The reasons for accepting the amending bill in preference to this however, were more complex. In the first place it was thought that politically the amending bill would be more acceptable. It was also felt that care should be taken to avoid overlap and inconsistency between legislation and that it was important that child welfare legislation should reflect modern concepts and philosophies and form a coherent and integrated whole. Child maltreatment should not be regarded as an issue separated from the whole area of child welfare. The decision in favor of the amending bill was also influenced by a desire to avoid diffusion of authority over the child. This would have undesirable consequences including confusion in the minds of the public which in turn would not be inducive to the formation of good relationships between the public and government agencies. It was also felt that diffusion of authority could provide agencies with an excuse to deny ultimate responsibility for a child if jurisdictional boundaries were blurred, and would be wasteful of resources.

No direct action to implement any of the recommendations made by the workshop has yet been taken. However there is presently sitting a Legislation Committee which is to advise the Attorney General on the Children's Court Act and *inter alia* to consider the Workshop Report in that respect. The Central Implementation Committee of the Committee of Inquiry into Child Health Services in Victoria is also considering the report as part of its brief to develop an overall policy for Victoria on family welfare and an interdepartmental committee comprising representatives of the Departments of Health and Social Welfare has been established to coordinate existing services and advise on necessary additions to them.[51] These activities are linked with a program of restructuring the administration of social welfare services throughout the state. Although the Victorian government could not be accused of acting precipitously in the matter of legislative and administrative reform, the danger is that a morass of committee reports and recommendations may unduly delay reform in an area where there is a real toll in terms of daily human suffering.

1. Community Welfare act 1972-1976 (S.A.); Child Protection Act 1974 (Tas.); Child Welfare Amendment Act 1977 (N.S.W.); Child Welfare Act (No. 2) 1947-1976 (W.A.).
2. S. 31. "Every child or young person under seventeen years of age who answers to any of the following descriptions shall be deemed to be a child or young person in need of care and protection, that is to say:—

Every child or young person:

(a) found begging or receiving alms or being in any street or public place for the purpose of begging or receiving alms or inducing the giving of alms;
(b) found wandering, abandoned, or sleeping, in any public place;
(c) who has no visible means of support or no settled place of abode;
(d) who is in a brothel or lodges or resides or wanders about with known or reputed thieves drunkards vagrants or prostitutes whether such thieves drunkards vagrants or prostitutes are the parents of the child or not;
(e) who (not being duly licensed pursuant to the provisions of Division 9 of this Part) is employed in street trading in contravention of that Division or the regulations after a member of the police force or any person authorized in that behalf by the Governor in Council has (whether orally or otherwise) warned the child to desist from such trading and (where the parent or guardian of the child can be found) warned such parent or guardian that the child should desist from such trading;
(f) who is not provided with sufficient or proper food, nursing, clothing, medical aid or who is ill-treated or exposed;
(g) who takes part in any public exhibition of performance referred to in Division 9 of this Part whereby the life or limbs of the child taking part is endangered;
(h) who is in the care and custody of any person unfit by reason of his conduct or habits or incapable by reason of his health to have the care and custody of the child or young person;
(i) who is lapsing or likely to lapse into a career of vice or crime;
(j) who is exposed to moral danger;
(k) who is required by law to attend school and who without lawful excuse has habitually absented himself from school and whose parent has, in respect of such absence, been convicted under Part IV, of the *Education Act* 1958."

3. Only two persons have been authorized under the Act. They are officers of the Children's Protection Society. One is based in Melbourne, the other is based in Geelong, 40 miles from Melbourne.
4. Children's Court Act 1973 (Vic.) s. 6 established a court consisting of up to three children's courts magistrates (i.e., in effect stipendiary or police magistrates), or in some situations of two or three justices of the peace.
5. Children's Court Act 1973 (Vic.) s. 22.
6. These points are made in the Report of the Child Maltreatment Workshop (Melbourne, 1976) p. 39. See note 49.
7. Child Protection Act (1974) (Tas.) s. 2(6) provides that:

"For the purposes of this Act, a child may be regarded as having suffered cruel treatment notwithstanding that the treatment was not intended to be cruel or was not intended to result in injury to the child; and the neglect, or failure to perform any act required for the welfare of the child may constitute cruel treatment of that child."

8. Child Protection Act 1974 (Tas.) s. 3.

377 Some Legal Aspects of Child Abuse in Australia

9. *Ibid.* s. 5.
10. A notable omission from this group is members of the Police Force. In a paper delivered at the first National Conference on the Battered Child (Perth, August, 1975), Professor Ian Lewis, Professor of Child Health at the University of Tasmania and a member of the Board, suggested that they were omitted because many health and welfare officers felt "rightly or wrongly" that they were heavy handed and punitive in their dealing with abusing families.
11. *Ibid.* s. 11(1). Professor Lewis in the paper cited in note 10 above observed that the reasons for selecting the age of twelve years were "completely illogical".
12. *Ibid.* s. 11(2). In the Child Protection Order (No. 2) of 1975, the following classes of persons were specified:

"Probation officers appointed under the *Probation Offenders Act* 1973. Child welfare officers appointed under the *Child Welfare Act* 1960. Welfare officers appointed under the *Alcohol and Drug Dependency Act* 1968.

Persons holding children's boarding home licences or day nursery licences under s. 54 of the *Child Welfare Act* 1960.

Persons holding office under the *Education Act* 1932 who are principals of primary or infant schools, mistresses in charge of infant schools, teachers in charge of kindergartens, or officers engaged primarily in welfare work.

Psychiatrists, social workers, and welfare officers, appointed under the *Mental Health Services Act* 1967, who are primarily engaged in welfare work.

Medical practitioners registered under Part III of the *Medical Act* 1959."

13. Child Protection Act 1974 (Tas.) s. 8(3).
14. *Ibid.* s. 9(1).
15. *Ibid.* s. 9(2).
16. *Ibid.* s. 10(1).
17. *Ibid.* s. 10(2).
18. *Ibid.* s. 11(1).
19. Child Welfare Act 1960 (Tas.) s. 34.
20. Child Protection Act 1974 (Tas.) s. 11(2).
21. Child Protection Act 1974 (Tas.) s. 16(1).
22. *Ibid.* s. 10(3).
23. This information was provided by Mr. W.H. Goudie, the Chairman of the Child Protection Assessment Board. He provided the following additional information: the sources of reports in 1976 were as follows: Hospitals 16; Police 2; Dept. of Social Welfare 13; Doctors 12; Public 23; Schools 12; Probation Service 2; Child Health Service 1; Life-Line 2. In four cases in 1976 a child was declared a Ward of the State on the application of the Board.
24. Juvenile Courts Act 1971-1977 ss. 9, 10.
25. *Ibid.* ss. 12, 14.
26. *Ibid.* Part III, ss. 17*ff.*
27. 'Neglected' is defined in accordance with Community Welfare Act 1972-1976 s. 6(1)

"neglected child means a child who:

(a) is under the guardianship of any person whom the court considers unfit to have the guardianship of that child;
(b) has apparently no sufficient means of support, and whose guardians or near relatives are unable or unwilling to maintain him or are dead or unknown or cannot be found or are detained in a prison or home;
or

(c) has no guardian, or is not cared for or maintained adequately, or is ill-treated by his guardian and in need of care."

28. Juvenile Courts Act 1971-1977 ss. 3, 56; Community Welfare Act 1972-1976 s. 3.
29. Community Welfare Act 1972-1976 s. 82a.
30. *Ibid.* s. 82c.
31. *Ibid.* s. 82e.
32. *Ibid.* s. 82d.
33. The offence referred must be that encompassed by s. 82e.

"82e. (1) Any person having the care, custody, control or charge of a child, who maltreats or neglects the child, or causes the child to be maltreated or neglected, in a manner likely to subject the child to unnecessary injury or danger shall be guilty of an offence and liable to a penalty not exceeding five hundred dollars or imprisonment for a period not exceeding twelve months."

However, it is not made perfectly clear who is intended by the phrase "person in charge of that hospital". Compare the recently amended Western Australian provisions; Child Welfare Act (No. 2) 1947-1976 (W.A.) s. 29 (3a) and (3b).

"(3a) Where a child under the age of six years is admitted to a hospital and there are reasonable grounds to suspect that the child is a child in need of care and protection, the Medical Officer in charge of that hospital, or his deputy, may order that the child be detained in hospital for a period not exceeding forty-eight hours for the purposes of observation, assessment or treatment, but shall thereupon give notice to the Department in the prescribed manner.

(3b) Where a child is detained in a hospital pursuant to subsection (3a) of this section, on the expiration of the period of detention that child shall:

(a) be discharged from the hospital; or
(b) remain in the hospital with the consent of a parent or guardian; or
(c) be apprehended and dealt with in accordance with the provisions of this section or of section forty-seven B of this Act,
as the case may require."

34. These points were made in a number of papers reproduced in "The Battered Child, First National Conference, Perth, August 1975", Department of Community Welfare, Western Australia, pp. 116-122.
35. See for example Social Welfare Act 1970 (Vic.) s. 81; Community Welfare Act 1972-1976 (S.A.) s. 82e; Child Welfare Act 1960 (Tas.) s. 66.
36. This is the intention of the Community Welfare Act 1972-1976 (S.A.) s. 82e.(2) in respect of proceedings for an offence under that section.
37. It is beyond the scope of this chapter to discuss fully the evidence and arguments concerning penal sanctions as effective deterrents to criminal behavior. It should be noted however that the complexity and interrelationship factors found to exist in cases of violence in the family would tend to suggest that behavior of this type would respond poorly to deterrents.
38. Both Tasmania and South Australia have imposed a duty to notify on specific classes of persons including medical practitioners, as discussed in notes 12, 32. On March 24th 1977 legislation to amend the Child Welfare Act of N.S.W. was passed. It largely followed recommendations made by the Muir Report on the Child Welfare Act and a report by the N.S.W. Child Welfare Legislation Review Committee, both published during 1975. The amendment involves placing a new provision into the Child Welfare

Act which compels any doctor or other presribed person to report cases of suspected child abuse and provides for limited protection from civil liability for any person who reports alleged child abuse cases where there are reasonable grounds for suspicion. The reports are to be made to the Director of Welfare, and failure to comply is an offence against the Act.

39. See notes 2, 7 and 27.

40. The Murray Report analyzed the response to the compulsory notification provisions passed in South Australia in 1969 and incorporated into the Community Welfare Act in 1972. The number of reports recorded in the central register of the Department was 23 in 1972, 18 in 1973 and 24 in 1974. The survey undertaken by the Committee of Enquiry made it clear that these figures are not a true reflection of the number of cases of non-accidental physical injury which occur and are actually detected in various settings in that state.

41. Murray Report *op. cit.* pp. 46-47. This suggested definition does not seem to have been implemented in legislation to date.

42. See note 38. s. 132, Child Welfare Act 1939 (N.S.W.) provides that the penalty for an offence under the appropriate division of that act is a fine of $1,000.

43. Compare Child Protection Act 1974 (Tas.) s. 8(3) and Child Welfare Act 1939 (N.S.W.) s. 138B with Community Welfare Act 1972-1976 (S.A.) s. 82d(5). The two former enactments provide for protection from three specified heads of civil liability: these are defamation, malicious prosecution and conspiracy. Both enactments also provide that the making of such a report or notification shall not be held to be a breach of professional ethics or a departure from accepted standards of professional conduct. On the other hand, the latter enactment provides . . . S. 32d(5) "Where a person acts in good faith and in compliance or purported compliance with the provisions of this section, he incurs no civil liability in respect of that action."

The House of Lords decision in *D.v. N.S.P.C.C.* [1976] 3 W.L.R. 124 was the culmination of lengthy litigation turning on a procedural issue but indirectly involving the possibility of civil action for negligent misstatement arising out of a report made to the N.S.P.C.C. This head of liability would not be covered by the exemption provisions in either Tasmania or New South Wales.

44. For example, a medical practitioner has given the example of a child admitted to hospital with extensive bruising. The casualty personnel in the hospital concerned assumed that the child had been beaten and notified the police. The child was ultimately found to be suffering from a rare blood disorder.

45. See text accompanying notes 16 and 33. The time periods in Australia vary from 48 hours in Western Australia to 30 days in Tasmania.

46. In a conversation with the writer Ms. Margaret Sitlington. Secretary of the Childrens' Protection Society (Victoria) and the only 'authorized' officer operating in Melbourne under the existing legislation, expressed the opinion that a formal right of entry was unnecessary. She had never been refused entry to a house.

47. "Criminal Investigation" (1975), 2 *Australian Law Reform Commn.* 94.

48. A different opinion was expressed by Loretta Re in a comment on the Victorian Child Maltreatment Report (see note 49 below). (June, 1977), 2 *Legal Service Bulletin* No. 7, 233.

"It could be argued that many abusing parents with insight into their problem would welcome the calls of a home visitor to counsel them whereas parents who are persistently uncooperative with doctors or who could only be described as brutal to their children (or step children) have forfeited the right to care for them without this degree of intervention."

49. Report of the Child Maltreatment Workshop, Melbourne 1976, Victorian Government Printer 1302/77. The Report was submitted to the Minister for Health in November 1976 but was not released and published until May 1977. In fact this delay was the first

indication of the difficulties envisaged by the Department in impelementing the recommendations of the Workshop, and the problems of its political acceptance.

50. It is worth noting that at the Perth Conference in August 1975 an informal vote put to the delegates on the question of mandatory reporting resulted in approximately 65 percent voting in favor of some sort of mandatory reporting system.

51. Victorian *Parliamentary Debates* Legislative Assembly 18th October 1977, 10449.

Chapter 25

Aspects juridiques des sévices à enfants en France

M.J. Gebler* et G. Deschamps†

1. La prévention et la détection des sévices

Parmi les éléments de la politique générale de protection de l'enfance sur le plan médical et social, quels sont ceux qui peuvent contribuer à prévenir et à dépister les sévices? Si en effet cette politique n'est pas orientée spécifiquement *vers* les sévices, les rencontres qu'elle suppose entre familles, travailleurs sociaux et médecins peuvent être *l'occasion* de découvrir des mauvais traitements.

Dans chaque département français, la mise en oeuvre et la coordination des actions de prévention incombe, sous l'autorité du Préfet, à la direction des affaires sanitaires et sociales (D.A.S.S.), service extérieur du Ministère de la Santé. Le personnel de la D.A.S.S., composé de médecins, de travailleurs sociaux (assistantes sociales, infirmières, puéricultrices, sage-femmes, éducateurs, travailleuses familiales) et d'administrateurs, collabore avec les juges des enfants en ce qui concerne la protection des enfants en danger.

Le code de la santé publique (art. L. 164) prévoit que "jusqu'au début de l'obligation scolaire, tous les enfants sont l'object d'une surveillance sanitaire préventive et, le cas échéant, d'une surveillance sociale". Ainsi les structures de santé publique notamment peuvent contribuer à la prévention et au dépistage des sévices, en assurant une surveillance systématique de la population des jeunes enfants.

(A) Sur le plan médical

En théorie, la médecine préventive est bien organisée car 20 contrôles obligatoires sont prévus avant que l'enfant n'ait six ans. Neuf pendant la première année, trois pendant la deuxième année et deux par an au cours des quatre années suivantes (décret no. 73-267 du 2 mars 1973). Autant d'occasions par conséquent de découvrir les sévices, spécialement, si le médecin, travaillant en liaison avec le service social, connaît la situation de la famille.

---

* Faculté de Droit et des Sciences Economique de Nancy.
† Centre Hospitalier Universitaire de Nancy, France.

En pratique, il n'est pas certain que l'objectif poursuivi sera toujours atteint. Le problème général des sévices à enfants, sous ses aspects divers, ayant déjà été exposé, il ne nous a pas semblé utile de l'"introduire" de nouveau. Notre objectif a simplement été d'examiner, à partir d'une législation donnée, comment la question a été posée, quelles solutions étaient proposées et quelles améliorations pouvaient être envisagées. D'une part l'enfant peut ne présenter aucun symptôme inquietant lors de l'examen medical. La date des examens est fixée avec une relative précision car elle correspond à certaines périodes importantes dans l'évolution de l'enfant (par exemple: au cours du neuvième mois ou du vingt-quatrième mois). Il est possible qu'au jour de la visite les sévices n'aient pas encore eu lieu ou que les traces aient disparu. D'autre part les sévices peuvent ne pas être reconnus par le médecin. Les examens pouvant être pratiqués par tout médecin choisi par la famille, dans une structure publique ou en cabinet privé, il est possible que le médecin examinateur ne connaisse pas l'enfant et sa famille, et manque ainsi de la continuité d'observation souvent nécessaire au diagnostic de mauvais traitements ou de négligences graves.

Enfin les examens, en fait, n'ont pas toujours lieu. Si l'enfant est victime de mauvais traitements, il est fréquent qu'il soit soustrait aux visites médicales: elles ne sont pas toutes assorties de sanctions, et de sanctions efficaces. Parmi les vingt examens en principe obligatoires (et gratuits), trois seulement comportent un risque immediat pour les parents qui s'y deroberaient: ceux qui ont lieu dans les huit jours de la naissance, à neuf mois, à deux ans (décret 2 mars 1973). Ils donnent lieu à la rédaction d'un certificat de santé envoyé à la D.A.S.S. par le médecin, et à la rédaction d'une attestation transmise par les parents à l'organisme de sécurité sociale qui verse les prestations familiales. L'absence d'attestation entraîne la suspension des versements. Cette menace devrait, à priori, être dissuasive. En réalité, elle ne l'est pas toujours, soit que les parents n'aient pas droit aux prestations, soit qu'ils puissent équilibrer leur budget sans cette aide, soit qu'ils ne prévoient pas la sanction (on ne pense pas beaucoup aux prestations quand on bat l'enfant).

Il faut aussi noter que, dans le cadre de la prévention, un médecin est normalement amené, à deux autres occasions, à rencontrer le jeune enfant. Dans les deux premières années de sa vie, l'enfant doit subir obligatoirement plusieurs vaccinations (variole, diphtérie, tétanos, poliomyélite). Deux sanctions sont prévues en cas de négligence des parents: ils encourent une peine d'amende ou de prison et ils ne peuvent faire admettre l'enfant dans une école ou dans toute autre collectivité d'enfant (art. L. 5 à 7-I C.S.P., arrêté du 19 mars 1965, décret no. 73-502 du 21 mai 1973). Mais en fait les vaccinations sont pratiquées lors des examens préventifs cités plus haut: il faut donc faire à ce sujet les mêmes réserves.

Au cours de la première année d'école maternelle et d'école primaire (vers trois ans et vers six ans), l'enfant fait l'objet en classe d'un bilan de santé très complet accompagné d'un bilan social (décret no. 64-783 du 30 juillet 1964). L'efficacité de ces dispositions est toutefois limitée par le fait qu'à l'époque du premier bilan, l'enfant peut ne pas encore être scolarisé. De plus les sévices sont surtout fréquents dans les toutes premières années de la vie, avant même l'entrée à l'école maternelle. Enfin, les parents auteurs de sévices s'abstiennent volontiers d'envoyer l'enfant en classe lorsqu'il présente des traces de coups.

(B) Sur le plan social

La surveillance sanitaire s'accompagne d'une surveillance sociale, spécialement lorsque l'enfant a moins de six ans (art. L. 164 Code de la santé publique).

(a) Comment se réalise la surveillance sociale?

Elle est confiée à des assistantes sociales et à des infirmières-puericultrices attachées à la D.A.S.S. (service de la protection maternelle et infantile).

Deux points paraissent importants en ce qui concerne la manière dont l'assistante sociale remplit son role: D'une part elle se rend au domicile des parents. Elle voit donc l'enfant dans son milieu naturel et peut ainsi apprécier quelles sont les conditions de vie habituelles de la famille, le mode d'existence quotidien des enfants, l'atmosphère du foyer etc. D'autre part le nombre et la date des interventions des assistantes sociales ne sont pas règlementes. L'assistante sociale se rend dans les familles sans avoir à annoncer sa visite, à n'importe quel moment. Les parents ne peuvent donc pas "s'organiser" en fonction de cette venue, il leur est plus difficile de dissimuler la situation réelle ou de se séparer par exemple de l'enfant battu.

Toutefois si les avantages des "visites surprises" par rapport aux "voyages organisés" à l'exterieur du foyer sont evidents en théorie, il n'en reste pas moins que le systeme n'est efficace que si les visites ont effectivement lieu et permettent une rencontre avec l'enfant battu. Or certaines familles refusent d'ouvrir la porte quand l'assistante sociale se présente, ou refusent d'ouvrir la porte de la pièce dans laquelle se trouve l'enfant, ou encore prétextent toujours que l'enfant est absent. D'autre familles ne reçoivent jamais la visite d'une assistante sociale. Il s'agit souvent des familles les plus défavorisées ou au contraire de familles aisées dans lesquelles le problème des sévices reste longtemps méconnu.

En principe chaque assistante sociale a la charge d'un secteur qui couvre de 3 à 5000 personnes. En fait elle doit souvent s'occuper de 8 à 10.000 personnes. Dans ces conditions le "quadrillage systématique" devient très difficile. Le 7ème plan (1976-1980) prévoit d'ailleurs dans ses programmes d'action prioritaire que l'accent devra être mis sur la prévention sociale précoce. "Le service sociale polyvalent de secteur sera renforcé, dans les 200 zones à haut risque retenues, par une diminution de la taille des secteurs (3000 habitants au plus, au lieu de 3000 à 5000) et par le doublement du nombre d'assistants de service social (2 au lieu d'un par secteur)".

Malgré ces imperfections, la coexistence des deux moyens de dépistage des sévices par les autorités responsables semble utile. La surveillance médicale et la surveillance sociale se complètent. La surveillance médicale est organisée de telle manière qu'en principe peu d'enfants devraient en être écartés, quel que soit leur milieu d'origine. Encore faut-il cependant que les sévices soient visibles au jour précis où a lieu la visite médicale, que des symptômes puissent être relevés.

La surveillance sociale est moins systèmatique mais étant aussi moins ponctuelle et plus continue, elle permet peut-être davantage de prévenir et de découvrir "par hasard" les sévices.

(b) Quels sont les moyens mis en oeuvre pour faciliter l'exercice de cette surveillance sociale?

"Afin de permettre la surveillance à domicile des enfants", les officiers d'état-civil adressent un extrait d'acte de naissance à la D.A.S.S. de la residence des enfants (décret no. 62-840 du 19 juillet 1962, art. 8). La D.A.S.S. connaît donc l'existence de tout nouveau-né. Il est rare que la mère ne reçoive pas la visite d'une assistante sociale ou d'une infirmière-puéricultrice peu de temps après son retour de maternité, une visite qui généralement sera considérée comme normale par les parents. Ils s'y attendent, savent qu'elle aura lieu et par conséquent l'acceptent assez volontiers.

Or, dans une perspective de prévention des sévices, l'intervention du service social est particulièrement importante au moment des maternités. Une enquête faite en hôpital à Nancy entre 1972 et 1975 montre que dans un cas sur deux une naissance était survenue dans l'année précédante les sévices. Il semble donc qu'une surveillance accrue soit nécessaire pendant les périodes de vulnérabilité qui entourent la naissance. Non seulement la mère est alors plus fatiguée ou plus nerveuse, mais l'accouchement nécessite souvent le placement des autres enfants et, au moment de leur retour, les risques de sévices s'accroissent. De même le nouveau-né doit faire l'objet d'une particulière vigilance s'il ne revient que tardivement au foyer (cas de l'enfant prématuré et fragile qui reste longtemps à hôpital puis est placé en pouponnière et devient finalement étranger à la famille. Une enquête faite à Paris entre 1972 et 1975 montre que 26% des enfants battus étaient d'anciens prématurés).

Dès lors l'information systématique du personnel social en cas de nouvelle naissance est importante. Ce n'est toutefois qu'un premier pas. Les interventions doivent continuer. Mais elles deviennent difficiles si les parents déménagent ou si le couple se dissocie. Juridiquement aucun texte n'impose de signaler un changement de residence. Même si le changement est connu, le transfert de dossier d'une D.A.S.S. à une autre ou d'un secteur social à un autre prend du temps.

Or, sur le plan des sévices, les périodes de déménagement, tout comme celles des naissances, sont considérées comme des périodes de vulnérabilité car dans les deux cas un evenement vient modifier le cours de la vie des parents et de l'enfant. Dans l'enquête faite à Nancy, plus d'un tiers des familles avait déménagé dans l'année précédante les sévices. Dans l'enquête de Paris, un quart avait déménagé plusieurs fois. La protection devient ainsi plus difficile à organiser au moment précis où l'enfant et ses parents en ont le plus besoin.

Un texte de 1962 (art. 8-I du décret précité du 19 juillet) impose aux assistantes sociales de faire porter tout spécialement leur effort sur certaines familles qui, en raison de leur passé ou de leur situation actuelle, peuvent être considérées comme des familles "à hauts risques".

Le texte cite notamment le cas des parents qui "recoivent un secours ou une allocation exceptionnelle de l'Etat, des collectivités ou des caisses de sécurité sociale", "ont subi un traitement dans un hôpital psychiatrique", ont été condamnés pour ivresse ou coups et violences, sont connus du juge des enfants en raison du prononcé d'une mesure d'assistance éducative ou de tutelle aux prestations familiales.

Comparons ces critères très généraux susceptibles d'orienter les démarches prioritaires des assistantes sociales, avec la situation des familles auteurs de sévices. Les familles qui "n'ont jamais fait parler d'elles" sont rares (mais il resterait à déterminer si les classes moyennes ou aisées n'ont pas davantage de moyens pour dissimuler les sévices et si leur situation sociale ne rend pas plus difficile la croyance et la révélation de l'existence des sévices). L'enquête precitée montre que l'ethylisme existait dans 42,5% des cas, les troubles psychiatriques — au sens large du terme — dans 36% des cas et qu'un père sur quatre avait été condamné pour des causes variables.

Pourrait-on aller plus loin et élaborer une grille des risques spécifiques de sévices portée à la connaissance de tous les intervenants au cours par exemple de leur formation? Il ne semble pas que l'on puisse s'orienter dans cette direction. Une tentative a été faite en ce sens à Nancy, à partir de nombreuses observations d'enfants victimes de mauvais traitements. Une liste d'indicateurs ou de facteurs a été dressée (antécédents des parents, couple actuel, fratrie, enfant), chaque élément étant affecté d'un indice. Mais il s'avère finalement que cette grille n'est pas vraiment spécifique des sévices (sans compter le danger que présenterait son utilisation sans précaution). Elle pourrait, à la limite, servir d'outil de travail à toute personne concernée par l'aide aux familles en difficulté (ce qui montre d'ailleurs bien que le problème des sévices ne peut pas être résolu par des mesures ne concernant que les sévices). Elle met cependant en relief l'existence de périodes de vulnérabilité au cours desquelles les risques de mauvais traitements s'accroissent. Les enquêtes de Paris et de Nancy montrent par exemple que dans 35 à 40% des cas, les enfants battus avaient été antérieurement placés. Un tel chiffre peut conduire à renforcer la surveillance à ce moment précis de la vie de l'enfant (et aussi à s'interroger sur l'opportunité du placement et sur les conditions de la restitution).

2. La dénonciation des sévices

Une constatation s'impose: les sévices sont rarement portés à la connaissance des autorités publiques. Avant d'examiner quel peut être le rôle du législateur en ce domaine pour inciter ou contraindre les témoins à parler, il est indispensable de s'interroger sur les raisons psychologiques qui rendent difficiles la dénonciation.

(A) Les difficultés d'ordre psychologique.

Elles sont nombreuses et profondes. La première difficulté résulte de la répugnance instinctive de toute personne à reconnaître la réalité des mauvais traitements exercés sur un enfant. Accepter leur existence est un premier pas difficile à franchir. D'une part, chacun a peur de se tromper. Quelle signification donner à la gifle trop forte mais peut-être accidentelle, ou à des ecchymoses d'origine douteuse? "Les symptômes de l'enfant battu sont parfois difficiles à identifier comme tels et plus encore à interpreter, sauf cas flagrants: leur simple examen ne permet pas généralement de conclure à l'existence et à la gravité d'un danger" (Question écrite no. 22132, Journal Officiel, Débats parlementaires, Assemblée Nationale, 5 février 1977). D'autre part, cette démarche intérieure (admettre l'existence des sévices) est particulièrement difficile pour les travailleurs sociaux qui sont souvent impliqués depuis longtemps dans les mesures de protection et d'aide à une famille et pour lesquels la survenue des sévices signifie un échec de l'action menée.

La seconde difficulté trouve son origine dans la crainte des conséquences de cette dénonciation. Pour le voisin ou la parenté, ce sera le souci égoïste de ne pas se "mêler des affaires des autres", de ne pas s'attirer d'ennuis, la crainte aussi d'être reconnu par l'auteur des sévices comme le dénonciateur, la peur enfin des réprésailles (parent violent). L'opinion publique est prompte à s'émouvoir quand l'affaire éclate ou est jugée, mais réticente à agir quand les sévices concernent les voisins.

Pour attenuer ces difficultés, plusieurs solutions sont concevables. Mais il faut avant tout que cette "dénonciation", terme pejoratif qui choque, puisse être considérée non pas comme une démarche punitive à l'egard des auteurs de sévices mais comme un premier pas vers la solution d'un problème trop douloureux pour être traité sans passion. Des campagnes d'information s'organisent en France et ailleurs. Elles peuvent avoir, à long ou à moyen terme, une importance certaine, à condition toutefois de présenter une image juste de situations dans lesquelles les auteurs de sévices sont eux-mêmes victimes d'un lourd passé, à condition également d'éviter les risques de zèle intempestif aboutissant à des calomnies lourdes de conséquences.

Des formules souples permettent de trouver des solutions discrètes qui conservent l'annonymat de l'informateur et donnent les moyens de s'assurer de la realité des faits avant d'engager une action qui pourrait être préjudiciable à la famille. Le magistrat, le médecin, l'assistante sociale sont tenus au secret professionnel et n'ont pas à révéler le nom de leur informateur. L'instituteur ou des associations de sauvegarde de l'enfance peuvent jouer un role d'intermédiaire. Le médecin ou le travailleur social peuvent résoudre le problème par le biais d'une *hospitalisation* en essayant de convaincre les parents de la nécessite de soins plus intensifs. Le prétexte, bien souvent, ne sera pas difficile à trouver car dans les familles démunies l'hospitalisation est un moyen assez ordinaire de soigner un malade. L'équipe hospitalière est en mesure de bien évaluer la situation et de faire le signalement aux autorités compétentes sans que la responsabilité des travailleurs sociaux ou du médecin traitant soit mise en cause.

(B) Les problèmes juridiques

Pour que l'existence des sévices soit plus sûrement portée à la connaissance des autorités, il a paru nécessaire de créer des textes spéciaux. Le droit commun ne protège pas suffisamment l'enfant, l'enfant n'est pas une victime comme les autres. La non-dénonciation des mauvais traitements est une infraction pénale, une infraction pénale autonome particulièrement intéressante à étudier quand elle implique une violation du secret professionnel.

(a) Les personnes non tenues au secret professionnel

Sont concernés par exemple, les parents ou les personnes qui vivent avec l'enfant, les voisins qui savent, les amis qui passent au foyer, l'institutrice qui voit les plaies ou les ecchymoses. . . .

Depuis longtemps, la non-dénonciation des crimes aux autorités administratives ou judiciaires est en droit commun une infraction pénale. L'article 62 al. 1 du code pénal punit celui qui n'avertit pas les autorités "aussitôt" qu'il a connaissance du crime ou de la tentative de crime, "alors qu'il était encore possible d'en prévenir ou d'en limiter les effets ou qu'on pouvait penser que les coupables . . . commettraient de nouveaux crimes qu'une dénonciation pourrait prévenir". En cas de sévices, l'acte coupable est très rarement unique, isolé de sorte que cette condition (renouvellement prévisible de l'infraction) sera aisément remplie. Sévices et récidive sont liés (l'expérience montre d'ailleurs que bien souvent l'enfant victime a déjà été hospitalisé, en principe pour d'autres motifs, ou encore qu'un frère ou une soeur est antérieurement décédé pour des raisons inexpliquées).

Si la victime est un mineur de 15 ans, l'obligation de dénonciation s'étend à un cercle plus large de personnes: elle pèse, contrairement au droit commun, sur les parents et alliés des auteurs ou complices du crime. Les peines prévues sont un emprisonnement de un à trois mois et une amende de 360 à 15.000 francs.

Une loi du 15 juin 1971 (art. 62 al. 2 code pénal) sanctionne de la même manière toute personne qui a "connaissance de SEVICES ou de privations infligées à des mineurs de 15 ans" et n'informe pas immédiatement "les autorités administratives chargées des actions sanitaires et sociales". Tout citoyen au courant de mauvais traitements, qu'il ait été ou non le témoin direct des scènes de violence ou du manque de soins, risque donc la prison, s'il s'abstient de le signaler. Il importe peu que ces mauvais traitements soient juridiquement qualifiés de crime, de délit ou de contravention. Le nombre de situations à dénoncer est ainsi plus grand lorsque la victime, en raison de son âge, dispose de peu de moyens de défense.

Le texte n'exige pas une démarche auprès de la gendarmerie, de la police ou du juge. Il suffit d'avertir "les autorités administratives chargées des actions sanitaires et sociales". Cette disposition s'explique en partie par un souci d'efficacité. On prévient plus facilement l'assistante sociale qu'un représentant de l'ordre. L'assistante sociale ne fait pas remplir de papier, "on" la connaît bien, "on" la rencontre souvent. Le policier en principe dresse un procès-verbal et le fait signer, bien qu'il puisse aussi ouvrir une enquête à partir d'informations anonymes. Cette possibilité d'éviter le circuit judiciaire ou policier traduit aussi la volonté du législateur de mettre l'accent sur la victime plutôt que sur le coupable. Les sanctions interviendront peut-être, mais plus tard. C'est l'enfant qui compte d'abord. En allant trouver l'assistante sociale, le témoin aura davantage le sentiment d'agir pour sauver l'enfant. En allant trouver un gendarme, il participe au système répressif, il agit contre quelqu'un et non pour quelqu'un, il accuse, il dénonce au lieu d'informer.

(b) Les personnes tenues au secret professionnel

Parmi les personnes tenues au secret professionnel, nous ne retiendrons que le cas des médecins et des assistantes sociales (art. 378 code pénal, art. 225 code de la famille et de l'aide sociale).

Le problème se présente sous deux aspects. La violation de secret professionnel est une infraction pénale. Peut-elle être retenue lorsque le médecin ou l'assistante sociale révèle ce qu'il a appris dans l'exercice de ses fonctions? (délit par commission). Inversement peut-on invoquer le secret professionnel pour refuser de dire ce que l'on sait? (délit par omission pour non dénonciation de sévices ou pour refus de témoigner en justice).

(i) *Le délit par commission.* Le médecin ou l'assistante sociale qui révèle aux autorités l'existence des sévices, ou qui témoigne en justice à leur sujet, peut-il être poursuivi pour violation du secret professionnel?

Le législateur est intervenu, depuis quelques années, pour supprimer sur ce plan la plupart des obstacles juridiques qui s'opposaient antérieurement à certains signalements d'enfants maltraités. En effct, dans deux hypothèses, l'article 378 du code pénal et l'article 225 du code de la famille et de l'aide sociale relèvent du secret professionnel les personnes qui y sont normalement soumises. Lorsqu'elles informent les autorités médicales ou administratives chargées des actions sanitaires ou sociales des sévices ou privations dont sont victimes des mineurs de 15 ans (ou même 18 ans si le signalement émane d'une assistante sociale: art. 225 C.F.A.S.). Lorsqu'elles témoignent en justice dans une affaire de sévices ou de privations sur la personne d'un mineur de 15 ans. Elles sont "libres de fournir leur témoignage sans s'exposer à aucune peine". Le médecin ou l'assistante sociale qui, sans être à l'origine du signalement d'un cas douloureux, a été amené à constater l'état déplorable de l'enfant pourra, sans risque pour lui, décrire ce qu'il a vu, au cours, par exemple, du procès pénal engage contre les parents.

Le problème est plus délicat, lorsqu'une personne tenue au secret professionnel a informe les autorités judiciaires (et non plus administratives ou medicales). Un texte de 1959 (ordonnance no. 59-35 du 5 janvier 1959 insérée à l'art. 225 C.F.A.S.) précise que les assistantes sociales ne s'exposent alors à aucune sanction. Mais il n'existe aucun texte analogue pour les médecins. Il semble donc que des poursuites soient théoriquement possible contre les médecins, alors qu'elles sont impossibles contre des assistantes sociales. Toutefois, à notre connais-sance, aucune procédure n'a jamais été engagée dans ces conditions. De plus, en cas de péril "imminent et constant". (L'enfant est par exemple en danger de mort), l'obligation de porter secours — qui sera étudiée ultérieurement et peut prendre la forme d'un avertissement à la police — s'impose à tous, y compris aux médecins. Il ne peut alors y avoir violation du secret professionnel.

(ii) *Le délit par omission.* Deux sanctions risquent, à priori, de frapper le médecin ou l'assistante sociale qui, ayant connaissance de sévices ou de mauvais traitements, se tait: le refus de témoignage et la non dénonciation de sévices.

L'infraction de refus de témoignage a déjà été envisagée. L'article 378 du code pénal prévoit que toute personne tenue au secret professionnel est libre, dans les matières qui nous intéressent, de fournir son témoignage "sans s'exposer à aucune peine". Si elle le fournit, il n'y a pas violation du secret professionnel. Si elle ne le fournit pas, l'infraction à laquelle s'expose normalement le témoin qui régulière-ment cité, refuse de comparaitre ou de déposer, n'est pas constituée: le secret professionnel est un fait justificatif qui neutralise un élément légal de l'infraction.

Le délit de non-dénonciation de sévices ou de crime peut-il être retenu contre le médecin ou l'assistante sociale qui n'avertit pas les autorités? En d'autres termes, il s'agit de savoir si les personnes tenues au secret professionnel ont *l'obligation* de dénoncer les sévices dont elles ont connaissance dans l'exercice de leur profession. Cette obligation pèse sur les personnes privées, mais l'article 62 code pénal est-il applicable aux médecins et aux assistantes sociales? Ces personnes sont, à priori, soumises à deux devoirs contradictoires: parler (art. 62 c.p.) et se taire (art. 378 c.p.): dans ce conflit de devoirs, il faut donner priorité à l'un ou à l'autre. La législation française nous impose de distinguer le cas des assistantes sociales et celui des médecins.

Les assistantes sociales doivent rendre compte aux autorités administratives de tout mauvais traitement qui compromet la santé de l'enfant (art. 166 code de la santé publique). Le secret professionnel n'existe donc pas dans les relations entre les assistantes sociales et les autorités administratives ou médicales dont elles dépendent. Leur silence serait considéré non seulement comme une faute professionnelle, mais aussi croyons-nous comme une faute pénale. Elles ont le devoir de parler.

Pour les médecins il n'existe aucune règle analogue à l'article 166 C.S.P. Aucun texte ne les oblige, de manière précise, à dire ce qui'ils savent. Tout dépend de la combinaison que l'on propose entre l'article 62 c.p. (obligation de denoncer) et l'article 378 c.p. (obligation de se taire). La cour de Cassation n'a pas pris position et la doctrine est divisée. Il ne paraît pas utile d'exposer ici les arguments en faveur de telle ou telle solution.

3. La sanction des sévices

Nous envisageons ici les sanctions pénales susceptibles de frapper les auteurs des sévices et les personnes qui, ayant connaissance des mauvais traitements, ne sont pas intervenues pour les empêcher ou pour éviter leur renouvellement. Il s'agit de punir directement ceux qui ont agi ou qui ont laissé faire. Le problème se pose par rapport au coupable que l'on veut sanctionner et non par rapport à la victime dont on cherche à préserver l'avenir. Le législateur ayant dissocié le sort du coupable et celui de la victime, nous le suivrons dans cette voie, mais en soulignant au préalable la liaison étroite qui existe entre ces deux types de mesures. Le père qui est condamné pour sévices (sanction pénale) peut de ce fait être déchu de l'autorité parentale, ce qui rend possible l'adoption (solution pour l'enfant). De plus, et surtout, toute condamnation ou même toute inculpation conduit à une cassure dans les relations parents-enfants: l'enfant est responsable des "ennuis" de ses parents, il est celui par lequel le scandale arrive, il sera rejeté.

Plusiers remarques préliminaires s'imposent. Les violences à enfants sont spécialement réprimées par le code pénal. Depuis 1898, des dispositions particulières ont été prises pour renforcer la répression lorsque la victime est jeune. Les sanctions prévues sont lourdes, plus lourdes qu'en droit commun et les condamnations principales peuvent être assorties de condamnations annexes: interdiction de sejour dans certains lieux (art. 44 c. penal), déchéance de l'autorité parentale (art. 378 et s. c. civil), retrait des "droits civiques, civils et de famille" (art. 42 c. pénal: droit de vote, qualité de fonctionnaire, etc. . . .)

Les tribunaux ont tendance à se montrer plutôt timides dans l'application des textes (malgré les 1.085 condamnations prononcées en 1974 pour coups à enfants). L'effet dissuasif de la sanction est faible. Le parent (ou le tiers, car les mauvais traitements ne sont pas toujours infligés par le couple parental; par exemple, la nourrice), qui bat son enfant est insensible au risque (pénal) qu'il prend. Il ne calcule pas, il agit sans se soucier de la suite de ses actes. Dans la "meilleure" des hypothèses, il prend conscience de la gravité de ses agissements, quand il redoute une issue fatale. Il conduit alors l'enfant à l'hôpital, à la dernière limite, espérant dégager ou atténuer sa responsabilité. Mais la perspective d'une éventuelle sanction n'empêche pas les sévices. Dès lors, il est difficile d'espérer trouver une solution dans l'accroissement des pénalités et c'est avec un certain scepticisme que nous abordons ce probleme des sanctions.

(A)Les sanctions prévues contre l'auteur des sévices.

Outre les textes de droit commun qui sanctionnent de manière générale les coups et blessures volontaires ou involontaires, la code pénal a créé deux infractions spécifiques qui s'appliquent lorsque la victime est un mineur: article 357-I 3° et article 312 al. 6 à II (les violences sexuelles font l'objet d'un rapport particulier).

Le premier de ces textes (art. 357-I c.p.) édicte des pénalités faibles (un an d'emprisonnement au maximum) à l'encontre des père et mère (à l'exclusion de toute autre personne) qui "compromettent gravement par de mauvais traitements . . ., par un défaut de soins ou par un manque de direction necessaire, soit la santé, soit la securité, soit la moralité, de leurs enfants". Il n'est pas necessaire que les parents aient agi volontairement. A titre d'exemple, un concubin, père naturel de l'enfant, a été récemment condamné dans les circonstances suivantes (cour de Cassation, chambre criminelle, 16 janvier 1974: Gazette du Palais 1974, I, 210). Il quitte sa maîtresse en lui laissant leur enfant commun. Il revient après huit mois d'absence, ayant cependant maintenu des contacts avec sa compagne. Il fait alors hospitaliser la fillette de 28 mois qui présente à l'évidence des troubles anciens de sévices "révélateurs d'un défaut de soins prolongés".

Le second de ces textes (art. 312 al. 6 à II code pénal) est plus souvent appliqué. Il concerne tous les auteurs de sévices (même s'ils sont juridiquement étrangers à l'enfant) et les penalités sont plus lourdes. En revanche, il suppose un acte volontaire. Entrer ici dans le detail de la réglementation (notamment les pénalités) ne paraît pas utile. Nous mettrons seulement l'accent sur certains points.

(a) L'âge de la victime

L'article 312, (al. 6 et s.) n'est applicable que si le mineur a moins de 15 ans. Le jeune âge de la victime est un élément constitutif de l'infraction. Quinze ans peut paraître un seuil relativement élevé, specialement depuis que la majorité a été fixée à 18 ans.

(b) La notion de sévices

Sont considerés comme des sévices les blessures et les coups, tout acte de violence ou toute voie de fait qui compromet la santé de l'enfant. Sont exclues les "violences légères": la fessée raisonnable, la gifle salutaire, mais modéréé. Traditionnellement un certain droit de correction, dont les limites ne sont pas précisées, est reconnu aux parents.

Les actes positifs brutaux et instantanés ne sont pas seuls pris en considération. Certaines abstentions sont des sévices. L'article 312 al. 6 cite la privation d'aliments et le defaut de soins (ex: medicaux ou affectifs) qui compromettent la santé de l'enfant. Le facteur temps, durée intervient. Les omissions, les actes anodins deviennent dangereux et graves s'ils se multiplient et empêchent le développement normal de la victime. L'abstention peut être aussi coupable que l'action.

(c) Les pénalités en cas d'infraction simple

S'il n'existe aucune circonstance aggravante, l'auteur des sévices risque de subir un emprisonnement de I à 5 ans et de devoir payer une amende de 500 à 5,000 F (art. 312 al. 9 c.p.). La durée minimum de l'emprisonnement est telle que l'infraction est nécessairement considérée comme un délit et non comme une contravention.

En droit commun, au contraire, les coups et blessures ne sont considéres comme des délits que s'il en est résulté une incapacite de travail supérieur à 8 jours. Une telle réserve n'existe pas en matiere de sévices a l'enfant. Maltraiter un enfant n'est jamais une contravention, alors que maltraiter une personne de plus de 15 ans peut l'être. Le coupable sera toujours jugé par le tribunal correctionel ou la cour d'assises et non par le tribunal de police.

Parmi les circonstances aggravantes, certaines sont classiques: les pénalités augmentent pratiquement toujours en cas de préméditation ou de conséquences graves pour la victime. Il est assez logique de sanctionner plus sévèrement celui qui a calculé son action ou celui qui a provoqué la mort de sa victime.

En matiere de sévices, tout comme en droit commun, cette augmentation des pénalités existe. Toutefois, en matière de sévices, le délit de base étant plus sévèrement sanctionne, il en résulté qu'en cas de circonstances aggravantes cette différence de pénalités sera accentuée, par exemple, en cas de mutilation ou d'infirmité permanente (perte d'un oeil), le coupable risque de 5 à 10 ans de réclusion en droit commun, de 10 à 20 ans, si la victime a moins de 15 ans.

Etudions maintenant les circonstances aggravantes qui sont propres aux sévices a l'enfant: la qualité d'ascendant et l'habitude. Les pénalités sont accrues, lorsque des liens de parenté ou d'autorité unissent le coupable à la victime. L'article 312 al. 8 cite "les père et mère légitimes, naturels ou adoptifs, ou autres ascendants légitimes ou toutes autres personnes ayant autorité sur l'enfant ou ayant sa garde" (notamment un concubin ou une nourrice). Les magistrats sont ainsi autorisés à faire preuve d'une plus grande sévérité, lorsque le coupable est précisément la personne qui est censée protéger l'enfant. En cas de délit simple par exemple, la peine prévue est un enprisonnement de 3 à 10 ans si le coupable est un ascendant (ou personne assimilée). Si le coupable est un tiers, cette même peine n'est applicable que si les sévices ont entrainé pour l'enfant une incapacité de travail de plus de 20 jours.

L'habitude est une circonstance aggravante, inconnue en droit commun, mais qui est retenue lorsque les sévices ont entraîné la mort, même sans intention de la donner. Ainsi le père qui, sous l'emprise de la colère ou de la boisson, frappe l'enfant avec une telle force que la mort s'ensuit, risque la réclusion à perpétuité (art. 312 al. 9). Mais il risque la peine de mort si son geste, au lieu d'être isolé, unique, s'inscrit dans un contexte habituel de violence (art. 312 al. II). La preuve — souvent malaisée — de l'intention homicide n'est pas nécessaire à partir du moment où il est établi que la répétition des sévices a occasionné la mort de l'enfant.

Aux actes de violence proprement dits sont assimilées les "privations habituel-lement pratiquées". En cas de décès de l'enfant à la suite de privations prolongées, l'auteur du crime est passible de la peine capitale, même s'il n'a pas voulu le décès: il suffit qu'il ait prévu (ou même peut-être qu'il ait dù prévoir) que son attitude aurait des conséquences fâcheuses sur la santé de l'enfant. A titre d'exemple, la cour de cassation (chambre criminelle II mars 1975. Gazette du Palais 1975, 2, 507) a récemment approuvé les motifs donnés par une cour d'appel pour retenir la qualification la plus sévère contre les parents qui avaient laissé mourir leur enfant de 18 mois né prématurément: "l'état de santé de cet enfant aurait dû imposer à ses parents des soins vigilants et le recours à un medecin"; il y a eu de leur part "avec conscience, connaissance et prévision qu'il en résulterait un mal pour l'enfant, une privation habituelle et prolongée d'aliments et de soins, ayant entraîné la mort sans intention de la donner".

(B) Les sanctions prévues contre les personnes qui ne sont directs des sévices

Le recours au droit commun permet de sanctionner dans certaines conditions les personnes qui, sans avoir personnellement participé à l'infraction, en ont eu connaissance et se sont abstenues d'intervenir.

Nous avons deja examiné le délit de non-dénonciation de sévices aux autorites administratives ou judiciaires. Il s'agit maintenant d'une autre forme d'infraction par omission, punie plus sévèrement (la durée de l'emprisonnement peut atteindre cinq ans): le refus d'assistance à personne en danger (art. 63 code pénal). Le législateur sanctionne le spectateur qui, volontairement, ne s'oppose pas au délit contre l'intégrité corporelle qui est sur le point ou en train de se commettre. Est également sanctionnée la passivité de celui qui, face à un péril déjà réalise, ne porte pas secours à la victime. Le danger doit être imminent et constant, une intervention immédiate serait indispensable pour éviter que le risque ne se réalise ou pour limiter les effets nefastes de l'atteinte à l'intégrité corporelle. Encore faut-il cependant que le tiers ait eu conscience du danger (exemple: on croit endormi un enfant qui est dans le coma).

L'intervention du témoin peut prendre la forme d'une action personnelle directe ou d'un appel à des tiers, afin de provoquer les secours nécessaires. Cette seconde manière de porter secours à la victime est interessante dans la mesure ou l'infraction n'est constituee que si l'intervention du témoin ne comporte pas de risque pour lui (ou pour les tiers). Or s'il peut être difficile de s'opposer par la force à un parent violent, il est sans doute plus aisé de lancer des appels au secours ou de quitter les lieux pour prévenir les voisins ou la police. L'inaction sera coupable dans les deux cas. Peuvent ainsi être poursuivis sur la base de l'article 63 du code pénal. Le conjoint ou le compagnon qui n'appelle pas un médecin à temps ou assiste passivement aux scènes de violence (s'il en est l'instigateur, s'il a aidé l'auteur des coups en tenant par exemple l'enfant ou en tendant le fouet, il sera condamné comme complice des sévices). Le voisin qui, sachant ce qui se passe à côté de chez lui, néglige de répondre aux cris de l'enfant (mais il est vrai que l'enfant habitué à souffrir manifeste moins sa douleur).

En théorie, le cercle des personnes susceptibles d'être poursuivies pour non assistance à personne en danger est relativement large. Mais il semble bien, en pratique, que les poursuites (notamment contre les voisins) ne sont pas fréquentes. L'entourage, trop souvent silencieux par insouciance, par égoïsme, par crainte ou par pudeur, reste généralement étranger à l'enfant et inconnu de la justice.

4. Les solutions pour l'enfant

Devant l'existence des sévices, ou une forte suspicion, deux impératifs apparaissent. L'un est immédiat: soustraire l'enfant au danger, l'autre est second: assurer l'avenir de l'enfant, sa sécurité future.

Nous avons plusieurs fois entendu des médecins dire: "Heureux est l'enfant qui a la chance d'être battu car il a peut-être un espoir de s'en sortir". Reflexion évidemment paradoxale et déconcertante, mais qui conduit à se demander quels moyens sont prévus par le législateur pour que, dans l'avenir de l'enfant, les sévices puissent être considérés comme une "chance".

La protection des mineurs est assurée en droit français à la fois par l'autorité administrative (la D.A.S.S. s'occupe essentiellement de prévention et utilise les services de nombreuses assistantes sociales) et par l'autorité judiciaire (representée notamment par le juge des enfants, juge du tribunal de grande instance). Entre elles, une différence est importante: l'autorité administrative ne peut agir qu'avec l'accord des interesses (les parents), l'autorité judiciaire en revanche peut imposer ses décisions. Les textes obligent le juge à rechercher l'adhésion de la famille (art. 375 — I c. civ.), mais non pas à l'obtenir. Le juge peut intervenir même si les parents s'y opposent, l'administration ne le peut pas.

Malgré cette différence, des liens étroits unissent les deux institutions. L'objectif poursuivi est le même: prendre une mesure de sûreté dans l'interêt de l'enfant et non sanctionner les parents. Sans doute la mesure sera-t-elle le plus souvent vecue comme une punition, ce qui ne facilitera pas la reinsertion future de l'enfant, lorsque elle doit avoir lieu. Mais cette restriction des "droits" des parents sur l'enfant, quelle soit proposée ou imposée, n'est qu'un moyen et non une fin. Par ailleurs en pratique la mesure prise est souvent la même, qu'elle soit ordonnée par le juge ou par l'administration (par exemple le juge confie fréquemment l'enfant à la D.A.S.S.).

(A) Premier problème: La sécurité immédiate de l'enfant

Le premier objectif à atteindre est de soustraire l'enfant au danger et de lui assurer les soins médicaux nécessaires.

Dans de nombreux cas la réalisation de cet objectif suppose le retrait (plus ou moins prolongé) de l'enfant de son milieu de vie actuel. Toutefois dans les hypothèses les moins graves le maintien de l'enfant dans sa famille peut être envisagé, à condition que certaines précautions soient prises.

(a) L'enfant est retiré de son milieu

(i) *Retrait volontaire.* Il intervient à la demande d'un parent qui conduit l'enfant à l'hôpital ou le confie à la D.A.S.S. à titre de recuelli temporaire (l'administration prendra alors les mesures qui s'imposent sur le plan médical). L'hospitalisation spontanée de l'enfant par ses parents n'est pas exceptionnelle. Elle est parfois immédiate: dès que la "crise" aigue est passée. Elle est plus souvent différée de quelques jours: lorsque les parents constatent une anomalie persistante de l'état de l'enfant (ce retard à la consultation constitue pour le médecin un élément de diagnostic important).

L'hospitalisation volontaire peut aussi être "provoquée" par le médecin appelé en consultation, l'assistante sociale ou la puéricultrice. Elle est motivée par les lésions patentes de l'enfant ou par un état général déficient (qui servira plus ou moins d'heureux prétexte pour permettre le rétablissement de la santé de l'enfant). L'hospitalisation peut être assortie immédiatement d'une mesure autoritaire prise par le juge des enfants pour empêcher la reprise de l'enfant par ses parents.

(ii) *Retrait forcé.* Une solution autoritaire est indispensable lorsque toute collaboration du milieu familial est exclue, l'enfant restant exposé à de nouveaux actes de violence de la part de son entourage.

Le juge des enfants a le pouvoir d'ordonner des mesures coercitives, contre la volonté des parents, dès que la santé ou la sécurité de l'enfant sont en danger (art. 375 c. civ.). Il ouvre une procédure d'assistance éducative, ordonne une enquête, entend les parents, confie provisoirement l'enfant à la D.A.S.S. qui le soignera ou demandera son admission dans un service hospitalier (art. 27 du décret no. 74-27 du 14 janvier 1974 relatif aux règles de fonctionnement des hôpitaux).

En cas d'urgence le juge des enfants peut, pratiquement sans formalité contraignante, prendre les mesures qui s'imposent.

(b) *L'enfant est laissé dans son mileu*

La solution peut être retenue pour les cas les moins graves. L'état de santé de l'enfant ne rend pas l'hospitalisation indispensable. Le contexte familial n'est pas trop déficient. On peut raisonnablement espérer que les soins necessaires seront donnés et que les sévices ne continueront pas. Il faudra cependant prendre un minimum de garanties pour l'avenir.

Certaines assistantes sociales ont parfois une très grande influence auprès des familles. La confiance et le prestige dont elles jouissent, les pouvoirs (à la fois réels et imaginaires) qu'elles détiennent peuvent suffire à convaincre les parents de la nécessité de faire soigner l'enfant, spécialement si ce "conseil" s'accompagne de visites et de contrôles fréquents et si la famille a le sentiment de "jouer sa dernière carte" avant les mesures coercitives. L'affaire doit cependant être de bien faible importance pour que soit pris le risque de la regler ainsi, presque "à l'amiable".

Parfois la saisine du juge des enfants est préférable. Il est averti par une assistante sociale, un médecin, la police, un tiers etc. . . . Certaines familles ne prennent conscience de la gravité des faits et des risques pris que si le processus judiciaire est entamé. Ce processus judiciaire n'entraine pas nécessairement le placement de l'enfant. Le juge des enfants peut mettre le mineur sous assistance éducative (puisque sa santé est compromise) tout en le laissant dans sa famille. Mais le magistrat subordonnera alors le maintien du mineur dans son milieu de vie actuel à des "obligations particulières" (art. 375-2 c. civ.) dont le contenu précis n'est pas prévu par le législateur et qui peuvent donc par exemple prendre la forme de visites médicales régulières destinées à vérifier l'amélioration de la santé de l'enfant. La menace du retrait de l'enfant au cas où ces prescriptions spéciales ne seraient pas respectées consitue parfois un moyen de pression suffisant sur les parents. Parallèlement une prise en charge sociale est ordonnée.

(B) Deuxième problème: Le devenir des enfants

Dès que la sécurité immédiate de l'enfant est assurée, le problème de son devenir se pose. Dans la meilleurs des hypothèses les conséquences physiques des violences vont disparaître. Mais si l'enfant est guéri, sa famille ne l'est pas. Le problème reste entier.

Personne ne devrait prendre le risque, par insouciance, par ignorance ou par optimisme irréfléchi, de laisser l'enfant revenir purement et simplement dans sa famille sans que les parents soient soutenus, aidés et controlés. Les mauvais traitements sont la manifestation aigue d'une situation familiale plus ou moins profondément perturbée. C'est dans la compréhension de ces perturbations (leur genèse et leur mécanisme) et dans l'évaluation des ressources positives de chacun des parents que se trouvent les éléments de solution.

L'avenir de l'enfant doit être envisagé à moyen et si possible à long terme afin de lui assurer la stabilité et la sécurité indispensable à un développement physique, moral et affectif normal. Plusieurs éléments paraissent fondamentaux dans le choix d'une solution.

La première qualité de la décision sera peut-être sa stabilité, sa permanence. Les intervenants-juge, travailleurs sociaux, éducateurs, médecins doivant avoir un projet sur l'enfant et être animés par le désir et la conviction d'une réussite possible. Même si la solution retenue n'est pas idéale (on choisit le "moindre mal"), il faut oser trancher, ne pas pratiquer une politique sans cesse remise en question ("attendre et voir") et tout mettre en oeuvre pour favoriser la réussite de la solution choisie.

La deuxième qualité de la décision est davantage liée à son contenu. Il faut choisir entre deux optiques diamétralement opposées: réinsertion de l'enfant dans sa famille — soit immédiatement, soit en passant par l'étape d'un placement temporaire le plus bref possible — ou rupture définitive entre parents et enfant s'il n'y a aucune chance raisonnable d'évolution favorable. Un placement prolongé aboutissant finalement à une reprise de l'enfant par ses parents présent de nombreux inconvénients: pendant la durée du placement l'enfant est en situation extrêmement instable, ensuite les parents risquent de reprendre un enfant qu'ils ne connaissent plus, enfin la prise en charge de la famille par le sang est difficile si l'enfant vit ailleurs.

Les autorités administratives et judiciaires disposent en principe des moyens juridiques nécessaires pour proposer ou imposer les solutions les mieux adaptées à chaque cas (soutien la famille, placement temporaire de l'enfant, rupture définitive des liens parentaux, adoption). La législation ne présente pas, semble-t-il, de graves lacunes. Mais les principales difficultés résultent de la lenteur des différents organismes dans la mise en oeuvre des mesures, du manque de personnel, de l'insuffisance de formation des intervenants, de l'absence de coordination entre les diverses instances, d'une mauvaise appréciation de la situation.

(a) Le rôle de l'administration

La D.A.S.S. est chargée "d'exercer une action sociale préventive auprès des familles dont les conditions d'existence risquent de mettre en danger la santé . . . de leurs enfants" (décret no. 59-100 du 7 janvier 1959). Elle dispose a cet effet d'un personnel spécialisé: assistantes sociales, éducateurs . . . qui "suscite de la part des parents toutes les mesures utiles et notamment, s'il y a lieu, une demande de placement approprié ou d'action éducative".

Parfois les parents se séparent volontairement de l'enfant qui est pris en charge par la D.A.S.S. et placé dans une famille nourricière ou dans une institution. Parfois l'enfant reste ou revient chez lui, mais le groupe familial, sur décision du directeur de la D.A.S.S., est soumis à une mesure de protection sociale, d'action éducative. Cette mesure peut être suffisante en cas de sévices légers ou occasionnels (manque de soins appropriés, absence d'hygiène, violences "accidentelles" liées à un énervement passager). Le soutien prolongé et intense de l'assistante sociale, de la puéricultrice, du psychologue, de l'éducateur ou de la travailleuse familiale, la résolution des problèmes matériels (financers, conditions de logement, surcroît de travail à l'occasion d'une naissance ou d'une maladie etc. . . .) permettront à une famille fragile mais non perturbée en profondeur de passer le cap difficile.

(b) Le rôle de la justice

La justice intervient dans l'avenir des enfants battus par l'intermédiaire, soit du juge des enfants (assistance éducative) soit du tribunal de grande instance ou d'un tribunal répressif (déchéance de l'autorité parentale).

Nous avons déjà envisagé le rôle du juge des enfants, personnage central en matière de protection de l'enfance, qui peut notamment soustraire l'enfant à son milieu de vie en cas de danger immédiat. Il peut de même, toujours au titre de l'assistance éducative, (a) empêcher les parents de reprendre l'enfant guéri en ordonnant le placement du mineur chez un membre de la famille ou un tiers digne de confiance, dans un établissement spécialisé, à la D.A.S.S. ou (b) rendre l'enfant à ses parents en ordonnant une mesure d'action éducative en milieu ouvert. Les modalités concrètes de cette "protection judiciaire" seront éventuellement identiques à celles prises par l'administration en cas de "protection sociale" (intervention des assistantes sociales de la D.A.S.S. par exemple).

Le juge n'est parfois informé qu'au moment de l'hospitalisation. Lorsque les relations entre le personnel hospitalier et le personnel judiciaire sont confiantes, il n'est pas rare que le médecin avertisse le juge dès que la cause de hospitalisation se révèle être liée à des sévices. Les textes permettent, en cas d'urgence, une simplification des formalités. Concrètement, le juge est averti par téléphone, il vient lui-même constater sur place les sévices, et prend immédiatement une mesure provisoire pour éviter, notamment que les parents ne reprennent trop rapidement l'enfant.

Lorsque la situation est irrémédiablement compromise, la déchéance de l'autorité parentale est prononcée par une juridiction pénale (tribunal correctionnel ou cour d'assises) ou par une juridiction civile (tribunal de grande instance) art. 378 et 378-I c. civ.

Dans le premier cas, (art. 378), les père et mère ont été pénalement condamnés en raison d'un "crime ou d'un délit commis sur la personne de leur enfant". La condamnation pénale pour sévices peut ainsi s'accompagner d'une déchéance de l'autorité parentale, prononcée par la même instance. Le second cas (art. 378-I c. civ.) est indépendant de toute condamnation pénale. Les poursuites pénales peuvent ne pas avoir été engagées ou n'avoir pas été suivies d'effets en raison par exemple de l'état mental des intéressés.

Le comportement des parents peut cependant mettre "manifestement en danger" la sécurité ou la santé de l'enfant notamment par "un défaut de soins". La déchéance est alors une mesure, autonome et non accessoire, prononcée par une juridiction civile (mais souvent vécue comme une mesure répressive).

La déchéance fait perdre aux parents les attributs de l'autorité parentale. Les "droits" sur l'enfant se concentrent sur le parent non déchu ou sont transférés à un tiers qui peut être l'aide sociale à l'enfance (D.A.S.S.). Un tribunal statuant en formation collégiale peut donc, dans les cas de sévices les plus dangereux, interdire aux parents toute intervention dans l'avenir de leurs enfants. La rupture avec les père et mère est généralement totale et définitive. La perspective d'une adoption est le but second de la déchéance (du moins si l'enfant est confié à un tiers).

Toutefois la restitution de l'autorité parentale peut être demandée, un an après la condamnation définitive, en cas de "circonstances nouvelles" justifiées et à condition que l'enfant n'ait pas déjà été placé en vue de l'adoption (art. 381 c. civ.). De plus certains attributs seulement de l'autorité parentale peuvent être retirés aux parents, notamment le droit de garde, ce qui laisse subsister le droit de consentir à l'adoption et s'accompagne éventuellement d'autorisations de visites. La situation est proche de celle qui résulte de la délégation de l'autorité parentale (art. 377 c. civ.): dans ce cas, les parents renoncent volontairement, sous contrôle du tribunal, à l'exercice de leur autorité qui est transférée à un tiers. Le droit de consentir à l'adoption n'est jamais délégué. Formules hybrides et souvent dangereuses qui conduisent l'enfant à s'installer dans un "statut d'incertitude".

(c) L'adoption

Lorsque l'enfant victime de sévices est profondément rejeté par sa famille, il ne faut pas écarter la possibilité de lui redonner d'autres racines, spécialement s'il est jeune. La formule du placement nourricier ou institutionnel n'est bonne que si elle est temporaire: le temps d'une guérison complète, le temps d'aménager d'autres relations parents-enfant etc. . . . et non pas le temps de laisser l'enfant s'enforcer douloureusement dans le statut incertain de "gosse de l'assistance". Il faut parfois oser prévoir, avec réalisme, que la situation n'évoluera pas favorablement dans un avenir proche et envisager alors sérieusement l'adoption.

L'évaluation de la situation et la prise de décision doivent être assez précoces pour que l'enfant ne soit ni trop âgé, ni trop perturbé.

L'adoption est irrévocable (adoption plénière). Tous les liens avec la famille d'origine sont rompus. L'enfant refait sa vie, il change de nom en changeant de parents, il n'est plus le fils de ceux qui l'ont engendré. Les parents, adoptifs peuvent donc avoir sur lui un projet et un désir qui sont les stimulants les plus profonds pour sa réussite. Un tel projet n'est au contraire guère possible en cas de placement nourricier. L'insécurité fait partie de la vie quotidienne de l'enfant. L'enfant peut brusquement être retiré à la nourrice qui de son côté peut aussi s'en séparer et le rejeter. La famille nourricière n'ayant aucune certitude quant à la durée du placement peut difficilement intégrer l'enfant à part entière en son sein. De plus elle est souvent insuffisamment préparée à son métier.

L'adoption n'est pas un remède miracle, mais seulement une solution qui permet de donner à l'enfant une perspective d'avenir. Trois moyens sont possibles pour parvenir à l'adoption.

(i) Les parents consentent volontairement à l'abandon et à l'adoption. Dans les trois mois qui suivent, ils peuvent, sans autre formalité qu'une simple lettre, reprendre l'enfant. Au-delà de ce délai s'engage normalement le processus devant conduire à l'adoption. Ce premier moyen est le plus simple. Encore faut-il qu'il ait été suggéré aux parents et que ceux-ci se soient laissé convaincre. Un consentement à l'adoption doit être préparé, puis soutenu.

(ii) Un enfant peut être déclaré judiciairement abandonné lorsque ses parents se sont manifestement désintéressés de lui pendant un an, c'est-à-dire lorsqu'ils "n'ont pas entretenu avec lui les relations nécessaires au maintien de liens affectifs" (art. 350 c. civ.). Un abandon de fait prolongé conduit, sur décision d'un tribunal, à un abandon juridique, prélude possible à une adoption. Ce moyen est retenu par exemple quand les parents ne rendent jamais visite à l'enfant placé après les sévices, ne lui écrivent pas, ne demandent pas de ses nouvelles.

Il appartient à la personne ou à l'institution qui a recueilli l'enfant d'être particulièrement attentive aux marques d'intérêt émanant des père et mère, afin de saisir le tribunal de grande instance dès que le silence et l'inaction des parents ont duré un an (il arrive aussi que certains services s'empressent de provoquer des visites dès qu'approche la date fatidique. . .).

(iii) Enfin, la déchéance de l'autorité parentale peut être à l'origine de l'adoption, notamment si le jugement a transféré à l'Aide Sociale tous les droits sur l'enfant. L'enfant devient pupille de l'Etat (art. 50 code de la famille et de l'aide sociale) et il est normalement placé en vue de l'adoption. Le placement empêche les parents de demander la restitution de leurs droits sur l'enfant (art. 381 c. civ.).

En conclusion, on pourrait se demander quel est l'importance du rôle du législateur en matière de sévices. Une législation solide et serrée est indispensable: multiplier les contrôles préventifs, obliger chacun à denoncer les mauvais traitements sous peine de poursuites, permettre le retrait immédiat de l'enfant, si des soins sont nécessaires, prévoir des sanctions sévères contre les auteurs des coups ou des privations, autoriser une rupture totale des liens parentaux, organiser un soutien efficace des familles en difficulté. Il faut que toutes les personnes amenées à intervenir disposent de textes, de soutiens juridiques leur permettant de mener à bonne fin leur entreprise. Une législation bien adaptée est la première condition pour permettre une action efficace.

Mais, remarque banale, ce n'est pas une condition suffisante et nous voudrions souligner trois points. Une "bonne" législation en matière de sévices n'est pas seulement une législation qui concerne les sévices. Le problème est global, il se situe en amont et en aval des sévices, avant et après le passage à l'acte, autour de ce qui n'est qu'une manifestation de difficultés relationnelles graves au sein de la famille.

Lutter contre les sévices passe par une politique d'ensemble énergique en faveur de l'enfance et de la famille (les auteurs de sévices ont généralement eux-mêmes eu une enfance et une adolescence perturbées, le poids du passé est lourd), par une lutte efficace contre l'alcoolisme, par un meilleur traitement des troubles psychiatriques, par une prévention des grossesses non désirées, par une amélioration des conditions de logement etc. Aucun de ces éléments ne suffit à expliquer les sévices, mais tous y concourent.

La législation existante n'est pas toujours appliquée dans des conditions satisfaisantes. Les dispositions assurant la protection sanitaire et sociale pourraient constituer d'excellents moyens de prévention et de dépistage. Le juge des enfants a pratiquement tous les pouvoirs nécessaires pour agir sur le sort de l'enfant. Les tribunaux répressifs peuvent sanctionner sévèrement les auteurs de sévices ou les témoins muets.

Sans doute peut-on encore améliorer la législation existante. Mais à quoi bon si certaines difficultés actuelles, qui ne sont pas essentiellement liées aux textes mais à leur application concrète, subsistent. La prévention doit se faire dans un réel souci d'aide aux familles en difficulté, de même que la prise en charge des familles où des sévices sont survenus.

Les possibilités de suivi des enfants et des familles paraissent souvent limitées. L'insuffisance numérique et l'instabilité des personnels impliqués dans cette tâche, à tous les niveaux de responsabilité, tant dans les structures médico-sociales que judiciaires, jouent ici un rôle important. Ces deux éléments sont à l'origine de nombreux inconvénients: retard de dépistage, évaluation hâtive des situations, insuffisance ou brièveté du soutien apporté aux familles, absence d'une politique suivie à leur égard, inefficacité des mesures prises.

En matière de sanctions enfin, certains s'étonneront du petit nombre de poursuites pour non dénonciation de sévices, ou souligneront la relative clémence des mesures judiciaires prises à l'encontre des auteurs de mauvais traitements. Dans tous ces cas, un changement de législation serait sans portée réelle.

Enfin parmi les personnes qui interviennent actuellement dans l'histoire de l'enfant battu, il arrive que chacune d'elles ait plus ou moins le sentiment que son rôle est terminé quand elle a signalé le cas, ou soigné l'enfant, ou ordonné telle mesure. Dés lors on peut se demander s'il ne conviendrait pas, dès que les sévices sont soupçonnés, de donner à l'enfant une sorte de tuteur, d'avocat, une personne — et une seule — qui, sans prendre les décisions à la place des autorités compétentes et sans les exécuter directement sauf cas exceptionnel, deviendrait responsable du mineur, servirait d'interlocuteur et d'intermédiaire face aux autorités, coordonerait les actions, centraliserait les informations, ferait avancer le dossier, aurait un projet d'avenir pour le mineur.

Sans doute ne peut-on envisager d'introduire une personne supplémentaire dans un "circuit" déjà encombré. Il faudrait peut-être par l'information et la formation des personnels administratif, judiciaire, médical, des travailleurs sociaux, susciter une prise de conscience telle que l'un d'entre eux accepte ce rôle de responsable du mineur. Sans doute aussi peut-on trouver d'autres formules que celle de ce "tuteur-avocat" au service de l'enfant. Mais il me semble qu'il faut se poser une question: les droits de l'enfant, victime de violences au sein de sa famille, sont-ils véritablement reconnus et défendus?

RÉFERENCES

Chazal, J., "Les droits de l'enfant", presses universitaires de France, coll. Que sais-je, 1969.
Colloque des 6 et 7 mars 1970 à Charleroi "Les enfants victimes de mauvais traitements", Bruxelles, Centre d'étude de la délinquance juvénile.
Couderc, M., "Dispositions nouvelles pour la protection de l'enfance en danger: abstention délictueuse et secret professionnel" (Commentaire de la loi du 15 juin 1971) Dalloz 1971, Législation, p. 396-I.
Deltaglia, L., "Les enfants maltraités. Dépistage et interventions sociales" Ed. E.S.F. 1973.
Desmottes, M., Rapport général présenté à la session d'études sur les enfants victimes de mauvais traitements 16 au 19 déc. 1974 — Ecole nationale de la santé publique.
Doll, P.J., "Une nouvelle atteinte au secret médical en vue de la protection des enfants maltraités", Gazette du Palaise 1971, 2, 415. Commentaire des articles 62 et 63 du Code pénal au Juris classeur pénal (abstentions délictueuses).
Franklin, A.W. (ed.), Concerning Child Abuse. London, Eng.: Livingstone Churchill, 1974.
Fournie, A.M., "La protection judiciaire de l'enfance en danger" 1971 Ed. techniques.
Girodet, D., "Les jeunes enfants maltraités", Etude médico-sociale de 110 observations hospitalières. Thèse de médecine, Paris, 1973.
Hallie-Bonnier, A.J., "La protection de l'enfance martyre aux Pays-Bas", Tribune de l'enfance, février 1977.
Henry, M. en collaboration avec Girault, H., et Chirol, Y., "Les jeunes en danger", Champ d'application de l'assistance éducative 1972 Vaucresson Coll. Enquêtes et recherches.
Joliot, E., "Rôle du travailleur social dans le cas des jeunes enfants maltraités" (1976) Journées parisiennes de pédiatrie 426 à 431.
Kreisler, L., et Straus, P., "Les auteurs de sévices sur les jeunes enfants. Contribution à un abord psychologique" (1971), 28 Archives françaises de pédiatrie 249 à 265.
Legeais, R., Commentaire de l'article 378 du Code pénal au Juris classeur pénal (Violation du secret professionnel).
L'Hirondel, J., "1936, une grande date: naissance des comités de vigilance pour la protection de l'enfance", Tribune de l'enfance janvier 1977.
Levasseur G., Commentaire de la loi du 15 juin 1971, Revue de science criminelle et droit pénal comparé 1971, p. 970.

Manciaux, M., et Deschamps, G., "Les mauvais traitements envers enfants", rapport d'enquête du Comité technique pour l'enfance et l'adolescence inadaptée et du Ministère de la Santé, Direction de l'action sanitaire et sociale, Nancy, 1972-1975.

Manciaux, M.; Deschamps, G.; et, Klein, O., "Prédiction des sévices", International congress on child abuse and neglect. Genève, 20-22 sept: 1976.

Mellennei, J., et Sicard, P., "Secret professionnel et médecin poursuivi", Gazette du Palais 1974, I, Doctrine, p. 84.

Neimann, N., "Les enfants victimes de sévices" (1968), 6 Journal d'actualités médicales et thérapeutiques 69 à 79.

Neimann, N., "Les manifestations cliniques des sévices" (1976) Journées parisiennes de pédiatrie 404 à 409.

Neimann, N.; Manciaux, M.; Rabouille, D. et, Dohm, J.P., "L'avenir des enfants victimes de sévices", Congrès international de pédiatrie, Vienne, 1971, Rapport p. 195 à 199.

Neimann, N., et Rabouille, D., "Les enfants victimes de sévices" (1969), 23 Revue du praticien no. 27.

Parisot, P., et Caussade, L., "Les sévices envers enfants" (1929), 9 Annales de médecine légale 398 à 426.

Pierson, H., et Deschamps, G., "L'adoption des enfants maltraités" (1976) Journées parisiennes de pédiatrie 426 à 431.

Rabouille, D., "Les jeunes enfants victimes de sévices corporels", Thèse de médecine, Nancy, 1968.

Rateau, M., Manuel de droit pénal spécial. Crimes et délits contre les enfants et les mineurs. Imprimerie du progrès, Tours, 1965.

Rouyer, M., et Kreisler, L., "L'enfant victime de sévices". Aspects psychologiques, (1976) Journées parisiennes de pédiatrie 410 à 415.

Saunier, F., "L'enfant et ses droits", commentaire de la déclaration des Nations Unies. Ed. Fleurus 1970.

Soule, M., "Les placements d'enfants dits cas sociaux. Bon air ou désadaptation? De l'obligation de réfléchir avant de prescrire ces placements" (1971), 93 Concours médical 1261 à 1266.

Straus, P. et coll., "Les enfants maltraités (à propos de 40 observations)" (1967), 24 Archives françaises de pédiatrie 1075 à 1076.

Straus, P., "Recherche sur les enfants victimes de mauvais traitements", Rapport d'enquête du Comité technique pour l'enfance et l'adolescence inadaptée et du Ministère de la Santé, Direction de l'action sanitaire et sociale. Paris 1972-1975.

Straus, P.; Girodet, D.; et Delaunay, C., "Perspectives actuelles du problème des enfants maltraités. Nouveaux axes de recherche" (1976) Journées parisiennes de pédiatrie 432 à 437.

Straus, P., et Kreisler, L., "Le jeune enfant brutalisé" (1972), 79 Gazette médicale de France no. 14, 2319 à 2336.

Straus, P., et Wolf, A., "Un sujet d'actualité: les enfants maltraités" (1969), 12 Psychiatrie infantile no. 2, 577 à 628.

Tardieu, A., "Etude médico-légale sur les sévices et mauvais traitements exercés sur les enfants" (1960), 13 Annales d'hygiène 361.

de Touzalin, H., "Le refus de consentement à un traitement par les parents d'un enfant mineur en danger de mort", Semaine juridique 1974, I, 2672.

Umdenstock; Ribardiere; et Ronayette, "Très jeunes enfants victimes de sévices", Tribune de l'enfance, Octobre 1974.

Underhill, E., "Pourquoi les enseignants et les professionnels médico-sociaux restent-ils silencieux devant les parents qui maltraitent leurs enfants?" (mai, 1974) Revue internationale de l'enfant 16.

Vandermoot-Le Grossec, M.P., "Les enfants maltraités: 60 observations médico-légales", Thèse de médecine, Lille, 1970.

Van Ries, "L'enfance martyre aux Pays-Bas", publication de Vereniging tegen Kinder-mishandeling, Mars 1977.

Verdier, P., "Rôle de l'aide sociale à l'enfance" (enfants maltraités) (1976) *Journées parisiennes de pédiatrie* 422 à 425.

Verdier, P., "Guide pratique de l'aide sociale à l'enfance", *Le Centurion* 1975.

Vesin, C.; Girodet, D.; et Straus, P., "Les sévices exercés contre les jeunes enfants", Etude clinique de 110 observations. (1971), 4 Médecine légale et dommages corporels, Paris, 95 à 107.

Vincent, M., "Les enfants victimes de sévices", Thèse de médecine, Grenoble, 1975.

Chapter 26

Legal Aspects of Child Abuse in the Practice of Custody Courts in the Federal Republic of Germany

*Gisela Zenz**

1. Child Abuse in West Germany

Child abuse would appear to be a 'marginal problem' in West Germany. Criminal police statistics in 1975 list 1662 cases.[1] Figures are similar in previous years. In about 200 to 300 cases per year there are criminal sentences.[2] The unreported number of cases, of course, is estimated to be high — though the basis of such estimates is unclear.[3] It is easy to see even in the isolated publications of the Youth Offices' (Jugendamter) yearly reports that the officially known cases alone are much more numerous than the police statistics indicate.

There is, moreover, no law in West Germany which requires the reporting of possible cases and no systematic registration of cases which might surface, *e.g.,* in hospitals, doctors' offices, or parents' counseling offices. A drastic increase in the figure for revealed abuse cases has been demonstrated in countries which have introduced required reporting and central registers.

So far, no case of child abuse, no matter how cruel and even if fatal, has made more than a day's sensation in the press. Public involvement, such as was triggered by the case of Maria Colwell in England (1973) or by the New York cases of Roxanne Felumero (1969) and, a century earlier, of Mary Ellen (1894), followed by private campaigns, far reaching official investigations, political activities, and legal initiatives, has not occurred in West Germany.

In West Germany there has hardly been any scientific work in this field. Isolated attempts by pediatricians and child psychiatrists receive almost no attention. In the context of forensic medicine, the focus has been concentrated mainly upon the elaboration of psychiatrically oriented classifications of criminals.[4] It is hardly necessary to add that neither adequate statistics nor information are available for research purposes nor are there specific programs for prevention and treatment. A

---

*Forschungsgruppe Familienrecht, Fachbereich Rechtswissenschaft der Johann — Wolfgang — Goethe — Universität, Frankfurt (Main), W. Germany.

suggestion for the establishment of a special child shelter center in Berlin has still not found financial support. The handling of child abuse cases lies in the hands of the police, the criminal courts, the custody courts (to the extent that parents' rights are affected in order to protect the child) and Youth Offices (Jugendämter) whose staff members 'take care of' families with or without court orders.

While in some countries efforts have already been made to avoid emphasizing child abuse *per se,* and rather to understand child abuse merely as one phenomenon within the framework of a more general individual and societal failure with respect to the basic needs and opportunities of children, in West Germany child abuse has really not yet been recognized as the most obvious link in this chain.

This situation, which can probably also be found in other countries, leads to several reflections of a legal and political nature as to how the consciousness of the public can be raised and a readiness for attacking the problem can be awakened. Experiences from abroad have proved, however, that political measures are inadequate if, having mobilized the public, the numbers of reported cases are increased but mechanisms for constructive action are not created.[5] The moral legitimacy as well as the economic rationality of all legal and political 'campaigns' count for naught unless the exposure of 'problem cases' in fact makes it possible for those involved to deal with their problems in a better way. Their purposes are perverted if increased reporting results only in official registration, indictments, and social discrimination. In practice this means that mandatory reporting and registration systems cannot be the main subject of legal and political initiatives so long as there are no appropriate mechanisms to deal with cases which are already known and model programs, from which certain perspectives could be obtained, have not been developed and tried. Models from abroad cannot simply be imported. They can only provide inspiration in finding domestic resources to be utilized and further developed in the framework of the existing legal and social environment.

2. The Custody Court in West Germany

One of these 'resources' in West Germany is the institution of the custody court. An analysis of its functions and potential is instructive in various respects. First, its traditional responsbility to 'help to solve problems' delineates what is considered the most important feature of social response to child abuse. The custody court is not an agency for sentencing; its job is rather the protection of the child from dangers within the family, and at the same time the protection of the family from governmental power. A court institution of this kind seems unlikely to be abandoned in the foreseeable future. At least its abolition has nowhere been seriously considered, no matter how far solutions to these problems may be sought in preventive programs and extra-judicial measures and no matter what view is taken of the function of the law and the courts in this regard.[6]

The question dealt with here, therefore, is how the institution of the custody court reacts to cases of child abuse. The primary matter for the lawyer is to ask to what extent the procedure, organization, tradition, and standards for decisions of this court facilitate or hinder a rational practice. At the same time it cannot be overlooked, however, that the law and the courts can at best play only a modest role in the efforts effectively to protect children. Social welfare laws, social work, parents' education and counseling and schools and therapeutic institutions play a far more important part. Shortcomings in these 'extra-judicial' areas, however, in turn affect the judicial practice, the examination of which cannot, therefore, be limited simply to legal issues, but must at the same time be illuminated by the limitations and barriers which result from the interplay of legal and social structures which are imposed on the judge's endeavours 'from outside'.

Initially, the legal framework in which the custody courts in West Germany operate must be briefly sketched. This framework is characterized mainly by a wide-scale deformalization of procedure and by broadly defined standards for intervention into the family. The custody courts are subdivisions of the local 'Amtsgerichte' (district civil and criminal courts of the first instance). The custody court judge is a fully trained lawyer. He alone makes the decision without jurors or legal assistants. In the case of a smaller, usually a rural Amtsgericht, the custody judge is often the same judge who hears civil and criminal cases.

For most of the cases pertaining to family law, the custody court is in the first instance responsible. The legal basis for a decision in cases of child abuse is para. 1666, article 1 of the BGB.

If the mental or physical well-being of the child is endangered by his father or mother abusing the right to care for the child, neglecting the child or engaging in dishonest or immoral behavior, then the custody court must discover the means necessary to avert the danger. Specifically, the custody court can order that the child be placed in an appropriate family or foster home for his upbringing.

As interpreted by the courts, the text of this law demands proof of the parents' guilt in each case. A reform proposal, presently under discussion in parliament, seeks to eliminate this questionable 'guilt principle'. The proposed text for para. 1666 of the BGB would read: "If the personal well-being of the child is endangered, and if the parents are not willing or not able to avert the danger, the custody court must order the necessary measures . . ."[7].

It needs to be emphasized that neither text determines more precisely the measures which the custody court judge 'must order'.

The custody court is not bound by decisions of other courts. So it can, for example, take measures to protect the child even after an acquittal in criminal proceedings for child abuse. The procedural standards allow the custody court judge a much wider scope of discretion than a criminal or civil judge in a trial. Para. 12 of the applicable law of procedure (Gesetz uber die Angelegenheiten der freiwilligen Gerichtsbarkeit (FGG) von 1898) provides: "The court has the official duty to arrange for such investigations as are necessary to find the facts and to collect the relevant evidence."

The judgment as to which investigations are 'necessary', which evidence is 'relevant', and in what manner (written, oral, by telephone) the evidence is gathered lies in the discretion of the judge. He is not bound by requests from the family members. They must, however, be given the opportunity to comment on the results of the investigation; this can be done in writing. It is left to the judge to decide to whom he wishes to speak personally, and, specifically, if he wants to see the child. There is no provision for a lawyer or legal aid in some other form for the parents or the children. The custody court judge is obliged, however, to request an opinion from the Youth Office (Jugendamt).

If one tries to obtain information about family law practice pertaining to child abuse cases, one might think they posed no special problem. There is no special literature in this field. It is true that the relevant textbooks and commentaries have always cited child abuse as a typical example of the 'abuse of parental custody rights' in the sense of para. 1666 of the BGB, but simply as a statement of fact and without elaboration. Only a few published decisions are cited. The following observations and reflections, therefore, will rely on the empirical case studies which have been conducted as part of a more extensive research project at Frankfurt University. The subject of the research was the term 'the child's well-being' ('Kindeswohl'), and the use of this term by custody courts. The central part of the study is an analysis of the files of the courts with respect to cases involving custody and visitation rights after a divorce, adoptions, and intervention according to para. 1666 of the BGB.[8]

Within this last group of cases child abuse is but a small subgroup of 12 cases and one cannot claim to be able to determine the actual conduct of the courts in child abuse cases from this small sample. However, one can assume that the typical tendencies and conduct of custody courts in cases not involving child abuse will reflect the practice in child abuse cases. The cases arose in courts in Frankfurt and its rural surroundings from 1970 - 1975.

3. The Custody Court and Its Interaction with Other Institutions

The Custody Court and Criminal Proceedings

It seems to be more of an aspiration than the reality that custody courts should decide independently from parallel criminal proceedings. In the majority of the cases studied, the results of the custody courts' investigation bear a close resemblance to and sometimes even apparently copy those of the criminal investigation, and their decisions are likewise practically identical. In several cases the custody court proceedings were explicitly postponed until the criminal proceedings were over. The files were then consulted, the expert testimony was used and frequently the investigation results were relied upon. In one case the child was taken out of the foster home and sent back to his family without further investigation by the custody court because of an acquittal in the criminal proceedings, despite the fact that some allegations had not been cleared up.

There are several objections to such a practice.[9] First, the proceedings should be shaped according to their different purposes i.e., in the form and content of the relevant evidence. The testimony of witnesses and the individuals involved may sound differently in a 'criminal' trial from that in 'child protection' proceedings, and it could also take on a different relevance or a different meaning. This is true at least to the extent that the proceedings in the custody court place emphasis on providing help for the child and the family. To copy the investigation results from criminal proceedings is therefore most questionable. Also, one would have to ask if facts that have not been proved in a criminal trial should be inadmissible in the custody court. Theoretically, the answer to this question is in the negative — only, however, to the extent of the operation of the principle of 'free evaluation of evidence', by which each judge can evaluate evidence in each case independently. The question, nevertheless, must be broadened to include whether or not the difference in the purposes of the proceedings does not imply different standards regarding the evidence. This will be discussed later.

Finally, grave objection can be taken to the delay which is regularly caused by waiting for the result of the criminal proceedings. Recently it has been emphasized again, on good grounds, that decisions in custody matters have to be regarded as urgent, *i.e.* that they have to be expedited as much as possible.[10] This is equally, if not especially, important in child abuse cases, not only because the children are made to feel deeply insecure in their emotional relationships and therefore so much more urgently in need of stabilization, but also because proceedings often start with a placing of the child in a home,[11] which, no matter how justified, constitutes an additionally heavy burden for the child (and for his family), which should be appraised as soon as possible. It should, therefore, be considered whether paragraph 12 of the FGG should be sharpened by introducing an explicit obligation for an immediate, independent fact finding conducted by the custody court judge himself with greatest possible speed.

From this a series of new problems emerges which needs to be carefully considered. 'Double' investigations do not only constitute a heavier financial and work load for the judicial system (should, for instance, psychological and psychiatric evaluations be made independently in each instance?), but they also present particular problems for the individuals involved. A special problem is raised by the repeated interrogation of the child by different institutions: police, Youth Office, custody court judge and criminal trial judge. At the same time the threat of a criminal proceeding could destroy all efforts by the custody court judge to enter into a 'helpful' discussion with the family, because the individuals involved may justifiably fear that the file might later be consulted in a criminal trial in which the custody court judge might be a witness. A law however, which would prevent the criminal judge from obtaining information from the custody court (or for that matter from the Youth Office) would probably not easily be accepted in West Germany because it would violate the principle of mutual cooperation between courts.

The Custody Courts and the Youth Offices

Para. 48a of the youth welfare law (Jugendwohlfahrtsgesetz) requires that the custody court judge has to get an opinion from the Youth Office before making a decision about the personal conditions of the lives of children, and this would appear to suggest something of an advisory function for the Youth Office. This would, however, be an insufficient description of the real function of the Youth Office. In practice the Youth Office regularly initiates the proceedings and it provides the information on the case and its background. This information is generally accepted by the custody court judge without verification. Often, but not always, the custody court judge personally talks to the parents,[12] but he hardly ever speaks to the child,[13] and rarely to neighbors or other informed individuals. Also, the opinions of psychological experts are rarely obtained.[14] If the parental authority is removed, custody is usually transferred to the Youth Office, which can then choose a foster family or a foster home. Thus, in practice, the Youth Office plays a decisive role in custody court proceedings, without this role being governed by legal standards.

The influential role of the Youth Office mainly results from the greater familiarity of the social worker with the case and from a trained competence in these matters which the custody court judge normally lacks. This is, of course, an undeniable benefit to the families involved. On the other hand, it should not be overlooked that the Youth Office is an institution with bureaucratic interests of its own which are not always identical with the interests of the children and families. Especially when, as is often the case in child abuse cases, there have been past contacts between the Youth Office and the family, the Youth Office is put into a situation where it has to justify its previous work or explain or at least describe its 'failure'. Also, in selecting a boarding place for the child, financial considerations play an important role, and the interests of publicly financed homes are as important as the worker's effort to find for the child a good foster home or a place in a special educational institution.

The question which arises from this is whether possibilities for judicial control and guidance of the Youth Office should be improved in order to protect the interests of the child and his family. Here too, however, solutions are hard to find. It seems doubtful that a 'formal fact finding procedure' to verify the findings of the Youth Office (as is done to verify the findings of the state prosecutor in a criminal trial) is necessary or appropriate. Also the selection of homes and private foster families cannot simply become the custody court judges' responsibility. Rather, forms of cooperation should be found which allow an optimal utilization of the specific possibilities of both institutions in the interest of the children and their families.[15]

4. Fact Finding — Legal Questions of Evidence

Difficulties in introducing evidence in abuse cases, especially where the children themselves are too young to testify, have been the subject of discussions for a long time, though in West Germany, only among criminal lawyers. As indicated above, it remains to be determined whether the different objectives and aims of the criminal and the custody court proceedings should also have consequences for the presentation of evidence. Several American states have decided that the evidentiary requirements should be different. Whereas in criminal proceedings evidence 'beyond a reasonable doubt' is required, in neglect or abuse proceedings the standard is 'a preponderance of the evidence'[16], a standard of evidence which has been used in other areas of the American civil law for a long time. The starting point of this rule is the justified belief that the risk of an unjust conviction in a criminal trial is much graver than the risk of an unjust acquittal, while in proceedings in which the main objective is the security and safety of the child, the risks of misjudging an abuse as an accident are as high if not higher than those of a falsely adjudged abuse.

In the German judicial tradition there is no differentiation as to the sufficiency of the evidence required. Like the criminal judge, the custody court judge must be fully convinced of the existence of child abuse if he wants to take measures for the protection of the child. In the judicial practice and in the literature, the judge is granted a certain discretion in determining the degree of probability upon which he makes his conviction.[17] But there is good reason to believe that custody court judges, just as criminal court judges, usually demand a 'probability bordering on certainty', *i.e.,* proof of child abuse 'beyond a reasonable doubt'.

The cases studied revealed the following incidents. In one case the child was sent back to his family after the mother's acquittal, despite a remaining suspicion. Two years later severe abuse was proved which demanded a new, and this time, final placement in a home. In the meantime, however, the chid's disturbed behavior had become so drastic that the foster home in which she had earlier been placed would not accept her. The placement in a foster family was out of the question. Severe damage was caused to this child because of a delay in court intervention which should have been avoidable. In other cases in which the evidence was insufficient in light of the strict standards of proof, the judge ordered supervision by the Youth Office, that is, that they should take 'informal measures', which, while having no strict legal basis, nevertheless constituted a severe interference in the autonomy of the family.

It is known, however, through the practice of the Youth Offices that they try to avoid, if possible, involving the custody court. When a child seems endangered but the evidence is unlikely to reach the standard required by the court, understandably enough, the Youth Offices will try to make the parents agree to a 'voluntary' placement in a foster home or to accept supervision, using the possible threat of court proceedings as pressure. Social workers themselves refer to 'blackmail' and can find themselves in situations of severe conflict.

This makes it clear that the law governing the burden of proof is out of step with the demands of reality. The consequences of this are that children are avoidably put in jeopardy, intervention is concealed and coercion takes indirect forms. This results in a loss in legal protection for the children as well as the families. Consideration should be given to revising the law. It would be desirable in so doing to draw on American experience with the 'preponderance of evidence' rule in neglect and abuse proceedings. The use of legal presumptions and the principle of *'res ipsa loquitur'* should also be considered. Such principles are recurrent in West German law, not in the connection with family law, but mainly in the law of damages and compensation. Since they are also regarded as functional equivalents of rules governing the sufficiency of evidence, they would have to be included in a discussion of the law of evidence.[18]

5. The Significance of the Social Situation of the Family

Although there are considerable differences of opinion regarding the evaluation of socio-economic conditions in studying the genesis of child abuse, there is general agreement that the problems which result from extremely adverse social conditions are one of the factors which trigger crises. Of these, financial difficulties, insufficient living space and social isolation are specially important.[19]

Nevertheless, in the course of legal proceedings, full investigations are rarely made and social aspects are rarely taken into account when the court makes its prognosis or disposition of the case. One often searches in vain for exact information regarding occupation, education, income and housing conditions of the parties. Their social contacts with relatives, friends and neighbors are hardly mentioned. One can gather from the information found in the Youth Offices' reports that the cases dealt with concern individuals from the lower income groups or from fringe groups of society which are anyway the center of official attention.[20] A concrete picture of the family situation, however, rarely emerges, and its significance in explaining the child abuse remains vague. The judges' decisions hardly ever consider it.

Here the traditional judicial thinking in one-dimensional causal connections certainly plays a part. It is expressed typically in the current version of para. 1666 of the BGB: that the child's welfare is endangered *by* the abuse of the parental custody right. The family's interaction with the social environment and the social biography of the family, in short an 'ecological dimension',[21] are seemingly without significance for judicial purposes. The new language suggested in the reform proposal would end this misleading and simplistic approach by directing attention to the endangerment of the child as such and to ways in which the family can escape that situation. Certainly such new language would not in itself be sufficient to achieve a new orientation in judicial practice. The proposals must reach further, for even today it is not the text of the law that hinders a judge in including social factors in his decision. Rather, the hindrances can be found in the general structure of the custody courts' practice. That will be discussed later.

6. Psychodynamic Aspects

Both early and more recent research leaves no doubt that psychological abuse causes as severe damage to children as physical abuse and that, moreover, physical abuse will also always result in psychic damage.[22] Often the psychological results are longer lasting and harder to correct than physical injuries. There are by now extensive studies on the psychological structure and dynamics of abusing parents, as well as on psychotherapy and social and educational measures taken to treat the abusing parents.[23]

However, judging from the cases we studied, psychodynamic considerations are in practice almost always treated as being of no importance. In no case we studied did psychological abuse alone constitute the reason for bringing the proceeding in court. In so far as the reports of the Youth Offices pay any attention to behavioral abnormalities or developmental deficiences, rather than simply to signs of physical abuse, usually the genesis of those disturbances and their connection with the family dynamics and with abuse remains unexplained. Information regarding the most important relationships of the child within or outside the family, is rarely included in the reports, even though generally the question is whether the child should be removed from the family or not. The court investigations hardly pursue these questions, and psychological evaluations are exceptional. Opportunities for the parents to be heard by the judge personally are not always provided and contacts between the judge and the children are quite rare, even when the children are beyond toddler age.[24] In the judicial decisions expressions of the necessity for psychological or educational testing or for a specific form of placement (foster home or foster place in a family) are hardly ever found, and the proper conditions and time for the return of the child to the family are not explored.

The cause for these deficiencies can only partially be found in specific legal provisions or principles, or the lack thereof. Simplistic ideas of action and causality as reflected in para. 1666 of the BGB, as well as the fault principle, do not correspond to modern understanding of the psychology of family dynamics and psychological development. Nevertheless, the 'psychic' welfare of the child is mentioned explicitly in the law as a separate entity to be protected in addition to the 'physical' welfare.

The law of procedure sets certain limits on the court's powers: a psychological examination of the child requires the parents' consent, although under certain circumstances the parents' consent can be supplied by the court. An examination of the parents is never possible without their agreement.

The courts, however, even within these restrictions, make very limited use of the opportunities for comprehending the psycho-dynamics of a given case. The reasons for this must again be seen in more complex institutional and extra-institutional conditions. Studies in this area were conducted in the course of the Frankfurt research project which, as mentioned earlier, involves custody decisions in a broader sense. After it became apparent that investigations and decisions for the child's 'welfare' in all areas concentrate almost exclusively upon the material aspects of physical health and care, while the psychic dimension of the child's welfare is neglected, an attempt was made to find explanatory connections between this tendency and the organizational structure of the custody courts and the education and self-image of the judges. Only some of the resultant theses, which will be explained and documented more closely in a final report, can be briefly introduced, and these should mark the starting point for further research.

(a) In several cases reports or evaluations by the Youth Office concerning the psychic situation of the child or indicating psychic disturbances or conflicts in relating were not taken note of by the judge and they were not considered in his decision. One reason for this could be the insufficient or often total lack of training of the judge in psychology, thereby impeding his ability to understand the significance of such reports or evaluations and to react accordingly.[25]

(b) Only rarely does a communicative situation emerge in pretrial interviews which would enable the exchange of relevant information pertaining to the child's psychic condition or difficulties in relating, and which would enable the individuals involved to develop their own 'problem solving behavior'. Here too the lack of training on the part of the judge could play a part (especially in interviews with children). Further reasons for the difficulties in communication could lie in the legal and procedural position of the parents, which is closer to that of 'objects' or 'passive subjects' of proceedings between the judge and the Youth Office rather than to that of 'participants' in the proceedings.

(c) The custody court judge, if possible, seems to avoid involvement in the psychic dynamics of the case. The material here is more apt to involve him personally than in the average civil proceeding. The result is a fear that his ability to make a proper judicial decision might be impaired; his judicial objectivity might be threatened.

(d) The narrow scope of the judge's action, whether limited by legal procedure or practical considerations, for the most part prevents individualized measures and puts in doubt the objective sense as well as the subjective willingness of judges to make differentiated psycho-diagnostic analyses.

These theses, however, must be seen in perspective. Para. 1666 of the BGB provides that the judge can take the 'necessary measures' to avert the danger to the child and therefore it would seem that the judge is granted whatever power is necessary to achieve this end. It is questionable, however, to what extent the judge can in fact go further than to use immediately child-related measures — by for example, ordering psychotherapy for the mother of an abused child. Other equally 'necessary' precautions will often doubtlessly exceed the limits of his legal powers. Some of these measures could be a change in the housing conditions, a special advantage in school for the child, not to mention the procurement of a job or other improvements in the financial situation of the family. In addition, the range of legally possible measures is further limited by practical conditions: there are neither enough therapeutic homes nor enough educational counselors or child therapists. The judge's scope of action may in fact be reduced to the alternatives: placement of the child in a home or a foster family or leaving the child in his family without any help worth mentioning. (In the child abuse cases we studied we did not find any other measures being used). The risk of (further) psychic damage is nevertheless high, in either of these alternatives, and they do not really provide reasonable options. Under these circumstances a more differentiated examination of the psychic needs of the child would merely illustrate so much more the discrepancy between what is necessary and what is possible, and would probably only additionally burden the judge in his work.

7. Conclusion

After a short survey one can say that the conduct of the custody courts in child abuse cases is not so free from difficulty as the lack of problem-consciousness in this area and in legal decisions would suggest. In practice many defects become apparent which are only partially due to the judicial system or those specific legal provisions which have not been adjusted in light of new developments and insights, as has been done with parts of the law of evidence and procedure. More seriously, judicial practice has not found a means by which to deal with the psycho-social determinants of child abuse, and there are no adequate remedies available when abuse is found. If, therefore, the resources of the institution of the custody court are truly to be used to solve the problems involved in child abuse cases, measures must be taken which go far beyond merely changing individual paragraphs of the legal code.

NOTES

1. Polizeiliche Kriminalstatistik BRD, herausgegeben vom Bundeskriminalamt Wiesbaden, 1976, these define child abuse in terms of para. 223b of the Criminal Code, *i.e.,* torture, cruelty and wilful neglect resulting in damage to health to children under 18 inflicted by a person having custody of them.
2. Statistisches Bundesamt Wiesbaden, Bevölkerung und Kultur, Reihe 9 Rechtspflege.
3. *Cf.* Mende, and Kirsch, *Beobachtungen zum Problem der Kindesmisshandlung* (Forschungsbericht des Deutschen Jugendinstituts) München, 1969; Petri, and Lauterbach, *Gewalt in der Erziehung,* Frankfurt M., 1975; Bast; Bernecker., *et. al.* (eds.), *Gewalt gegen Kinder, Kindesmisshandlungen und ihre Ursachen,* Reinbek bei Hamburg, 1975.
4. *Cf.* documentation by Biermann, *Kindeszüchtigung und Kindesmisshandlung,* München, and Basel, 1969; The first attempts to extensively inform the public — mainly using sources from abroad — are made in the volumes of Bast, Bernecker; *et al.,* and Petri, and Lauterbach (note 3). See also Fontana, *Somewhere a Child is Crying: the Battered Child.* New York, New York: Macmillan, 1973, p. 228*ff.*
5. Oviatt, After Child Abuse Reporting Legislation — What? in Kempe, and Helfer (eds.) *Helping the Battered Child and His Family.* New York, New York: Lippincott. 1972; Paulsen, Monrad, in (1966), 13 *Children* (cited from Fontana, 229); Besharov, Duryea, Report of the New York State Assembly, April 1972, App. C in Kempe, and Helfer (eds.), *The Battered Child* (2nd. ed.) Chicago, Illinois: University of Chicago Press, 1974.
6. *Cf.* Delaney and Polier, Wise, in Kempe, and Helfer (note 5); several contributions, among others by Paulsen, M., in Rosenheim (ed.) *Justice for the Child,* 1962; Wald, Michael, "State Intervention on Behalf of Neglected Children: Standards for Removal of Children from their Homes, Monitoring the Status of Children in Foster Care and Termination of Parental Rights" (1976), 28 *Stanford L.J.* 623.
7. Proposed Bill by the fractions of SPD and FDP. A new proposal to regulate the rights of parental custody, Bundestagsdrucksache 8/111 of February 10, 1977.
8. The file analysis (371 cases) was supplemented by interviews and group discussions with custody court judges and by questionnaires concerning the court organization and training of the judges as well as by an analysis of the contents of their decisions.
9. In the following reflections we assume that in the foreseeable future the notion "to eliminate criminal penalties against parents or, at a minimum, make prosecution subject to the approval of the juvenile court", will not gain acceptance, as Wald demands (see note 6).
10. Goldstein, Freud, A; and Solnit, *Jenseits des Kindeswohls,* Frankfurt, 1975.
11. In 9 out of the 12 cases studied by us this was the case — in 5 of these cases the provisional decision for placement outside the home was revoked in the course of the proceedings — after 6 weeks in three cases, 3 months in one case, and 6 months in one case.
12. In 4 of the 12 child abuse cases the judge personally spoke with both parents; in 4 further cases with one parent; in the other 4 cases a personal talk did not appear in the records. In all the cases studied in the course of the Frankfurt research project including custody misuse as well as decisions concerning custody and visitation rights

after a divorce (n = 236), only in 25 percent were both parents heard; in 18 percent one parent was heard; and in 57 percent of the cases there was no face-to-face hearing with the judge.

13. Only in 3 of the 12 child abuse cases did the judge himself speak to the child. In all 3 cases the children were more than 12 years old. In all the cases studied by the Frankfurt research project children were heard by the judge himself only in 7 percent of the cases — although about 60 percent of all children involved were more than 6 years old and about 30 percent of the involved children were more than 9 years old.

14. A psychological or psychiatric examination of the child took place in 2 of the 12 abuse cases (both at the request of the Youth Office), and an examination of the parents did not take place in any case. Altogether only 12 psychological or psychiatric evaluations were requested by custody court judges in all the cases studied by the Frankfurt research group.

15. See Handler, J., *The Coercive Social Worker*. New York, New York: Academic Press, 1973.

16. A summary is given by Katz, Sanford N.; Howe., and McGrath, "Child Neglect Laws in America" (1975) *Family Law Quarterly* Vol. IX, No. 1.

17. Maassen, B.M., *Beweismassprobleme im Schadensersatzprozess,* 1975.

18. For a discussion of evidential issues in child neglect cases, see Eekelaar, J.M., "The Protection of the Child's Welfare in Custody and Care Proceedings", in Bates, F. (ed.) *The Child and the Law,* 1976.

19. *Cf.* among others: Gil, D.G., *Violence Against Children.* Cambridge, Mass.: Harvard University Press, 1970., Light, *Abused and Neglected Children in America: A Study of Alternative Policies* (1973), 43 *Harv Ed. Rev.,* Steele, B.F., "Violence within the Family," in Helfer and Kempe (eds.), *Child Abuse and Neglect. The Family and the Community.* Cambridge, Mass.: Ballinger, 1976., Young, L.R., *Wednesday's Children: A Study of Child Neglect and Abuse.* New York, New York: McGraw-Hill, 1971.

20. This impression was caused mainly by frequent earlier contacts of the family with Social Offices (Sozialbehörden) as well by their social conspicuousness' (alcoholism, prostitution, previous convictions, psychiatric confinement). A special group of 'socio-cultural outsiders' are foreign families (especially Turks and Yugoslavs), in which teenage daughters were abused when they tried to break away from the traditional life style of their parents.

21. Richmond, J., *cit.* from Newberger, E., "The Myth of the Battered Child Syndrome" (1973) *Current Medical Dialog,* Vol. XXXX, No. 4.

22. Hetzer, H., "Psychologische Begutachtung misshandelter Kinder" (1973) *Zeitschrift für angewandte Psychologie und Charakterkunde* 50.

23. *Cf.* Kempe, and Helfer: *Helping the Battered Child and his Family, supra,* note 5., and Helfer and Kempe: *Child Abuse and Neglect, The Family and the Community, supra,* note 19.

24. *Cf.* notes 11 and 12 for the number of personal contacts.

25. One example: considerable retardation and malnutrition were found in a pair of two year old twins and their three year old brother in the children's hospital. The report of the social worker also points out that the two year old children were unable to sit up, that they "throw their heads and upper bodies constantly from one side to the other", that they were 'unapproachable" and did not react to the visit, and that their faces seemed 'rigid and expressionless". Upon talking to the mother, it was discovered that she hardly ever takes the children out of their beds. With respect to the three year-old brother the social worker surmises a "considerable delay in intellectual and emotional development". The judge urged the mother to follow the dietary instructions of the hospital and to keep in touch with the Youth Office. The drastic symptoms of damage in the psychological development of the children and the apparent problems of the mother in dealing adequately with the specific developmental needs of the children were not cause for specific investigation and consideration as to which helping measures beyond supervision of the children's diet were necessary to prevent further psychic damage to the children.

Chapter 27

The Police Role in Child Abuse

*R.C. Holmes**

1. Rural Police in Canada

In developing an explanation of the rural police role in the enforcement of laws relating to the battered child, it is important to understand the difference between urban and rural policing.

In a period of a few hundred years, Canada has moved from an undeveloped frontier to an industrialized and urbanized country. Since the majority of people live in urban or semi-urban areas, it is difficult, for those who seldom travel in rural areas, to truly appreciate Canada's size. With a land mass of 3,851,809 square miles[1], and a rural population of 5,157,525,[2] it can be generalized that there is an average of less than two persons per square mile. Considering this low density of population, it is physically impossible to supply easily accessible social services to the rural populace.

Over the years rural people have grown accustomed to calling the police for every type of problem. In fact the only agency in rural Canada that is available in most areas on a 24-hour basis are the police. This means police officers are responsible for resolving many problems often defined as social problems. One such problem is that of the 'battered, abused, and neglected child'. In large centers, these cases are most often dealt with by social workers, psychologists, family counseling centers, school crisis centers or hospitals.

In rural areas, because there are most often no other social agencies to deal with these problems, the child's protection depends directly upon police officers responding to reports or suspicions of an abused child.

Rural and urban police are mandated under provincial laws to report all suspected cases of child abuse and neglect to the proper provincial authorities.

---

* Royal Canadian Mounted Police, Ottawa, Canada.

2. Police and the Law

Modern society trains its police to enforce a multitude of laws. The Criminal Code of Canada contains numerous laws related to behavior described in literature on the abused, neglected or sexually assaulted child.

S. 168 (1) states:

Everyone who, in the home of a child, participates in adultery or sexual immorality or indulges in habitual drunkenness or any other form of vice, and thereby endangers the morals of the child or renders the home an unfit place for the child to be, is guilty of an indictable offence and is liable to imprisonment for two years.[3]

S. 197 (1) states:

Everyone is under a legal duty (a) as a parent, foster parent, guardian or head of a family, to provide necessaries of life for a child under the age of sixteen years.[4]

S. 200 states:

Everyone who unlawfully abandons or exposes a child who is under the age of ten years, so that life is or is likely to be endangered or its health is, or is likely to be permanently injured, is guilty of an indictable offence and is liable to imprisonment for two years.[5]

Other offences which are not intended to distinguish between a child or adult but that equally apply to conditions described within definitions of the battered child syndrome are described under a number of headings from assault to murder.

S. 204 states:

Everyone who by criminal negligence causes bodily harm to another person is guilty of an indictable offence and is liable to imprisonment for ten years.[6]

S. 205 (1) states:

A person commits homicide when, directly or indirectly, by any means, he causes the death of a human being.[7]

Murder, manslaughter and infanticide, sections 212, 217 and 216 respectively, are all charges that can be related to the death of a child where abuse is supected.[8]

Occasionally a form of child abuse has been the administering of a noxious substance. S. 229 states:

Everyone who administers or causes to be administered to any person or causes any person to take poison or any other destructive or noxious thing is guilty of an indictable offence and is liable (a) to imprisonment for fourteen years, if he intends thereby to endanger the life of or to cause bodily harm to that person; or (b) to imprisonment for two years, if he intends thereby to aggrieve or annoy that person.[9]

Various forms of assault, whether it be physical or sexual assault, are described within the Criminal Code. Although these charges are laid primarily in cases of adults assaulting adults, they apply equally to children.

The one section that provides for force to be used in child correction is s. 43 which states:

Every school teacher, parent or persons standing in the place of a parent is justified in using force by way of correction toward a pupil or child, as the case may be, who is under his care, if the force does not exceed what is reasonable under the circumstances.[10]

Regardless of this authority, s. 26 of the Criminal Code states:

Everyone who is authorized by law to use force is criminally responsible for any excess thereof according to the nature and quality of the act that constitutes the excess.[11]

Apart from this array of charges that cover nearly every conceivable type of physical abuse to a child, there is in every province a Child Welfare Act. These acts provide authority for police and welfare workers to remove children from a home where, upon reasonable grounds, child abuse is suspected. Considering the number of charges relating to these laws, it is easy to believe that every child is fully protected by the state. Yet overwhelming evidence shows that very few cases of child abuse, in relation to their actual number, are reported.

All laws are made in an attempt to control anti-social behavior. The majority of people view the reporting of criminal offences as part of their civic responsibility. However, when it comes to reporting offences perpetuated against a child, the majority of people do not fulfill their civic responsibility and become filled with doubt and uncertainty about what to do.

While social scientists have attempted to explain this failure of action, theories about why people do not report these crimes against children do little for the child being dehumanized by abuse. It is expecially difficult to accept the fact that many thousands of children have been and will continue to be physically maimed, emotionally destroyed and even murdered because otherwise rational, loving and concerned human beings do not report offences against children.

3. Reporting of Crimes Against Children

The law and the criminal justice system are constructed on the principle that a complaint will be made in respect of a violation. Young abused children are incapable of filing a complaint and older children in most cases are unwilling to do so. Adults, even those in professions that have the most contact with the battered, abused, neglected or sexually assaulted child, have repeatedly failed to accept their responsibility and report offences to the police or provincial authorities. It is important for all people to understand that without the active participation and assistance of the public, few crimes would be solved. For that matter, few would ever come to the attention of the police. In the case of abused children, the word public includes all those professionals most likely to come in contact with a battered, abused or neglected child, such as doctors, dentists, teachers, clergy and social workers.

Most citizens call the police when they observe a robbery in progress, a street fight or an adult being severely beaten. But seldom would the same adults report even a very severe assault by the parent on a juvenile. It is not uncommon to hear, in casual conversation, about adults who assault their children. However, an official complaint is rarely made.

Perhaps the most surprising fact to police officers working on child abuse cases is the failure of many members of the medical profession to cooperate. First by not reporting suspected or confirmed cases of child abuse, and second by their reluctance to give police investigators information or professional diagnoses that provides medical evidence necessary to complete the case under investigation.

To some doctors, the fact that prosecution will not bring back a dead child or may hinder the rehabilitation of an abusive parent seems a logical reason not to report or cooperate with an investigation. But, the investigation and prosecution of a serious violation of law is a requirement police are mandated to fulfill. In the case of a violent death, even where a child's death is unintentional, the police must investigate.

The most socially revealing tragedies are those where more than one child in a family is killed. Very often in these cases authorities are well aware that prior to the first death and certainly before the second, severe family problems existed. Still no reports, investigation or corrective measures were taken. As researchers study the records, a surprising number of such cases are revealed.

This brings to mind a case recounted by a close police officer friend. Twenty years previous he investigated a traffic accident. A child was killed and he was required to attend the autopsy. In the hospital morgue were the bodies of two children. When the doctor was questioned as to the identity of the second child, the officer was told the child died in the hospital as a result of an accident in his home. The constable looked at the second body and found it covered with bruises. On closer examination my friend recognized the child as a member of a family with whom he had had a number of official police contacts. His suspicions aroused, an investigation was launched and eventually charges were laid against the mother for murder.

The investigation revealed a sad story. This was the third child in the family to die over a period of sixteen months. No previous investigations had been made, because the deaths were never reported to the police. When the situation was reviewed following the disposition of this case, the police officer could only conclude what any reasonable person would under the circumstances. Had there been a better reporting system, previous investigations and better cooperation between the medical profession, social welfare and the police, the second and third child might not have died.

Even under our present system there is no accurate estimate of how many children are killed each year from abuse. Even less is known about the number of children who are physically and emotionally injured, often permanently. Literature on child abuse also stresses how often children are returned home after being beaten or severely punished, only to undergo further beatings that result in either more serious injury or death.

Until a police officer is aware of an offence, investigation is impossible. When citizens believe a crime has been committed, they report to the police what they have seen or heard. Statements are taken and physical evidence is gathered. The facts are compiled to get a clear picture of the offence. A major part of nearly every investigation is public support for the police both in reporting an offence and testifying as to what was seen or heard.

An exception to the usual public support of police occurs when criminal acts are perpetrated against children. This is especially so when the public is aware that the criminal act is committed by parents or guardians.

4. Police Discretion

Police discretion is an accepted law enforcement principle. Funk & Wagnall's *Standard College Dictionary* defines discretion as: "Freedom or power to make one's own judgment and decisions and to act as one sees fit".[12] Police officers use discretion daily in most of their activities, including those responsibilities related to the investigation and prosecution of criminal offences.

Discretion works on a sliding scale. In serious offences, few or no individual options are possible. As offences become progressively minor, a wider variety of options exist. In practice this means that in offences such as petty traffic violations, complaints bordering on civil action, or lesser victimless offences, the discretion of the individual officer plays a greater role in the decision-making process.

In the past, when using discretionary powers in child abuse cases, the police first decided if the complaint was serious enough to warrant an investigation. Was the abuse of a physical nature? Were there any injuries? The greater the reported physical damage inflicted on the child, the more likelihood of police intervention. However, if the complainant was vague about the extent or kind of injuries, or doubtful about how the injury was inflicted, the officer decided whether or not the report justified an investigation.

In the past, when enforcing the law in matters of child abuse, police officers reflected the social values of the community. Therefore, where there was community apathy it was reasonable to expect police apathy. Police apathy in the past must also be considered in relation to a professional community that should have shared inter-disciplinary responsibility for the protection of children.

Police officers have a legal responsibility to investigate violations of the law. School systems are responsible for the welfare of children under their care. Social agencies have a continuing responsibility to families and a legislated concern for the welfare of children. Doctors have medical, legal and ethical responsibility for the health and well being of their patients. Yet individuals in each group did and do fail to take appropriate action when child abuse comes to their attention. This apathy is not only the failure of individuals but the failure of a society that accepts and condones this lack of concern.

Today, however, there is a deeper professional awareness of child abuse. New provincial laws reflect a greater understanding of what failure to respond can mean to the safety of a child at risk and require that all suspected abuse be reported to provincial authorities. This means that police are also mandated to report all suspected cases to social welfare agencies.

5. The Prevention Side of Police Work

Long before the first government-operated social service agency was started, the police were often required to fulfill a social worker role as part of their duties. The evolving profession of social work has now taken over many functions that were previously police responsibilities. Traditionally, a part of police work is the role officers play in prevention through counseling. In this work police officers interact with juveniles and adults who are on the verge of breaking the law; or when there is insufficient evidence to support a charge but the officer feels the individual should be made aware that subsequent acts could lead to prosecution and a possible jail term. No doubt over the years the presence of police and the warnings given for acts now termed child abuse, have played some part in the prevention of serious injury or death to children.

The problem now is to develop and professionalize the police role in the field of child abuse. In concert with other responsible agencies police can work to provide a consistent, mutually-complementary approach to reduce and prevent the abuse of children.

6. Inter-Agency Conflict

Many police officers believe that present social work policies often destroy personal incentive, add greater numbers to welfare roles and make police work more difficult. Misconceptions and biases are also harbored by some social workers who have differences of opinion with police officers. These are some of the reasons for the misunderstandings between the two agencies.

Unfortunately, antipathy leads to communication breakdown and lack of co-operation in cases where both agencies should be cooperating in efforts to reach their common goal, the protection of children. The methods each agency uses to reach this goal, however, often cause problems between them. In recent years a great deal of effort has been made by responsible people in both agencies to understand each other and to work together on problems of mutual concern.

Future measures to resolve problems concerning the home and the abused and battered child will have to be multidisciplinary in approach. These measures will involve not only the police, social workers, doctors and the courts, but also government, private and community agencies that are established to provide help.

7. Legal Authority for Action

All provinces in Canada have Child Welfare Acts that provide police, social workers and welfare officials with the authority to remove children from homes where child abuse is suspected. The investigation and successful resolution of offences pertaining to child abuse, however, often pose problems for the police because there is no clear delineation of responsibility.

Too often the question of who is responsible for the case interferes with the action that should be taken. Very often a social worker is unable to remove a child from the home without police assistance. The police, on the other hand, may not act without the participation of a social worker. Often, however, these agencies are at odds. Obviously there is a clear need for cooperation between helping agencies working on behalf of a child at risk.

The present trend in the treatment of child abusers is family counseling. There is, however, no legal authority that makes counseling treatment mandatory. The family court could perhaps order counseling as an alternative to a sentence, but the programs and personnel necessary to provide such treatment are not often available. Time, personal contact and compassion are the important elements of successful treatment. At present the legal and social system is not meeting these treatment requirements.

As society moves toward greater legal protection for all individuals, it has become apparent that more time is required to present a case even in the traditionally informal family courts. In matters of child abuse a number of people are involved in the decision-making process. Increased professional involvement produces a greater variety of opinions and recommendations about what should be done. Clear options between criminal charges and actual treatment programs designed to treat and rehabilitate the parent should be available. It is important that future legislation provide family courts with the authority to sentence child abusers to a rehabilitation center or agency designed to treat abusive parents.

Police will continue, as they must, to be the investigating agency, both in urban and rural areas. The function of police is by definition to enforce existing laws through the laying of criminal charges. Without a clear legally-mandated treatment option, the present role of the police is difficult.

Current research on child abuse stresses the need to develop a variety of community-based treatment programs. This would suggest that for best results, a decision regarding prosecution or referral should be made before a case is brought to court. Implementation of these options could be decided through inter-disciplinary consultation. However, until legal alternatives are available, the police must operate within existing judicial parameters. This fact often places a strain on police-social agency cooperation.

8. Steps to be Taken

Researchers agree that the development of an efficient accurate reporting system is crucial. Therefore, mandatory reporting by doctors, nurses, hospitals, teachers, principals, social workers, police and others likely to come into contact with abused children is essential. The law must provide some form of penalty for failure to report including, as it presently does, a clause that protects those who report from civil liability. To maintain an efficient and accurate reporting system, all reports should be made to a central registry. I believe this registry should be national in order to prevent breakdowns in communication that can occur if each province establishes its own system. Security of information should be ensured, but records must be accessible to investigating agencies or qualified researchers. Without accurate statistics and information, research is of little value.

Widespread public knowledge of a reporting system is essential. Often citizens who are aware of abused children fail to report because they do not know how or to whom they should report. The same may hold true for professionals who have experienced the 'buck passing' that can occur when there is no clear line of action. Zenith numbers are presently used in the U.S.A. for the reporting of suspected child abuse.

While preparing this chapter, I spoke with an officer whose wife is a school teacher specializing in problem children. Recently she arrived home, broken-hearted over a youngster she had attempted to help. The child, about six years old, was poorly nourished, improperly clothed and severely bruised. She was informed that the parents had frequently disciplined the child because the youngster was difficult to handle. The woman related, however, that as she read to this little girl the child lay its head on her knee, obviously wanting and needing the feeling of closeness and affection. The school principal was informed, as was the Department of Welfare. However, no action was taken.

This case illustrates the problem for both social workers and the police who have the authority 'upon reasonable grounds' to remove a child from his/her home. What constitutes reasonable grounds is, of necessity, broad and hence vague. Action depends a great deal on individual discretion. Because of the range of professional opinions as to what is more harmful to a child, removal from its natural parents or the danger of either physiological or psychological injury as a result of leaving the child in the home, often no action is taken. Opposing views are not only confusing to officials who want to take remedial action on behalf of the child, but they also engender and maintain inaction. Compounding this is a lack of proper facilities to maintain and treat abused children.

Who can be held responsible for the lack of response or delay to a child's needs when every possible alternative move is questioned? There are problems with the institutional care some children receive when removed from their homes. In such cases, a logical solution would be to examine and, where required, correct or change these institutions. The alternative, leaving the child in an abusive home without providing protection for the child or treatment for the parents, is a poor one. Some researchers claim that removal of the child from the home may result in psychological damage. However, to allow a child to remain in an abusive home without protection or treatment negates the intent of all child abuse protection laws and leads to further physical and emotional damage or death.

9. Police Needs

It is necessary, not only for the police officer in rural areas but for all police officers, to place child abuse in its proper perspective. The law must provide a single definition of the offence. The definition must be clear and precise, with a physical description of what is meant by child abuse. The 1973 U.S. Child Abuse Prevention Act decreed that the term 'child abuse and neglect' means:

The physical or mental injury, sexual abuse, negligent treatment, or maltreatment of a child under 18 by a person who is responsible for the child's health or welfare is harmed or threatened by . . .[13]

With a definition similar to this as a starting point, individuals in Canada most likely to come in contact with abusive parents and abused children, such as doctors, nurses, teachers, welfare workers and police, could be trained to recognize these conditions and understand what options are available when dealing with the problem. The attitude of the law toward child abusers must also be clearly delineated. There is presently a transition in society from a punitive philosophy to a concept of rehabilitation as a means of dealing with offenders. This is so not only for criminals but for anyone classed as a deviate. Therefore, this concept should include those who abuse children.

Alternatives to incarceration must be both realistic and enforceable. It is not enough to say that an individual requires medical help, counseling, group therapy, *etc.* There must be ways and means of ensuring that people who need help actually receive it. This is particularly true in rural areas where most often no facilities are readily available and no alternatives are possible. Concern must be generated at all social levels to ensure the cooperative effort necessary to produce reasonable alternatives to incarceration.

This means developing a wide range of programs that provide for:
(a) referral by the police or the agency responsible for investigating initial complaints before the case enters the criminal proceeding stage;
(b) referral by the court once the case enters the criminal proceeding stage; or
(c) penalties, including incarceration, consistent with the factors surrounding the incident.

Another important step is the legal designation of one agency to be responsible for all the actions to be taken. This responsibility should not be divided, even though other agencies may be involved in the ultimate solution. The primary concern must be the protection of the child from future abuse. Divided responsibility is a sure way of clouding the main concern, the protection of the child.

Once the problem of the child's security is resolved, emphasis can then properly be placed on the search for preventive measures. Prevention of child abuse is everyone's concern and responsibility. The community must be aware of the problems and involved in the search for solutions.

Although those concerned with the problems of child abuse almost totally agree that the prosecution of offenders has had little effect in preventing child abuse, there is, at present, still a shotgun approach to alternatives. Legal and enforceable alternatives acceptable to the general public must be developed. Professionals recognize that programs of psychiatric treatment, family counseling and Parents Anonymous organizations do help the child and the abusing family.

Unfortunately, the public as yet does not necessarily agree with professionals. While the professionals and the public disagree, child abuse continues. It may be sometime before the average citizen no longer considers punishment the only way to deal with child abuse and the many other problems of anti-social behavior.

It is generally recognized among professionals that child abuse is not only a crime but a social problem that must be resolved by solutions other than prosecution. But social scientists, professionals, interested agencies and governments must consider the impact that punishment, and the belief in punishment, has on our present social structure. I am not suggesting that court and gaol are the answers. I do believe, however, that this alternative cannot be overlooked if we are to deal realistically with public opinion and the laws as they presently exist in the area of child abuse. Incarceration for crimes of violence against adults has been a long-accepted solution and, where no other suitable alternatives exist, this must ultimately be considered as part of the protection of children.

A workable plan can be formulated to identify and hopefully prevent all aspects of child abuse. In the meantime, existing laws and public opinion stress the need to stop the abuser from a pattern of continuing abuse against the child.

10. Present Trends

Current trends in police work indicate that police officers of the future will be socially motivated by a greater awareness of their role in a system of criminal justice whose goal is increased protection and security for all people. Officers will have broader discretionary powers that permit alternative action in many areas, particularly when dealing with youth.

The Law Reform Commission of Canada, in its Working Paper on Diversion, says:

The assumption is that police and prosecutors should continue to exercise discretion not to lay charges in proper cases, and that such use of discretion should be increased.[14]

Police education and training aimed at social responsibility is increasing. Behavioral training, psychology and sociology, crisis intervention, studies on minorities, prejudice, motivation and the problems of alcoholism, are subjects that broaden the knowledge and perspective of young police officers. The basic sensitivities necessary for handling family and youth problems in terms of a changing police role are being developed at all stages of police training. It is evident from this added training that the police are endeavoring to adapt to an evolving society.

Senior police officers are presently participating with all the agencies that make up the Criminal Justice System to formulate new legislation responsive to the needs of the community. Citizens are once again involving themselves with the police in the prevention of crime. I can foresee the day when there will be greater citizen participation in the prevention of child abuse.

11. Conclusion

In summary, the problem of child abuse has as its first priority the establishment of a reliable reporting system. With fuller research into the causes of child abuse, treatment methods can be developed to reduce and eventually eradicate the problem. While these efforts are being made, the immediate concern must be with the abused child. I feel certain that all police officers will support any program that first *protects* the child from adult abuse. Because violence breeds violence, the cycle must be broken. The last thing our society needs is more violence.

NOTES

1. *Canada Yearbook*, (1974).
2. *Statistics Canada: Annual Report*, (1974).
3. Annual Crim. Code of Canada, s. 168(1) (Martin 1975).
4. *Id.*, s. 197(1).
5. *Id.*, s. 200.
6. *Id.*, s. 204.
7. *Id.*, s. 205(1).
8. *Id.*, s. 212, 217, 216.
9. *Id.*, s. 229.
10. *Id.*, s. 43.
11. *Id.*, s. 26.
12. Funk and Wagnall, *Standard College Dictionary*, (Canadian ed. 1974).
13. Child Abuse Prevention and Treatment Act, Pub. L. No. 93-247 (1974).
14. Working Paper 7 *Diversion*, Law Reform Commission of Canada, 1975.

Chapter 28

Child Abuse: The Policeman's Role: An Innovative Approach

W. Johnson* and J. Thompson†

1. Introduction

Definition

> Considerable variation exists regarding definitions of child abuse. Nonetheless, there is increasing recognition that physical injury of children is only the tip of the iceberg of a wider spectrum of abuse.[1] Physical and sexual abuse is readily identifiable and is therefore more accessible to intervention by law enforcement or social welfare professionals. However, emphasis should be placed on the entire spectrum of child abuse, which encompasses also the difficult to identify children who suffer from non-physical insults such as emotional maltreatment or deprivation, deprivation of food, and social or intellectual neglect by parents or caretakers. These forms of neglect can be equally as damaging as physical abuse.[2]

Child Abuse Legislation

> The Child Welfare Act, s. 41 (Ontario) 1965 states:

> (1) Every person having information of the neglect, abandonment, desertion or physical ill-treatment of a child shall report the situation to a Children's Aid Society or Crown Attorney.
> (2) Subsection 1 applies notwithstanding that the information is confidential or privileged and no action shall be instituted against the informant unless the giving of the information is done maliciously or without reasonable or probable cause.

> The Canadian Criminal Code, s. 197, could be used to prosecute parents (or guardians) for failing to provide the necessities of life for any child under the age of sixteen. Furthermore, it is a criminal offence to assault or cause bodily harm to any person.[3]

---

* Chief of Police, London, Ontario.
† Research Co-Ordinator, Family Consultant Service, London Police Force, Ontario, Canada.

Incidence

There is no accurate estimate available on the incidence of child abuse and neglect in Ontario. In 1975, there were 769 cases reported to the Central Register of Child Abuse. However, due to the difficulties in detection and definition, and a failure to report cases, this figure is low in the context of the overall picture of neglect.[4]

Changing Role of the Police Officer in the Protection of Children

It is important to note that Ontario is the only province to legislate that reporting of cases of child abuse be directed to one of *two* sources — the Children's Aid Society or the Crown Attorney. All other provinces require reports to be directed *only* to the appropriate child welfare authority. Often it is assumed that these two authorities sit on opposite sides of the table with respect to their views and approaches to child abuse. The focus of the Children's Aid Society is on therapeutic intervention, *i.e.,* "to protect the child involved with proper regard to assessing the family dynamics, and providing supportive and rehabilitative assistance".[5]

On the other hand, the traditional police role in child abuse cases involves the receipt of reports, investigation, detainment and prosecution — an authoritative and, in many instances, a punitive approach. Furthermore, police officers tend to lose their objectivity when involved in cases of crime against children and punishment of the abuser can become a desired end. The involvement by police of child welfare personnel or the laying of charges typically requires the kind of justification observed in blatant and readily identifiable, physical abuse cases.

In recent years, however, law enforcement agencies have been re-examining their responsibilities in the area of child protection. Police officers are becoming sensitized to the problem. Greater understanding of the causes of child abuse shift the emphasis from the incarceration of the parent to the treatment and care of both the parent and children in the context of the family unit.[6] The police department has the capacity to respond to emergency calls where children are endangered, as it provides continued around-the-clock service and has the means to move into such situations without delay. Furthermore, some studies have estimated that close to 80 percent of the policeman's role overlaps with that of the mental health professional. Nowhere is this trend more apparent than in the area of domestic disputes, where the majority of cases of child abuse surface. An officer investigating a family crisis is in a good position to recognize the signs of child abuse and take the appropriate steps to alleviate the situation. Thus, it is apparent that the roles and approaches of both the police and the child welfare agencies are converging towards humanistic and supportive viewpoints. This development bolsters the resources for dealing with child abuse and neglect.

2. The Need

There is a need for early recognition of the abused or neglected child for the purpose of reducing the frequency of repeated abusive episodes. Professionals estimate that more than 50 percent of the children who are abused will be abused again if there is no intervention.[7] To this end, general awareness of the signs of abuse or neglect is needed for identification of all forms and stages of both physical and non-physical insults to the child. Furthermore, as physical punishment of a child is commonplace and acceptable in our society, guidelines are needed to identify what constitutes excessive discipline and hence, abuse.

The focus to date deals with instances of child abuse and neglect after the fact. The optimal goal is to prevent abuse from happening, *i.e.,* to diffuse the explosive elements in a potentially abusive family situation so that violence does not occur.[8] Prevention of child abuse can occur through the recognition and identification of three elements which can predispose a family to violence — the parent, the child, the crisis situation.

The high-risk parent has a tendency to abuse from having been abused him/ herself and, therefore, learning this abusive behavior from his/her parents. The parent tends also to be socially isolated or alienated with no close family ties.[9]

The high-risk child who produces stress within the family is usually illegitimate, unwanted, one of many or a problem child, *i.e.,* colicky, premature, physically handicapped, *etc.*[10]

The crisis factor may be any immediate life stress confronting the predisposed family. Situational indicators of potential crisis may be unemployment, financial difficulties, sexual or emotional problems, marital discord and so on.[11]

In summary, recognition and identification of family problems as potential indicators of abuse and their alleviation would aid in the prevention of child abuse.

There is presently a program in operation with the London Police Force, Ontario, which attempts to fulfill these two needs.

3. The Family Consultant Service

History

The idea for a Family Consultant Service with the London Police Force was born out of discussions in late 1970 between the present Chief of Police, Walter T. Johnson and Willard E. Reitz, formerly Director of Clinical Psychology Training at the University of Western Ontario. These discussions were stimulated by local newspaper accounts of the alarming number of police calls to handle family conflicts without the needed professional back up. In fact, family crises accounted for four percent to five percent of the police department's dispatched calls, or approximately 4,000 per year. Most of these calls originate in the evening hours or on weekends between 8 p.m. and 1 a.m. At these times, community social agencies are not open, with the exception of hospital emergency departments. Police officers feel they have neither the time, competence nor societal mandate to deal with such problems. Moreover, domestic disputes are amongst the most dangerous calls that police make.

A solution that seemed the most feasible and also coincided with the possibilities that the police force had explored was a training program on family crisis intervention. Funds received from private foundations were utilized to set up such a training program for police officers in 1972.

The Family Consultant Service was planned for 1973, following the training program, and was designed to provide 'around-the-clock' mental health consultation for officers. The Consultants became a specialized civilian branch of the force geared to assist officers in providing the best possible service to families and individuals in times of crisis.

Private funding dwindled in the spring of 1974. The Solicitor General's Department at the Federal and Provincial levels, recognizing the value of continuing the project as a possible model for police forces across the country, invested funds for a two year period to maintain and foster the development of the program. The number of Family Consultants expanded to five in 1975 and the service has remained an active and integral part of the London Police Force. As of April, 1976, the Family Consultant Service has been solely funded at the municipal level, although research funds are still provided by the Solicitor General of Canada.

The service operates directly out of the headquarters of London police department and provides service from 9 a.m. to 4 a.m. weekdays and noon to 4 a.m. on weekends. This seven day a week schedule optimizes service availability and program costs vis-a-vis community and police needs. The Consultants, who are in constant radio contact with the communications center for the police, are mobile and can therefore provide immediate assistance to police crisis calls. Approximately 10 percent of all the calls received by the police relate to matters within the domain of the Family Consultants (*e.g.,* domestic disputes, juvenile trouble, suicides, *etc.*). Of these, about one quarter result in an officer's request for assistance from the Family Consultant Service.

Philosophy and Goals

The philosophy and goals of the Family Consultant Service are:

(1) To assist officers by providing immediate assessment and intervention of crisis situations and supplying information about or arranging referrals to appropriate community resources,

(2) To aid in the prevention of serious social and/or emotional dysfunctions through early detection and intervention,

(3) To facilitate increased understanding and cooperation between mental health and law enforcement professionals,

(4) To increase community awareness of the social role of the police force,

(5) To provide a model of human services to other communities through careful documentation and evaluation, and

(6) To provide informal in-service and field training for police officers in the area of crisis intervention.

Family Consultant Role in Child Abuse

Police officers are not sufficiently skilled, nor do they have the expertise, to identify subtle signs of actual or potential abuse. Even in cases of blatant abuse or cases where the officer suspects physical abuse or neglect has occurred, they are often uncertain of the best disposition of the case. It is in these instances that the officer requests assistance from the Family Consultant.

The Family Consultants, through their experience and training, are able to go into domestic crisis situations and recognize physical, sociological and psychological precursors of violence. They are alert to family stress and are skilled in assessing family problems, communication and interaction patterns, parent-child and spousal relationships and the impact of environmental stress.

The Consultants have the capacity to respond immediately to crisis situations, and have direct and legitimate access to homes where crises have occurred. Through their early intervention, and their ability to identify family dysfunction, treatment can often be initiated prior to actual abuse and possible family disorganization.

Before the advent of the Family Consultant Program, police officers were left to their own resources to resolve crisis situations, as family disturbances occur when most existing social service agencies are closed. Also, heavy caseloads prevented agency workers from providing immediate assessment. The Family Consultants provide this immediate assessment and involve the appropriate agency for the crisis resolution. The five courses of action implemented by the Consultants in resolving the crises encountered are (1) referral of a family/individual to an appropriate agency for ongoing counseling or support, (2) recontact of an agency already involved with a family/individual and informing the worker of the situation, (3) arrangement for immediate psychiatric assessment in a local hospital, (4) involvement of a physician, clergyman, lawyer or justice of the peace, and (5) Consultant mediation alone. The role of Family Consultant as liaison between the police and social service agencies has increased communication and cooperation between the two, which is critical for the prevention of child abuse.

Training Police Officers as Casefinders

Given the extent and the nature of police services within the community, the police are in the best position to detect abusive families. It seems mandatory to capitalize on this capability of the police. Through training, police officers can be sensitized to the signs of abuse and neglect, as well as to the recognition of potentially abusive situations. Family Consultants, through their day to day contact with officers, provide informal instruction of this nature. Officer observation of Family Consultant intervention, explanation of the situation and its resolution, as well as informal discussion of cases give officers additional perspectives on child abuse. Further training is necessary, however, at a more formal level, particularly in police academy curricula.

Family Consultants, through example, train officers to be non-judgmental in their approach. They illustrate that abuse can be a function of situational or interpersonal stresses or crises faced by parents. For this reason, criminal sanctions are a poor means of resolution of the child abuse situation. Fines or imprisonment can often destroy, rather than benefit, the family relationships. In this context, officers may regard a referral to a Family Consultant as an alternative to laying charges.

Officer awareness of the problem will undoubtedly lead to greater community awareness and understanding. As long as the approach to abuse is punitive, the incentive of parents and the public will be limited to reporting only extreme cases, which is contrary to prevention.

It must be remembered that officers refer only approximately 20 percent of their family disturbance calls to the Consultants. The remainder are resolved by the officer, either by means of his mediation alone or by a direct referral to a social welfare agency. Therefore, both formal and informal training of officers is necessary for maximum prevention of abuse.

Overview of Reports to the Consultants of Child Abuse or Neglect

From July 1, to December 31, 1976, there were 69 cases of actual of potential abuse brought to the attention of the Family Consultants by police officers. These reports were directed to them in three manners, as follows: a) actual child abuse was detected or observed and the officer requested the assistance of the Family Consultant for appropriate resolution of the situation, b) the officer suspected some form of abuse or neglect and wished further assessment by the Consultant, and c) the Consultant was alerted to early stages of abuse or potential abuse during a domestic crisis.

Every domestic crisis, particularly those involving a form of abuse, is invariably laden with a complexity of underlying issues. In the 69 cases cited, at least three of the following issues were involved: poor supervision of children (62.3 percent), fear of violence (36.2 percent), complaints regarding another's activities (34.8 percent), problems related to custody or separation (20.3 percent), parents' negligence of home responsibility (17.4 percent), child demanding greater freedom (14.5 percent), money problems (13 percent), sexual problems (7.2 percent), psychological dysfunctioning (5.8 percent) and unemployment (4.3 percent). Alcohol was related to the dispute in approximately one third of the cases. These issues support the contention that child abuse is a multi-dimensional problem.

Behaviors displayed by disputants in the context of these disturbances are verbal (53.6 percent), child abandoned or unattended (39.1 percent), physical (30.4 percent), abusive (23.4 percent), misbehavior or unmanageability of a juvenile (17.4 percent), destructive (10.1 percent) and self-destructive (4.3 percent). This suggests there is a considereable range of behavioral pathology in which the Consultants lend their expertise.

An actual family assault occurred in less than one third of the cases. Of these 20 cases, six assaults were between spouses and only 12 cases involved an assault on a juvenile. This indicates that the abuse or neglect was of a more subtle nature.

Charges were pending or laid in approximately 10 percent of the cases, indicating the importance of resolution avenues other than the criminal justice system.

In resolving domestic disputes related to child abuse, the Family Consultant involves community social service agencies for counseling and ongoing support in two thirds of the cases (in 24 cases there was a direct referral to an agency and in 22 cases recontact of an agency already involved was made). The following community agencies were contacted: Children's Aid Society (80 percent), family counseling services (10 percent), public health nurse (5 percent) and children's treatment centers (5 percent). Six percent of the cases required emergency psychiatric assessment at a hospital and in one case a Justice of the Peace was contacted.

Only one fifth of the cases were resolved by Family Consultant mediation alone. This form of resolution is implemented in one third of all other cases. This illustrates the importance, felt by the Consultants, of involving community resources in the early stages of abuse or in potentially abusive situations for the prevention of abuse.

Case Studies

(1) A uniform officer was dispatched to a residential address. A neighbor had called the Police Department to report hearing a child's screams. The mother was surprised to see the officer at her door, but didn't hesitate to invite him in and tried to explain what had happened. She claimed that her four year old daughter had misbehaved and had been punished with several lashes of a belt. She admitted that this had happened in the past, but pointed out that the child was not hurt. The officer conferred with the woman and then called for the Family Consultant to assist in assessing the situation. The Consultant came and was briefed by the officer. She approached the woman in a delicate manner as not to arouse a defensive stance. The woman talked freely about her parenting and several concerns she had about her four year old daughter, her only child. The woman said that she only used the belt as punishment when the girl wet the bed although she felt the problem was getting worse. The Consultant discussed some of the issues that might underlie the bedwetting and asked the woman if she would be interested in learning new techniques to handle the problem. The following day arrangements were made for a public health nurse to make visits to the home to assist the mother. The Children's Aid Society was notified and maintained a supervisory role for a short period to ensure the well being of the child.

(2) Late one evening, a distressed woman called the police emergency number complaining of being beaten by her boyfriend. An officer was detailed to the home to investigate the dispute. Before his arrival, the boyfriend had left the premises. The woman was in her late teens and was eight months pregnant. It was apparent to the officer that the woman had been beaten due to various bruises and welts about her face and arms. The officer requested the assistance of a Family Consultant, who was immediately dispatched to the address. Through discussion with the woman, it was determined that the boyfriend did not wish the responsibility of a child and rejected and abandoned the woman due to her pregnancy. There was no hope in the mind of the woman of repairing the relationship between the two. In viewing the apartment, it became apparent to the Consultant that no preparation had been made for the upcoming arrival of the baby. In pursuing this with the woman, it was learned that the woman blamed the child for the deterioration of her relationship with her boyfriend. She expressed doubts of being able to cope with a baby on her own and resented leaving her job. Due to a strong family influence, adoption of the child was rejected. The woman, however, was open to seeking assistance for her problems. The Family Consultant assessing the situation arranged for a referral for the next day with the Children's Aid Society. In talking with the worker, the Consultant filled him in on the issues surrounding the crisis, outlining the woman's need for support and guidance in resolving her feelings toward the child and her relationship with her boyfriend. The family physician was also notified to ensure that the woman got into pre-natal classes on the care of the mother and baby. A Red Cross homemaker was requested to visit following the birth of the child to help the mother to understand the care and behavior of babies, and make certain appropriate day-care was arranged to promote the woman's return to work.

(3) An officer was dispatched to a family dispute after a complaint to the police headquarters by a neighbor. Upon arrival, the officer observed that the husband had been drinking heavily all night and was sitting on the porch in a drunken stupor. The wife explained to the officer that the husband had been both verbally and physically abusive to her over her alleged leniency in the disciplining of their six children. The officer requested the assistance of the Family Consultant. The officer remained at the scene for fear that violence would flare up again. The Family Consultant, through discussions with the wife, ascertained that the children (age 8-15) had been drinking beer at the request of the father and when the eight year old boy became ill, the father spanked him severely for his unmasculine behavior. It was also learned that the husband had been unemployed for several weeks and that they were suffering from financial difficulties. The Children's Aid Society was already involved with this family and the Consultant phoned the worker involved to share information about this particular occurrence. It was decided that further intervention was needed by the agency in the area of family counseling to improve communication patterns between the spouses and the parents and the children. The husband had been referred to Alcoholics Anonymous but had not been attending meetings. The woman was also encouraged to become involved in services for wives of alcoholics.

These case studies illustrate the Consultants' involvement at the time of crisis, their capacity to act as catalysts in the process of prevention and their interventions with multi-problem families already involved in the 'helping system'.

Due to their ability to recognize signs of abuse or neglect and to identify high risk situations, intervention by the Family Consultant and subsequent involvement of appropriate agencies appears to lead to the prevention of child abuse.

4. Summary and Conclusions

(1) Emphasis should be placed on the entire spectrum of child abuse, which

encompasses not only blatant physical abuse but also the more subtle forms of abuse such as emotional maltreatment, food deprivation and social or intellectual neglect.

(2) Law enforcement agencies have been re-examining their responsibilites in the area of child protection. Given the extent and the nature of police service in the community, they are in the best position to detect abuse. The roles and approaches of both the police and child welfare agencies are converging towards humanistic and supportive viewpoints, a development which bolsters the resources for dealing with child abuse and neglect.

(3) There is a dual need in the area of child abuse. At the secondary level of prevention, there is a need for early recognition of the signs of abuse for the purpose of reducing the frequency of repeated abusive episodes. At the primary level, there is a need to recognize and identify family problems as potential indicators of abuse and, through early intervention, prevent abuse from occurring.

(4) The Family Consultant Service was instituted to assist officers by providing immediate assessment and intervention in crisis situations and supplying information about or arranging referrals to appropriate community resources.

(5) The Family Consultant Program provides crisis service at times when most other agencies cannot. This, together with the immediacy of the Family Consultant intervention, increases the likelihood that adaptive changes will result from the crisis. This is particularly important in the area of child abuse and neglect.

(6) The Family Consultant Service, by acting as liaison, facilitates increased understanding and cooperation between community social services and the police department.

(7) Through informal training by Family Consultants, police officers can be sensitized to the signs of abuse and neglect, as well as to the recognition of potentially abusive situations.

(8) Domestic crises, involving abuse or potential abuse in which the Family Consultants intervened, were laden with a complexity of underlying issues and a considerable range of behavioral pathology. This supports the contention that child abuse is a multi-dimensional problem.

(9) Due to their ability to recognize signs of abuse or neglect, and to identify high-risk situations, intervention by the Family Consultants and subsequent involvement of an appropriate agency presents a model to aid in the prevention of child abuse.

NOTES

1. Greenland, Cyril, *Child Abuse in Ontario*. Toronto, Canada: Ministry of Community and Social Services, 1973; *Guidelines for Practice and Procedure in Handling Cases of Child Abuse*, Ontario Association of Children's Aid Societies, July, 1976; Segal, Sydney, "A Medical Overview of Child Abuse in B.C." (1976), 18 *The British Columbia Medical Journal* no. 2, 40-44; and see also *The Abused and Battered Child: A Report*, Federation of Women Teachers' Association of Ontario, August, 1976.
2. See *Guidelines for Practice and Procedure in Handling Cases of Child Abuse*, *op. cit.*; *Child Abuse and Neglect*, report to the House of Commons, Standing Committee on Health, Welfare and Social Affairs, First Session, Thirtieth Parliament, 1974-75-76, Ottawa. (Supply and Services Canada); and see Leavitt, Jerome E., *The Battered Child: Selected Readings*. Morristown, New Jersey: General Learning Press, 1974.
3. Greenland, Cyril, *op. cit.*, note 1.

4. *Child Abuse and Neglect, op. cit.,* note 2; Dawson, Ross, "Current Issues in Child Abuse in Ontario" (Nov., 1976), 9 *Journal of the Ontario Association of Children's Aid Societies* no. 19; *Guidelines for Practice and Procedure in Handling Cases of Child Abuse, op. cit.,* note 1; Hepworth, Philip H., "Services for Abused and Battered Children", *Personal Social Services in Canada: A Review,* Ottawa, Canada: The Canadian Council on Social Development, 1975; and see also *Position Paper on Service Delivery Systems,* presented at the Inter-professional Seminar on Child Abuse, Ministry of Community and Social Services, Ontario, Feb., 1976.
5. Dawson, Ross., *op. cit.,* note 4.
6. *Child Abuse and Neglect, op. cit.,* note 2; Dawson Ross, *op. cit.,* note 4; and Pitcher, Rudolph, "The Police" in Kempe, C., and Helfer, R. (eds.) *Helping the Battered Child and His Family.* New York, New York: Lippincott, 1972.
7. Justice, Blair and Rita, *The Abusing Family.* New York, New York: Behavioral Publications, 1974; and Segal, Sydney, *op. cit.,* note 1.
8. *Child Abuse and Neglect, op. cit.,* note 2., and *the Abusing Family, ibid.*
9. *The Abusing Family; Position Paper on Service Delivery Systems, op. cit.,* note 4.; and Steinmetz, Suzanne K., and Straus, Murray A., *Violence in the Family.* New York, New York: Dodd Mead, 1974.
10. *The Abusing Family, op cit.,* note 7; Segal, Sydney, *op. cit.,* note 1; and *Violence in the Family, ibid.*
11. Blumberg, Marvin, "Psychopathology of the Abusing Parents" (1974), 28 *American Journal of Psychotherapy* 21-29; Gil, David G., "A Conceptual Model of Child Abuse and Its Implications for Social Policy", in *Violence in the Family;* and see *The Abusing Family, op. cit.,* note 7.

REFERENCES

A Fifth Step: A Report on an Inter-professional Seminar on Child Abuse, Ministry of Community and Social Services, February, 1976.
Carter, James E., and Drescher, Lynne, "A Community Response to Child Abuse" (1976), 18 *The British Columbia Medical Journal* 45-46.
Elmer, Elizabeth, "Child Abuse: A Symptom of Family Crisis", in Pavenstedt, E., and Bernard, V. (eds.) *Crisis of Family Disorganization: Programs to Soften Their Impact on Children.* New York, New York: Behavioral Publications, 1974.
Fontana, Vincent, *Somewhere A Child is Crying: the Battered Child.* New York, New York: Macmillan, 1973.
Frazer, F. M., "How to Proceed" (1976), 18 *The British Columbia Medical Journal* no. 2, 53-54.
Gelles, Richard J., "Child Abuse as Psychopathology: A Sociological Critique and Reformulation", in Steinmetz, S., and Straus, M. (eds.) *Violence in the Family.* New York, New York: Dodd Mead, 1974.
Lieber, Harry, *Obstacles to the Identification and Reporting of Child Abuse,* Social Policy and Research, United Way of Greater Vancouver, 1977.
Morris, M.; Gould, R.; and Mathews, P., "Toward Prevention of Child Abuse" (Mar.-April, 1964) *Children.*
Rubin, Jean, "The Need for Intervention", in Leavitt, J. (ed.), *The Battered Child: Selected Readings.* Morristown, New Jersey: General Learning Press, 1974.
Smith, David F., "Child Abuse Health Centre for Children OPD" (1976), 18 *The British Columbia Medical Journal* no. 2, 47-49.
Swanson, Lynne D., "Role of the Police in the Protection of Children from Neglect and Abuse", in *The Battered Child.*
Von Stolk, Mary *The Battered Child in Canada* (1972).
Wasserman, Sidney, "The Abused Parent of the Abused Child" (Sept.-Oct., 1967), 14 *Children* 175-179.

437   Child Abuse: The Policeman's Role: An Innovative Approach

PART FIVE

SPECIAL ASPECTS OF
FAMILY VIOLENCE

On one of the coldest days of the English winter of 1977/78, an eight year old boy, Lester Chapman, ran away from home for the fifth time. The family's problems were known to the Social Services Department and Lester had been considered to be at risk of non-accidental injury. Over a month later his body was found in waste land a mile from his home. He had died from exposure. Was his death really an accident? In her analysis of children's suicide (Chapter 29), Professor Rood de Boer uncovers one of the most disturbing and least understood manifestations of family violence. For there can be no doubt that, as children are almost always born into families, a child's suicide, attempted suicide or suicidal behavior is evidence of profound family failure. Yet, as Professor Rood de Boer shows, social and psychological mechanisms operate to keep children's suicide at a very low level of visibility. While it is clear that it poses special difficulties with regard to detection, prevention and response, Professor Rood de Boer's conclusion that a child's suicide is usually rooted in a background of highly disturbed family relationships sets even this 'mysterious' phenomenon in the same context as child abuse and other manifestations of violence in family life.

Incest, too, has been, and still is, considered a bizarre phenomenon associated with extreme moral and social deviation. These may, indeed, be features of those cases of incest which are processed by the legal system and in this respect it is interesting to compare the judicial experience of Judge J.P. Peigné (Chapter 32) with the clinical evidence of Dr. Ingrid Cooper (Chapter 34). Dr. Cooper explains that incest, as legally defined, is just the extreme point of a continuum of possible physical-erotic contact between parents and children, much of which may be considered normal and healthy within a family. As Dr. Anthony Storr has pointed out,[1] incest between parent and child is objectionable primarily because it destroys the true nature of the parent-child relationship. This, of course, is possible although the physical contacts stop short of consummated incest. As in other forms of physical abuse, sexual abuse again appears as a symptom of severe malfunctioning of family relationships. It is therefore interesting to observe that Belgian criminal law, like that in some other European countries, tends not to punish incest as such but sees it more in the context of abuse of authority (see Chapter 35).

The response to sexual abuse raises the same tensions between the punishment the 'treatment/management' models relevant to other forms of family violence, particularly between spouses. Mr. Anthony Manchester's account of the history of the legislation on this topic in England shows the repressive instincts of society channelled into its criminal law (Chapter 33). Mr. Manchester refers to the State interest to punish 'flagrant breaches of the law'. Yet one may wonder whether Dr. Cooper would agree that criminal prosecution was the best course in some of the cases described in Mr. Manchester's survey. How important is it that communal denunciation of incestuous behavior should be manifested through the public criminal process? As Judge Peigné points out, strict proof is necessary because of the dangers of false accusations. If feelings of expiation should be exacted from the offender, is this process the right way to do it? Both Dr. Cooper and Mr. Manchester recognize the necessity of flexibility in response. But it is surely a matter of public interest to know on what grounds the discretion to prosecute is exercised and it is crucial for the welfare of the families concerned that this discretion is exercised on the basis of the fullest understanding of the family's psychodynamics.

While suicide by children and incest are regarded as highly deviant forms of family behavior, aggressive acts between siblings are usually regarded as normal. Indeed, as Mr. Manchester shows, reaction to sibling incest is less severe than to parent-child incest. Dr. Suzanne Steinmetz's research (Chapter 30) reveals the extent to which, in the United States at least, sibling aggression assumes violent forms. We seldom believe that social or legal intervention is appropriate in these cases though it is interesting to reflect why this is so. Is there a causal link between the violence experienced between siblings in their family settings and violent conduct in later life as is claimed in the case of children who have suffered violence from their parents? Is it significant that Dr. Steinmetz found that the highest level of sibling violence occurred between children of the opposite sex?

That sibling violence may be rather less profoundly affective than disturbances in relationships with parents may be suggested by the evidence of Professor Cormier and his colleagues (Chapter 31) that it is rarer for siblings to kill one another than it is for them to kill a parent. In discussing matricide and patricide, he and his colleagues describe a phenomenon which may provide an important clue to the apparently baffling behavior of many individuals caught up in family violence and to the reasons for the dilemmas over society's responses to it. This is the 'lockage phenomenon'. A person may find a relationship destructive to the point of intolerability and yet may be so locked into it that to break it appears equally unbearable. Violence may be an outlet for individuals caught in this vice. Others, equally trapped, cannot bring themselves to escape from the violence they suffer. In extreme cases the only solution is murder or, conversely, suicide. Is it perhaps the presence, to a greater or lesser degree, of this phenomenon which makes the criminal law model of response seem so inappropriate? And is not the special character of legal and social responses to violence within a family setting determined by the recognition that, if the intolerability of the relationship cannot be mitigated, the 'lockage' must be eased open so that the persons concerned can be given the opportunity and the means to recover their individuality and personal integrity?

NOTES

1. Storr, Anthony, *The Integrity of the Personality*. Harmondsworth: Middlesex: Penguin, 1970, pp. 96-7.

Chapter 29

Children's Suicide*

M. Rood de Boer†

1. Introduction

It may be asked why a lawyer should pay attention to this subject — so full of emotion and mystery. Does the phenomenon of children's suicide actually belong in the field of juridical investigation and research? I believe that this question must be answered in the affirmative, with the qualification that children's suicide needs to be viewed from many different scientific angles. This subject has, however, received very little attention from lawyers and there is very little literature on it.

From my own professional standpoint, children's suicide indeed does not merely have a juridical-theoretical dimension. The Chairs which I hold as an extra-ordinaria at the Rijksuniversiteit of Utrecht and the Katholieke Universiteit of Tilburg are named 'Child Law and Child Protection' (Kinderrecht en Kinderbescherming). The terms of reference of the teaching with which I am charged therefore do not only concern teaching and research into legal rules with regard to minors (or the non-existence of such rules) in the field of civil law, penal law and administrative law, but also the study of the application of such (absent) law in practice. My assistants and I are concerned with the problems of children and young people, especially those who, for one reason or another, have gone wrong, or are in danger of going wrong. There is no doubt that a child who kills himself or who wishes to do so, is a child with problems.

There is another reason for undertaking the research. From the time when, as a young girl, I became involved in the practice of child care and protection I have

* This chapter could not have been written without the cooperation and assistance of many. In the first place I would like to thank Dr. J.A.C. Bartels, who performed an extensive research into the literature. I also want to thank Dr. M. Golshani-Bovy who assisted me in collecting the literature and the statistical material and Dr. W. Strubbe whose practical experience and knowledge has been very helpful. I would also like to thank the staff of the sections 'Kinderrecht and Kinderbescherming' of the Rijksuniversiteit Utrecht and of the Katholieke Universiteit Tilburg.
† Rijksuniversiteit Utrecht, Willem Pompe Instituut, Netherlands.

been especially struck by stories of the deaths of children who were in the care of the child protection institutions. Were the stories of suicide in children's homes only rumors? Were they really accidents? Or had the phenomenon of the suicides of exactly those children who were apparently protected children cast a spell that attracted the rumours to me? Later, when I attended professional meetings abroad, I heard of an 11 year-old boy who 'for a joke' shot himself through his head in the presence of the entire group and its leaders; and about a 13 year-old girl who locked herself in the toilet and hung herself. The phenomenon of suicide in children's homes appeared to be not only a Dutch problem. It exists in all countries of the Western world. Furthermore, for many years I have been troubled by the question whether children with respect to whom there has been juridical intervention regarding the parental authority are perhaps more suicide prone than other children.

2. Concepts

A. Suicide

The Dutch author Speijer[1] (1969) gives the following definition of suicide:

One may speak of suicide when a person performs or omits an act, which involves his death, if such effect has been aimed at or accepted by him.

With regard to very young children, Speijer observes that information on the subject is often conflicting. As his own point of view he says that "with very young children, under the age of ten, there is almost never the question of suicide, but of an accident or of imitation." The real reason is that this group of young children has as yet no real consciousness of death. Therefore the fatal act of this age group would not fall within his definition of suicide; he prefers the expression 'self-killing'. I found that many authors hold that children only begin to understand the meaning of death from about the age of 8-10 years.[2]

In a recent publication, four Dutch psychologists, Diekstra, et al.[3] (1976) see suicide as 'problem-solving' behavior. Death is not the intended purpose. The purpose is, rather, to reach a desired state through death. By this reasoning, suicide can be seen as a form of socially-taught behavior which, in certain situations, is assumed to lead to the desired change. The writers do not mention in their study suicide among young and very young children. In any event, they prefer the word *somacide* to suicide.[4]

A fair number of foreign writers have proposed (slightly differently formulated) definitions. I prefer not to repeat these here since they are to be found in the relevant literature. More specifically, with regard to children's suicide, Mangold and Seidl[5] (1976) make the following statement:

Der Selbstmord ist der letzte verzweifelte Versuch einer Begegnung mit den Eltern. Er ist der letzte verzeweifelte Versuch, Anerkennung und Liebe zu bekommen. (Suicide is the last desperate attempt to reach the parents. It is the last desperate attempt to be approved and loved).

In what follows I propose to view suicide in the light of those three definitions, in which the self-killing is regarded from the standpoint of its *purpose* (Speijer), its *means* (Diekstra a.o.), and its *reasons* (Mangold and Seidl). These three conceptions each illuminate different aspects of the phenomenon and provide an acceptable starting point.

In the foregoing I have not tried to give a definition of a suicidal *attempt*. Especially where it concerns young children, there does not seem to be much sense in distinguishing between suicide and suicidal attempts. I do however wish to quote the Dutch psychiatrist Bloemsma[6] who gives a classification of suicidal acts:

1) *suicide.* The intention to commit suicide and the result is suicide;
2) *abortive suicide.* The intention to kill oneself, and the result is to stay alive;
3) *suicidal attempt.* The intention to undertake an attempt of self-killing and the result is that one stays alive.
4) *abortive suicidal attempt.* The intention to undertake an attempt and the result is an (effective) suicide.

The Swiss author Waage[7] (1966) considers that with children there can only be suicidal attempts and abortive suicidal attempts. For the present, in view of the sparse literature with regard to self-killing of children, I suggest that a line can scarcely be drawn between suicidal attempts and suicide. Hereafter I shall refer only to suicide[8] of children.

B. The Child.

This study deals with the self-killing of minors up to the age of 15. The researches studied do not always use the same terms. Reference is made sometimes to children, sometimes to adolescents and sometimes to juveniles. The reason is that often different age groups have been studied. In order to avoid inconsistency, this chapter will deal only with children who have not yet reached the age of 15. This is not a position of principle, but a pragmatic one; I am following the lowest age category the Dutch criminal (judicial) statistics use with regard to established suicide. (I regret that medical statistics give slightly different figures with regard to children in this age group). But doing this introduces a different problem. The group of minors aged + 8 to 15 does not represent a heterogeneous group. It would be better to deal separately with the group of + 8 to 12 year-olds and thereafter with the 12, 13, and 14 year-olds whose problems are likely to be different. However this division between very young children (under 12 years) and children in the pre-puberty stage (12, 13 and 14 years) cannot be made here, because neither statistics nor researches have made that division, nor does it appear in the very sparse literature.

3. Statistics.

A. Statistical records

"Suicide is a phenomenon which does not limit itself to any particular age. Statistics show suicide as an ever-increasing proportionate problem with the advance in age, the phenomenon occurring in all ages from the young child to the very old adult".[9] Although children almost never leave farewell letters which can be treated as evidence that their deaths are suicides, the absence of such letters does not appear to be the only reason why official information on the number of suicides of young people often looks contradictory. Speijer[10] is of the opinion that "the drawing up of statistics (itself) for very young ages seems to be less reliable than for the more advanced ages".

The records published by the World Health Organization[11] in which under-15-year-olds have not been inserted as a separate category prove how difficult it is to obtain reasonably reliable information with regard to suicide. The report of the W.H.O. (1973) states[12]: "The real extent and magnitude of the suicide problem is hard to measure. The definition of the term 'suicide' varies in different countries, whether by law or by custom. Different methods of certifying death causes, registration, classification and other coding procedures and factors make international comparisons hazardous".

Not only are statistics incapable of comparison internationally, but also national official registrations in all probability do not approximate the actual number of suicides. Nobody can give an estimate of the 'dark figure'. With regard to children's suicide, it seems likely that the real numbers are even more hidden than is the case with adults' suicide. *Tables* 1-4 show the numbers of registered suicides in the Netherlands in absolute numbers and in percentages from 1965 to 1975. It will be seen that only a very small number of (registered) self-killings of children are recorded. Hence Ringel[13] states that "suicide of children is really very rare". I doubt however whether the problem is in reality of such a minor order.

B. Does it Really Happen?

Somewhere in a medium-sized town an 11-year-old boy is being badgered in school because he cuts a bad appearance in school sports. When he is not allowed to play football in the street after school, he says to the other boys that he may not be any good at football, but he can fly! They laugh at him. He takes them up in the elevator of a high apartment building where his parents live. As soon as the group has arrived at the top, the tenth storey, he climbs on the railings, cries: "Look, I am flying" and jumps down.

In a children's hospital a doctor sits stupefied next to the bed of a 12-year-old Moroccan girl, just recovering from unconsciousness. In a clumsy way she says that a year ago she and her mother and brothers were allowed to join her father

Table I
Registered suicides in the Netherlands
(Absolute numbers)

| | Children up to 15 years | | Age 15 years and above | | Total |
	Boys	Girls	Men	Women	Total
1965		1	581	347	929
1966	4		608	354	966
1967	7	2	549	307	865
1968	3		563	343	909
1969	8		620	399	1027
1970	9	1	710	438	1158
1971	3		724	489	1216
1972	5		735	480	1220
1973	12	2	726	533	1273
1974	8	1	807	544	1360
1975	8	1	802	532	1343

Source: C.B.S.
Monthly Statistics, Police and Justice

Table II
Registered suicides of children up to 15 years in the Netherlands (in percentages)

	Boys	Girls	N:
1965		0,107	N: 929
1966	0,414		N: 966
1967	0,809	0,23	N: 865
1968	0,33		N: 909
1969	0,77		N: 1027
1970	0,77	0,08	N: 1158
1971	0,24		N: 1216
1972	0,40		N: 1220
1973	0,94	0,15	N: 1273
1974	0,58	0,07	N: 1360
1975	0,59	0,07	N: 1343

Source: C.B.S. Monthly Statistics
Police and Justice

Table III
Registered suicides in the Netherlands (Absolute number)

	Children up to 15 years		Age 15 years and above		Total
	Boys	Girls	Men	Women	Total
1965		2	524	324	850
1966	3		550	328	881
1967	7	2	491	284	784
1968	3		502	298	803
1969	8		575	366	939
1970	8	1	639	402	1050
1971	3		641	446	1090
1972	3		660	431	1094
1973	12	2	650	500	1164
1974	8	1	735	503	1247

Source: C.B.S. Yearly Statistics, Health Department 08.03.1977.

Table IV
Registered suicides of children up to 15 years in the Netherlands (in percentage)

	Boys	Girls	N
1965		0,24	N: 850
1966	0,34		N: 881
1967	0,89	0,26	N: 784
1968	0,37		N: 803
1969	0,85		N: 939
1970	0,76	0,1	N: 1050
1971	0,28		N: 1090
1972	0,27		N: 1094
1973	1,03	0,17	N: 1164
1974	0,64	0,08	N: 1247

Source: C.B.S. Yearly Statistics, Health Department, 08.03.1977.

who had already been working for some years in a factory in Central-Holland. The family originated from a small village in Southern Morocco. In the neighborhood where her father has rented an apartment there are no other Moroccan girls. In her class at school there are many younger children who laugh at her because she has less knowledge than they have, speaks Dutch poorly and wears different clothes. At home she found a box with sedatives her father had used when recovering from an accident at his work. She was brought to the hospital unconscious.

In the German weekly *Spiegel* (nos. 8 and 23), 1976 the same horrific photograph is reproduced as an illustration in two articles regarding school life in West Germany. The picture shows a boy of about 12 who has hung himself in a wood because he had a bad school report and did not dare to go home. In that same period, within ten days, three schoolboys died in Southern Germany, each, it appeared later, out of despair on receiving inadequate school results.

An American boy said[14] about his father: "When he used to come home, it was like a dark cloud coming over the house. What happened was, I came home from school and him and my mother had an argument. That day I was in a very good mood, everything seemed to go okay in school, but then I came home and he started yelling at me very military, that I should do this and that and it just got me to the brink of, well, what the hell, I'm not one of his little soldiers . . . so I went to the bathroom and swallowed some iodine. Then my mother rushed me to the hospital. . . . One time I had a little banty rooster as a pet. We were going to be moving, so my father went out and chopped its head off and plucked it and cooked it and tried to serve it for dinner and my whole family sat down and we realized it was my rooster and I went screaming into the bedroom."

Professional literature on children's suicide is not a recent phenomenon. Some 50 years ago the *Zeitschrift fur psychoanalytische Padagogik* edited an issue on suicide (August/September/October 1929, nos. 11/12/13). Several writers, *e.g.,* Friedlung, Leuthold and Pipal[15] made extensive reports on the thoughts and attempts of suicide of children from the age of seven onwards. Do such things really happen? Statistics say: hardly. The cases say: yes, in the whole of the Western, industrialized world the phenomenon of self-killing of children exists. The few examples given above could be multiplied. There is a discrepancy between the statistical registrations and the cases people whisper about.

4. The Veiled Problem

A. Taboo and Stigma

When we try to investigate suicide, we face mysteries and uncertainties. Unreliability of the statistics is only one aspect of the obscurity of the phenomenon.

"For a long time prejudices have confused the issue of suicide. These prejudices can be traced back to a series of factors, including the taboo and stigma associated with the phenomenon of suicide", says Van de Loo[16] (1971). "This taboo results in an unfortunate avoidance of the subject with the dangerous consequence that a frank confrontation with the tabooed phenomenon does not take place. It is important that as a result of the taboo a suicidal person was classified into three stigmatizing categories: either as a lunatic, or as a criminal, or as a sinner".

B. Denial

It is unlikely that people would generally dismiss children who have committed suicide with the oversimplification: 'the child was a lunatic, a criminal or a sinner!' With children, the problem is even harder to analyze. There is an element of taboo about it, but not so much because these children would be placed in any of those stigmatizing categories. Here the problem is more veiled, for it is one which is denied in our society.

In the search for an explanation of the denial of the actual occurrence of such events, we are first of all confronted with functional and rather trivial problems connected with the not always optimal communication between the various divisions of the health care services.[17] If the child recovers after emergency treatment in a hospital, he goes home, with or without the intervention of the family doctor. And that's that. A great many cases are dismissed from the hospital without psychiatric/psychological help. If the child had died without being admitted to hospital, it will depend upon the statement of the family doctor whether his death will be recognized as suicide or not.

If the child recovers and is asked what happened, he will probably deny what he really aimed at. Bergsma[18] remarks on the inability of people who are recovering in hospital from a suicide attempt to recollect what happened before they were admitted. We almost never hear the real cause of the act. Moreover, it is precisely in cases where children are concerned that expert assistance is seldom sought, the more so because the parents are inclined 'now that everything has ended well' to give as little visible attention to it as possible.

Among the many medical and psychiatric practitioners with whom I have spoken in connection with this research, only a few told me that they had encountered the suicide of a child. The rest claimed not to have heard of such a thing. They thought it was no real problem.

Haim[19] explains the denial as being a result of fear. He says that young people represent for adults the joy of living, and are *par excellence* the symbol of uncomplicated happiness. If a young person speaks of dying or killing himself, we blame him for it. His thoughts should be far removed from death. Therefore the thought of a child committing suicide is completely intolerable. The reason for the denial is *the fear of death of the adult himself,* against which a classic attitude of defence is usually adopted. The self-sought death of the child shatters this defence.

The denial of children's suicide can also partly be explained on the basis of a *sense of shame.* The adults around the child feel ashamed towards the outside world that they were not able to give their child a sufficient feeling of security and safety to keep the child from this final solution. Where feelings of shame play a role in the denial of the suicide-event to the outside world, *feelings of guilt,* which are of a more internal nature, can be a reason for those immediately concerned to be silent about what has happened and to disguise it to themselves as an accident. It is also possible that in some cases there can be feelings of genuine guilt because the parents did not take the child's complaints seriously for what they really were: desperate expressions of unhappiness. If the child kills himself, the adults have every reason to feel guilty and to keep their silence. In some instances children's suicide can evoke angry, *aggressive feelings* in adults towards the child that has dared to do it. These aggressive feelings themselves give rise to further guilt feelings. The child's suicide confirms as it were the failure of the surroundings in a starkly definite way. Not only has one failed in the education and care of the child; the child's signals of unhappiness were not received.

The outside world can probably identify more easily with the feelings of shame and guilt of those immediately concerned than with those (unspoken) feelings of the child and will keep silent. It will want to protect those who are already suffering so much. This silence of the outside world confirms the denial of the parents, brothers and sisters, management and group-leaders in the children's home and so on.

C. Veiling of the Problem

Experts assure us that as young children do not as yet have a sense of death, children's suicide does not or hardly happens. But is this thesis not a rationalization of these denials? I agree with Bianca Gordon[20] who says that more scientific research will be required in order to find out what children think about death. But we should also know more about how society thinks of and reacts to the death of very young people. We must recognize that with regard to children's suicide, there is a threefold denial: first, the most prominent scientific research workers say that children do not have any knowledge of these things and the judicial and medical authorities hardly register it; second, the defensive attitude of adults, based upon their own fear of death, makes them close their eyes to the real extent of the problem; third, the complex feelings of shame and guilt of all people concerned are conducive to the silence which surrounds children's suicide.

5. Conceptions and Explanations of the Suicide Phenomenon of Young Children

Within the framework of this necessarily restricted research, some observatory and explanatory theories on the suicide phenomenon will be reproduced. At the same time I shall try to investigate how far these opinions are relevant with regard to the group of young persons in the age group up to 15 years. In the following the approach of Speyer[21] (1969) has been largely followed. He distinguishes between sociological, psychological and psychiatric researches and theories. To this will be added the observations of pediatricians, for they form an essential complement to that information.

A. Sociological Explanations

Durkheim[22] (1897) introduced the sociological approach to suicide. By distinguishing factors which could lead to suicide and by his typology of persons who commit suicide, he greatly stimulated ideas about suicide, although in later years his conceptions have been disputed as being too speculative and too little based upon empirical research. But some of the connections he tried to make between for example, the rate of integration of certain social groups in society and suicide and between passing through a crisis and suicide, are still of relevance. With regard to children Durkheim remarks: "Il ne faut pas oublier en effect, que l'enfant, lui aussi est placé sous l'action des causes sociales et qu'elles peuvent suffire à le déterminer au suicide". But he states also: "Le suicide est extrêmement rare chez les enfants". In his statistics the category under 16 years does not occur.

In the Netherlands, Kruyt[23] (1960) has extensively considered suicide-confirming factors in society. His sociological explorations also cover adolescents. As regards children between 10 and 14 years, we find only some summary remarks. For example, he states that, for this group, a possible suicide-motive may be 'bad school results'.

Along with Douglas[24] (1970) (who takes a critical attitude towards Durkheim's findings) I would like to state that a statistical-sociological approach to the suicide phenomenon is bound to remain unsatisfactory. I think that this is especially true with regard to young children where the registered figures are too small to justify generalized conclusions. Those socially determined factors which indicate certain explanations for children's suicide generally relate only to school problems. But school problems are so interwoven with general family problems, *i.e.,* with (social)-psychological questions about the attitude of the family, that those sociological factors considered alone are unhelpful.

Otto[25] (1969) considers that the role of the school has not yet been studied sufficiently. A certain relationship between the increase of the number of suicides of very young people and too far-fetched expectations of the parents on the one hand and restricted opportunities for admission to certain kinds of education, (for example, the *'numerus clausus'* which is used in some school systems) on the other, must regretfully be admitted.[26] In view of the sparsity and unreliability of the data, it is impracticable to attempt to correlate children's suicide with such factors as religion, size of the household or the time or place of its commission.

B. The So-Called Werther-Effect

In 1774, when Goether was 25 years old, he wrote his novel *Das Leiden des jungen Werthers* at the end of which the young hero commits suicide. It is said that this publication led to imitation throughout Europe. Durkheim (1897) discussed the literature with regard to this imitation-effect; he thought that the suggestive effect of a book such as this was much less than generally accepted. Philips,[27] (1974) on the contrary, has shown that, in any event in the United States and in England, the number of suicides increases considerably after a suicide story has been published in the newspapers. The rate of suicides also increases in proportion to the extent of the publicity.

It seems that Philips has pointed out a phenomenon which can also be observed in other western countries and one on which television has an extra impact. After Jan Palach, the young Czechoslovak student, had burnt himself alive on 16th

Janurary 1969 next to the statue of Saint Wensislaus in Prague, similar suicides followed not only in Czechoslovakia but also in other places, like Northern France. The motive of Palach was political. The high school youths in Lille protested against all kinds of violence, the wars in Biafra, in Vietnam, in short against 'les guerres, la violence et la folie destructice des hommes'. These young people used a method that had been used by Vietnamese monks: self-immolation, which the press and television of the entire world had reported. It cannot be stated with certainty whether suggestion might provide a clear explanation for the suicides of very young children. The registered numbers are too small and, moreover almost all communication media have maintained a great reserve in reporting self-killing of children.

C. Psychiatric Explanations

Just as suicide cannot be understood from a sociological standpoint alone, neither can it be only from a psychiatric view. Moreover, in the multitude of published psychiatric observations on suicide, those dealing with young children are not only very few, but also contradictory.

De Sanctis[28] (1922) states that suicide by children is always produced by a pathological condition; Kanner[29] (1957) on the other hand is of the opinion that only in a very small minority of the cases can mental diseases like schizophrenia or depressive psychosis be held responsible. Still he states that children who show signs of deep depression ought to be carefully examined, because in those cases he does not exclude a suicidal tendency. Also Schrut (1964) and Shaffer (1974) draw attention to this.[30]

Anthony and Scott[31] (1960) state that depressive reactions of the manic depressive kind are very seldom found in children. Connell[32] (1960) has pointed out how this has led to the following contradiction:
(a) schizophrenia and/or depressive psychosis are rarely causes of children's suicide; but
(b) assuming young children do not have depressive feelings, their suicidal tendencies, when present, are not recognized.
In general, the authors, including Otto (1969), are of the opinion that *exogenic* factors seem to play a greater role in children's suicide than *endogenic*.

Winn[33] (1969) has published a study in which he describes the residential treatment of emotionally disturbed children who had been received in residence because of suicide attempts. Although the article mainly deals with adolescents, Winn also writes about the young children he observed who had experienced hallucinations leading them to believe that they had to kill themselves. These children experienced 'good' and 'bad' voices contradicting themselves. The voices came from within them. Eggens[34] (1974) has tried to trace the motivations of the suicidal behavior of psychotic children on the basis of longitudinal (an average of 15, maximum of 40 years) research on 57 patients who suffered from schizophrenia which had manifested itself before the fourteenth year of their life. He mentions that a number of suicidal attempts by children are undertaken under the influence of *acoustical hallucinations*, without any clear motives being apparent. To the group of children described in this paragraph, Speyer's definition of suicide as an intentional act with death as the intended result is applicable.

D. Psychological Explanations

Diekstra[35] (1974) states: "Somacidal thinking is very often reported by young adults having psychological problems and "somacidal thinking is generally connected with the existence of psychological problems".

People who have studied the suicide of young people are of the opinion that problems with relationships constantly appear to be the foremost factor. Relationships with parents are decisive. Jacobs[36] (1971) concludes that each case of suicide by a child is one of *a lonely child without friends and without firm ties with his parents*. He says that only in a few instances can the fatal act be attributed to a unique crisis. Suicide usually constitutes the final phase of a process of accumulating problems starting in early childhood. Waage[37] (1966) has extensively examined some 18 suicide cases in the age group of 8 - 15 years. One of his conclusions is that most important factors are related to the fact that the child does not feel safe or loved. Zumpe[38] (1966) also arrives at the conclusion that children's suicidal behavior must not be considered as an isolated phenomenon but as a "Signalsymptom einer seit längerer Zeit bestehenden Fehlentwicklung" (definite signal of a very dangerous development that has existed for some time). She found that almost all the 34 children and young people in her research group lacked love and security in their early years. They were experiencing difficulties in communication and feelings of isolation.

More than 100 years ago Durand-Fardell[39] (1855) wrote: "the world of the child consists of his family. All his strongest feelings, sorrow and joy are concentrated on and in the family. His emotional and physical development are stimulated by nourishment from the family circle". Mangold and Seidl[40] (1974) are also of the opinion that "Die Problematik des jugendlichen Suicid-Patienten vorwiegend in einer tiefgreifender Kommunikationsstorung zwishchen Eltern und Kind liegt". (The problems of a young suicide patient can be found paramountly in bad relations between him and his parents). The members of the conference (1974)[41] organized by the regional European bureau of the W.H.O. with regard to "Suicide and Attempted Suicide of Young People" came to the conclusion that "the break-up of the family unit had an increasing effect on the risk of young persons committing or attempting suicide" and that "parents may be very unsure how to handle their children and may need support".

Most writers who have thoroughly studied this problem seek the explanation for children's suicide in the first place in psychological terms and especially in problems of relationships.[42] If this is correct, it could provide an answer to the question: Are 'child-protection' children more suicide-prone than other children who live 'ordinarily' with their parents? So many times children are described as having lost a parent by death or divorce, or having frequently been moved from one institution to another at a very young age, or having been placed in a foster-family where they had failed to develop ties with the foster-parents. Juridical measure of child protection had not always been taken with respect to these children. On the other hand, with regard to 'child protection' children, a juridical measure has almost always been taken, at least in the Netherlands, because the child was experiencing problems in its relationships. From this perspective, then, 'child-protection' children would form an 'at risk group', precisely because they were experiencing difficulties in their existing relationships.[43]

The explanations given in this paragraph of suicide by children concur with the definitions of Mangold and Seidl that suicide is the last desperate attempt to reach the parents and to be approved and loved by them.

E. The Experience of Pediatrics.

One of the saddest things in our society is the death of young children who suffer from a fatal disease. Sometimes the attitude of the parents towards the illness of their child gives rise to ambivalent feelings. Strubbe[44] (1977) describes the tragic case of a gravely ill seven-year-old boy who was hardly ever visited by his parents. Notwithstanding the efforts of the hospital and the social worker, the parents had already as it were, passed through the mourning procedure. At home, in the family they acted as if he was not there any more. His playthings had been locked away and his bed brought to the attic. The parents had already reported to the boy's school that he would not return again.

Strubbe writes that this is, fortunately, a rare case. Nevertheless great tact and flexibility is required in guiding gravely ill children and their parents. Veeneklaas[45] (1975) describes the anxiety and disorganization of the parents and the contradictory feelings which they experience towards themselves, towards the medical personnel and towards their child. But Veeneklaas, who was a professor in child medicine at the Rijksuniversiteit of Leyden for 25 years and who pioneered the exploration of psychological aspects of child medicine in the Netherlands, also says that children from three to four years can be aware of their approaching death and can sometimes talk about it. He writes: "Death troubles sick children a lot. This leads to *depression,* heavy *anxiety* and rages. *Rage* can lead to scolding and reproaching in older children. These can be directed against parents and against the doctor and nurses."

Even if the nursing personnel is doing its utmost and if parents succeed in co-operating as well as possible, it may be that the child conceives the curative methods as a punishment and develops feelings of enmity towards those who are doing these things to him.[46] Bruch and Hewlitt[47] (1947) have written about the 'sabotage behavior' sometimes found in diabetic children who refuse to be cured in order to oppose their parents. It might be that the sabotage behavior slowly becomes suicidal behavior. The more the child becomes aware of the seriousness of his illness and feels increasing fatigue, pain and helplessness the more he could desire his own death.

To those who surround the child with daily care, the behavior of the dying child who cannot stand it any longer can be extremely confusing. It seems to happen that children in this situation (actively) commit suicide, sometimes in a gruesome, impulsive way, but it may also be that, by refusing all further treatment, they (passively) commit suicide. What should be the attitude of the medical personnel and the parents who see and experience all this? What should we do with regard to a young child who does not want to live any longer, knowing that in any case he does not have long to live? In this situation the problems around *suicide* and *euthanasia* overlap.

This 'pediatric category' mentioned here is not mentioned in the literature on children's suicide. Strubbe[48] (1977) writes that in the Netherlands in 1972, about 1500 children between five and 15 years died, a great number of them in hospital, most of them from a serious illness. How many of them died from the illness, or killed themselves by refusing to cooperate with treatment, is not known. It might well be that in this group more suicides are committed than we are prepared to believe.

For this category of children, Diekstra's definition of suicide as 'problem solving' behavior is applicable. By committing suicide the child aims at reaching the desired state of relief from pain, diets and operations.

6. Children's Suicide and the Law

A. General

A few authors have given some attention to a juridical approach to the problem of suicide. For instance, Silving[49] (1957) makes an extensive survey of legislation in different cultures over the centuries. The legal reaction to suicide depended on prevailing ethical standards, sometimes prohibiting and punishing, sometimes operating with great care, seeking only its prevention. Silving does not mention juridical measures concerning children who have committed or attempted to commit suicide. Speyer[50] (1969) has a chapter on 'suicide and the law', but he too does not mention any special rules with regard to children.

Since the Council of Arles (452 A.D.), legislation in the Western world slowly became infused with a religiously based rejection and condemnation of suicidal behavior. The results can be seen both in criminal law and sometimes in private law (for example, in the invalidity of the last will of a person who committed suicide). Only after the French revolution did the secularization of suicide-legislation slowly begin.

B. Suicide and Penal Law

Speyer remarks that "times with a simple morality and a complete condemnation of suicide (and therefore with more severe punishment) interchanged with times of a morality more *nuancée,* where there existed a more differentiated opinion (with light or almost non-existent punishments)". It is evident that at the moment we live in a period in which we see so many different approaches to the problem of suicide that no reasonable person could plead for its solution by penal provision.

In the Netherlands neither suicide nor attempted suicide is punishable. Article 294 of the Penal Code (since 1886) reads: "He, who intentionally induces another person to suicide, assists him thereto, or procures means, will, *in the event the suicide thereupon follows,* be punished with a detention of a maximum of three years". This criminal offence has therefore the peculiarity that the fact itself, the suicide, is not punishable,[51] but only its procurement, if the suicide results.

I believe that it is an inalienable right of every person to decide for himself whether and when he should die. On this reasoning, there is no place for punishing suicide or attempted suicide, nor for punishing another person who provides the means or information to terminate the life of the suicide, *provided that this is preceded by the express wish of and careful discussion with the person who wants to commit suicide.* Since in suicide situations it cannot completely be excluded that third parties may not have false intentions I would propose that article 294 Penal Code be maintained but that an exception should be added to it to cover *bona fide* assistance of a suicide.

This assistance to suicide at the explicit request of and in careful discussion with the person concerned, comes very close to euthanasia. There is much recent literature on this problem, in which the general view is to repeal the prohibition contained in article 293 of the Dutch Penal Code. Whether opinion in the Netherlands would be inclined to support the suggested exception for assistance to suicide seems for the moment very doubtful. Only a few persons are presently actively concerned with this problem.[52] However illogical it may seem in view of the foregoing, I find it very hard to suggest that the proposed exception for assistance to suicide should apply when the potential suicide is a child under 18 years. Perhaps this is largely an emotive response. Nevertheless, in my view, in that case the adult(s) concerned should be held responsible as if they had committed euthanasia.

C. What Role for the Lawyer?

Lawyers with specific conceptions, which, roughly, relate to *justice and injustice.* It would be extremely useful if lawyers, with their characteristic skills, would pay attention to the problem of suicide, but not only from the point of view of the criminal law. At the moment, solutions, if they can be found, are primarily being sought through the medical profession, which categorizes in terms of *health* and *illness,* and through psychiatrists, who categorize in terms of *mental health* and *mental illness.*

But in investigating the problem of children's suicide, we encounter facts. Lawyers can be helpful in examining them if they realize at an early stage the far fetching consequences some fact-situations can have. For example, certain kinds of educational legislation, by strongly emphasizing results, tend to oppress those who are already in a weak position.

By examining consistently and critically whether typical juridical conceptions like *fairness, carefulness* and *reasonableness* are maintained in the legislative process and are not sacrificed to electoral considerations, economic interests or the quest for power, the suicides of children triggered by 'rigid' laws might be prevented. Of course, suicide, especially of very young persons, would not be eliminated by lawyers reacting more promptly and perceptively to legal proposals. The problem however is so very important that it must not be left only to doctors, psychologists and psychiatrists. Both in the formulation of laws and in their execution, lawyers have a role to play.

It might even be more important if lawyers would realize that children who commit suicide almost always are *very lonely children,* without strong ties with others.[53] Kamaras[54] (1973) made an investigation about symptoms of poisoning in children who during 10 years were received in the largest children's hospital of Budapest. Among the 6900 cases there were 1112 cases of suicide. As many as 284 of the suicides, *i.e.,* 23 percent, had been educated outside their own family and were living apart from their natural parents. It seems urgently necessary that lawyers should think more creatively about how this group of children can establish new relationships, for example, by widening the rules for adoption, by establishing certain criteria allowing them to be carefully placed in foster-families, by enhancing the security of children placed out for adoption and so on.

D. The Role of Those who Execute and Maintain the Law

Hardly any literature can be found about the way in which people who apply the law and maintain public order react to the suicide phenomenon.

Vink,[55] in three articles on the role of the police in relation to suicide places great emphasis on the assisting duty of the police and on the eventual opportunities for the police to act preventively. Within the framework of his study he held a small poll among 30 members of the personnel of the executive departments of the city police in The Hague. In some of the answers to the questionnaire the ambivalence of our society with regard to suicide is clearly shown. When Vink asked his subjects whether the committing of suicide is a fundamental right of each man, more than 40 percent agreed and about 27 percent disagreed. But when he suggested that the individual responsibility of each policeman was to offer more structured help, 87 percent fully agreed. In other words, our society recognizes the right of (adult) persons to commit suicide, but on the other hand it is of the opinion that help must be rendered. The research of Vink, however, did not concern children. Of course, the police only become involved when suicide has been committed or is likely to be committed. For really preventive work the police do not appear to be the right institution.

7. Conclusions

In the foregoing I have tried to approach a veiled problem, especially through the literature. I think that each person who literally applies the maxim *mori licet cui vivere non placet* should realize that by doing so he also commits an act of violence against his family, friends and neighbors. Whichever definition of suicide we use, the closest members of the family are deeply affected by it. For the child this includes all the persons in his school, in the institution of child protection and friends and neighbors who were concerned with him. How all of those must live on with this subtle form of violence committed against them, is a separate problem. In a case of a child's suicide attention must be given in the first place to the brothers and sisters, the school-mates and the members of the children's home who witnessed his act. The literature[56] describes for how long feelings of guilt can remain with brothers and sisters, and how depression and sadness can lead to poor school performance and fears about which they cannot speak to their parents, teachers or group leaders. Even if we sometimes have to accept that a young child voluntarily chooses death, we should in any event try to prevent other children being drawn after him in a spiral of self-inflicted violence.

NOTES

1. Speijer, Prof. dr. N., *Het Zelfmoordvraagstuk, een samenvattend overzicht van de verschillende aspekten van de zelfmoord*, 1969, pp. 25 and 125.
2. *Vide*, especially parts 1-3 of the article "L'enfant et la mort", by Michaux, Leon (1970) 37 *Acta Paedopsychiatrica* 137 *et seq*. Also Col., C.,and Launay, C., "Suicide et tentative de suicide chez l'enfant et l'adolescent" (1964) *La Revue de praticien* 619 *et seq*.
3. Diekstra, Dr. R.F.W.; van Erven, drs. T.C.J.M., Oomens, drs. J.C., G.J.; Verstralen, drs. H.H.F.M., "Zelfmoord en zelfmoordpoging. Naar een rationeel humanistiche benadering", in Intermediair 17th December 1976.
4. A slightly different definition is given by Diekstra in his thesis "Crisis en gedrags-keuze", 1973. He states: (p. 33) "Suicide as the disposing of one's own physicality is then an intentional act whereby the expected and intended outcome of the act is something other than biological death".
5. Mangold, Burkart, and Seidl, Josef E., in "Der Suicideversuch als Kinder-psychiatrischer Notfall" (1975) *Praxis der Kinderpsychologie und Kinder-psychiatrie* Heft 6, p. 233 and following.
6. Bloemsma, F., "Depressie, zelfmoord en poging tot zelfmoord", in Van Praag, H. and Rooymans, H. (eds.), *Stemming en ontstemming*. Rooymans, 1974.
7. Waage, Gunnar, "Selbstmordversuchen bei Kinder und Jugendlichen" (1966) *Praxis der Kinderpsychologie und Kinderpsychiatrie*. This concerned research by the University of Basle regarding 18 children between 5 and 15 years who had tried to kill themselves.
8. It appears from the very clear article of Stengel, E., M.D., "Definition and classification of suicidal acts" in the Costs of Crisis, Proceedings of the Symposium on Prevention of Suicide, Nijmegen 1971, ed. 1972, p. 140 *et seq*. that much more could be said of the definition of suicide.
9. "Suicide and Age", in Farberow, Norman L., and Schneidman, Edwin S., (eds.), *Clues to Suicide*. New York, New York: McGraw-Hill, 1957, p. 41 *et seq*.
10. Speiger, *op. cit.*, p. 123.
11. *Vide* World Health Statistics Report, no. 6, 1968, Special Subject, "Suicides"/ "Suicides".
12. World Health Statistics Report, Special Subject "Suicides by Means Used, 1950-1969", no. 3, 1973.
13. Ringel, Erwin, *Selbstmord — Appell an die Anderen*, 1974.
14. Alpert and Leogrande, *Second Chance to Live*. New York, New York: De Capo Press, 1975.

15. Friedlung, Josef K., "Zur Kenntnis kinderlicher Selbstmordimpulse"., Leuthold, Hans, "Eine Schülerin denkt an Selbstmord"., Pipal, Karl, "Zwei unterbliebene Selbstmordversuche".

16. van de Loo, K.J.M., "Suicidal Behavior as Interpersonal Communication" in "The Cost of Crisis", proceedings of the Symposium on Prevention of Suicide, Nijmegen, 1971, ed. 1972.

17. *Vide* also for England: Connell, P.H., "Suicidal Attempts in Childhood and Adolescence" (1964) *Acta Paedopsychiatrica* 403.

18. Bergsma, "Suicide and Suicide Attempts, Especially With Juveniles in the Netherlands", (1966) *Tijdschrift voor de Psychologie* 245*ff.*

19. Haim, Dr. André, *Les suicides d'adolescents,* 1969.

20. Gordon, Bianca, "Een interdisciplinaire benadering van het stervende kind en zijn gezinsleden", in *Afscheid van een kind,* 1976 (Care of the child facing death, (1974).

21. Speyer, N., *Het Zelfmoordvraagstuk,* 1969.

22. Durkheim, E., *'Le Suicide' Etude de sociologie,* 1897. Recently a new edition was published, 1973 by Presses Universitaires de France.

23. Kruyt, C.S., *Zelfmoord, statistisch-sociologische verkenningen,* 1960.

24. Douglas, J.D., *The Social Meaning of Suicide,* 1970.

25. Otto, U., "Suicide Attempts Among Swedish Children and Adolescents" (1969) *Adolescence, Psychosocial Perspectives.*

26. *Vide* the recent French edition with the case histories of Denis Langlois, "Les dossiers noirs du suicide", 1976, in which the rhetorical question: (page 55) "Oui ou non, l'école peut-elle traumatiser un élève au point de l'amener au suicide? Oui ou non, le système des notes et des devoirs surveillés, le bachotage intensif, peuvent-ils tuer".

27. Philips, D.P., "The Influence of Suggestion on Suicide. Substantive and Theoretical Implications of the Werther Effect" (1974), 39 *Am. Soc. Review* 340*ff.*

28. de Sanctis, S., "Infantiele Selbstmorden" (1922) *Zent.Bl.ges.Neur. und Psychiatrie.*

29. Kanner, L., *Child Psychiatry,* 1957.

30. Schrut, A., "Suicidal Adolescents and Children", Dig.o. Neur. and Early Adolescence (1974) *J. Child Psychology and Psych.* 275.

31. Anthony J., and Scott, "Manic-depressive Psychosis in Childhood" (1960) *J. Child Psychol. and Psychiat.* 53.

32. Connell, P.H., "Suicidal Attempts in Childhood and Adolescence" (1964) *Acta Paedopsychiatrica* 403*ff.*

33. Winn, D.A., "Adolescent Suicidal Behavior and Hallucinations" (1969) *Adolescence, Psychosocial Perspectives.*

34. Eggers, C., "Das Suicid-Risiko im Verlauf kindlicher Schizophrenien" in Proceedings of the 7th International Congress on Suicide-prevention, 1973, ed. 1974.

35. Diekstra, R.F.W., "Somacidal Thinking Among Young Adults, An investigation Into its Occurrence and Meaning" in Proceedings of the International 7th Congress on Suicide Prevention, 1973, ed. 1974.

36. Jacobs, J., *Adolescent Suicide.* New York, New York: Wiley Series on psychological disorders, 1971.

37. Waage, G., "Selbstmordversuch bei Kindern und Jugendlichen" (1966) *Psych. Praxis* Heft 39.

38. Zumpe, L., "Selbstmordversuche von Kindern und Jugendlichen, Personlichtkeitsmerkmale und Entwicklungsverlaufe anhand von 34 Katamnesen" (1966) *Psychol. Praxis,* Heft 39.

39. Durand-Fardell, M., "Le Suicide chez les enfants" (1855), *Ann. Med. Psych.* 61-79.

40. Mangold, B., and Seidl, J.E., "Der Suicidversuch als Kinderpsychatrisher Notfall" (1974) *Praxis der Kinderpsychologie und Kinderpsychiatrie* 233*ff.*

41. Report on a conference, "Suicide and Attempted Suicide in Young People", Regional office for Europe, W.H.O. Luxembourg, 19-12/8/1974.

42. *Vide* also Corder, B.F.; Shorr, W., Corder, R.F., "A Study of Social and Psychological Characteristics of Adolescent Suicide Attempters in an Urban, Disadvantaged Area" (1974) *Adol.* no. 9, 1-6.

43. Rosenberg P.H., and Latimer, R., "Suicide Attempts by Children" (1966) *Mental Hyg.* 354*ff.*
44. Strubbe, W., "Eerlijk duurt soms niet het langst" (Jan., 1977) *T.M.W.* no. 1, 16. Theme number on "Stervensbegeleiding".
45. Veeneklaas, G.M.H., "Het sterven van een kind" (1975) *Het naderend eind* 53*ff.*
46. Burton, L., "Het gezin met een kind dat een intensieve medische behandeling moet ondergaan" (1977) *Afscheid van een kind* 95.
47. Bruch, H., and Hewlitt, I., "Psychological Aspects of the Medical Management of Diabetes in Children" (1947) *Psychosomatic Medicine* 205-209.
48. Strubbe, W., *supra,* note 44.
49. Silving, H., "Suicide and Law", in Farberow, N.L., and Schneidman, E.S. (eds.), *Clues to Suicide.* New York, New York: McGraw-Hill, 1957.
50. Speyer, N., *Het zelfmoordvraagstuk,* chapter III, pp. 69, 169 and Stengel, E., 1967, pp. 62*ff.*
51. Remmelink, J., *Het Wetboek van Strafrecht* Tome II, p. 951.
52. See the forthcoming report (1978) to be published in the next months of the Euthanasiacommission of the Vereniging voor vrijwillige euthanasie.
53. I was very much struck by the recently published book in the Netherlands of Keuls, Yvonne, *Jan Rap en z'n Maat,* 1977, in which countless cases are described of boys and girls who were received in a modern (crisis intervention) home in The Hague. Among them was an extremely high number of children with repeated suicidal behavior.
54. Kamaras, I., "Die Prevention der Jugendlichen Suicidien als Pädiatrisches Problem", Proceedings 7th Int. Conf. for Suicide Prevention Amsterdam 1973, ed. 1974, pp. 156-164.
55. Vink, C.G., "Politiële aspecten van zelfmoorden en zelfmoordpogingen" (1977) *Alg. Pol. Blad* nos. 4, 5 and 6.
56. Cain, A.C.; Fast, I., and Erickson, M.E., "Children's Disturbed Reactions to the Death of a Sibling" (1964), 34 *Am. J. of Orthopsychiatry* 741-752. Roberts, R., "Children's Reaction to Sibling Death", Proceedings of the First Int. Conf. of the Ac. of Psychosomatic Medicine, Int. Congress Series, No. 134, 1966., MacCarthy D., "The Repercussions of the Death of a Child", (1969), 62 *Proceedings of the Royal Soc. of Medicine* 553.

Chapter 30

Sibling Violence

*Suzanne K. Steinmetz**

1. Introduction

A definition often acts as a window through which one can gain insights regarding a society's feelings about a phenomena. Walters and Parke (1964) suggest that a physical abuse is not a set of behaviors and their outcome, but rather a culturally determined label which is applied by an observer according to socially defined judgments of the behavior and its outcome. Sibling violence is the most prevalent and most accepted form of family violence, and is possibly the most potent form because it represents the child's first experience of using violence to resolve conflicts among peers. However, unlike child abuse and wife beating, which have been referred to as the hidden or unreported crimes, sibling violence is readily acknowledged as a normal aspect of family relationship. That families do not see it as much of a problem is suggested by the following quote:

"Before breakfast Nancy and Fanny had a fight about a shoe brush which they both wanted. Fanny pull'd off her shoe and threw it at Nancy, which missed her and broke a pane of glass of our school room. They then enter'd upon close scratching &c. which methods seem instinctive in women." (Fithian, 1945:85).

This quote from the 18th Century diary of Philip Fithian, a tutor for the children of a colonial Virginia family, is not very different from what could be said of modern families. One mother in a recent study (Steinmetz, 1977b), when asked how her children got along, reported:

Terrible! They fight all the time. Anything can be a problem. . . . Oh, its just constant, but I understand that this is normal. I talk to other people, their kids are the same way.

Another parent elaborated on the conflicts between the siblings by noting:

I think they all went through periods where they hate each other. Right now the 15 year-

---

* Individual and Family Studies, University of Delaware, U.S.A.

old son hates the 21 year-old son. The older one doesn't hate the younger one. The girls get along pretty well.

While still another noted:

Its a wonder they're not all bruised and bloody. They must get tired of yelling at each other.

2. Frequency of Sibling Violence

Since parents seem to consider fighting between siblings as normal, it is interesting to see just how common this fighting is and how violently they fight. Steinmetz, (1977b) in an examination of physical violence between 88 pairs of siblings from 57 randomly selected families with two or more children between 3-17, found that high levels of physical violence were used by siblings to resolve conflicts. The study found that 70 percent of the young families (mean age of all children eight or younger) used physical violence to resolve conflicts, most of which entered around possessions. Sixty-eight percent of the adolescent families (mean age 9-13) also engaged in physical violence. Among this group, conflicts tended to revolve around personal space boundaries, touching or 'looking funny' at each other. Even among teen-age families (mean age 14 or older) who fought over responsibilities and social obligations, 63 percent used high levels of physical violence, a finding consistent with Straus (1974) who reported that 62 percent of a sample of college students used physical force on a brother or sister during the past year. Further analysis of these data revealed that although male sib pairs more often threw things, pushed and hit than did female sib pairs (60 percent against 49 percent), the highest use of physical violence occurred between boy-girl sib pairs of which 68 percent engaged in high levels of violence (see *Table* I). There are also differences in the use of physical violence based on the ages of the sibs. The data in *Table 2* suggest that older sibs are less likely to use physical violence to resolve conflicts than are younger sibs.

Table I.   The Sex Composition of Sib Pairs who Engage in High Levels of Physical Violence

	Throwing Things	Pushing	Hitting	Combined Physical Violence
	%	%	%	%
Girl/Girl (27)	37	59	52	49
Boy/Boy (22)	54	73	57	61
Boy/Girl (39)	55	88	69	68

Table 2   Age of Sib Pairs and the Methods Used to Resolve Conflict*

Age	Throwing Things	Pushing	Hitting
	%	%	%
9 Years or Under (9)	78	78	100
9-13 years (15)	80	100	100
11-13 years and 14 or above (17)	82	82	76
14 years and above (27)	61	74	61

* Five sib pairs 11-13 and 8 or younger, one sib pair 8 or younger and 14 or above, seven sib pairs 9-11 and 14 or above and seven pairs 9-11 and 8 or younger are not included in the above analysis because of large differences in ages of sibs involved.

In another exploratory study, composed of a broad-based but non-representative sample of individuals between 18 and 30 years, 72 percent of the respondents reported using physical violence to resolve a conflict between siblings (Steinmetz, 1977a). Preliminary data from a nationally representative sample of 2,143 families (Straus, Gelles, Steinmetz, 1977) are also revealing. During the survey year (1975) 1,224 pairs of siblings between 3-17 years of age used the following methods to resolve conflicts (See *Table* 3).

Table 3   Methods used to resolve Sibling Conflicts

Method	Percent
Pushing and shoving	60
Slapping	45
Throwing	39
Kicking, biting, hitting with fist	38
Hitting with an object	36
Beating up	14
Threatening to use a knife or gun	0.8
Use of knife or gun	0.3

Although the three-tenths of one percent using a knife or gun on a brother or sister may not seem high, when one applies this rate to the 46 million children in the United States, there were an estimated 138,000 children who had actually used a knife or gun on their brother or sister *during the survey year*. Furthermore, the 14 percent who beat up a sibling is consistent with Weston's (1968) reports that 14 percent of the battered children examined had received the battering from a sibling.

When the question regarding the method used by sibling to resolve conflict was asked as *ever* happening, rather than just during the *past year*, 18 percent reported

462   Family Violence

having beaten up their sib, and 5 percent had actually used a gun. Based on these figures, about 8.3 million children in the United States have been 'beaten up' by a sibling and 2.3 million children at some time used a gun or knife on a brother or sister.

Although national statistics are not available for sibling homicides, over 3 percent of the homicides between 1948-1952 which occurred in Philadelphia were sibling homicides (Wolfgang, 1958). Three percent of the homicides in New York City in 1965 were also sibling homicides (Bard, 1971). Although these studies do not constitute nationally representative samples, the 3 percent rate of sibling homicide appears to be stable over time and at least represents the rates for two large cities. Although these data may not represent the percent occurring in other parts of the country, if we take a few liberties with these samples and apply this 3 percent to the number of homicides which occurred in the United States during 1975, approximately 615 individuals were killed by their brother or sister in a single year.

Although the number of sibling homicides is less than the number of marital or filial homicides which occurred during that same year, when additional measures of severe violence, such as 'beating-up' or using a knife or gun are included, sibling violence exceeds the level of violence parents use on children or that which spouses use on each other.

During 1975, 3,077 spouses killed each other, 2 million 'beat-up' each other, and 1.7 million faced a gun wielded by a spouse (Vital Statistics Reports, 1976; Straus, Gelles, Steinmetz, 1977). In that same year 2,000 children were killed by their parents (Besharov, 1975), 1.5 million were brutally beaten-up, and 1.2 million were attacked by their parents with a lethal weapon (Straus, Gelles, Steinmetz, 1977).

Violence between spouses and between parent and child has received extensive media coverage and has been the topic of much research. It is labeled as heinous and criminal (though under-reported). However, sibling violence, which accounted for 8.3 million children being beaten-up, 2.3 million facing a gun, and 615 homicides during 1975 is considered by most parents to be a normal part of family interaction and not a serious problem.

3. Conclusion

The complacency over sibling violence must be seriously questioned. Violence used by siblings to resolve conflicts represents a training ground — an opportunity to practice physically violent interaction with peers. The training prepares them when they marry to use physical violence on their spouses to resolve marital conflicts, and when they become parents, on their children to discipline them. Studies have suggested that the patterns of conflict resolution used by family members are transmitted for over three generations (Steinmetz, 1977a, 1977b). These studies suggest that the methods used by husband and wife to resolve marital conflict are then used to discipline their children, and the children imitate these methods when attempting to resolve conflicts with their siblings. When these children marry, they used the methods learned during their childhood to interact with their spouses and children, thus continuing the cycle. The impact of witnessing violence between parents and experiencing violence in the form of severe physical discipline has been found to characterize the background of child abusers (Bryant, 1963; Wasserman, 1967; Zalba, 1966), murders (Bender, 1959; Sargent, 1962; Sadoff, 1971; Tanay, 1975), rapists (Brownmiller, 1975; Hartogs, 1952), and those who committed political assassination (Fontana, 1973; Steinmetz, 1977b). In a less dramatic context, the mother's use of physically violent methods of discipline accounted for over 25 percent of the variance in predicting physical violence between siblings, based on a regression analysis.

Since sibling violence represents the child's first opportunity to engage in violence which had been witnessed and experienced, it is, therefore, a very critical link for understanding and attempting to break the cycle of violence in the family. The practice of viewing sibling violence as a normal part of growing up simply reinforces the acceptability of using this method of resolving conflicts and provides an early opportunity for children to practice that which they have observed and experienced.

REFERENCES

Bard, Morton, "The Study and Modification of Intrafamilial Violence", in Singer, Jerome L. (ed.), *The Control of Aggression and Violence.* New York, New York: Academic Press, 1971.

Belder, L., "Children and Adolescents Who Have Killed" (1959), 116 *American Journal of Psychiatry* 510-513.

Besharov, J.D., "Building a Community Response to Child Abuse and Maltreatment" (1975), 4 *Children Today* no. 5, 2.

Brownmiller, Susan, *Against Our Will: Men, Women and Rape.* New York, New York: Simon and Schuster, 1975.

Bryant, H.D., "Physical Abuse of Children: An Agency Study" (1963), 42 *Child Welfare* 125-130.

Fithian, P.V., *Journal and Letters of Philip Vickers Fithian, 1773-1774.* Princeton, New Jersey: Princeton University Press, 1945.

Fontana, Vincent J., *Somewhere a Child is Crying: the Battered Child.* New York, New York: McMillan, 1973.

Hartogs, Renatus, "Discipline in the Early Life of Sex-Delinquent and Sex Criminals" (1951), 9 *Nervous Child* 167-173.

Sadoff, R.L., "Clinical Observations on Parricide" (1971), 45 *Psychiatric Quarterly* 1: 65-9.

Sargent, D., "Children Who Kill — a Family Conspiracy?" (1962), 7 *Social Work* 35-42.

Steinmetz, Suzanne K., "The Use of Force for Resolving Family Conflict: The Training-Ground for Abuse" (1977a) *Family Coordinator; The Cycle of Violence: Assertive, Aggressive and Abusive Family Interaction.* New York, New York: Praeger (1977b).

Straus, Murray A., "Leveling Civility and Violence in the Family" (Feb., 1974), 36 *Journal of Marriage and the Family* 13-29.

Straus, M.A.; Gelles, R.A.; and Steinmetz, S.K., Press Release, American Association for the Advancement of Science Annual Meeting, Denver, February 25, 1977.

Tanay, E., "Reactive parricide" (1975) *Journal of Forensic Science.*

Vital Statistics Reports (1976) *Annual Summary for the United States,* vol. 24, no. 13, Washington, D.C. National Center for Health Statistics.

Walters, R.H., and Parke, R.D., "Social Motivation, Dependency and Susceptability to Social Influence", in Berkowitz, L. (ed.), *Advances in Experimental Social Psychology.* New York, New York: Academic Press, 1964.

Wasserman, Sidney, "The Abused Parent of the Abused Child" (Sept.-Oct., 1967), 14 *Children* 175-179.

Weston, J.T., "A Summary of Neglect and Traumatic Cases", in Helfer R.E., and Kempe, C.H., *The Battered Child.* Chicago, Illinois: University of Chicago Press, 1968.

Wolfgang, M.E., *Patterns in Criminal Homicide.* Phil., Pennsylvania: University of Pennsylvania Press, 1958.

Zalba, S.R., "The Abused Child: A Survey of the Problem" (1966), II *Social Work* 3-16.

Chapter 31

Adolescents Who Kill a Member of the Family

B. M. Cormier; C. C. J. Angliker; P. W. Gagné, and B. Markus*

1. Introduction

This chapter describes a research project on adolescent homicide conducted by the McGill Clinic in Forensic Psychiatry. The project constitutes a longitudinal study of adolescent murderers who have been charged under the Juvenile Delinquents Act with causing the death of an individual, who have appeared before the Social Welfare Court of the Province of Quebec, and who have been kept in that court or been deferred to the adult court. An inventory is being made of all cases of adolescent homicidal violence in the Province of Quebec covering a period of a quarter of a century, from 1950 to 1974. Consequently this longitudinal approach will allow us to study (1) a certain number of subjects who have returned to society after incarceration, (2) others reaching the end of their sentence and awaiting freedom, (3) some serving their first years of sentence, and (4) those who remained under the jurisdiction of the social welfare court until the age of 21. In studying these four groups simultaneously, we can immediately use for the latter groups and for future cases the knowledge acquired from the previous ones.

Among other results, our investigation should permit us to define the evolution of the homicidal process during adolescence; to determine the area of family, social and temporal influences in the formation of these processes; to isolate and diagnose the symptoms which precede the criminal act and to clarify the psychological and psychiatric state consecutive to the act as well as their effect on ulterior social behavior of the young murderers.

In a previous study on homicide, we have defined three types of relationship between the murderer and his victim, namely, specific, semi-specific and non-specific.[1] When there is a relationship between offender and victim and the homicide results from a conflict within that relationship, it is said to be committed in a specific relationship. We will focus this presentation on homicidal violence in a specific relationship where the doer is an adolescent and the victim a member of his family, either a parent, brother or sister. As the incidence of sororicide appears

* Clinic in Forensic Psychiatry, McGill University, Montreal, Canada.

to be very much less frequent and mainly confined to children[2] in comparison with matricide, patricide, or fratricide, this facet will not be discussed here.

2. Incidence

Within the family group, the incidence of adolescents who kill a sibling seems low compared to adolescents who kill a parental figure. This can be explained in terms of our culture where brothers and sisters are either close to each other or very far apart. When close they share a lot and discover a lot together. When they are apart they tend to live the full experience of adolescence within their peer groups rather than within the nuclear family. Bad or conflictual parental figures often unite adolescent siblings rather than increase the conflict among themselves. This binding together of adolescent siblings promotes the discharge of aggression against the parents rather than amongst themselves. Conversely, good relationships with parental figures ultimately favor normal detachment of children from the family unit, so that in either good or bad parental relationships, adolescents are somewhat protected against homicidal aggression against each other. Thus, the lower incidence.

In a previous paper we summed up the cases in a number of studies on homicide and included our own cases.[3] In comparison with the other types of homicide committed by adolescents, the combined incidence of matricide, patricide and fratricide is less frequent. In our own series of 26 adolescents who have killed, the ratio is approximately 1:5 while in another series of 50, the ratio is 1:7.[4] In covering some of the literature on homicide, out of a total of 100 cases described, including our own, there were 14 cases of matricide,[5] 11 cases of patricide,[6] and two cases of fratricide.[7] Only three cases were adolescent girls,[8] all of whom killed their mother. It is interesting to note that some authors[9] state that the ratio of matricide over patricide is in the region of 2 to 1. However, in the literature cited in this chapter, the ration is almost equal. The reason for this appears to be that in adolescence the ratio is equal whereas when one does not take the age of the perpetrator into account, the frequency of matricide is higher.

Table 1.   Comparison of Adolescent Murderers in the Literature

	Bridge-[10] man	Briguet-[11] Lamarre	Brown[12]	Carek,[13] Watson	Duncan,[14] Duncan	Malm-[15] quist	Mc-[16] Knight et al.	Medli-[17] cott	Scherl,[18] Mack	Forensic Clinic	TOTAL
Total number of cases	4	50	1	1	5	4	4	2	3	26	100
Matricide	1	1	1	-	1	-	4	1*	3	2	14
Patricide	-	5	-	-	2*	1	-	-	-	3*	11
Fratricide	-	1	-	1	-	-	-	-	-	-	2

*Partnership

On the report on Homicide in Canada published in June 1976[19] statistical data reveal that during the period from 1961 to 1974 there were 735 homicide suspects between the ages of 7 and 19 years. Two hundred of these suspects killed in the context of a domestic relationship defined in Statistics Canada as members of the nuclear family, common-law family and other kinship. There were 63 between the ages of 11 and 15, and 137 between 16 and 19. These figures of course indicate to what extent homicidal violence is carried out within the family in general but do not specify the incidence of matricide, patricide and fratricide.

3. Psychodynamics Found in Adolescent Murders

A. Murder within the Dynamics of Adolescence

In studying individual and social behavior, the particular conflict experienced by the person at the moment of serious delinquent action, especially when it involves a loss of life, is of special concern. Until recently most adolescents accused of murder were treated by the judicial process as adults.[20] Although initially arrested under prevailing juvenile procedures in North America, most cases in the past have been transferred to the adult court, although provisions generally exist to keep these youths within the juvenile social welfare courts or their equivalent in the different states or provinces. The nature of the offence was sufficient reason to have most of these adolescents answer for their act in the same way as adults do. Since most adolescent murderers had been sentenced to adult penal institutions it is not surprising that we did not know much about adolescents who kill.

The cases which are known were those who were observed in an adult institution by professionals, and many of our 26 cases belong to that group. However, a trend is developing of keeping these adolescents within the juvenile court system, generally up to the age of 21, so that it is becoming easier to know about them and their problems of reintegration into society. The most recent cases we have known belong to this latter group.

In describing the many psycho-sexual and psycho-social tasks that adolescents must face and resolve before becoming young adults, Erikson offers a good frame of reference for studying the psychopathology of adolescents who kill. He has said that adolescence is not an affliction but a normative crisis; that is, a normal phase of increased conflict characterized by a seeming fluctuation in ego strength and yet also by a high growth potential. Within this normative crisis, the adolescent ultimately comes to define his identity as a young adult.[21] In trying to understand part of the psychopathology of some adolescent murderers one should recall that many of the problems and tasks encountered in adolescence are not only solved within the nuclear family, but also in the peer group. It is one of our contentions that amongst those adolescents who kill within the nuclear group, there is an inability to displace the problems encountered with the parents on to a broader group, such as their peers, where the problems can be defused and new gratifications experienced.

In dealing with violence against parents in a family, two factors are evident: an existing family relationship and, within this family conflictual psychological links between the parents and the children. A homicidal process occurs when the unresolved conflicts reach their peak. Psychological conflictual or ambivalent feelings, even aggressive and deadly in content, start early in life. A child going through a normal psycho-sexual and psycho-social development has fantasies about his parents' death such as being an orphan or of the parents being victims of an accident. These are usually short-lived and reactive to frustration or other emotional occurrences in parent-children relationships. We must remember that such affects as homicidal moods and fantasies co-exist with opposite affects such as the child feeling comfortable with the parents. When there is a balance of these opposite moods, there is no danger of an homicidal act either by parents or their offspring.

Death wishes and fantasies featuring the parents as objects in the complex love-aggression-frustration conflicts between children and parents are manifested in some form of psychomotor activity such as temper tantrums, punching or beating. This form of aggression may have deadly dimensions in a young child's fantasies but in reality his actual ability to inflict damage on an adult, because of his physical incapacity or his ignorance of weapons, for example, reduces his omnipotent fantasies to an illusory strength. However, the emotional states that would later permit such homicidal acting out against parents derive partly from unresolved conflicts of the early formative years which are carried over to the next phase of development, taking new strength and dimensions in pre-adolescence, adolescence and early maturity, when deadly conflicts do occur.

For the purpose of this chapter we will define the end of adolescence as the eighteenth birthday. However, it must be added that we find 18 and 19 year-olds and even young men in their 20's who are involved in patricide or matricide as a result of conflicts and emotions which in fact are symptomatic of a retarded or prolonged adolescent syndrome.

Looking at the problem in an overview, when sons and daughters kill their parents, whether they be adolescents or adults, it is generally in very conflictual family relationships that cannot find their normal resolution. Although other motivations and aetiologies may play a role, it is the abnormally strong conflictual emotional ties between parents and their offspring that are at the nucleus of the act. In discussing the psychodynamics involved in the homicidal process in adolescents we will attempt to describe some of the patterns that emerge. Some of these exist in other homicidal acts committed in specific relationships and are not necessarily particular to adolescents although they acquire in adolescents a special emotional tone.

B. Lockage Phenomenon and Overkill

Literature, both ancient and modern, is rich in examples illustrating the conflicts between parent and child, such as Oedipus, Orestes and Electra, to name but a few. The conflicts described in these Greek tragedies are bound to each other in such a way that death is the only solution. In modern psychiatry, this pathological link has been termed a 'lockage' phenomenon, where homicide results when "a relationship can no longer be sustained but also not given up."[22] Whereas in many other crises within the family, adolescents may have left home permanently, the adolescent offender who has killed has been unable to unlock himself from the bond between himself and his family. We have described this same phenomenon in the psychodynamics of homicide committed in a marital relationship characterized by "an inability to live together and an inability to part" and in the end, "the murder occurs at a point of intense emotion and the feeling that to continue is inconceivable and to give up impossible."[23]

In referring to the violence that occurs beyond death, Mohr and McKnight were of the impression that this was not "the result of explosive rage but rather of panic and fear of not having completed the task."[24] This fear and panic is in our view explained by the fact that it is the omnipotent father (or mother) who is killed and thus 'overkilling' is a reassurance that this omnipotent parental figure will not get up and retaliate. Features that make these bonds unbreakable are also related to fixation of the adolescent at Klein's paranoid and depressive positions characterized by the split in object relationship as well as the presence of mechanisms of introjection and projection dealing with the anxieties that are characteristic of these two positions.[25]

This lockage phenomenon as well as the overkilling and the mechanisms involved in both are well described by the words of an adolescent murderer who, many years afterward, came to explain with great insight the killing of his father: "My father was the victim of the fear of him he had created in me."

C. The Adolescent Murderer and the Incestuous Conflict

The syndrome that most illustrates the total involvement of the family is father-daughter incest, which has been aptly named, 'a family affair'.[26] The incestuous relationship that is acted out rather than remaining in thought and fantasies is generally limited to a period which usually ends before the end of adolescence. Incestuous daughters ultimately liberate themselves from the father as sexual objects, in contrast to daughters who live without acting out, having neither insight into nor solving their incestuous desires and fantasies. Some of these daughters may, paradoxically, have more difficulty in liberating themselves from their father or father-substitute. However, a real sexual relationship between father and daughter cannot survive the testing of reality, which ultimately leads the daughters to liberate themselves from the incestuous father. The actual sexualization of incestuous fantasies contributes in the end to destroying the belief that the father is ideally good and omnipotent.

Incest is a family affair since the three participants in father-daughter incest, namely mother, father and daughter are all involved in complex dynamics. The daughter becomes for her father a mother-substitute and, by paradox, his 'wife'. On the other hand, the mother of the victim becomes in many ways the equivalent to the eldest daughter of the family.[27] Father-daughter incest is more frequent than mother-son incest. Although the incestuous attachment between mother and son is well known, actual consummation is less frequent. In either relationship the incestuous attachments and links go deeper than the oedipal or pregenital phase of development. One of the major conflicts found in homicide against parents by adolescent children is the unresolved incestuous conflict. It is almost always present. A relationship between incestuous conflicts and homicidal acts committed in the family was found in most cases that we have seen and in cases reported in the literature.

In one of our cases the paternal figure was at the same time feared and loved, feared because he was a tyrannical father and loved because in his tyranny he had some good wishes for his son. In the years prior to the murder of the father, the son had a recurrent nightmare in which he was walking with a girl, the only person with whom he had succeeded in establishing some attachment, one he could call a girlfriend, no matter how superficial the links in reality were. Then the father appeared and took away the girl. This adolescent nightmare is practically a paradigm of the omnipotent father of the primitive horde who forbids his sons to approach the daughters.

If incest has been called a family affair, the killing of the parents can be referred to as a family drama and at times more accurately as a 'family conspiracy'.[28] The relationship between incest and conflicts involving parents and children in families appears to us so important in the drama of adolescents who kill parents that it will be elaborated on further in the research project.

D. Other Dynamics Involved in Adolescent Murder

Some authors believe that the explosiveness in the homicidal process has or appears to have an organic quality to it and has been compared with seizure activity in the brain. Menninger and Mayman have described this as an outburst of primitive, disorganized violence which may be self-directed or assaultive; the term they used in describing this pattern of behavior in which there is a damming up of tension followed by a sudden breakdown or discharge of impulses was *episodic dyscontrol.*[29] Bender and her associates[30] on the other hand, took into consideration a number of factors, organic, social, and dynamic, which in combination could be considered dangerous. Some of these dangerous symptoms were: organic brain damage with an impulse disorder and an abnormal E.E.G. and epilepsy; schizophrenia; compulsive fire-setting; severe reading disability; unfavorable home conditions and a personal experience with violent death.

Wertham explains the violent act as a 'catathymic crisis' which he views as a "transformation of the stress of thought as the result of certain complexes of ideas that are charged with a strong effect. . . ". The process begins with a traumatic psychogenic experience that precipitates an increasingly unbearable inner tension. The person blames the external situation for his inner tension and becomes more and more egocentric. A peak is reached in the idea that the violent act is the only solution to the unbearable inner situation. The crime is followed by release of tension and a superficial establishment of an inner equilibrium which leads to insight, and the realization that response to the crisis was far out of proportion to the situation. In regard to personality development, Wertham is of the opinion that the violent act becomes a 'rallying point' to preserve the patient's mental state from otherwise progressive psychopathology.[31]

Malmquist feels that homicide can serve the illusory function of saving one's self and ego from destruction by displacing onto someone else the focus for aggressive discharge.[32] His premonitory signs of homicidal aggression are object losses, somatization, an emotional crescendo, and homosexual threats.

It becomes evident that there is not any compact or unitary theory of homicide but that it is multifactorial and takes into account not only the data mentioned above but others, such as the easy accessibility of a weapon and a lack of protective supervision, not to mention the irritant effects of the victim upon the adolescent. However, when one studies cases of matricide, patricide and fratricide, there do appear to be observable trends and patterns between these three types of homicide, particularly when one examines the behavioral components, the personalities of the individual members within these families and the interplay between them. Usually, the interaction is triangular, that is, between mother, father, and son or daughter, with a shift in the degree of interactional psycho-pathological behavior between the family members, depending upon whether it is matricide, patricide, or fratricide.

4. Matricide

The cases described in the literature and those in our study have in common a history of severe early maternal restrictiveness with alternating deprivation, provocation and harshness, extending into adolescence. The mother-child relationship was intense and conflict-laden, and, with few exceptions, the mother was brutally killed.[33] The fathers, on the other hand, were uniformly passive and remained relatively uninvolved in the mother-child interaction by being either emotionally or physically absent. Any involvement would be in the form of placating the mother while at the same time being non-supportive of the son or daughter.

The son's role in this situation is a sado-masochistic one vis-à-vis the mother in which there is also a very strong erotic component supported by the mother. In a few cases described in the literature,[34] including one of our own, the mothers' seduction of the son was most prominent, for they would often expose their bodies in front of their son in a most provocative way, which would then be followed by brutal treatment. Tragically, in comparison with most adolescents who find themselves in conflict with their parents, these adolescents only make half-hearted attempts at escape. They may run away but they are either easily caught or return home of their own volition, only to be met with further beatings. There is an almost complete absence of other outlets, of other gratifications and opportunities for tension discharge outside the family. A question is therefore raised whether delinquency, destructive though it is from the point of view of society, serves as an adaptive phenomenon for the individual adolescent who strives to find external objects toward which he can discharge the sexual and aggressive tensions that are stimulated in the home. A model for these boys is set either by parental example or by approval. Many of the boys had a collection of knives and guns which they were allowed to retain and to augment even after there were several episodes of extremely violent and menacing behavior.[35] The parents either covertly or overtly expected them to be physically violent and antisocially aggressive.

In discussing the mother-son relationship, incest has been alluded to. In only three cases, our own plus two others,[36] was there actual intercourse, whereas in the remainder it was all but consummated or fantasized. Brown[37] vividly described the incestuous relationship between a mother and son and the conflicts, such as guilt, that arose following intercourse. Although there was not the same degree of chronic violence as in the other cases, the relationship did, nevertheless, end in matricide, such was the pathological degree of the neuroticism of the pair. It is tragic to note that, had the incest taboo not prevented them from consummating their relationship without such guilt, no great harm would have been done. It is of note, too, that during his trial the question of incest was never introduced, for, had it been, he would not have been branded, as he was, "a ruthless fortune-hunter who struck down in cold blood the one person who loved and cherished him in order that he might inherit her millions."[38] This case demonstrates how interlocking and complementary are the many motivations behind a crime. In this case, neither had deliberately set out on a pattern of wrongdoing; both had been caught in an inextricable web of passion from which they could find no escape.

5. Patricide

In cases of patricide, the scene changes. The interactions within the nucleus shift, roles change, and communication between its members differs in quality and quantity.[39] Whereas in matricide the mother is the dominant figure, in patricide she takes a back seat. She presents a weak, helpless, and passive figure who is dependent upon and/or protective of her son. The father is, in contrast, often found to be cruel, critical, and competitive with his sons, and it is not uncommon to find varying degrees of jealousy of his son's attachment to the mother, something akin to an inverse oedipal complex. Often in these families the husband is extremely brutal towards his wife, with the son witnessing the beatings. As a result of their violent behavior, some of these fathers have a criminal record, usually being charged with assault.

The son in this battle-torn family is very different from his counterpart in the matricidal group. Here he appears more timid, inhibited, and, strangely, despite his father's character and temperament, he strives to seek recognition from his father, but to no avail, for his father is too caught up in his own psychopathology and has become blind to his son's reaching hand. A point of no return is reached when the crescendo of paternal brutality is such that intervention is necessary. It is at this point that the son intervenes and kills his father. The son thus acts as the 'justice maker' or 'protector' of his mother and, following the murder, his reaction to having killed his father is often one of justification.

Homosexuality between father and son is rarely acted out in fact, although in one reported case it was overt.[40] In this case the relationship between father and son was similar to that of Brown's case, for death occurred when the son realized 'there was no way out', a typical case of lockage phenomenon.

6. Fratricide

Although the sibling rivalry of brothers is known to all, only rarely does it culminate in fratricide. The reported incidence is low, and we could find only two cases.[41] However, the true incidence may be somewhat higher, for the deaths of siblings may often be reported as 'accidents' in order to cover up and protect the child from legal and psychological sequelae. This has also been noted in cases of sororicide.[42]

Of the two cases reported, one boy was aged 17 and mentally retarded, while the other was aged 10.[43] In these youngsters, one is impressed with the air of helplessness, of economic and psychological depression, and a certain distance between the individual family members, with a hesitancy towards intimacy. It is very different from the seductiveness, turbulence and brutality that is present in the cases of matricide and patricide. Both boys demonstrated an episode of impulsive and irrational behavior as the result of experiencing a sense of helplessness or fear of not being accepted. They became enraged at their own impotence. In one of the cases,[44] the parents, too, would react in a similar fashion.

7. Partnership

In comparison with other types of homicide, partnership is not a common finding in the death of a family member. Killing in partnership is more commonly found in youth gangs where death results from rivalry or as the result of an acquisitive crime, such as armed robbery. We found four cases, two of our own and two others in the literature.[45] Two partnerships involved brothers while the other two involved their friends.

The family dynamics do not appear vastly different from the other families already mentioned. The differences seem to be within the adolescents themselves, for, amongst the partners they appear to be drawn together to form a pathological relationship or cohesion where one needs the other in order to carry out the deed. There is an element of conspiracy, one in which they talk freely and openly about committing the act, and when the murder is about to be committed, the fact that they are in partnership may have a disinhibiting effect. We feel that without a partner these deaths might not have taken place: the partners seemed to have been linked together as the result of some common crisis each was experiencing at that period in life. An excellent example of this type of pathological partnership between two girls was described by Medlicott.[46] This was a retrospective study of the development of *folie à deux,* culminating in the death of the girls' mother.

It is interesting to note that in these four cases there appeared a pattern regarding the seriousness of pathology amongst the partners. In the two cases where the partners were not related, the children of the victims were the stronger and more influential, but more psychologically disturbed, whereas in the related partners (all brothers), the younger members were more disturbed, while the older brother was the stronger as well as being the instigator.

8. Suicide

In contrast to the killing of one adult by another in the course of an intimate relationship, where there is immediate grief following the death of the spouse, the adolescent experiences a sense of relief or liberation. Mourning is postponed and the risk of suicide is, therefore, markedly reduced. The reported incidence of attempted and successful suicides is low.[47] This is quite the contrary to the adult murderers, where attempted and successful suicides are far from unknown,[48] as is also suicide in non-homicidal adolescents.[49] We feel that the type of adolescent we are studying has been deprived of the ability to form a gratifying relationship with either or both parents and there is not, therefore, the same fear or threat of loss of an object as there is in marital homicide.

9. Management and Treatment

Unfortunately, the prodromal signs of homicide are all too often missed, even though several agencies may have been involved with the youth and his family prior to the incident. The youth himself may have gone to the authorities and requested that he be taken out of the home, only to be told to go back, or be taken back, to the inferno from whence he tried to escape. Here the adolescent is pleading for some external controls to be placed on him, but the paternalism that exists in our various professions dictates that at all costs a child should live with his right and lawful parents. So a tragedy that might have been averted occurs, following which, and only then, all our energies and systems, both moral and judicial, are mustered into action.

If such a case presents itself before the fact, it should be insisted upon that the whole family be involved in therapy.[50] Often these youths present special treatment problems, not only because they are subject to violent outbursts, but also because they are adolescents with all the attendant adolescent turmoil, identity diffusion, and ambivalent needs for independence. The essence of the therapeutic process is primarily to deal with the regressive transference of the patient's symbiotic relationship with the member of the family with whom he is in conflict. From there the therapist should partially enter into this 'oneness' with the patient, but he must be able to withdraw gradually so that the patient does not feel abandoned and thence retaliate. If the therapist can withdraw from this symbiosis and at the same time allow the patient to discover two separate people instead of one, then contact will have been made with reality.[51]

Further problems are encountered following the adolescent's arrest, namely, whether he or she will remain in the jurisdiction of the juvenile court or be sent for trial in the adult court. In the adult court they are disposed of according to whether or not they fit the criteria of the M'Naghten Rules.[52] Thus the adolescent is more often found to be sane under the law and subsequently convicted and sent to a penal institution, where he is left without help.

Prognosis is generally good, for the risk of further homicide is very low indeed in these cases. The process wherein murder is committed during adolescence is self-limiting and is not necessarily part of an on-going delinquent or psychopatholo-gical process. However, several authors, ourselves included, are at variance from the point of view of psychological morbidity. This seems to be dependent upon where the cases have been isolated. A high percentage of those described by McKnight, *et al.,*[53] were diagnosed as schizophrenia of one type or another, whereas in our group the incidence of severe mental illness was not as apparent. The reasons for this were that the McKnight cases were in a mental hospital, in contrast to ours, who were or are in prison and were not found legally insane.

10. Summary

In summary, some of the literature has been covered concerning the death of a family member caused by an adolescent. In all, 100 cases were reported, out of which a total of 27 adolescents committed matricide (14 cases), patricide (11 cases) or fratricide (2 cases). Although a unitary or compact theory of causation is not possible, precursory signs were noted. However, definite patterns and trends were observed in these families regarding their interactional behavior and psychopathology.

As to prevention and treatment, both these issues pose grave problems, for the premonitory signs are often ignored, to the detriment of those concerned. But the adolescent's problems do not end here, for many juvenile courts respond to the public's consternation regarding the offender by evading their responsibilities and remanding him as quickly as possible to the adult court, where, more often than not, he is sent to an adult penitentiary.

In comparison with adult murderers, suicide amongst these adolescents is comparatively rare. Instead, the adolescent experiences a sense of relief or liberation following the murder. The sense of liberation, however, does not prevent a delayed reaction that influences subsequent adjustment to life.

Finally, the prognosis for these adolescents rehabilitation is good, both from the point of view of recidivism and of any psychopathological state that underlies the homicidal act. As the offence is committed in a specific conflict within the family, it is self-limiting and it is not among these adolescent murderers that we usually find an on-going delinquent process.

NOTES

1. Cormier, B. M.; Angliker, C. C. J.; Boyer R.; Kennedy, M.; and Mersereau, G., "The Psychodynamics of Homicide Committed in a Specific Relationship" (Jan., 1971), 13 *Canadian Journal of Criminology and Corrections* no. 1, 1-8; Cormier, B. M., *et al.,* "The Psychodynamics of Homicide Committed in a Semi-Specific Relationship" (April, 1972), 14 *Canadian Journal of Criminology and Corrections* no. 4, 335-344; and Cormier, B. M., *et al.,* "The Psychodynamics of Homicide Committed in a Non-Specific Relationship" (unpublished paper).

2. Bender, L., "Children and Adolescents Who Have Killed." Bender, L., and Curran, F. J., "Children and Adolescents Who Kill". Both articles appear in (April, 1940), 1 *J. Crim. Psychopath.* no. 4.

3. Angliker, C. C. J.; Cormier, B. M.; and Gagné, P. W., "Death of a Family Member — The Adolescent Who Kills", paper presented at the 7th International Congress of Criminology, Belgrade, Yugoslavia, Sept. 1973.

4. Briguet-Lamarre, M., *L'Adolescent meurtrier.* Toulouse: Ed. E. Privat, 1969.

5. Briguet-Lamarre, M., *ibid;* Bridgeman, O., "Four Young Murderers" (April, 1929), 13 *J. Juv. Res.* 90-96; Brown, W., *Murder Rooted in Incest.* New York, New York: Ace Books, 1970; Duncan, J. W., and G. M., "Murder in the Family: A Study of Some Homicidal Adolescents" (May, 1971), 127 *Amer. J. Psychiat.* no. 11. See also, McKnight, C. K.; Mohr, J. W.; Quinsey, R. E.; and Erochko, J., "Matricide and Mental Illness" (Mar./April, 1966), 2 *Can. Psychiat. Assoc. J.* no. 2; Medlicott, R. W., "Paranoia of the Exalted Type in a Setting of Folie à Deux. A Study of Two Adolescent Homicides" (1955), 28 *Brit. J. of Med. Psychol.,* and Scherl, D. J., and Mack, J. E., "A Study of Adolescent Matricide" (Oct., 1966), 5 *J. Amer. Acad. Child Psychiat.* no. 4.

6. Briguet-Lamarre, M., *op. cit.,* note 4. Duncan, J. W., and G. M. *ibid.* and Malmquist, C. P., "Premonitory Signs of Homicidal Aggression in Juveniles" (Oct., 1971), 128 *Amer. J. Psychiat.* no. 4.

7. Briguet-Lamarre, M., *op. cit.,* note 4. Carek, D. J., and Watson, A. S., "Treatment of a Family Involved in Fratricide" (Nov., 1964), 2 *Arch. of Gen. Psychiat.*

8. Bridgeman, O., "Four Young Murderers"; Medlicott, R. W., "Paranoia of the Exalted Type . . ." and Scherl, D. J., and Mack, J. E., "A Study of Adolescent Matricide", *op. cit.,* note 5.

9. Mohr, J. W., and McKnight, C. K. "Violence as a Function of Age and Relationship With Special Reference to Matricide" (1971), 16 *Canad. Psychiat. Assoc. J.*

10. Bridgeman, O., "Four Young Murderers", *supra.*

11. Briguet-Lamarre, M., *L'Adolescent meurtrier, supra.*

12. Brown, W., *Murder Rooted in Incest, supra.*

13. Carek, D. J., and Watson, A. S., *op. cit.,* note 7.

14. Duncan, J. W., and G. M., *supra.*

15. Malmquist, C. P., *op. cit.,* note 6.

16. McKnight, *et al.* (Mar./April, 1966) 2 *Can. Psychiat. Assoc. J.* no. 2

17. Medlicott, R. W., *supra.*

18. Scherl, D. J., and Mack, J. E., "A Study of Adolescent Matricide", *supra.*

19. Statistics Canada. *Homicide in Canada: A Statistical Synopsis.* Ottawa, June 1976.

20. Russell, D. H., "A Study of Juvenile Murders" (1965), 9 *J. of Offender Therapy* no. 3, and Malmquist, C. P., "Premonitory Signs of Homicidal Aggression in Juveniles", *supra.*

21. Erikson, E. H., "Identity and the Life Cycle, Selected Papers, Monograph I" (1968), 1 *Psychological Issues* no. 1, 176-178. (New York: International Universities Press).

22. Mohr, J. W., and McKnight C. K., "Violence as a Function of Age and Relationship With Special Reference to Matricide", *op. cit.,* note 9.

23. Cormier, B. M., "Psychodynamics of Homicide Committed in a Marital Relationship", (1962), 8 *Corrective Psychiatry and Journal of Social Therapy* no. 4.

24. Mohr, J. W., and McKnight, C. K., *supra.*

25. Klein, M., *et al.* (eds.), *New Directions in Psycho-Analysis.* New York, New York: Basic Books Inc., 1955.

26. Cavallin, H., "Incestuous Fathers: A Clinical Report" (1966), 122 *Amer. J. Psychiat.* 1132-38.

27. Cormier, B. M.; Kennedy, M.; and Sangowicz, J. M., "Psychodynamics of Father-Daughter Incest" (Oct., 1962), 7 *Can. Psychiat. Assoc. J.* no. 5, 203-217; and see Cormier, B. M., and Kennedy, M., "Father-Daughter Incest: Treatment of a Family", *Interdisciplinary Problems in Criminology: Papers of the American Society of Criminology,* 1964. Columbus: Ohio State University, 1965, pp. 191-96.

28. Sargent, D., "Children Who Kill: A Family Conspiracy?" (1962), 7 *Social Work* 35-42.
29. Menninger, K., and Mayman, M., "Episodic Dyscontrol: A Third Order of Stress Adaptation" (July, 1956), 20 *Bull. Menninger Clin.* no. 4.
30. *Op. cit.,* note 2.
31. Wetham, F., "The Catathymic Crisis. A Clinical Entity" (April, 1937), 37 *Archives of Neurology and Psychiatry* 974-978.
32. Malmquist, C. P., *supra.*
33. *Op. cit.,* note 5.
34. Scherl, D. J., and Mack, J. E., *supra.* Easson, W. M., and Steinhilber, R. M., "Murderous Aggression by Children and Adolescents" (Jan., 1961), 4 *Archives of General Psychiatry.*
35. Easson, W. M., and Steinhilber, R. M., *ibid.*
36. Briquet-Lamarre, M., *supra,* and see Brown, W., *Murder Rooted in Incest, op. cit.,* note 5.
37. Brown, W., *ibid.*
38. *Ibid.*
39. *Op. cit.,* note 6.
40. Malmquist, C. P., *supra.*
41. Briguet-Lamarre, M., *supra* and see Carek, D. J., and Watson, A. S., *op. cit.,* note 7.
42. Bender, L., and Curran, F. J., "Children and Adolescents Who Kill" (April, 1940), 1 *J. Crim. Psychopath.* no. 4.
43. *Op. cit.,* note 41.
44. Carek, D. J., and Watson, A. S., *supra.*
45. Duncan, J. W., and G. M., *supra* and refer also to the article by Medlicott, R. W. (1955), 28 *Brit. J. of Med. Psychol.*
46. Medlicott, R. W., *ibid.*
47. Bender, L., and Curran, F. J., *supra;* Briguet-Lamaree, *L'Adolescent meurtrier,* and McKnight, C. K., *et al., op. cit.,* note 5.
48. West, D. J., *Murder Followed by Suicide.* Cambridge, Mass.: Harvard University Press, 1966.
49. Toolan, J. M., "Suicide and Suicidal Attempts in Children and Adolescents" (Feb., 1962), 118 *Amer. J. Psychiat.* no. 8
50. Carek, D. J., and Watson, A. S., *supra.*
51. Smith, S. "The Adolescent Murderer. A Psychodynamic Interpretation" (Oct., 1965), 13 *Archives of General Psychiatry.*
52. *Ibid.*
53. McKnight, C. K., *et al., supra.*

Chapter 32

L'inceste: problèmes posés et point de vue d'un juge

*J.P. Peigné**

Le statut particulier des Juges des Enfants en France fait que si l'institution a été créée en 1945, pour juger et assurer le mieux-être des jeunes délinquants avec un rôle très particulier (puisque nous suivons la procédure, jugeons le mineur, assurons l'éxécution de nos décisions, et pouvons à tout moment les modifier pour mieux les adapter aux besoins en évolution de jeune concerné), nous avons reçu en 1958 une nouvelle tâche considérable; celle d'assurer, dans le cadre de procédures d'Assistance Educative, la charge, avec l'autorité administrative, de la protection des jeunes en danger. Cette tâche absorbe maintenant les deux tiers de notre activité, avec des techniques similaires à celles créées en 1945 pour les jeunes délinquants. A ces titres, et surtout comme Juge de l'Assistance Educative, Juge de la Protection de l'Enfance, j'ai eu à connaître tant en province (en Normandie) que dans la région parisienne de nombreuses situations où l'inceste était établi, et poursuivi, ou de nombreux cas où il était seulement envisagé, ou même présumé.

Tout fait de violences est déplorable, surtout quand les jeunes en sont les victimes, mais il s'y ajoute en matière d'inceste un profond sentiment de dégoût; un tel comportement ne peut engendrer que la sanction et le malheur: Oedipe ayant épousé sa mère s'est crevé les yeux. A vrai dire ce sentiment de dégoût laisse les sociologues un peu indécis; il est lié au problème du Tabou mais résulterait plus d'une évolution de la civilisation que de raisons valables. Pour Lévi-Strauss l'inceste est prohibé par une démarche culturelle; pour Altavilla "les rapports sexuels avec un proche parent ne sont en opposition avec acune règle biologique, et c'est seulement l'évolution du sentiment éthico-familial présent chez l'individu moyen, qui rend l'acte répugnant".[1]

Il est certain qu'à tout moment de l'histoire de l'homme et de sa sexualité on retrouve cette ambiguité en ce qui concerne l'inceste. Selon Germaine Tillon,[2] dans la société très primitive l'endogamie qui aurait été la pratique antérieure, a cédé la place à l'exogamie, qui ne serait donc pas un fait naturel mais serait née de l'obligation pour les premiers hommes d'assurer la sécurité de leurs zones de chasses. Nous retrouverons une idée analogue dans la culture chrétienne sous un concept proche. Egyptiens et Iraniens connaissaient l'inceste, et également les

---

* Vice-Président, Tribunal de Grande Instance de Créteil, France.

empereurs précolombiens, Osiris et Isis étaient frère et soeur avant de devenir mari et femme, et toute l'humanité serait issue de cet inceste illustre.

Le droit du mariage de l'ancienne France, très marqué par le droit Canon, le droit de l'Eglise, n'a connu en ses débuts, à l'encontre des incestueux que des sanctions spirituelles; un Capitulaire, dit de Verberie, prévoyait en 758, la simple interdiction de contracter mariage. Les livres de pénitence de la vieille église romaine, souvent peu connus des criminologues, contiennent des renseignements précieux: essentiellement des sanctions spirituelles; on nous a signalé, relevée dans un manuscrit Irlandais ou Gallois du IX° siècle, la phrase suivante "frater cum frater naturale fornicatione par commixtionen carnis, XII annos ab omni carne abstineat" ainsi l'homosexualité entre "frères" était sanctionnée par un régime végétarien.

Dans la vieille Europe, et en tout cas en France, le droit de l'Eglise a pratiquement exclu toute intervention des pouvoirs politiques jusqu'à la Renaissance, et à l'affermissement du pouvoir royal à la fin du moyen-âge. La centralisation des Rois Capétiens au XVI° siècle et la réaction après le Concile de Trente devaient renforcer la répression dans notre domaine. Le 2 Décembre 1603 en place de Grève, à Paris, étaient décapités un frère et une soeur; Pierre de L'Estoile, qui a laissé un journal fameux, a assisté à l'éxécution et a écrit "Ils étaient si beaux, qu'on eût dit que la nature avait pris plaisir à les former pour faire voir un de ses miracles". Les enfants du sieur Ravalet, seigneur de Tourlaville, près de Cherbourg, moururent ainsi. Le Roi Henri IV ne put les gracier, mais accepta de veiller à leur inhumation en terre chrétienne, et les magistrats par compassion, selon Philippe Erlanger, voulurent bien qu'ils soient décapités, et non brûlés, selon ce qu'aurait exigé la coutume. Le sieur de Tourlaville se voyait par ailleurs chargé d'assurer l'éducation de son petit-fils. Les amours prétendus du Régent Philippe d'Orléans avec sa fille, après la mort de Louis XIV, firent scandale mais rien de sérieux ne fut prouvé.

Phénomène de tous les temps, difficile à interpréter, reposant sur une certaine ambiguité, l'inceste reste présent dans notre monde, encore que dans certaines cultures il soit à peu près inconnu, notamment dans les pays de tradition musulmane.

Quelle est son importance dans les pays de culture occidentale? Il est évidemment difficile de donner des chiffres. Les études faites pour le Colloque d'Evreux en 1973 permettaient de penser que de tels agissements, dans la mesure où ils sont connus, d'après les chiffres de l'activité judiciaire dans ce domaine, concernent à peu près 300 cas par an en France, soit 6 cas pour un million d'habitants. Cette proportion paraît finalement très proche de celle relevée à l'issue d'études parallèles concernant d'autres pays de niveaux socio-économiques comparables du monde occidental.

Le "chiffre noir" est certainement fort important. Selon Di Tullio: "l'inceste est un délit très important en raison de sa diffusion, qui est certainement supérieure à celle que donnent les statistiques". Ces agissements sont liés au cadre familial, et souvent avec, nous le verrons, la complicité consciente ou non du groupe. Pourtant on peut penser que le "chiffre noir" n'est pas excessif du moins dans les campagnes où beaucoup de choses finissent par se savoir, où chacun est au courant de l'essentiel de ce qui se passe chez le voisin. Le chiffre noir est sans doute beaucoup plus important dans les villes, dans l'entassement anonyme des grands ensembles d'habitation, où chacun reste chez soi et ne connaît même pas ses voisins de palier.

Certains ont voulu également user d'un "chiffre gris" en parlant de ces situations préincestueuses fréquentes, connues par tous les travailleurs sociaux; leur rôle de prévention est alors essentiel.

En France même des différences appréciables peuvent être décelées selon les régions; curieusement les régions du Sud où depuis toujours est exploitée la vigne, qui suppose d'ailleurs une véritable spécialisation professionnelle un travail de tous les jours, sont beaucoup moins affectées que les régions très urbanisées, industrielles et surpeuplées du Nord, ou que les régions de l'Ouest où dominent l'élevage d'un part et la culture du pommier. Des recherches plus précises seraient sans doute à faire sur ces questions, qu'il faudrait relier peut être à la fréquence et au mode des suicides. Des collègues magistrats du Parquet du Procureur de la République ayant exercé d'une part en Normandie puis dans le Midi nous ont fait part de leur étonnement en constatant la rareté des incestes dans cette dernière partie de la France.

Dans certains pays, l'inceste est puni en tant que tel (voir article 564 du Code Pénal Italien). Il est punissable d'une peine d'emprissonnement de 1 à 5 ans, encore faut-il qu'il résulte des faits "un scandale public". C'est dans ce droit une infraction contre la morale familiale. Le droit français plus ancien à cet égard considère l'inceste comme une infraction essentiellement contre la morale sexuelle. Ce sont des infractions considérées généralement comme des "crimes", c'est à dire, comme de la plus extrême gravité, par rapport aux contraventions et aux délits. Il faut bien distinguer le sens du mot "crime" en droit français. Il est sans lien avec la notion du droit anglosaxon où ledit mot concerne toutes les infractions. En tant que crimes, les faits d'inceste sont jugés par la Cour d'Assises, et sont réprimés non en tant que faits incestueux mais en tant qu'infractions à la loi sexuelle pour l'application desquelles on prend en considération l'âge de la victime (plus ou moins de 15 ans, l'existence ou l'absence de violences, l'existence s'il y a lieu d'un lien de parenté avec l'auteur des faits, ou la situation d'autorité de celui-ci par rapport à la victime; par exemple le beau-père sur l'enfant de sa femme né d'un autre mariage). Des peines (articles 332 et 333 du Code Pénal) dans la dernière rédaction de 1863 vont jusqu'à la prison, à perpétuité: (attentat avec violence, sur mineure de 15 ans par ascendant).

Dans la pratique et devant le caractère peut-être excessif de ces peines le Procureur de la République négligera volontairement de retenir certains aspects des faits et ne retiendra que des infractions de violences sans préciser par exemple qu'il s'agissait de violences sexuelles; l'affaire sera jugée par le Tribunal correctionnel composé de trois magistrats professionnels, la répression sera plus stable, plus modérée et moins traumatisante pour la victime.

Comment sont déclenchées les poursuites pénales? Comment les faits viennent-ils à la connaissance de la justice? En Normandie on a constaté que dans 40% des cas la mère ou la victime ont porté plainte contre leur mari ou pére. En fait bien souvent elles se rétractent dans les jours suivants. Dans un tiers des cas la découverte est liée à des enquêtes administratives ou judiciaires sans lien aucun avec les faits d'inceste. J'ai connu des faits de nécrophilie qui ont amené l'arrestation du chef de famille, veuf, qui avait par ailleurs abusé de ces deux filles adolescentes.

L'inceste commis par un père, ou un beau-père sur une jeune fille est de beaucoup le plus fréquent; 75 à 80% des cas, et c'est de lui que nous parlerons surtout. Les incestes mère/fils sont rarement relevés, est-ce la force du tabou? Des cas d'inceste frère/soeur ne sont pas rares. Pour certaines psychiâtres ce seraient plutôt la continuation des jeux sexuels de l'enfance.

Quelles sont les conditions d'existence les plus fréquemment relevées et qui paraissent donc favoriser les faits? Le Professeur Kinberg, cité par les rédacteurs du rapport du groupe d'Evreux,[3] a étudié la situation en Suède et ses observations rejoignent exactement ce que nous avons constaté:

— isolement de la famille, sur les plans moraux, géographiques, ou sociaux;
— prédominance de cas dans la vie rurale;
— éthylisme, promiscuité, médiocrité intellectuelle et culturelle.

Il s'agit en effet dans le cas le plus fréquent de familles rurales; l'habitat dispersé dans l'Ouest de la France, le paysage de "bocage", sont sans doute des facteurs propices; les groupes sont en effet assez isolés. Le logement y est souvent médiocre, parents, ascendants et enfants sont entassés dans une grande promiscuité. Dans les zones très urbanisées, paradoxalement un tel entassement dans la solitude peuvent se retrouver comme je l'ai indiqué: les communications dans les grands ensembles sont bien souvent inexistantes. La famille ne possède que des valeurs "a-morales", et bien souvent des faits identiques se sont produits sans incidents dans les générations antérieures. L'inceste est accepté souvent par le groupe familial comme normal sinon inévitable.

Comment se présentent les divers protagonistes de ce drame? Le père: il est très souvent alcoolique, soumis à des pulsions. L'alcool exagère les pulsions agressives, facilite le premier passage à l'acte, estompe les freins moraux acquis éventuellement par l'éducation. Sa femme est souvent autoritaire, sans tendresse et castratrice. Il cherche des compensations affectives auprès des enfants et surtout des filles, ou bien il veut faire montre à leur égard d'une autorité qui lui est étrangère. C'est généralement un homme fruste, plutôt que débile. C'est rarement un malade mental, parfois pourtant, un paranoiaque. Il est âgé de 40 à 50 ans. Il est souvent immature et demande à sa femme de jouer en réalité un rôle maternel. Il est souvent travailleur manuel modeste et régulier, et apprécié en tant que tel.

La mère: comme il a été dit elle est parfois d'une autorité écrasante, c'est elle qui commande; en Normandie elle assure la vie financière quotidienne de la famille par la traite régulière des vaches et dispose ainsi d'un budget autonome. En fait le plus souvent elle est absente soit physiquement — décédée, ou malade ou en train d'accoucher lors du premier passage à l'acte — soit psychologiquement. Elle craint de nouvelles grossesses, et préfère se consacrer aux enfants déjà présents; elle peut vivre par ailleurs une aventure sentimentale que peut justifier le comportement brutal et alcoolique de son époux. Souvent on a constaté qu'elle avait eu un rôle inducteur inconscient au début des relations entre sa fille et son mari. Elle peut être ambivalente pour d'autres raisons; l'enfant est né de relations antérieures au mariage avec un homme autre que le mari, celui-ci a reconnu et élevé l'enfant, mais ce dernier reste toujours la comme témoin d'un passé que l'on voudrait oublier.

La mineure: elle présente souvent des déficiences notamment intellectuelles, et elle paraît particulièrement suggestible, et même passive devant les exigences de son père. Bien souvent, à l'étonnement des enquêteurs, elle n'a pas découvert elle-même le caractère anormal du comportement de celui-ci. Elle ne s'en est rendue compte que longtemps après lors de conversations à l'école, ou à l'occasion du premier flirt. L'enfant victime de carences affectives du côté maternel a recherché des compensations du côté du père. Il faut d'ailleurs distinguer selon que la victime était prépubère ou adolescente. La signification de l'inceste et ses conséquences sont évidemment différentes. La première situation est grave et peut être assimilée à un viol, l'enfant alors agit souvent sous la menace de coups. Dans la deuxième situation on constate dans bien des cas que la jeune fille a voulu prendre la place de la mère absente ou pas assez présente; elle s'identifie à ce rôle de chef de famille. Elle gère l'argent, elle tire des avantages de sa situation privilégiée, soit pour se sauvegarder une liberté plus complète par ailleurs en faisant un certain chantage sur le père, soit pour exercer sa propre autorité sur la famille. On a pu constater parfois une attitude véritablement séductrice à l'égard du père. Pinatel aborde dans son traité le problème de la séduction de l'adulte par l'enfant. La mère ou la belle-mère pourra d'ailleurs être jalouse de la situation et sera à l'origine de la dénonciation. On a pu constater une véritable relation amoureuse entre les partenaires.

Le déclenchement des poursuites crée généralement un drame; quelquefois l'arrestation du père permet une véritable libération des uns et des autres mais cela reste exceptionnel. Intervention de la Police ou de la Gendarmerie; connaissance des faits par la presse; insécurite et traumatismes pour les enfants; railleries de leurs camarades d'école, généralement sans pitié; rejet du voisinage; audition de la victime, de autres membres de la famille; examens médicaux, comparutions multiples et spécialement à l'audience et arrestation du coupable. Comment réagissent les uns et les autres? Le père sauf dans certains cas, quand notamment il s'agit de personnalités paranoiaques, reconnaît généralement les faits mais il n'en comprend et n'admet que très difficilement le caractère répréhensible. Il n'a pas intégré certaines valeurs morales communes au groupe. La mère, au début, parle souvent de divorcer mais ne le fait que rarement. Elle est, selon l'expression populaire souvent entendue, alors "plus femme que mère". Elle a pu porter plainte pour se venger par exemple à l'issue d'une nouvelle scène de violences après boire, pour se rétracter ensuite. Sa position est difficile; en but aux commentaires du voisinage, elle est paniquée par le départ et l'arrestation de son mari, qui, malgré tout, travaillait régulièrement et apportait la paye dans le mènage pour élever les enfants. Elle présente souvent un sentiment de jalousie à l'égard de sa fille qui est évidemment plus jeune et bien souvent elle accusera l'adolescente d'avoir provoqué le père. Le Juge des Enfants devra intervenir et demander à un service social spécialisé de suivre l'évolution de la situation; il lui faudra parfois placer l'intéressée.

La mineure? elle devient le centre de la situation et peut jouer de ce rôle. Elle peut être l'objet de manoeuvres des autres membres de la famille pour qu'elle se rétracte; l'intervention judiciaire, même menée avec prudence, comme maintenant on s'y efforce, restera toujours traumatisante, les examens médicaux surtout. Les magistrats sont de plus en plus conscients de ces faits; voir les résultats des travaux d'un séminaire international tenu en mai 1976 à Genève sur le "problème de l'interrogatoire des mineurs par la police et la justice". Il faudra dans la mesure du possible avoir recours à des policiers du sexe féminin. Elle pourra subir des conséquences pendant longtemps des agissements paternels et de ce qui a suivi; frigidité surtout s'il y a eu véritablement acte de pédophilie de la part du père ou du beau-père. Parfois tendance à la prostitution, mais cette issue pouvait être le résultat d'une passivité antérieure à l'inceste et qui l'a provoqué dans une certaine mesure. Pourtant, dans la plupart des cas, heureusement et à la surprise des observateurs, les dégâts restent limités et l'intervention d'un service éducatif avec un équipement psychologique avec assistance d'un psychiatre suffisant pourra éviter des perturbations durables. Selon le Dr Blondel, "la pratique de l'inceste n'a pas habituellement les conséquences terrifiantes décrites dans les productions culturelles". Pendant la durée de la procédure, et pendant l'éxécution de la peine, le rôle du travailleur social sera fondamental: pour dédramatiser la situation vis à vis des intéréssés, réouvrir les contacts avec l'entourage, traiter ou placer la victime, régler les problèmes matériels.

Le retour du délinquant posera de nouveaux problèmes; la répression est souvent inefficace, le condamné n'intégrera jamais les valeurs qui l'aurait empêché de commettre les faits, ou très exceptionellement. Il n'admet pas la répression et la considère comme profondément injuste. Bien souvent les codétenus, condamnés pour d'autres infractions, par exemple contre les biens, se livreront sur lui à des sévices, et il faut envisager sa propre protection pendant sa détention. Un établissement a été spécialisé en France, en Corse, à Casabianda, pour recevoir les condamnés de ce genre à de longues peines. La pratique habituelle du sursis avec mise en probation permettra à un Juge spécialisée, le Juge de l'application des Peines de prendre en charge le libéré avant l'expiration de la totalité de la peine. Avec une équipe éducative spécialisée, il pourra imposer certaines obligations à l'ancien détenu; par exemple subir une désintoxication antialcoolique, qui en fait aura souvent eu lieu en détention, ou se présenter régulièrement à un dispensaire d'hygiène mentale, etc. Le problème de la remise au travail se posera, rendue difficile si l'intéréssé revient dans le même pays. La reprise des contacts avec les enfants, s'ils sont encore mineurs, notamment la victime, est préoccupante: vengeance éventuelle, parfois récidive. Il est arrivé que le père et la victime devenue majeure partent pour vivre ensemble. Le rôle d'un service social spécialisé, chargé d'une mission d'éducation en milieu ouvert, est toujours nécessaire.

Le problème délicat des fausses dénonciations doit être envisagé. Elles sont très fréquentes et posent des problèmes considérables au Juge, surtout quand la famille était déjà considérée comme suspecte. La dénonciation pourra être le fait de la jeune fille; elle est enceinte et refuse de dire de quel garçon malgré les intérroga-toires pressants et maladroits du père, peut être lui-même un peu jaloux, mais qui s'est abstenu de tout contact sexuel avec la mineure. La jeune fille veut obtenir plus de liberté, et nous rencontrons souvent des problèmes de ce genre avec des enfants de travailleurs émigrants des pays de la Méditérranée, par exemple du Portugal, où l'autorité masculine et paternelle s'exerce sans nuance. La mineure qui va à l'école avec de jeunes Françaises supporte de plus en mal la comparaison entre sa vie à la maison et celle de ses camarades. La famille étrangère, elle même isolée pour des raisons diverses, et notamment de langue, se trouve dépendre par ailleurs de la mineure qui a assimilé la langue française. La dénonciation mensongère émane souvent de la femme elle-même qui veut refaire sa vie avec un ami plus agréable et veut divorcer ou, qui, ayant divorcé, peut faire disparaître les droits de visite accordés à son conjoint par le jugement de divorce.

Dans tous ces cas l'intervention de services sociaux mandatés par le Juge des Enfants sera nécessaire et les Magistrats chargés de la répression devront faire preuve d'une très grande prudence. Bien souvent on évitera de poursuivre.

Que conclure? l'inceste est fréquent, souvent méconnu, il est le fait le plus souvent de personnes n'ayant pas intégré, pour diverses raisons, des valeurs que nous croyons naturellement acquises par tous. La répression est inévitable mais le plus souvent mal adaptée, et elle peut elle-même entraîner des perturbations tout aussi graves que le mal à l'origine des poursuites. Une liaison constante entre les autorités de répression, les magistrats chargés de la protection de l'enfance et les services sociaux spécialisés est indispensable, et le personnel de magistrats et de travailleurs sociaux doit être préparé à cette tâche, sans illusion excessive.

Oedipe s'est crevé les yeux; mais au fait pour quelles raisons? pour avoir épousé sa mère, ou pour avoir tué son père Laius, lui-même déjà condamné par les dieux pour avoir enfreint un autre interdit sexuel. Oedipe est-il coupable ou victime?

RÉFERENCES

1. Cité par Di Tullio, *Principi di Criminologia Clinica et Psichiatrica Forensi* (Rome, 1960); Voir aussi: Szabo, "L'inceste en milieu urbain: Etude de la dissociation des structures familiales dans le département de la Seine" (1937-1954), *Année Sociologique* (1957) 58.
2. Tillon, G., *Le Harem et les Cousins.*
3. (Oct.-Dec., 1974) *Rev. sc. crim. de dr. pén. comp.* 967. Compte rendu des journées régionales de criminologie (Evreux 6-7 Juill. 1973) L'inceste en milieu rural.

BIBLIOGRAPHIE

Maisch, Ouvrage, Traduit de l'allemend par Spivac, E., Paris, Laffont, 1970. *L'inceste.*
Thèse Amet, Commandant de gendarmerie, thèse de doctorat, Paris II, 1974. *L'inceste en milieu rural.*
Etude Lutier (Janv.-Févr., 1961) *Ann. de médecine légale* 80-83, "Rôle des facteurs culturels et psychosociaux dans les délits incesteux en milieu rural."
Etude Auclair (Avr.-Juin, 1966) *Rev. dr. de sociologie* 215-228 (bibliographic). "Meurtre, inceste et énigme." (Etude comparée de presse.)
Etude Rassat; Sem. jur. 1974, 2614. "Inceste et droit penal".
Etude Marc; Compte rendu des journées de criminologie d'Evreux, Avr. 1973; (Avr.-Juin, 1973) *Rev. pénit. et de dr. pén.* 211, "Le juge de l'application des peines et l'inceste en milieu rural."

485   L'inceste: problèmes posés et point de vue d'un juge

Flandrin, *Les Amours paysannes, du XVIe au XIX°*. Collection Archives.

Kinberg, *Le problème de l'inceste en Suède.*

De Greef, *Condamnés d'assises pour affaires de moeurs.*

Lafon et autres, *Aspects psychologiques et sociaux des attentats sexuels sur les enfants et adolescents* (1957).

Scherrer: *La sexualité criminelle en milieu rural* (1958).

Chapter 33

Incest and the Law

Anthony H. Manchester*

There is an extensive anthropological, medical and sociological literature on
incest. This chapter is concerned solely with the legal process of incest. Reference
will be made, however, to the results of a survey of cases of incest in England
which resulted in a prosecution: a full analysis of that survey is given as an
appendix.

The laws of most countries frown upon incest. Yet not all countries punish incest
as such penally and even those countries whose criminal law does punish penally
an offence of incest differ widely in their definition of incest.

Certainly French law appears to frown upon incest. Carbonnier describes incest as
"un des tabous les plus profonds de l'humanité" and he goes on to describe the
conditions in which an incestuous union is prohibited at civil law. Yet the Code
Pénal knows no offence of incest. However, at article 331 of the Code Pénal
we do find that an ascendant who commits an indecent assault upon a minor not
yet emancipated by marriage shall be punished by solitary confinement.[1]
Similarly, the law of the Netherlands knows no offence of incest as such. Yet at
article 249 of the Penal Code of the Netherlands we do find a prohibition, which
is couched in very wide terms indeed, and which includes within its terms,
therefore, forms of conduct which are no doubt incestuous. Like comparisons can
be made with other criminal codes.[2] It is at least possible, therefore, that even
those countries which do not punish incest as such within their system of criminal
law, in fact may well punish incestuous conduct within the limits defined by other
criminal prohibitions.

Indeed, when we turn to the criminal law of England and Wales we can note the
existence of offences other than incest which are in a sense co-extensive with
certain of the more offensive forms of incestuous conduct. For example, it is an
offence to have unlawful sexual intercourse with a girl under 16 years of age.
Similarly, it can be an indictable offence for any person to make an indecent
assault on a woman, and a girl under 16 years of age cannot in law give any
consent which would prevent an act being an indecent assault.[3] If force is used,
the defendant may be charged with rape.

---

* Faculty of Law, University of Birmingham, England.

However, our existing law of incest as a criminal offence does go rather beyond this. And we are not alone in this respect. For example, Scotland,[4] the Australian states,[5] Canada,[6] New Zealand,[7] the American states,[8] South Africa,[9] Austria,[10] the Federal Republic of Germany[11] and Sweden[12] all punish incest as a criminal offence. Indeed, it is possible to specify three factors which are common to all jurisdictions (certainly to the English speaking jurisdictions) so far as their definitions of incest are concerned. First, the parties must be within specified degrees of relationship. Secondly, one at least of the parties must have been aware of that relationship. Finally, sexual intercourse must have taken place between the parties. However, the jurisdictions do differ very considerably on the first point *i.e.,* as to just what relationships are to be regarded as incestuous at criminal law. Some (Scotland and California[13] are examples) cover a wide range of relationships. Others *e.g.,* Illinois[14] and South Australia[15] cover a limited range of relationships.

Such disparity means that there is little point in comparing the criminal statistics of the countries concerned with a view to casting some light upon the international incidence of incest. England and Wales, for example, do not regard as incestuous at criminal law, acts which the law of Scotland declares are indeed punishable as incest at criminal law.

In the light of such uncertainty regarding the proper bounds of incest as a criminal offence, or even whether it should be a special criminal offence at all, it is perhaps appropriate that in England and Wales the Criminal Law Revision Committee is examining the law in the context of a survey of sexual offences generally. Scotland, too, is presently re-examining the forbidden degrees of matrimony. In Sweden the Sexual Offences Commission has only recently made radical recommendations. The Canadian Law Reform Commission is considering the question of sexual offences generally, including incest: it is probable that the Netherlands will commence a similar survey quite soon. In Australia the A.C.T. has reviewed its law of incest and South Australia, although it rejected the advice of its law reform committee that the offence of incest be dispensed with altogether, it did alter its law of incest considerably.

1. The History of Incest in England and Wales

It was only in 1908 that incest became punishable as a criminal offence in the ordinary courts of the country and this new criminal offence was restricted to certain relationships *inter consanguines.*[16] A person who had entered into a marriage within the much more widely drawn prohibited degrees of matrimony had always been liable to be proceeded against in one of the country's numerous ecclesiastical courts. Proceedings for incest were regarded as a species of the spiritual jurisdiction of those courts; they were said to be proceeded upon in the way of criminal suits *pro salute animae,* and for the lawful correction of manners. It was the duty of the churchwarden to present alleged offenders to the ordinary.[17] Punishment, which was through the medium of what Blackstone described as "the feeble coercion of the spiritual court",[18] was by means of monition, penance, excommunication, suspension *ab ingressu Ecclesiae,* suspension from office and deprivation.[19] In the case of lay people the most appropriate of the punishments were penance and excommunication.

Such proceedings were very rare, however, even in the early nineteenth century. The Ecclesiastical Commissioners so reported in 1832 and went on to comment:

It may be greatly doubted whether any beneficial effects have resulted from these proceedings, or at least so beneficial as to counterbalance the odium they have excited, and the oppression which, in some few instances, has been exercised.[20]

Those comments went to the jurisdiction which the ecclesiastical courts exercised in cases of adultery and of fornication as well as of incest. The Commissioners went on to suggest that incest was "a species of offence of so aggravated a character, that some remedy ought to be substituted," if ecclesiastical proceedings were to be abolished, and they recommended that it should become an offence punishable by fine and limited imprisonment in the courts of common law.[21]

That recommendation was not accepted. In fact the country agonized over the question of the prohibited degrees, and most especially over the prohibition of marriage with the sister of a deceased wife, throughout the rest of the nineteenth century. In 1848 a Royal Commission noted that legislation had failed to attain its object in that it "has not prevented marriage with the sister, or niece, of a deceased wife from taking place in numerous instances."[22] After reviewing the arguments for and against the existing law, the Commissioners doubted "whether any measure of a prohibitory character would be effectual. These marriages will take place when a concurrence of circumstances give rise to mutual attachment: they are not dependent on legislation." Accordingly, the Commissioners were "not inclined to think" that such attachments and marriages would be extensively increased in number were the law to permit them.[23] Yet the majority opinion of the day was to permit no such reform, despite repeated attempts to change the law, until in 1907 the Deceased Wife's Sister's Marriage Act pemitted marriage between a man and his deceased wife's sister. Other amendments were made until the present position at civil law regarding the prohibited degrees was settled in 1949.[24]

The first attempt to make incest a crime punishable before the ordinary courts of the country was made in 1903, a second Bill was brought forward in 1907. Upon that Bill being reintroduced in 1908, it became law as the Punishment of Incest Act. That Act was repealed in 1956: the present law regarding incest as a criminal offence is as stated in the consolidating Sexual Offences Act of 1956.

The private member who introduced the Bill of 1903 said that he had been induced to do so by the number of such crimes being committed in the rural districts.[25] This view was supported by another member who said that careful inquiries which he had made led him to believe that cases did very often occur both in large towns and rural districts. He was impressed also by the fact that many American States and, more especially, Scotland recognized incest as a criminal offence.[26] However, the Lord Chancellor, the Earl of Halsbury, succeeded in having the measure withdrawn. He maintained that private inquiry was not the mode by which a complete alteration of the criminal law was to be justified. Moreover, he believed that some portions of the press would give publicity to reports of the trial of such cases although these were cases which it was inadvisable to bring into the light of day.[27] Yet when a similar argument was put to the House in 1908 — the House should hesitate, one member maintained, before making a sweeping addition to the criminal law at a late period on a Friday afternoon at the instigation of a private member — it was unsuccessful.[28] On this occasion it was clear that the government supported the measure. Thus the Under-Secretary of State for the Home Department commented:

The Home Office had been long aware from the reports they received from the police and other sources, that it was exceedingly necessary to add to the law provisions of the character proposed by this Bill. . . . He doubted whether anyone could say with any degree of certainty either that it was increasing or that it was decreasing, but it was quite certain that the offence was by no means rare, and it was essential that some steps should be taken by the Legislature to put a stop to it. It was not merely the case of a moral offence affecting grown up people, but it might entail consequences of a disastrous kind on the offspring which sometimes followed from such intercourse, and from that point of view society had a special interest that should lead to steps being taken to put a stop to it. Nor was it the case that in Scotland the law was a dead letter. Every year there were a small number of convictions — on the average six each year — which showed that the law was necessary and that it could be put into force. So far from there being a danger, through this Bill, of persons being accused of the crime without being able to disprove it, he was afraid that, on the contrary, the danger would be found to be the great difficulty in proving the cases.[29]

Another supporter of the Bill stressed the 'great frequency' of incest. Thus the National Society for the Prevention of Cruelty to Children was said to have informed the Home Office that during the previous twelve months it had had experience of 42 cases of incest, some of which were of the 'most appalling nature'. It also appeared, *inter alia,* that in 193 cases of rape and carnal knowledge of girls which came before the Home Office on petitions for remission of sentence, the criminal intercourse was incestuous in no fewer than 51 cases.[30]

It was suggested that the mischief was really very small and also that the spread of education would do away with 'this evil'.[31] Yet after little public debate upon what those members who did take part clearly saw as a distasteful topic, the measure became law. Perhaps the then Lord Chancellor, Lord Loreburn, best summed up the legislative attitude when he said:

The question is whether this will be an effective remedy. There is no other remedy known to the law except to punish people who commit acts which are considered to be crimes. I cannot help thinking that it is better that the community should stignatize as a crime that which is a crime in substance, seeing that it produces not only moral depravity but also physical deterioration.[32]

2. The Law

The Sexual Offences Act 1956 provides that it is an offence for a man to have sexual intercourse with a woman whom he knows to be his grand-daughter, daughter, sister or mother. In like fashion it is an offence for a woman of the age of 16 or over to permit her grandfather, father, brother or son to have sexual intercourse with her by consent.[33] The statute provides that 'sister' includes half-sister, that 'brother' includes half-brother, and that for the purposes of those subsections any expression importing a relationship between two people shall be taken to apply notwithstanding that the relationship is not traced through lawful wedlock.[34] Incest is punishable by imprisonment not exceeding seven years. Yet if the intercourse is with a girl under 13, imprisonment may be for life. The punishment for attempting to commit the offence is imprisonment not exceeding two years. However, no prosecution for incest or for attempted incest may be brought without the sanction of the Attorney-General, except by or on behalf of the Director of Public Prosecutions. Finally, upon a man having been indicted for incest, the jury may find the defendant guilty of intercourse with a girl under 16 years of age.

A. Preventive Administrative Measures in General.

Some years ago the Ingleby Report suggested that preventive work could be considered in terms of four quite separate stages, namely: discovery and referral, the recording of referrals, investigation, and enforcement.[35] In the light of suggestions that a coordinated approach be adopted, the Department of Health and Social Security in 1975 invited local authorities to encourage area health authorities and local authorities jointly to set up area review committees to coordinate action between professionals with regard to potential or actual cases of non-accidental injury to children, case conferences would be used to discuss individual cases. Some steps have been taken along these lines.[36] This emergent administrative procedure was designed to assist the physically injured child. Yet there is no reason why the name of a child under 16 years who is involved, or thought to be involved, in an incestuous relationship should not be placed on the register and this may already be done in some areas.

The success of such a scheme is dependent on several factors. A greater public and professional awareness of the problem and of how to deal with it must be encouraged: there is an especially low level of suspicion in cases of incestuous conduct. The law must respect the wishes of those *bona fide* informants who wish to remain anonymous.[37] Information available within the responsible agencies must be shared more readily. Social workers and police officers must be encouraged to cooperate.[38] Above all, perhaps, there should be effective, continuing monitoring of such arrangements. Certainly the position at present appears to be that the system is not working well,[39] and incest does not figure very much, if at all, within the area of suspicion.

It is the duty of the Social Services Department to investigate all cases of suspected incest, in the light of the statutory requirement that they inquire into all cases where information is received which suggests that there are grounds for bringing care proceedings.[40] So in the typical case of a father's incest with a young daughter, care proceedings could be brought on the ground that the daughter was in moral danger. If it seems that an offence may have been committed, the Social Services Department is under a duty so to inform the police,[41] whether it does so in all cases is doubtful.

In many other instances incestuous conduct is not prosecuted either because an individual police officer, social worker, or other potential complainant, including members of the family, reject that possibility. We must assume that, if the incidence of incest really is much higher than the criminal statistics indicate, very many families are prepared either to ignore or to live with the fact that incest has occurred. For example, one case in the survey only came to light when the 43 year-old father became angry at his 14 year-old daughter staying out late and slapped her. Thereupon the daughter informed her mother of the incestuous relationship. At a family discussion with her sons, aged 20 and 18, the mother said that they must live down the affair within the family. However, she also discussed the matter with a neighbor who informed the police. The father was sentenced to three years imprisonment. Yet the wife, who blames herself for allowing the incestuous relationship to arise, wants her husband to return home once his sentence is completed. In such chance circumstances do quite a few cases of incest come to light. Nevertheless, it is submitted that few would deny that it was right to prosecute the father in this particular case.

Upon a complaint being made, the primary concern in the typical case of father-daughter incest is to protect the child. It is possible through the medium of relatively informal procedures to remove the child speedily to a place of safety.[42] By far the more common practice, however, is for the father to be removed from the home. Typically, he will be granted bail on condition that he has no further contact with his wife and daughter before his case is heard. Alternately, but much more rarely, he will be remanded in custody[43] e.g., if there is a danger of a repetition of the alleged offence. The survey shows that in 63 cases of father-daughter incest the father was granted bail in 45 (71.4 percent) cases: bail was refused in 18 (28.6 percent) cases. Moreover 10 of those 18 refusals came in two groups of cases which made up 20 out of the grand total of 63 cases. By contrast, the practice in many American states appears to be for the child to be removed from the home despite an awareness that this can often be harmful to the child.

B. Roles of Police and of D.P.P.

Simultaneously, it will be the duty of the police to assess the credibility of the complaint and, possibly with the aid of a Chief Prosecuting Solicitor, to determine whether the case should proceed further. Many accusations are false.[44] Even if the complaint appears to have been made *bona fide*, it may be difficult to prove any charge which may be brought in the absence of corroboration of the complaint or of an admission on the part of the suspect, for incest is virtually unrivalled among the criminal offences in terms of the opportunity for its commission. In fact one noteworthy feature of the process is of the high percentage of defendants in cases of incest who plead guilty.

So in the survey, defendants pleaded guilty to incest in 66 cases (86.8 percent) out of 76. In cases of father-daughter incest pleas of guilty were entered in 53 (86.9 percent) cases out of 61; in cases of brother-sister incest pleas of guilty were entered in 11 (91.7 percent) cases out of 12. The Criminal Statistics for 1976 do not give the relevant figures for incest. However, they do show that in sexual offences generally 47 percent of persons accused pleaded guilty. It is also worth noting, even at this stage, that of the eight fathers in the survey who pleaded not guilty, only one escaped punishment completely. Five were found guilty as charged and two pleaded guilty to lesser charges. In 61 cases of father-daughter incest, therefore, only one accused person both entered and was wholly successful in his plea of not guilty. In his case the sole evidence had been the word of his 12 year-old daughter. The judge directed the jury to find him not guilty. Yet in quite a few cases the evidence in corroboration of the complaint of incest may be slight. That fact, together with the tendency of some girls to fantasize[45] in such situations, make the decision to prosecute a difficult one in some cases. Nor should we ignore the pressure to plead guilty which a defendant in such a case may feel, rightly or wrongly, that he is under. Courts, quite rightly, may take a poor view of the defendant who appears clearly to have been guilty and yet who required his daughter to appear in court in such circumstances.

That admirable aim of saving the child from what may be the harrowing experience of giving evidence in court fits in well with that well known feature of American criminal practice, the negotiated guilty plea. Some American communities go further. One American commentator praised the practice of a small number of communities in which a staff member of the local Society for the Prevention of Cruelty to Children appears in court with the child victim and family as *amicus curiae* and opposes:

. . . unwarranted defense motions for adjournment; [he] will seek to have the case heard in privacy of the judge's chambers; [he] may seek to have the general public excluded from the courtroom; and . . . will work the county prosecutor toward accepting a guilty plea from the offender. If a guilty plea is accepted, there will not be a trial and the child will be saved the ordeal of testifying in court.[46]

Yet there are dangers in the practice. An American critic concludes that, "the practice of the negotiated guilty plea is thus wholly unacceptable as a means of protecting child victims of sex offences. It provides no care for children who are called to testify in courtrooms, and it mocks the constitutional rights of defendants, tempting them to yield to the instruments and pressures promoting the negotiated guilty plea. Thus, the practice falls short of accommodating the conflicting interests of the accused and the victims."[47]

In England and Wales there is less scope for the negotiated guilty plea. Yet the courts have attempted to indicate the bounds within which consultations may take place.[48] And research has pointed to the possibility that abuse may occur in a small number of cases.[49] Courts already have the power to order the public to be excluded from court during the taking of evidence from a child or young person in proceedings in relation to an offence against or any conduct contrary to decency or morality.[50]

The survey does not purport to explain why so high a proportion of guilty pleas are entered in cases of incest. Possibly some guilty parents welcome the opportunity to confess. Quite possibly many other probable cases of incest are not prosecuted as such for lack of corroboratory evidence with the result that only clear cases of incest are so prosecuted.

If it appears that the facts may form the basis for a charge of incest, the advice of the Director of Public Prosecutions must be sought, for incest is one of the large number of offences which the police must report to the D.P.P. with a view to the D.P.P. alone undertaking the prosecution. Each year the D.P.P. deals in all with more than 14,000 criminal cases. To assist him in this enormous task, the D.P.P. has 55 professional officers who are grouped into eight divisions, primarily on geographical lines. In all cases the first task is to ensure that there is no defect in the police file submitted *e.g.,* lack of jurisdiction. Then the office considers whether the facts reveal that there is a reasonable prospect of a conviction. It will then consider whether it is in the public interest to institute proceedings. The general policy is said to be one of flexibility. The staleness of the case, age and infirmity, mental illness and instability, public expense, may each be relevant factors, in addition, there is a number of factors which remain confidential.[51]

In one case in the survey, a wife, after consultation with a social worker, alleged that her husband had committed incest with her daughter. The wife made this allegation to a solicitor as she was initiating divorce proceedings. Indeed a child was born of the incestuous relationship. However, the D.P.P. decided not to prosecute; apparently a relevant factor was that the daughter did not wish the father to be charged. The daughter has since married and her husband has accepted the child born of the incestuous relationship with his wife's father. Moreover, the wife did not proceed with a divorce; she and the father are still together. In so far as the D.P.P.'s decision not to prosecute may have been made not because of any question of a difficulty regarding proof but rather on the wider ground of public interest, this case does appear to have been a bold use of such discretion. On the one hand it may well have served best the personal interests of the individuals directly involved. On the other hand it could be argued that the State surely had an interest in punishing such a flagrant breach of the law; the daughter, after all, was pregnant by the father.

Yet other cases in the survey suggest that on occasion prosecutions are brought in circumstances in which it is submitted that the public interest is less than clear. For example, a 21 year-old daughter who stated that she had had an incestuous relationship with her father since she was 11 approached Social Services with a view to obtaining medical and psychological help for her father. Yet eventually a prosecution for incest was instituted which resulted in the father being sentenced to two years imprisonment, suspended for two years, together with a supervision order. In another case a youth aged 16 pleaded guilty to incest with his 13 year-old sister. According to her own statement she was a willing partner who 'enjoyed it'. Her brother was sentenced to a two years supervision order. In another case the defendant brother was 56 years-old, his sister, who does not appear to have been charged, was 45 years-old. The brother was sentenced to three years probation.

Are not these examples of cases which would have been better disposed of in the first instance by not instituting proceedings on the ground that it was not in the public interest to do so? Such cases could be dealt with rather through the medium of what an appellate court recently called the 'social processes'. Very probably the sheer pressure of work may prevent the D.P.P. from really exercising a discretion effectively. Equally, the divisional organization of the office by geographical area together with the fact that there are relatively few cases of incest probably militate against the gathering and applying consistently of a body of principle which might govern the exercise of discretion in cases of incest.

In what circumstances, then, may the public interest suggest that a discretion be exercised not to press a charge of incest in circumstances where there is a reasonable prospect of a conviction? It is submitted that there are five such possible sets of circumstances. There is the case in which the sentence is likely to be no more than a conditional discharge, probation or a suspended sentence. For example, if a father who was suffering from emotional stress, perhaps due to the recent death of his wife or to the fact that he had just learned that he was suffering from a serious illness, consummated one act only of incestuous intercourse for which he later expressed sincere regret. Similarly, if the offence is unlikely to be repeated and not to press a charge of incest would be more likely to keep the family together and so assist the child in the long term, it is submitted that it could be in the public interest, though not necessarily so, not to press a charge of incest. Thirdly, it may appear desirable to protect a child, especially a young and sensitive child, from what could be the traumatic experience of giving evidence in court upon a charge of incest by accepting a plea of guilty to a lesser charge *e.g.,* indecent assault. Fourthly, it may not be in the public interest to press a charge of brother-sister incest against the brother in a case where the two are young, where there is no great disparity in age between them and where the younger person may have been a wholly willing partner to the incestuous act. Finally, it already appears to be unusual to charge the younger consenting woman with incest. The basis upon which this discretion is exercised appears to be that in the typical father-daughter case, the daughter will be deemed to have acted under the influence of the father; it is a consideration which illustrates just how close in practice the theoretically distinct offences of incest and rape may be.[52]

C. The Substantive Law

The definition of incest makes it clear that in law it is incest for a man to have sexual intercourse with a woman whom he knows to be his illegitimate daughter.[53] In such circumstances the law looks to the biological reality. Yet the law of incest does not protect the adopted daughter. Nor does it protect the stepdaughter. Nor, in the case of co-habitation, does it protect the daughter of one of the parties or any other child who has been accepted into or treated as one of the members of the family.

So far as the requirement of sexual intercourse is concerned, the courts have pointed out that there is a distinction between submission on the one hand and permission or consent on the other hand.[54] Yet in particular cases it will often be difficult to determine whether or not there was true consent, especially in the typical case of the young daughter. The young daughter, who does not truly appreciate the meaning of sexual intercourse, may not understand exactly what her father is doing. At a later stage she may be too frightened of her father to offer any objection. The statement of a young woman in a case in the survey illustrates the point well enough. When asked why she had permitted the relationship with her father in the first place some years before, she replied: "I didn't like what my father was doing to me but I was too frightened to say anything." Unsolicited suggestions of duress did occur in a number of cases in the survey.

Importance may be attached to corroboration of evidence. Thus it is the duty of the trial judge to warn the jury that, while it may convict on the testimony of an accomplice, it is dangerous to do so unless such evidence is corroborated.[55] For example, in *R. v. Draper*[56] it was held that, if on any of the material dates alleged in the indictment for incest the female had reached the age of 16, she might be liable as an accomplice. Therefore, if she were a witness, her evidence must be corroborated. In fact in this case of alleged brother-sister incest, the only suggested corroboration of the sister's story was an alleged conversation between the appellant and his mother in the presence of his wife. Yet the defendant had denied the use of the alleged corroboratory expression and his wife was called for the defence.[57] The conviction was quashed.

A more thorny question still is the question of the admissibility of similar facts. In *R. v. Ball*[58] a brother and sister were charged with incest. Evidence was given to the effect that the defendants were seen together at night in the same house, which contained only one furnished bedroom and there was in that bedroom a double bed which bore signs of two persons having occupied it. The prosecution then tendered evidence to show that these persons had previously known each other carnally and had had a child. The object was to establish they they had a guilty passion towards each other, and that therefore the proper inference from their occupying the same bedroom and the same bed was an inference of guilt so that the defence of innocent living together as brother and sister ought rightly to fail. The admissibility of such evidence did not help to convict the defendants of the crime with which they were charged by proving that they had committed some other crime, said Lord Loreburn, rather did such evidence go directly to prove the actual crime for which the parties were indicted. In principle the distinction may be clear enough: in practice it may often be less so.[59]

Other legal systems are well aware of the problem. Yet in a comparative sense perhaps the most interesting points are the widely differing nature of the definitions of incest in so far as the forbidden relationships are concerned and, to a rather lesser extent, the problems which this could cause to visitors to a country. The forbidden degrees of relationship do vary enormously. Often such degrees may correspond, roughly at all events, with the degrees which are prohibited at civil law for the purposes of marriage. This is true of Scotland, of South Africa, and of a number of the United States. Other countries limit the forbidden relationships quite severely. This is true of South Australia and of the American State of Illinois. Other countries have taken up an intermediate position *e.g.,* various Australian states, Austria, Canada, England and Wales, the Federal Republic of Germany, New Zealand, Sweden, and some of the United States.[60]

One factor which has probably contributed to this wide variation in practice is that in many countries the law is based upon the Biblical prohibitions which are contained in the book of Leviticus. Indeed, Scotland's Incest Act 1567 was based expressly upon Leviticus, Chapter 18, verses 6-18.[61] However, Leviticus is itself rather vague in respect of its general prohibition that no person shall approach to any that is near of kin to him. Such vagueness leads necessarily to a process of interpretation, the results of which may well differ from country to country.

Such disparity can be noted, for example with regard to the questions whether the criminal law of incest protects either the illegitimate or the adopted child. With regard to the effect of illegitimacy, Scots law is not clear. It does seem, however, that with the two possible exceptions of mother and bastard son, and father and bastard daughter, there can in Scotland be no incest between bastard relations.[62] With regard to the question whether it is incest to have sexual relations with an adopted child, the position is even more uncertain. Clive and Wilson state that "intercourse between a man and his adopted daughter is not incest, even although marriage between them is prohibited." On the other hand Gordon states that in strict theory it is incest to have connection with an adopted child but that in practice such connections would not be prosecuted as incest.[63]

D. Relationship with other Jurisdictions

In a situation where there is such disparity between jurisdictions as to how far to extend the forbidden relationships at criminal law, it is clear that problems might arise in determining whether to prosecute incest visitors to a country who are lawfully married according to the law of their own country. For example Scotland, South Africa and some American states regard as incestuous and punishable at criminal law relationships which are perfectly lawful unions according to other legal systems. This is true of relationships between affines. May the partners to such a lawful union be prosecuted for incest, then, when they are present in Scotland, South Africa, or the American states in question?

The American state of Louisiana has provided specifically for this situation by providing that the incest provisions:

. . . shall not apply where one, not a resident of this state at the time of the celebration of his marriage, shall have contracted a marriage lawful at the place of celebration and shall thereafter have removed to this state.[64]

Yet American authority generally is divided. And a South African writer comments: "If we recognize foreign marriages of this kind we must decline to prosecute the parties for incest when they have sexual intercourse within South Africa. But if we decline to prosecute them, should we not cease prosecuting South African citizens for the same conduct:"[65]

This is surely very much an area in which apathy and the exercise of a discretion not to prosecute has ruled.

3. Punishment[66]

Usually the offending father is sent to prison. Some years ago Walker was able to demonstrate that, of all offenders, the person convicted of incest was most likely to be sent to prison.[67] In 1969 Thomas wrote that in all cases involving parents the Court took a stern view of the offence and that sentences in the region of six years imprisonment were common, sentences below that level were generally the result of exceptional mitigating factors, and longer sentences had been upheld in cases involving aggravated features.[68]

The survey of 57 cases of father-daughter incest showed that the guilty father was imprisoned in 52 cases (91.2 percent). We may contrast this with the figures for persons sentenced to immediate imprisonment for sexual offences generally. The Criminal Statistics for 1976 show that, of a total of 2,355 men and women sentenced for sexual offences in the Crown Court, 1,026 (43.6 percent) were sentenced to immediate imprisonment.[69] Similarly, the proportion of persons sentenced to imprisonment for all types of incest remains high. In the survey of 72 cases, immediate imprisonment was ordered in 58 cases (80.5 percent). In like fashion the Criminal Statistics for 1976 show that of 133 men and women sentenced for incest at the Crown Court 97 (73 percent) were committed to immediate imprisonment.[70]

Yet the survey of sentences imposed in 57 cases of father-daughter incest suggests that sentences in the region of six years imprisonment may be rather less common than they were when Thomas wrote of appellate cases. In only 7 cases (9.7 percent) was a sentence of six years imprisonment or more imposed, although it is true that in a further 12 cases (21 percent) a sentence of between five years and five years and eleven months imprisonment was imposed. On the other hand sentences of between two years imprisonment and three years and eleven months imprisonment were imposed in 22 cases (38.5 percent).

Of course particular cases may demand that a departure be made from the norm. In one particularly bad case a sentence of twelve years imprisonment was imposed. In that case the defendant had had incestuous relations with four daughters, had attempted incest with another and indecency with a sixth.[71] In the survey, the highest sentence imposed was one of eight years imprisonment. In that case a 23 year-old daughter complained to the police that her 44 year-old father was having an incestuous relationship with herself and her sixteen year-old sister. The father had had two previous convictions for incest, the second of which had resulted in a sentence of four years imprisonment. The survey showed just one case in which a sentence of seven years imprisonment had been imposed. Here a 37 year-old father pleaded guilty to incest over a period of time with daughters who at the time of the trial were aged 16 and 14 respectively. Counsel had considered a charge of rape at one time. The defendant had a number of previous convictions of a non-sexual nature, the most serious of which had resulted in three years imprisonment.

The survey also shows that in some instances a relatively light sentence may be imposed. For example, in 5 cases out of 57 (8.8 percent) a non-custodial sentence was imposed upon a father; in 2 cases (3.5 percent) less than one years imprisonment was imposed and in 6 cases (10.5 percent) sentences of between one and two years imprisonment were imposed.

Appropriate sentences in cases of brother-sister incest will depend very much upon their respective ages. Where a brother and sister are of mature years, lesser sentences have been said to be appropriate. In *R. v. Winch*,[72] the Court of Appeal expressed the view that incest was often difficult to deal with because it was an offence which had social implications and some incestuous relationships were better dealt with by social measures than by criminal process. So in one case in the survey a 45 year-old defendant pleaded guilty to incest on two occasions with his 56 year-old sister. He was placed on probation for three years.

4. Incidence

A number of attempts have been made to report upon the incidence of incest. The tendency was to assume that incest was very rare in all types of society.[73] More recently it has been suggested that 3.9 percent of the average population of the United States had experienced incest and that 13.1 percent of the prison population had done so.[74] Further studies have also tended to suggest that a higher incidence of incest may exist amongst the disturbed and among the prison population. Thus 26 cases of paternal incest were encountered among 650 unselected patients in Northern Ireland. This suggested that about 4 percent of female psychiatric patients in that area had had incestuous experience at some time in their childhood.[75] A further study of 118 female drug abusers found that 52 (44 percent) had been involved at some time in an incestuous experience.[76] Of course such findings do not necessarily give any indication of the prevalence of paternal incest among the general population of the country.

Even more striking is the success in bringing to light a much larger number of cases of incest of the Child Sexual Abuse Treatment Program (C.S.A.T.P.). The Director, Dr. Giarretto, writes that in 1971 just 35 cases of incest were referred to the program. In 1975, 180 cases were referred: in the first quarter of 1976, 102 referrals were made. That represents a change from a supposed rate, in the earlier studies, of as low as one or two cases per million inhabitants, to about 200 cases per million. Yet Giarretto believes that even that revised figure does not reflect the true prevalence of incest. Further, Giarretto reports that so far from the families referred to the program coming virtually entirely from the lower socio-economic groups, referrals constituted a cross section of the whole community.[77]

Such figures do suggest that, as has long been suspected,[78] the criminal statistics are of no value in determining the number of incestuous relationships which exist. They represent merely the tip of the iceberg. In fact the criminal statistics for England and Wales show that each year about 300 cases are reported as known to the police, of these about one half come to trial.[79]

Without doubt father-daughter incest is the type of incest which results most frequently in prosecution. So the survey of 85 cases of incest is made up of 66 cases (77.7 percent) of father-daughter incest, 16 cases (18.8 percent) of brother-sister incest, and 3 cases (3.5 percent) of grandfather-granddaughter incest. Of course, prosecutions do occur with regard to other forms of incest. The Criminal Statistics for 1975 show that nine females were found guilty in the Crown Courts of incest as contrasted with 172 men. Similarly, the Criminal Statistics for 1976 show that three females were found guilty in the Crown Courts of incest as contrasted with 130 men.[80]

Typically, the daughter is aged between 10 and 14 years. This was true of 44 out of 80 cases (55 percent) in the survey. A further 27 daughters (33.7 percent) were aged between 15 and 19 years. Of this group of daughters nine were either 16 or 17 years of age; accordingly, the law of incest afforded them a protection which the present law regarding unlawful sexual intercourse does not offer to young women of their age.

The overwhelming majority of such convicted fathers (47 out of 50 cases or 94 percent) came from social class 3 manual and from classes 4, 5 and the unemployed.

5. Effects

What are the effects of incest upon the family and upon the victim? Maisch has written[81] that psychological and psychiatric research has demonstrated that the harmful effects on the family brought about by the official discovery and punishment of the offence are more serious than those which might arise during the course of incest. The economic effects of the father's imprisonment may be serious for the family. The daughter might be sent to a children's home, society might discriminate against the family. Such 'psychological poisoning', by the legal process, as one critic put it some years ago, was more likely to destroy the family than to protect it.[82] On the other hand, Maisch also points out that most recent empirical surveys had come to the conclusion that incest was not a cause but a symptom or result of a family whose inner order was as a rule already disturbed before the offence. It is surely clear also that the bad effects which the family in question may suffer differ very little from the effects suffered by many families whose fathers are imprisoned, irrespective of the charge. So far as the effects upon the victims are concerned, Bluglass has written that there "is significant evidence to suggest that the daughters in these cases do not emerge unharmed."[83]

If the incidence of incest really is as high generally as the C.S.A.T.P. figures suggest that it may be, however, much earlier research will be outdated. All that we can attempt at present is to measure the effects of the legal process upon the families and victims concerned. We know nothing of the effects of incestuous conduct which is not reported publicly, except that three recent studies appear to reveal a relatively high rate of incestuous experience — when compared with quite a low expectation of the incidence of incest in the community generally — among some special groups.[84]

6. Rationale

The history of incest shows that the prohibition was based upon a number of factors. Incest was an offence against religion; it was morally wrong. The law's particular aim was to guard against the possibly 'disastrous' consequences of such a union and to protect the family. At the present day there would be little support for the criminal prohibition on the grounds of religion alone; a substantial body of public opinion also believes that it is not the function of the criminal law to support general public morality.

It is the genetic argument, which is based upon the view that certain diseases are more likely to occur in a child the more closely the parents are related to one another, which appears to be the primary rationale of the law. For example, an appellate court commented recently that "the gravamen of incest was that it might have a disastrous effect on children born to the parties."[85] It is a view which has received distinguished medical support. Indeed, it was one of the two reasons which the Royal College of Psychiatrists put forward when it suggested recently that incest should be retained as a separate criminal offence.[86] And many countries are said to permit legal abortion where pregnancy arises from incest, due to the fear of degeneracy in the offspring.[87] Yet the medical evidence is slight. Indeed a recent and authorititative Swedish survey challenges it.[88] In any event it is possible to argue that the law should reflect a different standpoint. For example, the South Australian Criminal Law and Penal Methods Reform Committee wrote recently:

It is not the place of the criminal law to penalize citizens merely for moral or intellectual deficiencies. . . . The law in South Australia does not intervene to prohibit the marriage and subsequent procreation of issue by persons who are not related but who both exhibit unhealthy traits, nor does it permit compulsory sterilisation of the unhealthy. It seems to the committee that the retention of the crime of incest cannot be justified on genetic grounds alone.[89]

The view that the criminal law of incest is protective of the family, and more especially of the child, retains considerable support. Thus the Royal College of Psychiatrists affirmed the view that in present day society incest still disrupted families, though not invariably. The Royal College suggested "that there is a strongly double feeling towards incest — a readiness to resort to it and at the same time a strong reaction against it. It is in just such an ambivalent situation that the law should if the objective is justified, throw in its weight and play its declaratory role."[90] American courts have been prepared to acknowledge such a role for the criminal law of incest. "The object of the statutes defining and punishing the crime", said one court,[91] "is to . . . promote domestic peace and social purity." Similarly, another American court commented: "The laws against incest are designed to protect the family relationship, and its rights, duties, habits and affections, from the destructive effect of family inter-marriages and domestic licentiousness.[92] On the whole, English and Welsh courts have been rather less ready to philosophize. However, the protection of the young child at all events is clearly uppermost in the judicial mind and the courts' sentencing policy does make it clear that they often take a stern view in cases involving parents.

Yet clearly some forms of incest are regarded as being far more serious than others. For example, sentencing policy shows that a far less serious view will be taken of a sexual relationship between adult brothers and sisters. So in *R. v. Winch*[93] the court commented that some incestuous relationships were better dealt with by social measures than by the criminal process, although it went on to point out that if the brother committed incest again, the law would have to take its course.

It is submitted that the law no longer protects the family as such. Adultery is unpunished enticement and restitution of conjugal rights no longer form part of the law of England and Wales. The actual practice of the courts indicates that in this context the aim of the criminal law of incest is, above all, to protect the young child.

7. Treatment

Once in prison little is offered to the prisoner by way of treatment in the prison system as a whole. Of course, it is not suggested that treatment would be appropriate in all cases. It might well be difficult to convince the adult brother and sister that they are suitable cases for treatment. Others might well be unsuitable for treatment on other grounds. Nor is there any evidence that treatment has been successful. For example, the many experiments in treating young offenders generally by various forms of psychotherapy and counseling have yielded only inconclusive results. Is such treatment likely to be more successful in the case of incest offenders?[94] Psychiatrists may take the view that sex offenders are more likely to respond to individual psychotherapy, yet undoubtedly such treatment is expensive. Such doubts make the results claimed for the Californian Child Sexual Abuse Treatment Program (C.S.A.T.P.) all the more interesting. The program provides immediate counseling and practical assistance to sexually abused children and their families, in particular to victims of father-daughter incest. The treatment model is said to be one which "fosters self-managed growth of individuals capable of positive contributions to society, rather than a medical model based on the vagaries of mental disease." Two self-help groups, Parents United and Daughters United, have also been formed to offer guidance to members. The Director of the project stresses that C.S.A.T.P. works closely with the criminal justice system. He continues:

In all cases the authority of the criminal justice system and the court process the offender must undergo seems absolutely necessary in order to satisfy what may be termed an expiatory factor in the treatment of the offender and his family. It appears that the offender needs to know unequivocally that the community will not condone his incestuous behavior and that it will exact a punishment. Victims and their mothers have also admitted to deriving comfort from knowledge of the community's clear stand on incest. All family members, however, will do their best to frustrate the system if they anticipate that the punishment will be so severe that the family will be destroyed and that they, in turn, including the child victim herself, will become 'victims' of the criminal justice system.[95]

The Director reports that no recidivism has been reported among the more than 300 families who have received a minimum of ten hours treatment and whose cases have been formally terminated.

8. Protection of Family upon Release of Prisoner

Both when a prisoner may be released early on licence and when he is about to be released, administrative procedures are designed to protect the family. For example, when a man may be released early on licence, answers to the following questions in particular are sought:

(a) Does the social services department feel there is a risk to the children in the home?

(b) If so, what action will be necessary to remove or reduce that risk to an acceptable level?

(c) Is it possible to take action and, if so, what effect will it have on the children?[96]

9. After Care for the Offender

The Probation Service and after-care committees will offer assistance to discharged prisoners and to their families as part of their general responsibility to offer all discharged prisoners friendship, guidance and moral support.[97] On occasion advice may be offered to a family even while the offender is in prison. If social services believe that upon the father returning to the home, the daughter is in danger of the offence being repeated, the child may be taken into care. Equally, the father may apply for such a care order to be revoked.

10. The Options for Reform

The suggestion that incest, and in particular father-daughter incest, may be far more common among all sections of the community than had been supposed hitherto is surely of key importance. Equally interesting is the suggestion, which is also derived from the C.S.A.T.P. experience, that it may be possible successfully to treat such offenders and to offer valuable support to their families. In addition, in cases of incest there is the ever present problem of proof and the effect which the legal process may have upon the 'victim' and, indeed, upon the whole family. It is important also to distinguish between the various types of incest and to assess separately the degrees of harm to which each may lead. Thus the policy considerations which support the criminal offence of a father's incestuous conduct with a young daughter may well differ from the policy considerations which govern incestuous conduct between an adult brother and an adult sister. Certainly the sentencing policy of the courts indicates that there is a difference of degree at least between such categories of incestuous conduct.

The essence of incest is that it is an offence within the family. Often existing marital disharmony may have contributed to the incest taking place. Might not the civil process and in particular a new family court contribute more fittingly than the purely criminal process to dealing with such problems? The concept of a family court, together with the ancillary services at its command, has been sketched in outline before, although none yet exists in England and Wales. Yet it is rare for a family court to exercise a criminal jurisdiction. It is all the more interesting to note, therefore, that the family court of the State of New York in the United States may even consider exercising a jurisdiction in cases of incest. New York's Family Court Act[98] states that its purpose is to offer practical help within a civil proceeding for dealing with cases of interfamily assault. It can authorize orders of protection and support and contemplates conciliation procedures. If the family court concludes that these processes are inappropriate in a particular case, it is authorized to transfer the proceeding to an appropriate criminal court.

As yet there appears to be some uncertainty as to the precise role which the family court is to play in the case of sexual offences and in particular as to whether the family court is to exercise an exclusive jurisdiction. For example, in 1970 it was held that in determining whether the procedures of the family court were appropriate to retain and treat incestuous conduct, each case must turn on its own merits. In that case, however, the family court did have initial jurisdiction over alleged incestuous conduct between brother, 16 to 17 years of age, and sister, 12 to 13 years of age. On the other hand in 1972 it was held that incest was not an act within the exclusive original jurisdiction of the family court under this section.[99]

If individuals are to come forward for treatment, on the assumption that suitable treatment is available, further information must be made available to the public. The C.S.A.T.P. experiments' insistence upon education is notable. For example, an information bulletin states:

Incest is a hidden family problem where the family members involved are afraid to seek help. The basis of this fear, which is often expressed, includes the feeling that their situation is unique and no one will understand: and they fear the effects on the family upon disclosure. They are unaware that specialized help is available to them. These people must be reached.[100]

C.S.A.T.P. states that increased referrals to it are due to such public education. Referrals came from the juvenile probation department, from 'hotlines', and directly from people who previously had been reluctant to report the problem.

It is suggested, therefore, that the education of both public and of interested professionals such as probation officers, police officers, social workers, nurses, doctors, marriage guidance counselors and lawyers is desirable. The measures which have already been undertaken in the context of the battered child and the battered wife afford a starting point in terms of publicity. The overall aim would be to achieve a far greater number of referrals for treatment, within the context of the legal, although not necessarily criminal legal, system.

A mandatory reporting system, effectively monitored, could also be of help, if it could be made to work effectively. Such a system must also ensure that the *bona fide* unofficial reporter, *e.g.,* a neighbor, is protected from legal action by a parent as a result of giving such information, even the name of the neighbor should be kept confidential, if the neighbor so requests.

Should the present criminal law of incest be changed? The present law may not be wholly adequate to meet the objectives assumed for it, as outlined above. For example, if the family is to be protected it can be maintained that at all events the children of the family, whether they be adopted, or step-daughters or simply accepted into the family, should receive the same protection as a natural child of the family. In any event it is suggested that in appropriate cases, in accordance with principles to be made public, a discretion conditionally not to prosecute might be exercised more often. Yet should incest remain a criminal offence at all? To ask the question certainly does not mean that one necessarily condones incestuous conduct but rather that, as a commentator upon the Swedish approach put it recently, "the fact that many people construe incest to be repugnant and immoral does not make a convincing reason for defining it as a criminal act." The same writer comments:

As a rule the abolition of penalties for offences such as adultery, sodomy and homosexual relations between consenting adults has not denoted any repudiation of those values which were the underlying basis for those penalties. If anything, the reforms should largely be seen against the background of a greater appreciation of the difficulties posed by trying to control the sexual acts of human beings through penal provisions. The provisions encompassed a great many cases where there was no victim, in a strict and literal sense, of the offence. If the police found out that an offence had been committed, this would be due to the operation of chance circumstances. In consequence the interventions of civil authority came to be regarded as capricious and unjust. They came to impair confidence in the administration of justice. It therefore became imperative to limit the rules to outrageous acts irrespective of personal codes of sexual ethics.

The proposals put forward by the Sexual Offences Commission take cognizance of the *de facto* development that has unfolded over a long period. In the Commission's view, the principal aim of legislation on sexual offences must be to safeguard personal integrity by punishing sexual outrages.

From the terminological aspects words or phrases which in Sweden are construed to be moralizing, or which make reference to a system of norms other than that of the law, should be abolished. Thus terms like morality, propriety and carnal abuse have been dropped, and title 6 of the Penal Code has been reworded from "On crimes against morality" to "On sexual outrages."[101]

That conscious move against morality as such in the law is evident in the South Australian committee's approach to the question of incest between adults, when it wrote that it was not the place of the criminal law to penalize citizens merely for moral or intellectual deficiencies. It can be argued also that in the case of so universal and so deeply felt a taboo as incest, the role of the law is in a sense irrelevant as public revulsion exists quite independently of the law's declaratory function. No doubt that is still true of most people. Others disagree. At a recent conference one speaker made a plea "not just for children to be liberated for sexual relations with adults (including incest), but also for 'affecting healthy erotica' involving children." At the same conference another speaker maintained that "media conditioning into paedophilia and incest is now leading . . . into child sadism." She points to the fact that a recent edition of American Forum carried no less than twenty accounts of child sex (from 8 to 12) in the first quarter of its pages. The issue then moved on to incest, which it has cosily familiarized under the title of "Home and Family Sex".[102]

Those who believe that such attitudes are harmful may well argue that the fact that incestuous conduct is punishable at criminal law reinforces the public revulsion against it, — the declaratory view of the law, as the Royal College of Psychiatrists puts it,[103] and so affords added protection for the family and for society. However, the tendency does appear to be to limit prosecutions in practice to a relatively narrow band of relationships. For example, the adviser to Sweden's Sexual Offences Commission, Professor Alstrom, is reported to have noted that:

. . . legal interventions against incest between adult relatives very seldom occur. In the overwhelming number of cases one of the parties is under 18. In the ten year period from 1965 to 1974 there were only three cases of intercourse with children of direct descent where the child was over 18.[104]

In Scotland, too, there appears to be a reluctance to enforce the law as a whole. The widely based Scottish law of incest affords two recent examples. In one case a man who was living with his adult step-daughter was convicted of incest but merely admonished. In the second case the jury refused to convict a man and his step-daughter who were living together openly as man and wife.[105] Similarly, although this goes to punishment rather than to prosecution, there has long existed a recognition in the United States that incestuous acts between affines were less blameworthy than incestuous acts inter consanguines.[106] And it is clear that in practice in England and Wales the great majority of prosecutions for incest relate to the father-daughter relationship.

How well, then, do the present criminal sanctions against incest in England and Wales support the supposed objectives of the law? Certainly, the penal sanction must support the genetic objectives of the law, in so far as the sanction is enforced adequately. However, as we have seen already, the genetic argument is not as strong as was sometimes thought, nor is it altogether acceptable in principle. Moreover, it can be argued that criminal sanctions, or at all events really punitive criminal sanctions, may discourage some offenders or potential offenders from seeking treatment. Thus the C.S.A.T.P. experiment suggests that the incidence of incest really is many times higher than the criminal statistics suggest. Are such people really going to seek appropriate treatment, are their families going to encourage them to seek appropriate treatment, if punitive sanctions are to be imposed? Many would think not. On the other hand the C.S.A.T.P. experience emphasizes the value of the criminal justice system in that it fulfils an expiatory role for the offender and that it encourages, or rather requires, him to complete a course of appropriate treatment. The role of the criminal law need not be solely punitive, therefore, it has a valuable 'supportive' function also.

Do the present criminal sanctions protect the family? At present in England and Wales it is clear that the family affected is protected only in the sense that the offender will probably be removed from the family and will be permitted to return only if the responsible authorities are satisfied that there will be no repetition of the offence. In many cases, however, the family will not want such a father to return, possibly because of the effects upon the family of the legal process. It is in such cases that the adoption of a modified form of the criminal process, perhaps along the lines of the C.S.A.T.P. experiment, would be appropriate for it might ensure that considerably more such families, spared the full rigor of the criminal process and assured of appropriate treatment, would stay united to the greater benefit of both themselves and of the state.

11. Conclusion

The legal process should recognize that incest is an offense against the family, most typically it is an offence against an underage daughter within the family. Therefore, incest should not be regarded as an exclusively criminal offence. A speedy, and in some ways more informal, procedure should seek to reconcile both the needs of the child and the rights of a defendant. Clearly defined guidelines should seek to ensure that so far as possible prosecutions were brought only in what are deemed to be appropriate cases. Punishments ought not to be harsh in the less serious cases; otherwise the typical family complainant may feel reluctant to make a complaint in the first instance. Overall the legal process should be seen in appropriate cases to be as supportive of the 'victim' and of the family generally as it is punitive of the defendant.

Yet should incest be retained as a separate offence at all? I suggest that it should. However, in future, it should be restricted to cases where one of the parties is a minor *i.e.,* under 18 years of age. That proposal would codify the essence of much of our present practice. It also offers to the daughter, and not least to the daughter over 16 but under 18, a mark of special protection which she may well need when she is subject to some duress. The law stresses the importance of such forms of classification. After all it could be argued that murder is merely a form of assault. Few people would suggest, however, that murder as a separate offence should be dispensed with but should be classified in future simply as an assault.

NOTES

1. Carbonnier, J., *Droit Civil* (1972), 52. Code Penal (ed. Dalloz 1973-74). *Cf* Article 333.
2. Draft for Revision of Penal Code, Article 301. *Cf* Turkish Criminal Code. Articles 415 and 417 in The American Series of Draft Penal Codes.
3. Archbold, *Criminal Pleading, Evidence and Practice* (39 ed.), London, Eng: Sweet & Maxwell, 1976, p. 1243. Halsbury's Laws (4th ed.) para 1238*ff.* Smith and Hogan *Criminal Law* (3rd ed.), London, Eng.: Butterworths, 1973.
4. Clive, E.M., and Wilson, J.G., *Husband and Wife* (1974)., Gordon, G.H., *The Criminal Law of Scotland.* Edinburgh, Scotland: W. Green & Sons, 1967.
5. Howard, C., *Australian Criminal Law* (2nd ed: 1970) p. 177., Watson and Purnell, *Criminal Law in N.S.W.* (1971); Finlay, H.A., and Bissett-Johnson, A., *Family Law in Australia* (1972).
6. Criminal Code s. 150.
7. Adams, F., *Criminal Law and Practice in New Zealand* (1964); Inglis, B.D., *Family Law* (2nd ed., 1968).
8. *Corpus Juris Secundum:* American Jurisprudence.
9. Hunt, P.M.A., *South African Criminal Law and Procedure,* vol. 2 (1970).
10. The Austrian Penal Act 1852 and 1945 as amended to 1965 s. 131: in The American Series of Foreign Penal Codes.
11. Section 173. And see Maisch, H., *Incest.* London, Eng.: Andre Deutsch Ltd., 1973, p. 69*ff.*
12. Swedish Penal Code, as amended to 1972, chapter 6, s. 5.
13. Covers persons within the degrees of consanguinity within which marriages are declared by law to be incestuous and void.
14. Perkins on *Criminal Law* (1969) (2nd ed.) 383.
15. Criminal Law Consolidation Act Amendment Act 1976, s. 72: *cf* Law Reform (Sexual Behavior) Ordinance 1976 (A.C.T.) s. 3(2).
16. Punishment of Incest Act 1908.
17. Burn, *The Justice of the Peace and Parish Officer* (16th ed: 1788), 97.
18. 4 *Commentaries* 64 (5th ed: 1773).
19. The Special and General Reports made to His Majesty by the Commissioners . . . into the Practice and Jurisdiction of the Ecclesiastical Courts . . . (199: 1832), vol. 1, p. 13.
20. *Id.,* p. 64.
21. *Ibid.*

22. First Report of the Commissioners into the State and Operation of the Law of Marriage (1848), p. ix.
23. *Id.,* p. xii.
24. See Bromley, P. M., *Family Law* (5th ed.) London, Eng.: Butterworths, 1976, p. 647 for a table of the prohibited degrees of kindred and affinity.
25. 188 Hansard's Parliamentary Debates (4th ser: 1903) 1683.
26. 125 Hansard's Parliamentary Debates (4th ser: 1903) 820-822. See Hall Williams, J.E. in Maisch, H., *Incest* (1973) p. 219*ff.*
27. *Id.,* p. 822-823.
28. 191 Hansard's Parliamentary Debates (4th ser: 1908) 278-281.
29. Samuel, H., *id.,* 284.
30. The Lord Bishop of St. Alban's, *id.,* p. 284.
31. Russell, Earl, *id.,* p. 278-281.
32. *Id.,* p. 1411.
33. Ss. 10(1) and 11(1).
34. Ss. 10(2) and 11(2).
35. Cmnd. 1191 (1960).
36. (1976), 6 *Family Law* 65.
37. *D v. NSPCC* [1976] 2 All E.R. 993: later reversed in the House of Lords, [1977] 1 All E.R. 589.
38. *The Guardian* (social workers and criminal records) April 12, 1977. Committee of Inquiry, Auckland, J. G. Generally see Borland M. (ed.), *Violence in the Family.* Manchester, Eng.: Manchester University Press, 1976; Carter, J., *The Maltreated Child.* Sussex, Eng.: Priory Press, 1974; Renvoize, J., *Children in Danger.* London, Eng.: Routledge, 1974. *Cf.* General Secretary of B.A.S.W.: *The Guardian,* 19 November 1976.
39. Freeman, M.D.A., (1977). 7 Family Law 53. NSPCC, *Case Conferences: a Cause for Concern?* (1976).
40. Children and Young Persons Act 1969, s. 2(1).
41. *Id.,* s. 1(2)(c).
42. Children and Young Persons Act 1933, s. 40., Children and Young Persons Act 1969, s. 28.
43. See Bail Reform (1976) by League, Howard, for Penal Reform and N.A.C.R.O., *cf.* Bail Procedures in Magistrates Courts (Report of a Home Office Working Party) 1974.
44. Gibbens, T.C.N., and Prince, J., *Child Victims of Sex Offences.* London, Eng.: Institute for Study and Treatment of Delinquency, 1973.
46. De Francis, V., *Protecting the Child Victim of Sex Crime* (1965).
47. Libai, D., The Protection of the Child Victim of a Sexual Offense in the Criminal Justice System" (1969), 15 *Wayne L.R.* 977, 1009.
48. Turner (1970) 54 Cr. App. R. 352.
49. Baldwin J., and McConville, M., *Negotiated Justice* (1977).
50. Children and Young Persons Act 1933, s. 37.
51. This account is based upon Barnes, P., *The Office of the Director of Public Prosecutions in the Prosecution Process* (1975) Institute of Judicial Administration, University of Birmingham. See also Edwards, J. Ll. J., *The Law Officers of the Crown* (1964).
52. See generally Wilcox, A.F., *The Decision to Prosecute.* London, Eng.: Butterworths, 1972 esp. at pps. 51 and 80. For an account of the American practice of diversion which is used in minor criminal cases see Zander, M., *Diversion from Criminal Justice in an English Context* (N.A.C.R.O.: 1975). There is a growing literature on the discretion to prosecute.
53. Sexual Offences Act 1956, ss. 10(2) and 11(2).
54. *R. v. Dimes* (1911) 7 Cr. App. R. 43.
55. 11 Hals. Laws 457.
56. (1929) 21 Cr. App. R. 147.

57. *Cf. R. v. Stone* (1910) 6 Cr. App. R. 89: the question whether she consented was never left to the jury at all. See *R. v. Dimes* (1911) 7 Cr. App. R. 43 (on corroboration).
58. [1911] A.C. 47.
59. *Cf. R. v. Flack* [1969] 2 All E.R. 784, 788. See generally Cross, R., "Fourth Time Lucky: Similar Fact Evidence in the House of Lords" (1975) *Crim. L.R.* 62.
60. Refer notes 3 to 18, *supra.*
61. Leviticus, 18:6-18.
62. Gordon *op. cit.*, note 4, pp. 841-842.
63. Clive and Wilson *op. cit.*, note 4, p. 374. Gordon *op. cit.*, note 4, p. 841. In South Africa it appears to be incest; Hunt *op. cit.*, note 9, p. 257. Yet this is not the case in all American jurisdictions, 41 Am. Jur. 2d 516.
64. Penal Code of Louisiana, Article 78.
65. 41 Am. Jur. 2d. 519., Hunt, *op. cit.*, note 9, p. 251.
66. See generally Thomas, D.A., *Principles of Sentencing.* London, Eng.: Heinemann Educ. Books, 1970, p. 111 *ff; cf.* Fallon, P., *Crown Court Practice: Sentence* (1975).
67. Walker, N., *Crime and Punishment in Britain.* (2nd ed.) Edinburgh, Scotland: Edinburgh University Press, 1968, p. 215.
68. Thomas, *op. cit.*, note 66, p. 111*ff.*
69. Criminal Statistics 1976 (Cmnd. 6909) pp. 286-287.
70. *Ibid.*
71. *R. v. Flack* [1969] 2 All E.R. 784.
72. (1974) *Crim. L.R.* 487 C.A., cf. Glynn (1970) *Crim. L.R.* 293 C.A.
73. Weinberg, S. K., *Incest Behavior.* New York, New York: Citadel Press, 1955, p. 39-40.
74. Gebhard, Gagnon, Pomeroy, Christenson, *Sex Offenders* (1965); Lester, D., "Incest" (1972), 8 *The Jo. of Sex Research* 268; Weiner, H., "On Incest, A Survey", 4 *Excerpta Criminologica* 137.
75. Lukianowicz, N., "Incest" (1972), 120 *Brit. J. Psychiat.* 301.
76. Benward J., and Densen Gerber, J., "Incest as a Causative Factor in Anti-Social Behavior" (1975), 4 *Contemporary Drug Problems* 323.
77. Giarretto, H., "The Treatment of Father Daughter Incest: A Psycho-Social Approach" (1976) *Children Today* 2; Giarretto, H., "Humanistic Treatment of Father-Daughter Incest", in Helfer, R. E., and Kempe, C. H., (eds.), *Child Abuse and Neglect: The Family and the Community.* Cambridge, Mass.: Ballinger, 1976, c. 8.
78. Evidence to the Criminal Law Revision Committee of the Official Solicitor to the N.S.P.C.C. (unpublished).
79. The number of cases of incest recorded as known to the police was: 1971—307; 1972—323; 1973—288; 1974—337. In 1974 the D.P.P. brought proceedings in 169 cases of incest: *Criminal Statistics* (1974) (Cmnd. 6168) pp. 12 and 238.
80. *Criminal Statistics* (1975) (Cmnd. 6566) p. 162; and 1976 (Cmnd. 6909) p. 226.
81. Maisch, H., *Incest.* London, Eng.: Andre Deutsch Ltd., 1973, p. 208.
82. *Id.*, p. 209.
83. Valedictory Address to Birmingham Medical Institute: Section of Psychiatry (1976), p. 13 (unpublished).
84. Bensen and Densen-Gerber, *op. cit.*, note 76; Gebhard *et al., op. cit.*, note 74,. Lukianowicz *op. cit.*, note 75.
85. *R. v. Winch* (1974) *Crim. L.R.* 487. There is an extensive anthronological and sociological literature. For example, see Bischof, N., "The Biological Foundations of the Incest Taboo" (1972), 11 *Social Science Information;* Ferracuti, F., "Incest Between Father and Daughter," in Resnik, H.L., and Wolfgang, M.E. (eds.), *Sexual Behavior: Social, Clinical and Legal Aspects.* Boston, Mass.: Little Brown & Co., (1972), p. 169; Shelton, W.E., "A Study of Incest" (1975), 19 *Int. Jo. of Offender Therapy and Comp. Crim.* 139; Bagley, C., "The Varieties of Incest" (Aug. 21, 1963) *New Society* 280; Cornwell, J., "Incest: the Forbidden Union" (Aug. 4, 1974) *Observer Magazine* 15.

86. Evidence to the Criminal Law Revision Committee regarding Sexual Offences.
87. Dickens, B. M., *Abortion and the Law* (1966), p. 167. In 1939 a British committee took the opposite view (Dickens, p. 140): yet in 1974 the Lane Commission paid virtually no attention to incest.
88. See note 10.
89. Report of the South Australian Criminal Law and Penal Methods Reform Committee p. 30. Their recommendations on incest were not adopted.
90. *Op. cit.,* note 86, p. 6. See generally Andrejew, I., "La Protection Pénale de la Famille," Extract des Rapports Généraux au VII Congrès International de Droit Comparé (1966). *Cf.* Brown, L. N., "The Penal Protection of the Family in English Law", (1968) *Estratto dall'Annuario di Diritto Comparato e di Studi Legislativi,* Vol XLII - Tomo 1, p. 36.
91. *Columbia v. Garcia* 335 A2d 217, 222: 42 C.J.S. 504.
92. *State v. Tucker* 93 N.E. 3: 41 Am. Jur. 2d. 512.
93. (1974) *Crim. L.R.* 487.
94. Feldman, M. P., *Criminal Behavior: A Psychological Analysis* (1977) 236-241. *Cf.* Tappan, P., in Radzinowicz and Wolfgang (eds.), *The Criminal in Society.* New York, New York: Basic Bks., p. 314.
95. See note 81.
96. D.H.S.S. Circular 75/3. *Cf.* prison circular 16/1965.
97. Jarvis, F. V., *Probation Officers' Manual* (2nd ed: 1974) p. 144. *Cf.* McLean J.D., and Wood, J.C., *Criminal Justice and the Treatment of Offenders* (1969).
98. Article 8, s. 811: McKinney's, *Consolidated Laws of New York* (Annotated).
99. *Id.,* p. 695; SVS, 1970, 63 Misc. 2d. 1. 311 NYS 2d 169.
100. Undated and bears no classifying mark.
101. Engstrom, L.G., *op. cit.,* note 16, p. 2. *Cf.* NCCL Report no. 13, Sexual Offences: Evidence to the Criminal Law Revision Committee p. 15. Since this essay was completed Sweden has rejected the recommendation of the Sexual Offences Commission.
102. Conference on Love and Attraction: University of Swansea, Wales; *The Guardian* Sept. 16 1977, p. 11.
103. *Op. cit.,* note 86 at p. 6.
104. Alstrom, C. H., "A Study of Incest With Special Regard to the Swedish Penal Code" (1977), 56 *Acta Psychiat. Scand.* 357. *Cf.* Engstrom, L.G., "New Penal Provisions on Sexual Offences Proposed in Sweden" (1976), 118 *Current Sweden* 1; Bishop, N., (1976), 9 *SOU* 21; Alstrom, C. H., "First Cousin Marriages in Sweden 1750-1844" (1958), 8 *Acta Genetica and Statistica Medica* 295.
105. Personal communication, Clive, E.M.
106. 42 C.J.S. p. 505. *See further,* Gibbens, T.C.N.; Soothill K.L., and Way, C.K., "Sibling and Parent-Child Incest Offenders: A Long-term Follow-up" (1978), 18 *Brit. J. Crim.* 40.

THE SURVEY

Table 1

Forms of Incest which Occurred in the Survey

	number of cases	percentage
(i) father/daughter	66	77.7
(ii) brother/sister	16	18.8
(iii) grandfather/granddaughter	3	3.5
total	85	100.0

Note: Information on all the matters which are covered in the following tables was not available in every case. This survey is based on a sample of recent cases in England which is taken from police, prosecution, probation and psychiatric sources.

Table 2 (i)

Who Complained?

Father/daughter cases	number of cases	percentage
(a) wife/mother	28	36.4
(b) brother/step-brother	2	2.6
(c) neighbor	5	6.5
(d) school	4	5.1
(e) Social Services	2	2.6
(f) aunt/relative	5	6.5
(g) victim	29	37.7
(h) Citizen's Advice Bureau	1	1.3
(i) Hospital	1	1.3
total	77	100.3

Table 2 (ii)

Who Complained?

brother/sister cases	number of cases	percentage
(a) mother	3	20.0
(b) father	1	6.7
(c) sister	4	26.7
(d) neighbor	1	6.7
(e) school	1	6.7
(f) N.S.P.C.C.	2	13.3
(g) victim	3	20.0
total	15	100.1

Table 2 (iii)

Who Complained?

grandfather/granddaughter cases

(a) mother	3
(b) victim	1
total	4

In *Table 2* all complainants are listed: in some cases there is more than one complainant.

Table 3

Bail Granted

	number of cases	percentage
(i) father/daughter cases		
(a) bail granted in	45	71.4
(b) bail refused in	18	28.6
total	63	100.0
(ii) brother/sister cases		
(a) bail granted in	9	60
(b) bail refused in	6	40
total	15	100
(iii) grandfather/granddaughter cases		
(a) bail granted in	2	66.7
(b) bail refused in	1	33.3
total	3	100.0
(iv) overall summary		
(a) bail granted in	56	70.0
(b) bail refused in	24	30.0
total	80	100.0

Table 4 (i)

Age of Defendant

father/daughter cases	number of cases	percentage
age in years		
25 - 29	2	3.4
30 - 34	9	15.2
35 - 39	18	30.5
40 - 44	12	20.3
35 - 39	18	30.5
40 - 44	12	20.3
45 - 49	10	16.9
50 - 54	3	5.1
55 - 59	3	5.1
60 - 64	2	3.4
total	59	99.9

Table 4 (ii)

Age of Defendant

brother/sister cases	number of cases	percentage
age in years		
15 - 19	11	78.6
20 - 24	1	7.1
25 - 29	1	7.1
30 - 34	0	
35 - 39	0	
40 - 44	0	
45 - 49	1	7.1
total	14	99.9

Table 4 (iii)

Age of Defendant

grandfather/granddaughter cases	
first case	54 years
second case	53 years
third case	57 years

Table 5 (i)

Occupation of Defendant

father/daughter cases	number of cases	percentage
social class		
1	1	2
2	0	0
3 non manual	2	4
3 manual	23	46
4	(	
	(12	24
5	(	
unemployed	12	24
total	50	100

Table 5 (ii)

Occupation of Defendant

brother/sister cases	number of cases	percentage
social class		
1	0	0
2	0	0
3 non manual	0	0
3 manual	1	6.7
4	(	
	(6	40.0
5	(	
unemployed	7	46.7
schoolchild	1	6.7
total	15	100.1

Table 6 (i)

Age of Victim

father/daughter cases	number of cases	percentage
age in years		
0 - 4	0	0
5 - 9	6	7.5
10 - 14	44	55.0
15 - 19	27	33.7
20 - 24	3	3.7
total	80	99.9

Table 6 (ii)

Age of Victim

brother/sister age in years	number of cases	percentage
0 - 4	0	
5 - 9	2	10.0
10 - 14	14	70.0
15 - 19	4	20.0
total	20	100.0

In one other case the sister was 45 years old.

Table 6 (iii)

Age of Victim

grandfather/granddaughter cases	
first case	6 years and 8 years
second case	1 year and 4 months
third case	5 years

Table 7

Plea

(i) father/daughter cases	number of cases	percentage
(a) guilty	53	86.9
(b) not guilty	8	13.1
total	61	100.0

(ii) brother/sister cases	number of cases	percentage
(a) guilty	11	91.7
(b) not guilty	1	8.3
total	12	100.0

(iii) grandfather/granddaughter cases	number of cases	percentage
(a) guilty	2	66.7
(b) not guilty	1	33.3
total	3	100.0

(iv) summary

	number	percentage
(a) guilty	66	86.8
(b) not guilty	10	13.2
total	76	100.0

Table 8 (i)

Sentence

father/daughter cases	number of cases	percentage
(a) imprisonment		
0 - 1 year	2	3.5
1 year - 1 year 11 months	6	10.5
2 years - 2 years 11 months	11	19.3
3 years - 3 years 11 months	11	19.3
4 years - 4 years 11 months	3	5.3
5 years - 5 years 11 months	12	21.0
6 years - 6 years 11 months	5	8.8
7 years - 7 years 11 months	1	1.7
8 years - 8 years 11 months	1	1.7

Note: Imprisonment occurred in three other cases: details regarding sentence are not available

	number of cases	percentage
(b) probation	2	3.5
(c) suspended sentence	2	3.5
(d) conditional discharge	1	1.7
total	57	99.8

Table 8 (ii)

Sentence

brother/sister cases	number of cases	percentage
(a) imprisonment		
0 - 1 year	0	0
1 year - 1 year 11 months	1	8.3
2 years - 2 years 11 months	1	8.3
3 years - 3 years 11 months	1	8.3
4 years - 4 years 11 months	1	8.3
(b) probation	5	41.7
(c) suspended sentence	1	8.3
(d) conditional discharge	2	16.7
total	12	99.9

Table 8 (iii)

<u>Sentence</u>

<u>grandfather/granddaughter cases</u>
first case   4 years imprisonment
second case   2 years probation
third case   3 years imprisonment

Chapter 34

Decriminalization of Incest—New Legal-Clinical Responses

Ingrid K. Cooper*

Incest is a form of human behavior that is capable of arousing man's strongest feelings of both fear and fascination.[1] Although many theories attempt to explain the nature of the taboo, its roots are essentially unknown and shrouded in mankind's early history. The strength and universality of the incest taboo is commonly accepted, but its universality can be questioned when one realizes that legal sanctions against incest have been in existence only a brief time. Incest was not generally treated as a crime in common law and only became an offence in England in 1908. Prior to this, incest was dealt with in the villages by the use of public opinion and church laws. This recent criminalization of the problem has occurred in most countries in Europe and North America where it is a criminal offence, punishable by imprisonment. Recent years have seen a substantial increase to an already large body of literature on incest, particularly its clinical and sociological aspects. While this increased exposure in popular as well as scientific journals has resulted in some demystification of the subject, there has been no appreciable change in society's harsh legal response to the problem.

Basing itself on the well documented clinical knowledge described in the literature and on the twenty years of clinical experience of the McGill Clinic in Forensic Psychiatry, this chapter will discuss an alternative legal and therapeutic approach to the problem of incest. After a brief review of the main clinical factors, concrete suggestions of a new, comprehensive legal-clinical response to incest cases will be described with the view to providing society with a less punitive, more clinically effective way of dealing with incest.

1. Legal and Clinical Incest

To have a realistic discussion of the problem of incest, it is important to differentiate between legal incest and clinical incest. Incest as a clinical reality requires a broader definition than that contained in the Criminal Code, which requires that consummation occurs. If the types of prohibited sexual behavior between family members are placed on the scale of a continuum, with

---

* Clinic in Forensic Psychiatry, McGill University, Montreal, Canada.

sexual intercourse at the end of the continuum, we realize there is a wide variety of types of sexual behavior that can occur before reaching consummated incest. Sexual play, for example, between a father and a daughter that consists of touching, fondling, fellatio and/or masturbation, but which falls short of full penetration, can be referred to as incestuous behavior. In both legal incest, which involves consummation, and incestuous behavior, the sexual activity differs only in the degree of physical intimacy, while the quality and the psychological reality of the two behaviors have common psychodynamic roots. Since the legal definition of incest creates artificial categories of behavior which do not reflect the total clinical reality, in this discussion of the social and psychiatric aspects of incest, consummated incest and incestuous behavior will be treated as a clinical entity with variations in its manifestation.

2. Clinical Incest

This chapter deals primarily with endogamic or intrafamilial incest, as classified by Weinberg, and on father-daughter incest, the most commonly reported type of this intrafamilial variety. In endogamic incest, the emotional, social and sexual relationships are confined to the family alone, and the daughter is the specific object choice for the father. Less frequent are the other two types of incest described by Weinberg. These are where the father suffers from psychosis or character disorder and is sexually promiscuous and the family members are merely additional sexual objects, and where the father is the psychosexually immature type who has paedophilic cravings and becomes involved with other children as well as his own.[2]

Other types of incest, which are less common than father-daughter incest, are homosexual incest, mother-son incest, and sibling incest. Many of the dynamics occurring in homosexual incest are similar to those apparent in father-daughter incest.[3] Sibling incest, the least reported form,[4] is possibly the most common type of incest and, according to some authors, the least damaging.[5] Mother-son incest is a relatively rare phenomenon and is viewed as more pathological than father - daughter; either or both of the participants tend to suffer from a mental illness such as schizophrenia.[6]

In the past few years, data from numerous studies have revealed as a myth that most incest cases come from rural areas, are the result of poverty, alcoholism and over-crowding, and are related to mental retardation.[7] We now know that, although these may be factors, incest exists to a large extent in working and middle class families where there is no problem of alcoholism or mental inferiority.[8] One of the main points to realize when assessing father-daughter incest is that the incest between the father and daughter does not take place in isolation but is carried out within the family dynamics. All members of the family play a role in the incest drama and are affected by it. Incest is a family problem and not simply a problem arising solely from individual psychopathology.

The fathers tend to be middle-aged, or in their late 30's or 40's and are beginning to realized that they are growing older without, perhaps, having accomplished everything they wanted to. They are more often than not of normal of above-average intelligence, tend to be good workers and are usually not involved with other criminal activities.[9] The marital relationship is usually poor and sexual relationships tend to be either non-existent or very unsatisfying.[10] There is little evidence of the father resorting to extramarital affairs.[11] The role of the wife is particularly important. The evidence indicates that she colludes in the incest and, although she frequently denies knowledge of it, is often aware of the relationship existing between her husband and daughter. By ignoring the situation she fails to fulfill her role in the family of protecting her children.[12]

The incest becomes a family 'secret' that is shared neither with ousiders or with each other. All family members work at keeping this secret for the purpose of maintaining the equilibrium of the family, despite the fact that the family is already destroyed.[13] There is emotional neglect of the sons in these families as the father either ignores them or is overtly hostile.[14]

In the majority of cases the daughter is at puberty when the incest begins, although some are younger when the father initiates sexual activity. This activity may consist of foreplay or actual intercourse. The incest tends to be protacted over a period of years rather than episodic.[15] The sexual attentions of the father may extend to other daughters, particularly when they reach puberty, and when he is beginning to lose control over the older daughter.[16]

The father plays a dual role with his daughter. On the one hand he is authoritarian, using his position as a means of controlling her behavior, of securing her developing sexuality for himself, and of protecting her from the attention of rival boyfriends. In addition, he is the awkward adolescent lover, plying her with presents, bribes and attention. The psychodynamic interpretation of the incest relationship has been described as follows: when the father chooses his daughter as the object of his sexual desires, she is a substitute for his wife and represents his young wife whom he courted as a young man. He has the illusion of himself as the young lover. There is further transformation in that the daughter also represents his early, giving mother. Although he may deny the incest for various lengths of time, he usually experiences strong feelings of guilt about his behavior, consciously or unconsciously. These feelings are particularly acute at the time of disclosure, when he experiences guilt towards his wife, his daughters and his sons.[17]

There have been few comprehensive studies of the personality of the victim. Although there is general agreement that the incest has a negative effect on the girl's development, the degree and nature of the after-effects of the trauma have yet to be confirmed.[18] Some suggest that the girl's later pathology is due more to the family's disorganization than to the incest itself.[19] In our series of incest cases, some of the incestuous daughters seem to have made a better social adaptation than their non-incestuous sisters.

There is a range of feelings the daughter may experience towards her parents and these feelings vary according to the phase of the incest relationship. Generally speaking, her feelings towards the father are ambivalent. At the beginning she may be highly affectionate and actually seductive with him. Towards the end of the incest relationship and as she matures, she tends to become angry and hostile, desiring to break away from her father's control. It is usually at this point that she discloses the incest, but not without a good deal of conflict. She often expresses guilt about the difficulty she has brought her father and family with her diclosure. Towards her mother there are ambivalent feelings of guilt, shame and fear of her anger.[20] There may also be anger towards the mother for her failure to protect her daughters. Some authors stress the girl's revenge wishes towards the mother because of a primary maternal frustration.[21]

3. Current Legal Treatment of Incest

In Canada there are two legal routes which a person accused of incest may follow. He may be charged either in the criminal court or the family court, with very different consequences. The attitude towards the offence, the atmosphere in which it is handled and most important, the sanctions in the two courts are very different. Section 150 of the Criminal Code of Canada prohibits sexual relations between parent and child, brother and sister, and grandparent and grandchild. Those found guilty are liable to 14 years imprisonment.[22] There are two provisos for incest dealt with in the family court. The father may be charged under section 33 of the Juvenile Delinquents Act[23] or under article 15 of the Youth Protection Act.[24] Section 33 provides a range of case disposal from probation to two years imprisonment.

Although the consequences in each court for the individual are very different, the factors determining in which court the incest offender is charged, are frequently quite arbitrary. There are two clearcut situations, however, which clearly determine the charge. First, the criminal court handles only those cases where consummation of the incest is suspected. Incestuous behavior, defined earlier, and which comprises the majority of cases, is usually dealt with in the family court. This does not rule out the possibility of cases of consummated incest also being dealt with in that court. Homosexual incest, however, is not defined as legal incest and is therefore dealt with under section 33 of the Juvenile Delinquents Act. Second, the nature of the legal relationship between the two participants in incest may determine the charge brought against the adult. Cases involving sexual relations between uncle-niece, aunt-nephew, step-parents and step-children, not prohibited in the narrow definition of section 150 of the Criminal Code, would be charged in the family court. Outside these two factors, clearly defined by the working of the law itself, the decision of which proceedings are brought against an individual appears to be a discretionary one.

Although the consequences in human terms are vastly different for the offender and his family, depending on whether he is tried in the adult or family court, there is no existing research on the nature of the arrest process or the factors determining which court is used. It is likely that this will depend on the person to whom the complaint is made, his experience with the problem and knowledge of resources. It is likely that most cases are reported to a policeman, although some social workers are probably also recipients of information. There is some evidence that, through ignorance of the problem and lack of clear agency policy, the social worker may decide to take no action; either legal or therapeutic. When treatment is initiated, it may not be based on sound knowledge of the subject.[25] It is highly likely that there are instances when a social worker, treating a family for other problems, becomes aware of incest and because of this she is a key person to consider when thinking in terms of prevention or early treatment. In the Montreal area in the past 20 years, there has been an increasing number of cases handled in the family court as opposed to criminal court. One of the reasons for this may be the work of the McGill Clinic in Forensic Psychiatry which has accepted referrals of incest cases for evaluation and treatment and made this service available to that court.

A significant development in Quebec in the area of child welfare occurred with the passing of Bill 78, a new amendment to the Youth Protection Law, and the establishment of the Committee for the Protection of Children.[26] This committee is empowered to investigate solutions of suspected physical abuse of children. In this process they encounter incest cases, which their current mandate does not oblige them to handle. Because of their non-punitive therapeutic approach and their natural accessability to incest cases, it would be of considerable value if their mandate were enlarged so as officially, and by definition, to include incest and other cases involving sexual behavior between an adult and a child. When the sexual behavior is not assaultive, paedophilia, like incest, is best handled in a non-punitive, treatment-oriented setting.

The current law concerning incest, as defined in the present Criminal Code, is a blunt, inexact instrument which misses the majority of cases. Those it does touch are handled inadequately, with no sensitivity to the psychological factors involved. The law is moralistic rather than practical and the present system neither prevents incest nor ameliorates it once it occurs. The Gigeroff report concluded that there is no indication that the existing Code either identified the problem or acts as a deterrent.[27]

The principal purpose of the law prohibiting incest is to protect children from the trauma of early sexual relations with close relatives and to protect their families from the pathology that results from it. Since the majority of cases are never discovered and do not reach a court, this protective goal is seldom fulfilled. In those cases where the father is incarcerated, the protective function of the law is accomplished, but not without a series of negative consequences of such severity that one must conclude that the law actually causes more harm to the family than it alleviates. Incarceration causes both economic and psychological hardship to the family which is broken up regardless of any potential for restructuring family roles and protecting the children. Despite his incestuous relationship with his daughter, in many cases the father provides emotional and financial support for his family which, with his incarceration, is frequently forced to undergo the difficult experience of living on welfare. The abandoned wife is left to undertake all of the tasks involving child rearing. The anxiety and guilt frequently experienced by the accusing daughter when she exposes her father, whom she often loves, is greatly exacerbated by his imprisonment which deprives these feelings of an opportunity for resolution. By going to prison the father loses his family, friends and job, and has little or no opportunity to gain insight into his behavior. Utilizing the criminal court in cases of incest ensures only that further incest does not occur for the period the father is incarcerated. There is no evaluative or support system built into the criminal court that ensures that the individual needs of the family members receive attention and, if necessary, treatment.

The 'tip of the iceberg' aspect of incest is generally well recognized.[28] Fear of punishment which disclosure would bring is, no doubt, a major deterrent for these families already inhibited from seeking help. A more tolerant approach by society would also enable people in a position to suspect incest (teachers, relatives, friends, doctors and social workers) to make the appropriate referral for help.

4. New Legal - Clinical Responses

The decriminalization of incest has social and clinical merit in that it provides protection of the physical and psychological well-being of children while avoiding the damaging effects of incarceration of the father and affords the means of offering treatment and rehabilitation of family members where indicated. An appreciation of these factors is reflected in the Gigeroff report on incest. This study, prepared for the Law Reform Commission of Canada, makes the clear, unreserved recommendation that cases of incest and incestuous behavior be adjudicated in the juvenile and family court.[29] The Law Reform Commission has hence recommended that the criminal law on incest be carefully reconsidered.[30]

A major clinical factor to consider when discussing legal and psycho-social alternatives for the problem of incest is that *recidivism of incest is rare, when properly handled at the time of disclosure.*[31] It is possible, with the help of proper controls and monitoring either to keep the father in the community or to return him to his family, without fear of incest recurring. In the past 20 years, the McGill Clinic in Forensic Psychiatry has dealt with approximately 100 cases of incest. Of these 35 percent were seen in the penitentiary and 65 percent were handled in the family court and treated on an out-patient basis. In the latter group, none of the fathers were sent to prison and although at least half returned to their families, there were no cases of recidivism. The few cases of recidivism that occurred belonged to the first group and were fathers who were incarcerated with no access to treatment either for themselves or their families. Maisch, referring to a number of studies, describes the rate of recidivism as ranging from 0.1 percent to 2 percent, depending on the type of incest.[32] The rarity of recidivism can be understood when its psychological dynamics are examined. The maintenance of an incestuous relationship depends to a great extent on the father's ability to distort reality and, in his courtship of his young daughter, he sees himself as a young lover. In this process the daughter becomes his young wife and also the mother of his childhood. When disclosure shatters this illusion and he sees his daughter as she really is, it is psychologically impossible for him to return to this relationship. Disclosure also liberates the whole family who, by finding other, healthier roles, prevent the incest from recurring.[33]

5. Case Disposal - Legal

All cases of incest can be handled without use of the criminal court, either exclusively in community agencies, or in the family court system. Without suggesting that the family court does not require further alteration, there is sufficient scope within the court, with its case disposal alternatives ranging from probation to incarceration, to deal adequately with incest cases. Incest can be broken down into various behaviors, the classification of which will determine the treatment. There can be a gradation of legal and social interventions, the choice dependent on the severity and complexity of the incest, with incarceration used only as a last resort.

Three broad legal-clinical classifications can be made. These are set out below. Once incest is disclosed, the preliminary decision of which category the case belongs in can be made by a specialized service, such as the Child Protection Committee. Dissemination of information about this service and incest in general, both to social agencies and the community at large, would facilitate these referrals. Since incest is primarily a family problem whose causes are rooted in family dynamics as well as individual pathology, this decision as well as the treatment plan must be based on a thorough psycho-social assessment of the family and its individual members. For this assessment, the members can be seen in various combinations; each individual alone, the marital couple, and the mother-daughter unit. It is probably least stressful for the family if, during the crisis period of disclosure, the father leaves the home, at least temporarily.

(i) Endogamic/Non-Court Cases

The majority of incest cases are of the endogamic, intrafamilial type and a large number of these can be effectively handled, without using the family court at all, in community agencies and clinics, applying a variety of therapeutic interventions. In these families, incest is a symptom of family disorganization as well as individual pathology and the legal removal of the father only causes additional stresses without affecting the more deeply rooted family problems. The father's denial of the incest can be worked through with relative ease and treatment of the individual and family problems that initiated the incest can begin. When denial is stronger, the fact that referral to the family court may be the next step would often be sufficient impetus to the family to begin to deal with their problem. The actual treatment can be carried out by community agencies which have access to a central body such as the Youth Protection Committee. The role of such a committee would not extend beyong ensuring that the case was receiving treatment.

(ii) Endogamic/Court Cases

Cases requiring stronger intervention and more supervised control can be referred to the family court. Factors indicating such a referral might be an extremely rigid father and/or a passive wife who cannot protect her children. Placing the father on probation, part of which may require attendance at a clinic for treatment, is usually sufficient to control the situation. An essential ingredient of this plan is a close liaison between the judge, the probation officer and the treating agency in the form of regular progress reports.

(iii) Other

More stringent measures can be used in those cases where it is felt that a more moderate approach would be ineffective in controlling the incest. This category includes the following situations:

(a) where the father is very rigid or exhibits poor impulse control, perhaps due to alcohol abuse; (b) where there is a question of mental illness, such as a psychosis, or mental retardation; (c) where the sexual relationship has more of the qualities of a sexual assault than an incestuous relationship; (d) where the father is psychosexually immature and engages in paedophilic activities as well as incestuous ones.

Legal removal of the father from the home through a court order might be indicated in these situations. This, of course, would be accompanied by a treatment program for the father and other family members. Depending on his condition, a psychotic father might be treated in a hospital or on an out-patient basis. A sentence of deprivation of liberty, the maximum provided for under section 33 of the Juvenile Delinquents Act being two years, should be considered *only as a last resort* and only when more moderate measures, such as probation, have failed. None of the 65 cases of incest assessed and treated by the McGill Clinic in Forensic Psychiatry on an out-patient basis, were evaluated as necessitating imprisonment as a means of controlling the incest.[34]

Hans Mohr, in his study on sexual offences for the Law Reform Commission of Canada, has suggested that paedophilia is a behavior which has similar qualities to incest and could probably be better handled in a family court where there is the possibility of treatment.[35] It is our clinical experience that cases of paedophilia and cases of incest where paedophilia also occurs, are amenable to therapeutic interventions and can be safely and more effectively handled through use of the family court, with the offender allowed to remain at liberty. Cases of mental retardation indicated a specialized approach involving re-education and the development of social and vocational skills.

6. Clinical Treatment

There is no standard formula for treating incest cases as each family is unique and must be assessed on its own merits. There is, however, a range of possible therapeutic interventions which can be used in various combinations depending on the assessed need in each family. Most important, the treatment plan must be flexible and change as the lives of the individuals evolve and the family situation is altered. At the time of disclosure and during the period of assessment which follows, one of the members of the triangular relationship should probably be removed from the home. This is usually the father, who may be facing a charge in the family court. The decision of whom to remove from the home and the duration of the removal is a clinical one. Temporary removal of the daughter may be indicated if the mother is extremely hostile towards her because of the child's displacement of the mother in the father's affections.[36] Since the daughter may interpret her removal as banishment and a punishment, such a move should be discussed carefully and worked through with her.

A major goal in the treatment of these cases is the re-establishment of the roles in the family. This can be accomplished in a variety of ways; individual counseling for the different family members, joint therapy for the couple, and/or brief task-oriented family sessions. In reference to the latter, one should be cautious in involving all members of the family in therapy as there is a danger of interfering with the rights of individual family members, particularly those not involved directly with the incest.

Individual counseling is indicated for the father, who, in most instances, is the member most motivated for treatment. This father, quite different from our old image of him as a primitive, amoral person, experiences guilt and depression. At the time of disclosure, the depression may be quite acute, particularly if his wife rejects him and in essence he loses his whole family.[37] It is our experience that, although these fathers do not actively seek treatment, once incest is disclosed they welcome the opportunity of having therapy and frequently continue their treatment after the probation period has ended.

The wife, the injured party, and in some sense the victim of the incest situation, plays a pivotal role in the family's ability to reorganize itself on a healthier pattern of functioning.[38] She is somewhat less motivated to seek treatment than her husband and finds therapy difficult as she must face her collusive role and her failure to protect her daughter. Furthermore, she can easily rationalize her lack of guilt because her unconscious denial of the incest before disclosure is a crime neither of commission nor omission. The sooner she shows sufficient ego strength to acknowledge her past role, the more positive the outlook for the whole family. Supportive counseling may be all that is required to work through her conflicts.[39]

If the wife cannot face the past and the couple cannot resolve a more sexually gratifying relationship, they must decide to separate permanently. This decision to separate should be based on a carefully worked out decision rather than on the immediate, highly emotional reactions of the time of disclosure. Joint therapy can help them either come to this decision or, if they decide to stay together, work on some of the basic problems in the relationship.[40] Therapy for the daughter should have as a primary focus the establishment and consolidation of relationships outside the family. Although the daughter experiences great anxiety at the time of disclosure because of her fear that she has put her family in jeopardy, her action is a sign of emotional growth and strength. Her feelings of self-debasement should be worked through in order to prevent possible later difficulties in her relationship to other men.[41] Supportive counseling can usually achieve this and it is helpful if the daughter, having established a good relationship with the therapist, can return in times of later crises.

7. Summary

Incest is a complex family problem which has the best chance of resolution if it is handled by society, by our family courts and/or social agencies, in a non-punitive, sensitive and realistic way. Whether the family endures the crisis of disclosure and emerges intact or is permanently broken up, the application of a treatment plan, sensitive to the needs of each individual, ensures that each person has an opportunity to emerge with the least possible emotional damage and the greatest chance to develop and evolve in a healthy way. These aims are best achieved outside the judicial process. Legal measures should be the exception and all of these legal measures should be within the system of the family court.

NOTES

1. Maisch, Herbert, *Incest*. London, Eng.: Andre Deutsch Ltd., 1973.
2. Weinberg, Keison S., *Incest Behaviour*. New York, New York: Citadel Press, 1955.
3. Cooper, Ingrid, and Cormier, B.M., M.D., "Homosexual Incest", paper presented at the General Meeting of the Canadian Psychiatric Assoc., Ottawa, 1974 (unpublished).
4. Karpman, Benjamin, *The Sexual Offender and His Offenses*. New York, New York: Julian Press, Inc., 1954.
5. Masters, William H., and Johnson, Virginia E., "Incest: The Ultimate Taboo", *Redbook Magazine,* April, 1976.
6. Unwin, J. Robertson, unpublished paper, "Consummated Maternal Incest", International Conference on Criminology, Montreal, 1966; and see Wahl, Charles W., "The Psychodynamics of Consummated Maternal Incest" (Aug., 1960) *Archives of General Psychiatry,* Vol. III, 183-193.
7. Weiner, Irving B., "On Incest: A Survey" (1964) *Excerpta Criminolgica* IV, 137-155.
8. Szabo, Denis, "Problems of Socialization and Sociocultural Integration: The Aetiology" (1968) 16 *J. of Am. Psychoanalytic Assoc.* 783-791; Maisch, *Incest, op. cit.,* note 1.
9. Cormier, Bruno M.; Kennedy, Miriam; and Sungowicz, J., "Psychodynamics of Father Incest" (Oct. 1962), 7 *Canadian Psychiat. Assoc. J.* 203-217; Maisch, *Incest, supra;* and Weiner, "On Incest: A Survey", *op. cit.,* note 7.
10. Henderson, J., "A Synthesis of Data" (1971), 17 *Canadian Psychiat. Assoc. J.* 299-313; Maisch, *Incest, supra;* and Weiner, "On Incest: A Survey".
11. Cormier, Bruno M. *et. al., op. cit.,* note 9.
12. Cormier, Bruno M., *et al., ibid.;* Karpman, Benjamin, *op. cit.,* note 4; and Rhinehart, John W., "Genesis Overt Incest" (1961) *Comprehensive Psychiatry* Volume II, no. 6, 388-449.
13. Cormier, Bruno M., *et al., supra;* and Karpman, Benjamin, *op. cit.,* note 4.
14. Cormier, Bruno M. *et al., supra.*
15. Maisch, *Incest, supra* and see also Henderson, J., *op. cit.,* note 10.
16. Cormier, Bruno M., *et al., supra.*
17. *Ibid.*
18. Karpman, Benjamin, *supra,* Henderson, J., "A Synthesis of Data", *supra.*
19. Maisch, *Incest, supra.*
20. Cormier, Bruno M., *et al., supra* and see also Kennedy, Miriam; and Cormier, Bruno M., "Father-Daughter Incest: Treatment of the Family" (Nov., 1969), 40 *Laval Medicine* no. 9, 946-950.
21. Rascovsky, Arnaldo and Matilda, "On Consummated Incest" (1950) *International Journal of Psychoanalysis* Vol. XXX: 42-47.
22. Canadian Dept. of Justice, Criminal Code and Selected Statutes, Vol. XVII, no. cc. 34, 73-74.
23. Canada, the Juvenile Delinquents Act. *Statutes of Canada.* c. 160, 1972.
24. Quebec, Youth Protection Act. *Statutes of Quebec* Vol. 14, George VI, no. 42 c., 1960.

25. Power, Anne B., "Incest: Casualty and Treatment" (Oct. 1976) *Research Report*, McGill University, Montreal, pp. 81-82.
26. National Assembly, *Bill No. 78* Charles Henri Dubé. Quebec Official Publisher, no. c 220, 1974.
27. Gigeroff, A.K., *et al.* Research Report Incest. *Sexual Offenses Under the Criminal Code of Canada Research Project* (July, 1975) Law Reform Commission of Canada and Clarke Institute of Psychiatry.
28. Maisch, *Incest, supra.*
29. *Op. cit.,* note 27.
30. Law Reform Commission of Canada Report, *Our Criminal Law.* Ottawa, Canada: Crown Copyrights Information Canada, Mar., 1976.
31. *Op. cit.,* note 20.
32. Maisch, *Incest, supra.*
33. Cormier, Bruno M., *et al.* (Oct., 1972) *Canadian Psychiat. Assoc. J.* 203-217.
34. Cormier, Bruno M., *et al., ibid.,* and see also (Nov., 1969) *Laval Medicine,* Vol. 40, no. 9, 946-950.
35. Mohr, Hans, "Report on Disposal of Cases of Sexual Offenses", Law Reform Commission of Canada, 1976.
36. Cormier, Bruno M., *et al.* (Nov., 1969), *Laval Medicine,* Vol. 40, no. 9, 946-950.
37. *Op. cit.,* note 33.
38. *Op. cit.,* note 35.
39. Cormier, Bruno M., *et al., supra,* note 32.
40. *Op. cit.,* note 33.
41. *Op. cit.,* note 35.

Chapter 35

Incest in Belgian Criminal Law

*Patrick Senaeve**

1. Introduction

Belgian law, like French and Dutch law, does not penally punish incest as such. The absence of any provision that punishes sexual intercourse between close relatives on the one side and the explicit prohibition of marriage between these closer relatives on the other (while it is evident that in reality it is the sexual intercourse which is thought objectionable)[1] may be considered a consequence of the notion that sexual intercourse can only exist within the framework of marriage. Apparently the legislator is of the opinion that the sexual intercourse can be prevented if marriage is prevented.[2]

Although it is true that, generally speaking, Belgian criminal law by-passes the general phenomenon of incest, nevertheless incestuous conduct is considered from various points of view. Sexual intercourse between close relatives does not concern the criminal law provided that the intercourse is with the consent of both parties and that these parties are of age; this is so even in the case of intercourse with a minor between 16 and 21 provided that the partner is not a blood-relation in the direct line. The criminal law does, however, take into account the incestuous nature of certain acts in the following respects: (a) as a constitutive element of a specific offence and (b) as an aggravating cirmcumstance in offences which can be committed by anyone.

2. The Legal Provisions

A. Incest as a Constitutive Element of a Specific Offence

In 1912 the Belgian legislator introduced into the Penal Code (art. 372, ss. 2) the offence of "indecent assault committed without violence or threats by any

---

* Instituut voor Familierecht, Katholieke Universiteit Leuven, Belgium.

ascendant upon the person or helped by the person of a minor, even when fully 16 years of age, but not emancipated by marriage". Such an offence did not exist before the law of May 15, 1912; it had even been firmly rejected when the Penal Code was established in 1867.[3] Under the previous legislation the offence of indecent assault without violence committed by an ascendant was the same as the one committed by any person, but the penalty was aggravated in view of the nature of the perpetrator.[4]

The Belgian legislator chose 16 as the age when a minor is in a position to consent validity to all intercourse of heterosexual character: he cannot be considered the victim of sexual intercourse in the absence of violence or threats.[5] Nevertheless, an exception was provided concerning sexual intercourse between a minor and his ascendant. The justification generally given for this does not lie in the incestuous character of the intercourse but in presumption of the absence of valid consent by the minor on account of their relationship with their ascendants.[6] This offence is only committed if the victim is over 16 and under 21 years of age. An indecent assault committed without violence or threats upon a descendant under 16 is covered by subsection 1 of article 372: in this case the fact that the perpetrator is an ascendant cannot be a constitutive element of the offence (although it will constitute an aggravation circumstance) since indecent assault committed without violence or threats is in any case punishable whenever the victim is under 16.[7]

If the minor descendant has been emancipated by marriage, no offence will be committed. The *ratio legis* of this provision was that a young married girl (the case the legislator had specifically in mind) has her husband as a protector against the influence of her ascendants, so that the presumption of non-consent to the incestuous intercourse is removed.[8] On the other hand an express emancipation (art. 477, Civil Code) does not remove the presumption because, it is said "an act of the will of the guilty father cannot eliminate his misdemeanour".[9]

The impunity of incestuous intercourse where the minor has been emancipated by marriage, and the punishment of the same intercourse where she has been judicially emancipated does not seem to be in accordance with the modifications to the civil law that have taken place since the law of May 15, 1912 was passed. The law of April 30, 1958 abolished the husband's authority over his wife; as a result a husband is no longer the legal protector or his wife. The law of April 8, 1965 concerning juvenile welfare, transformed express emancipation; it is no longer a prerogative of the parental authority[10] and consequently we no longer deal with a voluntary emancipation but with a judicial emancipation. Now requests for emancipation must be referred to the juvenile court and it is for the court to decide whether to grant it.[11] As a result of this modification, art. 372, ss. 2, Penal Code is no longer consistent with the provisions of civil law concerning emancipation. The punishment of incestuous intercourse, which is based upon the presumption of absence of the minor's consent, should be dropped as soon as the minor is emancipated, either by marriage or through the juvenile court, since parental authority is terminated in either case.

In 1975 a government bill concerning the lowering of civil majority to the age of 18 was introduced in the senate.[12] Following the example of most West European countries, it proposes to fix the age of civil majority at 18. Although this bill is confined to civil law, the lowering of the age of majority will have repercussions on some texts of the Penal Code whose specific aim is to protect young people against offences of which they are the victim. This will happen whenever reference is made only to the victim having reached the age of majority.[13] Among these offences is found the indecent assault of art. 372, ss. 2, Penal code. When the age of civil majority is lowered to 18, sexual intercourse between ascendants and descendants between 18 and 21 will no longer be punishable since the descendant will then be of age.[14] Moreover, the reasons for lowering the age of civil majority (the reduction of the duration of psychological maturation, earlier intellectual awareness, increased freedom, *etc.*)[15] are equally applicable in this matter.

The fact of being an ascendant is a constitutive element in the offence of art. 372, ss. 2 of the Penal Code. Here we are definitely dealing with the *punishment of one kind of incest,* since the intercourse would escape punishment if occurring between other persons.[16] The expression 'ascendant' has given rise to some difficulty. The provisions of civil law on the matter may be of limited relevance.[17] The term certainly covers all those who are related to the victim by blood-relationship in the direct line resulting from a legitimate marriage, irrespective of the degree of the relationship (parents, grandparents, great-grandparents). This applies also to the father, mother and ancestors of a legitimized child.[18] The expression includes *illegitimate* parents with respect to whom filiation is legally established. This applies also to illegitimate ancestors remoter than the father and mother, although Belgian law does not recognize a relationship in those cases.[19] This solution does not have to be justified by art. 161 of the Civil Code, which prohibits marriage between all illegitimate ascendants and descendants,[20] but by the fact that, in ordinary speech, which is how the penal law is interpreted, an illegitimate grandfather really is an ascendant.[21] On the other hand, the father of an illegitimate child with respect to whom filiation is not legally established is not covered by art. 372, ss. 2, Penal Code. For the relationship towards him is not certain.[22]

The provision relating to indecent assault in art. 372, ss. 2 of the Penal Code does not apply to *adoptive* parents, nor to those who have legitimized their child through adoption. Although adoption of minors and legitimation through adoption are not simply legal fictions and are normally accompanied by an educational program which treats the relationship as a blood-relationship,[23] the principle of legality requires that the provisions of penal law concerning the criminal prohibitions are strictly interpreted. Since the Flemish text of art. 372, ss. 2 of the Penal code uses the term 'bloedverwant' (blood-relation), and adoptive parents are not blood-relations, the criminal prohibition of art. 372, ss. 2, cannot be extended to adoptive parents.[24] Of course the expression 'ascendant' does not include *ascendants of in-laws.*[25]

B. Incest as a Aggravating Circumstance of Other Offences

The second situation in which incestuous acts taken into account by Belgian criminal law is when they are considered an aggravating circumstance of another offence.

Art. 372, ss. 1 of the Penal code punishes "each indecent assault committed without violence or threats upon the person or helped by the person of a minor of either sex, under 16 years of age". The Belgian legislator, having determined the age of 16 as the age of sexual self-determination, logically deduced that a child under 16 cannot give a free and voluntary consent to sexual acts. Thus, the criminal prohibition here is indifferent to who the perpetrator is.[26] It makes no difference if the sexual assault deeds are accompanied by violence or threats. Violent indecent assault and rape are criminally prohibited irrespective of the age of the victim and the relationship between offender and victim.

But if the relationship is irrelevant to the criminality of the act, it is nevertheless relevant to the punishment, for it may constitute an aggravating circumstance. While indecent assault without violence or threats upon a minor under 16 and indecent assault with violence or threats upon a minor over 16 incur solitary confinement (for 5 to 10 years), the same deeds incur forced labor for 10 to 15 years, if, under the terms of art. 377, "the offender is the ascendant of the victim". So also in the case of rape. The interpretation of the expression 'ascendant' in this context is of little practical importance because art. 377 of the Penal Code also prescribes an aggravation of the penalty if the offender "is among those who have authority over the victim". Since most people who could be arguably considered to be 'ascendants' will usually have authority over the victim, such people will be covered by that clause. Furthermore, the clause extends to people other than ascendants, such as the second husband of the mother, her cohabitee or siblings and so on. In determining whether people exercise 'authority' over the victim, both the legal and factual authority are taken into account.[27] It should be stressed that it is not the incestuous character of these acts which aggravates the penalty but the misuse of authority.[28]

C. Incest as an Indifferent Constitutent of an Offence Against Morality

Sometimes incestuous conduct is punished in the same way as any other illegal sexual conduct. Under Belgian law sexual deeds are punishable either because of the age of one of the partners, or because of the violence used, or because of its homosexual character. These provisions can of course be used when such acts are committed within the family, but then it is not their incestuous character which makes them punishable but because they are infingements against the ordinary law.[29]

As we have noted before, any indecent assault perpetrated even without violence or threats *upon a minor under 16 is punishable.* Similarly, *any* sexual act inflicted by violence or threats is punishable. Finally, the offence of *homosexuality*, introduced in the Belgian Penal Code by the law of April 8, 1965, prohibits homosexual acts committed by a person over 18 upon the person of or helped by a minor between the ages of 16 and 18.[30] Therefore the penalties of solitary confinement for six months to three years and of a fine can be applied, for example, to a man who has sexual intercourse with his minor brother under 18 years of age. Of course, the minor's emancipation by marriage does not prevent the application of these provisions.

3. Conclusions

Belgian criminal law is fairly tolerant concerning the punishment of incestuous acts. The scope of this tolerance will be expanded further when the age of civil majority is lowered to 18. In most other countries of Western Europe, with the exception of France and the Netherlands, the laws are more repressive. Most know a specific offence of incest which punishes the two partners even when they are of age.[31] It does not seem that Belgian law should become more repressive. Although sexual conduct between close relatives is not desirable, criminal repression is, without doubt, not the obvious way to deal with problems within the domestic circle. Detecting such offences is extremely difficult and in most cases they are only disclosed as an act of vengeance by one of the partners. Moreover, there is the considerable problem of false denunciation. Finally, increased repression in regard to sexual offences would not be in line with the current trends of Western legislation. I would propose a limitation of the punishment of sexual acts, in the first place by abolishing the specific offence of homosexuality, as has been proposed in a recent private member's bill[32] and secondly by lowering to 15 the age at which a minor is considered to be able to consent validly to intercourse, as is the case in France.[33] This age seems more realistic than the present. These suggestions, of course, go beyond the scope of incest, but a modification of criminal lelgislation in this direction would automatically influence the criminal prohibition of incestuous acts.

A father or mother sentenced to imprisonment for sexual intercourse with descendants may be deprived of parental authority. In the law of April 8, 1965 (concerning juvenile welfare) the loss of parental authority has become an exceptional sanction, which will only be applied whenever it is necessary to break the ties between parents and their children.[34] In the case of incest, such a measure, which is particularly repressive, will very often be inadequate, because the separation between the parent and the minor, and the consequent placing of the minor in an institution, will usually seriously disrupt the family. The minor in question often finds it hard to accept and considers it an undeserved punishment on himself. Such a situation, on the contrary, calls for the re-establishment of the disrupted family ties.[35]

In incest cases, the juvenile courts can also take measures respecting *the minor*, even if an intervention by penal law is excluded, *e.g.*, in the case of incest between brothers and sister. If such measures mean the removal of the minor from his family, it will still defeat its objective. In cases of incest, juvenile welfare measures will only have a positive result if they help the members of the family to overcome their psychological conflicts. To this end, treatment within the frame of the family is indispensable and should be provided by the social welfare services. Educational assistance may be ordered by the juvenile court (Law of April 8, 1965, art. 30-31), if the parties do not freely accept the intervention of the social welfare services.

1. See *e.g.* R.P.D.B., VII, Vo. Marriage, no. 39; Sohm-Bourgeois, no. 4.
2. Heyvaert, p. 77.
3. Nypels, p. 139, no. 9.
4. Biltris, p. 1021.
5. *Cf.* Rassat, no. 4 (in French legislation that age is 15 years).
6. *Cf.* Rigaux and Trousse, pp. 305-306.
7. Biltris, p. 1020-1022; R.P.D.B., I, no. 22. *Contra:* Rigaux and Trousse, p. 309.
8. Biltris, p. 1022; Rigaux and Trousse, pp. 309-310.
9. Garcon, no. 99.
10. See De Page, II, no. 252*ff.*
11. Before the Law of April 8, 1965 the judicial authorities, in this case the justice of the peace, were involved only to ascertain the declaration of the will and intention of the emancipator and not to bring about the emancipation. It was not in the power of this judge to keep a proper check on the motives of the father's decision. See De Page, II, no. 266; Kebers, p. 122.
12. *Parl. Doc.,* Senate, 1974-75, no. 673. See Pauwels, J., and Nuytinck, H., "Voorstellen betreffende het wetsontwerp tot verlaging van de leeftijd van burgerlijke meerderjarigheid tot 18 jaar" (1975-76) *Rechtskundig Weekblad* 1329-1339; Mahillon, P., and Lox, F., "L'abaissement de l'age de la majorité" (1976) *Journal des tribunaux* 145-147.
13. *Parl. Doc.,* Senate, 1974-75, no. 673, Explanatory statement, p. 12.
14. *Ib.,* p. 13.
15. *Cf. ib.,* p. 13. However the text speaks unjustly about the *aggravation of penalty* determined in art. 372, ss. 2, which will no longer be justified if the descendant is at least 18 years of age.
16. *Ib., Explanatory statement,* p. 2.
17. Rassat, no. 4.
18. See the article of Legros, pp. 143-176, who defends the principle of the autonomy of the criminal law in the cases where it punishes an encroachment on social morality (contrary to an encroachment on formal regulations imposed by the necessities of social life). According to him, the basis of this autonomy is to be found in the difference between legal and everyday languages; in these cases the judge of the criminal court is not strictly committed to the language of civil law; he does not give the words their technical meaning in respect of civil law, but their everyday, usual meaning, which is necessarily that of penal law (p. 175).
19. See Brussels, May 15, 1908, *R.P.D.,* 1909, p. 59 (case of rape of a man upon a child legitimized by marriage).
20. However, Belgian jurisprudence did recognize many legal consequences of illegitimate relationship beyond the first degree; see Rigaux, I nos. 3026-3028. A recent Government Bill proposes to abolish completely the discrimination towards illegitimate filiation in civil law: *Parl. Doc.,* Senate, 1977-78, no. 305.
21. As do a.o. Biltris, no. 88; Garcon, no. 101; Nypels and Servais, art. 377, no. 2; Delva, no. 319.
22. Legros, p. 156-157. According to him, to appeal strictly to civil law here would really be a diversion of the civil law.
23. Biltris, p. 1171; Delva, no. 321. In the meantime all these questions concerning illegitimate filiation lose a great deal of their importance if the facts are referred to the assizes, which is a court with a jury (the offence of art. 372, ss. 2 is a crime). The civil status is, in the assizes, a question fact, and it is for the jury to decide the question of kinship; see: Biltris, nos. 36 and 89; Rigaux and Trousse, p. 307.
24. Rigaux, I, no. 2441.
25. Delva, no. 325; *R.P.D.B.,* Compl. I, no. 63; Biltris, no. 90. Contra: Rigaux and Trousse, p. 308, and all French textbooks.

26. Rigaux and Trousse, p. 308.
27. See Biltris, nos. 25-28; Rassat, no. 8.
28. See Cass., 15 December, 1845, *Pas.*, 1846, I. 88; Cass., 19 March, 1866, I. 282; Cas., 25 June, 1866, *Pas.*, 1866, I. 286; Cass., May 24, 1954, *Pas.*, 1954, I. 828; and unanimous textbooks (Delva, references cited no. 331). Concerning all possible hypothesis, see Delva, nos. 332-35.
29. Rassat, no. 9
30. See Rigaux and Trousse, pp. 310-313. If the perpetrator is the ascendant of the minor, art. 372, ss. 2, Penal code has to be applied.
31. See "Les infractions contre la famille et la moralité sexuelle", National reports and general report of the IXe International Conference on criminal law organized at The Hague in 1964 (1975) *Revue internationale de droit pénal* 415-1090.
32. *Parl. Doc.*, House of Representatives, 1977-78, no. 177 (introduced by M. Glinne).
33. In Belgium the limit was fixed at 16 years by the law of May 15, 1912, but the legislator did not amend article 144 of the Civil code. Under this article, a girl may marry at 15. Thus the civil law grants her, the day she is 15, the capacity to assent to marriage, which implies the obligation of sexual intercourse, but the criminal law considers her unable to consent to a simple touch on her person! In France, on the contrary, this age is fixed at 15 years. See on this Biltris no. 15.
34. Piret, p. 153.
35. Van Heule, no. 37.

REFERENCES

Biltris, N., "L'attentat à la pudeur et le viol" (1925) *R.D.P.* 1002-1046 et 1161-1199.
Constant, J., "La protection pénale de la famille en droit belge", *Rapports belges au VIIe Congrès international de droit comparé*, Brussels, 1966, p. 481-509.
Declercq, R., "Les infractions contre la famille et la moralité sexuelle en droit belge" (1964) *R.D.P.* 503-550.
Delicten betreffende de seksualiteit, Deventer, 1968, p. 89.
Delva, J., "Aanranding van de Eerbaarheid en Verkrachting" (*A.P.R.*), Brussels, 1967.
De Page, H., *Traité élémentaire de droit civil belge*, T. I, Brussels, 1962; T. II. Brussels, 1964.
Garcon, E., *Code pénal annoté* (nouvelle édition par Rousselet, M.; Patin, M., et Ancel, M.), T. II. Paris, 1956.
Gendrel, "Les infractions contre la famille et la moralité sexuelle, sous l'angle des attentats aux moeurs entre membres de la même famille" (1964) *Rev. pen.* 31-53.
Heyvaert, A., 'Huwelijkstoestemming, verkrachting en eugenetica op zijn Belgisch', *Actori incumbit probatio*, Antwerp-Amsterdam, 1975, pp. 71-85.
Hudig, J.C., "Offences against the family" (1964) *Tijdschrift voor strafrecht* 259-266.
Legros, R., "Essai sur l'Autonomie du Droit pénal" (1956-57) *R.D.P.* 143-176.
Kebers, A., "Les dispositions de droit civil relatives aux mineurs" (1966) *Annales de droit* 85-126.
Nypels, *Légoslation criminelle de la Belgique*, T. III, Brussels, 1869.
Piret, J.-M., "Les mesures à l'égard des parents" (1966) *Annales de droit* 141-163.
Racine, A., "L'enfant victime d'actes contraires aux moeurs commis sur sa personne par un ascendant" (1958-59) *R.D.P.* 635-642.
Rassat, M.-L., "Inceste et droit pénal" (1974) *Jurisclasseur périodique* Vol. 1, 2614.
Repertoire pratique du droit belge, T. I, *Verbo* Attentat à la pudeur et viol, p. 557-567.
Répertoire pratique du droit belge, *Complément*, T. I. Brussels, 1964, *Verbo* Attentat à la pudeur et viol, (par Delva, J.), p. 326-354.
Rigaux, R., Les personnes, T. I. *Les relations familiales*, Brussels, 1971.

Rigaux, M., and Trousse, P.-E., Les crimes et les délits du code pénal, T. V. (par Trousse), Brussels - Paris 1968.

Sohm-Bourgeois, A.-M., Empêchements de mariage, (1971), *Jurisclasseur civil, Verbo* Marriage.

Van Heule, F., "Jeugdbescherming in de praktijk," *Kind en gerecht,* Leuven, 1978, pp. 36-74.

Appendix

Model Act To Free Children for Permanent Placement

*Sanford N. Katz**

In the past few years major efforts have been made in the United States to discover why thousands of children are living under the uncertainties of changing foster homes over extended periods of time. Two reasons have been cited. One, many of these children are in special circumstances and cannot be adopted without public financial assistance. Two, the foster children are often not legally free to be placed in a permanent living arrangement.

To meet the needs of children in special circumstances, the United States Department of Health, Education, and Welfare, Office of Child Development commissioned Professor Sanford N. Katz to draft a Model State Subsidized Adoption Act which would remove the barriers to the adoption of these children. This act was signed by the Secretary of the Department of Health, Education, and Welfare in August, 1975 and is now being disseminated throughout the United States. Over 40 American jurisdictions now have some kind of subsidized adoption program.

In order to solve the legal problem of children who cannot live in their own homes mainly because of child abuse and neglect and whose precarious situation needs immediate attention, the United States Department of Health, Education, and Welfare funded a study directed by Professor Katz which resulted in the formation of a Model Act to Free Children for Permanent Placement. This act was the product of months of meetings, correspondence and consultation with persons, including those from minority groups, who are intimately connected with the administration, interpretation and application of state laws on termination of parental rights. In addition there were consultations with workers and administrators from public and voluntary social service agencies, again including minorities, which deal with foster care programs. Adoptive and foster parents were also given the opportunity to provide input. Using the advice, criticism and suggestions from these various individuals and rewriting the act many times to accommodate the various interests represented, the following draft resulted.

The February 8, 1977 draft of the Model Act to Free Children for Permanent Placement is thus a statute which tries to balance the competing interests of the institutions and individuals concerned with the family nexus. The final version should be issued sometime during 1978.

---

* Boston College Law School, Newton Center, Massachusetts, U.S.A.

Appendix

Model Act* To Free Children For Permanent Placement — Revised as of March 8, 1978 — With Commentary

Draft — July 5, 1978

Sanford N. Katz†

Contents

---

* This Act was developed under a grant (OCD—DB—473) from the United States Department of Health, Education and Welfare to Professor Sanford N. Katz of Boston College Law School, Newton Center, Massachusetts, U.S.A. The Act has not yet been approved by the United States Department of Health, Education & Welfare. Therefore, it does not necessarily represent the official views of the Department.

† Project Director, Professor of Law, Boston College Law School, 885 Center St., Newton Center, Massachusetts 02159, U.S.A.

Section 1. Purposes of Act; Construction of Provisions

(a) The general purposes of this Act are to:

(1) provide prompt judicial procedures for freeing minor children from the custody and control of their parents, by terminating the parent-child relationship;

(2) promote the placement of such minor children in a permanent home, preferably through adoption or by vesting their *de facto* parents with legal guardianship; and

(3) ensure that the constitutional rights and interests of all parties are recognized and enforced in all proceedings and other activities pursuant to this Act.

(b) It is the policy of this State that:

(1) whenever possible and appropriate, the birth family relationship shall be recognized, strengthened, and preserved through efforts and procedures as provided for under [state] statute(s);

(2) removal of a child from his home shall occur only when the child cannot be adequately protected within the home;

(3) if a child has been removed from his home for one year and cannot be returned home within a reasonable time thereafter, the state should promptly find an alternative arrangement to provide a stable, permanent home for him;

(4) the interests of the child shall prevail if the child's interests and parental rights conflict; and

(5) because termination of the parent-child relationship is so drastic, all non-judicial attempts by contractual arrangements, express or implied, for the surrender or relinquishment of children, are invalid unless approved by the court.

(c) This Act shall be liberally construed to promote the general purposes and policies stated in this section.

Commentary

Three broad general purposes are stated in Subsection (a). The first general purpose of providing judicial procedures for the termination of the parent-child relationship is similar to the general purpose of all existing state termination statutes. The phrase "freeing minor children from the custody and control of their parents" is derived from *California Civil Code* §§232-239, entitled "Freedom From Parental Control and Custody."

Subsection (a)(2) declares that the intent of the Act is to promote the settlement of children in permanent homes, preferably through adoption or via vesting legal guardianship in *de facto* parents. This section reflects the philosophy that a child's ongoing needs for proper physical, mental and emotional growth and development can best be met when he is firmly anchored in a family of his own.

Paragraph (3) of subsection (a) addresses the constitutional requirement of protecting individual due process rights. In subsequent sections the Model Act provides for counsel for parents, appointment of guardians *ad litem* for children, minor or incompetent parents and adequate notice to all parties.

Subsection (b) articulates the key underlying policy principles that are to guide the state's approach to judicial termination of parental rights. In paragraph (1) the state pledges, whenever possible and appropriate, to recognize the birth family relationship and to strengthen and preserve that parental relationship through efforts and procedures mandated by other existing state statutes.

Paragraph (2) provides that the sole criterion for removing a child from its home is that the child cannot be protected within the home either by his parents alone or through the marshalling of community social services or court ordered protective supervision. This principle appears in some neglect laws, but is not generally found in existing termination statutes. The Model Acts's sole focus is upon protecting the child, while most state neglect statutes also refer to an inability to protect the public.

When a child has been removed from his home for one year, paragraph (3) of subsection (b) places an affirmative duty upon the state to ascertain whether the child can be returned home within a reasonably foreseeable time. The exact length of time will vary depending upon the child's age and the various considerations enumerated in Section 4. If a return to the birth family is not possible or appropriate, this paragraph requires that the state begin to take steps to provide such a child with an alternative stable, permanent home.

Paragraph (4) mandates that the interests of the child shall prevail. This represents a departure from the wording of most existing termination and neglect statutes. Only California's *Civil Code* §§232.5 directs that: "The provisions of this chapter shall be liberally construed to serve and protect the interests and welfare of the child."

The final paragraph in subsection (b) declares invalid all non-judicial attempts at severance of the parent-child relationship by contractual arrangements. Termination of a parent-child relationship involves a severe reordering of personal statuses and legal rights and obligations. A judicial proceeding is necessary to ensure that the constitutional rights of all parties are recognized and enforced in accord with the general purpose expressed in subsection (a)(3). The Model Act, in subsequent sections, provides for some accommodation to the administrative procedures of some states which permit agencies to accept voluntary relinquishments from parents or other caretakers. In some instances, the required judicial proceeding may be only to ratify the voluntary relinquishment and to certify the proposed plan for the child. *See* Sections 3, 10(d) and 15(a) *infra*.

The last subsection (c) is a directive for liberal construction of all provisions of the Act in order to accomplish the stated purposes.

Section 2. Definitions

(a) As used in this Act, unless the context otherwise requires:

(1) "Authorized agency" means a public or private non-profit social agency expressly empowered by law to place children for adoption or foster care.

(2) "Child" means a son or daughter, whether by birth or by adoption, under the age of 18 years.

(3) An "abused or neglected child" means a child whose physical or mental health or welfare is harmed or threatened with harm by the acts or omissions of his parent or other person responsible for his welfare.

(4) "Harm" to a child's health or welfare can occur when the parent or other person responsible for his welfare:

(i) inflicts, or allows to be inflicted, upon the child, physical or mental injury, including injuries sustained as a result of excessive corporal punishment;
(ii) commits, or allows to be committed, against the child, a sexual offense, as defined by state law;
(iii) fails to supply the child with adequate food, clothing, shelter, education (as defined by law), or health care, although financially able to do so or offered financial or other reasonable means to do so; for the purpose of this Act, "adequate health care" includes any medical or non-medical remedial health care permitted or authorized under state law;
(iv) abandons the child; abandonment is conclusively presumed if the child is found under such circumstances that the identity or whereabouts of the parent is unknown and has not been ascertained by diligent searching and the parent does not claim the child within 2 months after the child is found; or
(v) fails to provide the child with adequate care, supervision, or guardianship by specific acts or omissions of a similarily serious nature requiring intervention of the child protective service or a court.

(5) "Threatened harm" means a substantial risk of harm.

(6) "Physical injury" means death, permanent or temporary disfigurement, or impairment of any bodily organ.

(7) "Mental injury" means an injury to the intellectual or psychological capacity of a child as evidenced by an observable and substantial impairment in his ability to function within his normal range of performance and behavior with due regard to his culture.

(8) "Court" means the [_____] court.

(9) "Guardian of the child's person" means a person, other than the parent of a child, or an authorized agency appointed by a court having jurisdiction over the child, to serve as custodian and to promote the general welfare of the child, with the duty and authority to make decisions permanently affecting the child's health and development.

(10) "Guardian *ad litem*" means an attorney appointed by a court having jurisdiction, to represent a person: either the child, his minor or incompetent parent, or his putative father in a judicial proceeding brought to terminate the parent-child relationship.

(11) "Legal custodian" means a person, or an authorized agency to whom legal custody of the child has been given by a court having jurisdiction over the child.

(12) "Legal custody" means a status created by court order under which a legal custodian has the following rights and duties:

(i) to maintain the physical custody of a child;
(ii) to protect, nurture, train and discipline a child;
(iii) to provide adequate food, clothing, shelter, and education as required by law, and routine medical care for a child; and
(iv) to consent to emergency medical and surgical care; and to sign a release of medical information to appropriate authorities, pursuant to state law.

(13) "Minor" means an unmarried person under the age of 18 years.

(14) "Parent" means the birth or adoptive mother or father of a child, regardless of the marital status of the parent; but the term excludes a parent whose rights have been terminated by judicial decree.

(15) "*De facto* parent" means a person, other than a parent, legal custodian, or guardian of the person, such as a relative, stepparent, or foster parent, who has had continuous physical custody of a child for one year and with whom the child has developed significant emotional ties.

(16) "Parent-child relationship" includes all rights, powers, privileges, immunities, duties and obligations existing between parent and child, as defined by state law.

(17) "Party" includes the child, the parents, and the petitioner.

(18) "Protective supervision" means a legal status under which a court, following an adjudication of abuse or neglect, permits a child to live in his home, subject to the supervision of an authorized agency designated by the court and subject to return to the court at any time during the period of protective supervision in case of harm or threatened harm.

(19) "Relinquishment" means the informed and voluntary release of the physical custody of a child by a parent to an authorized agency for the purpose of freeing the child for adoption or other permanent placement.

(20) "Residual parental rights and responsibilities" means the rights and responsibilities remaining with the parent after the transfer of legal custody or guardianship of the person, including, but not limited to, the right to reasonable visitation, consent to adoption, and the responsibility of support.

(b) As used in this Act, pronouns of the masculine gender include the feminine.

Commentary

The 20 terms and phrases defined in this section can be divided into 3 categories. First, all the possible parties in a termination proceeding: such as "child," "parent," "de facto parent," "legal custodian," "guardian of the child's person," "guardian ad litem," "agency" and "court" are defined. The second category defines an "abused or neglected child," with specific examples of what consitutes "harm" or "threatened harm" to a child's health or welfare and includes definitions of "physical injury" and "mental injury." Third, various statuses and relationships such as "minor," "legal custody," "parent-child relationship," "protective supervision," "relinquishment," and "residual parental rights and responsibilities" are delineated.

The Model Act's enumeration of major parties is consistent with the definitions found in most of the existing separate state termination chapters. The definition of "child" follows the wording of the Uniform Adoption Act and the trend to recognize any person under the age of 18 years as a child.

It should be noted that the definition of "parent" encompasses any birth or adoptive parent without regard to marital status. This definition is viewed as a positive step toward the elimination of discriminatory distinctions based solely on the status of legitimate or illegitimate birth, and is an approach consistent with the Uniform Parentage Act. *See,* Uniform Parentage Act, Comment to Sections 1 and 2. This definition is also viewed as a necessary step to accord the unwed father an opportunity to receive "notice" and to be heard on matters concerning the custody of his child, as required by *Stanley v. Illinois,* 405 U.S. 645 (1972).

The Model Act includes one term, *"de facto* parent," that does not generally appear in termination statutes. This definition is derived from a concept found in the Uniform Child Custody Jurisdiction Act's definition of "person acting as parent." The Model Act introduces the term *"de facto* parent" to describe the person who has had continuous physical custody of a child in his home for one year and with whom the child has developed significant emotional ties, but who has no other legal status pursuant to court order. A *"de facto* parent" may be a relative, a stepparent, or a foster parent.

The Model Act requires that the guardian *ad litem* be an attorney appointed by the court to represent either a child, his minor or incompetent parent, or an unknown putative father. Limiting guardian *ad litem* appointments to attorneys is the most effective method of implementing the Act's general purpose to ensure that the constitutional rights and interests of all parties are recognized and enforced in all proceedings. *See* Commentary following Section 13, *infra* for further discussion of the duties and qualifications of the guardian *ad litem.*

The definition of an "abused or neglected child" is consistent with the Federal Child Abuse Prevention and Treatment Act of 1974 (P.L. 93-247) and the Code of Federal Regulations (45 C.F.R. § 1340.1-2) and with terms found in the Model Child Protection Services Act, developed under the auspices of OCD/HEW. "Harm" to a child's health or welfare may occur from five kinds of parental acts or omissions: infliction of physical or mental injury; commission of or allowing a sexual offense as defined by state law against the child; failure to provide adequate care although financially able; abandonment; or such failure to provide adequate supervision that child protective services must intervene.

"Physical injury" may mean death, permanent or temporary disfigurement or impairment of any bodily organ—broken limb or a damaged internal organ such as a kidney. "Mental injury" encompasses emotional harm. It must be evidenced by some observable and substantial impairment of the child's social and intellectual functioning. The court is directed to give "due regard to the child's culture" when weighing evidence to determine if a substantial impairment of ability to function within a normal range has occurred or is threatened.

The Model Act's definition of "abandonment" [(a)(4)(iv)] is a narrow one which addresses the situation of a "foundling" left without any clue to the identity of the parent and under circumstances that indicate a complete abdication of all parental responsibility for the child. (A phone call to authorities notifying them of the location of the child—in a phone booth, bus depot, or rest room, for example— would not rebut the presumption of abandonment). If within two months the parents do not voluntarily appear or cannot be located by diligent inquiry by the agency or appropriate law enforcement personnel, the Model Act views such parental conduct as a ground for termination of parental rights so that permanent planning for such an infant can proceed. The Model Act does not require a finding of an intent to abandon.

The status and relationship definitions found in the third category of terms are modeled after the DHEW Model Family Court Act, *Ariz. Rev. Stat. Ann.* § 8-531 and *Idaho Code* § 16-2002. These statutes closely follow the suggested language found in the 1961 Children's Bureau publication, *Legislative Guides for the Termination of Parental Rights and Responsibilities and the Adoption of Children* 38-40 (Reprint 1968).

The Model Act's definition of "parent-child relationship" incorporates by reference "rights, powers, privileges, immunities, duties and obligations" as established under state law. Parents traditionally have been entitled to the custody of their children, unless they are proven to be "unfit." The state has imposed upon parents specific minimum responsibilities for fulfilling certain basic needs of their children for financial security, health and education. These basic needs of children represent social values shared by a majority of the population in the United States, but to which some groups may give varying priorities depending upon class, race, religion or other factors. Clearly, the dominant societal expectation is that child-rearing will occur within the context of a secure and autonomous relationship — one basically free from governmental intrusion.

Governmental intervention into the privacy of the family unit has traditionally been justified under the doctrine of *parens partriae* which gives precedence to a child's right to life over his parents' rights to custody. If the court determines that the child is suffering "harm" or is "threatened with harm," as these are defined in the Model Act, the court may make various orders. *See* Section 16 *infra*. One possible order is for "protective supervision" which permits a child to remain in his home, but subject to the supervision of an authorized agency designated by the court. Such an order can be a positive step toward implementing the general state policy expressed in Section 1(b)(1) to recognize, strengthen and preserve the birth family relationship whenever possible. Such an order would be appropriate for a family which has been assessed to have more strengths than weaknesses and where it has been determined that the parents can benefit from individual casework services or perhaps can learn better parenting techniques from a homemaker placed within the home.

When it has been decided that a child cannot be adequately protected within his own home, the court may place the child in foster care and order a change of "legal custody" and appoint a "guardian of the child's person." The legal custodian is charged with responsibility for the day-to-day physical care of the child, while the guardian of the child's person has authority to make important decisions affecting the health and development of the child. (*See* Section 17, *infra.*) In some instances the custodian and the guardian of the person may be the same individual. In other cases an authorized agency may be appointed the guardian of the child's person and the legal custodian could be a relative or other interested party. Whenever the court transfers "legal custody" to someone other than the birth parent or appoints a "guardian of the child's person", certain "residual parental rights and responsibilities" remain with the parent until a final decree of termination of the "parent-child relationship." These "residual rights and responsibilities" remaining until termination generally include the right of reasonable visitation, consent to adoption and the responsibility for support. "Relinquishment" refers to any voluntary parental release of the physical custody of a child to an authorized agency specifically for adoption or other permanent planning. Such a release must be made with full knowledge and assumes that the parent intends to completely give up exercise of all parental rights and responsibilities.

Section 3. Grounds for Voluntary Termination of the Parent-Child Relationship

(a) If the court determines that termination of the parent-child relationship is in the best interest of the child, it may order such termination provided that:

(1) a parent either directly or through an authorized agency voluntarily petitions for the termination of the parent-child relationship; or

(2) a parent has executed an out-of-court notorized statement evincing to the court's satisfaction that the parent has voluntarily and knowingly relinquished the child to an authorized agency no earlier than 72 hours after the child's birth.

Commentary

Consistent with the mandate in Section 1(b)(5) that termination be judicially supervised, this section requires the court to decide upon all voluntarily sought terminations of the parent-child relationship by considering the best interest of the child. Two general types of circumstances are envisioned. A voluntary petition seeking the termination of a parent-child relationship may be filed by a parent either directly or through an authorized agency. Or, an authorized agency which has accepted a written relinquishment of a child from a parent may present it to the court. (*See* Section 9(c) *infra*.)

This section of the Model Act recognizes that in some states well established administrative procedures are utilized to accept voluntary relinquishments. The Model Act does not require that these be abolished, nor does it require that all relinquishing parents appear personally before the court. In the interest of meeting constitutional standards of due process and recognition of the constitutional right of family integrity, all administrative relinquishments must be presented to the court and found to have been voluntarily and knowingly executed. The Model Act thus requires that a notorized statement be attached to the petition. Agencies may need to rethink their procedures for accepting voluntary relinquishments, including the oral explanations of the significance of the parent's decision, the language of the form executed by the parents and the numbers and kind of staff present at the execution of the relinquishment.

Section 4. Grounds for Involuntary Termination of the Parent-Child Relationship

(a) An order of the court for involuntary termination of the parent-child relationship shall be made on the grounds that the termination is in the child's best interest, in light of the considerations in subsections (b) through (f), where one or more of the following conditions exist:

(1) the child has been abandoned, as defined by Section 2(a)(4)(iv);

(2) the child has been adjudicated to have been abused or neglected in a prior proceeding;

(3) the child has been out of the custody of the parent for the period of one year and the court finds that:

(i) the conditions which led to the separation still persist, or similar conditions of a potentially harmful nature continue to exist;

(ii) there is little likelihood that those conditions will be remedied at an early date so that the child can be returned to the parent in the near future; and

(iii) the continuation of the parent-child relationship greatly diminishes the child's prospects for early integration into a stable and permanent home.

(b) When a child has been previously adjudicated abused or neglected, the court in determining whether or not to terminate the parent-child relationship shall consider, among other factors, the following continuing or serious conditions or acts of the parents:

(1) emotional illness, mental illness, mental deficiency, or use of alcohol or controlled substances rendering the parent consistently unable to care for the immediate and ongoing physical or psychological needs of the child for extended periods of time;

(2) acts of abuse or neglect toward any child in the family; and

(3) repeated or continuous failure by the parents, although physically and financially able, to provide the child with adequate food, clothing, shelter, and

education as defined by law, or other care and control necessary for his physical, mental, or emotional health and development; but a parent or guardian who, legitimately practising his religious beliefs, does not provide specified medical treatment for a child, is not for that reason alone a negligent parent and the court is not precluded from ordering necessary medical services for the child according to existing state law.

(c) Whenever a child has been out of physical custody of the parent for more than one year, the court shall consider, pursuant to subsection (a)(3), among other factors, the following:

(1) the timeliness, nature and extent of services offered or provided by the agency to facilitate reunion of the child with the parent;

(2) the terms of any social service contract agreed to by an authorized agency and the parent and the extent to which all parties have fulfilled their obligations under such contract.

(d) When considering the parent-child relationship in the context of either subsections (b) or (c), the court shall also evaluate:

(1) the child's feelings and emotional ties with his birth parents; and

(2) the effort the parent has made to adjust his circumstances, conduct, or conditions to make it in the child's best interest to return him to his home in the foreseeable future, including:

(i) the extent to which the parent has maintained regular visitation or other contact with the child as part of a plan to reunite the child with the parent;

(ii) the payment of a reasonable portion of substitute physical care and maintenance if financially able to do so; and

(iii) the maintenance of regular contact or communication with the legal or other custodian of the child; and

(iv) whether additional services would be likely to bring about lasting parental adjustment enabling a return of the child to the parent within an ascertainable period of time.

(e) The court may attach little or no weight to incidental visitations, communications, or contributions. It is irrelevant in a termination proceeding that the maintenance of the parent-child relationship may serve as an inducement for the parent's rehabilitation.

(f) If the parents are notified pursuant to Section 10(a) and fail to respond thereto, such failure shall constitute consent to termination on the part of the parent involved. The court may also, pursuant to Section 12(c), terminate the unknown father's relationship with the child.

Commentary

This section is designed to provide greater specificity in the statement of standards in termination and neglect statutes. Subsection (a) sets forth three fact situations which, if proven to exist, may justify an involuntary termination if deemed in the child's best interest. The three situations are: abandonment, prior adjudicated abuse or neglect, and being out of the custody of the parent for a year if the conditions that led to separation or similar conditions of a potentially harmful nature still persist, there is little likelihood that the child can be returned in the near future, and continuation of the parent-child relationship greatly impedes chances for adoption or integration of the child into a stable and permanent home.

Subsection (b) establishes guidelines for the court's consideration if termination is sought because of prior adjudicated abuse or neglect. The emphasis is upon whether a parent's present emotional or mental condition or use of alcohol or controlled substances consistently renders the parent unable to care for immediate and ongoing physical and psychological needs of the child. Parental acts of abuse or neglect toward other children in the family must be considered in determining whether the child who is the subject of the petition is harmed or threatened with harm. A "spiritual healing" clause, (b)(3), exempts a parent from being deemed negligent for the sole reason that, in legitimately practicing his religious beliefs, he does not provide specified medical treatment.

In subsection (c) a number of factors are listed for the court to consider when a child has been out of the custody of the parent for a year because of either private placement arrangements made by the parent or under court order. In order to ascertain whether return is likely in the foreseeable future, the court is directed to explore (1) the timeliness, nature and extent of services provided to the parents; (2) the terms of any social service contract agreed to by an authorized agency and the parent; and (3) the extent to which all parties have fulfilled their obligations under the contract.

This directive to consider a social service contract is in line with current task-oriented, reality-based casework which has been proven to be helpful in improving the parenting capacity of borderline or character disordered parents. It is critically important that agency intake and service practices reflect an understanding of the psychodynamic functioning of families that abuse or neglect their children. Treatment services should be offered by workers who are trained in differential diagnosis and who have the capacity to encourage positive growth.

Subsection (d) requires the court to evaluate and consider the child's feelings and emotional ties with his birth parents. Whether the parent has made efforts to adjust his circumstances, conduct or condition to make it in the child's best interest to return in the foreseeable future must be weighed. The court must consider such matters as whether the parent has maintained regular visitation, assumed reasonable support and maintenance obligations and cooperated with the agency. These aspects are thought to be important indices of whether additional services are likely to bring about a lasting parental adjustment which will permit the child's return to the parent. In cases where parental contact has been sporadic, *i.e.,* merely a card at Christmas, and does not indicate any pattern or ability to sustain ongoing communication, subsection (e) permits the court to disregard such incidental contacts. This section underscores the Model Act's general purpose that to further the best interests of the child, it must be recognized that some children need the opportunity to grow and mature separate and apart from their birth parents.

Finally, subsection (f) provides that parental failure to respond to properly given notice, pursuant to Section 10 will constitute consent to termination or, pursuant to Section 12(c) the court may terminate the rights of the unknown father.

Section 5.   Jurisdiction for Termination of Parent-Child Relationship

The [*Juvenile/Family*] court has original and exclusive jurisdiction over proceedings to terminate the parent-child relationship.

Commentary

Although court structures vary, the Model Act does suggest that the juvenile or family court or division within a district or circuit court system have original and exclusive jurisdiction.

It is recommended that jurisdiction over termination proceedings be vested in a division of the court of highest general trial jurisdiction which also has jurisdiction over guardianship, custody, adoption, dependency and support, paternity, divorce and other family litigation. In some states it may be the probate court. In addition to having broad substantive jurisdiction over family matters, the court of original and exclusive jurisdiction over termination should also have access to appropriate social service resources and a clear-cut responsibility for related judicial administrative matters.

Section 6.   Retention of Jurisdiction

For the purposes of this Act, when a court has obtained jurisdiction over a child pursuant to this Act, the jurisdiction may continue until the child becomes 18 years of age, unless adopted or emancipated earlier.

Commentary

This section enables the court to have continuing jurisdiction until the child is adopted or emancipated and should encourage fulfillment of the general purpose of the Act to promote the placement of minor children in permanent homes. This language is consistent with both the Uniform Child Custody Act and the Interstate Compact on the Placement of Children which grant continuing jurisdiction to the court making the dispositional order.

Section 7. Venue

Proceedings under this Act shall be commenced in the court of original and exclusive jurisdiction sitting in the county either where the child resides, or the petitioner resides or does business.

Commentary

Proper venue is deemed to exist in the child's residence, or the petitioner's residence or place of doing business because it is assumed that these will be the places with the most significant contacts and the most interest in the case. Venue in a place devoid of significant contacts would drastically hamper compliance with later procedural requirements. See Section 14, *infra*.

Section 8. Persons Eligible to Petition

(a) A parent, either directly or through an authorized agency, may file a petition seeking voluntary termination of the parent-child relationship.

(b) A petition seeking involuntary termination of the parent-child relationship may be filed by:

(1) an authorized agency;

(2) either parent seeking termination with respect to the other parent; or

(3) a guardian of the child's person, legal custodian, the child's guardian *ad litem* appointed in a prior proceeding; or

(4) a *de facto* parent, as defined in Section 2(a)(15), of a child who has been in foster care for 2 years.

(c) An authorized agency having custody of any child conclusively presumed abandoned pursuant to Section 2(a)(4) (iv) shall file a petition seeking involuntary termination within 10 days after establishment of abandonment.

Commentary

Subsection (a) addresses voluntary petitions and enables a parent to petition the court directly or to have an authorized agency initiate proceedings in behalf of the parent. Subsection (b) deals with involuntary petitions to terminate the parent-child relationship and extends standing to an authorized child placement agency, to a parent seeking termination with respect to the other parent, and finally to a group of other persons deemed legitimately interested either because of their legal status as guardian of the child's person, legal custodian or guardian *ad litem*, or because they have actual physical custody of the child and are *de facto* parents as defined in Section 2. These provisions are derived from the 1961 *Legislative Guides for the Termination of Parental Rights and Responsibilities and the Adoption of Children* prepared by the Children's Bureau, and, instead of giving standing broadly to "any other person having a legitimate interest in the matter," specify alternative petitioners.

Subsection (c) requires an authorized agency having custody of any child conclusively presumed abandoned to file a termination petition within 10 days of the establishment of abandonment. This should accelerate permanent planning for such children.

A *de facto* parent, such as a relative or stepparent, is accorded standing to bring a termination petition with respect to a child in their continuous physical care at least one year when significant emotional ties exist. Foster parents may also be *de facto* parents, but paragraph (4) of subsection (b) limits their right to petition to children who have been in foster care for at least two years. This provision of the Model Act recognizes that in some instances the foster parent is in the best situation to know the child, the frequency and quality of his contacts with the parents and the efforts of the agency. It provides an advocate for the child in foster care for more than 2 years if he is forgotten by all others as the result of uncovered caseloads. Thus, if a foster parent brings a petition the court should be alert to investigate why a permanent placement has not been worked out for the child.

Giving foster parents standing to bring a termination petition should not be equated with awarding them permanent guardianship. The court must still make a final order that furthers the child's best interests. Recent court decisions have recognized that foster parents as "*de facto* parents" have standing to appear as parties and contest the removal of a child in their care. *See In re B.G.,* 11 Cal. 3d 1079 (1975); *Katzoff v. Superior,* 127 Cal. Rptr. 178, 54 Cal. App. 3d 1079 (1976); and *Cennami v. Department of Public Welfare,* 363 N.E. 2d 539 (1977). In *Smith v. Organization of Foster Families* 431 U.S. 816 (1977), the United States Supreme Court held that foster parents did not have a right to a full hearing to contest the removal of the child in their care. However, in so holding, the Court assumed that foster parents did have a constitutionally protected "liberty interest", *Smith* at 847.

The guardian *ad litem* mentioned in paragraph (3) of subsection (b) is not the guardian *ad litem* whom the court must appoint in a termination proceeding under this Act, but refers to a guardian *ad litem* appointed in a prior neglect, abuse or child protection proceeding as authorized in the DHEW Model Child Protection Services Act. This does not, however, prohibit the same person from serving in both capacities and in fact such a continuing role is preferable, since the attorney would be familiar with the previous court action.

Section 9. Contents of the Petition

(a) A petition for termination of the parent-child relationship shall be entitled, "in the Interest of _____, a person under the age of 18 years," and shall set forth with specificity:

(1) the name, sex, date and place of birth, and address, of the child;

(2) the name and address of the petitioner; and the nature of his relationship to the child;

(3) the names, dates of birth, and addresses of the child's parents;

(4) if the child's parent is a minor, the names and addresses of such minor's parents or guardian of the person;

(5) the names and addresses of any:

(i) guardian of the child's person,

(ii) custodian of the child, and

(iii) guardians *ad litem* appointed in a prior proceeding;

(6) the facts on which termination is sought the grounds authorizing termination, the effects of a termination decree as set forth in Section 18 of this Act, and the basis of the court's jurisdiction;

(7) the names of the persons or authorized agencies to whom or to which temporary legal custody or guardianship of the child's person may be transferred upon disposition.

(b) If the information required under paragraphs (2) and (6) of subsection (a) is not stated, the petition shall be dismissed; if any other facts required under paragraphs (1), (3), (4), (5) or (7) of subsection (a) are not known or cannot be ascertained by the petitioner, he shall so state in the petition.

(c) A copy of any relinquishment or consent to adoption, previously executed by a parent to an authorized agency, shall accompany the petition, pursuant to Section 3(a)(2).

Commentary

In this section the form and contents of any petition for termination under the Model Act are specified. All the requirements are consistent with the broad general purposes stated in Section 1(a) and (b)(4). In accordance with the Uniform Juvenile Court Act, the petition is entitled, "In the Interest of _____, a person under the age of 18."

Particular attention has been given to recent cases, such as *Alsager v. District Court of Polk County, Iowa,* 406 F. Supp. 10 (1976), which held the Iowa termination notice procedure violative of the parents' due process rights. Paragraph (6) of subsection (a) thus requires that the petition not only state the facts on which termination is sought, but must also refer to the particular legal standard from Sections 3 and 4 that apply. These requirements are designed to meet the new due process demands for precision in defining concepts like the quality of parental care and the meaning of neglect. (*See* Commentary to Section 4, *supra*). The assumption of subsection (a)(6) above is that these requirements for a new specificity in termination proceedings will prevent the issuance of termination decrees based on vague and undefined statutory generalities. Furthermore, compliance with the requirements of subsection (a)(6) will facilitate the emphasis placed by the Model Act on provision of right to counsel. (*See* also Sections 10 and 12, *infra.*) As a result of subsection (a)(6) counsel for either parent or the child will now immediately know the allegations on which the case for termination is based since these must be stated specifically in the petition. There is the further requirement that the effect of a termination decree must be clearly stated. If these data, the information identifying the petitioner, and the nature of the relationship between the petitioner and the child are not given, the court must dismiss the petition. Without such information parents whose rights to the custody and control of their children have been challenged cannot adequately prepare a defense.

Paragraph (7) calls for the names of the authorized persons or agencies to whom or to which legal custody or guardianship of the child's person may be transferred. It should further the general purpose of promoting the placement of minor children in permanent homes by requiring that the petitioner give careful consideration to a placement plan at the time of petitioning for termination.

The other paragraphs in subsection (a) ask for the names and addresses of other significant parties if they are known to the petitioner. This should facilitate the court's giving notice to all necessary parties. When a parent has voluntarily executed a relinquishment or consent to adoption form to an agency, this must be appended to the petition.

Section 10. Notice; and Waiver

(a) Within 10 days after the filing of a petition, the court shall set a place and time for the preliminary hearing, to be held pursuant to Section 12 of this Act; the preliminary hearing shall be held no later than 45 days after filing of the petition. The court shall cause notice thereof to be given to the petitioner, the parents of the child, any guardian of the person of the child, any person having legal custody of the child, and any guardians *ad litem* appointed in a prior proceeding. If the parent of the child is a minor the court may give notice to such child's parent or guardian if the court finds that notice is in the best interest of the minor's child.

(b) Notice of the preliminary hearing and a copy of the petition, certified by the petitioner, his agent or attorney, or the court clerk, shall be personally served on the persons named in subsection (a) at least 10 days before the hearing. The notice shall state that a party is entitled to counsel in the proceedings and that if a party is indigent the court will appoint counsel.

(c) If personal service on a parent, either within or without this State, cannot be effected, notice shall be given by registered mail sent at least 20 days before the hearing to his last reasonable ascertainable address. If notice is not likely to be effective, the court may order notice to be given by publication at least 20 days before the hearing. Publication shall be in a newspaper of general circulation, likely to give notice, in the place of the last reasonably ascertainable address of the parent, whether within or without this State, or if no address is known, in the place where the termination petition has been filed.

(d) At any time before the preliminary hearing, notice and appearance may be waived by a parent or a person described in subsection (a) before the court or in a writing attested by 2 or more credible witnesses who are 18 or more years of age and subscribe their names thereto in the presence of the person executing the waiver. The face of the waiver shall contain language explaining the meaning and consequences of the waiver and the termination of the parent-child relationship. A parent who has executed a waiver is not required to appear. If the parent resides outside this State, the waiver shall be acknowledged before a notary public of the foreign jurisdiction and shall contain the current address of the parent. The court shall review all waivers to determine their effectiveness. All waivers to be effective shall be found by the court to have been knowingly and voluntarily executed.

(e) If the petitioner has reason to know that a person entitled to notice is unable to read, such notice shall be given verbally. If the person is unable to comprehend English, all notices, if practicable, shall be given in that person's native language or through an interpreter.

Commentary

The Fourteenth Amendment of the United States Constitution provides that a state shall not deprive any person of life, liberty or property without due process of law. As noted earlier in Commentary to Section 1, judicial termination of the parent-child relationship is a serious intrusion into the privacy of the family unit and can be viewed as a deprivation of liberty—as interference with the right to have and raise a family. *Griswold v. Connecticut,* 381 U.S. 479 at 485 (1965). Therefore the Model Act strives to require procedures that will conform to constitutional due process standards.

The absolute essentials in any proceeding made subject to due process requirements are adequate notice of the proposed action and an opportunity to be heard. In *Mullane v. Central Hanover Bank Company*, 339 U.S. 306 at 314 (1950), the Court said:

An elementary and fundamental requirement of due process in any proceeding which is to be accorded finality is notice reasonably calculated under all the circumstances to apprise interested parties of the pendency of the action and to afford them an opportunity to present their objections. The notice must be of such a nature as reasonably to convey the required information and it must afford a reasonable time for those interested to make their appearance.

Subsection (a) enumerates the various necessary parties — petitioner, parents, guardian of the child's person, legal custodian or guardian *ad litem,* who after the filing of a petition seeking termination of a parent-child relationship, must receive notice of the preliminary hearing set by the court to occur within 45 days. In Section 2 (a)(14) the Model Act defines "parent" as including an unwed, putative father unless such a parent has had his rights judicially terminated. *See* Section 12(b) *infra* for procedures when the birth father's identity is unknown. Notice to a minor's parent or guardian is left to the discretion of the court.

Subsection (b) provides that each party enumerated in subsection (a) shall personally receive notice of the preliminary hearing and that a certified copy of the petition seeking termination must be attached. This subsection (b), when read in conjunction with Section 9(a)(6) which requires the petition to state with specificity the alleged statutory grounds for termination, goes far to ensure procedural due process to the affected parties. Each notice must clearly state that the party is entitled to counsel in the termination proceedings and that if the party is indigent the court will appoint counsel.

Subsection (c) addresses the manner of service of process when it cannot be accomplished personally. Registered mail is the preferred method. If this is not likely to provide notice, the court may order notice by publication in a newspaper of general circulation at the place of the last reasonably ascertainable address of the party. This section conforms with the requirements for reasonable notice articulated in *Mullane, supra.*

Subsection (d) allows a parent or a person described in subsection (a) to waive notice and appearance. It is anticipated that this section would be used in the case of voluntary terminations. The waiver may be before the court or in writing, attested by two or more credible witnesses, and the face of the waiver must contain language that explains the meaning and consequences both of the waiver and the termination of the parent-child relationship. This section is included to accommodate existing administrative procedures used by some agencies. The requirement for witnesses and a clear statement on the face of the waiver itself will provide protection for parents whose execution of the waiver must be based on informed knowledge of the consequences. Agencies might well choose to make counsel available to parents before accepting such a waiver.

Finally by requiring in Subsection (e) that notice be given in a "person's native language or through an interpreter," the Model Act introduces another mechanism that will help to ensure procedural due process. It is clear that additional efforts must often be made when parties are known to be non-English speaking or to be illiterate to ensure that they truly understand the significance of the notice and may prepare for their day in court.

Section 11. Hearings: Phases and Conduct

(a) All termination petitions, filed under this Act, shall be considered by the court in three distinct phases, commencing with a preliminary hearing, pursuant to Section 12, followed by the adjudicatory phase to determine the appropriateness of termination, and concluding with a dispositional hearing, pursuant to Section 16.

(b) All hearings shall be conducted in the manner of a non-jury civil trial. The proceedings shall be recorded. Only those persons whose presence is requested by persons entitled to notice under Section 10 or who are found by the court to have a direct interest in the case or the work of the court shall be present. Those persons so admitted shall not disclose any information obtained at the hearing which would identify an individual child or parent. The court may require the presence of witnesses deemed necessary to the disposition of the petition, including persons making a report, study, or examination which is before the court if such persons are reasonably available. A parent who has executed a waiver pursuant to Section 10(d) need not appear at the hearing. If the court finds that it is in the best interest of a child, the child may be excluded from the hearing.

Commentary

Subsection (a) refers to the three distinct phases of a termination proceeding: the preliminary hearing, as required by Section 12, the adjudicatory phase, governed by Sections 3, 4 and 15, and the dispositional phase, governed by Section 16.

Subsection (b) expressly incorporates many of the "typical" neglect hearing provisions found in existing state laws as analyzed in *Child Neglect Laws* 71. The termination hearing is to be heard by the court without a jury, conducted in an informal manner but transcribed, and closed to the general public except interested parties. The court may require the presence of witnesses and persons making any report, study or examination of involved parties. In addition, to provide a mechanism for simplifying a voluntary relinquishment, the Model Act does allow for excusing the presence of a parent who has executed a waiver pursuant to Section 10(d) *supra*. The Model Act dispenses with a jury trial in order to minimize criminalization of the termination proceeding.

Section 12.   Preliminary Hearing

(a) If a party appears without counsel, the court shall inform him of his right thereto and upon request, if he is indigent, shall appoint counsel to represent him. No party may waive counsel unless the court shall have first explained the nature and meaning of a petition seeking termination of the parent-child relationship.

(b) If identity of the birth father of the child is unknown to the petitioner, at the preliminary hearing required under Section 10(a) the court shall:

(1) Inquire of the mother concerning the identity of the father, but may not compel disclosure by the mother;

(i) If the mother provides identification of the father, the court shall immediately give notice to the father pursuant to the provisions of Section 10;

(ii) If the mother does not or cannot provide identification of the father, the court shall determine whether notice of the proceedings by publication or posting is likely to lead to the identification of the father and, if so, shall order such notification; but only upon the mother's written informed consent;

(2) If the procedures in (i) and (ii) above fail to provide identification of the father, then the court shall appoint an attorney as guardian *ad litem* for the putative father to conduct a discreet search for him and to report the results to the court no later than 30 days from the date of the preliminary hearing.

(c) If after acting upon the provisions stated in subsection (b), the identity of the father is not determined within 30 days following the preliminary hearing, the court shall immediately enter an order terminating the unknown father's relationship with the child.

(d) In all involuntary termination proceedings, the court shall appoint an independent attorney to represent the separate interests of the child and to serve as the child's guardian *ad litem*. The court, in its discretion, may appoint a guardian *ad litem* for the child in any voluntary termination proceeding pursuant to Section 3 of this Act.

(e) Upon a finding at the preliminary hearing that reasonable cause exists to warrant an examination, the court, on its own motion or on motion by any party, may order the child to be examined at a suitable place by a physician, psychiatrist, licensed clinical psychologist, or other expert appointed by the court, prior to a hearing on the merits of the petition. The court also may order examination of a parent or custodian whose ability to care for a child before the court is at issue. The expenses of any examination, if ordered by the court shall be paid by the [_____].

Commentary

This section of the Model Act introduces the important concept of a "preliminary hearing" into the termination proceedings. At the preliminary hearing it is the function of the judge to advise all the parties, before formal commencement of the proceedings, of their constitutional rights to be represented by counsel and to remain silent, to confront, cross-examine and subpoena witnesses. The judge must also ascertain whether any party appearing without counsel fully understands his right to counsel or to appointed counsel if indigent. Subsection (a) specifically prohibits any waiver of counsel until after there has been a full explanation of the nature and meaning of the termination of the parent-child relationship. Subsections (b) and (c) outline the steps that the court shall take at the preliminary hearing when the birth father's identity is unknown to the petitioner.

In all involuntary termination proceedings the court must appoint an attorney as guardian *ad litem* for the child to provide the child with separate and independent counsel. In the discretion of the court an attorney to serve as guardian *ad litem* may be appointed for the child when a parent voluntarily seeks termination, but such an appointment is not mandatory. As authorized under Sections 11 and 15 (a) of the Model Act, the court may adjourn the preliminary hearing to allow appointed counsel adequate preparation time. If all parties are fully apprised of all of their rights and are represented by counsel, the proceedings may go immediately forward into the adjudicatory stage.

The right to appointed counsel found in subsection (a) is an important feature that conforms to due process standards under the requirements of *Stanley v. Illinois*, 405 U.S. 645 (1972). This subsection rejects the distinction made by some courts that neglect or termination proceedings, although civil and not criminal, nonetheless do not require court appointed counsel for the indigent parent. Since

Stanley an increasing number of state supreme courts have held that an indigent parent involved in an involuntary termination proceeding concerning his child is constitutionally entitled to be represented by counsel.

Subsection (a) thus also adopts the view that a right to appointed counsel for the indigent parent is constitutionally mandated. The position advocated by some courts, which would restrict the right to appointed counsel for parents in termination proceedings on an *ad hoc* judicial estimate of the need for counsel, is rejected on the ground that it will encourage litigation and will fail to give parents necessary guidance and protection.

It should be noted that subsection (a) imposes an obligation upon the court to explain to the parent the significance of the termination proceeding. Such explanation is deemed essential because for many parents, the nature of the termination proceeding is unclear. The required explanation is intended to assure as far as possible that before waiving appointed counsel an indigent parent fully understands that the termination decree will permanently sever parental rights since otherwise the waiver may be made too casually. Furthermore, this subsection places the initiative on the court to inform the parent of a right to appointed counsel, and only after carefully explaining the nature of the termination proceeding may the court ask the parent if he or she wishes to waive that right. Deeming the right to counsel waived unless requested is expressly disapproved.

Subsections (b) and (c) of this section are a response to the declaration in *Stanley v. Illinois, supra* at 657, n.9 that unwed fathers are entitled to notice of adoption and custody proceedings concerning their children. Notice is required in order to permit such fathers to make a claim to the custody of their children and a showing of their competence to care for them.

Subsections (b) and (c) contemplate in the main a fact situation where the mother has relinquished or wishes to relinquish an infant for adoption and where either or both the identity and whereabouts of the unwed father are not known. The Model Act thus reflects a broad view of *Stanley* in requiring some reasonable but practical effort to find and reach the unwed father even if unknown. However, subsection (b) and (c) take the position that the effort to provide notice to unwed father, if futile, need not be pursued to the point that placement of the child involved is unreasonably delayed. While detailing some alternative modes of notice, the policy of the subdivisions of subsection (b) is to leave the determination of the form of notice, as well as whether notice may be dispensed with altogether, to the sound discretion of the court which has inquired into the matter. Such a procedure is designed to render proper deference both to the due process rights of the birth father and to a proper and sensitive concern for the future placement and welfare of the child.

Privacy interests of both mother and child support the philosophy of subsection (b)(1) that the mother should not be compelled to identify the father in order that he may be notified of a termination proceeding. Whether or not compelling the mother to identify the father is constitutional, the theory of this subsection is that strong policy considerations argue against such compulsion.

The effort to provide due process to the birth father, the natural mother, the child and, ultimately, the adoptive parents sometimes results in setting these rights in conflict. Accommodation of the competing rights can best be resolved by a wise use of discretion by the court making the termination decision. Subsection (b) tries as far as possible to fashion remedies that would give the birth father notice of the termination proceeding without rendering the pending termination and future adoption impossible. The court must first consider whether notice is in fact likely to lead to the identification of the father. Subsection (b)(ii) allows for a good faith effort to reach the birth father through notice of publication if the mother consents to the use of her name.

Subsection (b)(2) is designed to prevent the procedure for providing notice to the unwed father from becoming an empty formalism. Provision for appointment when necessary of a guardian *ad litem* may be a particularly effective notice procedure when the mother does not know the father's present whereabouts. The mother may not be willing to have her name included in a notice by publication in a newspaper but may be able to provide the guardian *ad litem* with clues to the father's whereabouts. In such circumstances, the appointment of a guardian *ad litem* to search for the father will protect the privacy rights of the mother and at the same time will be more likely to locate the father than mere newspaper notice.

If the court fails to reach the unknown birth father through the procedures set forth in subsections (b)(1) and (2) the court is empowered by subsection (c) to enter an order terminating the unknown father's parental rights and responsibilities 30 days after the preliminary hearing. This time period is prescribed to assure that at least some significant period of time is allotted for the notification of the unknown birth father in order to give him an opportunity to assert, if he wishes, a right to the care and custody of his child.

In summary, subsections (b) and (c), the "Stanley" provisions of the Model Act, attempt to assure a good faith effort to notify the unwed father even if his whereabouts and identity are not known. At the same time, these subsections authorize the termination of the parental rights of the unwed father, even if he has not received notice, if the court concludes that the process of searching for him is likely to prove futile.

Subsection (e) authorizes the court to order that a child, parent or both, prior to the hearing on the merits of the petition, be examined by a physician, psychiatrist, licensed clinical psychologist or other expert. And subsection (f) requires the court to order a psychosocial assessment of the child's needs, pursuant to Section 13.

Section 13. Psychosocial Assessment and Report

(a) The court, if it assumes jurisdiction at the preliminary hearing, shall order a psychosocial assessment of the child's needs in all involuntary proceedings. This study shall be made either by:

(1) social service personnel attached to the court;

(2) an authorized agency which is not the petitioner or a mental health agency; or

(3) an independent social work practitioner. An authorized agency which is the petitioner may make the assessment only upon court determination that none of the above alternatives are possible. The report shall be submitted within 30 days after the court directive, unless the court grants a request for an extension.

(b) The court, when it hears a voluntary petition brought pursuant to Section 3, may order a psychosocial assessment if deemed in the best interest of the child.

(c) The psychosocial assessment shall be based upon consideration of:

(1) the circumstances described in the petition;

(2) the present physical, mental and emotional conditions of the child and his parents, including the results of all medical, psychiatric, or psychological examinations of the child or of any parent whose relationship to the child is subject to termination;

(3) the nature of all past and existing relationships among the child, his siblings and his parents;

(4) the proposed plan for the child;

(5) the child's own preferences according to his maturity of judgment; and

(6) any other facts pertinent to determining what will be in the child's best interest, including, but not limited to the child's culture, such as services provided or offered by the [State Department of Social Services] or by any other agencies or individuals.

Commentary

The title of this section of the Model Act is designed to highlight the interdisciplinary judgments that should be weighed in an assessment of a child's current social, emotional and psychological needs and in an evaluation of the capacity of the parent to adequately nurture the child and meet those needs.

Subsection (a) requires that at the preliminary hearing of all involuntary petitions the judge order a psychosocial assessment of the child's needs to be done by social service personnel attached to the court or by an authorized agency not the petitioner or mental health agency or an independent social work practitioner. If an authorized agency is the petitioner, the court may direct that the psychosocial assessment be made by some other agency or by an independent social work practitioner to give the assessment the objectivity that is desirable. This section contemplates that social casework and other clinical services, organized and administered by an executive branch of state government may be available to the court. If such personnel are not attached to the court, the Model Act requires that the judge utilize other resources.

When the court hears a voluntary petition for termination, in its discretion it may order a psychological assessment, but this is not mandatory. See Sections 3, and 12.

Again this more permissive option is available to accommodate existing agency administrative procedures governing voluntary petitions for termination.

Subsection (c) spells out the considerations for the psychosocial assessment. This study is considered critical in helping the court reach a disposition that will further the best interests of the child. A carefully prepared psychosocial study by a professional social caseworker will describe where a child is developmentally, the quality of both past and existing relationships with parents and other current caretakers, and estimate the nurturing capacity of any adult whose parental rights are subject to termination. The proposed future plan for the child, adoption or long-term guardianship, can be evaluated in light of these assessments. For example, a plan that proposed adoption of the child by foster parents with whom strong emotional ties had developed might be deemed preferable to a plan that envisioned several additional moves for a child before any consideration of a permanent placement. The Model Act also requires recognition of a child's own wishes, depending upon his age and maturity of judgment.

Section 14.   Guardians ad litem

(a) During all stages of the proceeding, the child's guardian *ad litem* shall be the legal representative of the child, and may examine, cross-examine, subpoena witnesses and offer testimony. The guardian *ad litem* may also initiate an appeal of any disposition that he determines to be adverse to the best interest of the child.

(b) In addition, the guardian *ad litem* shall be an advocate for the child during the dispositional phase to ensure that the best possible permanent placement plan is made. To ascertain the child's wishes, feelings, attachments, and attitudes, he shall conduct all necessary interviews with persons, other than parents, having contact with and knowledge of the child and, if appropriate, with the child. In the case of an American Indian child, he shall report on the legal status of the child's membership in any federally recognized Indian tribe.

(c) The guardian *ad litem* for a child shall be an attorney, preferably one who is experienced in the field of children's rights.

(d) The guardian *ad litem* for other persons entitled to such representation pursuant to Section 2(a)(10) shall protect the rights, interests, and welfare of the party and may exercise the powers enumerated in subsection (a).

(e) The court shall compensate the guardian *ad litem* for services and related expenses according to the court's fee schedule.

Commentary

The function of Section 14 is to insure that counsel for the child and other parties play an effective role. The *Gault* case ushered in a new era of court appointed counsel for minors involved in juvenile proceedings.

Section 14(a) imposes specific legal duties on the child's court-appointed guardian *ad litem* in order to avoid a situation where such counsel would play a merely routine role on an assembly line basis for a minimal fee. The duties imposed on counsel of conducting investigations and personal interviews will enable the attorney to effectively participate in the adjudicatory stage of the termination proceeding. The guardian ad litem may initiate an appeal of any disposition that he views as adverse to the child's best interest. Subsection (b) contemplates that during the dispositional stage, the guardian *ad litem's* recommendations to the court will reflect not only his legal judgments but will also be informed by the psychosocial assessment prepared by social service workers. See Sections 13 and 15. It is expected that the guardian *ad litem* will be an advocate for the child.

The guardian *ad litem* is especially charged with reporting on the legal status of an American Indian child's membership in a federally recognized Indian tribe because of the special benefits that frequently accrue from membership, *i.e.,* eligibility to share in any judgment that might be awarded to a tribe by the Indian Claims Commission, receipt of tribal assets as they are periodically distributed to members, or preference for employment by the Bureau of Indian Affairs. *See* also the reference to American Indian children in Section 18(d) *infra*.

Subsection (c) makes an additional effort to implement, the overall purpose of Section 14, effective legal representation for the child, by requiring that such representation be entrusted to those who have already demonstrated experience in and commitment to the legal problems of children. The decision to limit appointments to attorneys was made because judicial termination is presently an adversarial rather than an arbitration/mediation proceeding. Separate and independent legal counsel for the child provided by lawyers experienced in the field of children's needs and rights is needed. Although a given locale may not presently have such a specialized bar, this model articulates the standard that should be sought.

The purpose of subsection (d) is to provide the same kind of useful and effective representation, as specified in subsection (a), from the guardian *ad litem* appointed on behalf of any other party in the proceeding as from the child's appointed guardian *ad litem*.

The purpose of subsection (e) is to make it clear that compensation for appointed counsel in termination proceedings must be forthcoming. The best interests of the child are best protected if appointed counsel in the proceeding can be sure of being compensated for his skill, time and effort. Furthermore, it is the assumption of this subsection that the most effective way to assure the payment of such compensation is to make it a judicial responsibility.

Section 15. Findings

(a) If a petition has been voluntarily filed under Section 8(a) and is uncontested, the court shall make its findings at the end of the preliminary hearing if all parties are then before the court; but if not all parties are present, the court shall continue the hearing to give the absent parties opportunity to appear. The court will also continue the hearing to give parties without counsel the opportunity to be represented.

(b) If an involuntary petition has been filed pursuant to Section 8(b), the court shall hold an adjudicatory hearing to commence within 15 days following the end of the preliminary hearing in order to determine whether grounds for termination of the parent-child relationship exist.

(c) All findings shall be based upon clear and convincing evidence and rules applicable to the trial of civil causes. If information contained in a court-ordered report, study, or examination is received in evidence, the person making the report, study or examination shall be subject to both direct and cross-examination. If a parent or child has been or is in treatment with a psychiatrist, licensed clinical psychologist, or social worker, a privilege shall be deemed to exist between the patient and the therapist. However, no existing physician-patient or similar privilege other then the attorney-client privilege may be asserted to exclude evidence of abuse and neglect of the child or his siblings or parental conduct or condition specified in Section 4 of this Act; nor does any privilege exist if a court has ordered an examination of a parent or child pursuant to Section 12(e) of this Act.

Commentary

Subsections (a) and (b) direct the court to employ different procedural time frames for voluntary and involuntary petitions. If a voluntary petition is filed pursuant to Section 8(a), *supra*, the court may make its findings concerning termination of the parent-child relationship at the end of the preliminary hearing. If an involuntary petition is before the court, there must be an adjudicatory hearing to establish whether grounds for termination exist that commences within 15 days following the preliminary hearing. The differing requirements of these subsections are consistent with earlier distinctions drawn in Sections 4, 12, 13 and 14. *See* generally Commentary to these sections.

Subsection (c) prescribes both the requisite quantum of proof that must be shown if a termination decree is to issue and other evidentiary matter that may be used. There are three choices for a quantum of proof in termination and neglect proceedings. One of the choices is the criminal beyond a reasonable doubt standard. The other two choices are civil standards: the preponderance of the evidence standard and the clear and convincing standard.

The Model Act, in adopting the clear and convincing standard as the quantum of proof, follows the trends in both state and federal courts which is to reject the two other alternatives: the beyond a reasonable doubt and the preponderance of the evidence standards.

Since the overriding consideration in termination proceedings is the welfare of the child, the fault or guilt of the parents is not a central focus. Thus, the standard of beyond a reasonable doubt used in the criminal process was deemed inappropriate for these proceedings. The preponderance of the evidence standard, used in some civil proceedings, was rejected because this lesser test would make it too easy for the state to separate a child from its parents. By choosing the clear and convincing standard, the Model Act tries to provide the fairest measure for weighing the claims of the competing interests.

The final sentences of subsection (c) deal with the question of privilege. First, traditional therapist-client privileges for past or ongoing treatment shall be recognized. But, second, no existing physician-patient or similar privilege can be a basis for "excluding evidence regarding abuse and neglect of the child or his siblings or parental condition specified in Section 4." This approach is consistent with a majority of the current state child abuse and neglect reporting statutes which commonly waive the doctor-patient privilege, the husband-wife privilege and either similar privileges or all privileges. See De Francis & Lucht, *Child Abuse Legislation in the 1970's* (rev. ed. (1974); *Child Neglect Laws* 43-45, 66. And, third, no privilege shall be recognized for any court-ordered examination of a parent or child.

Thus, the Model Act accords a parent who has been or is a patient the privilege to refuse to disclose or to prevent a therapist from disclosing any communication between the patient and therapist relative to treatment of his mental or emotional condition, except evidence regarding abuse or neglect may not be excluded. In making the distinction between patients already in treatment with a therapist and a court-ordered mental examination or investigation, the Model Act follows both case law and sound clinical practice. While the Model Act recognizes the necessity for preserving confidentiality in the treatment relationship, it also acknowledges the judicial need for important information derived from court-ordered examinations and investigations.

It should be noted that this subsection specifically covers the social worker-client relationship. In light of the policies articulated in Section 1(b) *supra* and considerations to be weighed by the court under Sections 4 and 16, it is reasonable to anticipate that parents involved in termination proceedings will have had substantial contacts with social workers.

Section 16. Dispositions

(a) After considering all the evidence, if the court finds that sufficient grounds exist for termination of the parent-child relationship, the court shall:

(1) Decree termination of the parent-child relationship and after having considered the psychosocial assessment and report elect one of the following alternatives:

(i) appoint an individual as guardian of the child's person and vest legal custody in that person; or

(ii) appoint an individual as guardian of the child's person and vest legal custody in another individual or in an authorized agency; or

(iii) appoint an authorized agency as guardian of the child's person and vest legal custody in that agency; or

(2) Not decree termination of the parent-child relationship and after having

considered the psychosocial assessment and report order that a long-term or permanent home for the child be provided by appointing as guardian of the child's person the present *de facto* parent if:

(i) it is deemed that the child would benefit from the continued parent-child relationship; or

(ii) the child is 14 or more years of age and objects to the termination of the parent-child relationship.

(b) Any person or agency appointed guardian of the child's person under subsection (a) shall report to the court within permanent placement plan for the child to the court within 90 days on a permanent placement plan for the child. Within an additional 90 days thereafter, a report shall be made to the court on the implementation of such plan.

(c) In making an order under subsection (a)(2), the court must specify what residual rights and responsibilities remain with the birth parent.

(d) If the court finds that sufficient grounds for termination do not exist, it shall dismiss the petition and under applicable statutory standards make an order:

(1) returning the child to the custody of his parents;

(2) placing the child under protective supervision or under guardianship of the person; or

(3) vesting or continuing temporary legal custody in an authorized agency or person.

(e) Any order the court makes under subsection (d)(2) or (3) shall designate the period of time it shall remain in effect, with mandatory review by the court no later than one year thereafter. The court shall also specify what residual rights and responsibilities remain with the birth parent. Any individual granted legal custody shall exercise the rights and responsibilities personally unless otherwise authorized by the court.

(f) Every order the court makes pursuant to this Section shall be in writing and shall recite the findings upon which the order is based, including findings pertaining to the court's jurisdiction. Every order must fix responsibility for the child's support. All orders are final, conclusive, and binding on all persons after the date of entry.

Commentary

This section of the Model Act should be closely considered in conjunction with the statement of purposes in Sections 3 and 4 *supra*. While Section 15 *supra* addressed the matter of adjudication of the petition on the merits to terminate a parent-child relationship, Section 16 focuses upon the range of dispositional orders that the court may make. It is during this phase of the proceeding that the court reviews the psychosocial assessment and the recommendation of the guardian *ad litem*. This section, in a general way, incorporates language found in

Section 9 — Decree of the Act for Termination of the Parent-Child Relationship suggested in the DHEW's Legislative Guides, *supra* at 44.

Subsection (a)(1) provides three alternative dispositions open to the court if termination is decreed. It should be noted that a present *de facto* parent could be appointed under this section. For example, under (a)(1)(i) a relative might be appointed guardian of the child's person and be granted legal custody. Under (a)(i)(ii) a foster parent might be granted legal custody while guardianship of the child's person remained with a relative or an agency official.

Subsection (a)(2) addresses those cases where the court may determine that sufficient grounds exist to justify termination, but because of other circumstances it may deem that a termination decree is not in the child's best interest. Again, this decision is made by the court after careful review of the psychosocial assessment and the recommendations of the guardian *ad litem*. For example, although an older child may have developed a sound relationship with the present *de facto* parent such as a foster parent or relative, close ties may still exist between the child and the birth parent. Adoption may not be desired by the child; the *de facto* parent may not be financially able to adopt if no subsidy is available. In such circumstances permanent vesting of guardianship and legal custody in the *de facto* parent may be the best plan. It should be noted that subsection (c) requires the court to specify the rights and responsibilities that remain with the birth parent if a termination decree is not issued.

Subsection (b) requires that any person or agency appointed pursuant to subsection (a) must report back to the court on the completed placement plan for the child. This mandate was added to ensure that following a termination decree a child *in fact* would be adopted or settled into a permanent guardianship. Authorization for such a mandatory return is provided by Section 6 — Retention of Jurisdiction, *supra*. By retaining jurisdiction, a judge has the power to hold a hearing and to make further orders should that be deemed necessary.

Subsection (d) provides the court with alternatives if sufficient grounds for termination are not found to exist. Consistent with the public policy stated in Section 1 (b)(1) *supra* to recognize, strengthen and preserve the birth family relationship wherever possible, the court under paragraphs (1) and (2) may return the child to the custody of his parents either with or without protective supervision. (See Section 2 (a)(13) and Commentary *supra* for discussion of the scope of protective supervision.) A court may find that a parent has been rehabilitated. Significant emotional ties may continue to exist between parent and child, or the court may deem a proposed alternative plan for the child, *i.e.,* to be temporarily placed with persons other than the birth parents, to be in the child's best interest.

Finally, subsection (e) requires that all orders be in writing, recite the findings upon which the order is based, and fix responsibility for the child's support. The requirement that the order be in writing and recite the findings upon which it is based should facilitate meaningful review upon appeal and hence furthers the general purpose stated in Section 1 (a)(3) *supra* of protecting the constitutional rights and interests of all parties. Also, all orders are to be final, conclusive and binding on all persons from the date of entry. This is a very typical provision and ensures that any party aggrieved by the order may initiate an appeal under Section 22 *infra*.

Section 17. Authority of Guardian of Child's Person

(a) The guardian of the child's person has the authority without limitation:

(1) to consent to marriage, enlistment in the military service of the United States, and any medical, psychiatric, or surgical treatment; and to represent the child in legal actions, unless another person has been appointed guardian *ad litem* to represent the child;

(2) to serve as custodian, unless another person or authorized agency has been appointed custodian by court order: and

(3) to consent to adoption of the child if the parent-child relationship has been terminated under this Act.

(b) The guardian of the child's person also has the duty of reasonable visitations when he does not have physical custody of the child, except to the extent that the right to visitation is limited by court order.

Commentary

Under Section 16(d) *supra* the court when not decreeing termination may order long-term placement and appoint a present *de facto* parent or foster parent as guardian of the child's person. The duties and authority of such an appointed guardian are defined in this section and correspond to the definition of "guardianship of the child's person" appearing in both the DHEW Model Family Court Act and the Children's Bureau *Legislative Guides for the Termination of Parental Rights and Responsibilities and the Adoption of Children* (Reprint 1968).

Section 18. Effect of Decrees

(a) An order terminating the parent-child relationship divests the parent and the child of all legal rights, powers, privileges, immunities, duties, and obligations with respect to each other, except the right of the child to inherit from the parent. This right of inheritance shall be terminated only a final order of adoption.

(b) The parent-child relationship may be terminated with respect to one parent without affecting the relationship between the child and the other parent.

(c) Any parent whose relationship with the child is terminated is not entitled to notice of proceedings for the adoption of the child by another, nor has he any right to object to the adoption or otherwise to participate in the proceedings.

(d) No order or decree entered pursuant to this Act shall deprive a child of any benefit due him from any third person, agency, state, or the United States; nor shall any action under this Act be deemed to affect any rights and benefits, that a child derives as a descendant of a member of a federally recognized American Indian tribe.

(e) If an order is made pursuant to Section 16(c), only those residual parental rights and responsibilities specified by the court remain. All custodial rights and duties are subject to the rights, powers, and duties of the guardian of the child's person and to residual parental rights and responsibilities not terminated by judicial decree.

Commentary

Subsection (a) follows the traditional approach of divesting both parent and child of all rights, duties and obligations toward one another, except that the child's right to inherit from the natural parent is terminated only upon a final order of adoption. This approach, admittedly weighted in favor of the child, is consistent with a public policy commitment to "the best interests" of the child.

Subsection (b) clarifies that a decree may terminate the relationship between a child and one parent without affecting the status of the child's relationship with the other parent. Subsection (c) underscores the finality of the decree and the fact that following termination a parent will have no standing to object to adoption or other planning in behalf of the child.

The wording of subsection (d) reflects a special concern for the unique position of American Indian children. It is also included to cover generally any Social Security insurance benefit or any other governmental or private assistance which if discontinued might seriously hamper effective permanent planning for the child. See generally DHEW, *Subsidized Adoption in America* (1976).

Section 19.   Contempt

(a) If, without reasonable cause, any person served with a citation within this State as provided in this Act fails to appear, or to abide by an order of the court, or to bring a child before the court if required by the notice of hearing, the court in its discretion may adjudicate the failure to be a contempt of court, as defined and punished by [the applicable state statutes.]

Commentary

The above section's inclusion in the Model Act is grounded in the general doctrine of *parens patriae*. There may be instances when, in order to best serve and protect the welfare of a child, the court will exercise its traditional discretionary powers to enforce its orders. Reference is made to existing definitions and sanctions as they may appear in other state statutes.

Section 20.   Records; Access and Confidentiality

(a) All court files and records of any proceedings conducted under this Act shall be kept in a separate locked file and withheld from public inspection, but on special order of the court shall be open to inspection by a party in the case and his attorney, an authorized agency to which guardianship of the person or legal custody of the child has been transferred, or by legitimate researchers if all identifying data is withheld unless the identifying data cannot be concealed, in which case the researcher has a duty not to disclose.

(b) As used in this section, the term "files and records" includes the court docket and entries therein, petitions and other papers filed in a case, transcripts of testimony taken by the court, and findings, orders, decrees, and other writings or evidentiary materials filed in proceedings before the court, other than social records.

(c) Social records shall be withheld from public inspection, but information contained in those records may be furnished to persons or agencies having a legitimate interest in the protection, welfare, or treatment of the child, in a manner the court determines.

(d) As used in this section, the term "social records" includes the psychosocial study and investigation reports required under Section 14 and other related papers, materials and correspondence, including medical, psychiatric, or psychological studies and reports, either in the possession of the court or an authorized agency.

(e) No person, official, or agency may make copies of the files and records or social records or parts thereof, unless the court so orders.

Commentary

The primary intent of both Section 20 and 21 *infra* is to remove court files and social records from public inspection, but to give all parties and their attorneys or any agency having legal custody of a child access to them. It should be noted that records may be open to "legitimate researchers" if all identifying data is withheld, *unless such identifying data cannot be concealed, in which case the researcher has the duty not to disclose.* (Emphasis added.) The underlined option is included because some court record departments may not have the capacity to provide researchers with data that are free from all identifying information. Thus, the Model Act imposes an obligation not to disclose upon the "legitimate researcher" who is granted leave by the court to use records. *See* Section 21 *infra* for possible sanction.

Section 21.   Penalties for Disclosure of Confidential Records

(a) Except as authorized under Section 20 and under a court order, it is unlawful for any person to disclose, receive, or make use of, or authorize, knowingly permit, participate in, or acquiesce in the use of any information involved in any proceeding under this Act, directly or indirectly derived from the files, records, or other papers compiled pursuant to this Act or acquired in the course of the performance of official duties.

(b) A person who discloses information or aids and abets another in gathering such information in violation of the provisions of this section is guilty of a misdemeanor punishable by [the applicable state statutes.]

Commentary

This section of the Model Act follows the policy expressed in Section 20, *supra* which is to carefully guard the confidentiality of court records in these cases. It thus provides a criminal sanction for violation of the confidentiality requirements of Section 20. It does not suggest any specific monetary amount for a fine, but rather refers to "relevant state statutes" for the sanction of unlawful disclosure or use of files and records. As noted in the preceeding Commentary to Section 20, legitimate researchers may utilize records if all identifying data are either withheld or not disclosed. The obligation of non-disclosure is thus imposed on researchers in view of some of the logistical barriers that might arise in the attempt to make the contents of files available to researchers without any identifying information.

Section 22.   Appeals

Any party aggrieved by an order, judgment, or decree of the court, within 30 days after notice of its entry, may appeal to the [_____] for review of questions of law. The procedure of an appeal is governed by the rules applicable to appeals from the [_____] court in civil cases. The pendency of an appeal or application therefor does not suspend an order of the court regarding a child, but a petition for the child's adoption may not be heard pending the appeal of an involuntary petition to terminate a parent-child relationship.

Commentary

In accordance with its general purpose of ensuring that all parties' constitutional rights are fully protected, the Model Act includes the above section granting the right of appeal for review of questions of law. This section, as in other instances, does not spell out an appeals procedure but rather incorporates by reference existing state procedures and rules applicable to appeals of civil cases. *See* Sections 1(b)(1) and 2(a)(4). However, because of the ongoing needs of a minor child for care and supervision, this section does not allow for any suspension of orders of the court regarding a child during the pendency of an appeal.

Section 23. Termination Decrees of Other State or Tribal Courts

If the parent-child relationship has been terminated by judicial decree in another state, the decree shall be accorded full faith and credit. Such termination by decree of a federally or state recognized Indian Tribal Court shall also be accorded recognition.

Commentary

Due to the increasing mobility of our American population, it has become increasingly important to recognize and anticipate that parties before the court may have been involved in proceedings in another jurisdiction. A parent and child relationship may have been judicially terminated in another state. This section of the Model Act articulates the policy mandated by the Full Faith and Credit Clause of the Constitution of the United States. The section also provides for recognition of termination decrees issued by courts of federally or state recognized Indian tribes. An intent of the section is to prevent forum shopping.

This section is thus very similar to sections found in other model and uniform laws. *See* generally Revised Uniform Adoption Act, and Uniform Child Custody Jurisdiction Act.

Section 24. Severability

If any provision of this Act or its application to any person or circumstances is held invalid, the invalidity does not affect other provisions or applications of the Act which can be given effect without the invalid provision or application, and to this end the provisions of this Act are severable.

Commentary

The above severability clause is commonly used to ensure maximum utilization of all the provisions of the Model Act in the event that any single section or portion thereof is held to be invalid. For similar clauses see Revised Uniform Adoption Act and Uniform Child Custody Jurisdiction Act.

Section 25. Priority

All termination proceedings under this Act shall be given calendar priority and handled expeditiously.

Commentary

This section is important in order to ensure that the decisional time-frame is responsive to the needs of children. It should also avoid long delays due to defensive motions. This section also reaffirms the spirit of earlier sections in which specific time limits are set. *See* generally Sections 1(b)(3); 4(a)(3); 8(c); 10; 12(c); 13(a) and 16(b) and (e), *supra*.

Section 26. Effective Date

This Act shall take effect on _____.

Commentary

Generally an effective date should be set at three to six months after enactment to afford sufficient time to adopt whatever administrative changes are necessary to implement the procedures mandated by this Act.

Section 27. Repeal

(a) The following acts and parts of acts are repealed as of the effective date of this act.

(1)

(2)

(3)

(b) On the effective date of this Act any pending termination proceedings are not affected thereby.

Commentary

Since many states already have numerous statutes dealing with child abuse and neglect, child protective services, foster care and adoption, each state should make a special attempt to be consistent in the use of definitional terms. Other areas that might need evaluation include prior legislative statements of general purposes and intent, sections covering conduct of hearings, the standard of proof, rights to counsel and appointment of guardians *ad litem*. Enactment of this Model Act should occasion careful review of other child welfare statutes.

ISBN 0-409-87460-4